A Step Beyond:

A Definitive Guide

to Ultrarunning

Edited by Don Allison

A Step Beyond:
A Definitive Guide
to Ultrarunning

Edited by Don Allison

UltraRunning Publishers
Weymouth, Massachusetts
www.ultrarunning.com

Library of Congress Cataloging-in-Publication Data

Allison, Don, 1955-
A Step Beyond: A Definitive Guide To Ultrarunning / Don Allison
p.cm.
Includes index.
ISBN: 0-9742311-2-6
  1. Ultrarunning

GV1061.5 .H46 2002
796.42–dc21   00-056690

Library of Congress Control Number 2002096748

ISBN: 0-9742311-2-6

Editor: Don Allison; **Graphic Designer:** Richard Doubleday; **Illustrations:** Richard Doubleday; **Printing:** King Printing, Lowell, Massachusetts.

UltraRunning Publisher books are available at special discounts for bulk purchase. For details, contact Don Allison at UltraRunning Publishing.

Printed in the United States of America   10 9 8 7 6 5 4 3 2 1

UltraRunning Publishers
Web site: **www.ultrarunning.com**

United States: UltraRunning Publishers, P.O. Box 890238,
Weymouth, Massachusetts 02189-0238
1-888-858-7203, e-mail:don-allison@comcast.net

All photographs courtesy of UlraRunning magazine.

Contents

Chapter 6: Philosophy

Chapter 7: Humor

Foreword

Ultrarunners are that small minority who are often thought to live in a different mindset, all their own. Most have experienced similar reactions when telling a "man on the street" about an upcoming 50 or a 100-mile race they are going to run. The usual reply is: "You're going to do *what?* You're crazy!" The mere thought of running that far is inconceivable to many; they just don't get it. "I couldn't run five miles," they'll say. In truth, chances are they couldn't run two miles without stopping to walk. But chances are they have the *potential* within them to run any ultramarathon.

The gap between our actuality and our potential is enormous. It's as great as the mismatch between our perceptions and reality. That's why experience, actual and vicarious by the example of others, is necessary to close the gap in order for our aspirations to become more realistic.

The person on the street, without trying, has no real concept of how *hard* it is to prepare for and run an ultramarathon. That being said, neither do they have a concept of what is *possible.* They see only a mystery in their minds that paints ultrarunners as being a bit weird. Truth be told, for a long time, so did I. I also did not understand. I didn't understand how it could be possible to run 100 miles and beyond. What could possess the human animal to do such a crazy thing without any apparent reward at the end? I didn't even have a sensual feeling of how difficult it is. But gradually my mind was stretched, by effort.

As kids we run routinely, but only short distances at a time, in play. Gradually we discover that we can run longer, but generally anything beyond what we currently run seems out of reach. I find that to be true even today, at age 62. My "normal" everyday life of the 21st century does not require me to chase down my supper, as my ancestors did several millions of years ago when they stepped out into the hot and sunny African plains to become human, to become endurance predators. My mind and body forgets about running when supper is regularly served to me on a plate. Every time I take up the banner of wanting to run a long race I find it a challenge to consistently run even five miles per day. It is only after I eventually run ten miles per day that I begin to look back with amusement at my former self, and look forward to other challenges that then become possible. It happens, one distance at a time, one footstep at a time.

The question our ancient progenitors never asked, but that we ask all the time is this: *Why?* The person on the street asks it. Our spouses ask it. We ask it ourselves and search desperately for an answer, in each training run, and especially halfway into a race. We are left largely clueless, because the answer is not in our proximate rationality. It is far beyond that, and deeper. The fact that we may get a T-shirt or a worthless trinket for finishing a race only confuses and demeans the effort—it's as if these nominal awards are designed to trick the rationality that the race *is* for something, regardless of how trivial and in a total mismatch between what we put in and what we received.

But we don't run for the baubles. We run long distances because in the deep dark recesses of our mind there still resides the instincts of our millions of years as running ape people. It's in our biological heritage to run distances.

That's how we came out of Africa, chasing the antelope and the mammoth. Its stamp is clearly visible in our biomechanical structure, our physiology, and our mentality. Our mind is our unique weapon—the ability in the hunt to perceive value far beyond the horizon, far beyond that which is visible.

Our primal ancestors were hunters. They made their living from running down prey that in the short run outran them with ease. The prey's strategy, which works with most predators, is to run so fast as to seem invincible. Only those hunters, whose mentality gave them pleasure in the chase as such, without immediate reward but with the vision of a possible payoff far ahead, would give chase, or "race" as it were. Only those with the mentality to endure would push the evolution of their physiology to match the required effort. That mentality allows us to endure, if not honor, voluntary privations.

There is no better proof of our running instinct, it seems to me, than our selective ability to forget. Any running animal will long remember the pain of stepping on a thorn; they will never repeat it if they can possibly avoid doing so. Yet, the pain and discomfort—if not agony that we may feel for hours on end during a run—is quickly forgotten or ignored, at least by us humans. Three days after the toughest race, we're eager to run again, as though the pain never happened.

We are born to run. And to run distance. To many that may seem like a moronic statement, given that so few of us currently *can* run long distance. But the paradox is that most of us now can't run distance precisely because we don't run, although in our evolutionary past we ran regularly. We had adapted to running, to the point of needing it. All of our physiological systems start to deteriorate as soon as we stop exercising, because we're not adapted to the physical rigors of being couch potatoes. We are not like bears that can lie down for more than half a year without suffering any muscle or bone degeneration, without incurring a pre-diabetic condition and hardening of the arteries. Psychology matches physiology. I can think of nothing lazier than a bear lying around in its lair all winter long. A bear has no urge whatsoever to get up and going in the wintertime. All bears that did so in the evolutionary past surely became dead bears, because they exhausted their energy reserves and starved. We're the opposite. We're more like the migrant bird, at times restless and itchy for travel, regardless how arduous it may be. As with the birds, it's because for millions of years that tendency conferred survival.

Since the invention of weapons that kill from a distance, and then the advent of agriculture, we have transformed not only the planet, but also our lives. We no longer need to run down our dinner. When we did so, we developed a most powerful weapon that we still use. We developed mind power—the ability to project far ahead to the prey that is out of sight and sound, to the finish line of a marathon or an ultramarathon. We started a long run for the thrill of the chase itself, and we pursued it beyond all reasonable immediate rewards, by mind power and imagination. We were not always successful. Many hunts ended in failure. But there was the chance of a payoff, that we might "bring home the bacon."

I often wonder how many ultrarunners there would be now if the plains and forests were teeming with game animals, if there were no "jobs" as we know them now, and if *all* of us were given the opportunity to chase down the Kudu, the wildebeest, or the deer. Imagine if you could put in a six-hour run through a beautiful pristine countryside among antelope and elk, and top that off with the strong likelihood that doing so would keep your kids from starving to death, make you a hero in the eyes of your fellows, and catch the eye of a sweetheart. How many of us would engage in ultrarunning then? How weird would it seem then?

We can't relive those times now. But the mindset is still there, and the body to back it up is built by the mind. To be an ultrarunner is not to be weird. It's to bear through the tough crust of customs, to the core of what makes us human. We're just following an ancient script to seek harmony with the conditions to which we're adapted. *A Step Beyond* can help us read and follow that script, a current-day manifestation of millions of years of our evolution. – *Bernd Heinrich*

Introduction

Ultrarunning: A Personal Journey of Discovery

The question so often asked about ultrarunning is this: why? Why run such long distances that will almost always result in long hours of pain and fatigue? Why participate in events that will yield little in the way of recognition from others? Like other complicated questions, the answers are many and varied. The most common reply is the lure of the challenge—each individual's search to find where the limits of their own endurance lies. The fact that ultramarathons are so difficult is exactly the draw. The possibility that an individual will not be able to complete the event—or will have to reach down the very depths of their physical, emotional and spiritual reserves to do so—is just the element of challenge and competition that many athletes are seeking as we begin a new millennium.

Ultra distance races are not a recent phenomenon; the history of the sport dates well back into the 19th century. Long before team sports such as baseball and football were around, "pedestrians" were competing for prize money in immensely popular challenge matches, running and walking events lasting for one or as many as six days. Thousands of spectators turned out at arenas around the U.S. and England to witness these amazing spectacles. Since that time, ultrarunning has maintained a decidedly lower profile; even today, many recreational runners are not even aware of that competitions beyond the standard 26.2-mile marathon distance exist.

Despite this relative anonymity, ultra distance racing has grown steadily during the past few decades. In the U.S. and around the world, the number of events and participants competing in races ranging from 31 miles to 3,100 miles has increased markedly. Perhaps the most significant development in ultrarunning has been the understanding and realization that almost anyone possesses the necessary physical ability to complete an ultra distance race. The myth that only super endurance athletes are able to run ultras has been largely erased.

Advancing technology has kept pace with this knowledge. This is an inevitable development, as the physical requirements placed upon individuals have demanded the most efficient and comfortable means of running for hours, days, even weeks at a time. Ultrarunning has pioneered several technological advances in running: in shoes and clothing, nutritional supplements, as well as heart rate monitors and altimeters.

In the current era, we have witnessed the evolution of ultras from a unique point of view. While much has changed in the sport, the one constant—the challenge of an individual versus pure distance—has remained. That challenge has been written about in almost every conceivable manner, from almost every angle. In *A Step Beyond*, we present a compilation of articles covering a wide range of topics.

The sport has been blessed with many colorful personalities throughout the years. The feats achieved by ultrarunners from all walks of life, from all around the world, borders on the unbelievable. Pushing the edge is an integral aspect of ultrarunning; many of those who have led the way throughout the years have become legendary. Of course, these amazing athletes have needed a forum in which to perform. Thus, races have developed and grown in tandem with the sport. There is hardly a city, state, province, or region that has not been the site of an ultramarathon. Like the runners who have competed in them, some events have become classics. Races, the people who run them, and the history created by them, are integral to the sport: we present the best articles on these subjects in those sections of *A Step Beyond*.

Of course any time there are races, there will be strategies on how to best prepare for and compete in these events. We have assembled a varied compilation of articles with advice on how to prepare for and run ultra distances. While there is no one "right way" to prepare for or complete an ultramarathon, many excellent training principles and racing strategies have been developed and refined, offering both the aspiring and veteran ultrarunner information that will help them on their personal quests.

Many articles through the years have dealt with the philosophical side of the sport. As mentioned at the outset, trying to answer the "why" of ultrarunning has provided many ultrarunners long hours of introspection and not surprisingly, some superbly written pieces. In reality, there as many reasons for attempting an ultra as there are people who attempt them. In the philosophy section of this book, we explore some of these perspectives, all of which offer thought-provoking outlooks on the sport and the activity that is ultrarunning.

While there is no denying the importance of the mental side of the sport, the fact remains that ultrarunning is a supremely physical challenge. The effects upon the human body under the duress of running extremely long distances are many. Numerous studies have been conducted on the physiological ramifications of running ultras, both by medical experts and by the most insightful and acutely aware experts—ultrarunners themselves. We truly are all "an experiment of one." In the section on physiology, we present articles ranging from normal physiological functions in running to the far-reaching and sometimes serious medical consequences resulting from pushing the body to its limits.

Ultrarunning by nature is a serious endeavor, but we can't forget the lighter side of the sport, and we have not in this book. Quite often, humor is the perfect anecdote for an ultrarunner. Levity can lift the burden, allowing a lighter and more free-spirited approach—just what is needed to balance the sometimes seemingly impossible demands of ultrarunning. To paraphrase a popular euphemism, "Ultrarunning is too important to be taken seriously!"

As with all growing entities, ultrarunning is constantly changing and redefining itself. As society evolves, so do all aspects of life, ultrarunning included. Inevitably then, the sport will be constantly examined and analyzed. With the aforementioned rapid development of technological breakthroughs and advancements, one's approach must change in order to keep pace. In a new century, the possibilities for achievement in ultrarunning by athletes of all abilities have never been more exciting. In that sense, this book is simply a snapshot in time, one that will hopefully offer a perspective on where ultrarunning has been, where it is now, and where its future lies.

The sport of ultrarunning is an integral part of many people's lives. For others, it is only a brief journey. In either case, there is much knowledge and wisdom to be gained by our own efforts. Ultrarunning is a wonderful tool for learning about ourselves—not only our physical abilities, but our motivations and inner psyches as well. If *A Step Beyond* can help you get started or move further along the road of your personal journey of discovery, we will have achieved our goal. We wish you good luck on that journey. – *Don Allison*

Training and Racing Advice

How Do You Do It?

For many long-distance runners the chasm between the 26.2-mile marathon distance and an ultramarathon can seem as wide and deep as the Grand Canyon. Most often, it is the final miles of a particularly painful marathon that come to mind when they think of attempting distances farther than that, even twice, three, or four times as long. It seems impossible.

Yet, thousands of folks do exactly that each year. Can you as well? While those ultrarunners who set records and achieve spectacular heights grab most of the headlines and attention in the sport, the majority of folks who finish ultras are not blessed with a superior genetic gift for running. Nor is ultrarunning a full-time pursuit. Yet, by utilizing proper training and racing principles they manage to finish ultra distances.

How do you run an ultra? The aforementioned intimidating magnitude of the challenge has led to a ream of advice having been handed down through the years on just how to conquer an ultra distance run. That advice has ranged from the simplistic (one step at a time) to the complex (detailed analysis of specific nutritional, physical, and mental requirements).

Like all sports, there are universal training principles that apply to all. You must gear your training towards the event you are planning to run. Thus, if it is a very long race, you must at some point run very long in training. In reality, however, no single training schedule or set of advice is applicable to all. There is not one "magic" method of training or racing that applies to all. Through the years, just about every imaginable training and racing scheme has been tested by ultrarunners. For certain runners on certain days, their system has worked magnificently. Likewise, for other runners on other days, nothing they tried worked out right.

The best approach to preparing for and running an ultra is to view your own mind and body as unique. You are a truly "an experiment of one," as the late running philosopher George Sheehan often intoned. The training that will optimally prepare you for an ultra is that which you can reasonably hope to accomplish and integrate into other areas of your daily life. Will it require a sense of purpose, a deep-seated desire to accomplish your goal? Definitely. Will you have to prioritize your life and make an occasional sacrifice in order to properly prepare? Most likely. Will you have to become a narrowly focused single-minded zealot, shutting everything else out for your training? Most certainly not. If there is one theme that runs through nearly all of the articles we offer in this section, it is that a well-planned and reasonable approach is usually one that yields the best results. While the distance may appear extreme, it is usually a sense of balance that will bring you to the finish line of an ultra, whether it is your first or your 100th race.

Of course, much "how to" advice is geared towards the beginning ultrarunner, and when taking the leap into the unknown, it helps to be armed with as much knowledge as possible. Peter Gagarin offers solid and practical advice on how to reach the finish line of your first ultra, while suggesting how you can weave a sensible mental approach into your effort. Of course, once you complete an ultra, despite declarations that you will "never do it again," many ultrarunners in fact do. With that in mind, we offer articles on a wide variety of topics that will help you run farther, faster, and perhaps more enjoyably in future ultras.

Kevin Setnes is recognized as one of the most knowledgeable and perceptive ultrarunners in the country. His performances reflect the well thought-out approach he takes towards training and racing. He offers much good advice on a number of areas in this section. Relative to training, he details how hills, speedwork, and scheduling mileage can produce better results. He also offers solid, practical advice on peaking, tapering, dealing with hydration needs, and many other pertinent topics. Shawn McDonald addresses weightlifting for runners, training the mind, the need for coaching, how to make the best use of aid stations, and off-season rest.

In addition to training correctly, race-day strategy can make an enormous difference for an ultrarunner. Karl King explains the physiological basis behind a planned walk/run strategy, one that has allowed many ultrarunners to go beyond what they thought themselves capable. A goal of many ultrarunners is to finish the Western States 100 Mile. John Medinger offers tips on doing that, while Peter Gagarin explains how to run on the rocks and how to stay on course.

Finally, ultrarunners often require the help of others to realize their dreams.

Bob Adjemian gets into the role an official pacer plays, while John Medinger's *Ten Commandments for Those Who Sit and Wait* is a superb article on crewing for an ultrarunner. Anyone who has done it can tell you is often as difficult as running the race! There is plenty of excellent advice in this "how to" section of the book. Remember, though, you are an "experiment of one."

A Beginning Ultrarunner's Guide to Running 50 Miles

by Peter Gagarin

Think back to a marathon, when you hit the wall at 20 miles and struggled to make it through the last six, and then imagine being told that you still had 24 more miles to go. The thought of doing 50 miles may seem incredibly painful, or just downright impossible. Yet many very ordinary runners manage to finish 50 miles. In doing so, more often than not they pass the marathon point in remarkable comfort, reflecting afterwards that 26 miles never felt so easy. What is the secret? Is there a way for ultra novices to prepare themselves so that their initial efforts at 50 miles will result in a greater amount of success and a lesser amount of pain?

I'm not about to claim to know all the answers, and certainly the answers can vary quite a lot from person to person, but I do think that there are some ideas and considerations that are applicable to most beginning ultrarunners regardless of how fast they may be and regardless of how much experience they have had at the sub-ultra level. Fifty miles is different from a marathon and it should be run differently. Much of the difference in how you prepare for the two distances is mental, not physical. It is not just a matter of training more miles; in fact, more miles may not be necessary. More important is the right kind of training and the right strategy during the race.

Training

There are various programs for training for a marathon for the average runner. Most require a training period of several months. Most also require reaching at least 60 miles a week for part of the period, require occasional long runs, and require some speed work. Add a taper during the last few days, a good night's sleep, and a sensible pace for the first ten miles, and the result should be a successful marathon. This approach seems to work for most runners.

How should this be changed if you are preparing for 50 miles? The answer lies in how you plan to "run" the 50 miles, and if you consider my advice on only one point, then think about the following: you should plan on "running" the 50 miles quite differently from how you run a marathon. Because they are quite different events, most marathons are run (or *raced*) as follows: you figure out what time you want to run, and from that you get the average pace needed; the first few miles are run at about this pace, or a little faster if you get carried away; the middle miles are hopefully a little under the pace, to put a little time in the bank; then the last few miles are a battle to keep from slowing down.

On the other hand, a first-time ultrarunner should run (and definitely not race) 50 miles as follows: forget about setting any time goal; just try to finish; run at a pace that is very comfortable, where conversation is easy; take regular walking breaks, starting as early as half an hour into the race; drink regularly and profusely and eat some as the day goes on; enjoy the company of your fellow runners; and with any luck, finish with a smile. Bearing in mind the different approach necessary for a 50-mile, my recommendations on training would be as follows.

Weekly Mileage

Whatever you are comfortable doing for a marathon should be sufficient to run 50 miles. Marathoners run anywhere from 30 miles up to 150 per week. So do ultrarunners. To a certain extent, more mileage helps, but more mileage can also wear you down and cause all sorts of injuries. Don't be a slave to mileage. If you are looking for a magic number ("Hey, buddy, just average 73 miles a week for six weeks and 50 miles is yours, no problem"), then I will disappoint you. The magic is in using your head to get the most out of what training mileage you can manage to do. As a rule, 30 to 40 miles a week is enough for some people, while 70 should be enough for almost everyone.

As or more important than your total weekly mileage is how you break it up day to day during the week. As a rule of thumb for any given weekly mileage, the more days you take off, the better. The worst way to do 50 miles a week is six runs of seven miles each and then a long one of eight miles on Sunday. You will get to be very good at seven or eight miles, of course, but it will not help you much to prepare for an ultra. A much better plan would be to cover the distance in only four days, with two relaxation runs of five miles each, a 15-mile, and a long outing of 25 miles. Don't feel guilty on the other three days. Rest, recover, spend some time with your family, and feel smart.

Speed Work

Repeat quarters? Repeat miles? Repeat 10-km runs? Take your choice; just remember to set your pace correctly. If you have a 3:30 marathon personal best and a 50-mile goal in the vicinity of nine hours, this translates to a pace of 10:48 per mile. Part of this will be walking, so while you are running your pace may be about 9:00 to 9:30 per mile. Your speed work should train you to be comfortable at that pace. That's probably about what your normal training pace is. The result is that you are doing your ultra speed work every time you run. More seriously, forget speed work. More important is "slow work."

Slow Work

The focus here, and I am being serious, is to practice running with minimal effort. Be smooth, be flexible, be relaxed. Much has been written about the importance of running relaxed in an ultra. This can be trained. On your easy training runs, think about running at a given pace with the least possible effort. Land gently on your feet, relax your upper body, and think about becoming a jogger instead of a runner. Anyone can be a jogger. Most of us would consider it an insult to be a jogger, but after 30 or 40 miles, you may be quite happy to be running like a jogger. Then you will wish you had spent some time training to run slowly and gently for miles and miles. So take advantage of your ultra training to run with someone slower than you for a change, and enjoy the slowness.

Really Slow Work

This is also known as walking. Marathoners hope to avoid walking, since it is seen as a sign of failure. So the last thing they do is practice walking. Ultrarunners look forward to walking, since it's seen as a sign of being smart. The smart ultrarunner incorporates some walking into his or her training. The easiest way to do this is to incorporate some walking into long runs.

Long Runs

Or, more accurately, long run and walks. Since you are going to take walking breaks in the ultra, you might as well train that way as well. How long should the long run/walks be? Rather than thinking in terms of miles, think in terms of time. You should probably have several outings in the range of three to five hours. It might be a good idea to do the first of these on a loop fairly close to home, since you will probably not yet be taking this walking stuff seriously. So you will run for two hours or two and a half, or maybe even three, and then you will crash, or bonk, or whatever you want to call it. You will feel awful and wonder why you ever wanted to run 50 miles. Welcome to the ultra blues. At least you will not have far to walk home.

Maybe the next time you will take regular walking breaks, every 20 or 30 minutes, starting right from the beginning, or every time your route heads up much of a hill. Also have plenty to drink and something to eat (because you are carrying the stuff with you). After three or four hours you will be tired. But you won't be dead meat. You will be a little smarter in the ways of ultrarunning.

The reason for specifying three to five hours is to make yourself go long enough that you cannot run that long comfortably on your existing glycogen stores. Out of necessity you will learn to walk more, learn to drink and eat more, and learn that going fast in the first couple of hours will only make you miserable later on.

It is also important to learn to walk well. Walking uses the muscles differently than running does; it also stresses the joints and tendons differently. If your body is not used to these stresses, it will get pretty sore, both during and after the race. Knowing that you will be walking a lot should make it obvious that you should spend some training time on your walking. Many ultrarunners do not.

Specific Training

Most marathon courses are paved and reasonably flat and straight. A few ultra courses are paved and reasonably flat and straight. Others are on tracks with never-ending left or right turns. Others are hilly (sometimes mountainous), with significant grades both uphill and downhill. Others are on all sorts of rough surfaces, or at altitude, or in very hot weather. Whatever the case may be for your first ultra, do some training specifically geared to the course you are going to have to do. If it is a trail ultra, train as much as possible on trails using the same guidelines as I suggested above (i.e. not only as many miles on trails as possible, but learn to run gently and efficiently on trails, learn to walk smoothly on trails, and take your long run/walks on trails). If it will be a hilly ultra, then train on the hills if possible. Walk up the hills, learning to walk quickly and efficiently, then run down, training your important downhill muscles, learning to descend as gently as possible.

Training to Eat and Drink

You are going to have to drink a lot, and probably eat some, so the good news is that this, too can be practiced. Take drinks and food on your long run/walks and partake of them regularly right from the start, rather than waiting a couple of hours until it is already too late. Try to learn what your stomach will tolerate and what it will not. Many people can tolerate drinks and food better in small doses, so sip and nibble as you go, in particular during walking breaks. Weigh yourself before and after these long runs. If you are losing several pounds, then you are not drinking enough. It may feel uncomfortable at first, but with some practice you can learn to put down a lot more fluids than you might think possible, and still keep moving.

For a change of pace go out for your long run/walk right after a big meal. You will probably want to walk a lot during the first hour, or at most run slowly and very gently. In other words, you will be doing exactly the right kind of ultra training.

Another significant thing you will be training is your ability to carry things.

If you are carrying a water bottle in one hand and a little food in the other, you will learn to carry them comfortably. If you strap a small pack around your waist, you will learn where it chafes, you will find out if the extra weight makes your lower back sore or bothers your hips, and you will see if the sloshing sound of half-full bottles drives you nuts. If any of these problems occur, shouldn't you be finding out about them during your training, when there is time to do something about it, rather than with 30 miles still to go in your ultra? After all, skin that chafes easily can be toughened, lower back muscles can be trained just like quads can, and sloshing bottles, well, you can even become used to that. Just don't try a fanny pack once, find it a little uncomfortable, and never try it again until the race because training is easier without it. You would not run an ultra in new shoes, would you?

Tapering

I have heard of several cases of people getting sick a week or two before an ultra and being unable to train, then getting very depressed, thinking their ultra dream was going out the window. Come race day, they ran a terrific race. Without realizing it, they had discovered an effective taper.

You can argue about exactly how much you should run during the last week, but I think in general less is better, and a lot less is a lot better. You will get no positive training effect from any running you do in the last few days before an ultra. You will just make yourself more tired. It is much more important to arrive at the starting line well rested, well fed, and well hydrated. Unless you are a compulsive "Type A" runner, that should not be so difficult.

Race Strategy

Eventually the day of the race comes, you are at the starting line, and someone says, "Go." You can have done all the right training but still blow the race. (Vice versa, the good news is that your training may have been lousy, but you can still pull it off with good race strategy.)

The key is to remember that you quite literally have all day, so what's the hurry? More ultras are ruined in the first 20 miles by impatience than in the last 20 by a lack of training. Forget the way you run a marathon, with the focus on mile splits and maintaining your goal pace until the finish or the wall stops you. Let the faster runners go, even if you know you can keep up with them. Sure, you may be able to for 20 miles, but then you will regret your exuberance.

Instead, your concern should be only on finishing, regardless of how much time it takes. This is more important than it sounds. If you focus on finishing, then you will not be worrying about how fast you are going. You will not be tempted to run faster than is comfortable just to match some predetermined pace. Your focus should be on running and walking as smoothly and relaxed as possible. If you are looking at your watch, it should only be to remind you that it's time to walk, or time to eat and drink some more, not time to hurry.

If you find you are breathing hard, you should slow down. You should have no trouble carrying on a conversation. If you cannot, you are running much too fast. It may feel fine right at that stage, but you will pay for it later.

It will feel very strange to slow down to a walk after only 20 minutes of leisurely running, but you will be thankful for it later in the day. Even just a couple of minutes of walking will loosen up your muscles and relax you. It will ensure that your running will feel leisurely for much longer than would otherwise be possible.

I don't think it is important exactly how often you walk, or what ratio there is between your walking and running. In any case, as the race goes on, you may wish to change the frequency of your walking breaks. The main thing to remember is to walk early and walk often. If you do, you will pass the marathon point wondering what happened to the wall; with any luck, you will get to 50 miles before any real pain sets in.

If you are the macho type who thinks walking is for sissies, well, that's all right. We need a few people like you to get ahead at the start. Then when you crash and burn at 30 or 40 miles, it will give us a real psychological lift to go cruising by. On the other hand, if you start slowly and just keep up the same pace, then you will pass many people in the last 10 or 20 miles.

The only place where I would suggest that you not be too leisurely is at the aid stations. Take the time to get what you need, of course, but do not linger too long. Ten minutes can pass in the time it takes to sit down, tighten your shoelaces, have something to drink and eat, and refill your water bottle. If there are a dozen aid stations, that's two hours gone, and it may put you in danger of not making cut-off times at some point. Furthermore, sitting down can feel awfully good, at least until you have to get up again and get going, and then it can be a real problem. You do not need to rush through the station, but if you just pick up some supplies and then eat and drink while walking further along the course, then your progress will be that much faster and less stressful.

Even if you do everything right, 50 miles will still seem like a long way. For some people it may seem so far that it seems impossible, and this feeling then becomes self-fulfilling. You doubt that you can do it, so at the slightest excuse you stop. Getting rid of these useless thoughts may be easier if you can concentrate on the course section by section. The 50 miles becomes a series of five or ten (or more) short distances, each one a goal in itself. The distance never seems insurmountable; the mind stays positive; and the completion of each section adds to your mental energy. Your legs may be doing the work, but the mind tells the legs what to do and the mind is capable of amazing things. Give it a chance to show its stuff.

Problems

Despite your best intentions, some things will go wrong. In fact, some things will almost surely go wrong. Your stomach may rebel, you may get sore joints or blisters, or you may just get really tired. What then?

Some feel the best way to learn to run an ultra is to simply run many of them. Each one is a learning experience. Various crises will occur, and the experience gained from dealing with them will make you better prepared the next time. That advice is of little use to people running an ultra for the first time, however.

But it may be more useful than you might think. If your training has gone well, you will have done several run/walks of three hours or more. You will have also probably run marathons in three or four or five hours or more. All of this is relevant ultra experience. Look back upon your successful run/walks as positive models for what to do; look back on the marathons where you hit the wall as models for what not to do. You may find that you have more experience than you think. In any case, what are some of the things that can go wrong and what can you do about them?

You Start Out Too Fast

Despite all my advice, you cannot keep from getting a bit competitive and, anyway, the first ten miles felt so easy. What to do? Sorry, on this one I can't help you much. The one positive thing is to think how good you are making other people feel as they go breezing by you later in the race.

Your Stomach Rebels

Sometimes there is no hope, but it is still worth trying a few things. Antacids help, but it is better if you take some before the problem gets too bad. So if you feel gastric distress, don't just tough it out; it will probably just get worse.

Changing drinks can make a huge difference. You have to drink a lot to stay hydrated, but after a gallon or two of a sports drink, it starts to taste pretty bad. Not only are your taste buds tired of it, so is your stomach. Changing to Coke, or just water, or soup, or anything else can sometimes bring about a miraculous improvement.

Likewise, if you have not been eating, sometimes food can settle your stomach by giving the acid something other than your stomach lining to go after. In any case, slow down. If you are running, walk for a while. If you are walking, walk slower. If you are in an ultra where your own crew is supplying you, make sure they have a variety of drinks and food. After a few hours on the go, your stomach may surprise you in what it will accept or reject. Old favorites may taste terrible, while something you might normally turn your nose at will hit the spot.

Sometimes it will just get worse no matter what you do, but other times you will get lucky and things will actually get better. Even if it does not get much better, ultrarunners have been known to go a long distance with lousy stomachs. So don't give up too easily.

Blisters

Much has been written about blisters, both regarding their prevention (through various combinations of socks, properly fitting shoes, grease, tape, and who knows what else) and their treatment (good medical care can keep you going even on badly blistered feet).

I am no expert on blisters so I will add only one thing. You can help postpone the onset of blisters by being kind to your feet. Use the standard preventative measures on known problem areas (known, because you discovered them on your long run/walks). Make sure your shoes are big enough so that when your feet swell after a few hours there is still adequate room for your toes. Run gently. Charging down hills may be fun, but it will blister your toes in no time, not to mention trashing your quads. You can run downhills just as fast by being quick and light on your feet, and your feet will thank you for it. If you feel your feet sliding in your shoes after impact, the problem is only partly poorly fitting shoes. You are also not running smoothly. Blisters will not be long in coming.

Biomechanical Problems

Joints hurt, muscles cramp, tendons complain. At a certain point, you cease to be a hero by fighting through the pain; the only smart thing is to quit and save yourself for another day. For a while, other things can be tried.

Cramps can be caused by nutritional deficiencies, so it is worth trying to eat and drink something salty. Stretching, changing shoes, and/or changing your stride a little may help a biomechanical problem, but I find the best help is a course that has some hills in it. Many biomechanical problems are caused by the repetitive stresses of running on a surface that never changes. A course with some hills is actually easier on your body than a flat course, since the stresses are continually changing. So before you automatically pick a flat course for your first 50-mile, consider one with some hills. Just make sure you do some training on hills beforehand.

Energy

You run out of gas. Everything says to quit, but that's when you should hang in there for a while. Sometimes you're suffering from low blood sugar, and drinking something sweet and eating something will get you going again in ten or 15 minutes. Sometimes you are dehydrated and you need to force yourself to drink a huge amount. Walk for a while; remember, in a marathon unplanned walking is negative because it means that you are failing further and further off your pace, while in an ultra it's positive since you are getting closer and closer to the finish.

Running out of gas can feel miserable. Suddenly the distance left seems immense while the progress you are making is imperceptible. Don't quit. Down periods are part of the ultra experience (and you don't want to miss out on any of that do you?). They usually pass. Any experienced ultrarunner can relate experiences of being dead to the world one moment, only to be full of energy a half-hour later. When you do get it back together again, it feels wonderful.

Summary

In conclusion, 50 miles is a long way and a sizable challenge, but it can be done— and enjoyed by very ordinary runners. It is logical to think of it as a primarily physical challenge, but this misses the whole mental aspect. Being smart, rather than being macho, will make the event easier and more fun, even if your running buddies still think you are just macho.

I have not yet mentioned two other resources available to help you in your first ultra. One is the amazing collection of aid station volunteers that seem to show up at ultras. They spend all day and sometimes all night in your service, feeding, nursing, encouraging, and sometimes even cracking the whip when necessary, all just to help you reach your goal. The other resource is your fellow runners. In shorter races people compete against each other. In ultras they compete *with* each other, helping each other through the bad spells. Enjoy your first ultra. Most likely it will hurt, but that will only add to the memories!

Deriving Benefits From Mileage and Long Training Runs

by Kevin Setnes

On the surface, a typical runner would assume that to prepare for ultras one must learn to run longer than the marathon distance. It is a natural assumption, since running long is the single most important training in preparation for the ultra distances. Weekly training mileage is directly linked to this training.

Recently, I read the very informative Western States 100 Mile booklet published by the race committee. It contained an interesting paragraph about the decline of performance at the event through the years. The explanation was that it was a case of overtraining. Runners would become hurt in the months leading up to the event or would simply be burned out come race day. In my opinion, the decline in Western States performances is in line with the general decline of running performances over the last ten years. Why the decline? Because there has too much emphasis on minimizing training mileage. "Getting by on less" does not always lend itself well to ultrarunning.

Weekly Mileage

Thirty years ago, the emphasis in training was on speed. With the running boom in full swing, Joe Henderson of *Runner's World* coined the term "Long Slow Distance" (LSD for short). Runners started training long distances with less emphasis on speed, as the marathon craze started to emerge. Ten years ago, the runner's training regimen somehow managed to get lost. It has been aimlessly wandering ever since. Runners' weekly mileage varied greatly, from 10 miles per week to 110 or more per week. What is the right amount of mileage per week for you? How much speed work should you do in a week? The answers are quite varied, and depending on the individual, can range from very few miles per week with no speed, to 110 miles per week with 10 to 20 miles at a fast pace.

Can an individual survive a marathon on 10 miles per week? Probably; but it will likely involve mostly walking and a great deal of suffering. Increasing mileage to 20 to 30 miles per week will ease the pain threshold and result in a faster finishing time. Increasing mileage further will add more benefits. Can one run ultras on 10 to 15 miles per week (with no cross-training)? It would be extremely difficult at best. You might be able to squeak by in a 50-km, but a 100-mile? You had better think again. There is a minimum amount of mileage required to complete an ultra within the allotted time. Finding the right amount to suit your own needs is the trick.

At what point does a runner's weekly mileage total begin to yield diminishing returns? Some say 60 to 80 miles per week. While this may be true in some cases, I believe weekly mileage is only part of the formula and, quite often, higher mileage is not really the problem. It is simplistic to say that too much mileage causes too many problems. The term overuse injury is itself overused. For ultrarunners, the benefits of running long distances are great. It's how your weekly mileage is distributed that really matters.

During the last couple of years I have met many ultrarunners and after learning more about their training patterns, have surmised that many simply don't put enough miles in during the week to properly prepare for the event they are targeting. I say this with some apprehension, because how much energy and effort one can devote to the sport, combined with home and work commitments, vary from runner to runner. However, ultra distance races, like marathons, are not easy. Why would one subject him or herself to such a demanding event without the proper preparation?

The answer may simply be that he or she does not choose to run 40 to 60 miles a week. For them, the ultra may be more of a trek, combining running with plenty of walking, which still allows them to enjoy all that is good about our sport and still realize the dream of finishing a distance like 100 miles. For these people, training takes a back seat to the camaraderie and joy they get out of ultrarunning.

However, if maximizing potential is important to you, then the key in training for ultra distances is extending your long run capability. Mixing weekly runs with ample rest, along with longer training runs, is the basis for any sound training program.

In the accompanying chart are examples of mileage programs for different types of runners. It should be noted that these charts are examples only; they do not take into account speed work or other training exercises. Speed sessions do count in the total aggregate mileage for the week. Example one is for a runner who has minimal time to train. Example two is for a moderate mileage program, and example three is for the individual who is putting in steady miles day after day. Each of the examples are based on an eight to ten-week period leading up to an ultra.

Level One (minimal training based on 25 to 40 miles per week)
Saturday   Long run: 18 to 24 miles.
Sunday   Rest
Monday   2 to 3 miles
Tuesday   Rest
Wednesday   8 to 12 miles
Thursday   Rest
Friday   2 to 3 miles

Level Two (training based on 40 to 60 miles per week)
Saturday   Long run: 20 to 28 miles
Sunday   Rest
Monday   4 to 6 miles
Tuesday   6 to 8 miles
Wednesday   10 to 12 miles
Thursday   6 to 8 miles
Friday   Rest

Level Three (training based on 60 to 100 miles per week)
Saturday   Long run: 20 to 34 miles
Sunday   2 to 6 miles easy
Monday   8 to 10 miles
Tuesday   8 to 12 miles
Wednesday   12 to 17 miles
Thursday   8 to 10 miles
Friday   4 to 6 miles easy

The common thread in each of the examples is the long training run. Long runs, it should be noted, should not be done every week. Running very long should be done approximately two out of every three weeks. Backing off with a shorter, quicker pace in the third week will vary your routine and help maintain speed. Running nothing but long slow distance will slow your overall pace in training or racing.

When increasing one's mileage, it is important to be consistent in the daily routine. Schedule runs so that they disrupt your life as little as possible. If rising at 5:30 a.m. is the only way to get your weekly runs in, then plan to run then. Set a goal of achieving this, making it a point to get to bed a half-hour earlier if need be. Is it possible to train at the lunch hour, then eat your sandwich later at your desk? This is another possible training time.

Be wary of too much pavement when increasing mileage. Concrete is much harder on the legs than asphalt. Run on even surfaces as much as possible. If you run on the road, realize that all roads have a crown of some degree; when running against traffic, it is easy to develop hip or knee problems from the unevenness of the road.

Soft surfaces save your legs immeasurably. Fine, crushed rock paths such as those designed for hiking or biking, are great places to do your runs. Trails are also excellent; while they are soft, they are also varied, strengthening different areas of the legs that otherwise would not be used on the roads.

The Long Training Run

Suppose a runner does a 25 to 30-mile training run. What is being trained during such a run? Are there other ways to achieve that training effect? How often should a runner attempt such a long run? If we understood the stress-adaptation mechanisms better, maybe we could train more effectively while reducing the chances of injury from overuse. Here is what is being trained in a long run:

- **The mind** is trained through a learning process involving subjection to major fatigue, and battling through the siren song of a dozen reasons to quit. It is difficult for a novice to appreciate this struggle, but once a runner has made it through, a powerful lesson has been learned. It is not necessary to repeat it every week.
- **The nervous system.** It is easy to run when your legs are fresh, but when glycogen stores are used up, feet are pounded, and the muscles are sore, it is important to run with an efficient form that squeezes as much propulsion as possible from what's left. You can improve your neuromuscular coordination by training under those conditions. You will never get that from running short distances. Consider, though, that you might get it from running a short race or time trial that burns up a lot of muscle glycogen, and then adding another six to ten miles. Often, running a marathon at a steady pace may provide a good opportunity to work on running smoothly when tired. Maintaining running form when tired is a skill gained only with practice while running long distances.
- **Muscle fiber.** Muscles have two basic fiber types: slow twitch (Type

I) and fast twitch (Type II). Type IIb is fast twitch fiber that begins life as a power producer, but can be persuaded by lots of endurance training to sacrifice power for endurance. If you have been running ultras for many years, you would probably find it difficult to match your 10-km personal best again. Is this muscle fiber conversion good or bad? It depends. If you are fast enough to make race cut-offs and only want to finish an ultra, then the conversion is beneficial. For this reason, if you are a competitive runner who wants to minimize time to the finish line (or win your age division), then it is bad. History shows that most top marathon performances are run by short distance runners who are relatively new to the marathon and have not had time to convert their Type IIb fibers away from speed and power.

- **Connective tissue.** Muscle fibers exert force through connective tissue. Connective tissue consists of skeletal muscles that contract to generate the motion necessary for running. They contain fast twitch and slow twitch fibers and an array of nerves and capillaries, which supply the muscle with oxygen-rich blood. If connective tissue is not strong enough to withstand the stress, efficiency will suffer after many hours of running. Part of training for ultras is to train connective tissue. While this occurs during long runs, it happens in shorter runs too, and also in cross-training such a weight lifting. Total weekly miles are more significant than long-run miles in achieving this training effect.

- **The endocrine system.** The mind, nervous system, muscle fibers and connective tissue can be trained for an ultra without doing long runs regularly, but it would be very difficult to find a substitute that would properly train the endocrine system, the glands which secrete chemicals into the bloodstream for affecting control in other parts of the body. Most runners have no idea what the endocrine system is, nor its significance to ultrarunning. An ultra places tremendous stress on the body. The endocrine system reacts to enable the body to respond to the stress. Without proper endocrine system function, completion of an ultra would be virtually impossible. That system is trained by repeated exposure to stress. That is the real reason for doing long training runs. There are many ways to stress the body, but only the long run elicits the range and coordination of responses necessary for ultrarunning. Multiple glands (pituitary, hypothalamus, adrenal) are active, and they secrete multiple chemicals (aldosterone, vasopressin, glucagon, insulin, adrenaline, cortisol, endorphins—just to name a few) that affect how we get through these long, stressful runs. The endocrine system is not fully stressed until the long run stretches over three hours. Therefore, your long training run should take you out past this point. If you train at ten-minute-per-mile pace, then 18 to 24 miles is suggested for your long training run. If you are in the eight-minute-per-mile range, then runs of 25 to 30 miles should be included in your training program. The endocrine system can strengthen with moderate training, but can also be pushed to the point of fatigue and collapse by too much stress. That is really what overtraining is all about. Muscles recover rapidly from an ultra, but the endocrine system takes many weeks to fully recover. Too many long runs in too short a time will push a runner into an overtrained state that will force rest, not so much for the muscles, but for the endocrine system.

Recovery

Recovery from ultras and long training runs is an area in which people often get into trouble. It is critical after having stressed the body over an ultra distance to recover properly. Don't be afraid to take occasional days off. I often take about five days off from running after an ultra, and instead will substitute walks with my dogs. After about a week I resume with an easy week of running at no more than an hour per day. If it is a long training run, recover by refraining from intense speed work in the following days. If you are a level two or three runner, then your daily mileage following a long training run should be at a pace that is significantly slower than your normal training pace. I know of some elite runners, who after running 30 miles on Saturday like to follow it up with 20 more on Sunday. The reason they can do this, is that:

- They are highly trained athletes.
- The second day is at a reduced pace (minute per mile less) and treated as a recovery run.
- They did not deplete their energy stores and replenished during and immediately after the 30-mile training run.

Summary

What are the implications for training? Short runs don't stress the body enough for much growth; consider them as stepping stones to longer workouts, or just for the joy of running. Short, very fast work sessions, while enhancing leg speed, running form, and strength, also create a very bad habit for ultrarunners: burning carbohydrates like a spendthrift. For this reason, speed should not comprise more than 10 to 15 percent of your weekly miles.

Strength and speed can be built into medium distance runs that don't stress the endocrine system. Runs of 10 to 15 miles with embedded tempo pace (after three to four miles of warm-up) pack a lot of training stimulus into a moderate distance.

The endocrine system is not heavily stressed until a run goes for many hours. Long runs, which only dip into this area, subject the body to a lot of mechanical stress without doing much to stress the endocrine system. Given the rate of adaptation of the body after a long run, it is probably better for most runners to do long runs in the range of three to four hours, but do them less frequently (every two to three weeks instead of weekly).

In the weeks leading up to an ultra event, refrain from long training runs. The last long run is typically three weeks prior to the event. If you run long two weeks before the event, it should be done at a reduced pace on a soft surface. Of course, all runners need an appropriate base before attempting such long runs, and novices need to work their way up with runs of intermediate distances.

Training mileage varies, depending upon one's level of commitment. Increasing mileage properly while minimizing the risks can bring added benefits. The single most important ingredient in any ultrarunner's training regimen is the long training run.

Hill Running
by Kevin Setnes

Encountering uphills on the run can either be an ultrarunner's worst enemy or a familiar friend he or she has come to know through training sessions. While hills are almost inevitable in trail ultras, they are non-existent in ultras run on the track or small paved loops in urban areas. Hill training, however, can be a key ally in attempting an ultra. Understanding how to approach hill training and its benefits will enable you to get through the climbs much more easily when you encounter them in an ultra.

The Benefits
Uphill training is really just the body working against gravity. We all know that climbing stairs, walking up a steep grade, climbing a ladder, or running up a hill creates a lot more work for the body. Breathing becomes significantly greater, muscles quickly begin to ache from the acidity being built up in the legs, and the heart rate begins to race upward. It is basic physiology, but going uphill is very hard work.

The benefits lie in the area of strengthening. "Strengthening your body's legs will improve your overall running form," says Owen Anderson, Ph.D., former editor of *Running Research News* and monthly columnist for *Runner's World*. Strengthening, specifically the tendons and ligaments, will also reduce your chance of injury in these areas.

"Hill training is probably one of the best single forms of strength training, as it forces the muscles in your hips, legs, ankles and feet to contract in a coordinated fashion while supporting your full body weight," says Anderson. He also believes that other forms of strength training, such as those found in training rooms, including knee extensions, leg curls, presses, and squats, are the *least* helpful routines for runners. He says, "It's true that these exercises will strengthen your quads (for example), and strong quads are needed for running. They are being done from a seated position in isolation from the other muscles and not with your full body weight." Thus, he has been known to state, "That's fine if you are training to run in a seated position."

Hill running incorporates all of the motions of running and strengthens your leg muscles, tendons and ligaments in concert with one other. Another benefit is the anaerobic conditioning that it brings. Studies have shown that hill training will adapt your legs for better running efficiency and that hill-trained runners have higher concentrations of "aerobic enzymes" in their legs, which allows them to run at higher levels and for longer periods without fatigue.

Types of Hill Training

There are three primary types of hill training routines. Each offers a different set of benefits. One is to run a course that is rolling to very hilly. This is probably the most enjoyable form of hill training and offers some flexibility in how you structure your workout. You can run the course by attacking the hills, incorporating a little fartlek when you feel like it. You can also "hammer the downs" to condition the quads for an upcoming event that may contain plenty of downhill running.

The second form of hill training is to run a series of repetitive climbs, manageable, yet difficult enough so that after six to eight you are left pretty fatigued, with a burning sensation in your legs. The length of the hills can be anywhere from one to three minutes in duration. This will build good stamina and speed, very beneficial to the ultrarunner. After each run up, the runner should gently jog back downhill to repeat the same routine.

The third form of hill training is more explosive, incorporating repeats of short, steep climbs, which will result in more power in your legs. Running up these hills requires great arm action and thus is anaerobic in nature.

Whichever type of hill training you choose and whenever you run hills, it is imperative to concentrate on proper form. This carries over to any form of strength training. Erratic form, especially when fatigued, causes inefficiency and adds to the risk of injury.

Hill running should be part of the base foundation phase of your training. Strengthening the legs through hill training will build efficient leg motion and allow for longer stride length, which equates to a faster running pace. It is imperative to note though that since hill training is strength training, it should be reduced well before your next major competition or event. Ron Johnston, an ultrarunner and running coach from New Hampshire, has studied strength training and how it affects endurance runners. He says, "You should cut out intensive hill training four to eight weeks prior to the event you are peaking for. Any strength training builds bulk muscle; you must stop it completely to allow the body to re-focus and learn to turn over (the running stride) at rates you'll encounter in competition."

Johnston concurs with Owen Anderson's belief that hill training is an excellent form of strength training, especially for endurance runners. He says, "A running motion that works all the muscles in concert is extremely effective for ultrarunners." His studies, which pertained to traditional strength training (in a training room or facility) showed an increase in running efficiency, with less oxygen consumed as the runner progressed.

How to Run Hills

Running hills correctly can make your next ultra much more rewarding. Running hills aggressively will not benefit you physically in any way. It may offer a psychological advantage, but that advantage will be short-lived.

Studies by a British doctor, Mervyn Davies, found that energy expended in an uphill is not gained back on a similar downhill. In other words, he was able to calculate the additional cost of running uphill and the energy savings of running downhill and found that the energy savings on the downhill equaled only half of the energy that would be lost when running on an equivalent uphill grade.

According to Tim Noakes, author of *Lore of Running*, running uphill increased energy cost by about 2.6 ml/kg/min for each one percent increase in gradient. Consequently, downhill running reduced the oxygen cost by about 1.5 ml/kg/min for each one percent of down gradient. Noakes points out the practical implication that time lost going uphill can't be regained by running an identical down gradient.

So how should a runner approach a hill? The key is efficiency. Run as efficiently as you can and listen to your breathing. Shorten the stride slightly and don't lean unnecessarily into the hill. This will better enable you to maintain form while going uphill. If you are wearing a heart rate monitor, try to not let your heart rate go up more than five to seven percent above the target rate you selected. For example, if you are running at a heart rate of 150, then try to keep your heart rate from going over 160 on an uphill. It is equally important to refrain from charging up hills that come up very early in an ultra. The Western States 100 Mile offers a good example. At the start, you begin an immediate ascent of more than 2,500 feet within the first four miles. It is fairly cold at this 5:00 a.m. start, you are not at all warm after standing around awaiting for the start, so the last thing the body needs is a jackrabbit start up a 2,500-foot climb. When I participated in my first Western States 100, it was comforting to see that most veterans took it at a very leisurely pace during the first hour. Charging up such a steep hill between 5:00 and 6:00 a.m. is the worst way to begin an ultra, unless of course, you are planning to set a course record.

Hills are an integral part of ultrarunning, especially on the trails. If you become familiar with them through proper training, you will then know how to approach them in an ultra, and can begin to use them to your advantage.

Running Style
by Kevin Setnes

Have you ever stopped to watch the wide array of individual running styles? Whether it is an ultra, a marathon or any other running event, running styles vary greatly from individual to individual. From male to female, young to old, running mechanics of running vary greatly.

The legendary Emil Zatopek of Czechoslovakia, who won three gold medals in distance running at the 1952 Olympic Games, was widely regarded to have had absolutely horrible running mechanics. Pictures often show him grimacing while in a hunched over running style. What Zatopek may have lacked in style, he more than made up for in a competitive drive that was hard to match. Add to that his incredible training regimen, which has taken on legendary status, and you have a champion for the ages.

Is there a proper running style that is more efficient than others? Is there a right or wrong running style? Should you try to change your running style? These are all valid questions worth exploring.

What is Correct?

Simply put, there *is* a correct way to run. Humans have evolved over time to become upright animals. We walk and run in an upright, mostly erect position. Have you ever heard the phrase "run tall"? The premise is that if you hold your head up and keep your back straight with a straight line down to your hips, which in turn should have a direct line to your foot strike, you'll have a mechanically sound running style. Keeping your feet underneath you is another way of stating it. This results in an economy in motion for distance runners. Frank Shorter has always been an excellent example of a runner with a correct running style. In fact, it may have been his most valued asset as a distance runner. It worked to his advantage so much that it led him to the marathon distance, where he enjoyed his greatest achievement in Munich, winning the Olympic marathon in 1972.

The best running style starts with the hands, extends to the arms, torso, hips and then the legs. Hands should be kept in a loose fist with the wrists fixed. Arm carriage should be level and shoulders should not sway. You should not have a noticeable forward lean and your torso should not sway from side to side. A perpendicular line should run from your head to your hips, to the ground where your foot strikes. Remember as a child being told to "sit up straight"? Think of standing up straight, and then think about running with this correct posture, standing tall and erect. If you do this, you are well on your way to improving your natural running posture.

Stride length should also be natural and only change with proper training. Simply trying for a longer stride will not help your running economy. If you keep the running posture upright, your legs should naturally land directly beneath you. Improving leg strength through proper training will extend stride length—and ultimately running speed.

Foot strike should occur after the foot has reached its farthest point forward and has begun its backward motion. When the foot strikes the ground, it should do so directly beneath your knee and center of gravity. Don't overstride. If your foot strike is too far forward, ahead of your center of gravity, it will result in a braking action, which can lead to all kinds of problems.

Don't bounce! Keeping as light on your feet is another thing to focus on. Looking straight ahead and keeping the horizon as level as possible when running is a good posture exercise.

What's Wrong?

It is easy to spot incorrect running style. The most noticeable error is keeping the head down, swaying from side to side. Another is arm carriage that is not symmetrical and often rigid. A bouncing appearance in the stride is an example of wasted energy. Both feet strike the ground unevenly in that case.

One's fitness level can have a dramatic effect on running style. If you are extremely fatigued and exhausted from a hard effort, it is very hard to hold good form for very long. This is especially true if you are undertrained and trying to accomplish a running pace that it is unreasonable. The heart does not lie; if yours is "racing," then you are going too fast. Ease back and concentrate on keeping good form.

Run within yourself as much as possible. Overstriding is very inefficient and will ultimately cause the ultrarunner to tire well before the finish line. It is better to understride than it is to overstride. A shorter stride is more efficient for an ultrarunner. Stride length should and will only change with an increase in training. The best advice is to simply not worry about stride length. Ultrarunners should instead focus on posture to run with better style.

Should You Change?

Most runners have some deficiency in their running style, so don't worry if your mechanics are not perfect. A perfect running posture is usually God-given, often seen only in exceptional runners. All athletes may achieve greater performance if properly trained and motivated. Remember that running mechanics are only part of the equation of good running performance.

Any runner can improve his or her running style by focusing on some simple techniques. It is important to point out, however, that dramatic changes in your posture should not be made. You are who you are, and trying to make wholesale changes may have a negative result.

They don't give points for style in ultrarunning and many of us don't necessarily look pretty when running such long distances; however, identifiable fundamentals of correct running style can be corrected. The following techniques may help you achieve better posture when running and ultimately better efficiency:

- Think tall and keep your head up.
- Keep your back straight by tucking in your butt.
- Keep your hands in a loosely clenched fist, with wrists fixed.
- Keep your arms low and gently swing them from side to side.
- Keep your facial features relaxed. Let the jaw drop and don't grimace.
- Keep the stride and length of it flowing naturally. Don't overstride!

Being relaxed and tension free leads to more effective muscle use. A grimace or rigid arm carriage works against the effectiveness of muscles working smoothly. Few of us are blessed with great running mechanics, but style isn't everything in ultrarunning. Training, running tenacity, and smart pacing can overcome an inefficient style. Thinking about your posture when running will benefit your running economy, however, and result in you becoming a more stylish and effective runner.

Using a Heart Rate Monitor in Ultrarunning

by Shawn McDonald

Introduction

Heart rate monitors are used by elite athletes in a number of sports to help them plan, conduct, and analyze training to sharpen fitness without overtraining. Runners at elite levels who compete in races on roads, on the track, or in marathons use these monitors to continually quantify the intensity and volume of their training sessions. Due to electronic advances and increased competition from the many current monitor manufacturers, the price of a basic heart rate unit has dropped in the past several years, down to the $50 range. New features are added each year, some of which are useful and some of which are not, at least for most runners. In this article, we will review current technology used in monitors, the basics of how to use a monitor in training and during races, and whether you really need a monitor at all. Sample workouts using a monitor are presented for both aerobic and speed training sessions.

Do you need to use a monitor?

There are many benefits to using a monitor in training and racing. It provides a continuous measurement of the work and intensity level of the runner during a workout or race. Using a monitor allows the athlete to take into account the effect of environmental factors such as heat, altitude, or a headwind, and to thus make adjustments to his or her pace, in order to maintain an even effort over many miles and hours of running. This allows one to complete long training runs with confidence and to run races as fast as possible, given one's recent training. The data from a monitor can also allow you to spot overtraining. For example, suppose you usually have a heart rate of 140 beats per minute while running at eight minutes per mile on flat ground. If while doing a long run you find your heart rate at 150 or 155 while running this pace and the weather and altitude are normal, you might want to shorten the planned run. To get out of the slightly overtrained state, you would then rest the next day or two to recharge your batteries, so you can return to running well in upcoming training.

A monitor can also help you to work hard enough during speed training or while doing hill repeats. You can learn what a hard, slightly anaerobic effort feels like and then duplicate that effort for each repeat or interval in a session. Using a monitor for higher intensity runs also allows you the freedom to run on a variety of courses (roads and trails) during these workouts. The heart rate data provides an exact measurement of running intensity without having to know the precise distance you are covering during each hill repeat, interval, or pickup. Keeping a close eye on your heart rate is a good way to ensure that your run or cross-training workout on the day after a long or hard run is done at an easy aerobic effort, helping you to complete "active recovery." Using a monitor can also tell the athlete his or her baseline fitness at the start of a training program and provide an increase in motivation and interest by offering a new perspective on training and recovery. As the runner becomes fitter, he or she will see the results in the heart rate and will be able to run faster at a given heart rate after a number of weeks and months of training.

There can be a few negatives to using a heart rate monitor. For some runners, the goals of a given run and focus on overall goals can be lost in the sea of numbers and data the monitor can generate. It is important to know the reasons you are doing each workout and how that fits into your overall preparation for an upcoming race. Runners using a monitor might be inclined to train less, feeling that other athletes might push them too hard or slow them down on a given run. In using a monitor, a runner might keep his or her eyes on the watch so much that he or she might trip and fall while running or fail to spot an oncoming car. The runner can also forget to drink fluids and eat regularly during a run because he or she is focused so much on their heart rate and maintaining a certain effort level, and thus be more prone to either dehydration or bonking. These are some of the pros and cons you should consider in deciding whether to purchase and use a monitor in your training and/or racing.

Technology

A typical heart rate monitor consists of a transmitter that is encased in a strap worn around the chest and a receiver that is similar to a wrist watch. The receiver processes the signal from the transmitter and displays heart rate and other data on the face of the watch. A few of the current monitors combine the transmitter and receiver into the watch and thus remove the need for the chest strap. The signal from the transmitter is updated every second or two, so the monitor picks up changes in heart rate fairly quickly. There will be a delay of a few seconds between when you start to run faster and when you see an increase in your heart rate on the receiver. Try to ensure that there is a good contact between your skin and the chest strap when you put on the heart rate monitor. Otherwise, the monitor won't start to pick up your heartbeat until you have exercised for a few minutes and have sweated enough to form a skin-tight contact.

The transmitter in a monitor runs on the power of a battery; a few recent models allow the monitor owner to change the battery. This can be a benefit in that you will not have to send the transmitter back to the manufacturer or make a trip to a service center to have a new battery installed. To avoid being without a working monitor, you might want to have a second transmitter strap to use if your primary model runs out of power. Additional transmitters can be purchased separately from a monitor for a cost of about $10. The typical battery life for most models is several hundred hours of use, or one to two years for most runners. Batteries for self-installation models cost a few dollars.

In the last few years, a number of manufacturers have entered the heart rate monitor market. Most makers offer a few models of monitors, from a basic unit with few special features all the way up to a top-of-the-line unit that will store data from many workouts and allow the download of data to a computer or even a cell phone. Top manufacturers include Polar (one of the oldest makers), Nike, Reebok, Timex, and more recently Garmin (which combines their units with GPS capability to measure distance and speed). To compare features, ease of use, and quality measurements of different models and manufacturers, the reader can look up a variety of organizations such as *Consumer Reports*, *Runners World*, and *UltraRunning*, which have tested monitors in past years.

Monitor features

Some of the most useful features to look for when selecting a monitor include an out-of-zone alarm with re-settable limits, a workout and time-in-zone timer, an average heart rate mode, and a dual display of heart rate and percent of maximum heart rate. For some monitor models, an alarm (beeping) will sound when the heart rate is either below the lower limit or above the upper limit that the athlete has previously set. Average heart rate is one measure of the quality and effort level of a given run and can be recorded in a runner's training log to track progress and training load. Measuring time spent in various heart rate zones can help runners complete most of their mileage at quality effort levels, as well as track how much of their training is done at upper effort levels, to allow for steady increases in aerobic endurance. If you will be sharing use of the monitor with a friend or spouse, it is helpful to get a monitor that allows two or more series of settings to be saved and recalled at the start of your workout. On these models, the maximum heart rate and the heart rate that corresponds to 70 percent of maximum can be pulled up for each runner. If you want to save heart rate data to a computer, you will want to purchase a monitor that has one of a variety links that will connect the receiver of the monitor to your computer for data download. There are a number of computerized running logs that allow for input and analysis of this heart rate monitor.

Use of a monitor in training

For long training runs, the runner can set the upper and lower alarms on the unit at 65 and 75 percent of their maximum heart rate. The formula used would be: lower limit = 0.65(maximum minus resting) plus resting; and limit = 0.75(maximum minus resting) plus resting, where maximum is your maximum heart rate and resting is your heart rate when you awake in the morning before you get out of bed. For speed workouts, the athlete can put the monitor into the percent of maximum heart rate mode and then seek to run each interval at a pace where he or she hits a particular percent value (such as 90) over the second half of each interval. Recovery jogs between each interval or repeat would be of sufficient duration and at a slow enough pace to allow for the recovery of heart rate back to 65 percent of maximum.

A narrow range of heart rate (say plus or minus three beats per minute) can be a goal of the runner completing a tempo run. The athlete can use the alarm feature of the unit and attempt to run the tempo segment of the workout without hearing the alarm beep at all while keeping the heart rate in the range of 85 to 89 percent of maximum, for example. Alternatively, the runner can use the monitor in normal mode without the alarm turned on, then try to keep his or her heart rate and effort constant by viewing the monitor receiver watch every ten or fifteen seconds during any tempo segments of the run. The key to running a good tempo is to run a constant effort over the entire segment, making adjustments for running uphill versus downhill, or into a headwind or downwind. These adjustments can be difficult to gauge unless the runner has a good sense of different effort levels.

For an easy recovery run, the athlete should set the upper alarm limit at 70 percent of maximum heart rate and the lower limit at 55 percent of maximum. If the runner starts to put in too much effort during such a recovery run and hears the alarm, he or she should then either slow the pace or walk for fifteen to thirty seconds and then resume running at a slower pace. Running too hard on recovery days is one of the most common mistakes that runners new to ultras make in training.

Maximum heart rate

You can determine your maximum heart rate using two common methods. The first methods are linear formulas based on your age. The standard formula is: MHR = 220 minus age, where MHR is the maximum heart rate of the athlete who is "age" years old. This formula is good on average for running, although for individual runners it can be off by several beats per minute (as could other formulas). A research-based formula developed by Londeree and Moeschberger (1982) is: MHR = 206 minus 0.771 x age. A more recent formula developed by researchers Miller et al. (1993) is: MHR = 217 minus 0.85 x age. For a runner who is 50 years old, these three formulas give MHR values from 170 to 177. Slight adjustments can be made if you have been sedentary lately (add a few beats per minute) or if you are fit and over 50 years old (see the on-line article by Brian Mackenzie on maximum heart rate).

A fitness stress test administered by a doctor or sports physiologist is the other major way to determine an athlete's maximum heart rate. As the athlete works at harder and harder levels during the test, the heart rate will increase and then plateau at a value that is the maximum heart rate. Note that the maximum heart rate is sport specific, so runners should have the test done while running on a treadmill. The maximum heart rate for the same athlete while cycling will often be about three to four beats per minute lower than when running, and while swimming would be about twelve to fifteen beats per minute less than while running. A self-administered test for runners who are fit and have had a recent physical checkup by their doctors is the following: run a warm-up of two or three miles at an aerobic effort level, then run a series of half-mile intervals (probably four to six total) as fast as you can. Do a minute or two of easy jogging between each interval. Note the heart rate reading over the last minute of the third, fourth, and fifth intervals and figure out the average heart rate over this period. This is your maximum heart rate. Note that maximum heart rate will not change much over a short period of time, such as a few months, and its value will slowly decrease over the years as you age.

The other part of the equation to calculate the heart rate zone (or percent of maximum heart rate) for a given running pace is the athlete's resting heart rate. This value can be measured each morning when you awaken, before getting out of bed. Take your pulse for 15 seconds and then multiply by four. An average value over the course of a week should be figured, since your resting heart rate can vary from day to day, depending on how well you have recovered from previous training. In addition, your resting heart rate will change with fitness level as you progress in your training program, and could decrease by several beats per minute or more as you go from unfit to very fit states. Thus, you should determine your resting heart rate every few weeks throughout the year.

Use of a monitor during an ultra

A heart rate monitor can be used as a guide in setting your pace during an ultra, whether you are running uphill, downhill, or on level ground. Based on your measured maximum and minimum heart rates, you should decide a few days before a race at what average heart rate you will attempt to run the race. The average value will depend on the length of the race as well your perceived effort during and after long training runs completed at various average heart rate values. Set the alarm limits on your monitor at five to ten beats per minute above and below this average heart rate value and try to maintain your effort during the first two-thirds to four-fifths of the race without the alarm sounding. You will want to use a narrower heart rate range if you are running a road ultra on flat terrain than if running an ultra on mountain trails, where it is harder to maintain a constant effort.

As an example, lets suppose a runner has a maximum heart rate of 180 and a resting heart rate of 50. If he or she decides the goal is to run an upcoming 50-km race at a 70 percent heart zone value (see the book by Edwards for an explanation of different heart zones), this would correspond to an average heart rate of 141 (calculated as 0.7[180 – 50] + 50). This heart rate is just below 80 percent of the maximum for this athlete. If the race route is fairly hilly, the runner might set the lower and upper alarm limits at 134 and 148 beats per minute, respectively. If the same runner were competing in a 50-mile race, he or she might set the average heart zone value in the middle 60s (about 75 percent of maximum heart rate), or a value near 133, with lower and upper limits of 125 and 140.

If you hit your upper heart rate limit, slow your running pace for a few minutes or walk for a minute or two to return your heart rate to the middle of your goal range. If you bump up against your lower limit and the terrain allows (if you are not on a steep rocky downhill for example) try to increase your forward pace and leg turnover for a minute or two to push your heart rate up by a few beats per minute. The alarm is most likely to go off when you are heading up or down a steep hill. In this case, aim to mix in walking or adjust your pace before your heart rate climbs or drops and the alarm sounds. Late in the race you can turn off the alarm on the monitor and aim to increase your effort as you push on towards the finish while moving at a pace where you can run all or most of the remaining terrain.

At some point during an ultra you might find you are unable to maintain your heart rate in the goal range, even when on flat ground or on an uphill. This could be a sign that you have low blood sugar and thus should eat a small snack to gain energy to resume a stronger running pace. It could also signal that you are dehydrated and should drink a quart or more of water and sports drink over the next hour. The cause of the lower effort could also be mechanical damage to your leg muscles. If you have been drinking fluids and eating regularly then the latter cause is likely the problem, and the muscle soreness and tightness can be abated to some extent by getting a massage or doing a few minutes of stretching during a rest break off the trail or road or at the next aid station.

Sample workouts using a monitor

To complete an interval workout using a heart rate monitor, first decide the number and length of intervals you wish to complete and your target heart rate (percent of maximum) for each interval. For example, for a runner with a maximum heart rate of 180 who wants to run three repeats of one mile length each at 90 percent of maximum, the target heart rate is 162. This runner should aim to complete each of these mile repeats at a pace where he or she hits the target heart rate about a quarter of the way into each interval and maintains that heart rate plus or minute three beats per minute. Recovery jogs between each interval would be of a duration and at a pace to allow recovery to 65 percent of maximum, or a value of 120. This runner would complete a warm-up and cool down running (about two to three miles each) before and after these intervals at 70 percent of maximum heart rate, or a value near 125. For a hill repeat workout, first decide the number and duration of hill repeats you want to complete. Aim to run each uphill at a pace where your heart rate is 85 to 92 percent your maximum heart rate over the last half to three quarters of the hill, depending on whether the repeats are long (lower end of this range) or short. Jog back down the hill to allow your heart rate to recover into the range of 60 to 70 percent of maximum.

The process of using a monitor during a long run is similar to that used during an ultra. Decide on a goal heart rate (probably near 70 percent of maximum) and then set the alarm limits several (five to ten) beats per minute above and below this value. Adjust your pace during the run and mix in walking breaks (usually on uphills) to maintain your effort and heart rate so that the monitor alarm does not go off or only sounds briefly during your run. Aim to run 95 percent or more of the workout in your goal heart rate range. After the run, if your monitor has such features, you can view how much of the run you were in your goal heart rate range and note this in your training log, as well as examine a graph of your heart rate on a computer after downloading the data.

Summary

Use of a heart rate monitor in training can help an athlete train more consistently with a reasonable amount of high intensity work, while avoiding overtraining. During races, a monitor acts as a guide to help the runner adjust effort levels so that he or she can run as fast a possible given current fitness. Heart rate information can help a runner adjust pace to match environmental factors such as heat, altitude, or a head wind. The most useful features of a monitor include upper and lower limit alarms, a heart rate zone timer, stopwatch, and ability to recall or store heart rate data from the previous one to several workouts. The athlete should still rely on signals from the body to make pace adjustments during a run and to make decisions about volume and intensity for planning future training.

Reaching a Peak
by Kevin Setnes

Peaking for top performance in an ultra requires skillful planning and specific training that follows the principles of periodization. Runners seeking peak performance sometimes need to separate themselves from the recreational side of ultrarunning in order to be truly competitive at a higher level.

Runners should not kid themselves into believing that they can sustain a high level of ultrarunning performance for a long period of time. In a sport that is so physical and where mental toughness is a prime factor in completing the event, the human body is only able to perform at its peak for a relatively short period of time. This time can vary, but rarely lasts longer than a couple of months.

Ultrarunners who enter an event every month are either not achieving their true potential or are reaching plateaus that result in a level of inconsistency. This is no different than in other sports, in which champions rise to the top when the prize is greatest. Tiger Woods primes himself for the major championships of golf. In baseball, the Yankees' record improves in the playoffs and World Series. The Lakers peak to absolutely dominate the NBA in the championship playoffs. Road cyclists such as Lance Armstrong gear their year around the Tour de France.

Planning your year well in advance is the best way to build peak performance. First, establish your base mileage buildup periods. Specific training, as well as taper periods, have to be considered for peak success. Link your events together such that they complement each other and allow for plenty of recovery time. Prioritize your events in order of importance and allow for a "down period" or season-ending vacation from training.

Planning

Establish a schedule a full year in advance and don't deviate from it, if at all possible. If the plan is not sound and thought out with clear objectivity, it will be compromised if changes occur on a whim. Establish two or three major events that you would like to peak for. Next, select three to four secondary events that can complement the major events, or act as mid-term goals. If a runner takes on much more than a half-dozen ultra events, races begin to have a recreational feel. There is nothing wrong with that, but a competitive runner needs to balance his or her needs in order to achieve his or her stated goals.

Buildup

Each event should have finite buildup period. In most cases this consists of a base mileage buildup that gradually incorporates longer runs on the terrain on which the race is to be contested. Base building is the foundation of any training program. Consistency is the key to successfully establishing this period of training. Six to eight-week buildup periods are usually long enough to bring one to a level of fitness, at which time the runner can begin to incorporate specific training that will allow him or her to accomplish the goals of the planned event.

Specificity Training

This period lasts usually three to four weeks and consists of your longest training runs, hill (up or down) training, speed, and technical trail preparation. Usually runners will back off their mileage during this period; however, much of the mileage will be done in their longest training runs. The main focus has to be quality, with sufficient rest in between sessions to allow for the intense effort required to achieve results.

Taper Periods

Tapering for an event is also important. Those who opt not to taper will likely experience inconsistent results and are not likely to achieve their true potential. While tapering for an event, the objective is to accumulate enough rest so that the mind and body can deliver the desired peak performance. The length of a taper is usually one to three weeks for most runners.

Links

Linking your events to one another when appropriate can be extremely beneficial. Ultra distance events vary greatly in distance and scope. Some runners excel at trails, while others are standouts on the road. Making the transition from one distance or type of event to another is easier for some, more difficult for others.

Trail races can provide strength for a road event later on. The trail 100-milers in North America require a great deal of patience and adaptability to changing conditions. Preparing for this kind of event, while quite a contrast to training for a road event, builds physical and mental versatility.

Using a shorter run as a buildup for a longer event is also a good way to try out techniques that you are experimenting with. A 50-km road event can be a great stepping-stone to a 50-mile or 100-km road race. Fifty-mile trail races leading up to a trail 100 are ideal. An example of this would be running northern California's Miwok 100 Km in early May, followed by the Western States 100 Mile in late June. The key is to treat the 100-km as if it were the full 100-mile distance. Resist the urge to race. Rather, focus on the technical aspects of the trail, and practice energy plans, pacing ideas, and other aspects that will come into play in the 100-mile.

Focusing Your Efforts

You can harness your competitive energy and use it to peak for a specific performance if you prioritize on a single goal. Most coaches suggest that you only have so much competitive juice and thus must use it wisely.

Mentally preparing for an event involves visualization. View the race in your head many times over in training. Remove yourself from many of the "busy activities" that surround you day-to-day and practice different relaxation methods. Psyching oneself is a skill that is one of the critical final pieces to peak performance. What inspires you to perform at your best? Why are you running this event? Think about the large investment of time and energy that brought you to the starting line.

Peaking for a performance is sometimes tough to do when we are lured in by so many events that crowd the calendar year. It is hard for many of us to resist the temptations of running any one of a number of events in our area, but those who do will develop the crucial ability to train for peak performance. "Carpe Diem!"

Tapering for Performance
by Kevin Setnes

If an ultrarunner's ability is primarily determined by the extent of his or her training, tapering goes a long way towards determining the actual performance achieved. It is one area of a runner's training that causes a lot of anguish, since it is usually a time filled with a series of doubts, primarily whether training has been satisfactory to his or her goals and needs. Have you done enough long runs? Have you put in enough strength training? What about your speed level?

These questions often cause the runner to cram more training in the final weeks than is necessary. This often results in a sub-par performance. Tapering is absolutely essential in order to reach a consistent level of performance.

Tapering involves resting the body (and mind) in preparation for a specific event. It is the gradual process by which the runner cuts back the training regimen to fully rejuvenate muscles and tissues, in order to perform at maximum capability. Precisely when and how much to taper is an inexact science, subject to much debate. While there is no exact definition of how to taper for an event, there are given principles that runners should strive to follow to achieve a consistent level of success.

In the book, *Lore of Running*, Tim Noakes devotes a chapter to Arthur Newton, an English runner from the first half of the century who helped revolutionize the way distance runners train and perform. He established nine rules of training that should be the foundation on any running program, for athletes of all abilities, from the world-class runner to the novice beginner.

In the ninth principle he states the importance of resting before competition. Up until this time few studies had been conducted on resting the body for competition. He stressed the importance of resting (tapering) prior to an event, eventually leading more runners and coaches to employ tapering as an integral part of their training.

In more recent times, a University of Illinois study (1981) showed that fitness levels remain the same, even though athletes reduced training volumes over a 15-week period.

Another study done at McMaster University in Ontario examined different groups of runners who each cut back their weekly training volume. The most extreme cutback was a 90-percent cutback in volume.

When subsequent performance tests were done, the 90-percent taper group showed the greatest performance improvement. Owen Anderson, publisher of *Running Research News,* points out that tapering is very important in determining performance. The key is to rest, with a reduction of volume, while at the same time increasing the percentage of intense running. Anderson sums up the importance of tapering by saying, "Tapering works by producing an incredible array of positive changes for athletes, including augmented glycogen stores, increased aerobic enzymes, expanded blood plasma, upgraded economy, better repair of muscles and connective tissue, improved neuromuscular coordination, and heightened mental confidence."

How to Taper

The key to tapering correctly is to accumulate enough rest, while at the same time sharpening the abilities that were attained in training, all to maximize running performance. The methodology of tapering varies from person to person, but assuming you have had a sufficient base to build up your fitness level, resting properly before your next event can do wonders for your performance.

Most taper periods are at least a week long, with most runners using a seven to ten-day rest cycle before their major events. I feel that an even longer taper cycle is better, up to three weeks, in which the runner gradually cuts back his or her quantity by 25 percent or more per week.

Take for example a runner who normally runs 60 miles per week in training. With three weeks to go before the major event, the runner would reduce that amount to 45 miles, followed by 30 miles, and lastly a 15-mile week before the event (Figure 1).

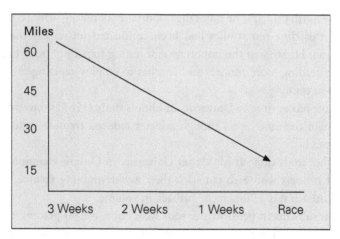

Figure 1

This tapering of mileage allows the muscles and connective tissue to fully recover from the rigors of training. Heavy training causes minor trauma to the body. Some call this trauma "micro-injuries." Needless to say, when training for a big event and putting in strenuous workouts and miles, you are tearing muscles down, straining ligaments, and stressing tendons. To heal these "micro-injuries," you need to interject sufficient rest. To recover fully you need to taper your training workload.

Tapering should not necessarily affect the intensity level of training. In fact, quite often, the intensity should be increased through shorter, faster sessions.

The result is that the runner begins to feel better with more and more "spring" in the legs, and the pace becomes quicker and easier.

Runners must back off long training sessions and strength training sessions during these taper periods. Runners should also complete their last long training run three weeks prior to an event. In addition, reducing strength training (such as weight work or hill repeats) during these weeks will allow muscles to fully recover from the repetitive work.

While some find tapering gradually towards an event greatly beneficial, others are uncomfortable with it. Some runners claim they are "out of sync" if they back off from their normal weekly training regimen. If this is the case, they must examine their training and resulting performances. Are they consistently meeting their goals?

If they are still uncomfortable in tapering as depicted in Figure 1, then they must incorporate periods of rest during the heavy training and sharpening phases of their preparation. All training programs should contain a pattern of "hard/easy" work. That is, the runner goes through a series of hard sessions, followed by a series of recovery sessions.

Some runners follow a program in which they alternate weeks, with one of heavy work, the next light work. Others may get their rest by taking in an easy training week once a month. Regardless, the bottom line remains the same: *Consistent high achievers know how to rest.* It is also the best way to avoid injury and mental burnout.

The Benefits of Tapering

1. **Improved running efficiency.** Increased muscle strength is gained. When backing off on mileage, the legs will gain strength. Stride length also increases. Mechanics improve when one is rested. A sure sign of a tired runner is the one who loses running form easily.
2. **Built up energy stores.** The natural way to carbo load is through tapering. Reducing training naturally increases glycogen stores. This

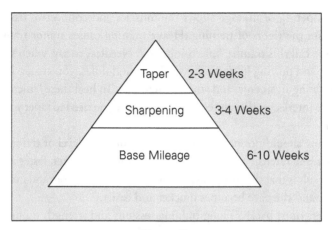

Figure 2

benefit has been well documented.

3. **An increase in speed and leg turnover.** When tapering, reduce overall mileage, but not the intensity of the workouts. Maintaining intensity (speed work) in training increases running pace. While a normal training pace might be eight minutes per mile, with a reduction in miles and higher percentage of "fast miles," that runner will find what was once a eight-minute-per-mile pace now becomes a seven and a half-minute-per-mile pace with little or no apparent increase in effort.

4. **Greater mental strength.** Heavy training loads create stress. When tapering, your mind eases back from the rigors of training and begins to focus on the task ahead.

The taper phase actually begins in the sharpening phase of the training pyramid (Figure 2). After the completion of base training, one should begin to cut back on overall mileage, while targeting specific workouts designed to achieve the desired goal (the upcoming event).

During this period you should begin to feel rested. Higher intensity workouts should be done when one is rested. If you are tired when running faster workouts, the chance for injury increases.

If you have any doubts as to whether tapering works, consider examples of a "forced taper" due to injury or illness. Tremendous anxiety builds within us when injury or illness strikes in the weeks prior to an event. Yet there are numerous examples of runners turning in great performances after being forced to rest due to injury or illness. Consider the case of Joan Benoit, in the spring of 1984, just prior to the Olympic Trials. Due to knee problems, Benoit underwent arthroscopic knee surgery. Being forced to refrain from running for about 10 days, she then went out and qualified for the Olympics and later went on to win the marathon gold medal at the Los Angeles Games.

Going back 50 years, the great Czech runner, Emil Zatopek was hospitalized due to illness for two weeks prior to the 1950 European Games in Brussels. Two days after being discharged he went out and won the 10,000 meters by a whopping one lap margin. This became known as the "Zatopek effect."

I had my own experience with a forced taper in 1983. With only three weeks to go before a big marathon, I injured my hip and was forced to sit out 13 days, yet went on to run my second best marathon ever. Did I experience some anxious moments? Yes, but I also learned a valuable lesson.

These examples are an extreme form of tapering. Hopefully, you will never have to go through this kind; but it should point out the clear importance of rest and backing off your training prior to a big event.

If you are undertrained or struggling with injuries, such that your training has been up and down, then the need for taper is less important. Your body is effectively undertrained and consequently has enough rest. In this case you can train as best you can with event specific sessions right up until your targeted event. Hopefully you will feel good during the event and avoid injury.

Summary

Tapering is absolutely essential to consistent running performance. The best taper is a gradual one. Tapering mileage while maintaining some intensity in training improves glycogen stores, increases leg strength, and improves running efficiency. Active rest is better than complete rest. A rested mind is as important as a rested body. The only way to get there is through proper tapering—one of the keys to successful ultrarunning.

Knowing When to Give it a Rest

In executing a proper training schedule for an important race, following the plan suggested by Kevin regarding a traditional taper is excellent advice. We have all learned through personal experience however, that things don't always go according to plan. Even the most well thought out training schedule can occasionally go awry for any number of reasons, from life simply getting in the way to the ups and downs of the human body.

Most often, problems crop up either because of overtraining and/or injuries. It can happen to anyone. With the race looming on the horizon, you just don't feel quite right. Where your training was rolling along fabulously a month ago, now with only three or four weeks before the big race, you are feeling totally flat and tired. You start to taper off slightly, but only feel worse.

If that scenario sounds familiar, perhaps your body is "over the edge," in a slightly overtrained state. A traditional taper may bring you back around in time for the big race, but then again it may not. After months of hard training, in which you have pushed to prepare as thoroughly as possible, your body is desperately seeking a respite. While your mind is saying "Now I will taper for the race and my body will respond by becoming stronger," your body is saying "Thank God—no more running!" Your body may then go into an extended recovery period that it may not come out of in time for the big day, on which you feel "flat" and do not perform as well as you hoped, or as well as your training indicated you might.

In situations such as this, I've learned that it can help to go immediately into a week to ten-day rest period, in which you cut your mileage drastically, as if the race were imminent. That way, you will reach your "low" point not on race day, but well before that. Then in the ensuing two weeks before the race, gradually build back up, not to a full training schedule, but to a little more than you might otherwise be running a week before the race. In this way, you are on the upswing when race day comes, feeling refreshed, not flat.

Conversely, every now and then you may be unable to do the necessary long runs or weekly mileage needed before a big race. But you have committed to doing the event, despite feeling woefully undertrained. This can happen when there is simply not enough time to train or because you are recovering from an injury. In such a case, you might try "rolling into" the race, putting some gusto into your training in weeks three and two before the big day, before scheduling a shorter taper period the week before the race. Without months of rigorous training behind you, the need for an extended taper is removed. In fact, such a long taper might prove detrimental to your chances of running the way you want to.

Sometimes, the perfect taper is a race, followed by recovery. While some ultrarunners are leery of taking much time off before a big race, they often go into an extended recovery period afterwards. Then a month or so later, they are running great again. This may indicate they are ready for another race! In effect, they have done a hard effort, then executed a taper. Many ultrarunners train by using race recovery as their taper period.

Like anything else, tapering is a learned technique, and it doesn't hurt to "practice" once in a while. This especially applies to those who run every day, or rarely take a day off. If you are not used to taking days off, doing so during a taper period can leave you feeling "out of synch." I have a friend who trains right up until the day before an ultra, just to avoid that "out of sorts" feeling.

While that is not recommended, you can indeed benefit by "practicing" your taper. Before a long run or a training race, allow a few days off in the week before the event, so that you can become accustomed to the down time that accompanies a taper period. Not only will you get practice for the taper, you often accrue the side benefits of having a good training effort and bouncing back quickly from it.

Obviously, in order to maximize your performance it helps to follow a solid training plan, one that includes a systematic taper period before the big race. But the body does always follow systematic rules, and if you try to listen to the signals it is sending and occasionally try a different approach, you'll be surprised how commendably it will perform.— *Don Allison*

Do You Need a Coach?
by Shawn McDonald

There are a number of reasons why an ultrarunner might seek out coaching. A coach can be a sounding board for training and racing ideas for an experienced ultrarunner, or can be a great source of information, experience, and wisdom for those new to the sport. A good coach can provide a jump start to the training program of a beginner, helping to motivate the runner. Veteran ultrarunners can benefit from the encouragement and positive feedback from a coach. The runner also benefits from the process of setting goals and planning a program. The coach will help the runner select goals that are both attainable and challenging, and to map out a plan to reach those goals. A coach familiar with and experienced in ultrarunning can also assist the runner in selecting races in which to participate and develop a detailed race plan once the event nears. The advice a coach provides to the runner can be invaluable in preventing overtraining and injuries. A coach who receives good feedback from the runner can suggest when to push training to higher levels and when to back off and take more rest.

You may have reached a plateau in your running, but want to continue to improve. A wise coach can help by trying different types of training than you have done in the past, which can help you reach higher levels of fitness and speed. A coach who is doing a good job will know where a runner is heading in his or her training program and be able to articulate what is trying to be achieved with each workout. The coach should keep track of the runner's training in detail (the runner can do this also in the form of a training diary or log book) and thus provide unbiased feedback to the runner in terms of training workload, speed work, hill running, and the like. Also, if the coach lives near the runner, he or she can provide direct feedback during training sessions regarding running form and fitness. A coach also helps in providing praise as new levels of fitness or racing goals are reached. A pat on the back and constructive feedback following a setback is also helpful. In working with a coach, ultrarunners will probably also find that training is more fun, in that they have a greater variety than when they were self-coached.

Where to Look for a Coach
Let's say you have decided you would like to work with a coach, but don't know any running coaches. There are a number of different places to look for information. One method is to ask partners or fellow competitors at ultra-distance races and marathons. Ask if they have had a coach, who it was, and if the experience was a

good or bad one. Some coaches have web sites, so you can do an Internet search for "running coach." Other places to seek out a running coach are at race clinics, training classes (for major marathons), running camps, or health clubs. Your local running store probably will also have an idea of who the running coaches are in your area, and may have contact information in the area of the store in which race entry forms are available. The local office of the Road Runners Club of America or USA Track and Field should have lists of running coaches in your area, and nationally as well.

Checking Credentials

Here is a key question: How do you find a coach who is both qualified and will help, rather than hurt your performance? The answer is not simple, but here are a few ideas to consider. First, in the sport of ultrarunning, experience is a great teacher. Thus, a good coach will likely have run ultras for a number of years, and have performed well at those races in which he or she has competed. You will also want to find out if a prospective coach has certifications from RRCA, USATF, or national exercise science governing bodies. These types of programs provide a basic understanding of physiology and proper running mechanics. Also ask about the individual's educational background and if they have a degree in physical education or exercise science, again for reasons of knowledge and an understanding of running.

Find out how long the person you might hire has been coaching, how many clients he or she has coached, at what level those runners trained and raced (such as beginner, intermediate, or national class) and the types of races they have run (such as long or short distance, on roads or trails). Ask if you can contact any of those runners to inquire about their experiences working with this coach. If possible, ask those previous clients how well they ran during the coaching period, compared with before and after the coaching, and if they were injured during the time they worked with the coach.

Other questions to ask the prospective coach include the following: What system or program does he or she use to train runners? Are there regular time commitments for runners in terms of group or speed runs and/or any team or group meetings? Will you meet regularly face-to-face or have contact mostly via phone, or email? You will also want discuss consultations you will have with the coach. Is coaching one-on-one or part of a group program? How much time does the coach devote to interacting with each runner on a weekly basis? Are scheduled appointments part of the contact time and if so, where will they take place and how are they scheduled? In addition, ask what the coaching fee is per month, and if you will be required to pay up front for a certain number of months before starting to work with the coach. The price will likely depend on the level of service the coach provides and how much time the coach spends with the runner. It is important to determine at what point and how you can terminate the coaching agreement should you become injured or not wish to continue working with the coach. Questions about coaching philosophy are relevant and appropriate. Does this coach stress high or low mileage training, regular speed work or hill running, or some other types of training ? There are many questions to ask, but you will be glad you asked them all before hiring a coach! The answers the coach provides will help you assess the quality of the coaching this individual might provide to you, and if their coaching style is a match for your training preferences, goals, and past running experiences.

Getting Started

There are numerous ways to exchange information with your coach once you start working together. Often, a coach will have you fill out an initial questionnaire or will ask you a series of questions during a free initial consultation. Topics on the questionnaire might include your past training and racing experiences, recent race results, your general health and running related injuries you have experienced, a self-evaluation as a runner (strengths and weaknesses), your nutritional practices in training and races, cross-training preferences, and if you have easy access to training partners, a local track, trails, or flat, marked road courses. The coach will probably also want to know if you have worked with a coach before, how you felt about that experience, and if you have any current concerns as the two of you get started. One of the first things that you and the coach will do as a team is to develop a set of short and long-term goals for your running. With the coaches' help, you can select goals that are realistic. Then the coach can develop individualized training plans that will help you to reach those goals.

The Runner-Coach Relationship

Over time, a coach will become a good sounding board for your training ideas, a trusted advisor, a motivator, and a friend. The key to the relationship is communication on a regular basis, in both directions. The exchange of training schedules, feedback after racing, and questions should be constant. The form the relationship takes depends largely on the coaches' style and perhaps on how many other runners he or she is currently coaching. If in doubt, ask as many questions as you can and give regular (at least weekly) feedback to your coach on your training. You should expect and demand longer or more frequent consultations as you approach an upcoming race.

Group Coaching

Coaching can be categorized into two general types: individual and group. Group coaching involves regular meetings for training and discussion (seminars, for example) for several to a few dozen runners who are coached by the same individual. These meetings might take the form of a once-a-week speed session at a local track and/or a once-a-week long run at a local park or trail system. As with individual coaching, you will want to ask the coach several questions about the details of his or her expertise and the services offered. There are some positives to group coaching, namely that you have built-in training partners and forms of encouragement in the other members of the group (this is particularly good if the runners who are selected by the coach are of roughly equal running ability and experience level) and that the training may be more enjoyable with the friendships that develop. The drawback of group coaching is that you might get less individual attention than if you were working with a coach one-on-one and/or that coach only had a few clients. You may also find that your running abilities and goals do not mesh with those of the other runners in the group and that the training methods employed do not benefit you in preparing for ultra-distance races. A period of a month or two may be necessary for you to determine if you are a good fit for the coach in this situation, and for the group dynamics.

Summary

Coaches are essentially resources, individuals who have "been there" and can offer you practical tips, planning, and support. Most coaches will provide all the information you need and will offer an initial free consultation to review your running background, racing history, and goals. Please remember that it takes time for any changes the coach makes to your running program to take effect, so be patient. Over the period of a few months you should see differences in how you feel during your training runs and in races. Finally, consider that coaching is not for all runners. It depends upon your personality to some extent, as well as your goals and experience. Obtaining the help of a coach is one way to gain experience, as well as to define and reach your goals, whatever they might be.

Training the Mind for Ultras
by Shawn McDonald

Introduction

It has been said by many ultrarunners that finishing an ultra requires a 10-percent physical effort; the remaining 90-percent is mental. The mind of a runner is very important in successfully running long races and overcoming and avoiding doubts and distractions during competition. In this column, I will review a few concepts of sports psychology, some recent research on mental abilities of top runners, and ways in which you can practice and apply a few of these mental techniques to stay relaxed, confident, and focused during your next ultra.

Mental Preparation

Studies of top athletes in a number of sports (*Rushall, 1979; Noakes, 1991*) have shown commonalities in mental preparation before and during competition. Top cyclists, runners, swimmers, gymnasts, and figure skaters are able to concentrate on a single goal during training. During the long months of training prior to a competition, they are able to stay focused on short and long- term goals, as well as to develop the ability to accurately judge how they will perform on race day. Through use of a variety of visualization, relaxation, simulation, and planning methods, they are able to quell excitation and anxiety before competition, as well as to adapt to unfamiliar circumstances. They use mental tools to reach an optimal balance of nervousness, confidence, and focus on technique, as competition commences. These elite athletes have detailed training plans and competitive strategies that give them high levels of confidence. As with the physical aspects of ultrarunning, each of these mental skills require time and practice to develop and master.

Sports psychology

Sports psychology involves the study of roles and function of the mind in the performance levels of athletes during sporting events. There are a number of tools that practitioners of sports psychology study and employ in coaching their clients to reach a peak performance. A few of these tools are described below, along with examples showing their application to ultrarunning. The details of how, when, and why to apply these tools are described in the references listed at the end of this column. Combining these tools, along with an evaluation of your current strengths and weaknesses as a runner, will help you design a well-balanced training program.

Goal Setting

Setting realistic but challenging goals in ultrarunning is important for each athlete. Short and long-term goals provide motivation to train on a regular basis, to get out on the trails or roads in bad weather, or when you are not feeling your best. These goals also serve as a guide as you develop a training plan for each week leading up to a key competition or series of races. A series of evolving goals can also provide a vision of where you want to go in the sport of ultrarunning and how to get there. Examples of short-term goals might be to train injury free for the next several months and to then complete your first ultra, or to improve upon your 50-mile time by 30 minutes at a race you ran last summer. Longer term goals might be to complete a 100-mile trail race (for a runner who has completed a few 50-km races), or to make the national 100-km team (for a runner who has been competing in ultras for a couple of years).

There are a few helpful tips you should keep in mind as you undertake the process setting goals. First, make sure the goals are those you truly hope to achieve. Don't chase after goals conceived solely by a spouse, parent, or coach. Make each goal concise and specific, for particular running events or with specific completion dates. This will help you see your progress toward each goal and allow you to measure your performance relative to each goal as you review each race. As you develop several goals, assign a priority to each one to help you focus on what will be most important in your training and during the competition. State each goal as a positive statement, such as "I will complete a 100-mile race in less than 24 hours." Do not use negative statements such as "avoid making the silly mistake I made in my last ultra of going out too fast at the start." Such a statement can be rephrased into "run the entire race with patience, poise, and control according to my race plan as much as possible." Be sure to write down your goals and share them with family, friends, and training partners. The goals will then be at your fingertips if you should need to make modifications due to a setback like an injury, or if you progress more quickly or slowly than you had anticipated in your training. Sharing goals helps make them more tangible and keeps them at the forefront of your mind as you continue daily training and develop a race plan to meet your set of goals.

Finally, make your goals incremental, by setting intermediate goals for a particular running event. For example, a novice runner might set a goal to complete a training run of four hours duration in three months time when their current longest runs are in the range of two hours. This runner might set this goal on the way to the longer term goal of completing a 50-km race by the end of 2006. Another athlete with more experience in ultras might aim for finishing times of 23, 25, and 27 hours at a 100-mile race they want to run in July, if they have completed the race in the past in times near 26 hours. By setting a number of incremental goals to tackle in the next one to three years, you increase the chances of meeting at least some of the goals and improving your confidence and self esteem. Set a mixture of performance (usually your finish time), outcome (winning the race or finishing place in your age group), goals. You will have direct control over the former type of goals but not over the latter, which involve performances of other runners. This goal setting system also lessens the chances you will overdo it in training and develop an injury or overtraining syndrome. Be sure to review your goals in the days and weeks after a race and how your performance compared with those goals. Were the goals too easy or hard? What successes did you have in training? What would you change for the next time? What did you do well and what areas did you struggle with in physical and mental terms during the race? Also give yourself a reward or two for any completed goals. Write down your answers to these questions in your training log or personal journal and review them as you start to prepare for your next race and draft a further set of goals.

Focus and flow

In your training runs or during a race, focus your attention on a number of different stimuli. Your focus can be on associative thoughts such as monitoring your breathing rate and depth, your running pace, personal commands, how sore or loose your leg muscles feel, and noticing any areas of your body that feel tight. Or you can put your attention on dissociative thoughts such as noticing spectators nearby or deciding what you are going to eat later for your dinner. You usually want to have associative thoughts during key training sessions and races, as these will help you adjust your effort level to test other nearby competitors and to respond to environmental conditions. Strive to notice any deficits during a race, such as not taking in enough calories or possible trouble such as developing heel blisters. During long training runs be sure to keep your focus on monitoring your body, how you feel at each moment, and on maintaining a good running form. Concentrate during each competition on your race strategy, on "staying loose," and on running efficiently by taking input from all areas of your body, including your breathing. If your thoughts wander, work at refocusing on the associative arenas and coming back to how you are doing relative to your goals by using positive statements or mantras.

"Flow" is a combined mental and physical state in which you are "in the zone," running with ease, confidence, and focused on the task at hand and your body signals. Flow can be most easily achieved by being relaxed (see imagery, simulation, and breathing techniques below), by having your full attention on performance and not on errors, and by keeping distractions under control. Flow is also assisted by thinking positive thoughts while eliminating all negative doubts and by practicing the focus of your attention solely on running, your body, and performance relative to your race goals as you complete each of your long training runs. Flow is inhibited by a strong desire to win, showing off to spectators, and trying so hard to achieve an appropriate state of mind that you lose attention on your performance and body signals. For more of the details on how to get into a flow state before and during a race, see the book by Jackson and Csikszentmihalyi.

Self talk and doubts

Ultrarunners go through a range of emotions during the span of long training runs and races. Their "self talk" during running will determine if they control and funnel these emotions. In contrast, rampant emotions could lead to a loss of concentration or self doubts that can eventually lead to dropping out of a race or not meeting goals, even if the runner was properly trained in a physical sense. Use of positive affirmations and a review of your training log in the weeks leading up to the targeted run are two ways to overcome negative self talk. Affirmations for ultrarunners include "I have trained well for this race, I have developed a realistic race plan, and I have the experience and emotional control to run well today and meet my goals." Affirmations work best when they are specific and are based in the present. Doubts about your ability to perform as a runner can also arise by comparing yourself to other training partners or to fellow runners when you are standing on the starting line of a race. Try to focus on what you have done to prepare for the race physically and mentally, and on your abilities to adapt and persevere during the competition. By setting realistic, achievable sub-goals that you meet during training runs and practice races leading up to a key competition, you can develop a substantial amount of self-confidence that will serve as a shield against doubts and negative thoughts.

Imagery and simulation

Imagery is the process of visualizing yourself during the course of an upcoming race, from the start, to the middle of the race, to the finish stretch. Your imagination is the engine that drives the process. You can start with a few minutes of imagery per day and build up to a 30 to 60-minute session during the week before a key race. Details to include in imagery include your pace and effort, tasks you want to complete at each aid station, and how you would handle unexpected events in a calm and confident manner. Also try to imagine how your legs will feel during the course of the race and any adjustments you might make in your pace and effort if you were to get ahead or behind your planned race splits. Using imagery is a great way to imagine yourself achieving performances that exceed those you have done in practice runs or past races. Imagery allows you to "pre-experience" the attainment of goals, which builds confidence that you can reach the goals you have set. You can also use imagery if you are injured and can't train, or if you are resting in the last week or two before a race and don't want to tire yourself physically. Specific neural pathways are created or strengthened in your brain as you perform imagery, and these pathways can be used to control your muscles and make wise decisions to adjust to changing race conditions. Aim to use all of your senses to create a particular set of images, and to imagine running "within yourself" and not from a perspective outside of yourself. These vivid images will be more effective at stimulating your neurons in the same ways as actual running.

Simulation involves actual physical training in the form of long training runs or practice races prior to a goal race. The aim of simulation is to create actual race conditions as closely as possible to train your body and mind to perform at high levels for many hours on end. Strive to match the terrain, weather, time of day, use of aid stations, effort level, and cheers from spectators and your crew, as well as to practice your pre-event routine. Simulation helps develop confidence since you are handling the actual difficulties of a race and can be a great tool to use in the last part of a training program as you make adjustments to your goals and race plan. You learn to push through fatigue and to maintain concentration on good running form when tired and sore. Simulation does take more effort to arrange and to carry out than imagery, but has the added value of being based in reality. Thus, imagery and simulation are complementary tools that can be combined to give you a double shot of confidence and stress control, developing a sense that you have "been there before."

Anxiety and bad moods: sources and control

Thoughts and feelings of anxiety or negativity can arise in your training program leading up to a race or just before the start of a race. These feelings can damage your motivation to train diligently as well as your self-confidence just prior to and during a race. Reasons for these feelings could include low blood sugar, overtraining, comparing yourself with top competitors, or unexpected events during a race, such as unusually hot weather or the loss of your luggage as you are traveling to a race site. Your aim should be to identify the likeliest causes of the bad mood or stress, and to make changes to eliminate the sources of the anxiety. Your mood can be improved by use of positive statements and affirmations (such as "I feel good") and relaxation techniques such as circle breathing and progressive muscle relaxation. (See the book by Kay Porter listed below). Other activities that reduce anxiety and improve mood include using imagery (remember back to a time when you were performing well at a race in the past and feeling good), reviewing your goals to get a shot of motivation, and flipping through your training log to remember at all the work you have done in the past several months. Remember to smile and laugh, which will reduce tension in your face and throughout your body and release chemicals in your body to lift your mood.

Hydration for Warm Weather Ultrarunning

by Kevin Setnes

Summer in North America means warm—and sometimes downright hot—running conditions for the majority of ultrarunners. The need for proper hydration in distance events is well documented; most runners understand the importance of drinking fluids prior to, during, and after long continuous periods of running. While awareness of hydration is important, it is also critical to understand some of the finer details of an ultrarunner's fluid requirements.

The body has a remarkable cooling system in the form of sweating and subsequent evaporation from the body surface, the skin. This cooling mechanism is only effective, however, if the body is adequately supplied with fluids—this is accomplished by drinking. The key to allowing this system to work properly is balance. Don't let yourself become dehydrated, but don't overhydrate either.

Dehydration

When we do physical work, the body generates heat and thus needs to be cooled. We sweat at a rate relative to air temperature, humidity, speed (work load), and body size. The more you sweat, the more you need to replenish. Studies show that during warm, summer-like conditions, an individual can sweat one to one and a half liters per hour. Sweat rates can exceed two liters per hour under extreme conditions, or for people who sweat profusely. Intake rates also vary by the individual and conditions; however, an intake of one liter per hour is about the most one can tolerate. Thus, the importance of staying hydrated prior to an event or long workout is critical to performance.

The key to preventing dehydration is to keep the pace moderate in extremely warm conditions, thus reducing the sweat rate. It also means drinking as frequently as possible, but at a rate the stomach can tolerate. Tied to this equation is the type of fluid you are drinking. Fluids with carbohydrates (such as most of the major sports drinks) should have no more than a seven to eight percent concentration. In addition, the drink should contain an adequate amount of sodium and potassium to ensure that the body maintains sufficient electrolyte balance.

Tim Noakes, in his book, *Lore of Running*, points out that an individual's electrolyte losses will vary by fitness and heat acclimatization. Electrolyte losses of fitter runners are less than those of lesser abilities. Gastric emptying (the rate at which your stomach can digest fluids) is tied to the air temperature and concentration of the fluid. For example, it is far easier to digest fluids in colder conditions than in hot weather. When running at a high intensity, blood is shunted away from the stomach to the working skeletal muscles for oxygen delivery, and to the skin for heat dissipation. This can leave the runner with a bloated feeling, as the gastric emptying process is slowed. The key is understanding pace, sweat rate and proper replacement.

Hyperhydration

Hyperhydration means storing greater than normal amounts of water in the body. The theory is that if you force a great amount of fluids (in this case water), the body will have an abundant supply going into a marathon or ultra event. This practice is flawed and can actually cause problems for many runners. If you overhydrate prior to an event with water only, your body has a mechanism in place to recognize this and promptly urinates the excess away. This can also disrupt the electrolyte balance of the body and adversely affect performance. Karl King, creator of SUCCEED! energy products, says this can have a significant effect on running performance. Overhydrating can cause hyponatremia, which means low salt levels in the blood. If you go into a competition with a diluted blood supply, you will have diluted hemoglobin, which affects the amount of oxygen your muscles receive.

If you are drinking only water in your long runs or ultra events, you may begin to feel confused, fatigued and nauseated. While many think that these symptoms are natural occurrences in ultrarunning (and to some extent they are), they may also be caused by hyponatremia. Matters may be made even worse when aid station volunteers mistake this for dehydration and then offer more water, when in fact what you need are more electrolytes.

The key to hydrating prior to performance is to practice moderation. Ensuring that you are not dehydrated is more important than trying to overhydrate. When drinking fluids prior to an event, make sure they contain some electrolyte and nourishment. I, like many other ultrarunners, have my own pre-race rituals. One of these is to consume 48 ounces of V-8 juice the day before an event. Mainly I like the healthy taste, but it is also high in sodium and potassium. The bottom line is that I never go to the starting line with low electrolyte levels. As for fluid intake, it is not more than normal.

Glycerin-Induced Hyperhydration

A popular product on the market nowadays is glycerin. The theory is that glycerin, when mixed with water, slows dehydration in runners. How does it work? Proponents say it increases fluid uptake prior to exercise or competition. While people who overhydrate end up going to the porta-johns or bushes frequently before an event, those who have taken glycerin with their water report *not* having to urinate as frequently before the start.

This modified hydration strategy is, according to David Martin's book *Better Training for Distance Runners*, a way for the water to be distributed to all compartments of the body, not just the blood plasma. It reaches two extravascular compartments, namely, the interstitial fluid between cells and the intracellular fluid within cells.

All these compartments contribute fluid to sweat, especially the extravascular compartments. The plasma volume is the smallest of these compartments, but its percentage of contribution is the greatest. Says Martin, "Glycerin-induced hyperhydration through the expansion of these two extravascular compartments provides a reservoir for maintaining blood plasma volume as fluid losses from sweating continues. In turn, this keeps the skin surface of the body cooler, maintains cardiac output, and delays the onset of fatigue." Dr. Martin, who has served as a national team coordinator and is currently chair of the developmental committee of Long Distance Running with USATF, has used glycerin for some of the marathoners on the U.S. team and reports positive results.

Studies have shown that when ingesting fluids with glycerin, the result is less urination, and thus lower body temperature, suggesting that glycerin serves to redistribute the water throughout the body and that plenty of fluid is available for use in evaporative cooling. It is very important to point out that glycerin should not be taken in its pure form. It must be greatly diluted with fluid, approximately 25 parts water to one part glycerin. Usually runners will ingest this mixture one to two hours prior to the run.

My only ultra racing experience with glycerin was at the World Challenge 100 Km in France. A teammate suggested I use it, so following his recommendation I took the appropriate amount and ended up running one of my best World 100 Km races. I have since tried it at a couple of marathons that were run as training runs, both with positive results.

There are more and more reports that indicate there may be something to this, which supports some of the studies completed. If you do choose to try it, you can find it in your local drug store, but again be careful. Mix at least to a 25 to one ratio (water to glycerin). You already have some glycerin in your body naturally, so a little more seems to do more good than harm.

As you prepare through the hotter summer months for an ultra, remember to not suffer from water intoxication and don't overhydrate with water only. Mix in some carbohydrates and electrolyte and perhaps look into experimenting with glycerin-induced hyperhydration.

Training for the Western States 100 Mile

By John Medinger

"Those who cannot remember the past are condemned to repeat it." - George Santayana

In developing a training program for Western States, it is instructive to look first at the reasons why runners do *not* make it to the finish line. The most common reasons are as follows:

- Heat and dehydration
- "My quads are shot"
- Nausea and vomiting
- "I'm completely out of gas"
- Bucklemania and other brain cramps
- Altitude problems and/or snow

Let's examine these items one at a time and get acquainted with what to do and what not to do.

Heat and Dehydration

This, by far, is the most common reason for "DNFs" (did not finish) at Western States. It is typically is very hot during the race. The average high temperature in Auburn at the end of June is 92 degrees F (34 C) and it is not uncommon for race day temperatures to exceed 100 degrees F. Remember too, official temperatures are measured in the shade. You will be in the sun much of the afternoon, and the June sun adds about 30 degrees F to the "feel" of the temperature. So, when it's 90 degrees F in the shade and you are in the sun, it feels much hotter.

The relative humidity at Western States is typically very low however, often less than 20 percent. This is good news, since it means that sweat will evaporate very quickly. It is this evaporation that cools your body. However, for those who are used to more humid climates, it may not seem like you are sweating all that much, since you won't be as wet as you are used to. This does not mean that you don't need to drink as much. How much do you need to drink? Everyone is different and some years are hotter than others. Having said that, most runners will need between one and two 20-ounce bottles per hour. This is a lot of fluid for your body to process. You will not be able to do it if you haven't practiced drinking this much in your training runs.

There are two clear indications of how you are doing on hydration during the run. One is your weight. You will be weighed on Friday before the race and should stay within about two to three pounds of your pre-race weight during the entire run. If your weight is lower than that, it is a clear sign that you are dehydrated. You should avoid this at all costs; once you get behind in your hydration, it is very hard to catch up. The other indication of how you are doing is your urine. You should feel a need to urinate at least once every two hours, and your urine should be clear or very light in color.

Some runners actually gain weight during the race. This is an indication that your system is not processing fluids as fast as you are taking them in. This is often due to an electrolyte imbalance. Taking in too much salt can cause your body to "bloat."

Maintaining a proper electrolyte balance is a very important factor in getting to the finish line. Too few salts, and you run the risk of cramping—or worse. Too many salts, and you may store fluids and gain weight, or worse, stop being able to process fluids entirely. Again, every runner has different needs and it will depend on how well heat trained you are. After about 10 days of training in hot temperatures (above about 80 degrees F), your body will automatically start holding on to salts more efficiently. It is simply one of the ways that your body adapts. For many runners in the race, finding a place to train in hot temperatures in late May and early June is easy. It certainly is the most desirable way to prepare for the heat during the race. For others who live in cooler climates, this may not be possible. For everyone, we recommend experimenting with electrolyte replacement strategies during training to find out what works for them. Most runners will need about 200 to 500 mg of salt per hour. You might be able to get these electrolytes from your sports drink and from salty foods such as pretzels, saltines, and the like.

Others prefer to take electrolyte supplements such as Thermotabs™ Buffered Salt Tablets, available in many drugstores, or SUCCEED! Electrolyte Capsules, available from Ultrafit, W5297 Young Rd., Eagle, WI 53119, email: ksetnes@aol.com. These supplements are very inexpensive; $10 worth will probably last you two or three years.

Another way to help alleviate the heat is to douse yourself with water at every opportunity. The Western States course has many small stream crossings; at each one, take your hat or a handkerchief and scoop some water, wetting down your head and neck. This will cool you in the same manner as sweating.

"My quads are shot"

Western States is a net downhill course. There are several very long downhill stretches, during which you may be running downhill for an hour or more. This is very abusive to your quadriceps muscles, which will absorb much of the pounding.

The only way to get your legs used to this is to train on long downhills prior to the race. Many local runners spend hours and hours in the canyons prior to race day. For those who live outside of northern California, it is recommended that you find a steep hill that is at least three miles long and practice running down. For those who live in an area that doesn't offer that kind of terrain, you may find that you can achieve some of that training effect with weight training specifically oriented toward your quadriceps.

On the long downhill stretches of your training runs, try to develop a fluid running pattern that allows you to run downhill in a very relaxed fashion. Concentrate on letting the energy of the pounding flow all the way through your body. Avoid at all costs the practice of using your legs as brakes to slow you down on the really steep pitches. Nothing will use up your quads faster than this style of running.

By the time you reach Foresthill (mile 62) during the race, you will be done with most of the tough uphill climbs. The stretch from Foresthill to the finish line is actually run on fairly gentle terrain. But you have to have enough left in your legs to be able to do something with it. Those who do well are the runners who are able to save enough on the downhills to have quads left and are able to run much of the last 38 miles.

Nausea and vomiting

This is a particularly vexing problem; nothing will shut you down faster than a bout of nausea. The causes of nausea are many. They include dehydration, running too fast (relative to your ability and training), electrolyte depletion, and sometimes, simple exhaustion.

In many cases nausea is simply your body's way of protecting itself. When the body gets into extreme situations, it automatically starts shutting down non-essential systems to protect the vital organs (heart, liver, kidneys, etc.). One of the first systems that it typically shuts down is the gastrointestinal tract. As you keep running, your muscles are calling for more energy and more fluids. So you continue to eat and drink. But as your gastrointestinal system is shutting down, it is no longer processing the food and drink (or is doing so at a significantly reduced rate). You will often experience a sensation that is described as a "sloshy" stomach. Eventually, all that non-processed food and drink has to go somewhere and so it comes back up.

How do you prevent bouts of nausea? There are no sure-fire cures. Directionally, it seems to help many runners to eat solid foods periodically from the start of the race. Upon the first symptoms "sloshy" stomach or queasiness, slow down. It is better to give up a few minutes during the next few miles than to spend hours later in a chair later on. Many runners have reported that taking additional salt at this point helps empty their stomach. Sometimes sucking on ice chips can help. Some report that eating something really bland, such as a couple of slices of bread, will help. Carbonated sodas such as 7-Up sometimes help. Burping or belching is generally considered a good sign; it's an indication that your stomach is working again.

What do you do after you have started throwing up? Again, there is no absolute consensus. Some runners recommend trying to get it all out of your system. Stop and sit for a while if you have to, but try to keep moving at whatever pace you can muster. Vomiting will empty your stomach of both food and fluids. At some point—the sooner the better—you will need to replace them. Energy gels—such as GU, PowerGel, or ClifShot—are designed to be eaten on an empty stomach. And your stomach will probably never be emptier than this! GU comes in an unflavored version, which may be the most palatable on a nauseous stomach.

It is important to try to start eating and drinking again as soon as you can. Once you have vomited enough to have emptied your stomach, you probably only will have two to three hours of energy left in your system; if you don't start generating new energy sources you will probably not be able to continue much beyond that. Some runners report that once they get everything out of their system, they start to feel much better in about an hour. Others take many hours to recover. Let's hope that if this happens to you, you are among the former! Gene Thibeault says, "If you feel good while running Western States, don't worry; you'll get over it."

"I'm completely out of gas"

This, generally, is one problem that can be fixed. Most runners will experience "flat stretches" during which they just don't have much energy. This is usually reflective of low blood sugar and can be remedied by eating and drinking. But beware of the quick fix. Simple sugars will make you feel better quickly, but are so quickly consumed by your body that you will often experience a crash a half-hour or so later. What is usually best here is a combination of quick energy and some longer-lasting food sources. Again, energy gels (such as GU) are designed to be eaten on an empty stomach and are effective at getting some energy into the body quickly. Combine a couple of packets of gel with a sandwich, soup, or some other food of substance. This combination will be the most effective means of giving you the combination of short and long-term energy sources you will need to make it to the finish. Many runners report that once they get behind in energy intake like this, it is difficult to catch back up completely. So, you might expect to suffer from the "low blood sugar blues" at periodic intervals for the rest of the race. Each time, the remedy is the same: eat and drink!

Bucklemania and other brain cramps

Many runners' focus is on that beautiful silver buckle, awarded to those that complete the race in less than 24 hours. Breaking 24 hours on this challenging course is a worthy goal. At the same time, it should be recognized that the primary objective is to make it to the finish line. Finishing Western States—no matter how long it takes—is a tremendous accomplishment! Recognize that typically fewer than 20 percent of the folks toeing the starting line at Squaw Valley will finish the race in less than 24 hours. If you do not typically finish in the top 20 percent of runners in other ultras, chances are you won't here, either. Setting an unachievable goal is a recipe for disaster in something as difficult as running 100 miles. Your number one goal should be to simply finish.

The first half of the race is mostly physical, while the second half of the race is mostly mental. If you spend the first half of the race worrying about splits, who you are ahead of and who's ahead of you, chances are you won't have the mental energy it takes to get through the second half of the race. Take the day as it comes and run your own race. Don't get too caught up in competing for position in the first half of the race. Instead, spend the first half of the race running well within your abilities, and concentrate on eating and drinking. You will be surprised how many runners you will pass later on. Experienced runners often say that the race really starts in Foresthill at mile 62. Heed their advice.

Injuries

Every year there are several runners who are unable to finish due to injury. Injuries can be separated into two categories: chronic and acute. Chronic injuries are the most common form for distance runners. They are usually the result of overuse. Many runners will stubbornly stick to their training programs and try to "run through" injuries. Sometimes this works, but often it does not. Among veteran runners, it is an axiom that it is better to show up at the starting line a little undertrained than it is to show up a little injured. Common runner injuries such as plantar fasciitis, patellar tendinitis, and iliotibial band syndrome are usually easier to deal with if aggressively treated in their infancy. Once they are well-established, they can be very persistent. It is better to take a few days off in April than to be hobbled at the starting line in June.

Acute injuries—those that occur during the race itself—usually take the form of sprained ankles and abrasions from falls. Check with medical personnel at the next aid station; they will help you make the determination as to whether you are doing any permanent damage or not by continuing. If you are risking permanent damage by continuing, by all means stop! There will always be another day. "Sometimes 'DNF' means 'did nothing fatal,'" says Suzi Shearer Cope.

Altitude problems and snow

Although the first 30 miles of Western States average about 7,500 feet of elevation, few runners have significant problems with the altitude at the race. Some runners may experience headaches, dizziness, or nausea in the early stages of the race, but there have been relatively few reports of serious difficulty with the altitude. If you have a history of problems at elevations in the 7,000-foot range, it would be a good idea to acclimatize at altitude for two weeks prior to the race, if at all possible. For most participants, the worst thing that will happen is that the altitude will slow them down a little.

Snow in significant amounts is a relatively infrequent visitor to the race. Since 1974, there have been three bad snow years (1983, 1995, and 1998) and two more years in which snow was somewhat significant (1982 and 1993). Race management will keep you posted during the spring as to expected snow conditions for the race. If it looks like it will be a significant snow year, it is a good idea to practice running in snow, since much of the first 25 miles may be snow covered. Running in snow is often treacherous; most runners will fall several times. Shoes with a very aggressive outer tread seem to work best. Also, runners will probably want to change shoes at Duncan Canyon; one of the effects of several hours of running in snow is that the mid-soles of your shoes will freeze and become rock hard, depriving you of the cushioning you will need once you get out of the snow.

Training

O.K., now that we've talked about all the things that can go wrong, let's talk about what you can do *right*, specifically training. First, you should start thinking in terms of hours instead of miles. Second, your training should be as specific as possible. Western States is a trail run, with many very demanding climbs and descents, usually run in very hot weather. The more that you can mimic these conditions in training, the better off you will be on race day. A training run on the course from Michigan Bluff to Last Chance and back might take you seven hours, even though it is "only" about 25 miles. This will do you much more good than a 30-mile run on flat roads that might only take you five hours.

One-hundred miles is a very long way to run. There is a temptation to think that you must do mega-mileage in order to be able to attempt running this far. You will hear stories of elite runners who train at 120 or 150 miles per week. But unless you are truly an elite runner, mega-mileage training is not recommended. Elite runners are elite because they are blessed with biomechanics that few of us can even dream of. This innate talent allows them to run faster and longer without becoming injured. When the average runner attempts a similar schedule, the results can be disastrous, usually resulting in serious injury. "Yeah, but I got my butt kicked by a 62-year-old!" said Scott Mills, after being congratulated for winning the 50 to 59 age division.

It is not necessary to run 100 miles per week to finish Western States. Many runners are able to finish on not much more than half this amount. Everyone has their own formula for what they consider optimum training. The key to most training programs is a weekly long run. It is important to stress your body (but not to the breaking point) and then allow it to recover before stressing it again. Reduced to its simplest form, training is all about stress and recovery. Everyone has a different breaking point, but it seems that many ultrarunners can handle up to about six hours of running without significantly breaking down their muscles. If you run longer than that, such as in a 50-mile trail race, you will find yourself stiff and sore for a few days. While this is occasionally acceptable or even desirable, it is not something that most runners can handle on a frequent basis.

It is a good idea to start your buildup in January, slowly increasing total time and distance during the first three months of the year. In order to be able to do the heavy work that is required during April and May, you will need to develop a significant base during January through March. A typical training program for the months of April and May might look something like this:

Monday	Rest, or 45 minutes easy
Tuesday	60 to 90 minutes
Wednesday	Two to three hours
Thursday	Rest, or 45 minutes easy
Friday	60 to 90 minutes
Saturday	Five to six hours
Sunday	One to three hours, slowly, even walking

Depending upon the terrain and your speed, this will give you somewhere between about 60 and 90 miles in a week. Once a month or so, it is good to attempt a 50-mile race or a longer training run of eight to ten hours. Use these longer efforts to simulate what you will want to do during Western States. Practice eating, drinking, changing shoes and clothes, etc. If you are running in a race, do not be too concerned about your competitive position. You may well be a little slower than normal, since you are in the middle of your heavy training period. Keep your eye on the big prize!

Other tips

Many runners incorporate a weightlifting routine into their training. It is important to have strong abs, and also strong arms and shoulders. Carrying a water bottle for 100 miles will definitely make your arms tired! Weight lifting should emphasize light weights with many repetitions. A rule of thumb says that if you cannot do three sets of 20 repetitions, you are using too much weight. Curls, bench press, upright rowing, lunges, and crunches are exercises that can be beneficial.

Train on trails whenever possible—the hillier and rockier, the better. Train in hot weather whenever possible. This should be obvious, but again, think specificity. Practice walking. Most runners will walk most of the uphills in the race and many runners will incorporate large amounts of walking toward the end of the race. Being able to hike aggressively will get you there a lot faster than walking slowly.

If you do not have any experience in running on trails at night with a flashlight, you should also practice this once or twice. This is also a good opportunity to test your nighttime lights. Some runners prefer headlamps, while others prefer hand-held flashlights. A few even use waist-mounted fluorescent lights. Each causes its own special problems. Whatever you use, we recommend strongly that you carry a spare light of some sort in your fanny pack, and place an additional spare light in each of your nighttime aid station drop bags. Virtually every experienced runner has "flashlight stories." Don't make the mistake of trying to save a few dollars by not having extra lights and risk ruining your race.

While blisters don't account for many "dnf's," they do cause many runners problems. They can slow you down significantly and create a painful aftermath. You should expect that the trail grit and dust will permeate your shoes and socks, even if you wear trail gaiters. This, combined with wet feet from stream crossings and from your own sweat, is a perfect breeding ground for blisters. In training, you should experiment with blister prevention techniques, such as putting Compeed™ or duct tape on friction points, ointments such as Vaseline or Bag Balm, frequent sock changes, etc. Many runners change shoes and socks at Robinson Flat at mile 30 (three miles after the Duncan Creek crossing) and at the far side of the Rucky Chucky River crossing at mile 78. You probably should plan to do the same, especially if you are blister-prone.

To the best of our knowledge, no one has ever finished Western States while sitting in a chair! If you must take a break at an aid station, allot yourself a modest amount of time (five minutes) and then force yourself to get up and leave. The longer you sit there, the better it will feel, and the more likely you won't leave the aid station. Some runners even practice sitting for five minutes and then getting up and going on in their training runs. Focus on relentless forward motion. When you can, run. When you can't run, walk. When you can't walk, walk anyway. "I hammered down the trail, passing rocks and trees like they were standing still," said Red Spicer.

It is recommended that you include a tapering period prior to race day, to assure that you are well rested and not overtrained on race day. Most runners start to taper their training two to three weeks prior to the race. Typically, the penultimate week should have a total mileage not more than half of what you have been doing in the previous couple of months (i.e., if you have been running 80 miles per week, this week should not be more than 40.) In addition, your longest run should not be more than about two hours. The week of the race itself, most runners like to do very little. Perhaps a 20 or 30-minute run or walk each day, just to burn off a little of the nervous energy that almost always precedes the race.

The day before the race, concentrate on drinking so that you go into the race very well hydrated. Remember that metabolizing all those carbohydrates that you are loading up with takes more water than you think.

Every runner has his or her own approach to getting mentally ready for a race. We wouldn't begin to tell you what might work for you or suggest that you change whatever your normal mental preparation might be. We only caution you to follow it. It is very easy to get caught up in all the excitement that surrounds Western States in the days immediately prior to the race and get away from your normal mental preparation. Try not to get too caught up in this and risk losing your normal focus.

Most runners find it much easier to assimilate the concept of running 100 miles by breaking the race into small segments. First, break the race into maybe four large segments: the high country (the start to Robinson Flat at mile 30), the canyons (Robinson Flat to Michigan Bluff at mile 55), the tough third quarter (Michigan Bluff to the River crossing at mile 78) and the victory stretch (the River crossing to the finish line). Develop a basic strategy for each section, such as this:

- High Country: Stay relaxed, take it easy, focus on eating a lot.
- The Canyons: Float on the downhills, hike hard on the ups, don't overheat, focus on drinking a lot.
- The Third Quarter: Don't stop eating! Concentrate on working hard, focus on pushing through the pain. The race truly starts here.
- The Victory Stretch: Keep moving forward, beware of the chair, smell the barn, and don't forget to drink!

Within each section, your mental focus should be on eating and drinking and making it from aid station to aid station. Constantly monitor your body and take the time to take care of any little problems before they become big problems. And don't forget to enjoy the scenery and the camaraderie of your fellow runners. After all, this is recreation! "You are tougher than you think you are!" says Ken Chlouber.

Competing in the Western States 100 Mile is a tremendous challenge. It will not be easy. It will test your physical and mental tenacity to its utmost. But with proper training and an intelligent approach, you can make it to the finish line in Auburn!

Some Different Training Ideas for 100-Mile Trail Runs

by Jim O'Brien

While I am certainly not claiming to be any sort of an expert on the training necessary for racing 100-mile trail races, I have formulated some strong opinions while attempting to correct the initial mistakes I had made previously. Please bear in mind that most of what I am relaying to you here is strictly my opinion, and due to the lack of reliable scientific studies conducted on ultrarunners, I will not be citing any specific research.

You may ask yourself, "Why on earth would I want to listen to this guy anyway?" Well, you might not want to, but at least read on and decide if what I say is of any value to you. Since there is relatively little scientific-based information on ultrarunning, it seems appropriate that we should share the "secrets" of our success. My own background in 100-mile races is as follows: Angeles Crest 100 Mile, 1987: third in 19:51; Western States 100 Mile, 1988: ninth in 18:33; Angeles Crest 100 Mile, 1989: first in 17:35.

Some of the things I say here will seem like heresy to many of you, because it goes against the grain of popular thinking. The theories I have developed are well thought out, but they are contrary to what most ultrarunners do. I hope that some of these ideas will contribute to your success in whatever race you choose. The following is a list of my recommendations with explanations for each one.

Train Like a Marathon Runner for Speed over Distance

In other words, be sure to incorporate intense runs on certain days and utilize interval training. Rather than becoming a "mileage junkie," you should be more concerned about the overall quality of those miles. For me, it makes more sense to run twice a day several times a week than to go out once for a longer period of time. The quality of my two runs will be higher and the benefits greater than if I went out only once at an average slower pace. This is not to say long runs are not important. The idea behind this method is simply to allow a runner to cover more quality miles and perhaps more total miles as well.

Limit the Long Runs in Training to No More Than 40 Miles

For my money, any training run that is longer than this distance is a total waste of time. I do not see the reasoning behind slogging through a 50-mile run for the sake of toughening yourself when the training is actually tearing you down. When you have to rest for a training run and then lose days of quality training while recovering from the run, something is seriously wrong. I would recommend limiting the "long runs" in training to somewhere between 30 and 40 miles. However, while running these long runs, you should be conscious of keeping the effort level up. You can get more benefit from a 30-mile run at a decent clip than from a 50-mile run at a relaxed pace. In addition, you spend less time and don't beat yourself to a pulp.

Utilize Therapy Regularly Throughout Training and During the Race

We all want to be able to train and perform at high levels of competency. Despite our best efforts at regulating our diets and meticulously planning our training schedules, we sometimes get into ruts and plateau for a while. With a regularly scheduled sports massage, you will be able to keep the body tuned and assist the recovery process. All the training required for 100-mile trail races exacts a toll on the body, with waste products building up in our muscles on a regular basis. Massage therapy is the answer. Besides the obvious effect of relaxation and refreshment of our systems, an added benefit of massage is in preventing injury or rehabilitating a previous one. During the race at specific aid stations, a quick massage can bring you back to a high level when things start slipping and performance has started to decline. Try it—you'll like it.

Limit the Number of Races During the Training Buildup for "The Main Event."

Concentrate and focus your efforts on this one most important race and, if you want to race during the buildup phase, then consider them "training races," in which you keep plenty in reserve. This way you are able to get right back into your normal pattern without losing time recovering from an exhausting effort. Probably four races of marathon distance or longer are plenty within the six months before the big one, and there would seem to be no reason in my mind to run any 50-mile races during this time. It is my belief that 50-mile races will detract from your ultimate performance over 100 miles if done too close to the race. Additionally, while there is surely a diversity of opinion on this subject, I strongly feel that one 100-mile race per year is all that we should race. I'm not sure the body is designed to run these 100-mile races at all, and we don't really know if there are any long-term negative effects from them. Train properly for one and allow the body a reasonable amount of recovery time before jumping into the next one. I personally believe that it is more rewarding to run one quality performance than several mediocre ones, and we have to allow our bodies the opportunity to perform without constantly beating them down.

Do Not Eat Any Solid Food During the 100 Mile Trail Race; Drink Liquids Only

I will make this explanation brief. Eating solid food during a race when your body is obviously under stress and the digestive processes are slowed is senseless and could very well be the reason for our energy problems during the race. It is my contention that we can eliminate the extreme highs and lows experienced during these long races if we simply eliminate the digestive blockage that inevitably occurs when eating solid food on the run. I suspect the body will work much more efficiently if we don't force it to utilize excess energy digesting food; Furthermore, I question whether the problems of dehydration experienced during the race are caused simply because the fluids we are drinking can't get through the stomach in order to be absorbed into our systems. The solution to this problem is to either get a blender and liquify your favorite foods or go with a pre-mixed food source and drink it at specific predetermined aid stations. It works for me, and I see no reason why everyone can't use this system for success.

I hope these recommendations are successful for you. Please remember that these are only suggestions and more importantly, they are merely my personal opinions. I realize that there are as many differing opinions out there as there ultrarunners. Good luck to you all.

The Advantage of a Run/Walk Strategy for 24 Hour Runs
by Karl King

In the Olander Park 24 Hour, which also served as the USATF National Championship, Kevin Setnes and Tom Possert waged a fierce duel, pushing each other to personal bests (160 and 158 miles, respectively) in the process. What was fascinating was that they used different strategies: Kevin alternated running and walking, while Tom ran continuously. Karl King, president of the company that makes SUCCEED! sports drink, and a sponsor of Kevin, reports on the various factors that led to the choice of Kevin's specific run/walk strategy.

Kevin Setnes and Tom Possert treated us to magnificent efforts at the Olander Park 24 Hour. Their methods raised the question of strategy for these events: run and walk, or run continuously. Tom ran continuously with an efficient form and a pace much slower than his normal training pace. Kevin opted for a 25-minute run at a relaxed training pace followed by a five-minute walk. The results were very close, so it can be argued that either method is good, especially for the right runner, but it is worth looking at the run/walk strategy in some detail, especially since Kevin used it to improve his personal best from 125 to 160.4 miles!

Might the run/walk strategy be better for the runner who does not specifically train to run at a slow pace? Here are some thoughts on this topic.

Energy considerations

There is not a lot of literature on the biochemistry of 24-hour runs because there is not great academic interest in it. Energy demands during a marathon are relatively well known, so we have at least a starting point for consideration of energy processing during long runs.

Muscle cells can burn carbohydrate, fat, or protein for energy, but for endurance events, most of the energy must necessarily come from fat burning. Carbohydrate provides much of the energy early in the run, but the body shifts the emphasis to fat burning as the run continues. Carbohydrate is needed to some extent for efficient use of fat. The challenge is to supply enough carbohydrate when the tendency is to run out long before the event is over. It is assumed that a runner will eat plenty of carbohydrate during the run.

Slow, aerobic running will automatically lead to fat burning, but there is a tendency in long runs for the pace to approach the lactate threshold where carbohydrate is burned in larger amounts. One's lactate threshold pace is not constant, but slows as fatigue sets in, making it easier and easier for the runner to overuse carbohydrate. As the main muscle fibers fatigue, others must work harder, approaching lactate threshold. Starting too fast, winding up the pace, and muscle fatigue all lead to burning carbohydrate too soon. Burn all your carbohydrate and you are reduced to the survival shuffle. Can walking help break those patterns?

Fat metabolism begins on one biomechanical path and carbohydrate begins on another. They join in a biomechanical process called the Krebs cycle. The two pathways are self and cross-regulated. Self-regulation prevents you from burning fuel faster than you need it. Cross-regulation prevents you from burning both fuels at maximum rate simultaneously.

The practical implication is that if you run slightly too fast, it tends to reduce fat burning at the expense of much needed carbohydrate. It does not hurt at all while it's happening, so great discipline is required for the continuous runner to hold a pace that does not burn carbohydrate too fast. Most runners, even excellent ones, tend to go out too fast and crash.

Walking for a significant time gives the body a chance to self-regulate the rate of carbohydrate burning without shutting down the fat burning, which is slower to start and slower to stop. That conserves carbohydrate and provides some time for carbohydrate to increase in the muscle fibers.

Many of the essential chemical reactions in the muscle cells and mitochondria are regulated by enzyme activity. The activity regulation occurs as a function of acidity, ATP/ADP ratio, and fuel concentration. Walking allows these controlling substances to be restored so enzymes work more effectively.

Timing

Kevin ran 25 minutes and walked five. Why run 25 minutes? Why walk five minutes? What about running five miles and walking one mile, a strategy popularized by Tom Osler in the late 1970s?

The run/walk concept is that the walk allows enough recovery to permit a relatively consistent running pace instead of the eventual slow shuffle. The splits from Olander showed that Kevin's average pace declined very little over the first 100 miles.

From a mathematical standpoint, we aim to minimize walking time and maximize running time, provided the running pace does not slow greatly. So, how long can the run time be and how short can the walk time be?

From Tim Noakes' *The Lore Of Running*, we have data suggesting that the most efficient use of aerobic energy is over periods of ten to thirty minutes of running. He does not apply this to ultrarunning, so the interpretation is somewhat debatable, but it suggests that long continuous running is not necessarily the most efficient method for aerobic energy production. This suggests that running five miles (45 to 55 minutes) is too long.

From David Costill's *Inside Running*, we have data regarding heart rate recovery from a fast running session. This illustrates that it takes about four minutes for significant recovery to occur. This result is far removed from slow-paced ultrarunning, but after many hours of running, it may be more applicable than one might first think. Again, it can give us an idea of what the body is normally capable of. It suggests that a walk of 30 seconds will not be long enough for adequate recovery. It also suggests that walking a mile (about 15 minutes) is longer than necessary, and thus concedes too much time to the slower pace.

Physiology

The non-walker must run a relatively slow pace in order not to crash badly. The walk/runner has to run a faster pace to make up for the walking break. In many cases though, that pace will be closer to the runner's most efficient pace. If you specifically train to run efficiently at ten minutes per mile, it will help, but most runners train for a faster pace and only occasionally compete in 24-hour runs. Ten minutes per mile is unlikely to be their most efficient pace.

The walking time may also relax tense tissues and allow fluids to circulate and carry away metabolites. That may lead to less fatigue from pounding, and less loss of elasticity. While running on a flat surface may seem advantageous, it is unrelenting on the muscles. Many prefer trail running because the hills give quads and hamstrings a chance to "relax." A walking break may provide a similar advantage because the muscles are being used differently during the walk.

Mental

The five-minute walk also provides a mental break. It is something to look forward to. On the negative side, starting up again may be a problem. According to Kevin, that was not a problem for him.

The continuous runner may see walking as negative, while the walk in the walk/run method is planned and is part of a pattern, rather than a concession to fatigue. The break is also a good time to eat and drink.

A walk also allows time for branched chain amino acid (BCAA) concentration in the blood to be raised, defeating the tryptophan/serotonin connection. BCAA is lowered by exercising muscles when energy supplies are low. When BCAA concentration falls, the amino acid tryptophan more readily enters the brain, where it is used to make the neurotransmitter serotonin. Serotonin promotes a relaxed, sleepy feeling. Combined with general fatigue, the effect is mind-numbing and very negative. Walking gives the body time to put some BCAA back into the blood, reducing the serotonin effect.

Summary

There are many reasons why the run/walk strategy is advantageous to the runner who does not practice a specific style for 24-hour runs. While the five-mile run and one-mile walk has been used before, the 25-minute run and five-minute walk may make more sense in consideration of the physiology and body chemistry mechanisms that are critical for success in the 24-hour. One of the beauties of this sport is that every runner can experiment and test the theories in actual practice.

How to Walk While Running
by Tom Kline

How do you run an ultra while simultaneously conserving energy, avoiding injury, reducing muscle fatigue and maintaining a respectable pace, all without having to stop? The answer: race walk part of the time.

Many outstanding multi-day runners incorporate walking into their race strategy. Various authors have also indicated some of the advantages to runners of taking walking breaks during ultras. As is often suggested, frequent walking is a smart thing to do, at least for most runners who are trying to cover a long distance. Even world class ultrarunners are now walking part of the time in long races. It is an intelligent race strategy.

Surprisingly, however, although many runners have discovered the benefits of walking, few know *how* to walk, at least not optimally. Consequently, most runners are not able to take full advantage of the time they spend walking in an ultra. Furthermore, their inefficient walking motions are fatiguing, require considerably more effort in order to maintain an adequate pace, and thus prevent the runner from taking full advantage of the psychological break from running.

Experienced ultrarunners may have spent years perfecting their running style. Arm positioning and movement, foot placement, stride, and posture are all important factors in achieving a good running style and reducing the chances of injury. The same goes for walking. There is an optimal style, one that can help ultrarunners move faster and longer and more comfortably, while also preventing injury.

The formal definition of race walking is "a series of steps so taken that unbroken contact with the ground is maintained." The two basic rules covering race walking are that one foot must always be on the ground and that the knee of the advancing leg must be "locked" for a moment. Admittedly, ultrarunners are not concerned about being disqualified in a race if these rules are not in effect. However, a highly efficient walking style for runners can still be derived from the techniques of race walking.

Many walkers become "sloggers" during their walking breaks. Slogging is nothing more than an inefficient way to walk fast. It is characterized by a forward lean of the torso. The head is bent down (with the eyes looking at the ground as if the runner is searching for money). The arms droop or hang at the sides. The elbows are straight and there is little or no rhythmic movement of the arms. Sloggers walk on their toes and their knees bend on every stride.

Walking can be significantly more efficient for runners when four simple techniques are followed:

- Keep the torso erect and perpendicular to the ground. Do not bend the head forward. Look up.
- Bend the arms at the elbow at about a 45-degree angle. The arms should be moved rhythmically across the center of the body while walking.
- Momentarily straighten the knee of the advancing leg. This will allow the muscles of the lower leg to be used to help thrust the body forward.
- Land on the heel of the foot, not the toes.
  These changes in your walking style are easy to master and will allow you to walk faster and farther with less fatigue.

The first photo shows the typical slogging style of walking. Note how the head and torso are bent. Since the head is one of the heaviest of the body's extremities, leaning it forward causes fatigue. Allowing the arms to hang at the sides is also tiring. A vigorous swaying of the arms helps to push the body forward when the elbows are straight. It is more difficult to move the arms rhythmically. This slows you down. Lack of arm movement also reduces stride length.

The second photo shows a more optimal walking style suitable for the runner.

Slogging Style of Walking   Optimal Walking Style

Note the erect torso, bent elbows, and the straight knee of the advancing leg. In addition, unlike running, the walker's foot lands on the outside of the heel, allowing the walker to thrust forward. A good way to master proper arm movement is to envision a piston constantly pumping. Try standing still and moving the arms vigorously across your midsection.

The cliché "practice makes perfect" certainly applies to perfecting a walking style. The best way to begin is simply to start walking, for about a half-mile at a time. Concentrate on the four elements of walking form. Is your head bent forward? Do your arms hang limply at your side? Are your knees bent? Do you walk on your toes? If so, you are a slogger. Then try walking the same half-mile optimizing your style and correcting each of these faults.

If you are training for a race of 100 km or longer, you should invest between 10 and 15 percent of your training miles in walking. In ultra races in which I have walked, people have often asked what my pace was. My answer is usually 13 minutes per mile. When a race goes beyond 50 miles, however, I may slow to a 17-minute pace. In training and racing I recommend that runners strive for a 12- to 14-minute per mile walking pace. Sound slow? If you could average this pace for 40 hours and also fit in six hours of running at an eight-minute-per-mile pace, then you would cover 227 miles in 48 hours and still have a couple of hours left for sleep. Race walkers are hip people. You can be too with a little practice.

How to Rest While Running
by Nathan Whiting

There are moments when the fatigue and pain are just too much, moments when you know you have to quit, moments when you can't think a positive thought, moments you are ten times more tired than possible. It is time to rest.

Rest is very simple, yet there is a sense of hurry that persists. Forget the competition. Often the one who rests first has the strength to win later. Forget the clock, anguish is not speed. A few minutes sitting is not eternity. Here are a few basic ways to rest in a long race.

Walk. You all know how to walk. Long strides are better than short steps. Stretching muscles helps more than letting them tighten. Deep breaths are important. A tired runner usually pants. Open the lungs and bring air in. Refresh yourself with air. Walk uphill, or on very steep descents. Don't walk into the wind when it's cold (you can chill easily). Don't walk where there is no wind on a hot day. You will boil. Use walking to regulate body temperature. Become aware of how your body feels walking and running. What is the difference? How do they help each other?

Stand. Find a flat place. Stand still. Close your eyes. Feel the movements your body is still making. Let each one calm down. Let your muscles hang. Your jaw, shoulders, arms, ribs, hip, rear end and leg muscles drop and relax. Take a deep breath in, then completely out. Widen your toes. Open your eyes slowly. Let the beauty of the world come in, don't reach for it. Smile. Run.

Sit. Find a chair or closest equivalent. Drink a lot. Eat. Massage your feet. Wear new shoes. Close your eyes for a few seconds. Feel dizzy. Find your strengths. Revise your race plan. Smile. Get up.

Squat. Find something to hang onto. Stretch your hamstrings a little if you want. Slowly squat. Relax and breathe as you go down. Keep your heels on the ground until you are down, then let them come up. Close your eyes as you rest on your toes. Put your hands on the ground. Let your head hang and pull you into a ball. Breathe into any stiff, tense or sore places, slowly and deeply. Look into yourself. See your heart, stomach, lungs. Let them become lights of strength. Find your strengths. Straighten your back. Open your eyes. Push up from your heels. Smile. Run.

Lie down. Find a place not too different in temperature from the race course (or you will never get up). Tell someone to wake you. Shoes off, rub your feet. Take some nourishment. Nap for a while, ten minutes to two hours. No more, unless it is a race longer than 48 hours. If you can't sleep, roll slowly from front to back a few times. Stretching any time it feels good. If cramping, drink. Breathe deeply and easily as you do. Lie quietly for a while. Think about someplace else. Get up slowly. Walk a while before you start to run.

The Lure of the Trail
by Don Allison

As evidenced by a shifting trend over the past two decades, trail ultras are becoming increasingly popular, especially 100-mile trail runs, which seem to be growing steadily every year. The lures of running on the trail are many: the chance to get closer to nature, a more forgiving running surface, and a heightened sense of adventure are just a few. The sense of satisfaction derived from having completed a difficult and beautiful course is what keeps runners coming back to trail ultras in droves.

The trail is not without its hazards, however. Although ultrarunners are a hardy breed of athletes, seemingly always ready to overcome any obstacles that get in their way, there are areas of concern that all ultrarunners should heed in both training and racing on the trails. Here are some of the issues ultrarunners should have knowledge of before heading out on the trail.

Footing

This is the most immediate and basic concern for a trail runner. The changeable surface underfoot is one of the most appealing aspects of trail running, but can present a formidable challenge for the beginning trail runner. Watching others effortlessly run over roots, rocks, and stumps, across streams, and up and down steep hills can be intimidating at first.

Like all skills, however, running on trails is a learned technique. Much like golfers and tennis players need to master hand-eye coordination to become more proficient at their sports, trail runners must learn to master foot-eye coordination in order to become more proficient trail runners. Gaining a "feel" for the trail will allow you to proceed with more ease, which is critical to becoming comfortable with trail running. In his article *Running on the Rocks*, Peter Gagarin offers insight into mastering the art of running on impediment-strewn trails.

Hills

Hills are as much a part of trail running as roots and rocks. Beginning trail runners are always amazed at the steepness and length of the hills, both up and down. Consequently, a strategy must be adopted that is different than one would employ in a road race, in which most runners try to power up and over any hills they encounter.

The primary concern on uphills is energy management. Over the long ultra distances, it is easy to squander precious energy reserves trying to get up and over a hill. Thus, most ultrarunners, especially those in trail 100-milers, walk many or all long, steep uphills. Developing an efficient uphill walking technique will save an ultrarunner a tremendous amount of energy, which can be then allocated over flat and downhill sections of the course, on which they will cover a far greater amount of ground for a comparable effort.

At first glance, running downhills would appear to be a piece of cake. Just take off and let gravity do the work for you, right? Well yes, in principle that is what you hope to do, although in practice it can be a more difficult skill than it first appears, especially on trails. The biggest obstacle is a runner's fear that he or she will trip and fall. This is a well-grounded fear (no pun intended), as there are few nastier experiences in ultrarunning than a bad fall on a downhill trail. Proper technique, however, will lessen the chances of that happening.

What is proper downhill running technique? The most important asset of proficient downhill trail runners is confidence, the belief that you can run a fast pace down rocky and root-filled trails without mishap. Like most skills, practice will perfect this technique. The key is to let gravity assist your effort. If you are able to do this on downhill sections of trail, the energy savings will be substantial.

Most beginning trail runners however, possessing a healthy fear of tripping and falling, will "put on the brakes," while running downhill, which will not only result in covering ground more slowly than more experienced runners, but will also use more of that precious energy, and perhaps worst of all make the upper quadricep muscles extremely sore and painful in later stages of an ultra. Learning how to proficiently run downhills is perhaps the one critical skill that separates those who are able to complete long trail ultras and those who are not.

Drinking Water

In training and sometimes racing, the availability of fluids is often a major concern. The best way to cope with this issue is to be as self-sufficient as possible. Although it may seem cool and shaded on the trail, you can sweat just as much as you do on open roads under the hot sun. The need to replace lost fluids is of paramount importance on the trail. You must calculate the availability of water along your route and how much you are able to carry on your own. Three miles to the next available water may not seem very far, until you have been out on the trail for hours and are bone dry and exhausted.

Some feel comfortable carrying water bottles, while others use waist packs. Sometimes a combination of both is best. Hydration packs allow for carrying even more water than the limited amount available in water bottles.

It is extremely risky to drink water from running streams in this day and age. However if you must do so, carrying a water bottle with a filter, such as those sold by

Oasis, and carrying iodine-based water purification tablets, will increase the chances of your escaping an aliment such as giardia from drinking impure water.

Poison Plants

Anyone who has suffered the effects of poison oak or poison ivy contracted along the trail knows just what an uncomfortable nuisance it can be. Individuals vary widely in their susceptibility to the poison plants, but everyone should be aware of preventive measures that taken in advance can save a lot of discomfort later on.

The most important preventative measure is knowledge, of just what poison oak, poison ivy, and poison sumac plants look like. Also be aware if the plants are in bloom at the time of year you are running on a particular trail. Of course, keeping susceptible areas of the body covered with clothing is great prevention, but not be a practical solution in warm weather. In the unfortunate circumstance that you acquire a rash from coming in contact with the plant, there are many over-the-counter products, such as Tecnu, that will help mitigate the itch.

Ticks

It is amazing that something so small and as innocuous as a tick can wreak such extensive damage on the human body, but recent history has shown that ticks can result in Lyme Disease, a malady that can end even the most promising ultrarunning career. Sadly, many running careers have been prematurely cut short, primarily due to not taking necessary precautions or ignoring the symptoms of Lyme Disease.

If you run on trails that are known to contain ticks, it is very important to inspect your body for ticks after a run. This should be done after every trail run, especially if you live in an area of the country known to contain ticks. Furthermore, symptoms that may be evidence of Lyme Disease should not be ignored.

Snakes

Yes, trails and wooded areas are home to those slithery creatures that Hollywood has used to scare moviegoers for years—snakes. Will you ever encounter a snake on the trail? There are areas of the country where this is a real possibility. If so, keeping watch is a good idea, if possible. Most snakes will avoid attacking humans, unless the individual comes directly in contact with them. Keeping a minimum distance of six feet between yourself and a snake should prevent the reptile from attacking.

Wildlife

Nature is not only the province of snakes, but to many other creatures of the animal kingdom as well. In many parts of the country, cougars and mountain lions populate the trail. The tragic death of a California ultrarunner from a mountain lion attack while out training on the Western States trail several years ago graphically illustrates the very real danger wildlife can pose for the trail runner.

To avoid problems, hike or run in small groups rather than alone. Individuals running or moving rapidly are at higher risk. Make enough noise to prevent surprising a creature; a sturdy walking stick could be useful in fending off an animal if necessary. Be alert to your surroundings, especially in dense cover and when sitting, crouching or lying down.

Running Alone

Ultrarunners by nature are self-sufficient. The ability to run extremely long distances in remote locales breeds confidence, in many cases to the point of cockiness. Ultrarunners often head out on the trail by themselves to tackle hilly, difficult trails in remote locations. Is this a smart thing to do? Is it safe? Certainly, becoming lost or injured on the trail while running alone is a real possibility.

As shown above, there are a myriad of potential dangers that could lead to trouble on the trail. Obviously, having someone else with you on the run or running with a group is the best insurance. Running with others may not help you avoid these dangers, but will certainly help you cope if you do encounter problems.

It's not always possible to run with others, however. If you must run alone, it's a good idea to plan ahead. The first precaution you should take is to make sure you do not get lost. Some trails have blazes or markings. Even so, they can become confusing if you lose your way. Carrying a map is imperative, especially if you are at all unfamiliar with the area. Also, keep track of where you have gone and where you are going. It's easy to daydream out in the beauty of nature and lose track of your surroundings. Global Positioning Satellite (GPS) devices have grown in popularity in recent years. Having such an instrument and knowing how to use it can also be of great help in knowing where you are on the trail.

You should be well equipped as well when you head out on the trail alone, especially for an extended period of time. You should carry supplies that will come to your aid in the eventuality that you become lost or run into trouble. Here is a list of suggested items that may come to your aid if things take a turn for the worse while running a remote trail alone. Decide which of the items will be most valuable to you and you are able to carry without too much inconvenience. You will very happy you did!

- Personal identification (with medical history)
- Water

- Fluid replacement drink
- Electrolytes
- Energy bar
- Ibuprofen
- Band aids
- Matches
- Knife
- Space blanket
- Map
- Compass
- Flashlight (with batteries)
- Adhesive tape
- Toilet paper
- Vaseline
- Money
- Water treatment tablets

Etiquette

One of the most appealing aspects of trail running is the ability to enjoy the beauty and quiet of nature. Common courtesy suggests that you do your part to keep it that way. Never, ever leave litter on the trail. No one is going to pick up after you, and you will only be destroying the environment and marring the beauty of the outdoors for others. Also, leave your aggression at home. You are sure to encounter others on the trail, be they other runners, hikers, or cyclists. They also have the right to enjoy the trail, so be considerate of their right to do so. It will make for a better experience for all.

Summary

After all of this, why would anyone ever venture out on the trails for a run? You might ask yourself that question, until you have effortlessly run alone on a beautiful trail on a clear day when all of nature's beauty is on display. Those who have experienced such days usually become converts to trail running. Add in the many and varied challenges that are offered by getting off the road and it is easy to understand why trail ultras have grown so quickly in popularity during the past several years. With knowledge, confidence, and a healthy respect for the trail, you will be able to fully immerse yourself in one of the great lures of ultras: trail running.

10 Tips for Downhill Trail Running

By Don Allison

Advice often given regarding improvement is, "Work on your weaknesses, not your strengths." It's good advice, which can be applied to running on trails, especially the downhills. For new or even experienced runners, dealing with downhills can be the most difficult aspect of trail running to master. If you are one those runners who usually passes competitors on the uphills, only to have them fly by on the downhills, here are a few tips to help you maintain that hard-earned lead, or simply to enjoy running on the trails without worrying about ending up face-first on the trail

Relax—and don't forget to breathe

Like anything else in life, learning to be a proficient downhill runner takes practice. Perhaps the most important aspect of downhill running on technical trails is to learn to run with ease and confidence, which results from letting go of unnecessary fear and tension and allowing your body relax. At first you will need to remind yourself to keep your body from tensing, by shaking out your arms, legs, and shoulders. With time, it will happen more naturally.

The focus, concentration and anxiety experienced by those new to trail downhills can also cause one to forget to maintain proper breathing—and it is awfully tough run well if you aren't breathing! Remind yourself to take deep, regular breathes. It will help your maintain a steady stride, conserve precious energy, and relax your body.

Assess the conditions

Weather affects everything, including downhill trail running. Dry trails are usually the easiest on which to run, but not always. Smooth rocks covered with slick, dry leaves can be as slippery as an ice skating rink. Similarly, humidity can make for very challenging conditions, adding a thin layer of slickness to roots and rocks. Conversely, pouring rain can be better than a light rain, as it can wash the humidity and slickness off the trail, roots, and rocks. If you are sure everything will be wet, it can make for easier negotiation, as illogical as it sounds. Of course, rain can turn a trail of pure dirt into a quagmire of shoe-sucking mud, which can make for very slow going, even on the downhills. And for those who traverse the trails in winter conditions, snow can be the biggest challenge of all, since it is slippery and obscures what lies beneath—often a layer of ice.

Learn to fall the right way

At one time or another, we are all bound to go from vertical to horizontal on the trail. Not all downhill falls on the trail are equal, however; some are more painful than others. Those resulting in broken bones and/or loss of consciousness are obviously to be avoided at all costs. So what should you do if you feel yourself careening out of control on a steep, rocky downhill? First, try to remain upright, and try not to panic. You might stagger forward for several strides, but will still be able to gain a solid foot placement that will keep you from tumbling onto the ground. Using a tree to arrest your forward momentum can work if you are not moving too quickly, but can result in injury if you are. At best, you will learn what it is like to be tackled a 250-pound linebacker!

If you feel you are going to fall and nothing you can do will keep you upright, there are two things you can do to limit the damage. First, try your best not to tense your entire body. Of course, that is easier said than done, when everything in your brain is preparing your body for the pain of crashing into the ground. But a tense body will almost always absorb more damage than a relaxed one. Second, try to roll into the fall if you can manage it. Let your body fall forward, landing with your shoulder and rolling onto your back, while protecting your head and arms. Of course, if you should land on a pointed rock, it will still be pretty painful. Trying to break your fall with your hands, knees, hips, or worst of all—your head, is an invitation to serious injury.

Better balance—it's not all in your legs

In all kinds of running, even on flat roads, the arms help balance the body, in order to allow for proper posture and a comfortable stride. Try running without your arms sometime to see just how much you use your upper body for balancing. This is especially true on the trail. Learn to use your arms and upper body in maintaining balance on downhill trails; it can add to greatly to your expertise.

Learn to feel the trail with your feet

Even if your eyes can't see exactly where or what you are landing on, your feet can. Practice and experience will help you learn to "feel" the trail with your feet. You will get to know by feel how solid or tenuous your foot placement is, and whether you can push off strongly with your next stride, if you need to chop it to regain your balance, or if you need to stop completely. Experienced trail runners know that feel is at least, if not more important than actually seeing where you are landing. Visually assessing the viability of each foot placement will make for slow going on the trail.

Let momentum be your friend

A key aspect of mastering any kind of downhill running is learning to run without the "brakes" on. This is especially true on roads, where there are no impediments to your forward progress, but is also important on trails. Leaning backwards can seem like the safest way to avoid falling, but in actuality it only makes negotiating the terrain more difficult. A far better running style is to lean slightly forward—not so much that your center of gravity is too far forward and you are out of control, but enough to let gravity help you. This, combined with improved footwork, will greatly enhance your speed on the downhill trails. Of course, it takes time to gain confidence in this kind of technique, so be patient and make small, incremental improvements in your downhill posture.

Obviously, gravity makes running downhills easier then going uphill. On those trails that feature switchbacks, maximizing your forward momentum can be a real energy saver. Maintain your pace right up until the turn on a switchback, and then plant your foot strongly as you pivot into the turn, without coming to a stop. On many switchbacks it is unnecessary to stop or even interrupt your pace in order to keep going.

All rocks are not created equal

There is a saying that the difference between trail running in the Eastern part of the USA, as opposed to the West, is that when you kick the rocks in the East, they don't move. Anyone who has felt the stinging pain of stubbing his or her toe on a sharp rock embedded in the ground knows how true this can be. The point is that you should know the general layout of the terrain on which you are running; it can and should affect your approach to downhill running. Scrambling down a pitch of loose rock and dirt is a lot different than hopping from big boulder to big boulder. Optimal technique will vary on each surface. Don't forget too, that just because you can't see it does not mean its not there. On some trails, rocks and other impediments are very will hidden in the underbrush and under trees and roots.

Getting to the root of the matter

In addition to rocks, many trails feature pesky tree roots, which as we all know, *definitely* do not move when you kick them. Sometimes they seem to be strategically placed to trip up an unsuspecting runner. Obviously, lifting the feet up and over roots will prevent such trips, but that is easier said than done. With practice, a combination of sighting and feel for the trail will allow you to avoid being tripped up by tree roots, without slowing your stride to "high jump" every root on the trail. In addition, roots can be as slick as rocks when wet with rain and/or humidity, so be careful when attempting to plant your foot on a root to push off.

Choose the right shoes

There are all kinds of trail shoes out there, and they make all kinds of claims as to what they can do. It is important to have a sturdy shoe in order to ward off unwanted sharp objects and to cushion hard blows to the feet. On the other hand, lighter, more flexible shoes will provide a better feel for the trail. It comes down to an individual choice. I have yet to find a shoe that will offer a completely sure grip on the slickest of rocks and roots, but perhaps someday one will be invented.

Enjoy the experience!

Downhill running can be an exhilarating experience. The feeling of moving fast and covering a lot of ground quickly can provide a big mental boost in both training and racing. Mastering the skill of negotiating tricky terrain can provide a real sense of accomplishment and make trail running much more enjoyable. So get out there and let the good times roll!

Staying the Course
by Peter Gagarin

Call it taking the wrong turn, losing the trail, or missing the streamers. Let's just call it getting lost. You can blame it on a poorly marked trail, on someone that led you astray, on fate, on bad luck, or maybe even on yourself. Let's just say, whoever or whatever is to blame, it happens to a distressingly large number of ultrarunners at a distressingly large number of ultras. What can you do about it? How do some people manage to stay on course while others get terribly lost?

Getting lost in ultras isn't limited to the frontrunners. In a 10-km, getting lost is seldom a problem. As long as the police car knows where it is going, slower runners can usually see runners ahead of them. But with the small fields in most ultras, you may be out of sight of other runners for most of the race. And with dozens of turns spread out over 30 or 50 or 100 miles, you can't expect course marshals to gently guide you around the course.

If you happen to get lost in a 10-km, it is disappointing and will probably get you pretty angry, but it's not the end of the world. There will be many more 10-km races, and the amount of time and energy you have wasted is relatively small.

Getting lost in an ultra is more serious. The extra mileage you end up running may be the difference between a good race and a poor one, between beating a time limit or not, between finishing or not. Mentally, it can be devastating. So many months of training, so much mental energy invested, the planning, the traveling, and all of the attendant costs—and all of a sudden you're out in the middle of nowhere, probably at night, and you've got no idea where the trail is. Ultras are long enough and hard enough without adding private side trips. What's to be done? How do ultrarunners deal with this potential nightmare?

Accept the Fact That Ultras are Different
Actually, the first thing to do is all in the mind, and it's already been mentioned— you can't expect course marshals to gently guide you around the course. You have to take some of the responsibility yourself. Trail ultras aren't like the New York Marathon. There is no blue line to follow from start to finish. No matter how well organized a trail ultra is, no matter how many people have spent time marking the course, you're still pretty much on your own. The key is to accept this fact. Once you accept the fact that staying on the course requires some effort on your part, that there won't be the equivalent of a police car or a long blue line to follow, then you will be way ahead of the game.

One way to tell if someone is really accepting some of the responsibility for staying on course is to listen to his or her comments afterwards. If all of the blame is put on the organizers, then you can bet that it won't be the last time that person gets lost. But if the person shoulders even a little bit of the blame, then progress is being made. You may think this is unfair, that it's the organizer's responsibility to mark the course. You may be right, but being right and lost still boils down to being lost. So you have to work at it, but how? It's easiest to break it down into two parts: checking out the course before the race, and employing tactics during the race.

Checking Out the Course in Advance

Ideally, you will have run every part of the course before the race. Not only that, you'll have done this in the dark, in the rain, and when you are really tired. But we usually can't manage any of these things unless the race is in our local area. But there is still a lot that can be done.

Most "trail" races have a surprisingly large part of the course on paved or dirt roads. The Leadville 100 Mile has 25 miles of pavement and another 20 miles of drivable dirt road. The Old Dominion 100 Mile has many back-country dirt roads that the course uses for a few miles at a time. While some of these may be closed to crew traffic during the race, they are usually open for checking the course a day or two earlier. Large parts of some trail ultras may be drivable with a four-wheel drive vehicle, if they are permitted. Even courses such as the Ice Age Trail in Wisconsin or the Laurel Highlands in Pennsylvania intersect roads every so often.

If I am investing the time, effort, and money to travel to a trail ultra, I will make sure I get there at least a day or two in advance. I'll spend that day or two driving to every point on the course that's accessible by car. What am I looking for? Problems. What sorts of problems? If the trail crosses a road, is it clear exactly where it goes back into the woods? Is it straight across, or will I have to turn left or right on the road for a while? Has the trail been marked by the organizers, and if so, how? What if it's dark when I get there? Next I'll follow the trail for 50 or 100 yards on each side of the road. Often a trailhead is the start for two or three trails, with a fork just into the woods. (The reason for only going 50 or 100 yards is that I'm trying to get as little exercise as possible.) If the trail turns and follows the road for a while, and then turns off into the woods again, I'll make sure I know where the turnoff is. Then if someone driving by happens to remove a couple of course markers, I'll still know where to go. The less left to chance, the better. If I'm lucky enough to have a handler, we will also make sure he or she knows where the course goes. It's not much fun, or good for the morale of either of us, if he or she becomes lost and misses a rendezvous point.

Another thing to check out is whether any parts of the trail have any marking system of their own, independent of the markings of the organizers. For example, the trail section of the JFK is on the Appalachian Trail, marked with small white rectangles painted on trees. One rectangle means the trail goes straight ahead; two means that a sharp turn or trail junction is coming and you should watch out. It's better to learn this ahead of time than to be asking at the finish, "Boy I had a hard time following the trail—what were those white marks I kept seeing?"

It also helps to check out the trail markings put out by the organizers. What color are they? How are they hung—high, low, often, rarely? Is the same color used throughout? Are they hung all along the trail, or just at intersections? Will they show up at night? At Leadville they placed three kinds of markers: orange pennants and orange surveyor's tape for daytime and yellow reflective tape for the night. It works great, except for the few people who don't realize that there were more than just the oranges ones marking the trail. Similarly, the Vermont 100 Mile uses arrowed pie plates for course marking and confirmation.

All of this checking takes time, particularly if you're careful about it (such as taking notes about any tricky places to help you remember them). I figure on one day for a 50-mile course, and two or more days for a 100-mile.

Most trail ultras have briefings before the race. I use these meetings as a chance to ask questions about parts of the course I'm worried about. I try to ask questions to lots of people—sometimes the organizers, sometimes other runners who have been out on the trail. The problem is that if you ask just one person what the trail is like, or how hard it is to follow, the answer you'll get depends on that person's frame of reference. A trail may be wet, rocky and easy to follow to someone used to running on vague desert trails. To someone from the Northeast the same trail may be dry, smooth and hard to follow. So I'll ask a number of people what the trail is like and where the tricky turns are. I learn a little from one, a little more from another. Overall, I'll be better prepared.

The final thing I should mention about checking out the course has to do with maps. Get the course map put out by the organizer. Get the state or county road maps and the Forest Service map if there is one. Maybe there are special maps of the trail, or special guidebooks to the trail (certainly true for races on part of the Appalachian or Pacific Crest Trails, but there are also locally available guides to a number of other trails we have ultras on, such as the Laurel Highlands Trail in Pennsylvania). Finally, get the United States Government Service (USGS) topographic map(s). If you can't read a map, get someone to help you. The more you learn about the course, the less the chance that five or ten or twenty hours into the race you'll turn down the wrong road. This goes for both you and your crew.

During the Race

Surprisingly enough, it's probably easier to go off course when you are running with someone else than when you are running alone. (The one exception to this would be when you are running with someone who knows the course extremely well.) Companionship on the trail usually takes your mind off what you're doing. It distracts you from paying attention to where the next turn is on the trail. It's as if your body and brain go on automatic pilot. In a physical sense it can be great; you "wake up" five, ten, or thirty minutes later and realize that the time and the miles have just been floating by. The problem is that sometimes you also realize that you've got no idea if you're still on the course or not.

Running behind others also tends to give you a false sense of security—just follow them, you think. No problem. So you "float." Meanwhile the runners in front of you are floating too—all except for the person in front of the group, who figures that if he or she takes a wrong turn, then someone behind will say something. It's the ultrarunner's version of the blind leading the blind.

This floating can happen when you're running by yourself, too. Call it daydreaming. Later in the race you can just call it getting tired, mentally tired. The challenge is to pay attention, to force yourself to stay alert.

It's hard to do this for the entire 50 or 100 miles, but often there are sections in which you can relax to some extent. Often these are on the road sections of these races. But even then you may have to watch out for tricky intersections. As a rule, all intersections can be tricky, particularly at night; however, some are easier to miss than others.

In drawing A, the course comes to a T-junction along the stem of the T. If you are floating, you should still probably wake up when you reach the junction, since you have to turn right or left. In drawing B, it's easy to float right along, wake up at some point further down the road, and have no idea whether the intersection is ahead of or behind you. This can happen on trails, or even on paved roads, particularly at night.

If I've checked out the intersection of type B in advance, at least I'll know to stay alert. I may also have found some other landmarks to help me spot the turn. Maybe there's a house across the road. (Will I see it at night?) Maybe it's after a steep downhill. (Is there more than one steep downhill on that part of the course that could confuse me?) Maybe it's just one mile from the previous intersection. (How will I know how far one mile is?) Intersections of type B are easiest to miss when you're turning off a larger road or trail onto a smaller one. It's so easy to cruise right by. But if you're paying attention, the problem is more than half solved.

One habit that you should get into, whether you're at a difficult intersection

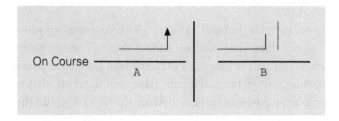

On Course

A   B

or just running along, is that of *looking backwards* regularly. This is particularly useful if the trail has regular markings (such as the Appalachian Trail). I'm subject to fits of insecurity during an ultra. Am I still on course? If I don't see a marker for a little while, I'll look over my shoulder to see if there are any markers visible going the other way. If so, I'm all right; if not, maybe it's time to start getting worried. If you're going to get off course, the sooner you find out the better.

The habit of looking backwards is just part of a more general habit of *looking*. Pick your head up, take in the view, look for trail markers. Don't just look at your feet and the five yards of trail in front of you. This can be hard to do, particularly if the footing is bad. Look up too much and you'll be flat on your face before you know it. Many Eastern trails are so rocky that runners will miss turns because they don't dare look up. If you have this problem, one of the benefits of training regularly on trails is that you develop the ability to look around from time to time without tripping every time you do it.

At night, looking is still necessary; it's just harder. But the habits should still be the same, still looking behind from time to time, still looking around in general. At night it's easy to become transfixed by the small ring of light right at your feet. It's a variation on floating—you're totally unaware of your surroundings. You got to force yourself to be alert, to break out of the trance that is just saying, "left, right."

One trick I use to stay alert, when needed, is to use my watch. If I know that it's, say two miles to the next landmark or intersection, and I'm plodding along at about 15 minutes per mile, then in about 30 minutes I'll expect to be there (i.e. in 20 to 25 minutes I'll tell myself that it's time to wake up and pay attention, and if I don't see anything in 40 minutes then it's time to get worried). The watch helps me stay a little more aware of my invisible surroundings.

The other thing to remember at night is that you can hear things that you can't see—roads (if a car goes by), streams, ponds (if the frogs are active), even power lines. At Leadville, the trail at one point turns to go under a power line. In the dark you couldn't see the wires or the towers, but you could hear the wires hum. The turn was hard to spot if you looked for it, but easy if you listened.

All of the above is written with trail ultras in mind, but much of it—the recognition that marshals won't be at every corner, that checking the course in advance can help a lot, that floating can still get you in lots of trouble—applies to road ultras as well. As for ultras held on a quarter-mile track, if you get lost in one of them, well...

Altitude Training for Improved Performance
by Kevin Setnes

When the Summer Olympics were held in Mexico City in 1968, the real impact of altitude and its effect on performance became readily apparent to the world. The results show that almost every medalist at distances from 1,500 meters and longer was from a high altitude environment, or at least resided and trained at high altitude. For Americans watching the 1,500-meter final, the way Kipchoge (Kip) Keino of Kenya ran away from Jim Ryun, arguably the best miler in the world, was simply incredible. Ryun would later admit to never having experienced such pain in the chest as he did during his kick to the finish that day. Kip Keino was born and raised in Kenya at an elevation of greater than 7,000 feet. Jim Ryun was from the heartland of America, Kansas, at an elevation of less than 1,000 feet. Mexico City is more than 7,000 feet. It doesn't take a rocket scientist to figure out which competitor was better adapted to perform in Mexico in 1968.

The higher you go, the less oxygen is available for the body to use. According to Tim Noakes' book, *Lore of Running*, one's VO_2 max decreases for every 1,000 meters above 1,200 meters (approximately 4,000 feet) by about 10 percent. Mountaineers on Everest, he claims, have an extremely difficult time climbing the last 400 meters, often taking up to five hours. That is with supplemental oxygen! The effect of altitude on human performance cannot be understated. There are two distinct differences in altitude training as it applies to ultrarunning. One is adaptation to higher altitudes. The second is training at altitude for improved performance at sea level events.

Some ultras in the United States have portions that far exceed the elevation of Mexico City. The most notable of these events are the Leadville 100 Mile and the Hardrock 100 Mile. Leadville averages more than 10,000 feet in elevation and Hardrock has sections that exceed 14,000 feet in height. The ultrarunner either needs to adapt to the lack of oxygen at these heights, or slow his or her pace down significantly to avoid altitude sickness, which often accompanies running at altitude.

The primary goal of this column is to look at the benefit of training at altitude, then relate that to performance at sea level events. Since distance running is primarily an aerobic activity, the need for oxygen is readily apparent to the athlete. A decrease in the availability of oxygen can result in a condition called hypoxia. The question arises then: How can one adapt to running with less oxygen available? One way to adapt is to simply live at altitude. Even a sedentary lifestyle (without training) can increase tolerance to the hypoxic stress of living at altitude.

Add training to the mix and you begin to stress the physiological abilities of the runner even more.

How does the body adapt to higher altitudes and the hypoxia caused by attempting to train? According to Dr. David Martin, (USATF's Long Distance Running Developmental Chair and notable author), "More enzymes are produced by the working muscles for oxidative metabolism. In particular, the skeletal muscle mitochondria, which increases in size and numbers. These working muscles also begin to rely on more fatty acids, rather than the more common glycogen for energy fuel. This results in less blood lactic acid buildup. When athletes immediately arrive at altitude, their maximum heart rates are unchanged, but reached at a much lower work level." He goes on to state, "The kidneys increase their output of the hormone erythropoietin, which in turn stimulates the bone marrow to produce more red blood cells, which contains hemoglobin".

Upon arriving at altitude, the blood plasma volume is reduced at once. After time, the blood plasma returns to sea level values. As this happens and as the red blood cell count continues to rise, the total blood volume will rise. Eventually, the blood's oxygen carrying capacity is increased.

If this increased oxygen carrying ability is true, does that mean the athlete returning to a sea level event will see an improvement in performance? The answer is not always clear. Jim Garcia, an elite ultrarunner from Massachusetts, won the inaugural Chancellor Challenge 100 Km at sea level in Boston in a personal best time of 6:55:27. This remarkable performance at the age of 41 was preceded by excellent efforts at local five-km and eight-km races. Garcia credited his success to training at altitude in Colorado prior to and during his Leadville 100 Mile, before his return to sea level performance.

Countless instances of other athletes achieving similar results are commonplace. Yet, the exact benefit is somewhat elusive, since there are many variables that comprise performance, which makes studying the phenomenon difficult. The difficulties of moving to an altitude training environment can be very stressful on athletes, thus negating any increased oxygen carrying capability that is achieved.

Another negative to overcome at altitude is a decrease in leg turnover, or quickness. To combat this, runners at altitude may shorten interval distances and lengthen recovery time. The individual may wish to return to sea level to regain the quickness with just a few weeks of speed training. The benefit achieved at altitude (increases in red blood cells and hemoglobin) is thought to be held for more than two months, plenty of time to recover leg quickness.

An ideal situation for maximizing the benefits of altitude training, without the stress that may accompany it, is to live there! Better yet, is to live at a high-altitude city, one that has freeway access that can zip you on down to lower levels for your faster training.

Martin says, "The optimal period of altitude residence is approximately four weeks. This increases red blood cell concentration in the bloodstream, thereby increasing oxygen carrying ability, and also permits an unhurried training block for the runner. The optimal time for return to lower altitudes and racing appears to be roughly two to three weeks. This is sufficient time to return breathing dynamics and acid-base levels to normality and to permit recovery from hard training at altitude."

Since VO_2 max decreases when running and training at altitude, it rises upon return to sea level and thus results in an increased capacity for enhanced performance. However, far too many runners have tried altitude training only to come away with mixed results when returning to the sea level events. They should give altitude training a second look or ask a qualified coach about the training experience. A sudden change in lifestyle (by going to altitude) can disrupt many other aspects of a runner's training habits. To quote a famous Dorothy: "There is no place like home." This is especially true as it pertains to optimal training. Martin offers these recommendations for runners thinking about incorporating altitude training into their preparations:

Seven Keys to Altitude Training:
- Don't wait until it's time to prepare for an important championship or event to try altitude training for the first time.
- Use laboratory physiological testing (if possible) before and after altitude training to quantify the extent of change in such variables as VO_2 max, anaerobic threshold, and hemoglobin.
- Don't go so high or train so hard that the altitude stress is excessive.
- Ensure that the terrain used for training permits the option for flat as well as hilly running.
- Stay long enough to acquire sufficient adaptation to make the effort worthwhile: at least three to four weeks.
- Create a homelike lifestyle and an entirely hospitable environment by thorough advance planning. Make an advance trip to familiarize yourself with the running areas.
- If the important competitions or events following altitude training are planned for sea level, return home early enough (roughly two weeks) to permit appropriate sea level ventilatory and neuromuscular adaptation before racing begins. (From *Better Training for Distance Runners* by David Martin, Ph.D., and Peter Coe.)

Racing at altitude and the impact it has on the ultrarunner is lesser than that on the middle distance runners (1,500 meters to the marathon). Any ultrarunner striving to cover 100 miles, especially over higher, rough terrain trail, needs to remain well within his or her lactate threshold or they may never see the finish line. A heart rate monitor can be an invaluable tool when trying to race at high altitude ultras. Keeping the heart rate down when working up steep grades or even especially high flat terrain will help immensely, as we sometimes lose track of just how hard our body is working.

The ultrarunner who successfully implements an altitude training program can realize substantial benefits when returning to a sea level event as well. The increased ability to run at a higher percentage of VO_2 max and higher blood lactate level should translate into a higher level of performance. This is especially true for ultrarunners, as their need for leg turnover speed is not as great as for shorter distance runners (marathon and below). This is perhaps why Jim Garcia had such a remarkable run at the Chancellor 100 Km. He probably returned to seal level in time to sufficiently train his legs for the critical turnover speed in racing so well at short distances, but still retained the benefits of altitude training in peaking for the 100-km.

With all due respect to our friends in Boulder, it is impractical for most of us to think that we will move to a higher altitude city to train full-time. For some of us, a summer vacation to the high country may be our only opportunity to experience altitude training. Whatever your experience may be, it is helpful to realize the potential benefits as well as the pitfalls of training at altitude.

Avoiding Problems at Altitude

There are several problems that can arise in extremely high altitude, such as pulmonary and cerebral edema. These maladies are normally seen at elevations of more than 14,000 feet. The single greatest risk for runners at Leadville and other high-altitude ultras, however, is acute mountain sickness (AMS). This condition can occur at altitudes as low as 5,000 feet.

In mild cases of AMS, the symptoms are headache, nausea, loss of appetite, insomnia, shortness of breath, and vomiting. In severe cases, fluid can get into the lungs or brain. This condition can be fatal if the individual does not descend to a lower altitude and/or is given supplemental oxygen at once. It can affect men and women of any age, even those who are in top physical condition.

Those who are at the greatest risk of developing AMS are individuals who move to altitude fairly quickly and then exercise. Thus, the best preventative measure is to allow time to acclimatize your body to higher altitude before undertaking exercise, especially as challenging as an ultra distance race. Physiologically, your body will adapt by increasing the number of oxygen-carrying red blood cells. This is the same theory behind training athletes at altitude in order to improve performance.

Mountain climbers have long ascribed to the motto, "Climb high, sleep low." This means that just being at high altitude will commence the acclimatization process. Then returning to a lower altitude to sleep will reduce the stress from the high altitude, allowing the body to rest, recover, and adapt. You should not attempt to train right away after arriving at high altitude, as this will increase your chances of incurring AMS.

In essence, the best plan would be to arrive at a high-altitude race site five to seven days before the race, climbing high during the days and returning to a lower altitude at night, thus allowing the acclimatization process to begin. By race day, most people will then be sufficiently prepared to undertake the race. Dedicating that much time may not be practical for some, however. If that is the case, it has been theorized that is it is better to simply arrive at the race altitude a day before the race, run, then return to a lower altitude at once right after the race. Allowing just a few days before the race may initiate the acclimatization process while leaving the body in a state of semi-breakdown.

Another concern at high altitude is dehydration. Because you are breathing harder and the air is drier, more water is lost in exhaled air. It's the same effect you feel on a "sneaky" dry day, one that appears to pose little threat of dehydration, but one in which sweat is whisked away by the dry air. Often on days such as these, you don't properly rehydrate. The risk for AMS goes up markedly with dehydration. So make sure to drink even if you are not sweating at all. Drugs exist that aim to prevent or reduce the effects of AMS. Their efficacy varies among individuals, and side effects can be a problem as well, however.

Can you run an ultra at high altitude? Unquestionably, a high-altitude ultra presents greater challenge than one at sea level. In order to prepare as thoroughly as possible, you should take the following steps:

- Train to increase VO$_2$ max to as high a level as possible before the race. Train on hills as much as possible.
- Allow at least five to seven says to acclimatize to the altitude at which the race will take place.
- Be conservative in getting up and over hills.
- Drink as much as possible during the event.

On the Edge: Avoiding Overtraining and Burnout

by Don Allison

Training for any athletic event involves following universal training principles. In that respect, ultrarunning is no different. Without following some sort of training plan, it is unlikely even the most gifted runner will be able to complete formidable ultra distances. A steady buildup phase involving a mix of distances and pace makes up a sensible training plan. It is only logical that we would want to prepare as best we can for an event. Ultrarunners are by nature overachievers—our sensibilities tell us to run in training as much as possible to be ready for an ultra.

But how much is enough? How much is too much? The answer to this question of course is *not* universal. The amount of training that will produce maximum training effect for an ultrarunner varies widely among individuals. Many factors must be entered into the equation in order to compute an optimal level of training: age, sex, recent racing and training history, other life commitments and stresses, and most importantly genetics, all factor into the equation and vary from individual to individual.

We all have heard stories of amazing feats by ultrarunners. In transcontinental races, competitors regularly complete a hard 40 to 50 miles of running day in and day out. Other ultrarunners have run several 100-mile trail races in one summer. That one individual can complete such a prodigious feat at one point in time does not mean we all should be capable of it as well. It does not even mean that we should be capable of even a fraction of such feats. While one runner races across the country with relative ease, another runner will have to carefully plot and plan in order to complete a 50-km race.

The penalty for overstepping our physical limitations is that our bodies will no longer respond by producing a training effect. Rather, a "negative" training effect will result in a reduction of fitness rather than a production of fitness. It is not always easy to determine exactly when you have overstepped the bounds, however. Being exhausted from a very long training run can be just the stimulus you need to produce the necessary adaptations in your body one day, while it will push you over the edge on another.

As a result, athletes sometime slip into an overtrained mode before realizing they have gone too far. What exactly happens? Usually, the muscle, nervous and hormonal systems are overloaded. These systems then stop working at a proper level of efficiency. Therefore, the ability of the body to recover from training or racing efforts is compromised. A vicious cycle develops, which in most cases results in a breakdown in the form of injury or illness, if the body is not allowed proper rest.

Allowing for proper rest, both during training and in recovery from hard racing efforts, is thus a key element in avoiding overtraining or burnout. A few days or even a week of reduced or no training may not be enough. Again, it all depends upon where you are in the large scheme of things. If you are only a few weeks or a month into a newly started training program, a couple of days may be all the refreshment your body needs. If you have been pushing through several months of nonstop training and racing, however, a full off-season may be required to get you back to baseline.

An off-season does not mean you have to cease and desist from training completely. Reducing training efforts to well below the threshold that will overstress the system is the key. It is often the endocrine system that crashes from hard ultra efforts. While your legs may bounce back relatively quickly, the endocrine system may take weeks to find its equilibrium. So if you stay away from runs long enough to overstress your endocrine system, you may be able to recover while running regularly.

How can you determine if you are overtrained? It is often a subjective process, but there are several objective signs: an increased morning pulse rate or a drop-off in performance are two critical signs. There are other more subtle signs as well: a change in appetite, sleep irregularity, and little physical injuries that keep popping up are all indications that you may be heading over the edge. In women especially, a drop in serum ferritin iron levels may precipitate burnout. Just because you have one bad race does not mean you are overtrained. It is a series of events which usually indicates you are headed in the wrong direction.

Your mood can often be an indicator as well. If you are feeling eager and anxious to get out and train, that's good. But if you find yourself frequently "not in the mood," it may indicate overtraining. Again, any one day does not tell the full story. It's the cumulative effect that counts. And make no mistake, ultrarunning does exact a cumulative effect on most of us. It takes extraordinary effort to push your body through the demands of 50 miles, 100, or even longer distances. You are "borrowing" on your body's reserves. Just how long it will take to "repay the debt," varies among runners. But if the debt is not repaid in full, there may be foreclosure down the road.

The best strategy is not to allow overtraining to take place to begin with. What preemptive measures can you take to make sure that you'll be in good graces with your running body? Here are some tips:

Ten Tips for Avoiding Ultra Burnout

- **Follow a routine.** The body and mind take comfort in the regularity of a training routine.
- **Change your routine.** Routine is good, but not too much! Every once in a while, do something different. Take a trip; run in a new area; run at a different time of day or with a different group; make your long runs an adventure.
- **Take a break after an ultra.** Don't be fooled by your "quick" recovery. The legs may come back quickly, but your system's equilibrium may take a good while longer to fully recover. If you don't feel fully physically and emotionally recovered from an ultra, err on the side of conservatism and reduce your training to a baseline level until you feel ready to train for another race.
- **Take a break for no good reason.** Even when in training for an ultra, you may need to give yourself a "breather" for a day, a few days, or even a week. Such a break may well leave you refreshed and ready to resume your training. In terms of overall fitness, this short of a break will not set you back.
- **Stay hydrated.** Chronic dehydration can lead to all kinds of physical problems that will lead you down the road to overtraining. Water is by far the most important nutrient, not only during a race, but every day, all day. You need to stay properly hydrated. Make sure to drink water regularly throughout the day.
- **Don't become chronically carbohydrate depleted.** Maintaining adequate carbohydrate stores is important to your physical well being as well. Repeated days of long and/or intense runs can deplete the carbohydrate stores, which can lead to fatigue. If you have scheduled one or more consecutive long runs, make sure to replace carbohydrate during and most importantly, immediately after the run. The first hour has been shown to be the optimal time for the body to replace carbohydrate. This will allow for a more complete recovery, thus not leaving your body excessively fatigued from the effort.
- **Do your own thing.** Trying to keep up with someone else's training program is a sure way to tire yourself out prematurely. In order to train at an optimal level, you must learn what training load your own body can take. Just because others follow a certain schedule does not mean it is the best one for you. It can be helpful to have training partners to push you every now and then, but not all the time.

- **Live your life.** Closing yourself off from other areas of your life in order to focus solely on ultrarunning is a prescription for burnout. Surely, training for and running an ultra is a major undertaking, but maintaining a well-rounded life will help your effort, not hinder it. The best way to integrate ultrarunning into your life is to make it a part of your life, not rule it. Involving others in your training and racing is a good way to maintain a healthy balance.
- **Stay tuned into the big picture.** While what kind of training you do every day has an effect on your physical condition, any one day of training is not critical in the long term scheme of things. If you have to miss a day of training, so be it—it is not the end of the world. Months down the road, even next week, it will not matter. Take a seasonal view as well. You don't have to do a race just "because it is there." Races will still be there when you are capable of running them. There is a time for hard training and racing, and a time for rest. Know when those times are.
- **Take an Eastern view.** Maintaining a calm demeanor and taking a spiritual outlook towards ultrarunning may seemed farfetched to some, but has helped many runners maintain a mentally and physically healthy approach to the sport. It may help you as well.

Making the Most of Aid Stations
by Shawn McDonald

If you really want to find out what is going on at most ultras, the center of the action and the buzz of activity can usually be found at the aid stations. This is where miles of relatively quiet running (and walking) is replaced by eating, drinking, clothes changing, and some very interesting discussions—just to name of a few of the activities that take place there. Aid stations are so ubiquitous at ultras that we sometimes take them for granted. But what exactly is the point of having aid stations? Primarily, it is to sustain runners throughout the race by the distribution of foods, fluids, first aid supplies, and moral support. They also offer a haven in poor weather and a place for an ill runner who is dehydrated, cramping, has blisters, or is suffering from an upset stomach to recover. The stations are also places to meet your crew and/or pacer.

Maximizing Benefits in the Minimum Time

So how can you, as an ultrarunner, maximize the benefits of aid stations at an ultra? Planning and practice will help you get the most out of the aid stations during a race. The first step is to find out what the various aid stations will offer in terms of fuel and fluids, as well as other supplies. Pre-race meetings usually provide this information in good detail. Aid stations come in different shapes, sizes, and with different levels of services offered. Then figure out what you will have out on the course with your crew or in drop bags. Draw up a race plan, outlining the aid station names and mileages, and what you hope to do at each one, in terms of food, fluids, clothes, shoes, an equipment change, and the like. If you think about it before the event, then you will be more likely to remember what you will need when you actually get to the aid station. Some reasonable goals for a given aid station stop are to: (a) get refueled; (b) attend to any medical concerns; (c) take a short rest; (d) find out what lies ahead on the next section of the race course; (e) change shoes/socks or clothing; and (f) start to get help from a pacer (if allowed by the race).

Practicing aid station stops can be done on your long training runs, by timing yourself as you refill water bottles with fluids and gather and eat snack foods you have left at certain points on the training route or that your crew person gives to you. You will be surprised at how fast a few minutes pass.

Once underway in the race, when you are about five minutes from an upcoming aid station (which is why it pays to have a good estimate of how long a given section will take to cover and to be familiar with the course if at all possible), think about what you want to do in the station, what help you need, and what food you are in need of. About a minute out from the aid station (when you can see the aid station table and hear the volunteers cheering you on) get your bottles ready by taking them out of your pack, drinking the rest of the fluid in them, and opening the lids. Ask the volunteers to fill the bottles (be clear as to what fluids and/or ice that should be put in them), head to the food table or drop bag area, get the food you want (put it in your shorts pockets, a plastic baggie, or just carry it if you just have a few items), get the clothes change done alone or with help from your crew or a volunteer, and then head out of the aid station at a walk or slow jog before transitioning back into running. Before you head out on the trail, make sure to thank the volunteers and your crew if you have one.

An efficient stop will be fluid; you will not feel hurried. Rather, you will move with purpose and direction. A stop just for fluids might take just a half-minute to a minute, or if you eat maybe a bit over a minute; a shoe or shirt change might add two to three minutes, but you don't need to do those too often. One reasonable goal to strive for is to establish estimated aid station times for races at 50 km to 100 km of 10 to 20 seconds per race mile, and 20 to 30 seconds per race mile in a 100-mile or 24-hour race. Most of my stops for aid stations for a 100-mile are in the range of one to three minutes in duration, with a few (perhaps three to five stops) in the range of four to seven minutes, when I plan a shoe or sock change, or take a longer time to eat.

If you still have food left from the aid station as you head out, then walk for a bit and eat, or carry it for a mile or two and eat it in small portions. The latter plan of eating may be better, as it distributes your energy intake more evenly. You don't want to be trying to wolf down food and fluids while you are at the aid station, since that can lead to digestion problems. Walking will help refresh your legs, and when you start running again you should feel better than when you entered the aid station. Remember that everyone at the station will be happy to see you, so be friendly, and use that enthusiasm and energy to your benefit. Being relaxed will help you conserve energy for when you need it later in the run.

To Sit or Not to Sit

An interesting question that has been long debated in ultrarunning circles is whether you should you sit down at each aid station, or at any aid station at all, and if so, under what circumstances? My thoughts, based on what I have seen at ultras, are that the only times you should sit down at an aid station are: (a) for a shoe change; (b) if you are dizzy or need to fix blisters; or (c) at the finish line.

Chairs have been known to suck runners right out of the race! Having a crew around if you do sit down may motivate you to get up—or it may not.

What are some strategies to try if you already know you spend too much unproductive time at aid stations? You might have learned this by viewing the aid station in/out times that some races provide with the race results, or by observations your crew makes in comparing your stops with those of other runners in the race. The key component in aid station efficiency is awareness during your stop, and having a fairly set plan for how to proceed into, through, and out of the station. I like to follow this plan at the aid station: first, take in fluids and get water bottles filled, then head to the food table to gather and eat food, then if necessary, take care of blisters, an upset stomach, chafing, or reapplication of sunscreen or insect repellent. If I have a drop bag at the aid station, I'll get that when I first arrive and do my clothing or shoe change and get the snacks out of the drop bag, all while the aid station volunteers are filling my fluid bottles. Then I head over to put some snacks into a plastic baggie, and exit the aid station. Another strategy that may help you from getting "trapped" at the aid station is to use the countdown timer on your watch (set for one or two minutes) and start it when you enter the aid station. When the timer is done and the alarm goes off, head out of the aid station. An alternative method is to be aware of other runners who entered the aid station when you did, then try to leave the aid station about the same time as they do.

Let's say you are at the opposite extreme and tend to rush through aid stations, and end up not getting what you need. As in the case of those that spend too much time at aid stations, having a plan also helps. Carry a three by five-inch card with a reminder list of key tasks to complete and questions to ask yourself while at the aid station: drink fluids, fill water bottles, secure foods, determine if you have blisters or chaffing, need more sunscreen, or want to change shirts or run packs. Or you can have your crew keep track of the list to make sure that each item is completed at each station. Using a list can also help you stay focused on the "here and now," if you tend to get distracted by all of the ancillary activity at the aid stations.

Information Please

Aid stations can also be a great source of information for you as a runner and competitor. You can ask the volunteers how far it is to the next aid station (in miles or hours) as well as the nature of the upcoming terrain and how many miles you have already completed. Sometimes this information is posted on a sign at the aid station. Volunteers can probably also tell you fairly accurately how far ahead the next runners are (especially if the volunteers you are asking are the ones keeping track of runners' split times), and maybe even if those runners looked good or were tired and spent a long time at the station. All of this information can help you to decide how much food and fluid to carry away from the aid station in order to have enough to get to the next station, as well as plan how hard you want to run the next few miles of the race, and if you have a chance to catch any runners currently ahead of you in the race.

Weather can and does have an effect on how you conduct your aid station stops. In cold weather I like to keep my stops short to keep from getting chilled. During hot weather I try to find a shady spot at the aid station to drink and eat, and use a sponge bucket to cool off if one is available. Ask for ice in your bottles along with fluids in hot weather, or warm water in cold weather. Also consider the effect of weather on the hygiene of the aid station. In hot weather, meat sandwiches may not stay edible for long, so if in doubt, ask a volunteer how long the food item has been out, and request they make you a fresh sandwich if possible. Batches of water and other fluids may not taste good or be cold, so ask for a fresh fill or batch rather than risk getting an upset stomach.

Expect the Unexpected

A couple of anecdotes about aid station stops highlight how the unexpected can happen. Several years ago at an aid station during the Angeles Crest 100 Mile, a runner took a food item from the aid table in near darkness and headed down the trail. The next day the aid station captain told us the story and we got a chuckle hearing that the food item taken and eaten was in fact a dog biscuit! So be warned, if in doubt about the identity of a food item or fluids at an aid station; speak up and ask a volunteer to identify that item. Be particularly careful if you have food allergies or easily get a queasy stomach.

The second story is from the Vermont 100 Mile, In one of the later aid stations, the eventual winner and his pacer arrived only to find the stations had not even been set up. The runner's pacer had to heft a five-gallon jug of water off the ground while the runner put the bottles under the spout to fill them. It was a humorous scene that shows just how resourceful ultrarunners can be. Both the runner and his pacer stayed calm, assessed what needed to be done, and got on with the work, getting through the station quickly while getting what they needed. With a little practice and planning, your aid station stops too can be thorough, efficient, and completed in less time than the average television commercial break.

Pacing in a 100 Mile: A Nice Way to Spend the Night

by Bob Adjamien

What is it like to run 100 miles? To get an idea without all of the effort, consider pacing someone in a 100-mile race. There are real benefits—you can run comfortably at an easy pace, enjoy the people and the scenery, and have a good training run. Most 100-mile events allow runners to be accompanied by pacers over the last 30 to 40 miles of the course.

The following is a guide for those who have never paced a runner over the last 30 to 50 miles of a 100-mile. Keep in mind that pacing should be fun. If you have never before run at night on a narrow trail, you are in for a treat. It will be a long night. You will develop an appreciation for the 100-mile distance, and despite your own fatigue while pacing, you might—after you have rested—be tempted to try one yourself.

The shared experience of the latter half of a 100-mile can create a close friendship between you and your runner. Only the basics of life are important during the run: surviving and moving towards the finish.

Qualifications

Ideally, the best pacer is another 100-mile runner who knows the course and understands through experience the moods of a runner going the distance. However, that should not stop you even if the 30-mile (or more) distance is new. If you know the course you will be running, so much the better. Otherwise, watch the course with extra concentration. The important thing is to pace someone within your abilities and training. Obviously, a 30-hour finisher will do more walking and go slower than someone who wants to break 20 hours. As a guideline, a runner who can complete a 50-mile trail race in less than 10 hours should be able to pace someone who hopes to finish 100 miles in less than 24 hours.

You should be able to pace someone if you can run the marathon distance. The main problem for a newcomer is knowing what to eat and drink, or more accurately, to eat and drink enough. Veteran runners will tell you to drink before you are thirsty and to eat foods with salt to help digest all the water you must consume. Be serious: 30 to 40 miles is not a 30-minute run. If you are prepared, stay well hydrated and eat enough, you will have fun and wish your runner would go faster. Ignore these guidelines, however, and you will be miserable.

Take two water bottles and food for your own use. For nighttime, bring a strong flashlight that uses D batteries and a halogen bulb. Also, take along a spare small flashlight or two, spare batteries, and bulbs. Even if you don't need the extra flashlight, someone else most likely will.

Eat a good meal the night before the race, and be properly hydrated before you start running. Remember the politician's motto—keep everything (including your urine) perfectly clear. In the same vein, lube your feet and wear the right socks. If you can't cover 30 miles without a blister, you are probably doing something wrong. The point is for you to be strong and alert during the run, so you can concentrate on helping the runner you are pacing. (A special note to experienced ultrarunners: you may know all that's needed, and have lots of experience, but you can still get into trouble if you're too casual about the distance. One year, two of my friends could not even finish as pacers at the Angeles Crest 100 Mile because, although they were well trained for the distance, they didn't take the distance seriously. One carelessly took only one water bottle for a dry stretch, "died," and had to let his runner charge ahead and win the women's division without him. The other didn't eat or drink properly the night before the race, and thus was not hydrated when he started running, and dropped out as a pacer.)

Duties of the Pacer

Every runner is different, so they will expect different things from a pacer. Generally, the pacer is a trail companion, a guide to keep the runner on the course, a safety expert who keeps a watch for any hazards that a tired mind may not notice, a psychologist to keep spirits up, and a coach to help the runner do his or her best. When the race is over, a pacer should feel they gave the race his or her best effort. The pacer is not a pack animal who carries the runner's supplies. The pacer should run behind or alongside the runner, except at night, when the runner may like the pacer to be in front for safety reasons.

What to Look for During the Run

At the proper intervals, remind the runner to eat and drink. As the race progresses, your runner will not feel much inspiration to do either. By then the sports drink tastes horrible, the stomach feels lousy. The runner should urinate on a regular basis. If they don't, there could be a kidney problem; at the very least, they are not drinking enough. One problem with covering long distances in warm weather is that the body will have problems assimilating the large quantities of water consumed. That is why aid stations have a supply of crackers, pretzels, and the like. Again, don't forget that you have to drink a lot, too.

Be sure your runner eats something solid. Once, my runner had a sour stomach and could only eat fruit. He was a vegetarian, so chicken noodle soup was out. Perhaps I should have pressured him to eat more, but you can't force a person to eat. The result was predictable; his quads gave out and he was reduced to a walk over the last ten miles. Had he eaten properly, he likely would have broken 24 hours, a tough task at Angeles Crest. (He was still under 25 hours, a most respectable time for the course.)

This brings up the art of pacing: knowing when to push your runner and when to hold back. Ultrarunners are not the most obedient people. Unless the race is obviously going well, the runner will at some point decide that he or she will just be satisfied to finish—period. He or she doesn't care about silver buckles, or people in front or behind. The runner will say, "I've run enough. I hate each rock on the trail. I just want to finish."

A classic example of this occurred at Western States when I was pacing my friend Steve in his first 100-mile. What with a bad ankle, on top of the normal problems of the race, Steve was not a happy camper. Yet ahead of us in equally bad shape were our friends Harry and Judy. It was not their day either.

"Come on Steve. Let's pass them. This is a good chance," I said.

"Forget it. I only have to finish." (We had about five miles to go.)

"O.K. Right now you may not care, but later on you'll be glad you beat them."

"(Grumble)" Steve did not like to be told what to do, so I couldn't say more. He was in no mood for another word. After a few minutes, he started walking faster and faster, almost running, fast enough to catch our friends on an uphill. We passed them, and to my surprise, he kept up the pace, and passed even more people.

Steve returned the favor to me the next year, again at Western States. I was quite content to walk in with about ten miles to go.

"Try running to No Hands Bridge, and you'll beat my previous time," he said.

"I could care less."

"Well, give it a try!"

"(Grumble)" I didn't like being told what to do either. Several minutes passed, and off I went. The legs had not informed my brain that I was quite capable of running, and I was astonished. The pace was not very fast, but I did it.

Other Ideas

After many hours of running, your runner does not want to think a single unnecessary thought. Consider it your responsibility to watch the trail for markings.

Be on the lookout for sudden uphill turns; they seem to be the easiest to miss.

Don't let your runner quit for anything less than something major. Fatigue does not count. The quads are supposed to hurt, and his or her attitude may at times get lousy. What I tell my runner is, "You're supposed to be hurting. Just keep moving." Let your runner know that you strongly want them to keep trying and to do his or her best.

Runners go through many ups and downs during the 100-mile distance. Perhaps the worst they will get is to swear they will stop running ultras. That feeling usually goes away within a week after the race. The important thing is to keep them going until they feel better. The beauty of the experience is in fighting through the bad spots and finding new strength. It may take ten minutes or two hours, but your runner will feel better.

Many runners experience sour stomachs and throw up several times—or wish they would. Bad food combinations or bad food choices often cause these problems. It is a normal part of the learning process for the runner. It may also be caused by drinking too much water and not eating something salty. Sometimes just a little bit of salt on the finger put on the tongue will help.

On the other hand, there are runners who should quit but won't, such as one runner at the Angeles Crest 100 Mile. She felt terrible pain in her leg on the descent from Mt. Wilson, caused by a stress fracture. Her pain was terrible, but this was one determined woman. Runners have to live with their decisions. It is their race. She finished two minutes after the final cut-off, but she finished.

Ideally, the pacer should not expect anything from the runner for pacing the distance. If you don't feel that way, be sure to express yourself. Some runners like to give their pacer a memento, such as a water bottle, a shirt, or a hat. There is no rule here, but again, it is better to be a purist and not expect anything. The experience is the reward. My preference is to at least buy the pacer a meal or two, and it is nice to cover their expenses if you can afford it.

If you live near a 100-mile race, call the race director and offer your services. There will always be someone from out of town who can use a pacer. Remember that you don't have to be fast. Some years ago, a slow runner at Angeles Crest was well within finishing in the required time, but by 70 miles he quit. He was discouraged and lonely after all the hours on the trail, and could not find someone to pace him. Surely having a pacer would have made a huge difference in his outlook at that point in the race.

No Pacers Allowed?

Some runners are hesitant to even have a pacer. One school of thought says the whole point is to pit your mind and body against the course. Why weaken the contest by having props for support?

There is something to that. That loner attitude reminds me of the time I was struggling alone to get to Newcomb Saddle late at night at the Angeles Crest 100. The night was foggy, I was hallucinating, I was alone, and it seemingly took centuries for this lone figure with a fading flashlight to get to the aid station. I finally I heard the beautiful sound of a Honda generator and saw a kind soul waiting for the next runner—me. The loner in me vanished. We are social animals, and I had to admit it then.

There is no shame to have someone pace you. It is a special experience to pace someone. If you want to run alone, go for it. For me, part of the experience of a 100-mile is running with a pacer through the night and enjoying the companionship. The camaraderie of our sport is what makes the distance so special. It is a special privilege to help other human beings, and a wonderful bonding experience.

Crewing: Ten Commandments
For Those Who Sit and Wait
by John Medinger

With the summer 100-mile races so popular now, it may be appropriate to review an element of ultrarunning that is often crucial but seldom discussed: crewing. While there are no hard and fast rules regarding the arcane but rewarding experience of assisting other runners, there are some simple elements that all crew members should keep in mind.

Be prepared. Talk things out in advance with your runner. Know what he or she will need and when it is needed. Pack a separate bag for each checkpoint. That way you won't have to fumble through a ton of paraphernalia to find what you are looking for. Err on the side of overpacking. If you are not sure, put it in. Nothing is more irritating than not getting that pair of dry socks you have been looking forward to for the past two hours, because the crew forgot to bring them.

Know the race course. Go over the course and access roads carefully. It can be easy to become lost, and sometimes it takes nearly as long to get from checkpoint to checkpoint by car as it does by foot.

In many races crew access is limited to designated spots. Race management may have had to limit access in order to obtain permits from park officials or other government agencies. Violating these rules jeopardizes the future of the race. Don't even think about it.

Be patient. Know about what time your runner expects to reach each checkpoint. Be there a good bit early just in case. Also know that runners are rarely early and often late.

Be impatient. There is a tendency for runners to waste incredible amounts of time at the checkpoints. They are glad to see you. It's good to talk to someone about how the race is going, and besides, it feels so damned good to sit down. Absent medical problems, however, there is no reason to stay more than five minutes at a checkpoint. Get them some food and fluids, a change of shirt or whatever, and then get them going again. An extra five to ten minutes at each checkpoint can cost a runner more than an hour or more in a 100-mile race.

Be positive. After a few hours wandering around in the wilderness, your runner's resolve may start to wane. Be cheerful; tell them how great they look. In doing so, you are probably lying; that's all right because they know they look terrible and that you are lying. It's all part of the game. The object here is to get them thinking positive thoughts again.

Take the blame. As the aches accumulate and the blood sugar level gets low, your runner will get cranky. Count on it. Because you are the first person he or she has seen in a long while, they are liable to take it all out on you. It may be *your* fault that it's too hot, that he or she has blisters, or that his or her left calf is cramping. This is part of the game too. They don't mean it and later will be sorry that they said it. Meanwhile, just smile and take it and accept the blame.

Make your runner drink. I cannot emphasize this enough. Every time you see your runner, remind them to drink. After they drink, make them drink some more. I would bet that dehydration causes more DNF's than everything else put together.

Don't forget the pacer. In most 100-mile and many shorter races, the runner is allowed to have a pacer in the latter stages of the race. In a 100-mile, this might mean that the pacer will run about 40 miles through the night and into the next day. The pacer must run at the other runner's pace, and will take a fair amount of abuse, both physical and mental (see above). While perhaps not as difficult as running the entire race, pacing is no easy feat. It's more than all right for the crew to ask how the pacer is doing and offer them some help too. It's also a good idea to have someone in reserve should the pacer falter. This can happen.

Keep a sense of humor. Runners in these long races develop a wonderfully warped and macabre sense of humor as the race progresses. This is truly one of the joys of the event and participating in this delightfully cynical humor lends a thread of sanity to the proceedings. In one of races, my crew said, "Smile, things could be worse." So I smiled and, sure enough, things got worse.

Have some fun. Save all the talk about personal challenges for the newspaper reporters. What these events are really about is having fun. Enjoy the scenery and that special ambiance that surrounds the event. Get to know the other crews; you will no doubt be seeing them again at other races. Trade gossip, lies, and old war stories. When the weariness sets in and you just wish it would be over, you can always take solace in the fact that it could be *you* who is out there running.

Planning for Off-Season Training and Rest

by Shawn McDonald

The Need for Rest and Variety

Most ultrarunners compete in a series of races and then plan a rest period of reduced, less intense activity. Training and racing at a high level will often tear down an ultrarunner's body, as well as his or her desire to train with concentration and intensity. The amount and type of rest and off-season training will depend on age, level of training and racing prior to the off season, individual differences in healing rates, and how many other stresses one has in his or her life. Older runners and those training at high volume levels will likely require a longer rest period with a reduced amount of activity, in order to achieve an effective recovery and healing. After focusing primarily on running for a number of weeks or months, most runners find they want to do more varied training in terms of location, activity types, and even the time of day of the workouts. This variety will help restore the desire to train for future races. After a good rest and recovery period the body and mind will be healed and refreshed, ready to devise a balanced plan for upcoming training and racing. A rest period also helps to extend the number of years one can run ultras, allowing for healing of minor aches and pains so they don't become larger problems, such as chronic injuries or structural imbalances.

Establishing Off-Season Goals

The off-season is an ideal time to work on overall fitness and supplement strength development with aerobic-based sports. The key is to reduce the amount of running significantly compared with peak levels during your last training program, usually in the range of 20 to 50 percent. Most days should not include running during the off-season, to allow for healing of the legs from the pounding of recent training and racing. A few days per week of cross-training will supplement your aerobic training during this recovery period, in the form of short, easy sessions. Ideal activities that are aerobic in nature and that work different and complementary muscle groups compared with running include cycling, rollerblading, stair-climbing, spin classes, swimming, and rowing. Weight training is not generally the best activity during a recovery period, as it is not aerobic in nature; rather, it is anaerobic and can thus delay recovery of muscle healing, particularly in your legs. A good goal is to keep all of your sessions in the off-season in your aerobic effort range, roughly between 60 to 70 percent of maximum heart rate, as determined by the age-based Karvonen formula. Generally this means exercising at an effort level during which you can easily converse with others, and at an intensity that feels similar to an easy run on flat terrain.

Scheduling an Off-Season

The timing of your off-season will depend in large part on your racing schedule for a given year, as well as the area of the country in which you live and your other life commitments. In colder climates, it is typical to take an off-season during the winter months, commonly December and January, with a transition period in February, leading into a training season from March to October, and races later in the spring or into the summer and fall. It is also common in the northern states to take a mini off-season of two to three weeks with reduced training following a series of spring races, prior to a summer training period and a series of races in the fall months. In warmer climates with temperate winters and good running conditions in the spring and the fall, such as in the Southeast or California, you may want to plan an off-season for the summer, when there may be fewer races on the calendar. In this case, the training and racing seasons may extend from February to June and September to November, with a short break in December or January, and an off-season in July and August. You may also want to plan an off-season in the summer, or during December, if you have plans for a family vacation or holiday festivities. If you have a key race, such as a 100-mile trail race or 24-hour run in September, then a good plan might include an off-season to rest and recover for the six weeks following that key race, and then plan for and start training for the next series of races starting in early November.

The Four-Week Recovery Plan

It is recommended that you complete at least a four-week off-season prior to starting regular, structured running training again for another set of races. If you are an older runner (over 50) or have been training at a high level (a ten-hour running week or more) for several months, you may want a longer off-season, perhaps lasting six to seven weeks. A typical four-week off-season might contain the following weekly components: two short, easy training runs (one hour maximum), three short cross-training sessions per week, and two off days of complete rest. The following chart details this schedule:

Week number	Number of days running	Number of days cross training	Number of rest days
1	1	3	3
2	2	3	2
3	2	3	2
4	3	2	2

The workouts should all be done at an aerobic effort; the total training time per week might range from three to four hours per week for most runners or about 30 to 50 percent of a typical training load during the training and racing season. Another component of the off-season is refueling and rehydrating your body. Thus, be aware of your intake of foods, carbohydrates, and fluids each day. You will find it easier to restore muscle glycogen and fluid levels due to the reduced training load of the off-season.

During the few weeks following this off-season, a runner should plan a balanced transition program consisting of four runs per week of short to medium duration (up to two hours), and two days of cross-training, with one rest day per week. By the conclusion of these bridging weeks, the runner will have transitioned back into regular running and should be prepared to increase the duration of the weekly long training run, as well as weekly mileage, while gradually cutting back on cross-training. It is important to include this transition period following the off-season, prior to starting regular training for a future race. The transition time will get the legs used to the pounding and stresses of regular running, in addition to preparing energy systems to hold up during subsequent long training runs and harder, more intense training of the strengthening and sharpening phases of your training plan.

To Run or Not to Run?

You may be wondering if you should run at all during your off-season. There are pros and cons on both sides of the ledger. If your legs are sore and drained following the racing season, then going a couple of weeks without running, substituting short cross-training sessions, might be the best way to allow for muscle healing and restoration of energy stores and electrolytes. If you know you have six months until your next race, then taking an off-season of two four-week periods, with the first containing no running, and the second having short runs of an hour (at most) would be fine, as you will then have time to devote two more months to building up your mileage and long run distance prior to the strengthening and sharpening phases. If your leg muscles heading into the off-season are not sore or overly tired, and you have only three months until you enter the next racing season, then you are probably better off taking a short off-season of four weeks, with running two times per week during the first two weeks, and then three to four times per week for the next two weeks, before entering into a regular training plan of four to five days running per week, one or two cross-training days per week, and one rest day a week. A plan of this type will help you rest while allowing you to return to regular running, with your legs ready for the rigors of a mileage buildup and increasing intensity.

A Sample Schedule
The second week in the off-season plan given in the four-week chart above would include two days of running, three days of cross-training and two days of rest. The principle to follow is to not run on consecutive days during the first two to three weeks of the off-season, and to spread the rest days throughout the week. This way your legs get optimal rest. There is still flexibility in how to arrange training and rest days to allow you to meet your family and work responsibilities. An example schedule would be as follows:

Monday: Rest day, hydrate regularly, and stay off your feet if you can.

Tuesday: Five to six-mile mile run on flat roads.

Wednesday: Cycling on roads with small hills, 15 miles at an easy spin.

Thursday: Five-mile run on trails with small hills.

Friday: Rest day, fueling up well with carbohydrates.

Saturday: Cycling on roads with moderate climbs, 75 to 90 minutes.

Sunday: Swim for 30 minutes.

The total training time is about three hours, 45 minutes for this week. The following two weeks of the four-week plan would involve adding 30 minutes per week to the training volume. The transition period might include weeks with five, six, seven, and seven hours of training, with a long run of about 1.75, 2, 2.25, and 2.5 hours duration, mixed in with shorter runs and cross-training sessions, in addition to one or two rest days per week. These four weeks would be a bridge into the start of a training period prior to running a few ultras with race dates two to four months subsequent to the end of the transition period.

Summary

A balanced off-season program contains ample rest days for recovery of muscle strength and flexibility, along with short cross training sessions two to three times a week, as well as short training runs two to three days per week, to keep up a base level of aerobic fitness. Individual differences due to a runner's age, level of prior training, and other time commitments will dictate the level of training during the off-season, as well as the number of times per week you run. These factors should be considered to determine if you can run on consecutive days or plan runs with two to three days of rest or cross-training in between to allow adequate repair and recovery. Your mental outlook and enthusiasm for future training and racing should also improve during and following a restful off-season period of several weeks duration.

Weightlifting for Ultrarunners
by Shawn McDonald

Introduction
In this column I will review the details of a weightlifting program that runners can use to complement training on roads, trails, and tracks. Certain runners aim to lift mainly during their off-seasons, while others lift regularly a few days a week throughout the year. I will discuss a number of types of lifts that are most beneficial for runners, as well as tips for novice lifters and specifications of equipment that can help you set up a gym at home. If you should have questions, consult with a trainer at your local gym or sports club, or seek out some of the references listed at the end of this column.

Benefits of lifting
Runners might ask, "why take the time to lift weights?" There are a number of benefits to regular weightlifting, including better hill running due to enhanced leg and upper body strength. The runner who lifts is better able to drive up hills using the pumping of his or her arms and stronger quad, hip, and butt muscles. Lifting weights can help prevent injury, as stronger supporting muscles are developed in the lower legs, leading to an improved sense of balance for the runner. This is particularly beneficial for runners training and/or racing on rough hiking trails. Lifting also can provide a better balance between muscle groups throughout the body. In particular, most runners have stronger muscles on the back of their legs (hamstrings, calves) compared with muscles in the front of the legs (shin, quadriceps). This muscle imbalance can lead to certain types of running injuries, including those of the knee, hip, and shins.

Athletes who add lifting to their workout programs can see an improvement in running economy (See research citations below). Those who live in areas that experience rain or cold winter weather can continue to train in inclement conditions by combining lifting with indoor aerobic exercise. Lifting can add variety to a workout routine, giving the runner a day off from the pounding of running and provide a mental boost due to the different routine of a lifting workout. A runner who lifts can also achieve body composition changes that will help combat the effects of aging. Athletes usually start to lose muscle mass as they near age 50 and beyond. Lifting also can lead to stronger bones to counteract the process of osteoporosis. This benefit is particularly relevant to older female runners. Lifting weights can also increase lean muscle mass, so that the runner gains less weight during the off-season when running less and maybe eating as much as normal.

Finally, weight work can help the runner maintain better form late in the race by using the arms to drive the legs. Stronger core (abdominal, lower back) muscles help maintain a relaxed, upright posture with a proper breathing rhythm after several hours of running.

Tips to get started

Athletes who are new to lifting or starting after time away from lifting should begin with a few weeks of easy workouts. Start with small amounts of weight for each lift, maybe 30 to 40 percent of the maximum you can lift for each exercise. After a few weeks, you can increase the amount you lift so that as you complete the last repetition of each set you feel you could not complete another repetition. Be sure to do a solid cardio type of warm-up to get your muscles ready for lifting, and then do a short set of stretches. Proceed after the stretching to complete your lifting session. Follow the lifting with a few more minutes of stretching. Do two sets of ten repeats (reps) for each type of lift. Seek the help of a trainer at a local gym or a runner friend who also has lifted for a few years to show you good lifting form (described below).

You may see some small gains in strength during the first few weeks, but most gains will not develop until you have been lifting for a few months. Gradually increase the amount of weight you tackle for each type of lift after you have been lifting for several weeks. You will notice that you are sore for a day after lifting when you first start to add these exercises to your workout routine. Thus, you should lift every other day to allow for muscle repair before your next weightlifting session.

Frequency and duration

Most experts suggest you lift every other day at most to allow for recovery and repair of muscles and connective tissue. If you do lift on consecutive days, try to work different muscles groups on the second day and decrease the amount of weight you lift for each exercise. The off-season is a good time to lift more frequently and develop more strength. During these few months each year you can lift three to four times per week. In the running pre-season (often the spring), as you start to build your running mileage, you can cut back your lifting to two sessions per week, usually on days when you are not running or just doing a short, easy run. This frequency is enough to maintain the strength you built during the off-season. Once you enter the racing part of the year, lift only once a week with an occasional week with two sessions. The two sessions can involve one with leg work and abdominal exercises, and one with upper-body and abdominal work, as well as a 30- to 40-minute session of non-running cardiovascular type of work.

The key is to not work your legs so much that you are sore or delay your recovery following harder running sessions or races.

How to fit lifting into a training schedule

You will usually want to lift on days you are not running or on days you run short mileage. If you are going to complete a medium-duration run on the same day as a lifting workout, run earlier in the day and then lift at noon or early evening. That will give your legs a little time to recover before you lift. Do not plan on working your legs as much as usual during the lifting if you did a medium-duration run earlier in the day. Instead, cut back on the amount you lift or the number of sets and/or reps you complete for each type of leg lift. Monitor your hydration level throughout the day for those times when you combine lifting and running on the same day. Remember that you may sweat more while working out indoors than when you run outdoors, particularly during the winter months. In addition, be sure to maintain a decent level of flexibility, as lifting tends to make your muscles tighter. If you are going to do a short, easy run on the same day as a lifting session, then you have flexibility in scheduling these workouts. You could lift in the morning and run later in the day or vice versa. Or you could lift and then run directly afterwards, as one workout should not interfere with the second workout. In order to allow for adequate rest and recovery, don't lift in the day or two before a long training run or race. A short, light lifting session the day after a long run or race may help with leg soreness, particularly if included with a short session of cardiovascular work, such as swimming or cycling.

Lifting form

Learning good form is a matter of timing and control. Seek to raise the weight for each lift on a count of three and lower the weight on the same count. Lifting the weights with a jerking motion is not as effective in working the muscles through a full range of motion, and increases the chance that you could develop a strain injury. Breathe in deeply as you lower the weight, and exhale as you raise the weight each time. Holding your breath as you lift can prevent you from lifting to your full potential and can lead to fainting. In addition, deep breaths oxygenate muscles and help clear out waste products, leading to enhanced recovery in the 24 hours after you lift. If you lift using free weights and are doing exercises such as bench presses, then learn proper spotting technique by working with experienced lifters at a local gym. Try to work through a full range of motion for each type of lift to maximize your strength gains. Make sure you are properly positioned on each apparatus if you use machines such as a Universal Gym, and adjust each machine to fit your size as well, and check the weight plates to ensure you are lifting the appropriate amount of weight.

Stretching

You should seek to stretch all the major muscle groups of your body in a short session (10 to 15 minutes) following each lifting session. Muscles to stretch include the hamstrings, quads, calves, butt, shoulders, chest, lower back, neck, forearm, and groin. Try to ease into each stretch for the first few seconds, then hold a fully stretched position for 20 to 30 seconds, and repeat one or two more times. You can also do a short bit of stretching after your initial cardiovascular warm-up and before you start to lift. In this case, aim to stretch muscles you will work in the lifting, and hold each stretch for just 10 to 15 seconds. The stretching will help counteract the tightening effect of weightlifting (which mainly occurs during the concentric contraction or down phase of each lift) so that you have the flexibility you need to maneuver around objects and negotiate hills when you run.

A sample lifting workout

You should always warm up before you start to lift. The warm-up may consist of 10 to 20 minutes of exercise that gets your blood flowing and heart pumping, such as stationary biking, brisk walking on a treadmill, or using an elliptical machine. This initial exercise prepares your muscles and connective tissue for the later work of lifting. Next, stretch the primary muscles for a few minutes. This involves the arms, shoulders, legs, and trunk. Then start to lift, doing upper and then lower body types of lifts (or vice-versa). The lifting part of the workout typically involves three to seven types of upper and lower body lifts, taking 30 to 40 minutes. Each lift consists of one or two sets of 10 to 15 reps each, depending on where you are in your training cycle. Finish the workout with 10 to 15 minutes of stretching major muscle groups.

Work major muscle groups with these lifts, including the shoulders, back, chest, quads, calves, hamstrings, hips, butt, and abdominals. The workout is concluded with a short cool-down of five to ten minutes of light cardiovascular work and 10 to 15 minutes of stretching. A sample workout is as follows: warm up for 15 minutes on a stationary bike, do upper body lifts, including lat pull down (two times 10 reps), shoulder press (two times 12 reps), bench press (two times 12 reps), bicep curls (two times 15 reps), dumbbell rows (two times 10 reps), tricep kickbacks (two times 12 reps); followed by lower body lifts such as squats (two times 10 reps), leg extensions (two times 12 reps), hamstring curls (two times 10 reps), calf raises (two times 15 reps), lunges (two times 15 reps); and then do abdominal crunches (two times 20 reps). During your racing season, you should just do one set of each of the above lifts, or cut back the number of reps to about seven to eight.

Free weights versus machines

Beginners are probably best off using machines to learn lifting technique and develop a sense of balance and timing, as well as to build up a base of strength. After a few weeks of using machines, these athletes can do most of their lifts using free weights. Free weights have the advantages of working muscles through a larger range of motion and also working supporting muscles as you balance during each type of lift. It is far less expensive to purchase a set of free weights, a lifting bench, and a few dumbbells, than it is to buy a lifting machine such as a Universal Gym or Bowflex. You will need to learn proper spotting technique if using free weights for certain lifts, and have a partner who can spot for you as well. Note that you will probably have to reduce the amount of weight you lift when using free weights as compared with most types of machines. Both of these types of lifting systems can be very effective at building strength if you slowly increase the amount of weight you lift and do not overdo your first few lifting sessions.

Tracking progress

You can include the details of your lifting sessions in your running log or in a separate notebook. Include information such as the date and time of the workout, your warm-up duration and intensity, the type and number of sets/reps for each type of lift, the amount of weight lifted, if you consumed any fluids during the workout, and stretches completed afterwards. Note also any signs of overtraining, such as lasting muscle or joint soreness, or if you have trouble sleeping or a loss of appetite. Also try to notice if you are more tired than normal during runs the day after you lift, as you may be overdoing the amount of lifting you do initially. Using a log book will help you determine which types and patterns of lifting provides the most strength improvements, while avoiding any combinations that result in injuries or overtraining.

Equipment

There are a few items you can buy at modest expense at your local sporting goods store or department store that will get you outfitted for lifting in your home. A weight bench with bar holder is an essential piece of equipment. The bench can be used in a flat or inclined position for a variety of types of lifts. A barbell with 100 to 200 pounds of weights (in five to 20-pound increments) is also necessary. The amount of weight you need depends upon your body size and whether you have been lifting previously. Dumbbells are used to do a variety of lifts for the arms and shoulders. Sizes in the range of 10 to 30 pounds will be most useful for most runners. Lower cost weights that can be used for lifts such as bicep curls and shoulder rows include large cans of soup, a five-pound bag of flour, and a laundry soap bottle filled with sand. A yoga type of mat is useful for crunches, pushups, and stretching. A step (like those used in aerobics classes) is needed for doing lifts in which you use your own body weight to work your legs and arms (see the on-line article by Walt Reynolds). These types of leg lifts are like a combination of bounds and squats where you step up onto the knee-high bench and then launch your body into the air above the step.

Summary

Weightlifting is one way to develop a stronger, less injury- prone body. For the ultrarunner there are a number of benefits of lifting, related both to running efficiency and power, as well as general health. Most runners can add two to three-hour lifting workouts (including warm-up, lifting, cool down, and stretching) to their training program without compromising the quality and quantity of their running. If you are new to lifting, start out slowly and learn proper lifting form by observing experienced lifters and asking for the help of trainers at your local gym. Allow time for muscle repair between sessions.

Cross Training and Fitness Equipment
by Kevin Setnes

"Cross training" is a popular buzz phrase that has been around for the last decade or more. At the same time, fitness equipment and other accessories have become commonplace in the repertoire of the distance runner. Both cross training and the use of fitness equipment show no signs of decline.

The growth in the popularity of these training methods and devices begs the question: How did we ever get along without them? The answer is simple: We got along just fine. But there is a huge difference between now and then. Prior to the birth of the running boom of the 1970s, a small percentage of the population actually ran for competition. While I have no concrete statistics, I would venture to say that it was less than five percent of the population (probably far less). Today, according to USA Track and Field and Running USA, the number of Americans running at least on an occasional basis is close to 30 million. Most of these people jog for basic fitness, but only about six to seven million compete in an organized run or event.

Prior to the mid-1970s, when the running boom started, there were relatively few organized events. Those events that were around had small fields numbering in the hundreds, not thousands. Those in attendance were mostly hard-core, competitive types, who were either in a competitive program or fresh from one. A minority of the field was comprised of so-called "recreational runners" who are so commonplace in today's environment. Runners competing typically immersed themselves in speed work, in addition to miles upon miles of training. For these runners of yesteryear, there was no substitute for pounding the pavement or grinding out laps at a track. For them, the extent of any cross training might have been the twice weekly visit to the weight room to work on strength with free weights.

Simply said, there is no substitute for running itself. If you want to succeed at running a road ultra, then you had better log substantial road miles. If you hope to conquer one of the long trail ultras, you had better find some trails on which to train.

Where does cross training and fitness equipment fit into an ultrarunner's training? Can we benefit from these training methods and devices? If so, to what extent? What should be used, and when?

Each type of cross training has its benefit. Each varies in cost and each may be more convenient than the next. What follows is a brief explanation and application of a variety of cross training methods and devices. While the list is certainly not all-inclusive, it does cover some of the most common activities and devices. You may apply them in different ways, which is fine, but the important thing to remember is that these are tools you should use to *supplement* your running. They should not *replace* running.

Strength Training

Strength training, in the form of free weights or machines that are designed to build muscle strength, is a staple in every health club in America. For the home user, it is relatively easy and inexpensive to get a set of free weights or dumbbells with which to work. Building muscle strength is good for ultrarunners. Building leg strength will improve your stride, through increased stride length and overall leg stamina. Increased strength reduces the stress that is put on your joints and other critical areas of the body. For example, strengthening the quadriceps helps the knees absorb the shock generated when running.

What type of strength training is best is subject to debate among fitness trainers. Distance runners are somewhat unique, in that they want to build strength, but not at the expense of adding weight, which building muscle tends to do.

Tip: Concentrate on doing routines correctly. Work with a health club specialist who is trained in the use of a machine or exercise. Focus on posture when lifting. Concentrate on repetitions versus weight. Heavier weights tend to build more mass; using lighter weights, but with a higher number of reps, translates to building more stamina.

Look for routines that focus on the leg motion. Stair step-ups with weights in hand are better than sitting routines. Routines that work muscles in a similar fashion to the running motion will better suit you as an ultrarunner. Don't forget the upper body, especially the arms, neck, back and abdomen. Lastly, schedule your weight or strengthening work for *after* your run and no more than two or three times per week. Abstain from extensive strength training routines at least two weeks prior to a major event.

Water Exercises

Swimming is excellent for building overall strength, especially in the upper body. Because there is no impact in swimming (unless you blindly crash into the wall), it is very easy on the joints. Aerobic benefits from this form of exercise are excellent, and it doesn't take long to get to that state. Anaerobic conditioning can also be accrued by restricting the number of breaths per stroke.

Pools are readily available at schools, Y's and health clubs. Another benefit is that pool running can be done without the use of much space. Water running with the use of a device such as an Aquajogger, a flotation device that keeps you upright in the water, is excellent for resistance training. This training builds strength with no impact. The running-like motion is also consistent with dry land running. If you are water running, keep in mind that the heart rate will be 10 to 20 percent lower for a perceived level of training and it will be difficult to match out of water "heart zones" due to the cooling effect water has on the body.

Tip: If a pool is readily accessible, consider investing in an Aquajogger for an excellent combination of aerobic and strength exercise. Use paddles or fins to increase the resistance against the water. When swimming, concentrate on form and using fewer strokes to improve your efficiency.

Cycling

Cycling is a good exercise. Like water activity, it creates no impact (again, unless you crash) on the legs and joints. Road cycling can be done most anywhere, so it is easy to fit into one's busy life. Off-road or mountain biking can also offer additional benefits. Recently I started riding a mountain bike, as the biking trails are within a mile of my home in the Kettle Moraine State Forest of Wisconsin. What I found quite remarkable was the conditioning it provided my upper body, especially the arms and shoulders. Working the hills on a bike is quite challenging; besides requiring some quick action with gear shifting, it has made "spinning" a term I am now very familiar with. Spinning (pedaling at a very high rate in low gear) is great work for the legs. The quadriceps work is good, as is the overall body workout.

Road cycling is better suited for leg strengthening. The aerobic work is fine for runners, but care should be given to not overdoing it. Cycling can be dangerous. As one friend told me, "You are either a cyclist who has had an accident or one that is waiting to have one." It seems that since this is almost inevitable, the need for protection, primarily in the form of a helmet, is paramount.

Tip: Whether you have a mountain (off-road) or road bike, make sure it is properly fitted and then adjusted for your body's frame. Have a bike specialist adjust the seat for height and have it centered properly. Improper fitting can lead to potential knee and leg problems with continual use. Try mountain biking for more overall body conditioning. Assume the risks associated with both road and trail and use the precautions, such as wearing a helmet.

Traditional or Mainstream Sports

Runners, especially long distance runners, are very one-dimensional athletes. We develop an efficient forward motion, one that is designed to move only in that direction. While stretching and other cross training routines may help with other body movements, such as vertical jump and lateral quickness, distance runners typically develop physically for that one sport only. A return to conventional sports such as basketball, football, or tennis is often accompanied by a difficult transition.

Mainstream sports usually involve more parts of the body when compared with distance running. While this is better for overall body fitness, it can be harmful if done suddenly. If a bunch of ultrarunners got together once a year for a game of touch football, I can guarantee you that almost everyone would be very sore in the days following. I can almost assure you of at least one or more injuries as well.

Since most of these other sports are played out as "games," the competitor in us is almost assured of coming out. Besides the unusual movements that these sports bring about, there is sometimes the inevitable collision, thus risking further injury.

Tip: If you want to get into the other sports and remain a healthy runner, participate in them on a regular basis. Avoid the once-a-year game or twice monthly pickup game. Get shoes or other equipment that are designed for that sport. Never wear running shoes when playing tennis or basketball, for example. Adopt a solid stretching regimen that will give you the added flexibility needed to play in such sports. Also, avoid rugby at all costs!

Treadmills

A treadmill, obviously one of the most popular training devices for the runner, can be an invaluable tool for ultrarunners. Treadmills come in many different makes and models. Some are cheap; some are not so cheap. Health clubs have models that typically run in the $4,000 to $5,000 range. Heavily advertised models for the home sells for less than $1,000. Finding a good one is important; how much money you spend depends on your usage.

An individual who wishes to walk at four miles per hour is probably well-suited for the less than $1,000 model. Ultrarunners, on the other hand, who aim to work on hills or a faster pace, are better off investing in a more sturdy (thus expensive) model. Options to be considered are the horsepower of the motor (1.5 horsepower or greater), options or programs available, and the vendor. Some manufacturers of treadmills make very good units that are of health club quality.

Treadmills allow you to run at varying speeds up to 12 miles per hour (depending on the model). Units with programs built-in offer a range of workouts that give the ultrarunner several alternatives, all within the friendly confines of a home or club. Treadmills may come with a heart monitor (see "heart monitors" later in this piece). These units allow one to work on hill running (uphill primarily), when one does not have hills to run outside. They allow faster tempo runs or even interval workouts, regardless of the weather outside. Living in the upper Midwest, we have a more difficult time getting in quality speed sessions in the dead of winter, especially if it is icy, snow covered, or extremely cold outside.

While treadmills are probably the single best device in which an ultrarunner can invest, there are adjustments necessary if he or she is to successfully incorporate such a device into a training regimen. The continuous motion of going nowhere is tedious to the mind. A runner also has to be mindful of the moving mat below them. This is uncomfortable for some and may require an adjustment period.

Tip: Spend money on a solid machine if you don't belong to health club or gym. Precor, Landis and LifeFitness make excellent units for the home user (in the $2,500 to $3,500 range). Position a mirror in front of the machine so that you can watch your footstrike as you run. This gives you confidence and allows you to stay on track of the moving mat much easier. This also allows you to examine your form and footstrike and, if necessary, focus on correcting errors.

Training applications that are good include hill training (either random or repetitive), interval training, tempo runs and heart or zone training. I don't like to run more then 10 miles on a treadmill, so instead will opt for a faster tempo to minimize the boredom of running in place. I also like to do hill repeats (most units go up to 15 percent in grade). Practicing power walking up steep hills is possible with a treadmill, even if you are an ultrarunner living in Florida.

Elliptical Trainers

Elliptical trainers or cross training machines have become quite popular during the last few years. Most health clubs are now equipped with them; they are almost as common now as steppers and treadmills. An elliptical trainer is a cross between a stair climber, treadmill and Nordic Track machine. It mimics running with an upward motion. The feet stay put in pedals, so there is no impact on the body. This is a great machine for runners recovering from an injury. It is designed with various routines, and can even comes with an upper body option, which allows you to push and pull with the arms, thus providing the ultrarunner an overall body workout.

An elliptical trainer allows for only one stride length and thus should not be used exclusively, but if you are recovering from a leg injury, there is probably no better piece of equipment available. These trainers also allow for reverse motion exercises. They work different sets of leg muscles in a different fashion. The cross trainer forward mode works the hip flexors, buttocks and hamstrings, while the reverse mode works the quadriceps and hamstrings.

Tip: Incorporate the elliptical trainer slowly into your training regimen, working up gradually in level of difficulty. Get the upper body option; this allows you to work on your front and rear deltoids, biceps, pectorals and back muscles. Use this as a tool to hasten your recovery from an event or injury.

Stair Climbers

An excellent aerobic device that is again commonly found in health clubs is the stair climber. If you like to "feel the burn," try climbing for an extended time. Like other machines, these usually have programs built in, allowing for various exercise routines. The stair climber as a home device is convenient, because it does not take up a lot of space. Costs can vary, as with any machine, but it can provide a worthwhile workout specializing in leg strength and cardiovascular work. Since many 100-mile trail runs involve climbing long hills—some with very steep inclines—climbers may be a good choice as you prepare for your next 100-mile.

Tip: Warm up before getting on a climber. If you are in a health club, start with a treadmill run to ease into your workout, switching to the stair climber only after you are warm. Work the interval or repeat programs, as this can be a very rigorous anaerobic workout. If you are purchasing a climber, take it for a test drive in the store in your workout clothes. Spend some time on it and stick with a better quality name brand. Follow up your stair climbing workout with a light cooldown on the treadmill.

Heart Monitors

Heart monitors have been around a long time and are widely accepted as a very useful tool for ultrarunners. In fact, some runners plan their entire training (and even racing) around the little devices. A heart monitor is mounted on an elastic strap that easily fits around the chest. A transmitter emits a signal to a watch that displays the heart beats (BPM). You can set up your heart monitor to beep on different heart zones or thresholds. Some ultrarunners use this tool to keep themselves below a certain heart rate when running ultras.

An important benefit of a heart monitor is that it can help prevent overtraining. People sometimes just don't know how to keep their easy runs *easy*! With a heart monitor, you can have the monitor watch your heart rate and alarm if you go over a certain rate. Typically, for recovery one should stay under 70 percent of their maximum heart rate. A maximum heart rate varies upon individual; but, in general, it can be calculated by subtracting your age from 220.

When training for speed, attaining a heart rate of 85 to 90 percent on tempo runs is considered ideal. Intervals require you to run at 90 to 95 percent of your maximum heart rate. If you are racing at shorter distances (less than a marathon), you should run between 75 to 90 percent of your maximum heart rate (MRH). The longer the distance, the lower the percentage of MRH. For ultrarunners, this means you want to target the 70-percent range of MRH (plus or minus five percent).

Tips: Use the heart monitor as a measure of fitness, by running a set course on a week-to-week basis. Understand that fluctuations may result from illness, overtraining, stress and possible dehydration. Temperatures also vary this reading, but in general, monitoring the heart rate is one of the key measuring sticks of fitness level. Use the heart monitor to keep under 70 percent of MHR for rest or recovery days. Use the heart monitor to prevent fast starts in ultras. Start out at rate that is no higher than 70 percent of MHR, gradually increasing as you warm up and cover the first couple of miles.

Ab Machines

Ab machines or devices that are designed to work the abdominal muscles have also been very popular sellers during the past few years. While no one should deny the benefit of good abdominals, using a device or machine is not necessary to get this job done. To be fair though, if it gets the individual doing the exercise on a regular basis with the correct posture, then it is probably worthwhile.

Ab exercising can be done with no equipment at all. In fact, a towel placed around your neck and held there can keep your hands and arms in the right place. In the end, this is as effective as an ab machine. Most abdominal devices are designed to keep an individual's posture correct when doing the exercise. The device keeps your neck and upper back from straining. This can make the exercise seem a lot easier when done correctly. Additionally, a roller cradles you on a crossbar between two rocker arms that provide support and alignment.

Tip: If you need an assist in getting you to do abdominal work, spend about $100 on an ab machine and you'll have something to remind you every time you look at it.

Summary

Cross-training and the use of fitness equipment is great for rounding out an ultrarunner's overall fitness. Ultrarunners tend to become very one-dimensional athletes; variety will help their muscles achieve better balance. Cross-training can also prevent the commonly occurring overuse injuries. Runners who are recovering from an event or injury can benefit greatly from cross training. By getting off the pavement or trail and working aerobically without creating that jarring impact that running produces, the runner will remain healthier.

While there is no substitute for pounding the miles out on the road or trail, there are great tools available for use in the home or health club that can supplement what you don't have or can't use outside. I look forward to the option of being able to do hill repeats in winter, late at night, while it is blowing snow outside with sub-zero temperatures.

Training for the Non-running Runner

Running, of course, is the best training for running, but there are times, especially for the aging athlete, when other forms of training are preferable, even more beneficial than running. I have been a long-time practitioner of cross training, even having completed the ultimate cross training event, the Ironman Triathlon. I've learned a few tricks along the way that have helped streamline my training. As an adjunct to Kevin's piece, here a few things I have learned:

Swimming. This is one tough sport! More than in any other endurance sport, proper form and mechanics are paramount in swimming. One should seek instruction if they have no background in the sport—or even if they do. Poor stroke mechanics can lead to frustration, wasted energy and other problems, such as biomechanical trouble that can carry over to your running if you are not careful. Your spinal column can get out of whack very easily with bad mechanics in swimming, setting you up for soreness, or worse, an injury.

Don't swim beyond the point when you are fatigued, even if this is only a few laps. Swimming when fatigued only leads to poor stroke mechanics. It is better to go shorter and concentrate on your stroke. Almost all swimmers train by doing intervals in lieu of lap after lap at the same pace.

Also, the shallow end of the pool is a great place to stretch after a swim. Your muscles are very pliable then, and the water helps facilitate stretching, even for those who are chronically tight and "never stretch."

Cycling. In road cycling, maintaining a proper cadence is important. Pushing too high a gear will slow that cadence. That will not be compatible with the quick leg turnover required in running.

Ride with a local cycling club. There is safety in numbers and you might get some tips as well. Getting a proper fit is critical. A local bike shop will help you with that. You can avoid accidents if you are careful, ride heads up, and avoid heavily trafficked areas. Aero bars will improve your speed, but may lead to a sore back and an encounter with a 2,000-pound car if you are not careful.

Do a short run after you complete a long bike ride, even if only for a few minutes. It will loosen up the muscles that have become stiff or sore from being in the cycling position for so many miles.

Weights. I sometimes do a "circuit" routine, an "aerobic" strength workout of sorts. I move quickly from machine to machine, keeping my heart rate up. I also mix in a stretching, as well as exercises done with my own body weight, such as crunches, dips, and chin-ups.

Also, a time saver is to combine running with weights. I live a mile from the gym, so I run perhaps five or six miles, do my routine, then run the mile home, slowly. That way, my last "muscle memory" is of running, but I still have done the strength workout without involving a separate trip to the gym. – Don Allison

Why Would Anyone Direct an Ultra?
by Don Allison

The timeless question of why we run ultras has long been the subject of conjecture, debate, and analysis. Although our motivation to run such long distances remains somewhat of a mystery, most of us, at least on some level, understand the fundamental nature of our pursuit and why we continue. Now, can we move on to a far more perplexing and mysterious question: Why in the world would anyone organize and direct an ultra for others to run?

We all know that without race directors there would be no ultras. Fun runs maybe, but not the events as we have come to know them in the past decade or so, replete with pre- and post-race gatherings, well-marked courses, ample aid stations, generous awards and prizes, and unstinting volunteer support. That such events now populate the ultrarunning calendar is as much a miracle as are those athletes who are able to transcend the normal boundaries of human speed and endurance, setting mind-boggling world records in those races.

One can (almost) understand those who stage short five and ten-km races. Although it may be a time-consuming process, at least the race-day task appears manageable. Even directing a marathon makes sense on some level, as many mid-size and larger 26-milers offer paid positions to those who are brave enough to undertake the job of moving runners along 26 miles of road. In addition to financial remuneration, there is a fair amount of prestige that goes along with heading up a marathon.

But an ultra? According to the year-end statistical compilation assembled for *UltraRunning*, the average sized field in North American ultras in 2006 was about 57 runners. That's hardly enough to garner public adulation or generate any kind of financial remuneration. Sure, there are a small handful of ultras that attract hundreds of runners, but what about all of the other events that go on year round, in every state and province in North America? Who are the driving forces behind these races? Why are they assuming such an apparently thankless task? Is there something deeper that is not evident at first glance about putting on an ultra? Could you too be a candidate for ultra martyrdom, otherwise known as race directing?

In order to solve these mysteries, I went to the source, to find out just how ultras race directors became ultra race directors, since no one—not even Norm Klein—majored in ultra race directing in college. At least I think he didn't. For most, it is a gradual process. Almost all race directors have first been ultrarunners, or at least associated with one, perhaps through a relative or a friend. Most, however, actually participated in a number of ultras before staging one themselves, which when you think about it is really crazy, as that means they at least had a rudimentary understanding of just how difficult it would be to direct one themselves.

But if hard-headedness and optimism in the face of impossibility are prevalent characteristics in ultrarunners, they are absolutely mandatory for race directors. Just thinking about the time involved on the day of the race alone is enough to scare most people off, let alone the complicated logistics most races present. But any race director will tell you that the time spent on the day of the race—even if it is all day and night—is merely the tip of the iceberg. Months of plotting, planning, and organizing are required before the runners are sent on their way. Then, of course, the possibility of something going wrong on the day of the race is geometrically higher in an ultra than in a shorter race. And this is not even to mention the potential nightmares of runners becoming lost or encountering serious medical problems.

So, why oh why do they do it? For many, it is a derivation on the old mountain climbing theme, "because it was there," while for others it is "because it wasn't there" and they thought it should be. In the former case, many assume directorship of an existing race by initially becoming involved on a volunteer level, then gradually assuming more and more responsibility, until one day they wake up, look in the mirror and say, "Guess what—I'm the race director." These individuals tend to be the level-headed, clear-thinking, somewhat cautious types. Other, more adventurous souls have a favorite route on which they would like to see a competition held, or see a void of racing opportunities in their area that they have a desire to see filled, so they create their own events. These are the real pioneers, the cowboys of the sport, those that embody the "never say never" attitude so many ultrarunners possess. Every event on the calendar today at one point started with someone or a group of people creating the race from scratch.

Margie Lopez, former director of California's Run on the Sly, is an example of the first type of race director. She explains how she came to direct this event: "I started out race-helping, for the purpose of giving something back to the sport (a common theme), and to encourage some non-runner friends to get interested—which most did. Through this I learned that, although it is a lot of work, there is nothing technically difficult about race directing, and I challenged myself to see if I could do one." She could and did, making the Sly a very successful and popular event.

Mark Dorion, who stages many low-key trail ultras in the El Paso area, epitomizes the latter type of race director. He says, "I got into race directing in 1990, because, after living in El Paso for eight years and waiting for someone else to put on an ultra, I realized most runners would rather complain about the lack of events than put one on." Thus, he offers frequent, low-key trail races in west Texas.

Are there certain characteristics or personality traits that might potentially lead one into the world of race directing? If so, which of these are most important for someone thinking of putting on a race? More than anything else, a race director must have the ability to lead. In all events, both runners and volunteers will be looking to the director for leadership. Thus, in order to engender confidence, a race organizer must assume a take-charge demeanor, since others will be taking their cue from him or her. Believe me, volunteers—and especially runners—can sense when a director does not have confidence in his or her own race. It is a recipe for disaster. In addition, as a race director you must be able to delegate responsibility well, generate enthusiasm, and remain cool under pressure or adverse circumstances. The ultimate race directors would also make good field generals in times of war. Viewing the film *Patton* provides a good primer for the potential race director.

Equally important are organizational skills. Directing an event is a complicated exercise in logistics. There are a number of different aspects to any race, many of which have to managed simultaneously. Entry forms alone create a myriad of paperwork. Staying organized is thus of paramount importance. There are many other skills that are useful to an event director. Some of those include: the ability to sell and negotiate (both to and with potential sponsors and runners), decisiveness, a knowledge of finance, a knowledge of meteorology, physical strength (heavy lifting is often involved!), endurance (forget about sleep the week before the race), and an optimistic nature, as you must believe your event will be a success for it to become one. Lopez explains it best: "You need to have heart. That is the most important thing, because if you really care about the experience you offer, then you will make it right enough (for the participants)."

Race directors must be keenly aware of just what it is that runners want out of a race. All ultras are not the same, so expectations vary widely. While in a large road ultra, an extremely well marked course and regular aid is critical, for a small trail race in a remote area that prides itself on a sense of adventure, these aspects may not be expected—or even wanted. The most critical point for a race director is that he or she must not promise what they cannot or will not deliver. "Caveat emptor" is applicable to ultras, but on the other hand, a director who does not make good on what he or she indicates will be available will not be a race director for long.

Scott Mills, an ultrarunner and director of the Bull Run Run, lists what he feels an ultra event director should provide for participants:

- Reasonable safety considerations (medical support and radio communications).
- A well-marked course.
- An appropriate number of well-stocked aid stations.
- A run that allows individuals a reasonable opportunity to finish, assuming they are adequately prepared.
- A thorough yet succinct handout covering all aspects of the event (i.e. directions to the event, course description/map, aid station information, local lodging information, crew rules/directions, etc.).
- A quality memento (apparel or other) recognizing each runner's accomplishment.

This seems to be a reasonable guideline, enough to avoid encountering potential problems. As long as there are races, however, there *will* occasionally be problems. The more difficult the logistics of a race, the more likely the chance that problems will occur. There is a special place in heaven for those who direct difficult and remote trail races. These events increase the complexity of staging a race geometrically, especially those that are held on point-to-point courses, as that brings the issue of transporting runners into play. In such races, if an ultrarunner becomes lost or suffers from medical problems, the consequences can be severe. Thus, the tracking and support of runners becomes of paramount importance. Participants in trail races must take proper responsibility for their own well-being. Want to really incur the wrath of a race director? Quit the race without telling anyone, suffer from medical problems you never told anyone about before the race, or fall behind the cut-offs and argue with volunteers to stay in the race.

Ironically, however, as we have seen in recent years, remote trail races are just the kind of adventurous races that ultrarunners are seeking nowadays. In addition to the sheer difficulty of putting on a trail ultra, the costs associated with staging such a race can be staggering. It is amazing that so many trail ultras are available and that directors are able to finance such events on what are usually very small budgets.

Regardless of how little money there is in directing an ultra, economics does indeed play a major part in making an event a going concern. Although a few lucky races are able to attract some sponsorship, most race directors rely primarily upon entry fees to subsidize the costs associated with an event. An entry fee must be enough to cover these costs, but not so high as to deter runners from participating. It can be a very fine line for many ultras. No director should have to pay out of his or her own pocket to make ends meet, but many end up doing just that. In an article many years, ago, author and director Gary Cantrell suggested that if race directors had to pay out of their own pockets to conduct an ultra, they should look at it as if they were throwing a party for their ultra friends and were simply paying to host the party. That is a generous view, but not a good strategy for the long term.

The basic laws of supply and demand apply to ultras, just as they do to every other part of society. There are a few select events in which the entry fee is not at all a deterrent to potential runners; these events will always draw big fields and fill up quickly. Those races are few and far between, however, so most race directors must have a keen knowledge of just how many runners can be drawn, and what entry fee is fair. The flip side of race income, of course, is race expenses. Managing a budget is critical in conducting a successful event. It is not a task most race directors enjoy, but one that must be addressed throughout the course of managing an event, in order to avoid piling up excessive "party" costs.

Regardless of how they got started, most race directors find that conducting an ultra turns out to be much more than they envisioned it would be. Given the multitude of concerns listed above, as well as the sheer magnitude and potential difficulty in staging an ultra, it seems even more amazing that anyone would dare try to put one on. But many do, and as I stated at the outset, there must be a reason.

In the end I think, what it really comes down to is that certain individuals are drawn to race directing, much as certain individuals are drawn to ultrarunning. It is the challenge they are drawn to, and the feeling that they are truly accomplishing something worthwhile. Completing an ultra is without question a terrific accomplishment, one that can serve as an inspiration to others. In that way, organizing and directing an ultra is an accomplishment on a higher plane, as even fewer of us aspire to and achieve that goal. In addition, directing an ultra does not just serve as an inspiration to others, it offers many ultrarunners the opportunity to achieve their own goals and garner a sense of achievement, all at the same time. That, I think, is the true feeling of satisfaction that allows race directors to overcome the mountains of obstacles they face in simply getting an ultra off the ground and running.

While, directors of ultras agree that the amount of work and effort involved in taking a race from the idea stage to an actual race is far greater than they thought it would be, almost all of these same directors feel that reward that results from of putting on an event is worth all of the required effort. Mills says, "What I didn't realize was the incredible amount of work involved in organizing all the logistical aspects of the run. But in most ways, yes, it has been all I thought it would be. For example, the sense of accomplishment, the gratitude of others, and the satisfaction of seeing the event grow in popularity were all things I hoped would be the outcome of race directing the Bull Run Run."

Ultrarunning is still a relatively small sport, one in which many of us consider ourselves uniquely invested. Many races are as much like family gatherings as they are athletic competitions. Fellow ultrarunners are not so much competitors as much as they are allies in the quest to test the limits of our endurance. Thus, staging an ultra is as much an act of friendship as it is work. This is an important concept to understand if you direct an ultra, or are thinking of doing so. Problems and hassles? There will be many. Money? There will probably not be enough. A sense of pride, satisfaction, and the feeling that you will be honestly helping other ultrarunners, while improving the sport? Oh, there will be plenty of that. Are those any kind of reasons to direct an ultra? You bet they are!

A Primer for Pessimists

by Don Allison

Race directing and Murphy's Law. Anyone who has directed an ultra will tell you they go together like, well...peanut butter and jelly. An optimistic outlook—along with a lot of planning and hard work—is a must for directing an ultra. But a hefty dose of pessimism can come in handy as well. Assuming that if there is a chance that something can go wrong that it probably will go wrong, has saved more than one ultra from near-certain ruin. From the prince of race directing pessimism then, a few tips.

Look over the race calendar carefully before you schedule your race date. In selecting your date, how close is too close, in terms of geography and date? If you put on a new ultra two towns over from an existing race two weeks before that race, are you encroaching on someone else's territory? Or is all fair in love and race directing? There are only 52 weekends in a year, so there is bound to be some overlap. Don't butt heads with an already successful race, however. At best it will hurt the turnout at your race; at worst it will turn you into an ultra pariah in your own region.

Assembling enough volunteers to properly conduct an ultra is positively critical to a race's success. But what do you do when you feel you just don't have enough volunteers to cover all bases? First, make sure to exhaust all of your possible resources. Potential volunteers can be found in places you might not ordinarily think to look. Local civic organizations and schools might be a possibility. I once covered an entire aid station by asking the local Boy Scout troop to help. The kids had fun and got credit for a civic project, and I got the help of the Scouts, as well as supervising adults.

If you are still short of help on race day, make an announcement at the pre-race gathering. Many times, spouses and friends accompanying runners will be willing to help, at least for a while. They may be looking for something to do but are afraid to ask. Volunteering can allow them to feel an integral part of the race. These folks have been some of the hardest working volunteers I have had at my races. As a last resort, prioritize. Make sure to employ the volunteers you do have at the most critical spots. Don't worry about someone recording an intermediate time split if you are still short of help at the finish line.

What about liability issues? What amount of medical coverage is enough? What if you can't get the Red Cross on site and can't afford an on-call ambulance? What about insurance? These issues are not trivial. Without being overly dramatic, this area of race directing can be the difference between life and death. Securing insurance through USA Track and Field is both reasonable in cost and broad enough to cover most any ultra. They also offer third party liability certificates for towns and other government agencies.

As for medical coverage, having the Red Cross and or an ambulance on hand is great, but if you can't arrange for that, at the very least brief all volunteers on potential medical concerns and know the location of the nearest hospital or other emergency medical help. In this day and age of instant communication, contact should be instantaneous, which can be a big help.

What happens when your race is two weeks away and you only have eight people signed up, when you expected 50? High expectations are the bane of race directors, so don't get your hopes too high. It's always better to be pleasantly surprised by a good turnout than be disappointed by a low one. This is a tricky area though, because you also don't want to come up short on race supplies on race day. Hell hath no fury like a runner denied a race T-shirt or a finisher's medal, because you "ran out." On the other hand, you will curse your high hopes every time you walk by those boxes of leftover T-shirts in your basement in the months (and years) following a race.

The best gauge for guessing the number of runners that might attend your event is history. Once a race has established a baseline number, the turnout in future years will usually be in that ballpark, unless you have struck gold and your race grows like wildfire. As for first-year events, the best strategy is to wait as long as you possibly can before ordering shirts and finisher's awards, and hope you are an accurate educated guesser.

Your race has started and the unthinkable happens: the runners have gone off course. This is a favorite race director's nightmare, so you surely want to go to great lengths to prevent this from happening, primarily by marking your route well and educating the runners as to how to follow the route, through maps and instructions. But sometimes, despite your best efforts, Mr. Murphy and his law intervene. What can you do?

First of all, know that all may not be lost, so don't give up hope. Getting the runners back on course is the first order of business. You don't want ultrarunners all over the forest or the neighborhood asking people which way the race goes (or went). The very long distances involved in ultras often means that a short detour off course will often not result in a significant disruption of the finishing times and places. Ultrarunners will try to make the best of the situation as well, so know that they too want the best outcome in this unfortunate occurrence. Do your best to get the race back on track. If it is only one individual or a few that have become lost, get them back on the right route and deal with the issues of time and place after the race is over. I participated in a point-to-point trail 50-mile few years ago, in which the individual responsible for marking the last several miles of the route never did so and never bothered to tell anyone she had not. So when we got past mile 40, we had no idea which way to go. We all spent various amounts of time wandering around trying to find the route to the finish. Remarkably however, after we did manage to do so, most of the talk at the finish line was of the beauty of the course. We all accepted what had happened late in the race and had factored it into our thinking of the final times and places, and that was that.

To paraphrase a certain former U.S. president, "You can't make all of the ultrarunners happy all of the time." What do you do when runner complaints come? Alas, it's inevitable. The best approach is to attempt to quickly and efficiently ameliorate a potential nasty situation, while trying to appease the runner and keep your focus on the event at hand.

The best way to avoid runner complaints is to be as clear and unambiguous as possible in the rules and regulations regarding the race. All rules should apply to all runners. Don't make exceptions. That applies to cut-off times and starting times. Making an exception may seem the easiest option in a time of crisis, but standing firm on race rules will serve you best over the long haul.

Most runner complaints come from an athlete's passion for the sport and that particular event. Runners invest a huge amount of training time in preparing for a race, so above all you must avoid appearing uncaring or nonchalant about his or her complaint. It is because they care so much that they are angry. If the complaint is well-founded and you truly did screw up, admit it. That many not fully assuage the runner, but sometimes it is the best you can do. You can offer them a refund or a free entry into a future race if you feel it is warranted.

If you feel the runner is out of line in complaining, don't stoke the fire by engaging him or her in an argument. Calmly let the runner know your position and say if he or she really feels the need to vent, it can be done after the race has concluded. By then the runner may have gained perspective and be seeing things more clearly. If the runner has broken a race rule and is still intent on continuing, let he or she know they are not a part of your event anymore and you will not be responsible for his or her actions. This is a last resort, obviously.

While on the topic of complaints, what if a third party has an axe to grind? I have been waylaid by more than one irate neighbor during a race I was conducting. Generally it stems from these folks not being in the mood for a bunch of runners invading their domain. Again, a friendly demeanor will serve you better than anger, no matter how groundless the person's complaint may seem. If a neighbor is complaining about the actions of one of your participants, tell he or she you will investigate the matter fully after the race is over and get back to them with your findings. Don't ignore those that complain. The reason they are complaining is that they want your attention, and they want it now.

O.K., here is the big one. What should or can you do if you have to cancel your event on race day or right before it? Sadly, this does sometimes happen, most often due to weather concerns and/or the shutting down of the race venue by a local or state government agency. As for the latter, don't assume that "things will work out on race day." Work with all agencies well in advance of the race to make sure you file for all the necessary permits. If you still encounter problems on race day, try to reason with the authorities; don't adopt a hostile attitude. Sweet talking is a skill, especially for those that can do so without betraying a hint of desperation. Telling the authorities, "Well, the runners are going to run anyway," may be a last resort, but rest assured that by issuing that pronouncement you have kissed goodbye any chances of ever having the race again.

As for weather, well, all we know who is in charge of that department. (Hint: it's not you.) Meteorological concerns dominate the thoughts of race directors during almost all waking hours leading up to a race. However, I know this much from my experience as both an ultrarunner and a race director: the weather always seems worse when you are directing. For the most part, ultrarunners are smart, resourceful and hardy. They will usually be willing to give it a go regardless of the weather, and will run accordingly. As a director, it is up to you to decide if the weather presents too great a danger to run. Some of those situations include: a hurricane, tornado, flood, or biblical-level lightning. It's not worth risking your life or the lives of others just to run a race.

On the other hand, extreme cold, rain or heat can be managed surprisingly well by ultrarunners. Remember that 100-mile races are held in the arctic north and the deserts on the equator. So your conditions may not be as bad as you think. In the Vermont 100 Mile in 1999, the temperature was near 100 degrees F during the day with oppressive humidity. Most television weather reporters were urging viewers to "stay inside and by all means do not exercise." But many of the runners ran all day and night, completing the 100 miles.

This list of potential problems could go on and on. As Karen mentioned, don't expect your race to be a money maker. If it turns out that way, all the better. But heed the advice given to first-time tourists gambling in Las Vegas: don't spend more than you can afford to lose. Oh, and one other tip: expect your own running to take a back seat for a while. Don't direct a race during a time that is critical in your own training for another upcoming ultra. Managing an event is enough of a physical and mental challenge. If you get some running in during the week or two leading up to the race, great. Don't expect volunteers to be happy however, if you ask them to work while you waltz off for your "important" training run.

All of the preceding warnings and suggestions should not obscure the fact that directing an ultra can be fun and rewarding. It's a lot like running a race: there will be good times and bad, but after it is over you will usually look back upon the experience with fond memories. However, knowing the potential pitfalls before you get going and being properly prepared is good advice for directing, just as it is for running. See you at the races. And remember, we're doing the best we can!

Physiology

The Ultrarunner's Body

Many of us have undertaken the challenge of running ultra distances in order to discover what our bodies are capable of achieving. In that quest to test our limits, we inevitably encounter the upper reaches of our physiological capabilities. The late author George Sheehan called all runners "an experiment of one." This is particularly true of ultrarunners. We are all given a body in which to live—and in which to run ultras. We quickly learn that managing our own physiology in an optimal manner will not only make the sport more enjoyable, but will extend our ability as well. No wonder volumes have been written about the ultrarunner's physiology. In this section of the book, we present a wide spectrum of articles on that topic.

When it comes to physiology, there are many unique concerns an ultrarunner must address. Foremost among these is nutrition. While runners competing in shorter distance events may not have to be too concerned with taking in fuel during a race, ultrarunners must. Kevin Setnes' article, *Eat, Drink, and Run Ultras: A Basic Dietary Guide,* along with several pieces by nutritionist Sunny Blende, examine the inner workings of the ultrarunner's body and how to best meet the special nutritional demands placed upon it. Charles Dumke undertook a study to determine how many calories you really burn un an ultra distance run. In addition, Karl King, who has made a science of understanding fluid replacement in ultras, offers suggestions in his article *Electrolytes and Fluid Replacement.* Also, Kevin delves into the often misunderstood world of vitamins and supplements, while Jason Hodde and Karl discuss the tremendous effect ultrarunning can have on the endocrine system and how to keep it vital and healthy. On the other hand, David Neiman looks into the question of whether ultrarunning can make you sick. Every individual is unique when it comes to their body's physiological response during the stress of running an ultra, but there are general guidelines and suggestions that will help us all. All of these authors and others stress that it is a matter of individual experimentation to correctly determine what works best. The famous quote, "One man's poison is another man's potion" applies perfectly when it comes to nutrition and ultras.

Certain areas of the body can be affected greatly by ultrarunning. As rudimentary they may seem, injured knees, hamstrings, or the low back can prevent ultrarunners from reaching their potential, and even stop us in our tracks. Jason Hodde presents sensible and straightforward advice on the inner workings of these areas and how to keep them healthy.

Ultrarunners can also be confronted more extreme medical issues. Doctor Robert Lind addresses the issue of muscle breakdown and its very real dangers. Jason Hodde adds his thoughts on hyponatremia. In a related piece, Jason Hodde addresses the use—and overuse—of NSAIDS. The lesson that extreme medical situations can arise in even the most prepared and careful ultrarunners is graphically portrayed in this article, as well as in Bruce Boyd's discussion of pulmonary emboli.

Kevin Setnes' article *The Agony of da Feet* and Jon Von Hoff's *Blister Prevention* are issues surely every ultrarunner can relate to. Who among us has not spent time during a race dealing with foot problems that will just not respond to any type of treatment? The physiology of the heart is also obviously very important to an ultrarunner. Dr. Barry Mink provides an overview in his article *Ultrarunning and the Heart.*

Eat, Drink, and Run Ultras: Basic Dietary Guides for Ultrarunners

by Kevin Setnes

There are few issues more critical to completing a successful ultra than what the runner ingests during the course of a race. Running any distance shorter than a marathon requires little more than water and perhaps some electrolyte mixed in a carbohydrate solution. In some of the cooler marathons, most runners are able to get by with this combination. Kenyans have reportedly run marathons without taking a single drink of water. While this example is rare and not recommended for the average runner, the point is that from the marathon distance on down, a runner's intake requirement is much less than what is required at the ultra distances.

Energy and fluid needs for ultrarunners far exceed those of the marathoner. This requires the runner to understand his or her own ability to ingest these solutions and the proper formulas needed to successfully complete an ultra. We have all witnessed severely depleted runners, exhausted from effort, sitting beside the trail, unable to go any farther. Battling the distance as well as the conditions requires high intake levels of fluids and calories just to survive, let alone run competitively. Show me an ultrarunner who ignores his or her body and fails to drink or eat adequately, and I will show you an ultrarunner who fades badly in the second half of an event or has a disappointing DNF (did not finish).

Eating and drinking remains one of the ultimate keys to success in running ultras. It is one of the most important factors in determining the outcome of a performance. Novices and veterans alike are vulnerable to missing an ingredient that can make or break their races.

Intake requirements for ultrarunners fall into in four categories: fluids, electrolytes, food, and other supplements. Runners should look at each of these areas in planning for an ultra. The four groups overlap and are normally used in combinations, but missing any single one can make for a miserable ultra.

Liquids

"Drink early and often" is standard advice for liquid consumption during an ultra. Runners can lose up to a liter of fluids per hour depending on weather conditions. Many studies have been done on sweat loss during exercise and replenishment of fluids. The general consensus is that a five-percent loss in body weight (mainly fluids) is the danger point, at which a runner should stop to replenish, returning his or her body weight to normal.

Many 100-mile trail runs in the United States require mandatory weigh-ins at specific points along the course. This is done in order to monitor weight loss. The Western States 100 Mile in California issues the following guidelines for monitoring weight loss:

- Three-percent loss in weight: The runner will be feeling fatigued and nearing exhaustion.
- Five-percent loss in weight: The runner is nearly exhausted and will be closely monitored by medical staff.
- Seven percent loss in weight: Results in mandatory withdrawal from the run.

The key to maintaining weight is to take fluids *early* in the race. How much is required? The answer varies depending on weather conditions, running speed, and body mass. Tim Noakes, author of *Lore of Running*, says the most important factor is the runner's metabolic rate, which is directly related to running speed. The rate at which we consume oxygen and use energy determines metabolic heat production. Since sweating is the primary method for dissipating heat, the faster the running, the greater the fluid loss.

Heat and humidity are other factors determining sweat rate. Adapting to heat and dressing accordingly helps the body dissipate heat. We all know that in warm and humid conditions the need for fluid increases. The average times in hot weather events are noticeably slower than in cooler temperatures. Again the need to ingest fluid is increased.

Karl King, former race director of the Ice Age 50 Mile Trail Run, says a typical ultrarunner needs approximately one liter of liquid per hour. This may increase up to two liters depending on heat and humidity. He also adds that water requirements increase after 20 miles of running, because water stored with leg muscle glycogen is no longer a significant contributor. Noakes often mentions 500 ml as the basic replenishment requirement, this amount for sub-ultra distances and training only.

Hyponatremia occurs when a runner takes in too much liquid. Although rare among ultrarunners, both officials and runners should be aware of the possibility of this occurrence. Hyponatremia is basically water intoxication and usually occurs in people who are predisposed to the condition. The runner will consume more than an adequate amount of fluid, only to dilute his or her blood sodium count to dangerous levels. This condition can be as harmful as dehydration and a trip to the hospital is often the result. Thus, the need for proper electrolyte replacement.

Electrolytes

Electrolyte imbalance does not only impact performance, it can be life threatening. Most people realize electrolyte replacement is important, but fail to realize how much damage an imbalance can cause in an ultra. Runners with an electrolyte imbalance can lose many of their motor skills and become disoriented. Electrolytes are essential to the function of all living cells within the body. Through sweat a runner loses many electrolytes; the failure to replace them truly can result in a loss of basic mobility and bodily function.

Noakes suggests electrolyte loss is about two grams per hour (assuming a sweat rate of about one liter per hour). In an ultra, this can result in a loss of 20 to 40 grams. The consequences of failing to replace these electrolytes are extremely high.

Energy drinks contain some amount of electrolyte. It's best to compare and choose one that supplies more than one that supplies little. Even these drinks cannot supply the total requirement. Foods such as crackers and pretzels, which are readily available at most runs, contain some salt, but too little to really add up to much.

The need for salt at aid stations in ultras is high, especially in 100-mile runs. Always check to see if the race will have salt available. If not, you can easily carry salt packets (convenient at any fast food establishment) in a pack. Salty potatoes and soup are quite popular in the longer ultras and the reason is simple; your body is low on electrolyte and craves it—so indulge.

Calories

When asked about calorie consumption, I often respond by saying, "I don't care where the calories come from, just get them in you right away." Calorie sources are wide-ranging. In a self-supported ultra, one can take in calories in almost any form. Aid stations typically provide the basic fare of energy drinks, pretzels, crackers, cookies, potatoes, candy, and a wide array of other food. There is always plenty to choose from; only through experience will you determine what works best and agrees with your system.

A constant battle for many ultrarunners is stomach distress during races. The reason it is such a common problem is the inability of the stomach to perform gastric emptying while running. Solutions vary, but the key is prevention. Understanding some basic requirements and rules goes a long way in helping run a better and more trouble-free ultra.

Draw out a plan for your energy requirements. Obtaining 50 percent of your calories from a liquid mix and 50 percent from solid food intake is a good starting point.

King suggests targeting a regimen of calories per mile equal to the distance of the run in miles. This formula equals 30 calories per mile for a 50-km, 50 calories per mile for a 50-mile, 60 calories per mile for a 100-km, and 100 calories per mile for a 100-mile run. Runners pushing a hard racing pace may have to settle for calories at a lower rate. The reason for this is that an increase in pace causes blood to be shunted away from the stomach to the working muscles, which are demanding more oxygen, hence requiring a larger blood flow. With less blood flow to the stomach, the digestive process will be compromised. Thus, the need for limited caloric intake.

Concentration levels of the energy drink should be in the seven percent range for optimum gastric emptying. Many of the energy drinks supplied at ultras are stronger than that, so be prepared to dilute the drink with water. This is also speed dependent. A longer event and slower pace allows for stronger concentration levels.

King also advises against relying purely on carbohydrates. Ultrarunners also need fat and protein in an ultra. For 50 miles and up, runners should include the following protein and fat in their energy plan: five to eight percent of calories from protein, 10 to 15 percent from fat, and the rest from carbohydrate.

Other Supplements

If liquids, calories and electrolytes are the staples for completing an ultra, what else could one possibly need? Vitamins, herbs, and painkillers are the most common "extras."

It is true that vitamins are lost in an ultra. Ultrarunners have requirements above and beyond the levels stated by the Food and Drug Administration (FDA), and mixing in some vitamins along with your food helps. Energy bars provide vitamin replacement, but examine the contents closely, as the amounts vary widely. Vitamins play an even bigger role after an ultra race. The immune system is weakened, thus consuming antioxidants will help ward off potential illness that sometimes follows an ultra effort.

Taking vitamin C, E and beta carotene can help neutralize the free radicals that are produced when exercising or running extremely long distances. Free radicals are unstable molecules that can cause muscles to be further damaged, as well as a weakening the immune system.

Amino acid supplements should in theory keep you more anabolic, versus catabolic, a state in which the body begins to break down. I have also seen people stage miraculous recoveries during the night of 24-hour runs, who, after consuming exclusively carbohydrates have taken protein or amino acid supplements, then suddenly sprung to life.

Caffeine is a drug found often in drinks. Colas and coffee are quick acting and can bring new life into a runner. While technically illegal by the United States Olympic Committee (USOC), the amount required to put one over the limit is extremely high (a ridiculous amount, such as 20 cups of coffee an hour). Some studies have shown that caffeine stimulates the central nervous system, boosts adrenaline levels and promotes fat burning.

Caffeine can also be detrimental in that it is a diuretic, causing water loss. Moderate doses of caffeine can boost performance, but overuse can be detrimental. For habitual daily coffee drinkers (four to six cups a day), the benefits are muted by addiction to the drug. Decreasing dependence on caffeine can be done in a matter of days through abstinence. Caffeine will then have a more pronounced effect in boosting performance.

Taking aspirin or ibuprofen is a common practice in ultras. It is not illegal or against the rules to use these items. However, to some, it is borderline and toys with ethical and moral standards. I think this stance is a bit extreme (I use them), but caution against abuse of these items is very important.

More is not better. Too often, under the stress of an ultra, a runner may be apt to consume too much pain medication, causing potential harm to him or herself. This harm results from masking the pain of a "real" injury, which might become very serious if the runner continues. Another real danger is kidney failure exacerbated by ibuprofen and other non-steroidal anti-inflammatory drugs (NSAIDs).

In summary, have a plan with built-in contingencies, practice moderation and variety, be acutely aware of danger symptoms and remain in control of your situation. This simple formula is the basis for successful ultrarunning.

Food in a Day of an Ultrarunner
by Sunny Blende, Sports Nutritionist

Does calorie-deprived, over-trained and chronically dehydrated, describe your nutrition habits? Are you a sports bar or protein supplement junkie? A fat-phobic? Do you train on empty and indulge in a nighttime feeding frenzy; gorging at dinner and into the evening? Do you have all the energy you need?

A well-designed food plan is the foundation for any ultrarunner's training program. The plan should meet your energy needs and incorporate proper timing of nutrients in order to optimize performance and enhance recovery. Research has clearly shown that ultrarunners as a group do not ingest enough calories and/or do not consume enough of the right type of macronutrients (carbohydrate, protein, and fat) and therefore do not always adapt to training and thus do not always reach their full potential.

General fitness athletes involved in 30 to 40 minutes of exercise per day, three times per week, can usually meet their caloric needs with a normal diet of 1,800 to 2,400 calories per day. Athletes performing a moderate level of intense training of two to three hours per day, five to six times per week, or a high level of intense training three to six hours per day in one to two workouts, five to six times per week, may need 2,500 to 8,000 calories per day. This level of intense exercise may use 600 to 1,200 calories per hour! Ultrarunners must maintain energy while running for hours and hours in order to perform at peak level, even if the intensity of the run is not extreme. Nutritional analyses of these runners' diets show that many are susceptible to maintaining negative energy intakes. Deficient calories leads to loss of muscle mass, increased susceptibility to illness, and overtraining. Although it may be difficult for you as an ultrarunner engaged in high-mileage weeks to consume enough calories, planning can make a real difference in both your health and your race performance.

Timing Your Food Choices
Your goal should be to remain consistently fueled. Ideally then, you'd be walking around with an IV drip in your arm, constantly injecting the amount of caloric energy you need for each activity you do. Since this isn't possible, you need to eat evenly throughout the day. Ultrarunners susceptible to negative energy intake must snack, eat four to six smaller meals each day and use nutrient-dense energy bars or higher caloric supplements such as Ensure. Concentrate on keeping your blood sugar level even and don't get hungry. Try to draw your calories at the beginning of the day. It takes four hours for carbohydrates to be digested and begin to be

stored as muscle and liver glycogen. Therefore if your run is in the afternoon, breakfast becomes your most important meal. And don't forget the 30-minute window following your workout to accelerate muscle glycogen re-synthesis and storage. Try to eat a half gram of carbohydrate per pound of weight. And a little protein in a ratio of one to four (one gram protein to four grams carbohydrate) will help with recovery as well.

The "big three" healthy and found-in-nature foods for training are fresh fruits, vegetables and whole grains. Let's look at the latest research and recommendations from the International Society of Sports Nutritionists. The overall findings show that athletes involved in moderate and high volume training may need greater amounts of carbohydrate and protein in their diets to meet macronutrient needs, and this may mean calorie dense foods that are in a processed or supplement form in addition to the three mentioned above.

Carbohydrate

Carbohydrates remain the cornerstone of any ultrarunner's diet. Whereas runners in a general fitness program may need three to five grams of carbohydrate per kilogram of body weight per day, athletes in moderate and high volume training may need as much as eight to ten grams/kg/day, respectively. For someone exercising three to six hours a day in one to two workouts, that could mean one to four pounds of pasta! It is difficult to eat that much carbohydrate and still find time (and stomach comfort) to run. Dense grains and sports nutrition products containing maltodextrin may help endurance athletes in getting enough carbohydrates.

Protein

The amount of protein needed in an athlete's diet remains one of the most debated subjects in sports nutrition. New research over the last ten years has shown that athletes involved in intense training, such as that of ultrarunners, requires one and a half to two times the RDA of protein (0.8 to 1.0 g/kg/day) to maintain nitrogen balance. A negative nitrogen balance can increase protein breakdown and slow recovery. Over time this can result in muscle wasting and poor training tolerance.

Not all protein is equal, however. The source, processing, and amino acid profile all affect the availability, as well as the rate of digestion. Protein choices should be high quality and low fat. The best sources include light skinless chicken, fish, egg white, and skim milk (casein and whey). The best sources in supplements are whey, colostrums, casein, milk proteins and egg protein.

Fat

Recommended fat intake for athletes is similar to that of non-athletes as far as general health is concerned. However, the goal of maintaining energy balance can be a reason for increased intake in an ultrarunners diet, beyond 30 percent of daily caloric intake. Replenishing intramuscular fat stores and consuming adequate essential fatty acids are also of importance. Data from recent research suggests athletes may need more fat when participating in a heavy volume of training. Testosterone suppression can occur during high volume training and higher fat diets maintain circulating testosterone concentrations better than low fat diets. On the other hand, athletes trying to decrease body fat should keep their level of fat to 0.5 to 1.0 gram per kilogram of body weight per day. The type of fat can be important as well. Omega three versus Omega six and monosaturated versus saturated animal fats can help decrease body fat.

Vitamins

Vitamins are essential organic compounds that regulate metabolic processes, neurological processes and help with energy production. Research has demonstrated that specific vitamins may possess some health benefits for ultrarunners, but not much ergogenic value. Vitamin C and E may help athletes tolerate heavy training by reducing oxidative damage and maintaining a healthy immune system. This effect may indirectly improve performance. Sports nutritionists as well as the American Medical Association now recommend that athletes involved in moderate to heavy training consume a low-dose, one a day multivitamin.

Minerals

Minerals are essential inorganic elements responsible for a host of metabolic processes. Minerals can serve as structure, components of hormones and regulators of neural and metabolic control. Mineral status can be compromised in response to heavy training and prolonged exercise, and in this case, exercise capacity may be reduced. Supplementation can positively affect exercise capacity and act as an ergogenic in some athletes, in contrast to vitamins. Minerals reviewed that seem to possess health or ergogenic value under some circumstances are calcium, iron, sodium phosphate, salt (sodium chloride) and zinc.

Water

When just two percent of an athlete's body weight is lost through sweat, performance can be significantly impaired, which makes water the most important nutritional ergogenic aid for any ultrarunner. Four percent of body weight loss during a run can lead to heat illness, heat exhaustion, heat stroke and even death. The normal sweat rates of athletes ranges from a half to two liters per hour, with temperature, humidity, exercise intensity and training level all affecting that rate. Ultrarunners should learn to use a scale to weigh themselves before and after a training run to learn their own personal sweat rates. Drink two to three glasses of water for every pound lost on a run. Preventing dehydration may be the single most important thing an ultrarunner can do for his or her performance and maintenance of exercise capacity.

Consult the Ultrarunner's Eating Plan (see the accompanying chart) and fill in the blanks for your personal food plan. Adapt the chart for your own needs; obviously if you do not run or exercise in the morning, you do not need both a pre-breakfast snack and a breakfast. You may only need an evening snack the day before a race or a really long run. Keep these things in mind. For a pre-breakfast snack, focus on fruit. Think sports drinks and gels just before your run. For breakfast, be sure to have some calcium-rich foods and consider getting some iron from fortified cereals. Your mid-morning snack should help you stabilize your blood sugar—that makes yogurt an excellent choice. Lunch can be a real variety depending on your personal tastes and the time of your run. Strategic afternoon snacking can also help with a late afternoon workout. Dinner should focus on fiber: vegetables and whole grains, and omega three-rich fish or some other low fat protein. Use some of the ideas from the list on the right hand side of the chart and add your own favorites. Even the process of writing food intake down for a couple of days will help you make positive food choices and become more aware of your energy level and caloric needs. Try it and see how much your endurance increases when you are fully fueled.

Sunny's Tips

Pre-Exercise (one hour or more): Bagel with peanut butter or low-fat cream cheese, toast w/jelly, breakfast bar, yogurt and lite granola, breakfast burrito (maybe a half).

Pre-Exercise (10 minutes before): Sports drinks, GU or raisins and water, banana.

During Exercise: Water, Gatorade, Cytomax, PowerAde, sports gel and water.

Post-Exercise: Rehydrate. Sports bar and water, PB&J, yogurt, nuts, fruit, breakfast bar.

Timing of Foods

1. Eat soon to avoid low blood sugar (any foods, but low glycemic Index foods will burn fat longer)
• Upon waking up
• Right after exercising
2. Do not spike blood sugar with high glycemic Index foods
• During the hour before exercise
• Right before you're going to bed/sleep

Insulin Spiking Issues

1. Avoid sugar from and hour to 10 minutes before exercise.
2. "Bad" carbs (high glycemic Index) become "good" carbs during exercise.
3. Make good use of the "30-minute recovery window," during which time the muscles can store up to two times as much carbohydrate right where it is needed for the next bout of exercise.

Hydration Issue

1. The higher the heat or intensity of training, the more dehydration occurs.
2. Sports drinks with electrolytes and carb calories help your body absorb more water and maintain blood sugar and stamina, especially if you are a heavy sweater or if it is a hot day. They may help you drink more.

To Help Burn Fat (increasing Metabolism)

1. Eat breakfast; it revs up your engine.
2. Include in each meal: unsaturated fats (nuts, vegetable oils, avocados, fish), moderate protein, at least one vegetable or fruit, a whole grain (100 percent grain bread or pasta, skin on potato, whole cooked grains or rice).
Eat low glycemic foods as much as possible. Think "close to the source." Good snacks include carbs with a small amount of protein.

Ultrarunner's Eating Plan

Pre-Breakfast Snacks:
Bananas; fruit juice with a piece of toast or breakfast bar; sports bar and water; sports drink

A.M. Workout
Breakfast:
Whole grain cereal with berries, nuts, raisins; yogurt and piece of fruit; waffles w/ fruit and sausage; bean burrito; egg omelet and fruit
Morning Snacks:
Yogurt (with grape nuts); nuts and fruit, cheese; bagel with peanut butter; breakfast or sport bar
Lunch:
Sandwiches: peanut butter or soy butter with jam; sliced turkey, cheese; humus and vegetables; tuna; all on whole grain bread
Soup: lentil, vegetable, broth based; all with bread
Salad: add protein source like beans, chicken, watch high calorie dressings
Afternoon Snacks: Same as morning

P. M. Workout
Dinner:
Vegetables (colorful and a variety); wheat pasta, 100-percent whole grains and breads, brown rice; beans; fish; skinless chicken; lean meat, hamburger; low-fat pizza; stews; salads; soup.
Evening Snacks:
Low-fat frozen yogurt with granola; chocolate milk; oatmeal-type cookie and low-fat milk; fruit and nuts.

(Pre-Race Day)
Supplements: Balanced multi-vitamin, possibly C, E, CA

Goal: Emphasize fruits, vegetables, whole grains, and fat-free or low-fat milk products in addition to including lean meats, poultry, fish, beans, eggs, and nuts. Try to not go too long without eating; at least eat a small snack. Every two to three hours is best.

Taper Week Nutrition

by Sunny Blende, M.S., Sports Nutritionist

You are standing on the start line of an ultra. All of the workouts are over and all the training miles have been run. You haven chosen your shoes, trail pack and hat carefully. Have you spent the same effort on your fueling? Negotiating your nutrition during the final two weeks before a big ultra can seem almost as difficult as that last long training run. Should you increase the calorie amount? Should you change the ratio of carbohydrates, fats and protein? What foods should you eat? When should you eat those foods? And what happens when you are traveling or changing time zones, or even changing cultures, and therefore food choices? Managing these issues will be easier when you understand the rationale behind fueling for an ultra.

Nutrition Goals

Ensuring that you have stored your body with the maximum supply of energy possible for running the ultra is the primary goal. Increasing carbohydrate stores in your muscles and maintaining muscle mass (and strength) can be accomplished by timing your food intake in the last few days before competition. You will also want to increase water storage to ward off dehydration. Staying lean and continuing the fat-burning metabolism will ensure that you do not tap into precious carbohydrate stores before the race. Increasing antioxidants to decrease oxidative stress caused by free radicals may also be helpful. And of course, avoiding stomach distress is critical to a successful ultra.

Just After Your Last Really Long Run

One of the most important meals you will eat is the meal following your last long workout. Don't miss this opportunity! Recovery after this run is a key to your race, as your pre-race muscle glycogen level is the most important factor for performance and this is the time to replenish it! Within 30 minutes of your run, consume a 200 to 400-calorie snack, followed by a full meal within two hours. Eating lower glycemic index foods will burn fat longer. Better yet, eat a full nutritious meal, consisting of complex carbohydrates and some protein (at a ratio of four parts carbs to one part protein) right after your run, before your shower. Trained muscles can store more glycogen than untrained ones, yet use less glycogen during exercise than untrained muscles. Training teaches muscles to use a higher percentage of fat as fuel and this diet manipulation can nearly double the amount of glycogen stored in skeletal muscles. This means running longer before the onset of fatigue or needing more fuel.

Two Weeks Before

You will want to continue your regular diet and the same calorie level at meals during this time, right up to your last real run a few days before the ultra. Familiar foods are best. You will be eating slightly less total calories because you are doing less training and you will not consume so much "during exercise" fuel. Again, you want to be very judicios in your food choices; this is your time for a full recovery from heavy training. Empty calories (foods with calories but little nutrition such as potato chips, most cookies and candy, fried foods) will just make you feel sluggish without adding to your fitness. Mental stress takes it toll too, so be sure to include a variety of fruits and vegetables for their antioxidant and vitamin protection. Don't catch a cold during this week. Ample carbohydrates will help with protein (muscle) rebuilding too. Studies show that muscle tissue better absorbs amino acids from the bloodstream for resynthesis and rebuilding with a steady influx of carbohydrates.

General Nutrition And Insulin

Stable blood sugar directs calories to muscles instead of fat cells. Eating three to four small meals and two healthy snacks a day results in lower blood sugar rise with each meal. This does not mean increasing the total amount of calories per day, only the timing of the calorie ingestion. Eat half of your lunch sandwich in mid-morning. Eat another low sugar snack mid-afternoon and make your dinner smaller portions. Insulin is secreted into the bloodstream in response to ingested sugar. The higher the concentration of sugar, the more insulin secreted, with the exception that the more trained the athlete is, the more finely tuned and accurate the insulin response will be. The job of insulin is to avoid wasting energy by carrying the sugar molecules into the fat cells for storage for future energy needs. This is fine, but it makes more sense for an ultrarunner's extra energy to be stored in his or her muscle cells to the maximum extent possible. To minimize the insulin response, include some fiber, unsaturated fat and a moderate amount of protein with each snack or meal. Emphasize whole grains such as whole wheat bread, whole wheat pasta, brown rice, couscous and other grains. Include low fat proteins such as beans, chicken, fish, legumes and lean meats. Fresh fruits and lightly steamed vegetables will help with vitamins, minerals and phytochemicals.

Carbo Loading After Your Last Run

The purpose of carbohydrate loading is to rest the muscles by cutting back on exercise and to supersaturate them with glycogen in anticipation of competition. Muscle glycogen stores in the body only consist of about 800 to 2,000 calories of energy; definitely not enough for an ultra. However, as much as carbo loading can increase endurance, not all aspects are beneficial. The effectiveness of the carbo loading is somewhat dependent on the carb depletion or exercise intensity that must be done prior to "loading." This can result in reducing recovery during the all-important taper phase. In addition, a "loaded" muscle will burn glycogen at a higher rate and reabsorb glycogen from the bloodstream (from calories consumed during the race) at a lower rate than normal. As long as you know whether you are "loaded" when you start, and therefore need to eat fewer calories per hour for the first one or two hours of the ultra, you will be fine. But if you did not carbo load, then you will need to consume carbohydrate calories earlier in the race. Just be sure to eat that carbo load meal within 30 minutes of your last run. Don't miss this opportunity.

Loading improves endurance, not speed. It involves increasing a 50 to 60-percent carbohydrate diet to 70 percent. You will still need to maintain 15 to 20 percent protein intake, so guess what you have to give up? Yes, that's right; fat. Be careful not to fat-load. This makes french fries a poor choice. Eat foods that are familiar and wholesome; close to their source. An orange versus orange juice versus an orange popsicle. Brown rice versus white rice versus refined rice cakes. Fiber-rich carbohydrates will keep your system regular. Drink extra fluids to hydrate your body while limiting dehydrating fluids such as caffeine-containing beverages. Remember, extra carbohydrates need extra water. For every molecule of glycogen stored, three molecules of water are needed. Extra water is good for hydration, but has a sluggish-feeling effect on muscles, so be ready for a slightly heavy-leg feeling.

Day Before Nutrition

The goal here is to top off your glycogen reserves and be sure you are fully hydrated. Be sure to stick with familiar foods and eat them in normal-size amounts. Graze or eat frequently throughout the day, so you don't feel as if you have to stuff yourself at the evening meal. Drink plenty of fluids throughout the day (expect to urinate frequently). Most ultrarunners experience stomach distress at some time in an ultra run. The act of running is causitive due to the high impact running places on the GI tract. Multiply that by 10 to 30 hours and you can understand the problem. Differences in digestion time, stress levels, hormones, pre-existing conditions like lactose intolerance, irritable bowel syndrome, and the amount of bacteria in the gut all add to stomach ailments. Avoid high-fiber foods such as raw fruits and vegetables with thick skins, bran cereals, nuts, and seeds on this day; they can cause cramping during a run. "White" carbohydrates will be digested more quickly and get through your gut before the start of the race, averting stomach distress. Avoid cruciferous vegetables containing raffinose (broccoli, cabbage, radishes) and other gas-causing foods like beans if you suffer from bowel problems. Lactose-free dairy products, or avoiding dairy (milk, cheese and ice cream) may help with quesy stomachs. Avoid sugar substitutes like sorbitol and mannitol (in gums, candies, and other foods), which may cause diarrhea, and avoid alcohol altogether. Sugar alcohol cannot be used in the muscles; it must be broken down in the liver and converted before being available to the muscles for energy. Fructose can be another problem so avoid foods or gels that list this as the first ingredient. Experiment with your diet the day before long training runs so you know what works best for your particular stomach and nutrition needs.

The Last Supper

Your last meal should be high in carbohydrates and contain modest amounts of fat and protein without much, if any, fiber. Try to eat two hours before bedtime and choose foods you feel comfortable with or that you believe enhance your performance. Pasta, low fat pizza, baked potatoes, or fish or poultry with vegetables and rice all make good choices if you have tried them in practice. Eat or drink a light bedtime snack to squeeze in a few more calories and help you sleep better if you feel you need it. Choose what works best for you. Sports drinks, bars, bagels, pretzels, cereal, rice foods or Ensure can all be good choices.

Breakfast, Sleep Or Both?

Choosing between sleep and getting up early enough to digest a meal (three hours for a full meal!) doesn't really sound like a choice. Most of you would choose sleep and you would probably get more benifit from that choice. If you have been eating healthy meals and replenishing your carbohydrates after your runs on a regular basis, you should have plenty of fuel to start your race and still have an hour or so before you will need to begin refueling. That said, there are some scientific reasons for fueling up in the morning. The primary one is to top off your store of liver glycogen before beginning your run. During sleep, it is your liver glycogen that maintains normal blood sugar levels and it is this that gets depleted, not muscle glycogen, which remains undisturbed overnight. It takes only a few hundred calories to accomplish repletion and those calories should be made up of easily digested complex sugars (an example is maltodextrin in sports gels and bars) with no fiber, simple sugar or fat and very little protein. Another reason to eat one to two hours before exercise is that it increases your ability to burn fat, a distinct advantage during an ultra. Possibly the best motivation is that pre-race nutrition significantly increases your brain function, allowing for greater mental focus and less hunger. Just finish eating or drinking your calories one hour before the start so as to not spike your blood sugar and use up your precious stored glycogen. Good choices are eating a high complex carbohydrate snack with minimul or no fiber, fat or protein one to two hours prior to race start. This may be a liquid sports fuel such as Sustained Energy® or a product such as Ensure®, potatoes without the skin or white bagels, bananas, rice, Cream of Wheat® or a low fiber bar.

Since you must allow time for digestion of pre-race food and you simply cannot do this, there are other options. These will work if you are a very nervous runner who prefers (or cannot) eat much or anything before running, or a runner who has had repeated stomach issues when racing. These include:

- Eating a snack before going to bed the night before the ultra.
- Getting up in the middle of the night, eating a light meal (200 to 400 calories) and then going back to bed. This works well for the restless runner who isn't sleeping anyway and who may benefit by food that induces sleep.
- Eating something within five or ten minutes of the start such as a sport gel with 100 to 150 calories or a liquid carbohydrate sports drink (six percent glucose solution). There is not enough time for an insulin release and once you begin exercise, this response is mostly shut off.
- Starting in with your race nutrition after you get into a groove of running. Just be sure and consume appropriate amounts as discussed in previous articles.

You're trained, your mentally focused and now you're fully fueled. Have a great race!

High carbohydrate, low fat meals
Bean and rice burrito with vegetables
Low fat chips and salsa
Low fat milk
Pasta with vegetables and chicken
Italian roll
Low fat vanilla milkshake
Spaghetti with tomato sauce
Garlic bread
Garden veggie salad
Lemonade
Pizza with mushrooms
Salad with veggies
Breadsticks
Low fat milk
Grilled chicken sandwich with greens and whole wheat bread
Low fat potato salad
Ice tea
Turkey sub
Low-fat chips
Apple
Sports drinks
Deserts:
Low fat frozen yogurt
Low fat vanilla milkshake
Sherbert
Oatmeal raisin cookie
Fig Newtons®

Traveling

Traveling to an ultra race can often disrupt a healthy eating routine. Whether by plane or car, take time to plan. Keep meals and snacks three to four hours apart. If it means carrying snacks, pack non-perishables like peanut butter and jelly sandwiches, nuts and fruit or low fat pretzels. And drink plenty of water or water-based beverages to stay well hydrated.

Road Trip: Take familiar food when you can. If you need to stop at a convenience store or road stop fast food, think healthy sandwiches that you can decide what goes on them, Gatorade®, low fat milk or chocolate milk.

Airport: Many of today's airports offer flavorful, lower fat options such as wrap sandwiches, packaged salads and fruit smoothies. Bananas and low fat yogurt are available almost everywhere.

Airplane: Tuck nonperishable snacks into your carry-on bag. Let the snack cart roll on by. Do order from the beverage cart. Try to have one cup of fluid per hour in flight. Ask for water. Dry, re-circulating air in a pressurized airline cabin is dehydrating, which in turn promotes jet lag.

Dining Out: The best way to dine out healthfully is to ask questions:

- Can sauces or salad dressings be served on the side?
- Are baked and broiled items basted while they cook?
- Are vegetables cooked in butter or margarine?
- May I substitute a high fat, high-calorie item with something that is lower in fat and calories? Fruit or vegetables?
- Is the fish grilled, broiled, breaded or fried? Is it cooked with fat?
  The horizons expand even further with ethnic and international selections.

Here are a few ideas:
- Chinese: egg foo yung or vegetable tofu stir fry
- French: ratatouille or vegetable quiche
- Indian: curried eggplant and potatoes
- Italian: pasta primavera, eggplant parmesan or involtini
- Greek: spanakopita and tzatziki
- Mexican: bean burrito and chiles rellanos
- Middle East: falafel, hummus and tabouli.

Electrolytes and Fluid Replacement

by Karl King

Frequent debate about the need for electrolytes has raised many interesting questions. What amounts are too much or too little? What is right for you? What are the dangers? These are all valid questions, but ones to which there are no right and wrong answers. Maintaining proper electrolyte levels in ultra endurance events is critical for optimal performance. There should be little debate about that. Understanding an individual's requirements is another matter. Every runner, from the race winner to someone struggling to make the cut-off times, needs to understand their nutritional needs. Some things are basic: the need for fluids, the need for calories, and the need to go at a pace according to one's individual ability level. When attempting to run very long distances, each runner's success is largely determined by how well he or she understands their individual needs and abilities.

Moderation should be one of the golden rules of ultrarunning. Practice it in everything you do, until you fully understand your personal needs as a runner. With electrolyte replacement, you need to understand your fitness level, your sweat rate, the weather conditions, and the content of the replacement you are taking. Practice electrolyte replacement in training, and continue it in ultra races. What follows is a primer for any runner wishing to understand electrolyte replacement.

Hydration and Electrolytes

We have been told for years how important it is to drink during an ultra in order to avoid dehydration, which degrades performance and can lead to collapse. Many 100-mile ultras weigh runners at medical stops to check for water loss, pulling runners who have lost too much fluid weight.

What we seldom hear about is how we need to pay just as much attention to our electrolyte stores during an ultra. Electrolytes are those salts that play a major role in the biochemistry and physiological processes of the human body. While dehydration is a serious problem, we see many cases of DNFs and death-march experiences because of electrolyte imbalance. You will enjoy your running far more if take care of your electrolyte needs, as well as your hydration.

Let's review where fluids are in the body, and their amounts. Sixty percent of body weight is water. Forty percent of that body weight is located inside body cells. Fifteen percent is in the space around the cells, and five percent is in the blood. Although the weight of the blood is minor, its water and electrolyte contents are critical for optimal performance. Running performance suffers greatly with increased dehydration. The following chart indicates just how much:

Weight loss	Consequences
0 to 2 %	Beginning thirst, performance loss at 1.8 percent.
2 to 3 %	Thirst, seven percent performance loss.
3 to 6 %	Cramps, strong thirst, 20 percent performance loss.
> 6 %	Severe cramps, heat exhaustion, coma, death.

Water is lost through the skin by sweating, the lungs by breathing, urination, defecation (possible diarrhea), vomiting and wounds. Except for the lungs, all those routes are also pathways for loss of electrolytes. The amount of electrolytes lost in sweat and urine is variable, depending upon fitness, body electrolyte content and acclimation to heat levels. Vomiting and diarrhea can lead to large electrolyte losses, and thus are serious problems during an ultra. The only significant route for water entry is your mouth—you must drink.

Sodium and Potassium

Sodium and potassium are the major electrolytes in the body. The fluid in body cells is high in potassium; 90 percent of the body's potassium is inside the cells. Other body fluids are high in sodium, as indicated by the chart.

Fluid	Sodium content	Potassium content
Blood	3,100 to 3,330 mg/L	137 to 200 mg/L
Sweat	575 to 1,725 mg/L	155 to 200 mg/L

The major route for sodium loss is sweat. Because potassium is contained inside the cells, it is not lost at high rates, provided there is adequate sodium in the body. Normal sweat rates can range from three-quarters to two liters per hour, depending upon conditions such as temperature, humidity, pace, clothing, and the degree of heat acclimation the runner has. A rate of one liter per hour is not uncommon for an acclimated runner. At that rate, typical electrolyte loss rates by sweat are 1,300 mg per hour for sodium, and 230 mg per hour for potassium.

Electrolyte Imbalance

The body is sensitive to the amount of sodium in the fluid outside the cells, and in the blood. If the blood sodium level falls much below normal, a serious condition called hyponatremia can result. The typical symptoms are headache, muscle cramps, weakness, disorientation, apathy, and lethargy. Those symptoms are often seen in the latter stages of an ultra. If blood sodium falls to less than 2,500 mg per liter, the result can be death. That, fortunately, is rare. The body has mechanisms to retain sodium when it is faced with sodium losses, but there is only so much compensation that can be done. If you keep sweating without replacing the salt losses, the eventual result will be electrolyte imbalance.

Because a runner loses and ingests both water and salt during a run, the situation can be complex. The body is sensitive to the ratio of sodium to water; the ratio can be raised or lowered depending upon the rate of intake, as well as the loss of both sodium and water. It is possible to see runners in the same event suffering from different forms of electrolyte imbalance.

Many runners drink too little water, consequently suffering from dehydration. A runner's body usually cannot absorb water from the stomach as fast as it is sweat out of the skin, so most runners end up with some dehydration in an ultra. Some back-of-the-pack runners may have enough time to drink more water than they lose, especially if they are walking a lot. Most runners do not fully replace the sodium they lose and thus create a deficit. Some runners may take electrolyte supplements, some may use a sports drink with electrolytes, and some may take salty chips or pretzels, while others may take no electrolytes at all. Runners may drink mineral-free water after the run and get dilutional hyponatremia even though they were fine during the run.

Since most runners are not physiologists or biochemists, we will not get deeply into the science, but let's look at what commonly happens in an ultra when insufficient electrolytes are taken. Early in the run, sweat rates and sodium loss rates are high. Urination amounts may be high too. As sodium levels fall, the body increases the level of the hormone aldosterone, which influences kidney function to slow sodium loss. As exercise continues and sodium is lost, blood pressure may fall. The body produces the hormone vasopressin to help maintain blood pressure. If exercise continues, with more water and electrolyte losses, performance begins to suffer and the runner slows down. Eventually things get ugly. Since sodium is important for the absorption of food and water from the digestive tract, what the runner eats and drinks is not absorbed. Nausea results. Even the sight of food may make one want to retch. This is your body's way of telling you, "Don't bother, because I can't process it even if you force yourself to eat." If you drink, the water will not be absorbed well and will slosh around in the stomach. What is absorbed cannot be retained and will soon be urinated out.

As the level of sodium in the blood decreases, the ratio of sodium to water decreases to dangerous levels. As a defense mechanism, water will be moved from the blood into the spaces around body cells. That is why hands and feet swell after many hours of running. When feet swell, the toenails are more susceptible to mechanical damage, resulting in lost or blackened nails. Loss of water from the bloodstream is equivalent to further dehydration, causing additional loss of performance. Such conditions lead to a DNF or misery all the way to the finish line.

A Plan to Avoid the Problems

First of all, you can reduce your tendency to lose sodium by what you do when *not* running. You can reduce the amount of sodium in your daily food. That will increase the level of aldosterone so that your body retains sodium better. Choose less salty foods. Use Morton Lite Salt in your salt shaker. That will reduce sodium and increase your potassium intake (as will eating fruits and vegetables). If you expect to run in the heat, get heat acclimated as soon as possible. That will reduce your sweat rate under hot conditions.

During an ultra, stay cool so that your sweat rate is lower. Wear light clothes, keep your shirt wet, and/or put ice in your cap. Consume supplemental salt or electrolytes during the run. Most sports drinks have sodium levels that are fine for marathon running, but inadequate for ultras. Most gel products have insignificant amounts of sodium. Many runners eat pretzels during a run, but they have far less salt than you might think. You would have to eat 30 pretzels per hour to meet your needs. To satisfy your needs in a hot ultra you can take sodium in different forms. The simplest is table salt (a pinch per hour). If an aid station has salt and boiled potatoes, you can dip a potato into the salt before eating it.

You can use a salt tablet such at Thermotabs. Some runners use Stamina Electrolyte Tablets but those are not a good source of sodium or potassium (they are a good source of calcium and magnesium). Some runners use SUCCEED! Buffer/Electrolyte Caps that are formulated specifically for ultrarunning to supply sodium, buffers, and sufficient amounts of potassium.

As always, you need to drink. Don't wait until you are thirsty; the human thirst mechanism is too slow and inaccurate. As the adage goes: Eat before hunger, drink before thirst. When you finish a long run or ultra, you will usually have a deficit of water, calories and sodium. You will have a much smoother recovery if you replace all of those promptly. Soon after finishing, you can take an electrolyte supplement, 200 calories of carbohydrates, and drink water until you are no longer thirsty, and are urinating again. In the days that follow, you will probably find that you have more energy and fewer aches and pains if you have promptly replaced water, carbohydrates and sodium after your run.

Electrolyte and Hydration Table

Hydration: LOW
Electrolytes HIGH
Hypernatremia with dehydration
Likelihood: moderate
Weight is down a few pounds or more.
Thirst is high, and salty foods taste bad.
Mouth and skin are dry.
Food acceptance is poor.
Absence of urination.
Causes: No access to water or voluntary restriction of water intake, body
    electrolytes concentrated by loss of water.
What to do: Get access to water and drink. Restrict electrolytes until weight
    is near normal.

Hydration: LOW
Electrolytes OK
Dehydration
Likelihood: common
Weight is down a few pounds or more.
Thirst is high, and salty foods taste normal.
Mouth is dry, food acceptance is poor.
Skin is dry and may tent if pinched.
May have dizziness on standing up.
May have cramping.
Mental performance may be affected.
Causes: Insufficient fluid intake.
What to do: Drink sports drink with electrolytes, or water.

Hydration: LOW
Electrolytes LOW
Hyponatremia with dehydration
Likelihood: very rare
Weight is down a few pounds or more.
Thirst is high, and salty foods taste good.
Mouth is dry; can't spit.
May have cramping.
Skin is dry and may tent if pinched.
May have dizziness on standing up.
Causes: Insufficient drinking, no electrolyte intake.
What to do: Take electrolytes and drink
    sports drink or water.

Hydration: OK
Electrolytes HIGH
Hypernatremia
Likelihood: rare, transitory if water available
Weight is normal.
Thirst is high, and salty foods taste bad.
Mouth is not very dry.
Causes: N access to water, or voluntary restriction of water intake, body
    electrolytes concentrated by loss of water.
What to do: Drink to satisfy thirst, so that excess electrolytes are removed
    by sweating and urination. Restrict salt intake until excess is urinated
    and sweated out.

Hydration: OK
Electrolytes OK
Proper hydration and electrolyte balance
Likelihood: common
Weight is stable or slightly down.
Stomach is fine, food acceptance is normal.
Mouth is moist; can spit and skin is normal.
Cramps: none.
Urination is normal.
Causes: Proper water and electrolyte intake.
What to do: Continue with hydration and electrolyte practice unless condi
    tions change.

Hydration: OK
Electrolytes LOW
Hyponatremia
Likelihood: mild form is common
Weight is normal.
Stomach is queasy, with poor food acceptance.
Wrists may be puffy.
Salty foods taste good.
Thirst is normal.
Mouth is moist; can spit.
May have cramping.
Causes: Insufficient electrolyte intake.
What to do: Increase electrolyte intake until stomach feels o.k.

Hydration: HIGH
Electrolytes HIGH
Hypernatremia with over-hydration
Likelihood: very rare
Weight is up a few pounds or more.
Thirst is high, and salty foods taste bad.
Possible mental confusion.
Hands may be puffy.
Shortness of breath, rapid heart rate.
Food acceptance is poor.
Causes: Over-consumption of salt, probably from a combination of sources.
What to do: Stop electrolyte intake, drink only to wet mouth until weight is normal.

Hydration: HIGH
Electrolytes OK
Over-hydrated
Likelihood: moderate
Weight is up a few pounds or more.
Wrists and hands are probably puffy.
Stomach is queasy.
Thirst is low, and salty foods taste normal.
Mouth is moist; can spit.
Causes: Fluid intake in excess of needs.
What to do: Drink only to wet mouth until weight is near normal.

Hydration: HIGH
Electrolytes LOW
Hyponatremia with over-hydration (dangerous!)
Likelihood: moderate
Weight is up a few pounds or more.
Wrists and hands are puffy.
Nausea, stomach sloshing, possible vomiting.
Thirst is low, and salty foods taste very good.
Athlete may show mental confusion, odd behavior
Mouth is moist; can spit.
Urination may be voluminous and crystal clear.
Causes: Over-hydration, insufficient sodium intake.
What to do: Drink only to wet mouth until weight is normal, then correct any
    sodium deficit.

How Many Calories are you Really Burning?

By Charles Dumke, Ph.D.

Most ultrarunners understand the impact of caloric intake on performance. But what should you base the amount of intake on? Ideally, ultrarunners should aim to take in enough calories to replace stored fuel utilized during the race. Energy taken in cannot completely make up for the energy cost of running an ultra; however, we cannot solely rely on stored energy either. There have been many formulas, prediction equations, tables, and assumptions made to estimate the energy cost of running. But are these assumptions correct, when you consider that you will be running slowly—in fact walking at times—over undulating single-track trails, often at altitude? Having spent time collecting data on nutritional practices of ultrarunners, I was curious about this question: How much energy does one *really* burn when doing an ultra?

Data in available literature is not helpful in answering this question. Most studies done in this area have focused on individuals running on tracks or otherwise predictable surfaces. It is understood that energy expenditure is a function of speed, body weight, duration, and to a lesser extent efficiency, or running economy. Everything else being equal, a heavier individual will burn more calories, since he or she must move additional weight through space. And although energy expenditure increases when intensity increases, it is believed that for a given distance it remains constant. For example, a 200-pound individual will burn more calories than his or her 150-pound friend when running with that individual. This can be expressed numerically, in calories per minute or hour. Let's say the 200-pound runner goes on a nine-minute-per-mile, four-mile run one day (a total of 36 minutes), and on another day the same person runs seven-minute-per-mile pace (28 minutes) on the same four-mile route. The total energy expenditure would be about the same for this individual. This can then be expressed as calories per mile, or total run. (By the way, "calories" in food are expressed scientifically as 'kilocalories' or kcal.) In our previous example the kcal-per-minute would increase with an increase in intensity, but the kcal-per-mile for this individual would remain the same. Many runners are aware of the universal assumption of 100 kcal-per-mile burned for a person running or walking. However, this is an assumption that may be misleading. It is predicted that a 120-pound individual will burn about 86 kcal-per-mile, whereas a 190-pound individual will burn about 138 kcal-per-mile when running on a flat, even surface. It is this assumption we set out to verify in ultra-like conditions.

Recently, portable metabolic systems have been developed. This device allows oxygen consumption and carbon dioxide production to be measured while in the field (see photo). An individual at the 2003 Western States 100 Mile (WS100) wore this

Table: Course, intensity, and energy expenditure data from the four field trials. Data are expressed as means ± SD.

	Pace (min*mi⁻¹)	HR (b*min⁻¹)	%HR max	VO₂ (ml*kg⁻¹*min⁻¹)	%VO₂ max	EE (kcal*min⁻¹)	EE (kcal*mi⁻¹)
WS100	10.67	131.8±9.1	75.3±5.2	34.0±6.8	51.0±10	12.6±2.5	133.9±27
Track	6.65	133.1±7.1	76.0±4.1	47.5±3.6	71.2±5.4	18.1±1.3	120.1±9
3-Up	7.33	NA	NA	44.4±2.3	66.6±3.4	15.8±0.8	116.3±6
6-Dwn	7.23	NA	NA	38.2±5.0	57.4±7.5	14.5±1.9	105.0±14

portable unit for the first 40 miles of the race. That allowed investigators to get an idea of oxygen consumption (VO_2), carbon dioxide production, the type of fuel utilized (carbohydrate or fat), breathing rate and ventilation, in addition to heart rate and pace. Oxygen consumption indicates energy expenditure during aerobic activities such as running. The same individual wore the portable unit on three other runs for the sake of comparison. The runner completed four miles on a track, three miles on a gradual uphill, dirt road (3-Up), and six miles mostly downhill on a dirt road (6-Dwn). The energy comparisons between these trials can be seen in the accompanying table.

The energy expended per mile (kcal/mile) under "normal" conditions of the track, 3-Up and 6-Dwn were similar to what would be predicted for an individual of this body weight (165 pounds). The 105 kcal-per-mile is likely lower due to the largely downhill nature of this particular six-mile run. However, surprisingly, the kcal-per-mile during the WS100 (134 kcal-per-mile) was much higher, compared with the other, more normal conditions. This was true even though the relative intensity (percent of VO_2max) was low (51 percent). In fact, there was a significant amount of walking and downhill running on this portion of the trail. The relative consistency for energy expended per mile for this individual was disrupted by the rough, undulating trail race.

These data have practical implications for an ultrarunner. Evidence in the literature suggests that participants in ultras do not take in adequate amounts of energy, or kilocalories. This is true even given the assumptions of what is now understood as underestimations of energy requirements. In situations of running for 12, 24 or 30 hours, exogenous nutrient intake is critical to performance. If the athlete in this study were to attempt a 100-mile race, that would add up to 13,400 kcal of energy burned! Under the previous assumption of 100 kcal-per mile, this would result in a potentially crucial 25-percent mistake in meeting energy needs. In the study, it was determined that this athlete was burning approximately 70-percent carbohydrate, and 30-percent fat. That would equate to 9,100 kcal of energy from carbohydrate for the entire race. A well-fed athlete can start the race with about 2,500 kcal of stored carbohydrate, which means that 6,600 kcal, or 1,650 grams of carbohydrates need to be taken in! This may sound daunting, however over 30 hours this equates to just 220 kcal-per-hour, similar to suggested intake during endurance exercise. Certainly, individuals differ in their ability to ingest fluid and fuel while running, but this is something that can be trained or learned. Runners should attempt to teach themselves to ingest while moving at a good clip. Many elite ultrarunners and triathletes are known to be able to take in more than 400 kcal-per-hour. Yiannis Kouros is famous for not only his running, but also the fact that he is able to ingest more than 11,000 kcal-per-day during a six-day, 600-mile run!

Of course most athletes are not counting calories during a race. But keep in mind that carbohydrate stores are limiting (muscle and liver glycogen), whereas fat stores, even in lean runners, are likely unlimited. Due to carbohydrate limitation, and reliance during exercise, carbohydrate intake should make up the majority of the energy ingested during an ultra. (Leave the low-carb products to the sedentary dieters.) This is why an individual's ability to intake and digest fuel sources during an ultra is so important to performance. Exercise physiology literature suggests that an individual can take in and utilize about one gram of carbohydrate per minute, or 60 grams-per-hour, or 240 kcal-per-hour. That is very close to our calculation above. This amount should be targeted by most ultrarunners (depending somewhat on body size).

What are the consequences of suboptimal nutrition? Most runners have heard of the "bonk," which happens when muscles run out of stored carbohydrate. In addition, even before the bonk, as stored carbohydrate becomes less available, an athlete's intensity is jeopardized as they are more reliant on fat and protein for energy. This all points to the suggestion that energy intake should be in frequent, small amounts, of mostly carbohydrate, and approach somewhere between 200 to 400 kcal-per-hour depending on body size and intensity. Because of these energy requirements, the accomplished ultrarunner is not solely rewarded for trained lungs, heart, and legs, but also for a well-trained digestive system.

Hyponatremia

by Jason Hodde, MS, ATC/L

Hyponatremia is a common electrolyte abnormality that can affect ultrarunners of all levels of experience and performance. While it can vary in severity, the worst cases can lead to coma, seizures, or even death. Sodium is the dominant electrolyte in the spaces surrounding all of the body's cells. Because all of the body's cells depend upon its presence in a tightly restricted concentration, its levels in the blood are carefully monitored and controlled by mechanisms involving thirst, antidiuretic hormone (ADH), and the kidneys. In ultrarunners, hyponatremia, or a lowered concentration of sodium in the blood, is due to inadequate intake of sodium, either in fluids or in food.

Hyponatremia can also be dilutional, caused by excessive drink, especially after a run. Too little sodium during the run followed by too much sodium-free fluid after the ultra can lead to dilutional hyponatremia and problems after the run has been completed. Dilutional hyponatremia appears infrequently in the general population, but may be more prevalent in endurance athletes due to impaired kidney function in the later stages of a race.

Symptoms

Symptoms range from visible swelling of the hands and feet, nausea and malaise, to lethargy, a decreased level of consciousness, headache, and possibly, seizures and coma. Shivering, even at normally comfortable temperatures is another symptom. You might not want to eat and your muscles may cramp. Rhabdomyolysis may also occur and should be considered if you are experiencing severe muscle tenderness or pain. Neurologic symptoms most often are due to a severe and sudden drop of the blood sodium level, resulting in cerebral edema (brain swelling). According to the experts, the most common sign of hyponatremia during an ultra may be excessive weight gain during a race.

Runners who develop acute hyponatremia (i.e., in a race of up to 48 hours in duration) are subject to more severe cerebral edema for a given level of serum sodium than if hyponatremia is allowed to develop over several weeks. The primary cause of death from this condition is compression of the swollen, vital midbrain structures against the skull.

Causes

While there are many potential causes of hyponatremia, the type of condition usually observed in runners reflects the inability of the kidneys to handle the excretion of free water to match oral intake and is called "hypotonic hyponatremia."

This condition can be caused by either too little sodium intake relative to the amount of fluid replacement (i.e., dilutional hyponatremia) or as a result of severe dehydration, which results in a decreased blood volume as fluids and sodium are lost through sweat.

In the case of dehydration, the decrease in blood volume causes the blood vessels to constrict in an effort to maintain adequate blood pressure. This constriction impairs blood flow to the kidneys, which has the eventual effect of turning off urine production in an effort to conserve water. Other hormones, such as ADH, are also produced in response to the decreased blood volume, which compound this water-sparing effect. These hormones are also potent stimulators of thirst, which, when satiated, acts to worsen the hyponatremia because free water excretion is already severely limited.

In the case of dilutional hyponatremia, an increase in total body water, and possibly, sodium occurs. Paradoxically however, a decrease in the effective circulating volume stimulates the same mechanism of impaired water excretion by the kidney that is observed as a result of dehydration. In ultrarunners, kidney impairment due to the rigors of the event and/or NSAID ingestion to control pain may further hinder normal kidney function and worsen the condition.

While determining the exact type of hyponatremia is limited to the emergency room and hospital laboratory studies, excessive swelling of the hands and feet during an ultra suggests dilutional hyponatremia, while dry mucous membranes, rapid heart rate, and diminished skin turgor (i.e., your skin doesn't return to normal immediately after being pinched) suggest hypovolemic hyponatremia due to excessive loss of body fluids.

Treatment

Rapid transport to the local emergency room is advised if a runner is experiencing the signs and symptoms of hyponatremia. At an ultra, this might be almost impossible, however. The important thing to remember in treating hyponatremia at an aid station is that the runner has a sodium imbalance that can be made worse by giving the runner plain water or other fluids that do not contain electrolytes. If a runner with hypovolemic hyponatremia is given large amounts of electrolyte-free fluids, the sudden drop in blood sodium level caused by rapid absorption of water can lead to shock. Gradual correction is less likely to produce acute problems. Treatment at an aid station on the course should involve an assessment of the cause of the hyponatremia. Is the runner dehydrated, or is he or she drinking water without taking in sufficient sodium?

Prevention

Hyponatremia can be prevented if an ultrarunner is careful to ingest adequate sodium during the run. Drinking fluids containing balanced electrolytes and eating foods containing salt can help minimize the degree of electrolyte depletion experienced during a race, but it is still easy to become depleted in the later stages of an ultra without ingesting electrolyte supplements in capsule or tablet form (i.e., SUCCEED! Buffered Electrolyte Capsules or Thermotabs), or by eating very salty food.

Elite Malady?

There is very little research available in this field to point to specific causes and incidence of hyponatremia in endurance athletes. Studies on runners are even less common than studies on cyclists.

Elite athletes might appear to suffer more frequently than everyone else, but I would guess this is more likely due to their rather limited food and fluid intake relative to their level of effort than anything else. Although slower runners might be exerting effort equal to that of elite runners, they are also more apt to visit an aid station for a bit longer, eat a little more, and take more time drinking than someone who is out to win the race.

Vitamins and Supplements: Do You Need Them?

by Karl King and Kevin Setnes

Vitamins

The body requires many chemicals for catalyzing the biochemical reactions that are necessary for life's processes. Most are made in the body; but a few are not. Those few we call vitamins. They must come from what we eat.

People speak of vitamins as if they were all somehow the same, but each is a unique chemical that accomplishes specific tasks in the body. Some are critical for running success; others are not.

Do we need vitamins? Absolutely. Do we need more than the government recommended daily amount (RDA)? In general, yes, because while the RDAs are enough to keep us out of the hospital, they are not sufficient for heavy training often undertaken by ultrarunners.

Can one get sufficient vitamins from a good diet? In theory, that should be the case. Runners in training have no trouble taking in 3,000 calories of food per day. That much food should provide the necessary vitamins. However, studies clearly show that most marathoners—and subsequently ultrarunners—are vitamin deficient despite ample meals. Either their bodies are using up the vitamins, or their food selections are poor in vitamins. The answer is to take a daily vitamin/mineral supplement as an insurance policy.

Are expensive vitamins better than the drugstore varieties? That is seldom the case. Buy name brands from stores with a good turnover so you know that the vitamins are not old.

If some vitamins allow you to run better, will you run even better if you take megadoses? No! In fact, you might run more poorly if you do. You need a minimum amount for proper functioning. Once you have more than the minimum, the excess is wasted. There are no reputable studies that show excess vitamins leading to enhanced performance. If a runner is vitamin deficient, correcting that may lead to better performance, but increasing the dose beyond sufficiency will not produce further improvement.

Vitamins A and D can be harmful if taken to excess. Some B vitamins may produce strange symptoms in large doses. B3 is known to reduce fat in the blood— *not* a good idea for an endurance athlete who needs that fat to burn in muscle.

Vitamins that are important during endurance running are B1, B2, B3, B5, B6, choline, biotin, C, and E.

Vitamins C and E are also antioxidants, therefore very important for recovery.

You take in extra oxygen and burn a lot of fuel during a long run, and that produces chemical combustion products, which pollute the body for many hours afterward. The antioxidant vitamins C and E, as well as beta carotene, can detoxify these oxidants. It is important to take both C and E, as C is water-soluble while E is fat-soluble. To get the antioxidant action throughout the body, you need both. Vitamin C is also important in the repair of tendons and ligaments, the connective tissues that suffer damage whenever you run long or hard.

If you take C before bedtime (a good idea after a long run), take it in a buffered form. Regular C is a moderately strong acid and can irritate the stomach if there is no food around. Buffered C reduces the acidity, just as it does in buffered aspirin. Regular C should be taken with meals. Some forms of C are claimed to be much stronger than regular C, but the claims are mostly advertising hype.

What has worked for me (since 1967) is to take a daily multivitamin and C at breakfast, lunch and dinner. I take E at breakfast and dinner. On training days, I take a buffered C at bedtime.

Supplements

"Should I take supplements?" This is a common question asked by runners. Supplement advertisements are common in the media; they imply that significant health benefits can be accrued from these products. Supposedly, these health benefits will translate to more effective training and racing. Runners are always looking for something that will enhance their performance, so these products can be alluring.

Upon a visit to a health food store that carries supplements, one often sees walls covered with racks of products, all touted to do something useful. The array is bewildering, but instinct tells you that some are "snake oil," useless products designed primarily to separate dollars from your wallet. Can you make sense of this situation? Could supplements actually be good for your health and performance?

First, let's review "normal" nutrition, without supplements. We need both macronutrients (the major components of the diet) and micronutrients (the very small components) in our diet.

Macronutrients include water, electrolytes, carbohydrates, fat, protein, and fiber. A general pattern for good health is to get plenty of water (dehydration is common in runners), avoid excess salt, eat low glycemic index carbohydrates for energy supply, eat medium to high glycemic index carbohydrates during or just after a training session, avoid large amounts of saturated or "trans" fats in your diet, get plenty of quality protein for body repair, and keep regular with plenty of fiber, preferably from whole grains, vegetables and fruits.

Micronutrients are vitamins and minerals. An athlete in training requires a significant amount of energy in the daily diet. In theory, if you get that energy by eating nutrient-rich foods, you will get all of the vitamins and minerals you need without supplementation. But studies show that runners often don't make the best food choices and thus end up short of B vitamins and minerals such as zinc and magnesium. Some vitamins and minerals should not be taken in excess (vitamins A and D, iron and selenium), while others should be taken in proper ratios (calcium and magnesium, for example).

Accordingly, one should determine his or her requirements for vitamins and minerals before supplementing the diet. There are many books on the market that will provide this information.

In the long run, it is probably a good idea to take a multivitamin and mineral supplement, to ensure that you are getting your micronutrients, regardless of the food choices in your diet. If you do, read product labels to see what dosage is suggested. In some cases the products are quite concentrated, thus you may not need to take as much as suggested.

Basic macro and micronutrients should keep you alive and healthy for decades. Why would you need anything more? Here are some reasons why:

1. Your food is insufficient in providing nutrients in required amounts.

   As we age, our digestive systems degrade in their ability to absorb the needed nutrients, so we may need supplemental nutrients to ensure we are getting necessary amounts delivered to the bloodstream.

   We may make poor choices of foods, or choose foods that are poor in nutrients. Snack foods can provide quick calories, but are frequently lacking in necessary vitamins and minerals. The fat content of fast foods is high, but lacks the essential fats our bodies need. The result is that although you have eaten a fatty meal, your body is still starved for fats not present in the food.

   Food processing may degrade nutrients that were originally present, or foods may have been grown on soil deficient in important minerals.

   Your training may also increase the need for specific nutrients. Your food choices may provide adequate nutrients for a sedentary person, but fall far short of providing what you need as an active athlete. Further, not everyone requires the same amounts. You might need more of a particular nutrient than another runner. For example, some minerals are lost in sweat. If you have a high sweat rate, your needs for those minerals are likely much greater than the needs of a runner with a low sweat rate.

An injured runner may need additional nutrients for body repair. Repair rates can be slowed if your diet is poor in the nutrients needed to rebuild body tissues.

2. Abnormal or compromised biochemistry

The human body is a miracle of biochemical processing. The complexity of what goes on inside is astounding, and there is much that science still does not fully understand. Many of the chemical reactions that go on in the body during exercise would not normally reach completion at body temperature. Complex chemicals called enzymes facilitate those reactions. Sometimes we need a number of enzymes for the multiple steps a reaction takes on the way to completion. If one of the enzymes is in short supply, the reaction is compromised.

It may be useful to supply nutrients in forms that are closer to the end product, so that reactions are not limited by intermediate steps. For example, your body can make glucosamine, but perhaps not at the rate at which you degrade it in training. Taking a glucosamine supplement may provide the amount your body needs for repair.

3. Drug effect

Some supplements provide chemicals that are not needed by the body, or provide needed chemicals in amounts far above those normally required. In such cases we should regard these supplements as drugs.

Obviously there are ethical considerations, in addition to the technical considerations. The Unites States Olympic Committee provides information on drugs banned from competition. Some supplements promise amazing benefits, such as dramatically raising the body's ability to burn fat. If the supplement or its ingredients are not banned from competition, you can probably infer that the controversial claims are not substantial.

A thorough discussion of drugs is beyond the scope of this article. It is in some cases a very gray area. For example, caffeine, aspirin, or ibuprofen may be available at some race aid stations. Is it unethical to use a drug when it is made available to all entrants? Is it unethical to use a drug or supplement in training? We do not propose to answer these questions here, but merely point out that use of some supplements raises questions about drug ethics.

Some products, such as energy bars, contain supplements in large amounts. That's fine if you're going to eat one serving per day, but if you down 15 servings during an ultra, you may overdose on some ingredients. As always, read labels so you know what you're ingesting and can avoid problems.

Some supplements, such as DHEA and "Andro," affect the body's hormonal balance in possibly dangerous ways. It would be advisable to have a blood test to confirm a real need, and discuss the results with your physician before experimenting with such supplements.

In some cases, supplements are fast acting and provide results right away. In other cases, the benefits are accrued over time. Ask questions so that you know what to expect.

The supplement industry is large and spends considerable money on advertising. Companies are always looking for a presentation that will move their products. Buyer beware! There are a lot of slick sounding sales pitches that appear to promise much, but are not backed by nutritional science. While there aren't many dangerous products on the market, there are many that, while harmless when used as directed, fail to provide much benefit. There are many "fad" products that you won't find on the shelf a year from now.

Quality control can be a problem as well, in that a product may not supply as much of the substance as claimed on the label. In that regard, it pays to purchase a brand that has been in the marketplace for number of years and has a good reputation.

Some supplements age on the shelf, so it pays to shop at places with a large turnover, and to read the labels to see if there is an expiration date for the product.

Some supplements possibly useful to runners include:
Amino acids: L-carnitine, glycine, HMB, L-tyrosine, OKG, and protein supplements.
Vitamins and related chemicals: lipoic acid, B vitamins, vitamin C, choline, vitamin E, and folic acid.
Minerals: chrome picolinate, zinc, magnesium.
Miscellaneous: CoQ10, glucosamine, pyruvate, DHEA.

Herbal Supplements

Herbal remedies and related supplements continue to reach new heights in the world of athletics and fitness. Advertising emphasizes herbal antidotes for just about anything. Do herbal remedies and supplements provide benefits for ultrarunners? It is a complicated question that can best be answered with a qualified yes.

I have been intrigued by herbal medicines and claims made by its advocates for quite some time. While I don't claim to be an expert on the subject, I do feel it is an area worth exploring. My main concern is how it will relate to ultrarunning, both in training and in performance. Here is some of what I have found.

Certain countries have found consistent success in their athletic endeavors, countries that are dwarfed in size by the United States, yet match and even outperform us in competition. It is often attributed to the culture, as many Americans lead sedentary lives. This is especially true today. In the "old days," we walked through ten-foot high snow drifts, ten miles to school, uphill both ways. Today, however, every schoolchild's house is a bus stop. A country's culture has a lot to do with its physical makeup; that makeup also includes the diet.

Other countries—China, Japan, Germany, Korea and Russia to name a few—have used herbal medicine for a long time. They are also some of the biggest proponents of herbal nutrition for ergonomic aid in athletic events.

During the last few years, I have read and seen numerous reports on the benefits of herbal remedies to support one's recovery or fitness performance. Are there appreciable benefits? While there always seem to be contradictory studies published, the vast number of years of use and experience with such herbal supplements is hard to deny. Like the old saying goes, "You cannot beat a few thousand years of Chinese experience." Have I tried herbal remedies or supplements? Yes, and with those I have tried, I have experienced noticeable benefits. One such product is an "energizer" product by Genesis. It is an "all natural herb stimulant." It contains guarana, kola nut, centaury, ho shou wu, cayenne and garlic. I primarily tested it as an alternative to the caffeine stimulants of coffee and colas during 24 and 100-mile events that lasted into the night.

The following are a list of uses for different herbs. The usages apply to areas ultrarunners experience. Again, I have not tried all of these, but I do find them of interest and worth noting.

Aerobic Support: eleuthero, ginko, alfalfa, spirulina, chlorella, pollen, ginseng, pine pollen.
Antioxidants: ginko, greens, spirulina, chlorella, rosemary, chaparral,milk thistle.
Blisters: calendula, echinacea, chamomile, comfrey.

Circulation: ginger, cayenne, ginko.

Endurance: eleuthero, schisandra, ginseng, ashwaganda, foti (ho shou wu).

Energy Releasers: ginseng, eleuthero, ginger, cayenne, damiana, rosemary, wild oats.

Muscle Spasms: valerian, Roman chamomile, California poppy, passion flower.

Sore Feet: lavender, rosemary foot bath.

Sore Muscles: essential oils such as wintergreen, chamomile, clove.

Stimulants: cola nut, ephedra (ma huang), green tea, coffee, yerba mate, chocolate.

Certain herbs have been proven to be effective and are widely supported. Eleuthero, for example, has been shown to help our cells utilize oxygen more efficiently, thus increasing stamina and endurance. Ginseng has also been widely reported to have beneficial effects.

Caution: While herbal supplements are legal and safe if taken in recommended dosages, some of them are on the international banned substances list.

In addition, athletic purists insist no supplements should be allowed. Some ultrarunners refrain from all caffeine and even pain killers such as Tylenol or Advil. It is believed that this crosses the line of ethics in sport. It can also be dangerous. The effects of too much Ibuprofen or other pain killers combined with the rigors of ultrarunning have been well documented and can be very hazardous to your health. These types of substances should *not* be supplied by any race or organized event. Taking these substances should be left up to the individual. Herbal supplements, while widely used and generally known to be safe, fall into a similar category.

Herbal stimulants that are alkaloid (originating from bitter organic bases, seeds, etc.) can have a negative effect on an individual who has a weak digestive system, as it misdirects the energy needed during an ultra. Also, those individuals who have certain health problems, such as high blood pressure, should avoid taking herbs that are stimulants.

Herbal supplements may improve one's health and offer remedies modern drugs may lack. They may also boost one's athletic performance, especially over ultra distances and for extended periods of time. Be careful, use them in moderation, and experiment in your next ultra. You may just find a missing ingredient that fits into that "magic formula" that we all are looking for.

Antioxidants and Ultrarunning
by Jason Hodde, MS, ATC/L

As ultrarunners, we appreciate the role nutritional supplementation may play in our diets and in helping us recover from the rigors of long races. New data from researchers at the Linus Pauling Institute of Oregon State University in Corvallis, Oregon, suggest that taking vitamin E before a grueling ultramarathon may lessen or avert some of the cellular damage it can cause.

In Corvallis, Oregon, contestants ran up and down 32 miles of steep hills, with an elevation gain and loss of 12,000 feet. Dr. Maret Traber and her group have worked with these runners, investigating the antioxidant effects of vitamins C and E and whether they can protect the body from oxidative stress caused by such extreme athletics. Dr. Traber is Principal Investigator in the Linus Pauling Institute and Professor in the Department of Nutrition & Exercise Sciences at Oregon State University.

She explains, "The body converts food energy into energy it can use, producing carbon dioxide and water. The process is similar to that of a log burning in a fireplace; you're burning energy in order to have enough energy to run your body. Energy conversion on the cellular level is not perfect; but it is efficient. But because it's not perfect, about one percent of energy escapes as free radicals like superoxide, a very toxic free radical that contains oxygen and that can initiate all kinds of damage. That's where you get into the damage caused by oxidative stress. We study this on the membrane level."

A few years ago her group published research that showed that despite the many known health benefits of exercise, endurance exercise is also associated with oxidative stress. They determined whether extreme endurance exercise induces lipid peroxidation, a type of cell damage caused by free radicals. In this study, 11 athletes (three females, eight males) were studied during a 50-km ultramarathon and during a sedentary protocol a month later. Baseline measures of oxidative stress and vitamin E were obtained, and changes in levels were measured following exercise. This first study showed that extreme endurance exercise results in the generation of lipid peroxidation and increases the rate of vitamin E disappearance.

More recently, Traber spoke at a health and science writers' workshop on vitamin E and health, held at the New York Academy of Sciences and sponsored by the Council for Responsible Nutrition. In Dr. Traber's newly released double-blind study, ultra-marathoners took either antioxidant vitamins C and E or placebo daily for six weeks, and then were evaluated for inflammation and oxidative stress on the race morning and every morning for the week after the 50-km. Inflammatory markers were increased in all runners, whether they received antioxidants or not. While antioxidants had no effect on inflammation, the nutritionist found no increase in cell membrane damage caused by oxidative stress in those runners who took antioxidants, although there was membrane damage in those taking placebo.

What the researchers found most interesting, however, was that although the oxidative stress markers for women on placebo went back to normal two hours after the race, men on placebo had elevated oxidative stress markers for a week after the event. The role that gender played in this study was unexpected. According to Dr. Traber, "Women are better protected from oxidative stress than are men. This was surprising. I wouldn't have guessed that there was a gender difference."

The nutritionist suggested that men who decide spontaneously to run a marathon and who haven't been training or planning ahead, can really can do some serious injury to their muscles and experience oxidative stress. This is especially true if they haven't had proper nutrition. Taking antioxidants, however, may help them recover sooner.

Runners in this study supplemented their diet for six weeks prior to the race with 1,000 mg vitamin C and 300 mg vitamin E acetate on a daily basis. For safety, the Food and Nutrition board suggests limiting your daily intake to less than 1,000 mg vitamin E. If you prefer to obtain your antioxidants in your food, consider the following sources. For vitamin C, choose a variety of fruits and vegetables, such as peppers, kiwis, oranges, grapefruits, or papaya. For vitamin E, also choose a variety of leafy green vegetables, oils, and nuts, such as wheat germ oil, almonds, sunflower seeds, peanuts, broccoli, or spinach.

Contributing Authors: Judy Blatman, M.J. Wyatt, Amy Briskin, and the Council for Responsible Nutrition

Supplements for Cartilage Damage: Glucosamine

by Jason Hodde, MS, ATC/L

Articular cartilage is the type of tissue that lines the ends of all long bones, such as the bones of the leg that comprise the knee and ankle. It is only a few millimeters thick, but possesses excellent wear characteristics and can withstand the extreme shear and compressive forces placed upon it. It is a highly specialized, nearly frictionless tissue structure that acts to cushion the bone ends, preventing the underlying bone from becoming damaged as a result of stress.

The smoothness and thickness of the cartilage determines the load-bearing characteristics and mobility of joints. Lesions on the cartilagenous surfaces of the joints interfere with smooth motion and can cause mild to significant symptoms of pain, instability and stiffness. Cartilage also lines the underside of the kneecap, or patella, and is the tissue structure that becomes damaged when an athlete suffers from chondromalacia patella, a condition popularly called "runners knee."

Articular cartilage can become damaged as a result of acute athletic trauma, such as when an athlete gets kicked by an opposing team member; as a result of repetitive stress, such as regular pounding on the joints caused by worn running shoes or excessive mileage on concrete; or as a result of degeneration (thinning of the cartilage), which occurs as a result of aging. Unlike some other tissues with an inherent capacity to regenerate following injury, it is widely thought that articular cartilage lacks the capacity to repair itself.

Traditional treatments for treating injuries of the articular cartilage include rest, ice, and anti-inflammatory medications. Strengthening of the muscles surrounding the affected joint, altering the stresses placed upon the joint by cross-training, modifying your running surface, and/or replacing worn running shoes, should also be first-line treatments to ease the pain and limit further damage to the cartilage.

Glucosamine sulfate can be thought of as a building block that helps restore the tissue structure of articular cartilage. Recently, nutritional supplements such as glucosamine sulfate have been touted in the popular press as safe and effective means of treating injuries to the articular cartilage, as well as to prevent the onset of cartilage degeneration as a result of aging. Beneficial effects of these supplements in the osteoarthritic population have been documented, but the effectiveness of these supplements in the athletic population has yet to be shown. Further, supplementation of glucosamine sulfate has not been shown to be an effective prophylactic measure against the onset of osteoarthritis.

Glucosamine is a building block for the structure of the articular cartilage.

Specifically, it is used in the synthesis of glycosaminoglycans, the carbohydrate-rich component of the cartilage that is responsible for absorbing shock and making the bone ends slippery. It is thought to be a safe and effective treatment for osteoarthritis, and supposedly stimulates the cartilage cells to produce additional glycosaminoglycans. In osteoarthritic joints, it has been reported to stimulate new cartilage formation.

Glucosamine supplementation by various methods has been tried experimentally. However, oral supplementation has been deemed most effective because all methods of supplementation result in rapid absorption into the bloodstream. This is stark contrast to chondroitin sulfate, which is not efficiently absorbed. Currently, the recommended dosage for the relief of osteoarthritic pain is 1,500 mg of glucosamine sulfate daily; this is generally divided into three equal 500 mg doses.

Glucosamine has mild anti-inflammatory activities, as confirmed in animal of models of inflammation and arthritis. It acts through anti-inflammatory pathways different from those utilized by NSAIDs (non-steroidal anti-inflammatory drugs, such as ibuprofen or Aleve), which might help explain its low incidence of toxicity and other side effects, such as gastro-intestinal bleeding, when compared to traditional NSAID drugs. Although side effects appear minimal, glucosamine supplements have been found to increase blood glucose levels in animals; individuals with diabetes should consult their physician before supplementing with glucosamine sulfate.

Studies comparing glucosamine sulfate to placebos in the osteoarthritic population have demonstrated significant reduction in knee pain, improved range of motion, decreased swelling, and improved function of the affected joint. Many studies, however, contain flaws in either design or analysis. At very least, it can be said that glucosamine sulfate supplementation does not appear to have any negative short-term effects, though long-term effects remain unknown.

Summary

Glucosamine assists the body in providing the body the components necessary to carry out articular cartilage synthesis. It appears to slow the process of cartilage degeneration and facilitate the recovery of normal joint mobility. While supplementation appears safe in the short-term, long-term safety has not been established. Glucosamine appears to have a positive effect on cartilage metabolism in the osteoarthritic population, yet its positive effects on trauma-related cartilage damage in the athletic population remain unproven.

Endocrine System Depletion
by Jason Hodde and Karl King

When ultrarunners think of running-related injuries, they usually think of conditions affecting the musculoskeletal system: the bones, muscles, and joints. Ultrarunning, however, is strenuous on other parts of the body as well, and can lead to deficiencies in immune function (increasing the risk of infection, flu, or colds), disturbances in the basic senses (temporary loss of vision), or problems in responding to the stress of everyday life.

The body's response to stress—from everyday, on-the-job stress to stress that results from running excessive mileage in training or racing—is made by the endocrine system.

In this article, we examine the normal function of the endocrine system, its role in the body's response to extreme endurance activity, and how the system gets "injured" as a result of extreme mileage. In addition, we present suggestions to treat an overtaxed endocrine system and offer tips on preventing endocrine system depletion.

The Depleted Runner

Let's look at the case of a mythical runner named "John." He is new to ultrarunning and is extremely enthusiastic about training and racing. He has set lofty goals, attempting to run at least 10 miles per day during the year. His weekly long run is 40 miles on Saturday, followed by 30 on Sunday, except for the one weekend a month when he races either a 50 or 100-mile.

John is pleased that he has been able to recover from his racing quickly. He is able to run 100 miles on the weekend and return to his daily 10-mile run on Monday without even missing a day. Just last month, he was extremely pleased to finish the Kettle Moraine 100 Mile in just over 18 hours and return to conquer the Mohican 100 Mile two weeks later in 19 hours.

After Mohican, his recovery seemed a little bit sluggish, but he was able to gut out his 70-mile weekend training ritual without problems. Things were going great, so he decided to enter the Finger Lakes 50 Mile (two weeks after Mohican) in New York to celebrate the July 4 weekend.

Ten miles into Finger Lakes, John felt sluggish, his muscles hurt, and his legs weren't able to respond to the hills. By 18 miles, John was reduced to a walk, felt like he wanted to sleep, and was unable to run, even though he had "carbo-loaded" for the run the night before.

Dejected and saddened by his failure on the course, John DNF'd for the first time in his short ultrarunning career.

Looking back at his training logs, John couldn't figure out what went wrong. He'd been training hard for months and was in the best shape of his life. "Maybe I need to train harder," John was overheard saying the next day.

The truth is, maybe he needed to train less—or at least alter his training program—to allow his endocrine system ample time for recovery from the stress of the high mileage and the hard racing.

Endocrine Function

The endocrine system is a collection of glands that produce a wide variety of chemical messengers called "hormones," necessary for normal bodily functions. Hormones regulate processes as diverse as metabolism, growth, digestion, sexual development, and the body's response to stress. The glands release the hormones directly into the bloodstream where they are transported to organs and tissues. At these "target" organs and tissues, the secreted hormone evokes a specific, pre-programmed response from the target cells.

The specific functions of the endocrine system include:
- Regulating the chemical composition and volume of the body.
- Regulating metabolism and energy balance, including digestion.
- Regulating contraction of smooth and cardiac muscle.
- Maintaining homeostasis even during "crisis" events.
- Regulating components of the immune system.
- Regulating the integration of growth and development.

Thus, the endocrine system is one way the body coordinates its actions with information collected from the environment.

Most runners think long training runs are needed only to build muscle for the hours of work they will do in an ultra. Actually, long runs are just as important for training other systems to respond to stress: the heart, lungs, liver, kidneys, digestive system, and the endocrine system. We often think of the surge of adrenaline we get when frightened, but to run an ultra, adrenaline is needed all day. The endocrine system is responsible for teaching the body to react to the physical, emotional, and mental stress of running an ultra. Most of its training is accomplished during very long runs.

Endocrine Anatomy

While the endocrine system consists of several different glands that secrete more than 50 different hormones, the hypothalamus and the pituitary gland control such a broad range of bodily functions (and other endocrine glands) that they are often referred to as the "master control center" of the endocrine system. The other endocrine gland critically important during ultrarunning is the adrenal gland. The following is a look at the components of the endocrine system:

Hypothalamus. The hypothalamus is found in the brain. It regulates many aspects of the body's internal environment, including heart rate, body temperature, water balance, and the amount of glandular secretions from the pituitary. It secretes hormones that help regulate the pituitary gland and also responds to their presence in a feedback mechanism.

Pituitary Gland. This small gland is tightly connected with the hypothalamus and secretes two hormones of particular interest to runners. Antidiuretic hormone (ADH) promotes water reabsorption in the kidneys and is released from the pituitary when sensors in the hypothalamus determine that blood is too concentrated (i.e., during dehydration). Adrenocorticotropic hormone (ACTH) stimulates the adrenal gland to produce cortisol. While the pituitary secretes numerous other hormones necessary for growth and survival, a full review of these substances is beyond the scope of this article.

Adrenal Glands. Each person has two adrenal glands, one on top of each kidney in the lower back. Each of these glands consists of an outer layer called the cortex and an inner core called the medulla. Secretion from the adrenal medulla is controlled via the nervous system, whereas ACTH controls secretion from the adrenal cortex.

The major hormones produced by the adrenal medulla are adrenaline (also called epinephrine) and a related hormone called noradrenaline (norepinephrine). These hormones cause the changes the body goes through during an emergency situation (the "fight-or-flight" response). Such changes include: increased heart and breathing rate, increased blood flow to muscles, cessation of digestion, and increased blood glucose levels and metabolic rate.

The adrenal cortex produces two main classes of hormones: glucocorticoids and mineralocorticoids. It also produces small amounts of both male and female sex hormones. The main glucocorticoid hormone, cortisol, promotes the breakdown of muscle proteins into amino acids that enter the blood. The resulting increase in amino acid levels in the blood then causes higher glucose blood levels when the liver breaks down these amino acids. Cortisol also favors metabolism of fatty acids over carbohydrates. This hormone thus works in opposition to insulin, raising blood glucose levels. In a different mode, cortisol counteracts the inflammatory response that can lead to the pain and swelling of joints in arthritis and bursitis.

The main mineralocorticoid hormone is aldosterone. When blood volume or sodium levels drop, a hormone called rennin is released from the kidneys and indirectly causes the release of aldosterone.

Aldosterone causes sodium re-absorption by the kidneys, resulting in increased water and blood volumes. The hormone also increases arterial constriction, which increases blood pressure.

Endocrine System Fatigue and Recovery

The endocrine system can become fatigued just like a muscle that is continually overworked. At some point it just can't produce the stress hormones like it should. A tired (but not damaged) muscle may recover in 24 to 48 hours, but an overused endocrine system takes weeks to recover.

The stress of running an ultra requires a major response from the endocrine system, but that system requires time to recover. Hormonal levels start to normalize in the hours after the run, but it may take days before excess hormones have cleared the system. It is not unusual to feel really "high" from adrenaline and endorphins for 24 hours after an ultra, but then physical depression often sets in.

During the ultra, cortisol serves the body well by mobilizing energy stores and reducing inflammation. Afterwards, it temporarily blocks the desirable effects of insulin, and repair of the body is slowed.

Even when the cortisol levels fall to normal after a few days, there are lingering effects from the disturbance of the endocrine system. Symptoms include apathy toward work or training, inability to concentrate, changes in sleep patterns, appetite suppression, reduced libido, increased thirst, diarrhea, susceptibility to colds, and menstrual disturbance in some women. If the body is called upon to respond to stress again, adequate levels of cortisol cannot be produced, resulting in a "crash" after too much running.

The broad and profound nature of these symptoms points to suppression at the level of the central nervous system hypothalamus/pituitary axis. That is, it isn't just one gland that isn't working right, or some simple nutrient deficiency. The driving force for the suppression is not currently known, but could be related to reduced blood flow, desensitization of the hypothalamus or pituitary caused by leg muscle breakdown byproducts, or down-regulation of axis function brought on by prolonged, abnormally high cortisol levels. Since the mechanisms are not known, there is currently no "magic bullet" that can be used to recover in a short time. Rest from stressful situations, training or otherwise, is needed. With rest, recovery times can range from three to twelve weeks. Note that this is longer than the time required for adequate muscle repair; the two may, in fact, be related. It makes no sense to have a strong endocrine response when damaged muscles are not prepared for an ultra effort.

The best way to reduce endocrine recovery time is to not stress it too hard in the first place. That implies being fully trained and rested for the event you are about to run, then minimizing stress during the run. It is relatively obvious from experience that those who have properly trained with long runs, speed work and weights are able to withstand the stress of an ultra better than those who run with minimal training.

During the run, one cannot avoid the course and its challenges, but one *can* reduce stress by proper pacing, and by maintaining proper hydration, caloric, and electrolyte status. Stress hormones are low when one is at the starting line. It's when we run short of water, short of blood glucose, and have electrolyte disturbances that the level of stress hormones increases dramatically.

There is a mental component as well. You are less likely to be stressed if you treat your run as a joyous adventure rather than a life-and-death struggle. You will get plenty of challenge from the course; don't add unnecessary excess baggage.

Prevention

The endocrine system needs to perform well during a run, so take good care of it. Train adequately without overtraining, run at a sensible pace, keep a good intake of water, food and electrolytes, and enjoy the experience as you go. Your endocrine system responds to stress from any source, so as much as possible, avoid stress at work and at home, as well as self-imposed stress such as performance anxiety. Expect to rest as long as it takes until your endocrine function is back to normal. Before you sign up for a bunch of ultras in a row, plan for adequate rest between each one. If you train heavily, plan a number of weeks to allow your system time to recover. You will know you are well recovered when your legs feel energetic in your training runs, and you have no hesitancy to run. Once you've built up a strong endurance base, you won't lose anything from a good rest.

Are odd things happening on your run? The endocrine system is highly active during and after endurance exercise. Here are some experiences common to ultrarunners and the endocrine system hormone(s) that may play a role in each of them. Note that some of these phenomena can have multiple causes, so a hormonal response may not be the sole cause of the experience.

Difficulty sleeping the night before	Adrenaline
Urination shortly after the run begins	Adrenaline
Increasing heart rate and respiration rate as the run goes on	Adrenaline
Hands and feet swell late in the run	Vasopressin, Aldosterone
Nausea when running only on carbohydrate	Gastrin, CCK
Elation after hours of running	Endorphins
Appetite suppression	Endorphins
Analgesia	Endorphins
Improved memory	ACTH
Inhibition of inflammatory response	Cortisol
Ability to run on low calorie input	Cortisol, Adrenaline, Growth hormone, Glucagon
Slow healing after the run	Cortisol
Healing during sleep	Growth hormone
Weak immune system response	Cortisol

Can Ultras Make You Sick?
By David C. Nieman

Introduction

The relationship between exercise and sickness, especially the common cold, evokes considerable interest among the general public and athletes alike. Many are convinced, according to surveys, that regular moderate training as protection against colds (and increasing evidence supports this assertion). On the other hand, when exercise is pushed too far, reports of increased sickness—sometimes for prolonged periods, are common.

Consider this letter from a runner in Canada that recently crossed my desk following an article in a running magazine. "I am an (avid) runner and have not had even so much as a reasonable season for the last three (perhaps four) years owing to colds and constant viruses! Two years ago I got glandular fever and took a year to get over the chronic fatigue symptoms, but have now almost returned to 'normal' training loads. (In recent years, I've been more sensible than perhaps I used to be, and allow more rest days in my schedule). But particularly the last two years (summer included), it is literally a bug or cold every two to three weeks. This has made life (never mind training) absolute hell. I tried four grams of vitamin C every day without it seeming to help. Right now as I write, I have a cold. This means that out of the last twelve weeks, I've been ill for about six or seven weeks. It's no fun, I can tell you. Any suggestions?" In this article, I will attempt to provide some answers for this runner and others on the complex topic of exercise and sickness, and review recent data collected on ultrarunners during the Western States 100 Mile Endurance Run.

Can Too Much Exercise Suppress Immunity?

Among elite athletes and their coaches, a common perception is that heavy exertion lowers resistance to colds. For example, Alberto Salazar, once one of the best marathon runners in the world, reported that while training for the 1984 Olympic Marathon, he caught 12 colds in 12 months. "My immune system was totally shot," he recalls. "I caught everything. I felt like I should have been living in a bubble." During the Winter and Summer Olympic Games, it has been regularly reported by clinicians that "upper respiratory infections abound" and that "the most irksome troubles with the athletes were infections." In a 1996 survey by the Gatorade Sports Science Institute of 2,700 high school and college coaches and athletic trainers, 89 percent checked "yes" to the question, "Do you believe overtraining can compromise the immune system and make athletes sick?"

To determine if these anecdotal reports were true, I studied a group of 2,311 marathon runners who ran a recent Los Angeles Marathon. During the week following the race, one out of seven runners came down sick, which was nearly six times the rate of runners who trained for but did not run the marathon. During the two-month period before the race, runners training more than 60 miles per week doubled their odds for sickness compared with those training less than 20 miles per week. Researchers in South Africa have also confirmed that after ultra-distance races, runners are at high risk for sickness.

I have studied the immune systems of athletes in my laboratory during prolonged treadmill running, and during marathon and ultras. A steep drop in immune function occurs, lasting at least six to 24 hours. Much of this immune suppression appears to be related to the elevation of stress hormones which are secreted in high quantity during and following heavy exertion. Exercise immunologists believe that this temporary drop in immune function allows viruses already in the body to spread and gain a foothold.

Results from the Western States 100 Mile

At the Western States 100 Mile Endurance Run (WS100), 45 runners agreed to provide blood and saliva samples the morning before the race, at the 50-mile aid station, and five to ten minutes post-race. The average subject had been training for 15 years, had finished 52 previous ultras, and took 27 hours to finish the WS100. Sickness rates during the two-week period following the WS100 were measured. Several immune measures, including inflammatory cytokines such as IL-6 and IL-10, rose to very high levels during the WS100, reflecting extreme physiologic stress and immune disorder. For example, the secretion rate for salivary IgA, an important immune defense mechanism in the throat, decreased by half during the WS100. One in four runners became sick after the WS100, and a low salivary IgA secretion rate was a strong predictor. This finding was confirmed in a larger group of 155 runners at the 2003 WS100.

These data have been submitted for publication in research journals and represent the first attempt to measure sickness rates and the immune response to running a 100-mile. In future studies, we plan to test the effectiveness of using various nutrients and drugs in countering the immune suppression experienced by WS100 runners.

Practical Guidelines to Lower Infection Risk

To low risk of immune suppression and sickness during heavy training and after competition, ultra-distance athletes can follow several practical recommendations:

- Keep other life stresses to a minimum. Mental stress in and of itself has been linked to an increased risk of upper respiratory tract infection.

- Eat a well-balanced diet to keep vitamin and mineral pools in the body at optimal levels. I have initiated studies to measure the influence of vitamin C and E supplements on post-race immune function in ultra-distance athletes, but more research is needed before recommendations can be passed on to the athlete.
- Avoid overtraining and chronic fatigue. Athletes are most susceptible to sickness and immune suppression when overtrained.
- Obtain adequate sleep on a regular schedule. Sleep disruption has been linked to suppressed immunity.
- Avoid rapid weight loss (which has also been linked to negative immune changes).
- Avoid putting hands to the eyes and nose (a primary route of introducing viruses into the body). Before important race events, avoid sick people and large crowds when possible.
- For athletes competing during the winter months, flu shots are recommended.
- Use carbohydrate beverages before, during, and after race events or unusually heavy training bouts. This lowers the impact of stress hormones on the immune system resulting in less immune suppression.

Rest or Exercise When Sick?

Athletes are often uncertain of whether they should exercise or rest during sickness. Animal studies generally support the finding that one or two periods of exhaustive exercise following injection with certain types of viruses or bacteria lead to more severe symptoms, and an increased risk of widespread infection to all parts of the body, including the heart muscle.

With athletes, it is well established that the ability to compete is reduced during sickness. In addition, several case histories have shown that sudden and unexplained downturns in athletic performance can sometimes be traced to a recent bout of sickness. In some athletes, exercising when sick can lead to a severely debilitating state known as "post-viral fatigue syndrome." The symptoms can persist for several months, and include weakness, inability to train hard, easy fatigability, frequent infections, and depression. Concerning exercising when sick, most clinical authorities in the area of exercise immunology recommend:

- If one has common cold symptoms (e.g., runny nose and sore throat without fever or general body aches and pains), intensive training may be safely resumed a few days after the resolution of symptoms.

- Mild-to-moderate exercise (e.g., walking) when sick with the common cold does not appear to be harmful. In two studies using nasal sprays of a rhinovirus leading to common cold symptoms, subjects were able to engage in exercise during the course of the illness without any negative effects on severity of symptoms or performance capability.
- With symptoms of fever, extreme tiredness, muscle aches, and swollen lymph glands, two to four weeks should be allowed before resumption of intensive training.

Closing Thoughts

Whether one gets sick with a cold after a sufficient amount of virus has entered the body depends on many factors that affect the immune system. Old age, cigarette smoking, mental stress, poor nutrient status, and lack of sleep have all been associated with impaired immune function, and increased risk of infection. Based on current knowledge, good immune function can be maintained by eating a well-balanced diet, keeping life stresses to a minimum, exercising "within yourself" while avoiding undue fatigue, and obtaining adequate sleep.

My experience has been that some runners have robust immune systems that can handle substantial training workloads, while others break down at much lower training thresholds. Each runner must find their own training threshold, and avoid pushing beyond that threshold (i.e., overreaching) into the zone of immune suppression and increased risk of sickness.

Ultrarunning and the Heart
by Barry Mink, M.D.

Running and racing ultra distances are not activities without medical risk. Ultrarunners accept this risk, but at times are either misinformed or not informed at all about the risks of dehydration, renal failure, hyponatremia, hypothermia, and musculoskeletal and myocardial damage. Medical research, although quite sparse on ultra-distance running, does provide valuable information that ultrarunners should spend some time trying to understand.

Several publications have considered the subject of cardiovascular risk and myocardial fatigue in the healthy ultrarunner. Does myocardial or cardiac fatigue and damage occur as it does in leg muscles when ultra distances are run? Anyone who has run 50 or 100-mile races knows the leg fatigue and pain that must be overcome in order to finish. Medical studies support these running experiments by revealing hundredfold increases in muscle enzymes that are measured in the bloodstream when muscle cells are injured and die. This muscular destruction obviously slows us down and can eventually stop us, but also causes the pain and stiffness that occurs following a race, as well as persisting muscle weakness that can last for several weeks. Ultrarunning efforts, fortunately, do not result in permanent deficits because damaged and injured muscle cells can regenerate back to normal in relatively short periods of time. In fact, if the injury to the muscle is not too great (hard to believe for most of our ultra efforts), then adaptation to and improvement of our abilities to tolerate long races eventually occurs.

Look at those who are able to run 100-mile races regularly, completing all four of the major 100-mile trail races with as little as two weeks in between each effort. Also, six-day runners can run 100-mile distances daily for up to five or six days at a time. Since it is well documented that muscular damage occurs and in the majority of cases is reversible, does the same physiology apply to the heart muscle with regard to ultra-distance running?

The heart pumps five liters of blood per minute at rest, and can increase this output to 20 liters per minute in trained athletes during exercise. With efforts lasting several hours or even days, one would expect the heart muscle to fatigue long before the leg muscles do. We cannot take a break and totally rest our heart as we can with our legs during training or racing efforts. Therefore, the question is often asked: Do we demand too much from our hearts in these ultra-distance races? Can we cause temporary, or even more important, permanent myocardial damage?

In 1971, Dr. Timothy Noakes, a noted South African physiologist and finisher of several Comrades Marathons, reported two cases of trained runners who went into pulmonary edema from heart failure after finishing the Comrades Marathon. Subsequent extensive medical testing of these individuals could turn up no underlying cardiac problems that would have predisposed them to this cardiac problem. Dr. Noakes postulated that the cause of their heart failure was cardiac muscle fatigue.

More recent studies by a Finnish group revealed heart-muscle fatigue after a 24-hour track run. By using echocardiography, the authors were able to demonstrate that the heart muscle fatigued and weakened as a pump, during and immediately after the long distance race.

Other studies in laboratory settings used subjects running on the treadmill and exercising to exhaustion, as well as studies of participants in the Ironman Triathlon, and revealed the same results: the heart muscle fatigues and weakens. How dangerous is this to the ultrarunner, and should there be precaution and concern for race directors and participants?

Answers to these questions are not complete, but some conclusions can be made. In all of the studies mentioned, the heart-muscle fatigue was only temporary, with no evidence that any permanent deficit was present when subjects were tested 30 hours after the race. This is similar to the observations made of the leg musculature mentioned earlier. The difference is that heart-muscle recovery occurs much faster than in the leg. Long-term damage to heart and leg musculature does not seem to occur. However, short-term and immediate muscle damage and stress do occur; they are a significant factors in one's ability to recover. If underlying cardiac disease is present, even to a mild degree, then the heart-muscle demands of running ultra distances will obviously jeopardize the individual with regard to a cardiovascular catastrophe. However, this can occur in any strenuous effort. Ultrarunners, through their own training and racing programs, usually would not have reached that point without cardiovascular problems occurring earlier. Races at the 1,500-meter and marathon distances have a much greater incidence of sudden death from cardiac causes. This is probably because ultrarunners have already "survived" races of shorter distances before attempting ultra distance efforts.

After reviewing this research, I recommend the prudent practice of obtaining a good medical evaluation, if cardiovascular risk is present, before attempting a training program for racing ultra distances. Even if you are not a beginner, if you are over the age of 45 you should have routine medical evaluations. Knowing practices of pace, terrain, food and fluid intake, and recognizing the point of having to stop, are all medical "musts" for the ultrarunner to master. Until more research is conducted, ultrarunning would seem to have no long-term or permanent detrimental effects on the heart, although there is definite jeopardy even to the healthy heart, because of myocardial and musculature fatigue that occurs during and immediately after a race. Survival depends upon the good use of supportive practices and understanding our limitations realistically and accurately.

The Ultrarunner's Knee
by Jason Hodde, MS, ATC/L

The knee is the largest and one of the most complex joints in the body. Because of its complexity, several different injuries to any one of numerous different structures can force a break from running. In order to understand what is likely to go wrong at the knee, it is important to understand the knee's structure and why injuries to the foot and ankle can also exacerbate knee pain.

Bones
The knee is comprised, technically, of just three different bones: 1) the tibia, or shin bone, 2) the femur, or thigh bone, and 3) the patella, or kneecap. The small bone on the lateral side of the leg, the fibula, is not part of the knee joint but is often involved in some occurrences of knee pain.

Each of the bones is lined with a smooth surface of articular cartilage (called hyaline cartilage) which protects the bone ends from trauma by absorbing shock and ensuring a smooth, lubricated surface upon which the bones can slide. One of the most common injuries in runners, chondromalacia of the patella (commonly called "runner's knee"), involves a softening of the cartilage on the undersurface of the kneecap.

Ligaments
Ligaments join bones together. At the knee, the ligaments can be within the joint (intra-articular) or external to the joint (extra-articular). The ligaments within the joint capsule are the Anterior Cruciate Ligament (ACL) and the Posterior Cruciate Ligament (PCL). The intra-articular ligaments prevent the femur from sliding too much on the tibia. The main supporting ligaments outside the joint capsule are the Lateral Collateral Ligament (LCL) and Medial Collateral Ligament (MCL). They lie to the sides of the joint and prevent it from opening too much when a direct blow strikes the knee.

Injuries to the ACL and PCL are common in non-contact sports like running because the limited space within the joint allows very little free motion. A rupture of the ACL, one of the more common knee ligament injuries in trail runners, occurs when an uneven foot plant forces the leg to rotate excessively at the knee.

Tendons
Tendons attach muscle to bone. Several tendons attach around the knee, and all of them can become injured as a result of overtraining. Some of the most debilitating

injuries occur to the hamstring tendons on the back side of the knee. The resulting tendinitis can make running impossible.

The patellar tendon holds the kneecap in place and acts as a pulley to make extending the leg and foot easier. Along with the quadriceps (thigh muscles) and the kneecap, the patellar tendon comprises the structure referred to as the "patellofemoral complex." Abnormalities in the patello-femoral complex can lead to several injuries, the most common being "runner's knee."

The iliotibial band (IT Band) is a thick band of connective tissue on the lateral side of the leg and knee. IT Band Syndrome is the inflammation of the IT band as it crosses the knee; it is one of the most common and painful injuries in ultrarunners and cyclists.

Menisci (Cartilage)

The medial and lateral menisci (singular: meniscus) are the main shock absorbers of the knee and lie on top of the tibia, an area called the tibial plateau. The menisci distribute forces throughout the underlying articular cartilage, thereby preventing injury to the ends of the bones. The menisci help compensate for the incongruence of the tibia on the femur and help insure a smooth gliding joint with some freedom of rotation. A twisting motion can injure the menisci, causing them to tear.

Kinetic Chain

The lower extremity is a multi-joint complex in which the foot, ankle, knee, hip, and low back work together to reduce and absorb shock during running and walking. Because the joints are linked together in a "kinetic chain," an injury to the foot can lead to ankle pain, ankle pain can lead to knee pain, and knee pain can lead to problems at the hip and lower back.

In addressing your knee pain specifically, you need first to address the cause of the problem that you are having. Pain at the knee joint is often caused by wearing excessively worn shoes or shoes incompatible with your foot type. It can be caused by a leg-length discrepancy, or may be secondary to another injury in the foot, ankle or leg.

As we progress through the myriad of injuries involving the knee, it is important to remember that the knee connects the hip and back with the foot and ankle. Forces are distributed from the ground through the ankle and the knee. If they are not dissipated effectively, pain may also occur in your hips or back. Therefore, the single greatest preventative measure of preventing all lower extremity and back injuries is to ensure that the shoes you are wearing are proper for your feet and have not exceeded their life expectancy.

Chondromalacia Patella

Chondro-what?

The very knee ailment known as chondromalacia patella is a quite common and chronic injury and is a major reason runners are advised by their physicians to stop running and take up alternative sports such as swimming or cycling. But what is it and how can it be avoided?

Chondromalacia of the patella is also called "runner's knee." A more current term is "patello-femoral syndrome" or PFS. It can be most easily described as a softening of the hyaline cartilage of the kneecap, resulting from an excessive load on the knee joint. Many scientists believe that there is a link between chondromalacia and eventual arthritis, but this association is still unclear and subject to debate.

In a normal knee, the bone ends of the lower leg (tibia), thigh (femur), and kneecap (patella) are lined with a smooth, shock-absorbing layer of hyaline cartilage. The cartilage lubricates the joint and protects the underlying bones from sheer and compression forces.

Normally, as the knee bends, the patella slides smoothly along a groove in the femur. As we age and run ultras, our knees are subjected to uneven forces that are transmitted through the joint due to genetic variations in our anatomical structure and the unevenness of the surfaces on which we run. The patella may be subjected to forces that are abnormal and prevent it from moving normally through the femoral groove during exercise. Abnormal tracking of the patella can eventually cause the hyaline cartilage to deteriorate. This deterioration in the cartilage lining leads to pain as the bone ends are forced to distribute more of the load associated with weight bearing.

Chondromalacia generally progresses from a minor problem, characterized by swelling and softening of the cartilage, to a more severe and extensive problem, characterized by cracking of the cartilage. Eventually, destruction of the cartilage with complete exposure of the underlying bone can occur. The earlier that this condition is recognized and treated by a sports medicine professional, the less chronic and debilitating the injury will be.

Causative Factors

Chondromalacia is very common in older runners because of the effects of aging. It is also common in young women shortly after pubertal changes have resulted in a broadening of the hips. The increase in hip width alters the pre-pubescent bony anatomy and can result in genu valgum (knock knees). It also increases a measurement called the "Q" (quadriceps) angle.

Factors that increase the Q angle increase the chance of incurring runner's knee.

The Q angle is an estimate of the effective angle at which the quadriceps (thigh) muscles average their pull. It is determined by drawing a line from the Anterior Superior Iliac Spine (the bump above and in front of your hip joint) to the center of your kneecap and a second line from the center of your kneecap to the tibial tuberosity (where the tendon below your kneecap inserts). A normal Q angle is less than 12 degrees (15 degrees for women); abnormal is greater than 15 degrees (20 degrees for women).

Often, adding to the strong lateral pull of the quadriceps is a weak vastus medialis muscle. This is the part of the quadriceps muscles that helps stabilize the patella on the medial (inner) side. It runs along the inside portion of the thigh bone to join at the kneecap with the other three muscles making up the quadriceps.

Other mechanical conditions that may contribute to chondromalacia include wide hips (especially in female runners), a subluxating patella, a condition called "patella alta" in which the kneecap does not slide normally over the end of the femur, weakness or tightness in the quadriceps muscle group of the thigh or the gluteal (butt) muscles, and excessive pronation of the feet.

Training errors that may contribute to chondromalacia include excessive hill running, stair climbing, or too much distance without adequate training.

Signs and Symptoms

When the knee is bent there is increased pressure between the joint surface of the kneecap and the femur. This places stress on the injured area and leads to pain. Runners with chondromalacia will often report pain near the kneecap, along the medial (inner) edge and below it. Pain is also felt after sitting for a long period of time with the knees bent. Running downhill and walking down stairs often exacerbates pain, as does stair climbing.

Compression of the patella while bending and extending the knee may elicit discomfort and a grinding sensation known as crepitus. In many people, however, crepitus is a normal finding in the absence of other signs and symptoms. If you look at your shoes, or have a gait analysis performed in a biomechanics laboratory, you might notice that your foot pronates excessively during running.

Treatment

The precise treatment depends on the severity of the injury and on its causative factors, but there are several treatments that can help alleviate the pain associated with chondromalacia. During the early stages of the injury, running should be decreased to lessen stress on the area and to allow healing to begin. Particularly, downhill running and repeats on stairs should be avoided because of the increased stress these activities place on the patello-femoral complex.

Generally, exercises performed with the knee bent should be avoided; if you lift weights, substitute straight leg lifts and terminal leg extensions (limit the range of motion to the final thirty degrees of extension) in place of squats and deep knee bends. Cycling, because of the repetitive motion around the knee, is often an ineffective substitute for running.

Treatment for chondromalacia also involves rest, ice, and anti-inflammatory medications. Patellar taping, when done correctly by an athletic trainer or physical therapist, can supply immediate pain relief and helps correct the abnormal positioning of the patella.

Because chondromalacia is caused by improper tracking of the patella in the femoral groove as a result of poor flexibility or strength, stretching and strengthening exercises need to be performed to return the tracking to normal. The exact stretching and strengthening exercises that need to be performed depend on what muscles are tight and weak, but the following areas should be addressed:

- The Vastus Medialis Muscle: This muscle lies on the inner thigh just above the knee and works primarily during the last thirty degrees of leg extension. It is the muscle that helps stabilize the kneecap medially and prevents it from shifting laterally and tracking improperly. Straight leg lifts strengthen the vastus medialis and do not significantly stress the undersurface of the kneecap. They should be done 10 times on each side. Start with five sets of 10 and work your way up to 10 sets of 10. Straight leg lifts are best performed lying on a firm, cushioned surface with the exercising leg held straight and the non-exercising leg slightly bent to relieve pressure off the back.

- The Iliotibial (IT) Band and Hamstrings: Tight hamstrings and a tight IT Band are often related to improper patellar tracking. When these structures are tight, the patella shifts to the lateral side of the knee, making it track improperly. Good stretches for these structures, performed three times a day, should be performed in sets of three stretches, held for at least 30 seconds each. – *Jason Hodde*

Hamstring Injuries
by Jason Hodde, MS, ATC/L

One of the most common injuries surrounding the knee joint does not actually involve the knee. It involves the insertion of the hamstring tendons where they attach to the top of the weight bearing bone in the lower leg, the tibia. This injury is called hamstring tendinitis, and sometimes "pes anserinus tendinitis," depending on the specific hamstring tendon (or anatomical area) that has become inflamed.

In addition to tendinitis, many ultrarunners will occasionally suffer from a hamstring muscle strain. While strains can occur in any part of the muscle, the most common places for strains are right behind the knee near the tendons, or high in the muscle, near the buttocks.

Anatomy
The hamstrings are a group of three muscles that all lie on the posterior surface of the thigh. They attach to either the medial (inner) side of the posterior knee or the lateral (outer) side of the posterior knee and function during running by helping to bend the knee and extend the hip.

The biceps femoris is the name of the hamstring muscle that lies on the outer side of the thigh. It attaches to the lower leg at the tibia and the lateral bump at the knee, which is actually the head of the second bone in the lower leg, the fibula. Often, direct trauma to the head of the fibula results in severe pain and inflammation that can involve the biceps femoris tendon.

The remaining two hamstring muscles attach to the medial side of the posterior knee on the tibia. These two muscles are called the semitendinosus and the semimembranous. If you feel behind the inside of your knee, you can actually feel these two tendons as they cross the knee joint. The semitendinosus feels like a pencil; the semimembranous feels like a broad band. If you pay attention to the structures you are feeling, you will notice that there is another, separate tendon in the area behind the medial knee. This muscle is called the gracilis, one of the adductor muscles. The gracilis attaches with the semitendinosus and another muscle, the sartorius, at the place on the tibia called the pes anserinus.

In addition to flexing the knee and extending the hip, all of the hamstring muscles help to stabilize the knee from rotary forces. Thus, their strength is important to ultrarunners trying to minimize pain and discomfort around the knee as a result of running.

Etiology

Hamstring tendinitis is a common injury in runners and cyclists because of the repetitive flexion and extension of the knee during training and racing. Tendinitis can involve any one or several of the hamstring tendons, either individually or as a group.

Traumatic hamstring strains often occur in sports that involve sprinting, but strains are common in ultrarunners as well. One of the reasons hamstring strains occur is because of the relative inflexibility of the hamstring muscles. Strains are not usually caused by weak hamstrings, but are common in hamstrings that were originally of adequate strength and length but have become shortened due to neglect in stretching the muscle. Frequently, a hamstring injury is the result of a muscle strength imbalance. That is, the quadriceps (thigh) muscle group is excessively stronger than the hamstring muscle group. Generally, this means the hamstrings are less than 60 percent of the strength of the quadriceps muscles.

In runners, a long stride length helps running economy for faster running. Many ultrarunners run too many long, slow miles and train slowly year after year. Repetitive, long, slow running results in an abnormally short stride. Many ultrarunners who have injured their hamstrings report that they have increased the duration of their long runs at the expense of their speed work. When they attempt to run fast in an ultra, they are predisposed to developing either hamstring tendinitis or a hamstring strain. Poor flexibility also predisposes runners to injury, especially if the race is over hilly or mountainous terrain.

Prevention

Don't neglect a regular stretching plan in your training. Only by preventing hamstring inflexibility will you minimize your risk of hamstring tendinitis and hamstring pulls. Should you decide to add speed work to your ultramarathon training plan, you should gradually increase your stride length. Remember to increase your leg turnover rate, rather than just increasing your stride length, to help minimize the risk of injury.

Many runners become injured because they are racing on terrain that is vastly different from their training terrain. Training on the flat, level ground of Indiana doesn't adequately prepare you to run the long, steep climbs associated with the Wasatch Front 100 Mile. Knowing your limitations when running on different types of terrain will help you prevent an early DNF.

Treatment

The standard "RICE" (rest, ice, compression, elevation) treatment applies to acute hamstring injuries. Ice will help limit the pain associated with inflammation, and compression of the muscle will give it the support it needs to heal. Anti-inflammatories can be used to limit swelling and break the cycle of pain and spasm. Most important to quick recovery, however, is adequate rest.

Rest is important in the initial treatment and rehabilitation of hamstring injuries and should be used along with very gentle stretching and then gentle strengthening before any vigorous exercise is undertaken. Hard speed work must be eliminated until the muscle has recovered. Care must also be taken to avoid re-injury of the muscle.

Hamstring injuries often take weeks to heal because the athlete often returns to vigorous exercise too soon. While the time needed for recovery depends on the severity, type, and location of the injury, a good rule of thumb is four to six weeks of reduced activity before returning to vigorous exercise.

A return to running will require you to shorten your stride and eliminate hill work until your strength returns to normal. A proper warm-up of slow running and stretching becomes more important than ever before if the injury is going remain at bay. You may consider using moist heat before a workout, to increase blood flow to the muscle, and ice after a workout, to reduce exercise-related swelling. This is a common practice, one that works well during the rehabilitation phase of a hamstring injury.

Hamstring injuries are common in runners because the combination of poor flexibility and weakness of the hamstrings relative to the quadriceps is a result of the high mileage associated with training and racing. By maintaining flexibility and adding gentle weight training exercises to your training program, you will help reduce the chances of incurring a hamstring-related injury in your next race.

A Different Approach

by Nathan Whiting

The following section includes four articles by Nathan Whiting, a former columnist for UltraRunning, *whose perspective always offered a different and thought-provoking point of view.*

Skeletal Thoughts

Runners tend to be muscle-oriented. We train muscles, recover muscles, massage, and study them. While muscles propel us and become tired and sore, most of our injuries occur in joints and tendons. We tend to blame these injuries on soft, elastic muscles rather than hard bones. Better form, greater freedom, easier cushioning, balance, and leverage can be discovered from the bones. Knowing how bones work also makes it easier to see how the muscles work. When we are aware of the skeleton, we become more internal and begin to see our bodies from the inside out. It is not the purpose here to be definitive, but to give some starting points for individual awareness.

Every bone is involved in running. The skeleton must be free to pass action efficiently and quickly to other parts. If muscles hold joints or bones rigidly, motion will tend to stop. Short-circuiting motion causes inefficiency and stress.

I begin with *the shoulders* because I see more problems here than in other parts of the body, especially in tight runners. The entire shoulder complex—arms, shoulder blades, and clavicles—attaches to the rest of the skeleton in only one place, under the chin where the collarbones meet the sternum. (You can feel where if you wiggle the collarbones a little.) The shoulders are not nailed to the ribs, as many ultrarunners seem to think. They have great freedom, flexibility, power, and buoyancy. They should move forward with the arm. They should move up and down with each step, and quite a bit on a jarring step. The up and down freedom of the shoulders absorbs perhaps ten percent of the total shock of a race and even more on trails. It is important to stretch your shoulders to develop their potential. Shoulders also propel the body forward, especially uphill or, as you tire, to rest the legs. You must keep them loose and floating as you do so to avoid jarring the rest of the skeleton.

The *skull* is remarkably balanced. The point of balance may be higher than you think. Feel in back behind your nose. Neck muscles should not hold it erect, but let it wobble slightly as stress passes through. Be free to look and listen. When tired, the skull tends to drop. This puts strain on the body. Think of the skull as lifting you as if pulled from the very top, above the ears, by a string, as if able to float and lighten the entire body

The *jaw* has one purpose: to hang open and let air in. Muscle tightness not only wastes energy, it also acts as a wall, which instead of letting shock pass up and out of the body, reflects it back down. Brush your face and jaw loose with your fingers.

The *arms* are more adjustable than any lamp invented. They are another pathway to let shock out of the body. They should not interfere with the shoulders by too rigid pumping. The elbows and wrists bend with each swing; arms fine-tune our balance. Feel the ability of the wrists and hands to control the body. A flick of the hand can correct an imbalance that would stress a leg muscle.

The *spine* straightens our long bodies, keeps us erect, but also gently curves to act as a kind of main spring or ride stabilizer. Tight muscles in the lumbar region of the lower back and the neck can lock the spine and prevent cushioning and natural movement. While the upper body rarely needs to rotate very far (it might on trails), it should turn back and forth somewhat, lengthening the stride slightly, balancing, adjusting and keeping itself free. While the individual vertebrae are linked together, it is useful to think of them as separated by puffs of air, light and floating upward.

The *ribs* open and close with each breath. Put your hands around them and feel this sensation. They are part of what fills the lungs. This does not mean we need to lift the ribs and push them forward. Let the ribs hang toward your toes and even let them reach inward towards your strong back. Therefore, the upper body has the head free, balanced, and reaching upward. Shoulders are independent, responding to each step, arms free, loose, and balancing. The ribs hang easily downward around a light, erect, limber spine. Ideally, you are as present in your back as in your front.

The *pelvis* is a wonderful and complex piece of architecture. Its many secrets of leverage and balance are beyond the scope of this article, but worth exploring. The stress from two off-balance legs is transferred to the single, central spine at our center of gravity. While the hips do not need to wiggle suggestively, there should be movement back and forth and up and down. No bone connects the hip blades to the rib blades.

It is useful to concentrate on the *tailbone*. Think of it as pushing the body forward, instead of the legs. There are strong muscles nearby, which have few nerves and are hard to feel. If you can see your tail propelling you instead of your legs, it is easier to "get on top" of and use your inner muscles instead of the more painful and less efficient outer muscles you are more familiar with. You can feel as if the bones themselves are moving you.

The *knee* is complex in the ligaments, not the bones. The femur rests on the tibia like two knuckles on an anvil. A great deal of shock can be concentrated here. Fortunately the bottom of the femur is rounded and can be rolled over instead of pounded into the tibia, which is why we keep our knees bent as we step and the foot strike quiet and rolling. The kneecap can be pulled out of place by tense muscles below or above. If you have a knee problem, check the kneecap's location, free it with the leg held straight, and massage tense muscles, which might be displacing it.

The *lower leg* is two bones, not one. A common cause of shin splints is the bones locking together. They should have some independent motion. It is possible to spread apart and free these bones with your own or a friend's hands, or even by moving your foot from side to side, and circling it.

The *foot* is many bones and they all play a role. For now, I will only say that cushion and support is better if you are allowed to spread and enlarge under each step. There are two things that prevent this: tense foot muscles and tight shoes. Don't forget that feet expand with distance and heat. It is a good idea to let the toe drop freely as it rises from each step to relax the leg muscles. Be careful not to trip.

Muscular Overbalances

A muscular overbalance occurs when a muscle is stronger than the muscle that counters it, such as on the other side of a bone, or where a group of muscles overpowers weaker muscles in another part of the body. Some of these are natural and useful. For instance, a finger needs more strength to bend toward the palm, to grip, than it does to straighten. Other imbalances can cause misalignment, fatigue, and injury. Any repeated activity develops some muscles at the expense of others. In running, the most common overbalances are back verses front, inner leg verses outer and lower body verses upper.

Running pushes the body forward. The big hamstrings, the back of the calves and the back of the upper body are all used to shove the 100-plus pounds of the body forward, while the front muscles are relatively passive. It is no surprise that our legs have heavy, dense, tight muscles pushing, while lighter more flexible muscles in front are needed only to fling the leg back for the next step. It is no wonder we get injuries to the front of the legs: shin splints, sight pulls, and the like.

There are two basic ways to deal with this overbalance. One is to strengthen the front muscles. Formal race walking, cross training with swimming or other sports, and using weights give legs better overall strength and toughness. Some caution is necessary. The front muscles need to remain flexible. They are like rubber bands and snap the leg back with stored energy. If these muscles are simply enlarged, they can become dead weight on the leg and make steps labored. Like all muscles, they need to be stretched as they are enlarged. To stretch the front of the legs, one must bend the opposite way from stretching the backs. A bow yoga position can lengthen and free these muscles.

The other approach is to simply accept the overbalance and treat it by massaging and stretching the hamstrings, back, and calves. You do not have to try to touch your toes. You should bend your knees a little. Relax as much as you can and simply hang for half a minute or so. Don't bounce, but do breathe deeply. You can move your hips around. Keep your head down and go into a squat. Massage is intuitive. Learn to loosen your legs with your hands. Be gentle, be patient, go with the muscle's length, not across. Feel soreness and elongate the muscle away from it. Breathe slowly and deeply into all stretches and massages. The back is more difficult, but you can learn to loosen, relax, and apply pressure, moving slowly.

The insides of the legs are very strong in most runners, while the outsides are skinny strings. This is a common weak point in very long runs, causing soreness and swelling on the outside of the knee, ankle, or shin. It is hard to strengthen the outer leg, although weights can be used. It is also a difficult area to stretch. A lunge with a twist can be used. Massage, lengthening the inner muscles, is best. It is also useful to free the kneecap and push it down slightly, and to allow the separate motion of the two bones in the lower leg by rotating and twisting the ankle before injury occurs.

Our upper bodies are not as weak as we think they are. In runners, the psoas and diaphragm inside the body are strong. The back muscles along the spine and between ribs are so strong they can inhibit breathing and body fluidity. The shoulders that swing the arms are big enough to pull the body into bad posture.

The problem is that our upper bodies are not developed evenly. Our abdominal muscles are weak. The pectorals are weak. Most upper body overbalance problems are simply the result of not relaxing. Learn to release and shake out the jaw, neck, and shoulders as you run. Wiggle the back all sorts of ways, now and then. Think of the front of the body lengthening and back softening at all times. Do not allow the chest's weakness to become something you collapse into. Because running does little to develop the upper body, many of the injuries and pains we develop are not from running, but from other stresses in our lives. I once had a shoulder pain I blamed on running, until one day while typing I discovered the real cause. Look at your whole life when tracing problems, not just the obvious strain of mileage.

So far what I have said is obvious, if a bit sketchy. You all have some idea of what I am talking about. I would like to finish with two concepts that are a little more advanced. They separate those who are sensitive to their bodies from those who merely run and hope.

The first concerns overbalances, which are caused by more separated muscle groups such as the left psoas muscle, behind the intestines, stressing the right knee, or a shoulder overpowering an ankle. Recently I traced an ankle weakness to a locked muscle at the base of my skull. Most people look for the cause of an injury where the injury is. This is often not the case. The cause can be stress or misalignment far from the harm.

The trick is in tracing the path. There is little established medicine or science here. Follow lines of energy and balance. Look for sore spots or still places, throughout the body. Stress moves up from the foot, knees, hips, into the body. It also comes down from arms, from the weight and twist of the hips into the legs and from leg to leg. We each stress in our way. Listen to the clues. Where is pain coming from? How is the body being pushed and landing? Where are we off balance and why? Where do we feel too strong?

The other overbalance is that within a single muscle. We tend to believe all of a muscle is equally strong, equally dense, and equally limber. Not true. A muscle can vary a great deal through its length. One part of a hamstring or abductor can be light and elastic. An inch or so away, a muscle can be dense and powerful and another part quick and elongating. Most muscles we use for running are long. Each operates over a variety of leverages, shoves, pulls and snaps back into place. When we feel a muscle is tight, where is it tight? When we feel a weakness in a muscle, where? Is it right below or above part of a muscle that is strong? Tendinitis (a tendon is an extension of a muscle) can come from differences in density in the muscle. Explore the whole length of the muscle around a problem Soften the parts too hard, lengthen those too short, and relax parts too tense or jittery. All of the body is intimately tied together. The runner needs to be aware of its powers, as well as ways to achieve the best balance possible.

The Ultrarunner's Back

Running is an odd sport. We use our muscles for one purpose—to push ourselves forward—then congratulate ourselves on our body awareness. Most of the muscles runners use are behind us, but since we are a face and hands-oriented species, our awareness is in front of us. True, we know when our legs get sore, but it's no surprise to have sore legs when you run 50 miles or more. A little lactic acid, some muscle fatigue? We're strong. We can deal with that. Sore feet? No problem, we're all postgraduate shoe and blister scientists. We can run forever. Yet one thing is left out—our poor, powerful backs.

Fatigue usually begins in the legs and spends an hour or two bothering the legs in our minds before we say to ourselves, "We're tired, but we can do it; we knew it would hurt, but our legs are strong." The collapse of a runner is more sudden and disastrous. The collapse usually begins in the back, but we are not always aware of it.

The back is a wonderfully complex weaving of capabilities and weaknesses. It contains the spinal bones, which are far more flexible than we think. Each can move separately from the rest—it's not a wooden rod. The spine stretches from the head behind your eyes all the way down to the tail at the top of your legs. The curve of the spine and pads between the vertebrae are essential for shock absorption. The back has the wing-like shoulder blades important in arm motion. It has the big arches of our hip bones for the attachment and leverage of many leg and hip muscles. Across the back are layer after layer of muscles that connect most parts of the body to the other parts of the body. They coordinate such disperse movements as the right index finger with the left little toe and organize the total movement of the body as it relates to the torso.

For any direction you can move, your back has its system of muscles. Muscles connect individual vertebrae, and in the expansion of ribs for breathing, connecting the top of the legs to the middle of the spine with surprising power. The layers pull in different directions: side to side, diagonally, up and down. Many of these muscles give our bodies buoyancy and strength to lift us off our legs with a sense of floating. Others push the hips forward, swing and extend the arms in any direction, help the diaphragm suck air and the stomach digest (or get upset). Most, if not all, are important in running and endurance. They give us the swings and rotations. They govern our balance. They service us. They push us.

Surely all this complexity is automatic and we can take it for granted. Not really. It works fine for a one-year-old, but adults have had habits. We have blockages, stresses, and odd postures, all of which create problems for the efficient working of the back. Also, stress, overuse, and imbalances placed on the back by extreme efforts on uneven surfaces and uneven temperatures can cause problems anywhere from the neck to the stomach to the toe. The back, like any part of us, needs to be monitored and understood.

Posture

Ideal posture is fairly simple to visualize. The hip joint should be on a line between the shoulders and ankle so the bones support you. You might want to stand and try this. Wiggle yourself tall. Then move your hips forward and back and feel what that does to the back. Then feel the balance point between where you are held by the bones and need little effort from the muscles. Slowly swing the arms a couple of times as if running. This is an efficient and protective stance for the back. The problem is to continue this "uprightness" as the ankles change places. The shoulders rotate, and you're tired. It helps to keep reminding yourself to be as tall as possible. The upper body opens like a fan skyward, with a floating energy. If you sense the tail sneaking back, the chest rolling down, or the head sagging, get back onto your bones. You'll use less muscle more efficiently and your feet will hit the ground lighter with each stride.

Tension and stress

Tension is caused by our lives, our jobs, our families, and so on. We all have it. The back has a notorious tendency to gather and hold tension and stiffen or "tense up" under anxiety or uncertainty. This tends to become habitual and define our posture. Any stiffness in the back forms blockages where the coordination of movement is interrupted. These are the parts of the back that tend to tire (and tire us) when running, leading to a loss of posture, happiness, and endurance. The first part to go in a runner is rarely the knee, hip, or ankle—it's the back. The leg receives the imbalance secondhand. The cure is to become aware of the places in your back, neck, jaw, and shoulders, where you hold tension and learn to let go of it. Rigid, erect posture is not the answer. You must relax and release. This isn't easy, because tension is so habitual and so familiar we often sense no problem. Expanding the breath to all of the back will begin to open the space. Lying on your back and taking inventory can help, dropping each bone, rib, and muscle. Take moments now and then to pause, relax. Classes in yoga or release-based dance can help.

Stress is what happens after a few hours of running in harsh weather over bad terrain. The little breaks and walks a runner takes are useful to relieve stress. When you take any kind of break (or even while running), wiggle and release any tension in your back. Regain your posture. Shake out the legs, arms, and head. Lengthen the head. Fill the lungs with air and stretch. When running, allow the back its complete and natural motion. Get a massage if you feel a pain or stiff area and someone will do it. It may only take a few seconds. Don't let your back beat you.

Weather

The body sweats. The wind blows. The back shivers. Even on a warm day, sweat (or ice water poured over the head) can cool one muscle to inertia while the next muscle is about to spasm from the heat, leading to stiff spots, tired spots, and a dangerous loss of efficiency that may be the cause of problems in the legs. "It's my knee." No, it's your back. Cold days are even more dangerous. You've run into the wind for a while. You turn a corner. Wind hits the sweat on your back. You may not even feel it before rigor mortis gets you. Wind from the side can cause a cold muscle to pull a warm muscle. Keep the shins dry and the back as uniformly warm as possible. Stretch, then breathe into and rub any cold area before it stiffens.

Therapy and exercise

A simple therapy for the back and a way to release tension and recover is to take two tennis balls and lie on your back on a rug or mat. Place one ball on each side of the spine. Begin at the back of your head and slowly roll over them until you get to your legs. If you find a stiff or slightly sore spot, rest a while, relax, and just hang into the floor. If you feel related twinges on your front side, massage those areas. Take your time. It may take a couple of tries to get used to it.

Most runners have stiff legs, which discourages stretching. This doesn't mean you can afford not to stretch the back. Leading from your head, slowly roll down one vertebra at a time towards the floor and hang, deeply and regularly. Bend your knees. Cheat all you want. You can also stretch the back in a squat. Let the head fall between the knees. You don't need to look around. A good stretch for the diagonals is to get on your hands and knees. Put the top of your head on the floor and explore it. See how many parts of your head and face you can touch or roll on the ground. You can adjust your legs. Remember to do all back stretches very slowly in a relaxed manner while breathing deeply. Don't do anything that causes sharp pains.

To feel the width and strength of the back and feel its presence, you can do a deep squat with your heels on the ground. Adjust your feet. Straighten the back as freely as you can. (Don't stay long.) Then rise and keep that wide feeling. Another way is to place your heels four or five inches from a wall. Bend the knees, lean back and let the back relax and widen. Then, keeping the sense of moving into your back, walk forward a few steps with the knees still bent. Try to sense moving forward by moving backward into the strength of your back. Try it a few times. There is more. Observe and experiment, and you will discover.

Breathing Beyond Distance

There are office workers sitting all day who breathe better than many ultrarunners. We think because we can talk and run at the same time that we have the right to pant, gasp, wheeze, and generally forget whether we are breathing or not. The lungs are the center of running. They touch and affect how our heart, stomach, liver, adrenals, kidneys, and intestines perform. They stretch across and affect three major energy and emotional centers of our bodies. If muscles weaken, our lungs can usually pull us through. If our lungs give out, our legs suddenly wobble and we collapse. More than half of the DNFs in ultras are not caused by the mind, but by the lungs. (We rarely blame either. "It's my ankle. It's my stomach," we say instead.)

The three lungs: Lungs use three sets of muscles. Very few of us use all three well. *The lower lung* is by our navels and is propelled by the diaphragm, which rests on and helps work the stomach. Steady breathing into this area can calm and control emotions, aid digestion, and help relax leg muscles. *The middle lung* is around the heart and is propelled by the rib muscles. Steady breathing into this area can improve mood, give a kindlier, more loving viewpoint, and slow and control the heart. *The upper lung* is propelled by the shoulders and higher back muscles. Steady breathing here can increase creativity, awaken and interest the mind, and relax and lower the arms. Try filling each area, one after the other, to feel its capacity and power. Ideally, the entire cylinder should fill with each breath.

The out breath: When short of breath or tiring, the natural urge is to breathe in. A potential result in a long race is to breathe into half-filled lungs with short gasps. Muscles used to breathe out, especially the diaphragm, are strong. Once emptied, the lung's leverage to breathe back in is greatly improved, and the volume of air exchanged increases. The muscles are used more efficiently and the limbering of the spine takes pressure off the legs. If you are tiring, panting, out of breath, or forced to walk hills, think *out-in, out-in* rather than *in-out.*

Breathing to a spot: Breathing is not only a source of air; it is a way to massage the body. A breath can be directed to a very specific place. Pains in the body can have many causes: glandular fatigue, tension, pounding, poor form. In most cases breathing directly into a pain or weak spot can have an immediate effect and help correct the underlying problem. Try taking a sharp breath to the very bottom of the spine. You should feel an instant relaxation and stretch of the hip muscles. With practice, you can learn to extend this effect to your knees and below. Try breathing into your shoulder, or placing a thumb on your back or chest and inhale directly to that spot. Feel the great precision and freedom of the lungs. A massage is a help, but can only reach so deep. Breath can massage you with hands from the inside and you don't have to stop to receive it.

Breathe to concentrate: A longer breath is more efficient than a short one. A little more than one second for each breath is minimal. A good steady long breath *is* concentration and becomes the basis for relaxed, steady and efficient pace (moving out by moving into yourself). One way to achieve this is to practice counting reps: two, three, or four steps for each breath in, and two or three steps for each breath out. This is useful on hills and can lead to shorter, efficient steps going up and longer, coasting strides down. It can also help you measure your pace as you run. *Warning:* Don't try this method for more than a half-hour at a time until you are in are condition and have practiced it. While records have been set using it, it can lead to an unexpected collapse. Another way to improve breath control and mood is to sing out loud while you run.

Walking: Walking is not a time to forget about breath. It is actually the time to remember it. Breathe forcefully and carefully when walking as you would want to when running. Good breathing and a long stride will speed your walking and aid your recovery for more running.

First aid: Weakening of the lungs and associated organs, tiredness of the upper body, or sudden loss of strength can often be improved by applying hard acupressure with a stiff finger, or a vigorous massage to spots along the lung meridian. Begin at the bottom of the sternum or breastbone, then a spot about one hand above the nipple, then a spot just under the clavicle or shoulder bone, then down the top of the arm to a spot about an inch above the wrist bone. Do the right side first. You may also need to work just under the ribs. The left side is the adrenal gland and the right is the liver. A good hard rub, if these areas are sensitive, can bring new energy to the body and strengthen the diaphragm.

Training: Good hard speed work once or twice a week at distances from 80 yards to a half-mile is the key for strong, deeply developed lungs. Racing five or ten km regularly is almost as good. Hill work, focusing on breath control, is good for power and concentration. Holding your breath while running a steady pace can help you discover and overcome hidden fears associated with breathing. Many of our problems are caused by panic and lack of confidence. Ultrarunning is essentially an inner growth of courage. Yoga classes that include breathing exercises are also useful.

Terrain: Be aware of changes in hill gradient. Run rolling courses by breath being used, not by speed of the legs or a watch. You can deplete a little on a long slow rise, a lot on a short steep climb, as long as you can make it up on the flats. Practice coasting, relaxing the hips and shoulders on downhills, regaining your breath and preparing for the next climb.

NSAIDS and Ultras: A Dangerous Combination?
by Jason Hodde, MS, ATC/L

Much as flashlights are considered indispensable for night running or extra clothes a necessity when running in the cold, many ultrarunners rely upon "the candy jar of little white pills" to get them through the later stages of a long event. The commonality of ibuprofen ("Vitamin I") in ultras almost makes it seem a prerequisite race-day preparation for many runners.

The goal of this column is to present accurate information about the use and abuse of non-steroidal anti-inflammatory drugs (NSAIDS) during endurance exercise. It is only meant to get you to think about the effects of NSAIDS on your body. While the information presented in this column is accurate and current to the best of my knowledge, it is important to realize that many medical professionals do not agree upon the level of risk associated with high-dose, short-term use of anti-inflammatory drugs. You will need to be the final judge and evaluate the risks with the benefits of using these drugs during ultras.

NSAIDS
NSAIDS are drugs that have anti-inflammatory effects. This class of compounds acts by inhibiting an enzyme in the body called cyclooxygenase. Cyclooxygenase catalyzes the formation of prostaglandin, a compound that enhances inflammation, increases blood flow to the kidneys under stressful conditions, and assists in protecting the lining of the stomach from acids.

The enzyme has two forms. Cyclooxygenase-1 (COX-1) has protective effects on the stomach lining, whereas cyclooxygenase-2 (COX-2) produces proinflammatory effects. Older NSAIDS, such as ibuprofen, inhibit COX-1 more than COX-2, whereas the newer class of NSAIDS, like celecoxib and rofecoxib, inhibit COX-2 predominately, decreasing adverse gastrointestinal effects. Many NSAIDS are available without a prescription (e.g., ibuprofen, naproxen sodium, and ketoprofen), but the newer, COX-2 inhibitors all require a physician's prescription in the U.S.

Acetaminophen and Aspirin
Aspirin is a salicylate drug with anti-inflammatory effects and is often considered as part of the NSAID family. Although effective to reduce inflammation and fever, it is the shortest-acting NSAID available and is therefore less-commonly used in ultra distance running. Aspirin use has been linked to the development of Reyes'

Syndrome in adolescents, and is therefore no longer recommended for anyone under the age of 18.

Acetaminophen, or Tylenol, is a common drug used to reduce fever. Unlike NSAIDS, Tylenol has no anti-inflammatory effects. Therefore, taking Tylenol to reduce pain due to inflammation during running is ineffective.

Cox-2 Inhibitors

This new class of NSAIDS has been touted during the last few years as having fewer side effects than the older NSAID medications. There are currently three drugs on the market that fall into this category. All are available by prescription only. They are: celecoxib (Celebrex), rofecoxib (Vioxx), and valdecoxib (Bextra). Because of their relative newness to the marketplace, few controlled studies have been performed to compare their effectiveness with incidence of side effects as compared with the older NSAID classes. While much more expensive than older medications, it is also unclear if they are more effective than aspirin or ibuprofen.

Use

It is estimated that the U.S. population alone ingests more than 30 billion NSAIDS annually. In one recent year, the American Association of Poison Control Centers (AAPCC) documented 52,751 toxic exposures to ibuprofen, of which 13,519 were treated in health care facilities. Four deaths were reported. As you can see, toxic overdose is rare, but it can occur.

Common Side Effects

The most common side effect of NSAID ingestion is dyspepsia, or "sour stomach," and has been reported to occur in four to sixteen percent of all patients taking ibuprofen, and up to 60 percent of all patients taking any NSAID, during controlled clinical studies. Stomach irritation can be mild to severe, but can often be minimized if NSAIDS are taken with food or milk.

Nervous system complaints are also quite common with NSAID use. (ibuprofen: three to nine percent.) They include seizures, hallucinations, changes in mood, and headache. These side effects are most common with NSAIDS that are fat-soluble, like ibuprofen (Motrin, Nuprin, Advil, etc.), naproxen sodium (Aleve), or ketoprofen (Orudis). It should be noted that these drugs are all available without a prescription.

Because NSAIDS have the effect of decreasing blood flow to the kidneys, kidney problems are also a side effect of NSAID use (ibuprofen: less than one percent). These effects include salt and water retention, hyperkalemia (increased potassium in the blood, which can lead to erratic heart rhythms), and acute renal failure. Other kidney problems can also occur, but they are not as common. The elderly and those with chronic kidney problems are particularly susceptible to these kidney complications.

Signs Of Toxicity

Toxic signs and symptoms can occur with relatively low doses of ibuprofen and other NSAIDS, as little as one or two tablets. For Ibuprofen, serious side effects start to be seen with doses of approximately 100 mg/kg taken over 24 hours. Practically, this is about 25 to 200 mg (regular strength) tablets for a 120-pound female or 35 to 200 mg tablets for a 154-pound male. It should be realized that lower toxic doses might be realized while you are running, due to increased levels of body stress and already reduced blood flow to the kidneys as a normal function of exercise. The most common signs of toxicity are altered breathing patterns, increased blood pressure, irritability, and difficulty concentrating. High doses of NSAIDS can also exacerbate the symptoms and severity of asthma.

Ergogenic Effects

An ergogenic aid is any substance or method that helps to increase work output by increasing strength, enhancing endurance, increasing concentration, decreasing pain, or delaying onset of fatigue. NSAIDS, due to their analgesic and anti-inflammatory properties, may therefore be considered "ergogenic aids." Runners may use NSAIDS for the following reasons: 1) To reduce pain and therefore allow them to train and compete when injured; 2) to decrease swelling due to injury, allowing a faster return to activity; 3) to prevent injury and reduce post-exercise muscle soreness; 4) to block the pain associated with running ultras.

The ergogenic benefit of NSAID use is still highly debated. The area that claims to have the highest ergogenic benefit is that the ingestion of NSAIDS prior to exercise can limit muscle damage, reduce post-exercise soreness and prevent injury. Studies examining the benefits of NSAID ingestion prior to, during, and after exercise have been either inconclusive or contradictory. While many ultrarunners use NSAIDS to block the pain of running long distances, there is no concrete evidence that this practice enhances performance.

Are NSAIDS Dangerous?

In the strictest sense, NSAIDS are generally safe drugs with few side effects. Most individuals can take them without experiencing kidney malfunction, stomach upset, or nervous system impairments. However, because they are safe for the general population does not mean that they are safe for use during an ultra. The stress placed on your body during an ultra is extreme. Blood flow to the kidneys is normally reduced during exercise, often compounding dehydration. Both of these effects of running long distances result in reduced kidney function and can cause acute kidney failure even in the absence of NSAID ingestion. Thus, adding yet another stressor that decreases optimal kidney function may not be the wisest course of action.

Many people tolerate NSAIDS without side effects. However, it is virtually impossible to determine in advance if you are one of them. Is the risk of trial and error and the need to finish worth the permanent damage that can be caused if you experience the side effects listed above? Acute kidney failure is a life-threatening side effect of NSAID use and can also occur during ultras if you do not remain fully hydrated.

Pulmonary Emboli: A Personal Struggle
by Bruce Boyd

I was diagnosed with "pulmonary emboli" in both lungs not long ago. While the condition is not common among active people, it is often difficult to diagnose and can be fatal. Also, there does not seem to be a large body of information about the illness and its course. It is therefore difficult to have a sense that you are healing at an appropriate rate. While the fitness level of ultrarunners may be better than average, there may be reasons that we are more susceptible to this malady than the public at large.

What follows is a collection of information I have read or obtained in discussions with doctors, nurses, and others with varying levels of knowledge about the illness. It is therefore anecdotal and not authoritative medical information. Disclaimers that could apply, do.

I initially experienced shortness of breath and elevated heart rate while running and a few days later severe pain in my left lower back and in the region of my left collarbone. It hurt to breathe and hurt terribly to cough or sneeze. An X-ray showed a slight shadow on my lung in the area of the pain. I had no other symptoms. The initial conclusion was that something had irritated that portion of my lung, but whatever it was it was no longer apparent. I was given an anti-inflammatory drug and we decided to monitor my progress over the next several weeks. The pain subsided immediately, but I noted a slight pressure where the pain had been and an elevated heart rate when I ran. I also experienced mild coughing and an increased need to clear my throat. My resting heart rate remained in the 45 to 55 range.

In my initial visit to the doctor he had asked if I had taken any prolonged plane trips. I had not, but I had driven to a 24-hour race and back, 750 miles each way.

During the next few weeks I monitored my heart rate; while I noted some improvement, it remained elevated. Five weeks after the initial episode I flew to a meeting and a few days later experienced pain in the lower back and collarbone again. I had severe difficulty breathing, but was not sure if this resulted from the pain breathing caused or some other factor.

Upon returning home I spoke to my doctor. He ordered a lung scan. Based on the result I was admitted to the emergency room where I was immediately given an intravenous solution (IV) of Heparin, a blood thinner.

I had what is known as a pulmonary embolism. This condition results from a blood clot that generally forms in the leg, then becomes lodged in the lung, where it can disrupt the flow of blood back to the heart and in severe cases the flow of oxygen to the brain. In time these clots dissolve or form scar tissue in the lung. The severity of the problem depends on the number and size of the clots and the overall physical condition of the individual.

What are its common causes? It is usually associated with advanced age, post operative conditions, trauma, prolonged immobility, dehydration and constrictive clothing.

At age 60 I guess I must begin to admit to advanced age. The trip to Toledo and back certainly fits the definition of prolonged inactivity, even though I did stop every hour or two. The flight, which preceded my second episode, was only two and a half hours, but at that point the formation of clots had already begun. While I don't tend to dehydrate during a race, the day was hot and in 24 hours dehydration was certainly a possibility.

The treatment I received was the immediate IV of Heparin followed by a prescription for Coumadin for six months. These are both blood thinners designed to prevent the enlargement of existing clots and the formation of new ones. As I understand it, the body takes care of existing ones.

During this period I was initially unable to run. It was not the exercise, but the jarring that could shake loose existing clots that was the worry. As a matter of fact, while in the hospital I walked a few miles each day in my hospital gown, rolling my I.V. stand. It looked like I was taking my mechanical stork for a walk.

I returned to running daily. My heart rate improved, but was still somewhat elevated for a time. I was about a minute slower per mile at my race pace heart rate than I was when the episode began.

I still have an occasional slight pain in my left collarbone region and pressure in my left lower back. My lungs still feel like I have cotton in them and I cough and clear my throat quite frequently. While I am not positive of the origin of my condition, I have learned some things that may prevent it from recurring. These may also help others prevent an initial occurrence. When I travel, I take frequent breaks—at least once per hour, preferably more frequently. It's amazing how this prevents stiffening up as well. I drink plenty of fluids and avoid alcohol when I travel, crossing my legs, and wearing constrictive clothing. Once off Coumadin, I started taking an aspirin per day.

There are a number of features of ultrarunning that could make us more susceptible to this condition than other people. These are pure speculation on my part. First, we go from prolonged activity to inactivity when we do an ultra. Many of us travel at least several hours to an event and often arrive just before the race and leave right afterwards. It is quite possible that the extreme change in activity level is the cause. In other words, we may be more affected by the inactivity of travel than a "couch potato" would be. Also, the change in heart rate from an active state to an inactive state is probably a much broader range than for most people. Is it possible that our heart rate or some other component of ultrarunners' circulatory systems makes us more prone to clots? Is there something about the need for our bodies to heal after a long race that could result in blood flow to the legs that may contribute? Could this be heightened by our need to devour large amounts of food after a race? Despite our efforts to the contrary, we all are susceptible to dehydration. Of course, there are many plusses to ultrarunning as well. Some may decrease the potential for clotting. Better circulation may be one.

When I began the curing process I tried to approach it like an ultra. I knew it would be a long haul. I tried to set realistic goals and I knew there would be bad times, but things would get better. I have found moderate success with this approach. Part of the problem is not knowing how long this "race" is or what goals are realistic. How can I expect to feel along the way? As in an ultra, only time will tell.

Ozone and the Ultrarunner: It's a Serious Health Concern

by Brent Backus

In California, May through October is commonly known as "smog season." The main component of smog is ozone. Ozone is a highly reactive gas that is a form of oxygen. Ozone and other photochemical oxidants are air pollutants produced in complex photochemical reactions involving sunlight and emissions of hydrocarbons and nitrogen oxides from motor vehicles and stationary sources of pollution. Ozone can have adverse effects on human health.

The lungs are ozone's major target. Medical studies show that ozone damages cells in the lungs, making the passages inflamed and swollen. Ozone is a strong irritant that can chemically burn and cause narrowing of the airways, forcing the lungs to work harder to provide oxygen to the body. Major airway restriction can occur in humans within one to two hours after exposure to ozone. Even short-term exposure to ozone over an hour or two can add stress to the body.

The effects of ozone include shortness of breath, nasal congestion, coughing, eye irritation, sore throat, headache, chest discomfort, fatigue, fever, dizziness, nausea, numbness, and convulsions. Ozone can damage alveoli, the individual air sacs in the lungs where oxygen and carbon dioxide are exchanged. Certain changes in the lungs take place with exposure to ozone, including increased inflammation and increased tissue scarring. At concentrations of 0.12 parts per million (ppm), the federal ozone standard, 10 to 25 percent of the general population experiences a decline in lung function after one to two hours of exposure. Some people experience lung function decline at ozone concentrations below 0.12 ppm.

Ozone can also reduce resistance to infections. Research has shown that immune system cells move into the lungs after acute exposure to ozone, producing a nine-fold increase in disease fighting cells. Short-term ozone exposure has also been shown to decrease resistance to bacterial pneumonia in animals.

Studies of the effects of ozone exposure on cells and tissues provide evidence that genetic material may be damaged by ozone, thereby increasing the risk of cancer. Ozone has the potential to contribute to cancer by more than one route; it might inflict damage on the respiratory cells by means of free radical reactions, which have been associated with cancer, and it might initiate increased cell reproduction.

According to the Environmental Protection Agency (EPA), even though a person may not show obvious effects of ozone exposure, this does not mean the person has adapted to ozone. Some evidence suggests that the ozone damage does not always go away when the ozone does. Recent research shows that lung injury continues during the time the ozone tapers off. The same effects observed after extended short-term ozone exposure are also seen after longer-term exposure. The effects seen over both time periods include nasal, tracheal, and bronchial lesions. The occurrence of these effects after long-term, low-level exposure to ozone suggests that ozone can initiate changes associated with the development of chronic lung disease. The long-term effects of ozone exposure can also include lung aging, a loss of elasticity, inflammation of small airways, and a decline in lung function. Results from human and animal studies indicate that repeated exposure produces an eventual reduced response to ozone.

The effects of ozone-induced inflammation are similar to those caused by cigarette smoking, although the effects of cigarettes can be attributed to direct toxicity of the inhaled products, as well as to the indirect effects of tissue inflammation. Research shows that lung tissue inflammation in young smokers occurs at the junction of the airways and in the gas exchange areas of the lungs. Chronic inflammation is considered responsible for the effects on lung structure and function seen in cigarette-related lung disease. Similar effects are found at the same sites in the lungs of ozone-exposed animals. The analogy of the effects of ozone exposure to those of cigarette smoking implies that humans chronically exposed to ozone at levels which cause lung inflammation should show greater deterioration of lung function than those who are not exposed to such concentrations. Preliminary research indicates that exposure to ozone may be associated with a decline of pulmonary function and an increased risk of chronic lung disease.

Athletes may be more healthy and physically fit than non-smokers, but they may be among the most vulnerable to the effects of inhaled ozone. The sheer physical effort they expend results in a higher volume of air breathed deeply into the lungs. Increased breathing rates can increase ozone exposure even during low ozone levels. Ozone interferes with lung function and can cause pain and discomfort at concentrations as low is 0.009 ppm.

In studies of people who exercise, normal lung function declined by 10 percent or more in five to 20 percent of subjects when exposed to ozone. Lung function was further reduced as the ozone level increased. At 0.20 ppm, lung function in about half the subjects decreased by more than 20 percent. The number of people affected and the severity of the effects rose at higher ozone levels. Heat and high humidity can make symptoms and lung impairment worse. High temperatures (87° to 104° F) and/or humid conditions combined with exercise during ozone exposure can reduce lung function more than similar ozone exposures at moderate temperatures and humidity.

Another study on ozone and exercise found that many athletes may develop symptoms (nose and throat irritation, cough, shortness of breath, headache, wheezing), reduced lung function, and reduced physical performance during endurance exercise with exposure to ozone. At 0.12 ppm exposure for one hour, lung function decreased by 16 to 21 percent and coughing increased. When the exposure included exercising at competitive levels, lung function decreased as much as 30 percent and chest tightness appeared. Endurance studies suggest that performance may begin to suffer at 0.12 ppm (the federal standard); other studies indicate adverse effects at 0.09 ppm (the California standard); it is very likely that there would be adverse effects at 0.20 ppm for most athletes exercising heavily for one or more hours.

So what are ultrarunners to do if we live in smoggy areas? We know that ozone reaches its highest concentration in the early to mid-afternoon, so we can train in the early morning or evening hours. Ozone also trends to peak late in the week (Thursday and Friday), although you should check with your local air pollution control agency. Not running or exercising during health advisories is also recommended.

So what are race directors to do if their race is in a smoggy area? Start the race early enough so that it is completed before peak ozone times. Most ultra races start early anyway. For 12-hour runs you might want to consider having the event during the smog off-season or during the night during smog season. For 24-hour runs or longer, I would suggest having the races during the smog off-season.

The Agony of Da-Feet

by Kevin Setnes

Foot problems affect just about all runners at one time or another. As ultrarunners, we must take extra care in recognizing and understanding treatment of foot disorders. Foot problems can be quite painful, whether they are irritating blisters or the very aggravating plantar fasciitis. Because of the constant repetitive nature of running and the critical foot strike, runners are frequent visitors at the podiatrist's office. Furthermore, foot problems are often the root cause of other injuries throughout the body. Nearly all veteran ultrarunners have experienced foot problems and have struggled in learning how to deal with them. Failing to understand the cause of foot discomfort can be frustrating for both veterans and newcomers alike.

On a positive note, nearly all foot problems can be prevented, provided that one understands the foot and how it strikes the ground. Ultras, often lasting up to 10, 20 or even 30 hours, place a huge demand on the feet. By learning the causes and preventive measures one can take, running with pain-free feet can become a reality, even given the punishment an ultrarunner puts on them. Here are some common problems found with ultrarunners' feet, and suggestions on how to handle them.

Blisters

Who among of us has not had a blister or two? Blistered feet are a common sight at the end of any ultra. How do some manage to escape blister-free? By simply avoiding them. As simple as this may seem, blisters are one of the most preventable foot problems.

Friction causes blisters. Cutting down on the abrasive sock is step one. Unlike years ago, today's market offers many excellent moisture resistant socks, specifically designed for runners. Next, make sure you have properly fitting shoes. A running store specialist will help ensure proper fit. Trail runners often experience more toe blisters as a result of the force that keeps the foot moving when trying to brake on steep descents. Examine the toe box very carefully. Your toes should not be touching the front of the shoe, but the shoe should provide a snug fit that allows for little movement. Also, monitor electrolyte intake. Swelling can occur when electrolyte levels fall off. If feet or toes swell, extraordinary friction occurs. In ultras, maintaining a proper electrolyte balance is important for many reasons—this is just one.

What about lubricating the feet? A common practice by many ultrarunners, it provides some means of prevention, especially for shorter events (marathon and 50-km distances). Vaseline is a good lubricant, but may not be the best choice for the feet. Its benefits are short lived, softening the feet, but absorbed by the foot and sock relatively quickly. Other lubricating products tend to be more effective for longer distances. If you are lubricating feet and toes, you may want to do so at regular intervals, especially if the race is 100 miles or 24 hours. Monitor "hot spots," and do not hesitate to check the feet. A regular change of socks can also help.

Keeping feet dry is recommended, if at all possible. However, do not be afraid to venture into water or douse your body with water in the event of hot temperatures. If the feet are sufficiently trained, and you have access to dry socks and shoes later on, don't worry about being wet. Cool water can even be refreshing to the feet.

Uneven surfaces such as trails or tight turns can also cause abnormal wear on the foot's skin. Try staying on as smooth a surface as possible and watch the crown in the road, concentrating on the smoothest, yet straightest path on the roadway. Trails require even more practice for the feet. Feet that are unaccustomed to the constant change in surface will be in for a rough time when the runner first hits the trail.

Lastly, a word about mileage. High mileage runners have far fewer blister problems than those who run less. They simply condition their feet with the constant daily grind of miles. Surely, there are hazards to big mileage, but a toughened foot is one benefit. Elite runners quite often do not bother changing shoes or socks during a race; they cannot afford the time if they are competing for a top finish.

Plantar Fasciitis

Plantar fasciitis begins with an ache at the heel, which usually comes and goes, depending on the time of day, and how much running one does. Eventually, the pain becomes even more prevalent. It is often worse in the morning, when the underside of the foot has been immobilized while sleeping and the tissue has tightened, or when first beginning a run.

The plantar fascia is a thick, fibrous sheet of tissue on the underside of the foot, which attaches to the heel bone. It is this sheet of tissue that gives the foot its characteristic arch. When the tissue becomes sore and swollen, it is called plantar fasciitis. Often plantar fasciitis results from the pulling forces on the plantar fascia, where it directly attaches to the heel bone. This can cause severe pain. The pain often worsens over time, and may eventually lead to heel spurs, due to formation of bone at the attachment of the plantar fascia to the heel. Running, which requires full weight bearing on the foot, and is extremely repetitive, is one of the most common sports in which plantar fasciitis occurs.

Check your running shoes! Seek out a sports podiatrist who has experience in dealing with runners and consult with a qualified running store, one that might help determine if the shoe you are using is the right one for you. Examine the width of the shoe and its arch support. Most running shoes have better arch supports than street shoes. Ask a podiatrist or running store specialist if an insert might help. Over the counter inserts might be beneficial and are often inexpensive.

There may be a need to be fitted with orthotics, inserts which are designed to stabilize weak or ineffective foot positioning. It is a more costly solution, but orthotics can correct a fair number of the footstrike problems encountered by runners. Many ultrarunners wear soft or hard orthotics. I would defer to your own trusted podiatrist's judgment as to which is best for you; but if they do fix the problem, they will become one of your more prized possessions.

What about surgery for plantar fasciitis? As with most sport injuries, surgery is usually a last resort, only after other treatments have failed. In rare cases, when rest, physiotherapy, home exercise, and anti-inflammatory medications are unable to relieve the symptoms, some runners may opt for surgery. Surgical treatment usually involves simply cutting the fascia, so that no stress is placed on the junction between the fascia and the heel bone. This will often leave the athlete more "flat footed" than before, but it may significantly relieve the pain. Due to possible complications from any kind of surgery, this should be done only after exhausting all other possible remedies.

Black Toenails

Black toenails normally result from the impact of the toe with the front or the top of the shoe. The greater the distance run, the more likely there will be the trauma to the toe. Downhill running, especially evident in trail running, is another contributing factor. Those sharp, steep hills so common in trail running are very hard on the toes. Jamming toes against the front of the shoe is a difficult thing to avoid in trail ultras.

Another factor may be the size of your shoes. It is very important to have properly fitting shoes. Runners should have their shoe size measured frequently, as feet can expand with years, even as middle-aged adults. You should also wait until mid-day before trying on new shoes, as your feet tend to expand during the day. One of the most important factors when selecting the right shoe is the toe box. Most podiatrists recommend a high toe-boxed shoe. The toe box varies greatly from brand to brand. It is simply a matter of trying on a variety of brands and finding the one that best fits your type of foot. Remember, the size and form of feet varies greatly among individuals.

Treatments for black toenails vary as well. First and foremost is prevention. Cutting toenails as short as possible is a good start. It is almost inevitable, however, that at one time or another you will encounter a black toenail. I have had them on occasion. Luckily, they caused me little or no problem. My own treatment is to let them take care of themselves. The toes are extremely resilient and sometimes the best policy is to keep hands off, letting nature take its course.

However, if the pressure underneath the toe (blocked up blood) is bothersome, it is possible to drain it yourself. One method is to heat a paper clip so that it is almost red. Then apply it to the toenail, actually melting a hole through the toenail, opening a hole for the blood to ooze out. It is painless, as the nail has no nerves. You have to be careful that you do not go too far through the nail. Black toenails can become thick and cause increasing pressure. In this case, it will be necessary to continually trim, clip and file the toenail to minimize its size and lessen the discomfort.

Another possible solution, one that a podiatrist may recommend, is to have the toenail surgically removed, which eliminates the problem forever. I had one toenail removed a few years ago and have not missed it at all. In fact, some people have even thought about having them all removed. The downside to this solution is that it must be removed by a doctor and they usually recommend not running for a few days to a couple of weeks. It also can be painful, so a local anesthetic is required.

Pronation and Supination

While watching other runners in action, one of the first things you notice is their gaits. Watch the legs and how the foot strikes the ground. It seems that each of us has our own "signature" gait. Many of us strike the ground and land on the inside of the foot, causing much of the weight to fall toward the inner side of the foot. It is a sure sign of weak or "fallen" arches. Pronation causes very uneven wear in running shoes, particularly on the inside edges of the bottom sole.

Pronation is fairly common in runners, to varying degrees. Excessive pronation can lead to arch, leg and back pain. For this reason it is important to monitor wear on the bottom of the shoe. Have someone who is experienced in running styles watch you run from behind. If you have problems, buy shoes that have greater support on the medial edges. Shoes come with many different features; those with support for pronation are readily available.

Supination means that you are landing with too much of your weight on the outer side of the foot. It is basically the opposite of pronation; but it too can create problems if neglected. Supinators wear down the entire outside edge of the sole of the shoe, and thus are susceptible to knee problems. Again, consult with an experienced running shoe specialist or ask a podiatrist for a recommendation.

Select the Right Shoes!

In the case of the previous four problems (there are others, such as Morton's foot, bunions, hammer toes and excess calluses), a critical preventive measure becomes the selection of proper running shoes. The right shoe can make a huge difference in how well you run. The wrong shoe can lead to injury. Understanding your stride, the foot strike, and basic bodily makeup will help in the shoe selection process.

It is most important to find a running store specialist. They see all types of runners and get constant feedback. A specialist will be able to assist you in shoe fitting and answer questions about the specific features of any given shoe. Remember though, there are few running stores that understand ultrarunning. They may be able to help you find the best fit, but they might not be able to relate to the aspect of running 100 miles through all types of off-road terrain. Thankfully, many manufacturers make trail shoes; you should be able to find them in most major running stores or mail order establishments.

Almost all ultrarunners spend the majority of their running time in training shoes. Only a small minority wear racing flats. Training shoes usually last anywhere from 500 to 1,000 miles. The outer sole wear is the first thing to watch. Abnormal wear in specific areas indicates a potential problem. Bring in your old pair of shoes when looking for a new pair. Shock absorption in the midsole starts to break down fairly quickly, often as fast, if not faster, than outer sole wear. If you have problems with bruises in the foot, then look for softer shoes. If your structural mechanics are unbalanced or you are heavier than the normal runner, you may want to avoid the softer models (this includes air soles). The toe box, as mentioned earlier, is critical to the ultrarunner. Keep in mind that swelling can occur in the later stages in an ultra and this only exacerbates the problems with the toes.

Flexibility is greater in racing flats than training shoes. As ultrarunners, you will probably want a more rigid, firm feel that will give you more support over the miles. If you are a stable runner with great mechanics (stride), then a lighter training shoe (or racing flat) will work. I happen to be one of those runners blessed with good stability in my running form; because of this, I can run in a racing flat during road ultras.

I do, however, follow a rule: I always run (racing an ultra) in a new pair, in order to obtain the best shock absorption possible. Too many runners log too many miles on their shoes. If they used a relatively "new pair" of shoes when running ultras, they would have better support and shock absorption. Your body will appreciate this and you will recover faster than if you wear an older, more worn pair of shoes. Try running your ultras in shoes with no more than ten percent of their life used. If you normally put 500 miles on a pair, than try to run ultras in a pair that has no more than 50 miles of wear. They will be plenty worn in, yet still have the better part of their shock absorption capability. Also, the outer sole will still be in fine shape.

It is a good practice to rotate your shoes, making sure to number them sequentially. This gives them a chance to dry out and allows you to use different shoes for different purposes. Gradually phase out the older pairs with the newer ones. I limit my racing flats to about 100 miles total, usually retiring them to track or speed workouts after one ultra. Racing flats have a shorter life span, as the midsoles break down faster than heavier training models. The vast majority of ultrarunners, however, are best served with a well cushioned training shoe that is relatively new when running an ultra distance. Only experience will tell if you have the right shoe for the distance and terrain you are running.

In summary, taking care of your feet is one of the keys to success in ultrarunning. Understand your footstrike, your stride mechanics and consult with an experienced running shoe specialist to find the shoe that best fits you. If you are prone to foot related problems, seek out a podiatrist who works with runners or specializes in sports-related injuries.

Components of Blister Prevention
by Jon Vonhof

Tim Noakes, M.D., in his book *The Lore of Running*, states his sixth law of running injuries, "Treat the cause, not the effect." He then goes on to talk about cause and cure. "Because each running injury has a cause, it follows that the injury can never be cured until the causative factors are eliminated." We who run ultras should heed his advice and start treating blisters as injuries. The problem we most often experience, the one that drives us crazy, costs us time, and in some cases unfulfilled dreams, is blisters.

In doing research for my book, *Fixing Your Feet*, the real eye-openers for me were these four findings:

- The extent of the problems so many runners have with their feet.
- That so many of these runners naturally expect to have problems, because what has worked for them in the past no longer works.
- What they see other runners do with their feet does not work for them.
- They do not know what options they have to fix their feet.

In light of these findings, what works? Will it work for you if it works for me? Blister prevention works through a combination of components that we will explore briefly. Each of these components may work alone or in combination with other components. We each must learn how to keep our own feet healthy and prevent blisters.

To understand blister formation, imagine a triangle with heat, friction, and moisture at its three sides. These three factors combine to make the skin more susceptible to blisters. Heat and moisture, in the presence of friction, lead to blisters. Dr. David Hannaford, a podiatrist who has twice earned the coveted silver buckle at Western States, stresses, "If you eliminate any one of the three factors, you eliminate the blister."

The triangle with these three factors—heat, friction, and moisture—sits on a base that has two levels. Each level of the base is a circle made up of components that can prevent these three factors from forming. Closest to the triangle is a top inner circle with the components of socks, powders, and lubricants. These three components form the first line of defense against blisters. Friction, which produces heat, can be reduced by wearing a sock with wicking properties—either alone or with an outer sock—or by using powders or lubricant. Moisture can be reduced with the wicking properties of certain socks and by using powders to keep the feet dry.

Socks are made of either single or double-layered construction. Some single-layered socks, particularly cotton or those without wicking properties, allow friction to develop between the feet and the socks, which in turn can create blisters. Double-layered socks allow the sock layers to move against each other, which reduces friction between the feet and the first sock layer. Most double-layered socks provide wicking properties. Newer socks that offer a blend of fabrics can increase wicking, are softer, and can help reduce blister formation.

Powders reduce friction by reducing moisture on the skin, which in turn reduces friction between the feet and the socks. Dry skin is more resistant to blister formation than skin softened by moisture. Some powders can cake up and cause blisters. Good powders will absorb many times their weight in moisture.

Lubricants create a shield, either greasy or non-greasy, to areas of the skin that are in contact during motion. This lubricant shield reduces chafing, which in turn reduces friction. Some lubricants may not work on your feet, but may work on other parts of your body. Any lubricant or powder must be reapplied at regular intervals in order to be effective.

At the bottom of the triangle base is an outer circle made up of components that play a strong supporting role in preventative maintenance. This outer circle is made up of several components, including skin tougheners, taping, orthotics, nutrition for the feet, proper hydration, antiperspirants for the feet, gaiters, laces, and frequent sock and shoe changes. Each can contribute to the prevention of blisters and other problems. You could argue that these outer components should be identified as major components. To some this may be true. Some components may be more important for particular individuals. The trick is to determine what we each need to keep our feet healthy under the stresses of our particular sport. Here are some of the components that comprise healthy feet, discussed in detail.

- Skin tougheners form a coating to protect and toughen. Most of these products also help tape and blister patches adhere better to the skin.
- Taping provides a barrier between the skin and socks so that friction is reduced. Proper taping prevents hot spots and blisters and adds an extra layer of skin (the tape) to the foot in problem areas. Improper taping can cause problems when the tape rolls and slides around on the foot. Learning how to tape your feet and what tape to use can be a lifesaver. I still thank Nancy Crawford for teaching me how to

duct tape my feet when I developed blisters 12 hours into the Gibson Ranch 72 Hour Run. Taping can also be a treatment if hot spots and blisters do develop.

- Orthotics help maintain the foot in a functionally neutral position so that arch and pressure problems are relieved. Small pads for the feet may also help correct foot imbalances and pressure points. Reducing these pressure points will help in reducing blisters.
- Nutrition for the feet includes creams and lotions so that dry and callused feet are softened. The result is softer and smoother skin, more resistant to blisters.
- Proper hydration can help reduce swelling of the feet, often common after hours of running, so the occurrence of hot spots and blisters is reduced. This means proper hydration, not just being well hydrated. Ultrarunner Jason Hodde notes that "As extra fluid accumulates in the tissues of the feet, from being well hydrated yet having low sodium, the likelihood of blister formation increases. When you become fluid deficient, the skin loses its normal levels of water and loses its turgor. Then it easily rubs or folds over on itself which leads to blisters." Karl King has studied the effects of low electrolyte and sodium levels in runners and developed the SUCCEED! Electrolyte Caps that are used by many runners.
- Antiperspirants for the feet help those with sweaty feet by reducing the moisture that makes the feet more prone to blisters.
- Gaiters provide protection against dirt, rocks, and grit. These irritants cause friction and blisters as shoes and socks become dirty. Gaiters have been proven as functional running gear that all dedicated trail runners should wear.
- Shoelaces often cause friction or pressure problems. Adjusting laces can relieve friction and pressure over the instep and make footwear more comfortable.
- Frequent sock changes help keep the feet in good condition. Wet or moist shoes and socks can cause problems as the skin softens, maceration occurs, and skin layers separate. Changing socks also provides an opportunity to reapply either powder or lubricant and deal with any hot spots before they become blisters.
- Something as simple as a crew member removing your shoes at an aid station can cause problems. Be sure your crew knows to untie your shoes and gently work them off your feet. Using a shoe horn

to put them back on can avoid putting additional pressure on hot spots and treated blisters.

Each runner needs to find what combination of these components works for them. Tim Twietmeyer has won the grueling Western States 100 Mile several times while accumulating more silver belt buckles for sub-24 hour finishes than any other runner. A week before running a 100-mile trail ultra Tim trims his toenails as short as possible. The morning of the run he coats his feet with lanolin to reduce friction, provide warmth if running in snow or through water, and make his skin more resilient to getting all wrinkled. Then he pulls on a pair of Thorlo Ultrathin socks. His strategy is, "The more sock you wear, the more moisture close to the foot. The more moisture, the more blisters and skin problems." He usually wears the same pair of shoes and socks the entire way. Tim acknowledges "My feet don't usually have problems, and when they do, I'm close enough to the end to gut it out."

We also need to understand the importance of other factors that contribute to preventative maintenance. Proper strength training and conditioning will help make the foot and ankle stronger and more resistant to sprains and strains. Quality insoles and orthotics can help prevent or relieve problems such as plantar fasciitis, Achilles tendinitis, heel pain, metatarsalgia, Morton's neuroma, Morton's foot, sesamoiditis, corns, and bunions. Properly fitting footwear will help prevent problems with toenails, arches, and blisters. In short, everything you put on or around your foot becomes related to how well your foot functions. We would be wise to heed the words of late ultrarunner, Dick Collins, who said, "Anything other than socks on (his) feet over time becomes an irritant."

Dealing with blisters before they develop is being proactive. Taking a proactive approach will mean less time being reactive to problems when you often do not have the time to spare nor readily available materials. The choice is yours. This means that before the competition we each must find what works best for our feet in order to manage them during the race. Dave Scott put it into proper perspective when he said, "When you do not take care of your feet during a long run or race, each step becomes a reminder of your ignorance."

It's All in Your Head—Or is it?

By Rick Lovett, courtesy of *New Scientist*

Timothy Noakes will never forget the day he encountered the hill from hell. It was 1976 and he was running in the grueling Comrades Marathon, an annual 90-kilometer road race between Durban and Pietermaritzburg in South Africa. About 20 kilometers from home he rounded a bend and saw a steep incline he hadn't known was there. Even before he started climbing, he suddenly began to feel overwhelmingly tired. At the time it was just a case of gritting his teeth. But Noakes, a professor of exercise physiology at the University of Cape Town, South Africa, soon came to see that hill as an intellectual mountain, too. Why had the very thought of it made him feel so tired?

Conventional wisdom on muscle fatigue can't explain what happened that day. For the better part of a century, scientists and athletes have presumed, not unreasonably, that fatigue originates in the muscles themselves. Precise explanations have varied, but all have been based on the "limitations theory." In other words, muscles tire because they hit a physical limit: they either run out of fuel or oxygen or they drown in toxic byproducts.

In the past few years, however, Noakes and his colleague Alan St Clair Gibson have taken a hard look at the standard theory. The deeper they dig, the more convinced they have become that physical fatigue simply isn't the same as a car running out of fuel. Fatigue, they argue, is caused not by distress signals springing from overtaxed muscles, but is an emotional response which begins in the brain.

The essence of their new theory is that the brain, using a mix of physiological, subconscious and conscious cues, paces the muscles to keep them well back from the brink of exhaustion. When the brain decides it's time to quit, it creates the distressing sensations we interpret as unbearable muscle fatigue. This "central governor" theory remains controversial, but it does explain many puzzling aspects of athletic performance, as well as suggesting some revolutionary approaches to training and offering tantalizing hints as to the cause and maybe even the cure of chronic fatigue syndrome.

The "hill from hell" might have set Noakes thinking about fatigue, but it was a more recent discovery that made him start researching it in earnest. He calls this the "lactic acid paradox." Lactic acid is a byproduct of exercise, and its buildup is often cited as a cause of fatigue. But when research subjects exercise in a decompression chamber designed to simulate high altitude, they become fatigued even though lactic acid levels remain low. Nor has the oxygen content of their blood fallen too low for them to keep going. Obviously, Noakes deduced, something else was making them tire well before they hit either physiological limit.

Noakes and St Clair Gibson decided to probe further. For their first study, published in 2001 (*American* Journal *of Physiology-Regulatory Integrative and Comparative Physiology,* vol 281, p R187), they recruited seven experienced cyclists and asked them to pedal 100-kilometer time trials on stationary exercise bikes. On several occasions during the time trial, they asked the cyclists to sprint for 1,000 or 4,000 meters. Throughout the experiment, the cyclists wore electrical sensors taped to their legs to measure the nerve impulses traveling to their muscles.

It has long been known that during exercise, the body never uses 100 percent of the available muscle fibers in a single contraction. The amount used varies with the length of the endeavor, but in endurance tasks such as the cycling test the body calls on about 30 percent, spreading the load by rotating in fresh ones as needed. And because separate nerve filaments send signals to each fiber, sports scientists can determine what fraction of the muscle is being used by measuring the electrical impulse traveling to it.

Noakes reasoned that if the limitations theory was correct and fatigue was due to muscle fibers hitting some limit, the number of fibers used for each pedal stroke should increase as the fibers tired and the cyclist's body attempted to compensate by recruiting an ever-larger fraction of the total But his team found exactly the opposite. As fatigue set in, the electrical activity in the cyclists' legs declined—even during the sprints, when they were striving to cycle as fast as they could.

Plenty in the tank

To Noakes, this was strong evidence that the old theory was wrong. The cyclists may have felt completely done in, he says, but their bodies actually had considerable reserves that they could theoretically tap into by using a greater fraction of the resting fibers. This, he believes, is proof that the brain is regulating the pace of the workout to hold the cyclists well back from the point of catastrophic exhaustion.

More evidence comes from the fact that fatigued muscles don't actually run out of anything critical. Muscle biopsies have shown that levels of glycogen, which is the muscles' primary fuel, and ATP, the chemical they use for temporary energy storage, decline with exercise but never bottom out. Even at the end of a marathon, ATP levels are 80 to 90 per cent of the resting norm. And while glycogen levels approach zero, they never get there. Post-marathon muscles also still have substantial reserves of other fuels, notably fat.

Still more evidence in favor of the central regulator comes from observations of the closing stages of distance races. Top athletes almost always manage to go their fastest (or at least faster) during the last kilometer of a race, even though, theoretically, that's when their muscles should be closest to exhaustion. In particular, Noakes says, the final sprint makes no sense if fatigue is caused by muscles poisoning themselves with lactic acid. If lactic acid buildup is the limiting factor, racers would progressively slow down and they would find it impossible to sprint for the finish line. But with the central governor theory, the explanation is obvious. Knowing the end is near, the brain slightly relaxes its vigil and allows the athlete to tap a bit of the body's carefully hoarded reserves.

The central governor theory however, does not mean that what's happening in the muscles is irrelevant. The governor constantly monitors physiological signals from the muscles, along with other information, to set the level of fatigue. A large number of signals are probably involved, but the ones Noakes is most sure about include the body's remaining stores of carbohydrates, the levels of glucose and oxygen in the blood, the rates of heat generation and heat loss, and the rate at which muscles are working. Where the central governor theory differs from the limitations theory is that these physiological factors are not the direct determinants of fatigue—they are just information to take into account.

Conscious factors can also intervene. Noakes believes that the central regulator evaluates the planned workout, and sets a pacing strategy accordingly. Experienced runners know, for example, that if they set out on a 10-kilometer training run, the first kilometer feels mysteriously easier than the first kilometer of a five-kilometer run, even though there should be no difference. That, Noakes says, is because the central governor knows you have farther to go in the longer run and has programmed itself to dole out fatigue symptoms accordingly.

This can be verified by putting people on treadmills and telling them they're going to run one distance, when in fact you have another planned. When the subjects are given the real story midway through the test, their reported levels of fatigue suddenly adjust to account for the new information. It also explains Noakes's experience on the hill from hell. "The central governor had been pacing me for another 20 kilometers," he says, "but it had presumed it was going to be flat. Now, it suddenly had to take the hill into account, and it forced me to slow down."

St Clair Gibson believes there is a good reason why our bodies are designed to keep something back. That way, there's always something left in the tank for an emergency. In ancient times, an emergency might take the form of a lion or pack of wolves at the end of a long, grueling hunt. Today, the "wolf" might be a mugger hiding In an alley, or a lightning storm near the end of a long hike. But the same concept applies: life would be too dangerous if our bodies allowed us to become so tired that we couldn't move quickly when faced with an unexpected need.

Drugs and hypnosis

The team also believes the central governor theory helps to explain why hypnosis helps block sensations of fatigue, allowing athletes to work harder. If fatigue were merely the result of reaching the muscles' physiological limits, this shouldn't be possible. But it is. Amphetamines have a similar effect, and again it could be due to the central governor. Blocking the sensation of fatigue with drugs, however, makes it much easier to work yourself to death. Normally, fatigue will force even the most iron-willed competitor to quit before they succumb to heatstroke, but this didn't happen for the British cyclist Tom Simpson, who died after taking amphetamine during the Tour de France in 1967, the year before drug tests started. Ecstasy, Noakes adds is an amphetamine-like substance that could have the same effect on young party-goers.

The theory could also help to unravel the mystery of chronic fatigue syndrome. Perhaps something has interfered with the brain's regulation of fatigue so that you always feel exhausted even though you are not. Successfully puzzling out the workings of the central governor theory might open the door to a long-awaited cure, Noakes suggests.

St Clair Gibson and Noakes are presently trying to find where the central governor is located in the brain by studying the electroencephalograms (EEGs) of tiring cyclists. "We're finding that a lot of areas of the brain are involved," St Clair Gibson says, "but we haven't yet found the stop switch." However, the mix of such areas is interesting, and includes the frontal lobe (which is involved in decision making), the parietal lobe (which is involved in sensation), and, for some reason, the visual and speech centers. The central governor theory has found favor with other exercise physiologists. You feel exhausted, but if a life-threatening danger suddenly appeared you would find the energy to run.

George Brooks at the University of California, Berkeley, for example, recently amended his textbook to include it. But for some it remains controversial. One critic is Jere Mitchell, a cardiologist at the University of Texas Southwestern Medical Center, Dallas. He points to treadmill tests in which people run up ever-steeper slopes while having their oxygen consumption measured. Shortly before the subjects collapse in exhaustion, their oxygen consumption reaches a plateau beyond which it won't increase, no matter how hard they try to work.

This maximum rate of oxygen consumption, VO2 max, can be boosted by increasing the number of red blood cells in circulation—for example, by re-injecting blood that was taken several weeks earlier. This proves that fatigue has nothing to do with any central governor, Mitchell argues. Instead, it kicks in at the point at which the body has bumped into a very real physiological limit the amount of oxygen the blood can transport. Peter Wagner of the University of California, San Diego, concurs. He has conducted treadmill tests in which athletes are tested under two different conditions: on normal air, and on pure oxygen. That is enough to produce an eight to ten-percent increase in the amount of oxygen going to the muscles, he says, producing a measurable increase the V02 max In well-trained athletes.

Noakes and St Clair Gibson, however, argue that the central governor theory can explain both studies. The brain, they say, senses the elevated amount of oxygen in the blood and then "resets" the pace to allow the athlete to work harder, while still maintaining a reserve. "So there is a ceiling of oxygen use," says St Clair Gibson, "but at a level decided by the brain, with a wide margin of reserve for error."

If the central governor theory does prove to be correct, can coaches use it to improve athletes' performance? Noakes's experience in the Comrades Marathon underscores the importance of knowing the course beforehand, particularly its later stages. Top athletes and coaches figured that one out many years ago. In fact, says Brooks, trainers are often ahead of the science. "Coaches, by experience, have discovered things which scientists take longer to understand," he says. But Noakes argues that the central governor theory helps make sense of interval training, a "sharpening" technique in which athletes do repetitive bouts of high-intensity exercise interspersed with recovery breaks.

In a recent experiment, Noakes took a group of cyclists who had never done intervals before and asked them to add them to their normal training, once or twice a week for six weeks. At the end of this program, the cyclists, who were fast recreational riders but not professional racers, had shaved a startling 15 minutes, or approximately 10 percent, off their previous times on a 100-kilometer time trial.

Similarly dramatic improvements are often observed when runners are introduced to interval training. Traditional theory says that the improvement is due to physiological changes in the muscle cells that make them better able to use oxygen or tolerate the buildup of metabolic waste products. But Noakes doesn't see how major physiological improvements can occur so quickly. And in any case, he says, interval training seems to induce very little, if any, biochemical change in the muscle. He believes that interval training works largely by teaching the central governor that going faster won't do you any harm.

Perhaps, then, the central governor idea can be used to give athletes an important mental edge. Simply telling them that even when they are feeling completely exhausted their bodies actually have a lot in reserve should provide an incredible psychological boost, says St Clair Gibson. "When athletes know that," he says, "it's going to be exciting."

Now I Lay Me Down to Sleep
by Gary Cantrell

At last, the bottom was falling out. After 21 hours of unbroken effort, with some 92 miles of running behind me, my long coveted 24-hour 100-mile race was in serious jeopardy. What was going to bring me down? Not my training: I was in the best shape of my life. Not the weather: I had already made it through the sub-freezing night; now the sun was re-warming my aching bones. Not even my legs: I had passed beyond the reach of cramps and pain hours before. No, none of those old familiar problems were going to get me. Rather, it was sleep that had come to terminate my try for a lifetime best.

I tried to struggle on, but even in motion (with my eyes open) my brain had reached a point of shutdown. Repeatedly my thoughts slipped into a dream state until reality was almost indistinguishable from dreams. Each time I would slow to a virtual halt before snapping back to consciousness. Soon it became painfully evident that if I continued this rate I would fail to break 24 hours.

Fortunately for me, the observations and experiences of multi-day running provided the key to salvaging my race. I headed to my tent and rousted my handler/spouse from the cot. "Wake me in 15 minutes, not a minute later." "You can't give up now. If you stop you will never get back up." "If I don't stop I won't make it in time." Face down on the cot I went, asleep even before my head touched the pillow.

It seemed instantaneous that a terrible, screeching pain, arising simultaneously in both knees and hips, awakened me. My first thought was that my handler had forgotten my time instructions. A glance at my watch told me I had been down a total of 12 minutes. I staggered to my feet and exited the tent (meeting my wake up call on the way out). Returning to the track, I found that my last little reserve was waiting and I easily cranked through the final eight miles to reach 100 in 23:04. For many runners that might be an average effort; for me it was a personal best that might last forever. But for my hard-earned knowledge about sleep, I would have fallen short.

The limitations imposed by sleep are subject to as wide a variation as those imposed by speed. For some runners, multi-day efforts must be done at high speed, due to an absolute inability to endure sleep deprivation. The human brain is perfectly capable of enforcing sleep, as happened to me in the race just mentioned. A handful of runners can either transcend the need for sleep (over astonishing periods of time) or can literally sleep on their feet. The vast majority of us fall somewhere in between.

While individual sleep requirements do force certain concessions upon us, much can be done to minimize the ultimate impact. Sleep limitations differ from speed limitations, in that we cannot train for them, but rather must rely on knowledge of the parameters of these limitations to overcome them.

The temptation to attempt to train ourselves to do without sleep comes with the nature of our sport. The belief that work and sacrifice are the keys to success is at the very foundation of our ultra mentality. However, just as we never push into certain levels of effort in training because we do not want to "go to the well" until it counts (since you only are allotted so many successful trips), the same applies to sleep. Self-denial of sleep is a serious manner and should be reserved for the races.

Altering your circadian rhythm for a race is a different matter. We all are slaves to the daily patterns of sleep and wakefulness, and at certain times we simply cannot resist sleep. The flexibility of this pattern is highly individual and the runner who intends to change sleep cycles had better practice the technique before it is needed in a race setting. Usually this is done for one of two reasons. The first is to move the "crash phase" of a 24-hour or 100-mile as close to the finish as possible. The other is to allow for night running in a hot weather multi-day. The technique is easy: Somewhere between a day and a week before the race, simply change bedtimes. For me one day is adequate to make the shift. That shift was why I crashed at 21 hours, well into the morning, instead of halfway through the event.

Most people need three to four days to successfully alter their cycle. In normal life we all seek an optimum amount of sleep that leaves us mentally and physically up to the daily demands of life. During races we aim to restrict ourselves to the absolute minimum amount of sleep on which we can survive. As a rule that will be roughly half the normal amount, although it can be less. Several methods exist for reducing even that limitation. I have found that in any individual sleep episode, any time over two hours actually has a negative impact on my returning pace. The popular theory is that sleep beyond a minimum level allows healing to begin, drawing your body's resources away from continued motion. Since that is insupportable as a daily average sleep, I compensate by running a schedule below 24 hours so that I can maintain that healthy three-hour average during the body of the race.

At the end of a multi-day, or after a 24-hour, or 100-mile, we wish to eliminate sleep to the maximum extent possible. That is when it comes in handy to realize that *falling* asleep is the critical factor when you hit that must-sleep phase. It seems that the brain lacks the ability to time sleep. While the failure to complete enough sleep will catch up eventually, you can buy a reprieve from enforced sleepiness by merely falling asleep, then getting up almost immediately. That is why I threw my handler out of bed and took a 12-minute nap. While it fixed me up for the last little stretch of the race, I crashed big-time within six hours after the race. Of course, at that point, I didn't care,

I would not advise just showing up at your next race planning to sleep exactly by my schedule. The odds of it working for you are small, but if you use the same principles and engage in a little pre-race experimentation to discover your own sleep guarantees, then you can plug in your customized times to the same techniques and squeeze every last drop out of yourself. Sweet dreams!

3

Making History

Like many sports, ultrarunning is rife with lore and history. Through the ages, legend has built up surrounding the characters and events that have woven an intricate story and laid the building blocks on which we all currently learn from and rely upon. It often seems as if the sport is just getting started, as growth in numbers is currently as strong as it has ever been. We learn from the historians of ultrarunning that this is simply not the case. The sport dates back not years or decades, but centuries.

Andy Milroy is the ultimate ultrarunning historian; he contributes several articles to this section. Milroy points out that the first ultramarathons were contested by the ancient Greeks, and in the late 20th century, it is another Greek born runner who has revolutionized the sport, Yiannis Kouros. In between Kouros and his ancestors is a wonderful history. Milroy delves back into ancient Greek times to challenge the legend of Pheidippides and the run from Marathon to Athens. You'll be interested to hear what he has determined to be the real story.

The 19th century was a grand time for ultrarunning. While six-day races flourished in the late 1800s, it was not only men who competed. There was also a subculture of all-female races. "The Pedestriennes," examines just why it was that women, who had not yet been given the right to vote or run longer than 800 meters in the Olympics, were performing Herculean feats such as covering hundreds of miles in a 144-hour period.

One of true characters in the history of ultrarunning was Captain Barclay. Living in an era when long-distance endurance events were almost unheard of, Barclay was literally larger than life and his legend has grown throughout the years. His performances would still rank among the elite nearly two centuries later. Andy Milroy provides a look into the life of Captain Barclay.

The lure to run from one side of a country to another has been around as long as there have been national borders. Dan Brannen's story of the "Bunioneers," a hardy group of men who raced across the U.S. in 1928 and 1929 is a fascinating account, one that reflects the socioeconomic conditions that existed at the time. Run 3,000 miles for a few dollars? There were many that did. A few decades later an end-to-end race in Britain was held. Andy Milroy tells the story of this race, one that was riddled with accusations of cheating. This race account, too, shows us that it even in ultrarunning, it is not always possible to escape societal ills.

Pheidippides—Marathoner or Ultramarathoner?
by Andy Milroy

This is the age of the marathon and to much of the general public, any road race from 10 km to 50 miles is a "marathon." The word has permeated everyday language to such an extent that any long drawn-out activity is now colloquially described as a "marathon." All this comes from the fact that an ancient Greek runner ran from Marathon to Athens and then collapsed and died. Or did he?

The famous legend that gave rise to the idea of the modern marathon is that a runner called Pheidippides was said to have run from Athens to Sparta to ask for help against the invading Persian armies. It was the year 490 B.C. and the Persian king was determined to crush the Greek city-states that had been supporting Grecian enclaves, resisting his role within his empire. The Spartans were unwilling to help the Athenians for religious reasons, so Pheidippides returned to Athens before joining the Athenian army on its journey to Marathon. The Athenians won the Battle of Marathon against the Persians and Pheidippides was sent to carry the message back to Athens. Upon reaching the city, the exhausted runner could only gasp out the words, "Rejoice, we conquer," before he collapsed and died. It was this legend that inspired Pierre de Coubertin, founder of the modern Olympics, to include a race from Marathon to Athens in the first Olympics in 1896. So much for the myth. But what is the truth? Was there really a Pheidippides? Who was he? What did he actually do?

The runner seems to have been a real person, but his name was probably not Pheidippides at all, but rather Philippides, which in ancient Greek means "the son of a lover of horses." Later Greek writers may have thought such a name was unsuitable for one of Greece's great heroes and changed it slightly.

The great Greek historian, Herodotus, recorded some details about the runner. He says that the Athenian generals, before setting out for the Battle of Marathon, sent "a herald, Philippides, an Athenian, a hemerodromes and an expert at it . . . . After being sent at this time by the generals, this Philippides reached Sparta on the second day out from Athens."

Philippides was therefore a hemerodromoi, which in ancient Greek means a "day runner," a runner who would run for a day or more. Such runners were used as messengers over the mountainous terrain of Greece. According to legend, "They were young men but recently out of their childhood, like those that wear their first downy growth of beard. Nought take they with them save bow and arrow, spear and sling, for these things are found to be of great service to their course." Such weapons would have been essential to ward off the wolves, wild bears and robbers that inhabited the Grecian Mountains then. It would seem likely that Philippides was older than most hemerodromoi because he is described as an expert.

He is said to have arrived at Sparta on the second day, that is, within 48 hours. The two cities were said by ancient Greeks to be some 1,200 stades apart (a stade being about 200 yards), which would be about 136.3 miles. Prior to a run from Athens to Sparta by a group of British Royal Air Force (RAF) runners, John Foden, helped by Colonel N. Hammond, a former Cambridge history professor, studied the possible routes taken by Philippides. (It was the RAF run that inspired the Spartathlon, which first took place over the same course in 1983.) Foden and Hammond took account of the writings of near contemporaries like Herodotus, and of the political relationships of the various Greek states, for several were allies of the Persians.

Their scenario for Philippides' run went something like this: He left Athens at daybreak and ran along the undulating Sacred Way to Eleusis, and then by way of the Coastal Scironian Way from Megara to Corinth. His journey would then have led him through fairly flat, fertile country, then along by the river through the Zapartis Valley. Rocky, stony paths followed, which would have led eventually to the top of the Parthenian mountain range. The remainder of his run is uncertain. He might have run across the hostile territory of Argos, but this would have meant taking in six ranges of foothills and five rivers, or perhaps taking a flatter but still undulating route before the final downhill to Sparta. Such a journey is reckoned by modern-day measurements to be some 155 miles. Philippides is reputed to have completed his run in less than 48 hours, probably in 41 to 42 hours—the time from sunrise on the first day to sunset on the second. That is far from impossible for an expert long distance runner, for all 15 finishers in the 1983 Spartathlon race over this course finished inside 36 hours.

Therefore, Philippides' run from Athens to Sparta would seem to be a matter of historical record. The same cannot be said for the dramatic tale of the runner's last journey on foot from Marathon to Athens and his subsequent death. Modern Greek scholars, having examined the various sources, have concluded that this is a later addition to the story. Herodotus, a near contemporary of Philippides, who lived from 484 to 425 B.C., would have been able to get information from elderly veterans of the Battle of Marathon. He does not mention Philippides, or anyone else running from Marathon to Athens. Not until 500 years later is the second run added to the story, and then only one of the writers says that it was Philippides who made the journey; others mention a Eucles and a Thersippus. It was not unknown for long distance runners to collapse and die after an arduous journey run. Woolley Morris and Gryffyd Morgan, two of the best British 10-mile runners of the 18th century, were two such fatalities. However, the demise of a runner after reaching his goal was not an uncommon addition to earlier Greek stories by writers retelling them in the Roman era. As well as the famous Marathon to Athens episode, a Euchidas was also said to have collapsed and died after a run from Platea to Delphi and back.

Thus it looks very much as if the whole story of the run from Marathon to Athens is just a late invention to add dramatic interest to a notable ultra distance run, and that the first run from Marathon to Athens took place not in 490 B.C. but in 1896 A.D.!

Thus, one of the first ultramarathon runners whose name has come down to us is Philippides, the Athenian. The modern ultrarunner follows a tradition of endurance that stretches back 2,500 years and beyond, to the nameless running messengers who journeyed on foot from one ancient city to another.

What of the much vaunted marathon? It was inspired by a run that never actually happened, and its legendary founding father would probably have disdained to run such an insignificant distance.

Captain Barclay: Nineteenth Century Super Ultrarunner

by Andy Milroy

Imagine a man capable of picking up a 250-pound man with one hand and placing him on a table. A man who was reputed to have walked 30 miles grouse shooting, then returned 60 miles home on foot to get on with his normal affairs, and who on the following day walked 16 miles to a dance and back, getting home at 7:00 a.m., and thereupon went partridge shooting. One hundred and twenty miles in 48 hours without sleep, just for fun. A man who is said to have driven a mail coach from London to Edinburgh in two days without giving up the reins for a single stage, only stopping for meals. Such a man was Robert Barclay Allardice, better known as Captain Barclay. It is hardly surprising that he was the most famous athlete of his day, perhaps of the whole of the 19th century.

Robert Allardice was born in August 1779, and his athletic career started a mere 17 years later. He entered a match to walk six miles in an hour, "fair heel and toe," for 100 guineas, which he won. He rapidly increased the distance of his wagers and three years later he successfully undertook the task of walking 150 miles in two days, from Fenchurch Street in London to Birmingham, by way of Cambridge. A few days later he returned to London, this time via Oxford, again in two days.

The following year Captain Barclay undertook his most important wager—he agreed to attempt to cover 90 miles in 21 and a half-hours for a bet of 500 guineas. A Mr. Fletcher, a well known sporting man, wagered against him and collected an easy 500 when Barclay caught a bad cold and could not start on the day appointed. Barclay was not discouraged and the following year he again wagered with Fletcher that he would complete the 90 miles within the alloted time. On this occasion the bet was for 2,000 guineas. The young Barclay reached 67 miles in 13 hours, but recklessly drank some brandy and became sick and conceded the bet. Unfortunately, after two hours rest he had recovered and could have easily completed the distance in the time left.

He still did not give up and decided to go into training. He undertook a time trial in very bad weather, with mud up to his ankles. Despite the conditions, he completed 110 miles in 19 hours and 27 minutes. Barclay decided he was ready. This time the bet was for 5,000 guineas. He and Fletcher arranged for a mile to be measured on the York-Hull road and a post was fixed. A pace and a half were needed to round the post, but this was not to be included in the distance. People were stationed at the post to note the rounds and ensure the feat was fairly performed. At 12:00 midnight on the ninth of November six stopwatches were set and put into a box, which was sealed. This was the signal for Barclay to start. He was never in difficulty and finished the 90 miles in 19:52:04.

In the next few years Captain Barclay proved that he was not only endowed with great stamina, but was a great all-around athlete, In 1802 he ran 440 yards in 56 seconds, and in 1804 he beat a swift runner, John Ireland, over a mile in 4:50. He also excelled at field events. Few men were able to match him at quoits, a discus type event, or at the Scottish heavy events of throwing the 56-pound weight both for distance and height. In the latter event he achieved 15 feet, which compares well with the current record of 17 feet, two inches.

However, it is his feats in ultra-distance events that are best remembered. His walking in these was not "fair heel and toe." It was accepted in those days for long-

Captain Barclay

distance walkers to run to ease cramps, so his progress would best be described as "go as you please." He can perhaps be regarded as a pioneer of the 100-km event, although he would not have realized that (the kilometer had only just been adopted by the French). In November 1800, he walked 64 miles (just under 103 km) in 12 hours in a time trial, and two years later covered the same distance, this time from Charing Cross to Newmarket, in ten hours for a wager. If the later time is correct, it was to be many years before the distance would again be performed at such a pace. In December 1806, he tackled 100 miles on what was reputed to be the worst road in the country. He went from his home at Ury (near Stonehaven) to Crathynaird (near Balmoral Castle) via Aboyne, then back again. He covered the first 28 miles to Aboyne in four hours, and then rested for ten minutes. He then proceeded to Crathynaird where he stayed for 50 minutes, before returning to Aboyne. He refreshed himself there for a half-hour before returning home, completing the whole distance in 19 hours. With him on his walk was his groom, William Cross, who was a noted pedestrian in his own right.

A 24-hour challenge

Barclay was also involved in what may have been the first 24-hour race. His opponent was the other great pedestrian of the period, Abraham Wood. Wood, of Mildrew in Lancashire, was the greatest long-distance runner of his day, being described not only as a swift runner, but also possessing "good wind and great bottom." He had run 20 miles in 2:05, and 40 miles in 4:56:30, the latter so quick that few horsemen could keep up with him. He had run without shoes or stockings, wearing just flannel drawers and a jacket.

When the match with Wood had first been proposed, Barclay refused, partly because Wood was a professional runner and partly because Wood had no one to put up big enough stakes. Eventually a publican came forward to back Wood with 150 guineas. The race was to be held on the Newmarket-London Turnpike. One mile was roped off and both competitors were to run on the same course. Barclay was to be allowed a 20-mile handicap and the match was for 600 guineas a side.

The event was looked forward to with great excitement. People poured into Newmarket the day before. All the inns were full and would-be spectators had to pay handsomely for accommodation, even in stables. In the weeks before the match, Wood had been the one-to-nine favorite, but just before the start Barclay had come to five-to-two in the betting.

At the start at 8:00 on the morning of October 12, 1807, both men were dressed similarly in flannel with no legs to their stockings. Wood went eight miles in the first hour, reaching 20 miles in 2:41. He had some refreshment at 24 miles, and then amid great controversy he resigned the match after covering 40 miles in 6:20. At that stage he had begun to make inroads into the 20 miles Barclay had been allowed. His retirement was apparently due to having been given laudanum by some "friends." His backer, the newspaper owner of the time, had never been known to wager 20 guineas before, let alone 150. On the day of the match he was putting money on Barclay to win, so it probably is not necessary to look too far to find the poisoner.

The whole unsavory episode cast a shadow over both men's reputations. Wood had been in very good form; he had gone 50 miles in seven hours in training in wet conditions before stopping while still fresh to avoid injury.

However, in the opinion of the experts of the time, it would have been very unlikely that Wood could have won. Remembering Barclay's walk in training for the third Fletcher match when he covered 110 miles in under 20 hours, they thought it probable that Barclay would cover 135 miles, thus forcing Wood to accomplish 155 miles to win, which would have been beyond him. Another match was arranged between the two men, but it never came off.

Before we look at Barclay's greatest feat, it is worth discovering how he trained. To start with, he benefited from the early conditioning that we now associate with African athletes. The runners of the early 19th century were used to traveling on foot from an early age, as it was only the favored few that could afford horses or coaches. It was said of Barclay himself that he preferred walking to any other means of transport and "except when hunting he is seldom on horseback." The training that Barclay underwent in preparation for his exploits was to be very influential and versions of it were used for more than a century. The athlete was first purged by drastic medicines, then he was sweated by walking under a load of clothes, and lying between feather beds his limbs were roughly rubbed. His diet consisted of beef or mutton, his drink strong ale, and he was gradually inured to exercise by repeated trials in walking and running. The sweating and time trials continued until the completion of training, and if considered necessary so were the purges. It is not surprising that one writer in 1890 commented, "Such training, if carried into effect, is calculated to send a man to his grave, rather than the cinder path." It is a testimony to Barclay's toughness that he thrived on such a regime. He took care over his dress for pedestrian contests. On his 90-mile walk he wore a flannel shirt, flannel trousers, and a nightcap, and took the time to change his clothes and refresh himself at intervals. He always took good care of his feet, shifting his woolen stockings frequently and wearing large, thick-soled shoes. His style of walking was economical, a sort of lounging gait, without apparently making any great effort, scarcely raising his feet more than two or three inches above the ground.

1,000 miles in 1,000 hours

On October 10, 1808, Captain Barclay made a match with Mr. Wedderburn Webster for 1,000 guineas to walk 1,000 miles in 1,000 successive hours. This may not seem a very arduous undertaking, but there was one condition that made it a very difficult feat—Barclay had to walk one mile in *each* and *every* hour for 41 and two-thirds days. Several famous pedestrians had attempted this exploit, to be defeated not only by the distance and the exertion, but by the lack of rest and sleep, which caused them to quit with swollen legs and loss of weight.

Barclay started the walk on June 1, 1809, on Newmarket Heath. The first 11 or 12 days proceeded without difficulty, but he began to get pains in his legs from the 13th day, slight at first, but gradually becoming increasingly painful. The bad pains in his legs were augmented by a toothache on the 23rd day, and by the 26th day he was very ill and very stiff. He found great difficulty in walking and complained much about the pain. By the 32nd day, after resting he could rise only with help, and he needed so much time to walk that he had little opportunity to rest. Two days later he could not move without crying out and walked in a shuffling manner, "and could not mend his pace if it had been to save his life." To have seen him on the 35th day, one would have thought it impossible to continue, he was so fatigued and in such agony. The spasmodic affections in his legs were particularly distressing. But Barclay was determined to finish. To show the state such stress can produce. Peter Van Ness, after finishing 1,718 half-miles (of the planned 2,000 in 2,000 half-hours) in 1879, shot his trainer in the arm and then fired at everyone he came in contact with before collapsing unconscious. He then went on to complete his task!

By the 41st day, it was clear that Barclay could not go on much longer, but fortunately his ordeal was to end the next day. A huge crowd was there at the finish to see him successfully complete the 1,000th mile in the 1,000th hour. The crowd was so large that it was necessary to rope off the ground and several pugilists who had been supported by Barclay to keep off roughs. His first mile had taken him 12 minutes. His last took 21. He had lost more than 35 pounds in weight, but he had won 16,000 pounds in wagers (which would be worth $360,000 nowadays). After the finish he had a bath and then slept for 17 hours, after which he got up and, free from pain, went for a long walk about Newmarket, including four hours on the race course!

The great pedestrians of this period—Foster Powell, Abraham Wood, and of course Barclay himself—did a great deal towards establishing many of the long distance events we know today. However, it was his 1,000-mile walk that was to be copied as often as any, with many variations. An exact repetition of his feat was called "a Barclay match." Wilson, Weston, and others attempted the 1,000-mile record; Eaton, Weston, and Gale tried to walk as far as possible in 1,000 hours. A few tough individuals attempted to repeat and surpass Barclay's actual feat: Richard Manks with one mile every half-hour for 1,000 miles, Peter Van Ness a half-mile every half-hour for 2,000 successive half hours, and William Gale one and a half miles every hour for 1,000 successive hours. Recently the "Barclay match" has been revived in Australia and England.

Captain Barclay's athletic career did not end with his epic walk—he was to run his last race in Hyde Park in 1813. The end of the great era of gentleman athletes competing for wagers was to follow soon after with the depression that marked the end of the Napoleonic Wars. Barclay was to live to see the next great age of long-distance endeavor in the 1840s. It is typical of the man that he would not succumb to the illness and old age that carry off most mortals—he died in 1854 at the age of about 75 after being kicked by a horse.

The Pedestriennes—Female Ultra Stars of the 19th Century

by Dahn Shaulis

Where the history of male ultrarunners from Pheidippides to the Bunion Derby races is long and fairly well known, the story of the distaff side is sparse and relatively obscure. One account that has been buried in running history is the story of the pedestriennes, female distance athletes who shared the sports scene with men from 1875 to 1896. While the great Edward Weston was walking for fame and fortune, women also competed in walking events held in the United States, Canada, England, Germany, and Australia.

The first contest in New York City in 1875 was more of a sideshow than a competition; in the "Monster Classical and Geological Hippodrome," William G. Harding defeated Madame Lola as part of a P. T. Barnum circus spectacle. But by 1876 indoor races became actual athletic contests, with hundreds and sometimes thousands of spectators on hand. In addition, betting made the races an exciting attraction.

The Second Regiment Armory in Chicago was the site of one of the first pedestrienne contests, pitting Bertha Von Hillern of Germany against Mrs. Mary Marshall. In the six-day battle, Marshall walked 234 miles to Von Hillern's 231 miles. The armory was crowded with paying spectators, but neither walker was able to complete the 300 miles necessary to take the $500 prize.

The rivalry between Von Hillern and Marshall continued at New York's Central Park Garden. Newspaper accounts of the contest included fashion statements about the pedestriennes. "Von Hillern was attired in a short yellow frock and blue jacket, with a jaunting Derby hat, and carrying a short riding-whip in her hand. Miss Marshall was dressed in somber brown and also wore a Derby hat, but carried no whip." Von Hillern won the six-day contest and $1,000, outdistancing Marshall, 323 miles to 281 miles. An editorial in the *New York Times* proclaimed the contest an initial step for women's rights, proclaiming, "The world moves, is moving. Today it is the walking match; next it will be the coveted entrance to the Bar. After that, who shall tell how soon the ballot will come."

A few days later, Mary Marshall affirmed this editorial by defeating Peter Van Ness in a series of 20-mile walks. Von Hillern continued walking, mostly solo against the clock, in Boston, Providence, Philadelphia, and Washington, D.C. The crowds were large, with 1,800 people at the close of her Philadelphia walk. At Oddfellows Hall in Washington, the spectators included "many persons of distinction."

An Elko, Nevada editorial ranked women's pedestrianism with transcontinental wheelbarrow racing and glass ball shooting as "a type of lunacy" that "will exercise a demoralizing effect upon the rising generation and ought to be summarily abated." Unfortunately for the editor in Elko, women's pedestrianism was flourishing. Kate Lorrence walked several times against the clock and against men in the nearby silver mining town of Virginia City. In a race against John Oddy, approximately $3,000 was bet. Newspaper accounts suggested that the race was fixed for the woman to win, but that Oddy broke the agreement during the race. In what was called ". . . one of the most disgraceful affairs that has ever been witnessed in National Guard Hall," Lorrence punched and slapped Oddy in the face. In defense of himself, Oddy threw Lorrence "against the chairs," possibly breaking two of her ribs.

In more civilized realms, the *London Times* of August 26, 1878, reported that a Madame Anderson walked a quarter-mile every five minutes for six days at King's Lynn. Later that year, Mme. Anderson would travel to America, billed in a *New York Clipper* advertisement as the "Champion Lady Walker of the World." Interest grew as the 37-year-old former "concert singer, actress, manageress and circus clown" continued to walk a quarter-mile every 15 minutes at the Mozart Garden, Brooklyn. Newspapers such as the *Chicago Tribune* and the *Rocky Mountain News* picked up the story of Mme. Anderson's "most wonderful" performance of 2,700 quarter-miles in 2,700 quarter-hours.

Anderson's performance included not merely walking, but singing several songs between walking bouts. According to the *Clipper*, "It is an unusual circumstance to find a woman who can shine alike on the walking track and the music-hall stage." The *New York Times* reported, "The women are so fascinated by the spectacle of a woman on the track performing a feat which the majority of men would be incapable, that they watch her for hours at a time, day after day, with unflagging interest." On the final night of her long walk, more than 2,000 people paid one dollar apiece and "jammed" into the hall. As Mme. Anderson completed her walk, it was reported, "Men shouted themselves hoarse, while hundreds of ladies clambered to the tops of their chairs, waving their handkerchiefs and cheering loudly."

Not everyone was entirely impressed with Mme. Anderson's accomplishment. A popular sports newspaper, *The Spirit of the Times*, stated that Anderson's performance ". . . had little merit as a purely pedestrian feat." However, the article acknowledged that Anderson's walk proved the thoughts of many eminent physicians . . ." that women are superior to men in the power of living with little or no sleep." A *New York Times* editorial called Anderson's effort an uninteresting and dangerous effort that should not be repeated. Editorial writers were not the only people unhappy with Anderson's performance. People who bet for Anderson to fail dropped bent pins on the track in an attempt to disable her, and there were rumors that chloroformed bouquets had been tossed onto the track. Rumors were also spread that a twin sister was put on the track at night to give Mme. Anderson time to sleep. Some religious leaders also spoke negatively about Mme. Anderson's performance. In a speech entitled "Evils of Pedestrianism," the Reverend W. C. Steele reported that ". . . ladies of the Temperance Union protested the open violation by that coarse rough woman Mme. Anderson."

In early 1879 the popularity of women's pedestrianism in the U.S. exploded. Women's contests were held from New York to San Francisco. Bertha Von Hillern had retired in Boston, but there were many others to fill her shoes. *The Spirit of the Times,* "The American Gentleman's Newspaper," reported, "The Madame Anderson fever has assumed a virulent epidemic form, and is making fearful ravages throughout the country." Regarding the unscrupulous managers of pedestrienne Annie Bartell, the article stated, "It is evident that the managers eat the chicken while the walker sups the broth."

Annie Bartell, "The Westchester Milkmaid" and others who did not live up to their billing were targets for newspaper satire. A cartoon in the *New York Clipper* featured a well-dressed woman ". . . who has taken the unprecedented task of walking 15 miles every quarter-minute. She promises to keep this up as long as her dress remains in fashion." And a verse of a poem in the *Clipper* stated, "Then one of gentler sex, within 3,000 quarter-hours, 3,000 quarter-mile essays to test her latent powers. But stops at half the distance for a 'public presentation,' then prone upon the track she drops for want of ventilation." Bartell's efforts to walk 4,000 quarter-miles in Philadelphia was condemned by the Philadelphia Medical Society as barbarism similar to The Inquisition. The *New York Herald* agreed with the doctors, hoping the police would step in.

Despite negative publicity, thousands of spectators filled halls in Boston, Chicago, and Washington, D.C., to watch women walk the sawdust circles. Madame Exilda La Chapelle's 2,700 consecutive quarter-miles at the Folly Theatre in Chicago was called "the greatest pedestrian feat ever attempted in the West." But Lulu Loomer's Boston performance set the record of 3,004 consecutive quarter miles. The *New York Illustrated Times* advertised Madame Anderson's walk with "two full page illustrations of her pedestrian efforts." Illustrations, or "cuts," of the women walkers were on sale in New York and through mail order. Said the *Times,* "Still the fever rages. Pedestrian vies with pedestrienne, but it is the latter who jauntily challenges attention on the billboards, and whose cuts are freely offered for sale or hire in advertising columns. The pedestrienne is the favorite attraction, for since the first pomological transaction in the first garden, woman has a peculiar drawing power."

Six-day walking contests replaced walks against time in popularity. The most competitive walks occurred in New York and San Francisco. The participants in the six-day race at Gilmore's Garden were described as "... young girls and gray-haired matrons, indigent and unfortunate, who grasped at this chance to earn bread for themselves and families." But two women in the race were said to "... own valuable real estate in New York City, live sumptuously on their rent-rolls and went into this contest . . . for fun and reputation."

More races were held in Baltimore, Cincinnati, Pittsburgh, Toronto, and many other places in North America. According to the *Territorial News* (Nevada) "This exhibition of female pedestrianism is quite instructive, particularly to the male portion of the audience. It shows them that women are not such feeble creatures as they have all pretended to be. Now let us set them to sawing and splitting wood, heaving coal and handling the rake and pitchfork!"

Six-day race records continued to progress, from Bertha Von Berg's 372 miles in April, 1879, to teenager Amy Howard's 409 miles in San Francisco in May, 1880. Spectator numbers were also enormous. The final night of the six-day contest at New York City's Madison Square Garden was witnessed by 5,000 people.

By 1880 women's pedestrianism was fading in popularity in New York, but detailed accounts of women's performances at Platt's Hall and Mechanic's Pavilion filled the *San Francisco Chronicle*. Headline letters on the front page of the *Chronicle* advertised the women's matches as "The Most Exciting Contest Ever Witnessed! See The Struggle Tonight!" In addition, the newspaper reported on the size and shape of the walkers, their personal histories and previous races, their diets and sleeping patterns, and the lotions that they used.

In one San Francisco race, four women eclipsed the 350-mile barrier. The *San Francisco Chronicle* reported that women's pedestrian contests were now fashionable to attend, even on Sunday. Comparing the six-day walkers of both sexes, the *Chronicle* remarked, "They do not complain half as much as the male fraternity, and are less cranky and immeasurably more pleasant to look at than the men." The last six-day race of consequence took place at Mechanic's Pavilion in July, 1880. The pedestriennes, however, were only permitted to walk 12 miles per day. Lead changes did not occur and therefore betting was infrequent and gate receipts declined.

There are few accounts of women pedestriennes after 1880. One woman, however, continued to walk throughout the 1890s. Former actress Zoe Gayton, her two managers, and her pet cocker spaniel walked across the U.S. during the winter of 1890-91, a distance of 3,395 miles, for a wager of a 31-stone diamond belt and a part in a stage show. According to the *Carson City News*, "She is a strong, hardy woman, and has many times proved to the world that a woman has great powers of endurance and can stand more hardship than most men . . . she can protect herself very well, as she carries a trusty 44 and knows how to use it." In 1896, Zoe Gayton was 41 years old, but she was still walking for wagers. In possibly her last "professional" walk, Gayton was reported to have arrived in Virginia City, Nevada, finishing a 680-mile walk that had started in Salt Lake City, Utah.

So far in my research I have been unable to trace the complete life of even one pedestrienne. Many were known only by stage names. Others married and changed names. They are all dead now, and many of their stories are buried with them. But their legacy to women's sports is beginning to be uncovered.

The Accuracy Of Our Forebears
by Nick Marshall

Some modern runners have expressed doubt about the performance totals credited to participants in six-day races during the pedestrian craze more than a century ago.

In light of how records have dramatically improved at all the shorter running distances, people have understandably wondered why the standards in this event established in the 1880s remain "world-class" in quality. More men surpassed 600 miles during that decade than in the modern era.

At a casual glance, something seems amiss. Didn't people back then have only a primitive knowledge of diet, and lack the benefits of present-day shoe technology and scientific training methods? So how did they manage to produce such tremendous athletic results?

I'm an extremely skeptical person about many things. Oddly, though, I've always placed a lot of credence in the validity of the claims made on behalf of the old-timers. To me, these claims could be categorized as "awesome, but plausible." That is, they make sense if you take some unusual factors into account—factors that have not been operative in other running events.

Paradoxically, the primary reason for believing the old accounts is because of the presence of money. While dollars can certainly be a corrupting factor (especially in terms of the way large amounts of cash could possibly encourage cheating), in this case it is more likely to have helped serve a regulating function.

To wit, the headline races of the golden age of pedestrianism were intensely scrutinized. They were professional affairs that literally offered extreme riches to the victors. For a brief period, this type of ultra distance contest could make a person wealthy. While people who run for fun may feel the lure of big money has an ignoble taint to it, there is no doubt that it can be a powerful motivator for individuals who may be talented but poor.

As professional affairs, such races were able to attract some of the most outstanding athletes of the day. While baseball was a popular pastime, basketball hadn't even been invented yet, and other modern sports were in their infancy, compared with foot racing, which had been around longer than recorded history.

The major six-day races received tremendous publicity. They were front-page stories, so the winners could achieve fame as well as fortune. Again, this was an extremely powerful motivator for someone to train as hard as possible for success, and then thrash themselves to the maximum in the event itself.

Still, while that suggests these were running events in which the competition was more deadly serious than anything modern ultrarunners experience, how can we be sure the results can be trusted in terms of their accuracy? The simple fact that they were held at indoor venues, on short tracks, the sheer volume of laps involved in someone's completing 500 or 600 miles offers plenty of room for errors. Many of us are all too familiar with how easy it is for lap counting mistakes to occur in long track ultras on quarter-mile tracks, much less shorter ovals.

Furthermore, I've heard modern doubters express concerns over the basic trustworthiness of the track lengths on which they performed their feats. After all, they lacked the rigorous course certification processes, which are insisted upon nowadays if times or distances in a race are to be accepted as accurate. How do we know they weren't sloppy in how they measured a venue? Done casually, one could give a distance for a lap that might easily be off by a few percent. Multiply that by thousands of laps, and you could end up with results that deviated from reality by many miles.

The issue of measurement is an interesting one. Decades after the fact, we end up mainly relying on trust that a particular race locale was truly what it was represented as. For instance, Jesse Owens set some of his world records during college track meets. I've never seen their veracity questioned and have no reason to doubt their accuracy. Yet at this late date, I suspect the paperwork proving the college tracks he ran on were correctly surveyed was lost to history long ago.

Stuff like that is a backbone of record keeping, yet it is one of those behind-the-scenes technical matters that rarely gets noted for the ages. Even more transitory is information on nuts and bolts items, such as officiating decisions or lap counting procedures.

However, in the case of the six-day races, press coverage at the time was so extensive that occasionally the reporting even included such esoteric topics as these.

I collect old newspapers; at an auction last year I was lucky enough to buy a big stack of issues from 1878 to 1884 of a rare weekly sporting paper called *The Spirit of the Times*. While I've been surprised in the past by how thoroughly some six-day races were covered by the general press of the day, I'd never seen any stories on these events that match the depth provided by this publication. Although *The Spirit of the Times* was mainly interested in horseracing, it would sometimes print columns of statistics on the big six-day races, with charts on things such as mile-by-mile split times, and hour-by-hour distance totals for the leaders. Nowadays, if you'd like to see what a Boston Marathon winner ran for their eighth mile, you would probably not be able to find that information in your local paper. By contrast, old-time readers could find out that Charles Rowell's time for his 447th mile was 13:04, and also discover that earlier he had been off the track for 23 seconds during his 172nd mile!

This amazing trivia showed up in *The Spirit* on March 22, 1879. The story on the Third Astley Belt Race at Gilmore's Garden in New York City the previous week gives the most detailed behind-the-scenes description I've ever come across on any race.

The extensive detail proves exactly how scrupulous officials were for this event, both in terms of the how the track was measured, plus the lap counting procedures that were utilized. It's nitty gritty stuff, the type of which you'd never see today. Yet it should lay to rest the doubts anyone might have about whether we can trust the results of these races from more than a century ago.

Following are extensive excerpts from the paper, providing details on these aspects of the race. (Plus a paragraph on a subject race directors today certainly never have to worry about—crowds of gate-crashing spectators that had to be brought under control by club-wielding police!)

The account should give modern readers an appreciation of how well the best of these six-day races were managed. They were definitely not conducted in a casual manner. Here is the excerpt:

"The track was exactly one-eighth of a mile in circuit, measured eighteen inches from the inner edge of the curb. It was staked out by C. H. Haswell, the well-known civil engineer, and to correct any error made by the carpenters in laying the curb, he resurveyed it just before the start, with the assistance of three of the judges. The straight sides were each 191 feet, 9.5 inches, the east half circle 138 feet, and the west half-circle 138 feet, 5 inches. To get this measurement it was found necessary to go out in some places two and even three feet from the pillars which enclose the inner circle . . . The track was ten feet wide, and a stout railing set back three feet from each edge, fully protected the contestants from any interference, either accidental or intentional.

"A huge blackboard was erected at the east end of the ring, and every mile made by either contestant promptly bulletined in figures plainly legible from the remotest corner of the building. Every spectator could see these figures, and there was no need to ask questions as to the score.

"Just across the track from the scorer's stand a place was railed off along the front of the boxes, on which each man's name was painted, with blank spaces for miles and laps. Whenever either contestant passed the score, men detailed for that purpose hung up cards showing the number of miles and laps finished. This enabled each competitor to know always exactly how far he had

traveled, and also to watch for himself that the record was correctly kept.

"The arrangements for the comfort and convenience of contestants, spectators, and reporters were better than at any previous race in New York City, and left little to be desired. An enclosure for the working members of the press was made just behind the scorer's stand, with accommodations for twenty writers at a time, and a duplicate copy of the tally sheets kept expressly for their use.

"The scoring was done by six of the amateur athletic clubs of this vicinity; each club serving one day. New York A. C., Monday; Brooklyn. A. C., Tuesday; Harlem A. C., Wednesday; Scottish American A. C., Thursday; Manhattan A. C., Friday; and American A. C., Saturday. Sometimes seven or eight, and never less than five, men were on duty at all times, and the tiresome work was done faithfully and correctly. Only one claim was made during the week, some parties thinking that Ennis had been marked one lap too many, but it is by no means certain that the claim was well founded. The thanks of the contestants are due to these young gentlemen, who, at great inconvenience to themselves, gave their time from day to day for the purpose of guaranteeing the score.

"There was no referee nor umpire, and the race was controlled by a board of eleven judges, five from the staff of many sporting newspapers, and one from each of the scoring clubs. Two or more of these judges were present at all times, and usually five or six were on duty. Some of them served a little time, some a great deal, and one, our neighbor of Murray Street, fairly lived in the building, and was on the track almost as many hours as the pedestrians. They took general supervision of the track and the contestants, and assisted in preserving order and ensuring a clear course. As far as deciding any claims of fouling or unfairness, their duties were happily light. Soon after the start Rowell passed O'Leary, and stepped in front of him, but seemed to think he had not sufficient lead to warrant this course, and immediately stepped out again. Just as he did this O'Leary stepped out to go around Rowell, and a collision resulted, but no claim was made. On the 54th mile, by direction of one of the judges, the scorers made this notation: "On the fifth lap O'Leary crowded Rowell out on the Madison Avenue turn, and nearly fouled." On the last day, when Harriman, with ten miles to go, came out of his tent, almost unable to move, Rowell and Ennis successively linked arms with him, and walked twice around the track. As the rules demanded 'traveling without assistance,' men who were betting against Harriman and Ennis reaching 450 and 473 miles objected to this performance, and an appeal was made. As regards Harriman, the claim was just, but the depth of stupid meanness *was reached in arguing that Ennis, who was stronger and fresher than on the first day, and had given, not received, assistance, should be penalized for a kindly act toward Harriman. Although denying the justice of this absurd claim against Ennis, the judges thought best to afford the betting malcontents no pretext for a quibble, and compelled both Ennis and Harriman to walk an extra quarter mile on account of the disputed distance.*

"The management was intelligent, untiring, and thoroughly impartial. The attendance was unexpectedly large, especially on the first night, and no preparations had been made to accommodate and control so great a multitude. But as soon as it was found that full houses would be the daily and nightly rule, suitable arrangements were made for the comfort of as many spectators as the building would hold. So great was the crowd on Sunday night, that the doors were closed before the start, and the several thousand men thus shut out became somewhat unruly, burst open the gates, and would have speedily overrun the track and stopped the race but for their timely though unnecessarily brutal repulse by the police. As is usual in such cases, the ringleaders escaped, while a few hundred innocent but over-curious citizens went home well clubbed."

One Mile Per Hour Isn't So Difficult—Or Is It?
by Joe Oakes

Young Violetta looked puzzled, afraid. All of this attention bothered her. And she was tired. Violetta knew that Papa was doing something very special, but why did it have to involve her? Oh, how she would have preferred to stay at home with Mama. Still, this was for Papa, and she was ready to do anything to help him to reach his goal. Such a strange and difficult goal!

Every day the newspapers reported exactly what he was doing. Every day someone was predicting that Papa would quit, become very sick, or maybe even die. But he didn't. And he would not. Papa would never, never quit, not her Papa. Now she was ready to do what he had asked her to do. She would run with him on his 615th mile.

The *Venice Vanguard* very proudly said today that it would be a world record, set right here in Venice, California. Funny, but just the other day the same paper had used the word "freak" when talking about Papa and his running. Fickle! Violetta would be very glad when this was all over. She would run this mile with Papa because he had asked her to, because he looked so piqued, and because she loved him so much. But she hoped he would never ask her to run again. Ladies did *not* run, and both she and Papa knew that.

The date was December 17, 1910. The place, Venice, California. Mr. Eugene Estoppey was in the process of breaking a formidable world record. He had committed to run 1,000 miles in 1,000 hours. By simple mathematics, that comes to one mile per hour for 41 2/3 days. If you were to run at three miles per hour, you could do it in eight hours per day and finish up in the allotted 1,000 hours. That is about the limit pace for the Trans-America Race, and they run a lot further than 24 miles a day. For a lot more days, too. Not such a big deal, 1,000 miles in 1,000 hours.

But wait just a minute. Look at this item from the *Los Angeles Times* a couple of weeks earlier: It says that Eugene Estoppey would, on a wager of $1,000, run 1,000 miles in *each* of 1,000 consecutive hours. *A thousand dollars. A thousand miles. A thousand hours—every hour. When would he sleep?*

While they have faded into the history hooks, all but unknown today, races at a-mile-an-hour were regularly contested in the early part of the 20th century. The supermen who did these events were not like the famed pedestrians, the prototypes of today's ultrarunners. No, they were milers. Every hour on the hour, they *raced*. They would take on all comers, sometimes winning, sometimes not, but always ready to go another mile in another hour. In December, 1910, the recognized world record in this event was 614 miles in 614 hours.

Going for the record Eugene Estoppey had bet that at the beginning of every hour from November 20, 1910, until midnight, December 31, he would run a mile. So far he was making good on his promise. At the beginning of each and every hour he would get a quick rubdown, run his mile, get another rubdown, then pass the time until the next time the big hand got reached 12.

For nourishment, he ate five times per day. While there is no record of what he ate, the papers said that he would refuse all food offerings except from trusted friends, a Mr. and Mrs. Fox. One can imagine that the gamblers might have loved the opportunity to add a little to his menu, considering the size of the wager, the times, and the potential for reaping a good profit from a bit of mild skullduggery in the form of food doctoring. No, he was very careful during this world record attempt. He did tell the press that he appreciated the offers of food from the fine ladies of Venice, but he would prefer flowers.

The question arose: When and how much did he sleep? The *Los Angeles Times* tells us that he never took more than 35 minutes of sleep at a stretch, and that his total sleep amounted to not much more than four hours per day in seven or more catnaps between runs. Most of the time he sat around, rested, wrote letters, signed autographs, and did what it took to maintain a generally jovial and pleasant demeanor. When he did put his head down to sleep, he was in the arms of Morpheus within three minutes.

Eugene Estoppey was a runner, and a very fine runner for his time. Keep in mind that Queen Victoria, that symbol of imperial greatness, was not yet a decade in her grave. It would not be until mid-1914 that the Archduke Franz Ferdinand would catch the bullet of a crazed Serbian nationalist in Sarajevo, setting off a very ugly World War in Europe. Just 39 years earlier, Estoppey was born on April 12, 1871, in Lausanne, Switzerland. At the age of ten his parents migrated to America. It was here that he learned to run.

How good a runner was he? His name isn't on everyone's tongue and it isn't clear that he was the best miler of his day. Still, he had a personal record of 4:40, and his hourly miles were done at a good pace. According to the papers, he reeled off the first of his hourly miles in 5:35, a respectable clocking in any era.

Let's look at how the papers covered the event: *Venice Daily Vanguard*, November 26: ".....completes 151 miles in six days.... one leg weakening . .. freak race. . .... on occasions when he feels especially gay, he covers the distance in well under six minutes."

December 8: "Footsore Estoppey Yet Runs. After 439 miles of dirt, asphalt, cement, boardwalk, and dance floor, Eugene Estoppey's feet were sore. In the opinion of Doctor LeFevre, who examines him twice daily, he would last no more than another 100 miles."

December 11: "Rounding his 500th mile . .. hundreds of spectators."

December 16: This was the day when 14-year-old Violetta would run a mile with her Papa. That mile, his 615th, would break the world record. Despite many attempts, no one had passed this barrier. It was said that previous failures were "mental," not physical. Twice, it was reported, men had ended up in insane asylums after such an ordeal.

Estoppey was different. He was enjoying it. Until that day he had run hourly sprints against various beach runners, *racing* every hour on the hour. This levity would now have to stop. He would now have to get serious. The world record was already his, to grow as far as he would carry it. Every hour, every mile, he drew closer and closer to that seemingly impossible goal of 1,000 miles in 1,000 hours.

An iron will, a sense of humor. Think about it. One mile per hour, every hour without stop. Food and rest have to be grabbed between runs, and your body has to do its best to put that food and rest to use in keeping the engine running. At what point does deep fatigue take over and shut the machine down? When does sleep deprivation become so severe that the body refuses to go on?

At first people thought it was weird, this oddball race. No one really expected him to be able to go very far. It all seemed to be just a lark. The discerning eye would, however, pick up a few clues. First, the wager. In 1910, 1,000 smackers was a very large amount of money. The second clue would have been apparent only to the few with the ability to look deep into a man and size him up. He was very obviously a runner, but more so, he was a man of very strong motivation, a fellow with a positive attitude and a will of iron. He was confident.

To watch him run was to feel his spirit. As he got further into the event, the *Los Angeles Times* attributed his success to his ability to remain lighthearted while under apparent duress. He took good care of himself, eating well, resting as he could, and joking with those around him. He changed his running costume frequently, showing a preference for what he called his "stars and stripes" outfit, and another emblazoned with the crest of his native Lausanne, Switzerland. He was as proud of his Swiss heritage as he was of his adopted America.

America had been good to him. In December of 1910, he was a 39-year-old family man, happy to be in California. Here in Venice, which was at that time almost as big in area as its neighbor, Los Angeles, he enjoyed a beautiful climate, crisp clean ocean air, and a good healthy lifestyle. Now, at almost 40 years of age, he was finally getting a chance at the recognition and fame he deserved. When he was done on New Year's Day, he would be a hero, known the world over as a great athlete, the first man ever to break the 1,000-mile barrier. If he could only stay with it.

And, of Course, a Little Hype

It did not hurt that the merchants and land speculators in Venice, California, were backing him with logistics and publicity. Although today it is only a small part of the Los Angeles megalopolis, Venice was in 1910 a separate entity, a sparsely populated piece of beachfront territory. The area was hungry for new people. This run would help to get "The Venice of California" publicized worldwide. The gold rush of northern California was already a half-century into the history books. The railroads were now offering good and regular service across the continent. Indians were no longer perceived to be a problem. Geronimo, one of the last and most fearsome threats, had died just the previous year, an old and broken man.

The land speculators were anxious to tell the tale of their little piece of paradise to anyone with a few loose dollars and a yen to travel. "Come West, young man," they shouted. The phenomenon of Hollywood was just a few years over the horizon, with untold millions of dollars to be made, and millions of souls yet to pour in to this great Los Angeles basin. If only they had known!

With stiff leather shoes and sore feet, Estoppey ran on. Every hour his rubdown of olive oil, alcohol, and wintergreen readied him for another mile, another addition to his new personal property, the world record. On December 19, the *Times* reported that, "A good-sized crowd had gathered at the dance hall" where he ran at night. It had been a rainy day, but he had run his 700th mile at noon. Now at night he was reported to he in good spirits, even confident. They were amazed that he had gained a pound since embarking on this trial.

The next day would mark one month that Eugene Estoppey had been running; one mile per hour, every hour for a month without missing a single one. Every hour, every mile, his world record became even greater, that much more difficult for future challengers. With every mile Estoppey became that much more confident of his ability to meet his goal of 1,000 miles in 1,000 hours. On December 20, he sent a postcard to a friend:

"Dear Theodore, Many thanks for your Christmas card and wish you the same. Go to the limit on your betting. Can't fail. Gene. P.S. Come and see me finish the 1,000th mile, please."

He was strong and confident, and he was urging his friends to place more money on him. "Can't fail."

On to 1,000 Miles

What the newspapers had called a freak event a few weeks before now became a cause celebré. The excitement of this great run was infectious. The *Los Angeles*

Times was giving him more coverage, including photos of him running, sleeping, and eating.

The newspaper reported, "Every hour between 8:00 p.m. and 7:00 a.m. the night patrolman at the beach town comes around to the little room in the hall where he sleeps, wakes him, and keeps time and the number of laps (at) the dance hall where he has a 12-lap track measured off. His muscles and spirits are in the best of shape. He seems likely that he will be able to accomplish the feat. He is eating pies and cakes and a number of dishes that an athletic coach would declare unfit for a man in training."

The next day the headline read, "No Faltering: Estoppey in Fine Condition," and it told about prizes which were growing in number every day:

"*The Police Gazette* has offered a valuable gold medal, and a number of his friends who had enough confidence in him to place bets (early) at the big odds which were offered are contributing liberally to the fund of prize money." They reported him running a 4:20 mile, "which is a coast record."

On December 31, 1910, a large ad appeared in the *Times* inviting southern Californians to come to the Venice Pavilion, where "Estoppey will run the Last Mile in his 1,000-mile Endurance Contest at Midnight."

The next day, January 1, 1911, the *Times* carried the following article: *Estoppey Wins! Venice, California, December 31.* "In a blare of brass and a blaze of pyrotechnics and electricity, Venice watched the old year out and welcomed the advent of the new. There was a concert and an Italian band, followed by a masquerade ball in the dance hall. Then, at he stroke of 12 there was a grand display of fireworks at the end of the breakwater. Simultaneously, the last mile of Estoppey's freak endurance race was run, the 1,000th mile and the 1,000th hour expiring as the last sheet on the calendar was torn away to reveal the first glimpses of 1911."

He had done it. He had bettered the world record by more than 50 percent. He had been the first, and perhaps the only man ever to run 1,000 miles in 1,000 consecutive hours. After more than 40 consecutive days of performing every hour on the hour, Eugene Estoppey was bone weary. What part of his body did not hurt, what cell of his body was not screaming for rest?

Young Violetta said, "Papa, you must come home and rest now. You need a good sleep." He replied, "Not yet my darling daughter. In the morning I must run one more mile in Pasadena at the Tournament of Roses. Then I will rest."

Across America on Foot: The Bunion Derbies of 1928 and 1929

by Dan Brannen and Andy Milroy

There was only one serious attempt in the 20th century to develop full-scale professional ultrarunning, and it was made in 1928. Perhaps inspired by the surge of noteworthy ultra performances in 1927, professional sports promoter Charles C. Pyle (better known among his detractors as "Cash & Carry" Pyle) decided to promote a footrace across the United States of America.

The controversial and flamboyant Pyle began his sports management career with immediate success on a grand scale. He signed on as an agent for the first superstar of professional gridiron football, Harold "Red" Grange. Pyle signed Grange to the Chicago Bears to an unprecedented, lucrative contract, thus effectively becoming a promoter, with equally unprecedented success, of Grange, the Bears, and the heretofore floundering sport of professional football.

Pyle then moved on to professional tennis, signing on to manage French phenom Suzanne Lenglen, the queen of Wimbledon. He created a virtual tennis circus with Lenglen as the star attraction, traveling around the U.S. with a portable tennis court. Again, he achieved unprecedented promotional success.

Pyle then decided to extend his sporting empire to new frontiers. Perhaps influenced by the country of Lenglen's origin, he took a close look at the Tour de France bicycle race, and then at a footrace which had its inaugural staging in 1926, the arduous, 500 km Paris to Strasbourg walking race. He decided to combine the two concepts and promote an extended coast-to-coast footrace, to be completed, like the great French cycling event, in daily stages. The fact that Route 66, linking Los Angeles and Chicago, had just been completed, gave Pyle an opportunity to latch onto the coattails of the publicity already generated by its opening. Here was a ready-made course for a Trans-America race.

Pyle was not the first to promote professional running in the 20th century. Following the excitement of the 1908 Olympic marathon, when Italian Dorando Pietri had been assisted and then disqualified while inside the stadium, a marathon craze swept America, but by 1928 most of the professional marathon runners of that era had long since retired. Pyle was probably aware of the recent American ultra marks, particularly those of native Americans, but he relied upon the lure of prize money, totaling an unheard of $48,500, to attract other competitors from around the world as well. It did. The announcement of the race was made in Hollywood, and newspapers carried the news worldwide.

A staue of Andy Payne, in his hometown of Foyil, Oklahama

Possibly the most prominent runner attracted by the money was already a professional. Willi Kolehmainen, brother of the great Hannes, who had won gold in the 1912 and 1920 Olympics, was arguably the greatest of the professional runners during the marathon craze 20 years earlier. Willi had set a world professional marathon record of 2:29 in 1912, a mark unmatched by any amateur until 1925. Willi Kolehmainen signed up for this race across America, as did several other Finns. (In the 1920s, the Finns were to long distance running as the Kenyans are today, the masters of the sport.) Another runner from the Baltic region with excellent credentials had also entered: Estonian Juri Lossman, the silver medalist behind Hannes Kolehmainen in the 1920 Olympic marathon.

Pyle's most brilliant coup, however, was to sign up the greatest ultrarunner of the era, Arthur Newton from Rhodesia, multiple winner of South Africa's annual Comrades Marathon (a 56-mile ultra), and record-holder of Britain's 55-mile London-to-Brighton.

The prospect of prize money also attracted experienced American runners, such as Lin Dilks, as well as notable Native American runners such as Nick Quamawahu, a Hopi Indian from Arizona. Quamawahu had defeated the world marathon record-holder, Albert Michelsen, over the 26.2-mile distance the previous year. Also entered were also former Olympic competitors Phillip Granville from Canada and August Fager, the latter a steeplechaser.

In addition, there was a hodgepodge of unknown quantities who were to make names for themselves in this inaugural great race across the American continent. The race called for daily stages averaging more than 40 miles for more than two months. Only a handful, however, had ever run 40 miles even once.

The 1928 Race

At 3:46 p.m. on March 4, 1928, 199 runners lined up at the Ascot Speedway in Los Angeles. The tall Pyle, swathed in a double-breasted overcoat with a fur collar, surveyed the field. Red Grange, by then an American icon, fired the starter's pistol and the world's longest footrace was underway.

The first 17-mile stage (of a proposed 3,100-mile route) was won by the 40-year-old Kolehmainen, but he had to run hard to win. The second stage of 35 miles told the same story. The Finn looked invincible, but the following day he ground to a halt with a leg injury. Nick Quamawahu, the diminutive, graceful, silent Hopi, held the lead briefly, but by the end of the fifth day, the 44-year-old Arthur Newton, the class of the field, had assumed the lead. Over the following days the lean Rhodesian moved gradually away from the field, usually winning the longer stages.

Behind the leader, other younger, less experienced runners were developing their own styles and tactics. Among the more successful, some, such as the 23-year-old Pete Gavuzzi, an Englishman of Italian lineage who had served as a waiter on the transoceanic SS Majestic, chose to run hard for a few days, then take an easy day to recover. Others, among them 20-year-old Andy Payne, an Oklahoma farm boy, and later Johnny Salo, a 35-year-old Finnish American shipyard worker from Passaic, New Jersey, chose to run more economically, effectively running themselves into shape, thus ensuring that they would invariably finish among the top five or six almost every day.

Approaching Flagstaff, Arizona after the first two weeks, Newton held an eight-hour lead over unheralded Payne. Nevertheless, the master was in trouble. He had started the race with a troublesome left leg, inevitably straining his right one in attempting to compensate. Sunburn exacerbated his problems and made massage impossible. On the 16th day, he was forced to retire. The Oklahoma farm boy, barely out of his teens, was now leading the world's preeminent footrace.

Although he had no basic speed to speak of, he could churn out mile after mile at a steady pace without difficulty, despite his relatively tender age. However, his lead was not to last long. During the seventeenth stage, he contracted an illness, which was to be diagnosed as tonsillitis. Feverish, he was reduced to a walk, which he would nonetheless maintain through that stage and the next. Arne Suominen, another of the Finns, assumed the overall lead. Pennsylvanian Lin Dilks, whose previous ultra exploits had helped to convince Pyle that there were runners who could indeed successfully complete the race, won that memorable day's stage.

Suominen was a Detroit physician who had given up his medical practice to compete in the race. Having taken the lead, he was to continue in that position for the next 19 days, running fluidly and relaxed. Behind him, Payne showed the remarkable resiliency of his young constitution by walking out his illness in a few days. Gavuzzi then became a factor, and the pair kept Suominen's lead pegged to about three hours. The trio was now some 20 hours ahead of the rest of the field.

Exposure to the elements was to mark many of Pyle's runners for life. One side of their necks and faces was constantly exposed to the beating sun and blistered badly. When the blisters burst, they became sores that in some cases would leave permanent scars.

As the race left New Mexico and entered Texas, the runners were faced with gale force winds and driving snow. The shifting running surface caused Suominen to tear his Achilles tendon. Thus, he was forced to retire. It now looked to be a race between Payne and Gavuzzi, with Johnny Salo emerging as the most likely threat from behind. Gavuzzi was a faster runner than Payne, with an unusually long stride for a man of his small stature. Like Payne, he had run intelligently, avoiding the rashness of the early leaders, maintaining his hard/easy approach through the daily stages. Some days he would cut loose and build a big lead, only to run with the pack and recover on the following day. Salo was a more muscular, strong runner who would come into his own in difficult conditions, or on the longer stages, some of which were more than 100 km.

Payne entered his home state of Oklahoma in the lead, some two and a half hours ahead of Gavuzzi, but the British runner began to press in earnest, taking big chunks out of the lead. Payne led as the race ran through his hometown of Foyil, but Gavuzzi was closing. In the 53rd stage, Gavuzzi took the lead and was now the class of the field. By the 59th day, he had built a lead of five and a half hours, but he too was harboring a skeleton in his closet.

Before the race Gavuzzi had suffered from toothaches and had received medical advice to have all of his teeth removed. Not wanting to take the risk of not being able to eat sufficiently, he had foregone the oral surgery. On the 59th stage his dental problem reemerged. Suffering, he pressed on with infected gums, but for the next ten days he was unable to take any solid food. Amazingly, he continued to draw away and by the 68th stage held a lead of six hours, nine minutes. But his condition was in steady decline.

Pyle then upped the stakes. In an attempt to reduce his expenses, he increased the length of each stage to move up the proposed finish date and to winnow the size of the field. Those who were no longer in contention for prize money began to form a bond of mutual encouragement and support in order to finish the considerable distance each day. Newton, then acting as a member of the race support staff, spent long hours on the road encouraging exhausted runners to continue. It was a poignant, at times pathetic entourage, but Newton's efforts were appreciated. At the end in New York City, the finishers gathered and presented him with a silver cup.

Seventeen days outside New York, two weeks without solid food finally caught up with Pete Gavuzzi. Rather than risk his health any further, he decided to retire despite still holding his six-hour lead. At this point only 56 of the 199 starters remained in the race. Andy Payne regained the lead, 24 hours ahead of Johnny Salo, who was gathering strength with each stage. Salo launched a sustained attack, which he maintained day after day. He took nearly six hours out of Payne's lead before blisters eventually forced him to drop back. Payne then retook an hour back from his determined pursuer. Upon reaching Salo's hometown of Passaic, New Jersey, the Finnish-American was made an honorary member of the city's police force. In the long term, it was to prove a dubious honor.

On May 28, the race arrived in New York City, finishing with a 20-mile run on the track at Madison Square Garden. The winner was Andy Payne with a final time of 573:04:34, ahead of Johnny Salo (588:40:13), with Canadian Phillip Granville third in 613:42:30. Irish American Mike Joyce was fourth and Italian Guisto Umek fifth.

Pyle was reckoned to be some $50,000 down on operating expenses even before paying out any prize money, but due in part to the largesse of the millionaire father of one of the competitors, all of the promised prize funds were paid. Payne received $25,000, Salo $10,000, and Granville $5,000 for their prodigious efforts. Such winnings were a considerable sum in that era.

Between The Bunion Derbies

During the race, the event acquired the popular moniker "Bunion Derby," although that name was never used promotionally by Pyle. Some of the "bunioneers" were able to make use of their newly found endurance. Tex Rickard promoted a 26-hour, two-man team event in Madison Square Garden, recruiting some 40 runners, mainly from the Pyle entourage. The race was won by the team of Phillip Granville and Frank Van Flute, over Newton and Gavuzzi. Following a prolonged bout of nausea, Gavuzzi had spent several hours off the track. He and Newton sprinted, alternating laps in the closing hour to close on the leaders, but the deficit was too great.

The success of this event persuaded Rickard, owner of Madison Square Garden, to promote another such race. Selected transcontinentalists were chosen to compete against the Olympic marathon champion, Boughera El Ouafi of France, who had been persuaded to turn professional. Two such races helped establish a livelihood for professional runners, while the possibility of another Trans-American race in 1929 was being worked out.

Another Pyle runner resorted to long solo runs to keep in condition. Lin Dilks made an attempt on the American 100-mile road best in November. He had set out to run from Newcastle to Erie, Pennsylvania, covering 63 miles in 9:57, and reached 82 miles in 13:14 before quitting.

C.C. Pyle's 1929 Trans-America race was to be organized differently from its predecessor. Competitors would be required to provide their own vehicles for their support crews. This reduced the field considerably. On the whole, entrants were experienced competitors from the 1928 race. As Pete Gavuzzi later stated the difference, "The 1928 race was an amateur race; the 1929 was professional." To Gavuzzi, being professional meant being well prepared and properly trained for the event.

The 1929 Bunion Derby

The 1929 Trans-America "Bunion Derby" ran from east to west, into prevailing winds. It started at Columbus Circle, New York City, at precisely 3:00 p.m. on March 31. It began with a short dash to the Hudson River ferry, which then carried the reassembled field of runners across the river to New Jersey, where they recommenced their footrace to the West Coast.

The early stages were dominated by those who thought the initial days' results were important, including a surprising number of veterans from the first race. By the ninth day, however, the experienced runners were all in front. Ed Gardner, a smooth-striding, 29-year-old black man from Seattle, led Salo by 35 minutes, with Gavuzzi two and a half hours back and Newton a close fourth. Andy Payne was not in the race, having decided to retire after his one and only ultra, taking his winnings back to Foyil, Oklahoma to get his family's farm out of hock.

Pyle expected the race to attract large crowds of people at each day's finishing town. He had brought together an elaborate assemblage of music hall acts to entertain what he expected to be a steady stream of paying spectators to nightly performances. This extended entourage was bused along the race route ahead of the runners each day. Foul weather and Pyle's overly optimistic assessment of the potential audiences meant that the salaries of the performers were soon to become a major drain on the race budget, rather than an enhancement to it. Almost from the outset, Pyle occupied most of his time during the race talking his way out of encroaching debt.

Heavy rains, the Allegheny Mountains, and early stages extending over 100-km showed just how remarkably tough the corps of runners was. The quality of the food available at race camp at the end of each day was to be yet another hazard. The iron stomachs of Gavuzzi and Gardner would soon prove to be a major advantage, as their main competitors were forced to spend time on urgent "pit stops." The arrival of Salo's wife and her personal cooking soon caused an upsurge in the Finnish-American's fortunes, and by the end of the first few weeks Gavuzzi, Gardner, and Salo were locked in combat at the front.

By the 21st stage the field had been reduced to just 31 runners. That stage marked the retirement of Arthur Newton (in ninth place), who was suffering with blisters. There is no better testament to the prowess and fortitude of the three leaders than the realization that Newton was never in contention. He was forced to retire when he was hit by a car, dislocating his shoulder. For the rest of the field, this turn of events almost assured the race would go to one of the three leaders.

Heading into the fourth week Salo moved into second place, but Gardner remained a threat. The trio watched each other carefully. Any move to strike out and gain a decisive advantage had to be matched. Any sign of weakness had to be hidden, injuries minimized, opponents' victory margins reduced to tolerable levels. One of the great, physical chess matches in the history of competitive sport was being played out across the American topography. Often the three men would jog in to complete a stage together, content to postpone the decisive moment for another day. Sometimes back markers would push hard for a surprise day of glory, particularly when approaching their hometowns. Such random extravagances could be ignored by the leading trio, secure in their comfortably large lead over the field. For nearly four weeks, the three were locked together. Then Gardner overextended himself and developed a leg strain, which caused him to fall back. By the 25th stage he was more than seven hours behind Salo, and thus quit the race. It became a two-man battle.

Just when things seemed less interesting, a third figure decided to make a bid for glory. Guisto Umek was a temperamental Italian, a formidable long-distance walker who had originally intended to complete the 1928 race by pure walking. Soon realizing he would be unable to compete effectively only by walking, he approached Gavuzzi and persuaded the amiable Italian-Englishman to teach him to run. A long-range ultra-endurance athlete by nature, the feisty Italian had surprised everyone by finishing fifth in the first race. With the demise of Gardner, Umek now moved into third place in this race. Unwittingly aided by Pyle's determination to cross the sparsely-populated areas as quickly as possible by lengthening the stages, the Italian came into his own over a six-day stretch including stages of 54, 74, 44, 60, 54, and 50 miles. He ran the 74-mile stage in 9:42:20, arguably the best single-day performance of the entire race.

Salo and Gavuzzi, who had come to be good friends, decided to respond to this sudden threat to their professional pride. They conspired, taking turns extending themselves to put the upstart in his place. Within three stages they had made it clear to Umek that they were the top men in the field. Nevertheless, the new three-way battle remained fierce. Approaching the 50th day Gavuzzi held the lead, and he decided to sit on it. Content only to match Salo's moves, he provoked the sometimes irascible Finnish-American into going beyond himself in his drive to take the lead. On the 48th stage, running with Umek for most of the day alongside a railway line, he succeeded in wresting the lead from Gavuzzi. The next day he extended it. For the next week, Salo and Gavuzzi were like two peas in a pod, inseparable. During the subsequent week they took turns pulling away from each other, Salo all the while maintaining the nominal lead. As they entered the Rockies, Gavuzzi surged and retook possession of the lead.

During the next few stages, the lead would swing back and forth between the two, but the Brit was confident that his superior leg speed would prove the trump card in the end, provided he could avoid injury and illness. On the 72nd stage he saw that Salo was in trouble with a stomach bug, so he struck. Finishing an hour and thirty-five minutes ahead of Salo, he now held a 45-minute lead with only six days left. In the remaining days across the Mohave Desert and over the coast range, the indomitable Salo worked for every minute, gradually whittling away Gavuzzi's lead. On the 76th stage Salo pulled out all the stops to try to seize the lead. Gavuzzi was unable to respond to the challenge, but Salo fell short by less than 10 minutes with a single stage remaining.

The final stage was to consist of a four-mile run into Wrigley field, where the race would end with a marathon run around the track. To this day, there remain conflicting reports as to what happened and why on that incredible final day's run. Most accounts agree that the impression was created that the four-mile jaunt to the stadium would be non-competitive, that the entire field (which was by by then reduced to 19 runners) would reconvene and start the final track marathon together.

Salo shot off with the leaders in a mad dash for Wrigley field, hoping to get an inside-lane draw for the start of the marathon. Gavuzzi saw no reason to hurry, and was delayed further by a train that crossed the course just ahead of him. When Salo and the other frontrunners arrived at the stadium, they were waved straight onto the track and the lap counting was begun. Salo assumed that each runner's marathon time would be taken individually, so he pressed on in the belief that the overall final time would be calculated after everyone had finished. He began the marathon run at 10.5 miles per hour, intent on reducing Gavuzzi's lead of nearly 10 minutes.

When Gavuzzi arrived at the stadium, he initially was thrown off guard by the sudden change in plans. Much of his lead was gone. Salo was running like a man possessed, his head cocked to one side. Gavuzzi regained his wits, still not knowing what was really happening, and moved onto the track, gradually increasing his pace. Ever calculating, he did not really begin to push until he saw Salo begin to slow. Gradually he cut down on his foe's apparent lead, but repeatedly Salo would rally to draw even, to the point where he could see his opponent across the track. Gavuzzi would eventually stop running nine laps after Salo, who had collapsed into his wife's arms. The world's longest footrace had ended, but who had won? No one knew. Confusion reigned. After a delay of a half-hour, the official result was announced. Johnny Salo had won the race by the slim margin of two minutes and forty-seven seconds.

Arthur Newton wrote afterwards in his autobiography that the official notice prior to the last stage had said that the Wrigley Field marathon race would start when all the competitors had reached the field. Despite that, Newton, like a typically stiff upper-lipped Englishman of the period, advised Gavuzzi not to contest the result. Gavuzzi had come to regard Newton as his mentor, and so accepted the counsel and raised no protest.

Harry Berry, in his definitive history of the Pyle races, *From L.A. to New York, From New York to L.A.*, estimates that Gavuzzi lost about six minutes to Salo on the track. Thus, if the race had started at Wrigley Field, the margin of victory should have been reversed in favor of Gavuzzi. So, what really happened? The most probable explanation is that the officials were confused, and thus misunderstood their instructions, and once the first mistake happened, were too embarrassed or unable to unscramble the whole result. As it was, it took them a half-hour to come up with some result, surprising when all that was necessary was to add on the individual elapsed times for Salo and Gavuzzi.

The official finishing times were: Johnny Salo, 525:57:20; Peter Gavuzzi, 526:00:07; Guisto Umek, 538:46:52; Sammy Richman, 571:29:29; Paul Simpson, 586:30:53; Phillip Granville, 618:54:23; Mike McNamara, 627:45:28.

Postscript

The story of the C.C. Pyle Bunion Derbies does not end there. Pyle faced a long line of creditors. Virtually all the way from New York he suffered from severe cash-flow problems. Claims were filed against him in courtrooms all along the route, and attachments were made against some of the race operations support equipment and vehicles. When Pete Gavuzzi went to meet Pyle after the race to receive his $10,000 prize money, he met Johnny Salo on the way out. Salo told him, "It's no good, Pete. There is no money." He was right. There was not.

Following an attorney's advice that documentary evidence was needed to back the runners' claims against Pyle, Sammy Richman, who lived in New York City, volunteered to run back along the course collecting evidence and statements. It took him 162 days and 19 pounds in weight. After all of that effort he still did not get a dime from Pyle.

Until the day he died, Pete Gavuzzi held the useless promissory note for his prize earnings, which Pyle had given him more than a half-century earlier. Johnny Salo left his job at the shipyard and, as an honorary member of the Passaic, New Jersey police force, was granted envious assignments. Not long after his historic, inspirational, double-transcontinental performances, he was assigned a security post at a local baseball game, where he was killed after being hit in the head by a foul ball.

The last known survivor of the C.C. Pyle transcontinental races was Harry Abrams of New York City, who was a finisher both years. Abrams died in the early 1990s as he approached his 90th birthday.

Britain's End-to-End: The Best of Races, The Worst of Races

by Andy Milroy

In February 1960, one man, with the resources to carry out such an undertaking, decided to put on a go-as-you-please race of nearly 900 miles—from John O'Groats, Scotland, to Land's End at the southwestern tip of England. Billy Butlin, owner of the Butlin Holiday Camps, advertised in eight national newspapers, inviting applications for entry into the race. More than 5,000 pounds in prize money was offered. Four thousand answered the ad and 1,500 sent in entry forms.

The interest in such journey walks had been engendered by an eccentric Russian-born scientist/dietician, Dr. Barbara Moore, whose aim was to show that such demanding activities could be accomplished on a diet of fruit juices, honey, and green vegetables. In the late 1950s, "Dr. Babs," in her red polka dot head scarf, black cardigan, and navy slacks, was a common sight on cinema and television news programs. She had started with "short" walks from Birmingham to London (110 miles), which she first completed in 27 hours, later in 26 hours. It was her 373-mile walk from Edinburgh to London in seven days that really caught the public's imagination. Following that walk a prize of 250 pounds for that particular journey walk was put up and won by a Tim Hayward in six days, one and a quarter hours. Dr. Moore immediately challenged the 22-year-old truck driver, who declined, wanting a cash incentive and time to recover. Thereupon the lady walker announced her intention to walk from John O'Groats to Land's End.

The national newspapers carried daily reports of Dr. Moore's walk. She averaged four miles per hour for eleven hours a day, completing the journey in 23 days. Almost immediately, a pair of walkers, Keith Symington and Peter Hoy (the latter a veteran of the Edinburgh to London race), finished in 19 days, 14 hours. Two sisters, Joy and Wendy Lewis, set out from Land's End a few days after Dr. Moore's arrival. Wendy Lewis was to figure prominently in the 1960 race.

This was the background when Billy Butlin decided to put on a race and perhaps "put an end to all this jogging up and down the country." The race was announced in early February and set for Friday, February 26, 1960. Conditions were not expected to be good—the chief constable of Caithness had even asked for the race to be canceled because of the weather. There were reports of ice twelve inches thick on the roads, with snowdrifts on either side. Two days before the start the race secretary's car skidded off an icy road and he ended up in the hospital with head injuries. Many of the competitors almost failed to get to the start in John O'Groats; then they had to contend with snow, very cold rain, sleet, and freezing conditions all the way to the finish.

At 5:00 p.m. on February 26, 12 rockets shot into the sky. The race had begun and 715 competitors ambled, marched, trotted or sprinted off on their journeys. The roads were clear with occasional icy spots and snowdrifts piled on either side. In the initial rush many competitors abandoned backpacks and equipment in an attempt to keep up with the frantic pace.

The leader after 20 miles was 28-year-old John Grundy, one of the favorites. John was an experienced ultrarunner; he had finished sixth in the London-to-Brighton the previous year and had followed that by winning a 48-mile race from Liverpool to Blackpool a month later. Wearing white shorts but otherwise warmly dressed, the Wakefield runner powered through the first 20 miles in two hours and twenty minutes. He stopped for the night at Dunbeath, 39 miles from the start. His plan was to run a set distance every day and sleep every night in a hotel or bed-and-breakfast accommodation. He planned to cover 70 to 80 miles per day comfortably, which he felt no one else in the field could equal. He had the confidence of 90-mile training weeks behind him.

In second place was Richard Penman, a 26-year-old distillery worker from Glasgow and a member of Bellahouston Harriers. However, the Scot had a stomach ulcer and the lack of regular meals on the road was to be his undoing.

During the night, one of the legendary figures of the race forced his way into the lead while Grundy rested. David Robinson was a 35-year-old research student from Bermuda. His incredible efforts were to dominate the first third of the race. He led through Drumnadrochit, with Penman second and Grundy third. By this stage, the field behind them was being decimated. Three hundred had retired and 100 more were disqualified for taking rides in motor vehicles.

By Fort William, the bearded Bermudan had extended his lead to fifteen miles over Grundy, who had overtaken Penman. The latter was in bad shape with stomach pains and had struggled into bed at Drumnadrochit. Grundy was soon to be in trouble too. Shin splints, the nemesis of all journey runners, caught up with him. He walked from Fort William to Gretna Green all day and most of the night with virtually no sleep to keep within distance of the leader. He knew if he could get running again he could still win. At Gretna Green, he was able to run again, but he carried this problem with him to the finish. He was still in second place, ten miles behind Robinson and ten miles ahead of Penman.

Robinson made the most of his pursuers' problems and pushed on strongly. On 4:00 p.m. on March 1, just under four days into the race, he arrived at Lochearnhead and left a mere two and a half hours later, following a meal and a brief rest. He looked very fresh despite the bad weather. Earlier that day he had had to face driving rain

as he ran and walked across Rannoch Moor, accompanied by a police escort. By now, Grundy was a distant second and Penman had dropped out with stomach trouble soon after reaching Glencoe. When Robinson reached Callendar, he had covered 260 miles in four days; John Grundy was 25 miles behind.

It was 3:30 a.m. on March 2 when Robinson left Callendar. When he arrived at Denny five hours later for breakfast, he was reported to be very tired. He stopped for six hours, his longest rest so far. For the first time, he had secured a support crew; one of the Scottish agents of his firm had joined him with a van.

Despite his weariness, the Bermudan extended his lead that day and by 10:00 p.m. went through Braidwood, Lanarkshire, nearly 50 miles in the lead. Behind him, Alf Rozental, a 31-year-old Hungarian-born miner at Crianlaish, had overtaken Grundy. Rozental was another of the favorites, an experienced race walker. At one stage, he closed to within 30 miles of Robinson. However, by Callendar the battling Grundy had regained second place. Depending on which walker/runner was resting or moving, the distances between them lengthened or shortened.

The lead was 40 miles by Beattock the next day with the real struggle being for second place. Rozental was a mere four miles ahead of Grundy. By the end of the following day, the leader was obviously tiring and the Hungarian had closed to 30 miles, four miles north of the Scotland-England border. The Bermudan had arrived at Penwith late at night and Rozental was at Kirkpatrick. Grundy was still third despite straining his ankle the day before.

It was at this point that Robinson showed he was human and the real effects of his fierce early pace began to show. He struggled on, handicapped by swollen ankles and using two walking sticks. However, it was not to be his perennial pursuers who took advantage of his problems, but a new figure, Keith Carrington, a 32-year-old chocolate factory worker. He grabbed a narrow lead from Rozental at Broughton, just north of Preston, but was unable to hold off the persistent Hungarian, who took the lead in Preston. At that point, another new combatant entered the fray. James Musgrave, a 37-year-old Doncaster glass worker, moved into second place on the tenth day of the race, twelve miles behind Rozental. The ever-present John Grundy was five miles behind Musgrave and Carrington, suffering from stomach trouble, but was dropping back. In fifth place was the amazing David Robinson, still determined to finish.

On March 8, Alf Rozental heard that he was no longer an amateur. The Midlands AAA had decided that by competing in a professional event previously, Rozental had forfeited his amateur status. Later in the day Rozental lost the lead as well. While he rested in Kidderminster, Worcester, John Grundy at last regained the lead. Musgrave was still third.

The race was heating up. Any one of the three could only keep the lead as long as he was moving forward. Any rest could put one back in second, even in third. Grundy lost the lead soon after Kidderminster but Rozental was forced to rest at Gloucester. While he slept in a hotel Grundy again went ahead. Musgrave was third and Robinson still clung to fifth.

On the morning of March 10, the leaders had breakfast together at Bristol. Grundy then took the lead, four miles ahead of Rozental with Musgrave farther back. The rest of the field was scattered all the way from north of the Scottish border to Bristol. On the following day the crucial blow that was to decide the race was struck. While Grundy was resting at Crediton, James Musgrave made his bid for victory. While his rivals were in bed he took only an hour's rest. Running most of that time, he built a comfortable lead.

The race was not finished there—Grundy and Rozental had come too far and fought too hard, to give in during the last 100 miles. Musgrave desperately ran and walked to keep a seven-mile lead on Grundy, while Rozental was only eight miles farther back. The strain on the leader was great. He almost gave up 40 miles from the finish, suffering from strained muscles. He stopped for tea, then decided to pack it in immediately. His team of pacers and helpers tried for a half-hour to persuade him to carry on, but he was adamant. Seven miles back Grundy was in a similar state. He had injury problems too and did not seem to be making any headway on Musgrave, no matter how hard he tried. He sat down on the edge of the pavement in the darkness and smoked some of his backup man's Capstan full-strength cigarettes—and he was a non-smoker!

One of Musgrave's scout cars reported that Grundy had also stopped, and that was enough to give Musgrave the strength to go on to win. He said later that he had covered the last 103 miles in 14 hours and 31 minutes, non-stop apart from a 15-minute rest. He had lost 18 pounds during the trip. He covered the full 851 miles in 15 days, 14 hours, and 31 minutes. His strategy had been to keep up with the leaders and average six hours sleep per night in Scotland, four hours per night in England, and three hours per night over the last 300 miles. He had eaten ordinary meals and plenty of chocolate, finishing each day with two good steaks.

Musgrave's win earned him 1,000 pounds; John Grundy won 500 pounds when he arrived at Land's End an hour and twenty-three minutes later. Rozental was third, finishing nearly six hours behind the winner. In fourth place was a 44-year-old telephone engineer named Benjamin Jones, who had walked the whole way in Wellington boots! David Robinson finally struggled to a nineteenth place finish after 19 days.

The ladies' race became a two-woman battle early on. A car had knocked down the experienced Wendy Lewis, an 18-year-old hairdresser, while in the lead, and she received bruises. Beryl Randle, 31, had overtaken her and held the lead until within 30 miles of the finish. There, Wendy overtook her and kept the lead until the finish. She looked very drawn at the end. Both women received 1,000 pounds in prize money. Wendy Lewis' time was seventeen days, seven hours, and 30 minutes, with Randle close behind her.

With such a large field and with so much money at stake, it was inevitable that cheating would occur. Billy Butlin put in extra, secret checkpoints to catch the cheaters. Officials, posing as motorists, would offer competitors lifts, but the well organized cheaters with cars of their own became wary of secret checkpoints. Their cars would go ahead, spot the checkpoint, then take the "competitors" to a spot a mile before the checkpoint. The entrant would then walk up to the checkpoint, get his or her race card stamped and initialed, and walk on a bit before getting into the car again.

Many genuine competitors gave up in disgust at the cheating. One competitor said that in hindsight, he was quite sure that it was possible for someone to stay a reasonable distance behind the leaders using a support vehicle, as long as they went through the checkpoints (28 to 30 miles apart) in a reasonable time for the distance, simply because the organizers could not watch everyone. If someone did this for 12 or 13 days, he would be in a very strong position at the finish. Naturally, there was a very careful watch kept on the leaders so such tactics could not be used at the front.

After the race James Musgrave went straight back to work, as he had used up all his holiday time. He had to finish when he did! John Grundy was one of the few athletes in the field with a normal running background. He said it took him a month to get back to something approaching normal, although of course he could no longer compete because he had been banned from amateur athletics. He still went out for runs, but nowhere near the 90 miles per week he had been doing. It took him about a week to recover mentally. He was quite a celebrity in his hometown of Wakefield; he was invited to many parties to meet the mayor and other dignitaries. He competed in the professional athletics circuit that still exists in the north of England and Scotland, but their events did not really suit an ultrarunner. The events were mostly sprints; half-mile and one-mile races, with an occasional three or four-mile hill race.

After giving this up, he still joined his former clubmates for training. He even ran in some road races, somewhat in the fashion of the most famous ghost runner, John Tarrant, who had been similarly banned from amateur events. Grundy would change in his car and run without a number, although he was careful not to interfere with the race or trouble the timekeepers. In 1963 John went to the United States and entered prospector events, where a series of burro or mule races were held.

One such race was from Fairplay to Leadville, Colorado, a 23-mile route over mountainous terrain at high altitude. A Denver policeman had trained himself and his burro for the event, but he developed a leg injury. He could not find any local runners to run his burro, but then he heard about the English runner who had run the length of Scotland and England. When he asked Grundy if he would like to have a crack at it, John agreed, and he and his burro finished second. He also tackled the famous Pikes Peak race and unofficially finished ninth. He has since been reinstated as an amateur athlete, but no longer competes.

The memories of that epic race so many years ago still live for those who saw the competitors, either in person or on the screen. In the words of Peter Lovesey, the snowbound north of Scotland witnessed the greatest gathering of eccentrics since Peter the Hermit's crusade. For months afterwards hospitals along the race route were littered with the human debris of Butlin's extravaganza. Billy Butlin paid out for many destitute competitors to return home. Questions were asked in Parliament about the cost to the public of all the injured, sick, or penniless race competitors. There was talk of holding a running race the following year, and banning support cars, but nothing ever came of these plans. Perhaps wisely, Billy Butlin thought that such a go-as-you-please event was basically unmanageable and perhaps simply too expensive to undertake.

An interesting footnote to the Butlin race is that it gave a good comparison between walking and running under reasonably fair conditions. Stage races favor runners, for it is the cumulative time taken for all the stages that counts. That format allows the runners time to recuperate unpenalized after gaining time on the slower-moving walkers. In a go-as-you-please event, the walker's more economical movement enables him or her to cover much the same distance per day as a runner by taking (and needing) less rest. In Butlin's race, the first two were runners; the next two were walkers. In the 1929 Trans-America race, which consisted of 78 daily stages, the Italian race walker Giusto Umek had to become a runner to be able to compete on equal terms with runners Johnny Salo and Pete Gavuzzi. Umek finished third.

Races and Places

Classic Races

Where do you start when talking abut classic ultras? As history has shown, you can go back to the time of the ancient Greeks to find foot races that have been held over extremely long distances. In modern times, perhaps the event currently being held that is most steeped in tradition is the Comrades Marathon in South Africa. It is not only the oldest, but also the biggest ultra in the world, and possibly the most competitive as well. Almost all ultrarunners hope to cover either the "up" or "down" routes at least once during their ultrarunning careers.

Of course one of the appeals of ultrarunning is the lure of completing long distances in far off, exotic locales. It doesn't get any more remote than Mt. Everest and the Himalayas. Patrick Johns tells of his five-day, 100-mile Himalayan trek. It can be cold in the Himalayas, but it is *really* cold in Alaska. Completing an ultra in the Alaskan winter has got to be one of the toughest challenges there is. Eric Clifton relates his chilling experience in winning the Iditasport race. If ultrarunners will brave the cold, they must also take on brutal heat as well. The Marathon des Sables through the sands of the Moroccan desert is just that kind of ultra, as is the legendary Badwater race in Death Valley, both of which are profiled in this section. The former race spawned a new kind of event, the multi-day adventure ultra. Gordon Wright explains the growth of this new kind of race. Long distance running began in Greece, and fittingly, one of the classic ultras, the Spartathlon, is held over 250 km from Athens to Sparta. Jackson Griffiths provides a Greek history lesson while recounting his experience in that race.

Also fittingly, the Spartathlon was where the world was introduced to Yiannis Kouros, perhaps the greatest ultrarunner in history. In the United States, any ultrarunning discussion has to begin with the Western States 100 Mile. Now more than 30 years old, the race is one that many American ultrarunners aspire to. The stunningly scenic course from Squaw Valley to Auburn, California offers all kinds of challenges to ultrarunners. In his article, Gordy Ansleigh describes the unusual circumstances in which this historic race got started. In addition, Jason Hodde provides commentary and advice on the other 100-mile races in North America.

There are many other historic venues for ultrarunning in the U.S. Not the least of these is New York City. One might not readily think of the metropolitan area as a hotbed of ultrarunning, but the fact is that more events have been run and history made in the Big Apple then perhaps anywhere else in the country. As famous as New York in its own way is the Appalachian Trail. David Horton for many years held the record for the fastest ever trek over the length of the 2,144-mile trail, stretching from Georgia to Maine. In his account of that experience, he tells us of the many obstacles he faced and how he managed to overcome them. Finally, there is the majestic Grand Canyon. Although no officially sanctioned ultra races are held there, it still draws ultrarunners like a magnet. Janice Anderson looks into its history, while Phil Lowry warns of the danger of long ultra distance runs and hikes in the "big ditch."

There is no way just one chapter of a book could encompass all of the classic ultras. With the sport now thriving in the 21st century, there are literally thousands upon thousands of races from which to choose. Ultrarunning and racing has truly become a global sport, one that is growing steadily. Each year spectacular performances are achieved and tradition builds. Each event thus develops a unique character, which helps weave the colorful fabric that makes up the sport of ultrarunning.

The Classics
by Don Allison

What makes a race a classic? While there may be no specific definition, the ingredients are pretty well known to all. The first requirement of a classic is time. A race needs to age well, like a fine wine. In that sense, it must have tradition and lore that has grown through the years. Equally important is quality. The event must be conducted in a first-class manner from start to finish. Recognition and stature in the running community are mandatory. A race can hardly be a classic if it is not known. Uniqueness helps to create a classic. Most "must-do" ultras are held on challenging and interesting courses, often point-to-point races defined by the unique geography of the region in which they are held. Size does not necessarily make a classic ultra, nor is it a requirement. Usually, however, if an event is that good, ultrarunners will learn of it and make it bigger. Mix all of these ingredients together and you have a recipe for a classic ultra. That's easier said than done, of course.

The lure to run one or more of these races is strong for those who have immersed themselves in the history and tradition of ultrarunning. Many ultrarunners make a lifetime pilgrimage out of completing one or more of these events. It can be both exhilarating and humbling to know that you are following in the footsteps of the legends in the sport by running from Pietermaritzburg to Durban in South Africa or from Squaw Valley to Auburn, California. While 50 miles is 50 miles or 100 miles is 100 miles no matter when, where, or how you run it, the distance seems a lot more meaningful when completed in one of these all-time events.

How many "classic" ultras are there worldwide? While everyone's list might be just a little bit different, here are 15 ultras from around the world that meet the criteria by almost anyone's definition.

1. **The Comrades.** 90 km; Durban, South Africa. "The" classic—the granddaddy of all ultras, the Comrades has it all. More than 75 years old, the race changes direction from "up" to "down" each year, in actuality making it two races in one. A roll call of the top ultrarunners of the 20th century have competed in this race, now along with more than 10,000 other ultrarunners from around the world annually, making it easily the biggest ultra in the world. The gold, silver, and bronze medal cut-offs add to the lore and lure of this event, easily the standard by which all others are measured.

2. **The Western States.** 100 miles; Squaw Valley to Auburn, California, USA. Now more than a quarter-century old, this event created an entire niche of ultrarunning, the 100-mile trail race. The quest for a Western States finisher's buckle is in the hearts and minds of almost all American ultrarunners, and now many from around the world as well.

3. **The Spartathlon.** 250 km; Athens to Sparta, Greece. Greece is the home of long-distance running, dating back thousands of years. This event is in keeping with that tradition. Fittingly, this race was where the legend of the world's greatest ultrarunner, Yiannis Kouros, began.

4. **London to Brighton.** 55 miles; London to Brighton, England. Much like the Comrades in its course and tradition, although much smaller and low-key. Many classic duels between England and South Africa's best have been waged on the hilly route to the shore of the English Channel. (Note: after the 2005, the London to Brighton was discontinued as an official race.)

5. **Swiss Alpine Marathon.** 75 km; Davos, Switzerland. Thousands flock each year to this beautiful trail race in the Swiss Alps. The competition is fierce as well.

6. **Del Passatore.** 100 km; Italy. Held in the true Italian tradition. Participants, eat, drink, sing, run and walk their way through the night. A scenic point-to-point course from Florence to Faenza.

7. **Marathon des Sables.** 146 miles; Morocco. A brutal stage race across the barren Sahara Desert in Morocco. Only the self-sufficient need apply, as runners must carry all their own provisions except water.

8. **The Two Oceans.** 56 km; Capetown, South Africa. Many in South Africa claim this race is superior to the Comrades. Like that race, the competition and organization are world-class. In addition, the scenery at the southern tip of the continent is spectacular.

9. **The Biel 100 Km.** 100 km; Biel, Switzerland. The original European 100-km, begun in 1959. Recently the race had nearly 2,000 runners.

10. **JFK 50 Mile.** 50 miles; Maryland, USA. Started more than 40 years ago, the JFK has become the USA's biggest ultra. A course combining trail and roads tests the complete skills of an ultrarunner.

11. **Winschoten 100 Km.** 100 km; Winschoten, Holland. A 23-year-old race, with at least one runner under seven hours in each of those

years. Winners read like a who's who in ultrarunning. Site of the World Challenge for several years.

12. **Lake Saroma 100 Km.** 100 km; Lake Saroma, Japan. Ultrarunning is a hugely popular sport in Japan, as evidenced by this race, which draws more than 1,000 finishers each year.

13. **Basel 24 Hour.** 24 Hours; Basle, Switzerland. More than a decade of top quality 24-hour running at this up-and-coming race.

14. **The Himalayan Trek.** 100 miles (stage race); Nepal. Held in the shadows of Everest, this stage race offers scenery and culture that no other event could hope to equal.

15. **The Kepler.** 67 km; New Zealand. A trail race from coast to coast, this race boasts the biggest ultra field in either Australia or New Zealand.

The Comrades Marathon: South Africa's Gem
by Don Allison

Most ultrarunners from the United States know of the Comrades Marathon in South Africa, especially in light of Alberto Salazar's stunning victory there in 1994. Most are also aware of the staggering numbers associated with the Comrades: roughly 13,000 starters, 10,000 finishers, and a full day of live national television coverage. The race is a front-page story in virtually every South African newspaper. Quite obviously, there is no point of reference for comparison in U.S. ultrarunning. There is however, a strikingly comparable event right here in the United States. That race is the Boston Marathon.

Like Boston, Comrades is its nation's premier road race, a tradition-laden event that has been held for the greater part of a century. Like Boston, its winners through the years are a who's who in running, including several larger-than-life legends. Like Boston, the course is as famous as those who have run it, a hilly point-to-point route between a small burgh and a city on the ocean. The course also features several well-known landmarks and fearsome hills. And like Boston, in recent years the event has grown in stature, drawing a top international field in search of prize money.

Also similar to Boston, the popularity of the Comrades is fueled by history and media attention. The race has been lucky to have had several legendary winners, from Arthur Newton in its first year to world record setter Wally Hayward in the 30s and 40s, to Bruce Fordyce, a nine-time winner in the 80s. In Boston terms, Newton is Clarence Demar, Hayward is Johnny Kelley (he ran Comrades 37 times), and Fordyce is Bill Rodgers. In reality, among the general public Fordyce's profile is more like Michael Jordan's or Tiger Woods' rather than Rodgers'. Women's course record holder Frith van der Merwe is the Comrades' Joan Samuelson. Her "down" course record of 5:54 is arguably the finest performance in the history of women's long distance running.

It's not as if the sport of ultrarunning is highly developed in South Africa. It's simply that the Comrades is so big that runners from all over the nation long to participate, much as Americans dream of making a pilgrimage to Boston. The fact that the race is 30 miles longer than the standard marathon distance doesn't seem to faze South African runners. They simply do the required training to finish the race. The Two Oceans 56 Km in Capetown is another large ultra, but mainly because it is a training event for the Comrades.

The Comrades' course runs between Pietermaritzburg and Durban, but changes direction each year, one of Comrades' unique characteristics. The "down" run from Pietermaritzburg, held in odd number years, is gradually uphill to halfway, then sharply downhill into Durban. The "up" run from Durban is uphill at the start and flat to gradually downhill to the finish. Each direction requires different strengths and exposes different weaknesses. While the up run favors a strong constitution, a set of steel quads is mandatory for success in the down direction. The actual distance of the race varies from year to year, allowing for small route variations. The up run is usually about three or four kilometers shorter. The distance of the "up" run is usually 53 miles or so, and the "down" 55 to 56 miles.

Where Comrades truly separates itself not only from ultras, but also from the world's other top races of any distance, is in its love affair between the race and the runners. All participants are made to feel integral to the race's success, not simply interchangeable parts in an organizational machine. The race number each runner is assigned is for life. Each year a new bib is issued containing the same number, the runner's name, and the number of Comrades completed. Oh, how important that last piece of information is! For anyone to have completed even one Comrades is an achievement. Incredibly though, many South Africans make the race an annual event, in hopes of someday joining the hallowed "green number" club.

A green number in Comrades signifies having completed the race ten times. This status is quite obviously hard-earned and highly coveted. A yellow number is issued for a marathoner's tenth Comrades. A special chute is set up at the finish line, whereupon finishing, the runner is escorted to meet a race official, who presents a handsome cloth green number to the athlete. Having attained this status, a runner is accepted into the race for life. Special privileges and clothing are available for these runners only. In effect, the race is taking these runners in as partners and giving them equity in the event. It's a wonderful tradition that greatly enhances the stature of the race.

Another unique tradition is the earning of finishing medals. Gold medals (solid gold!) are awarded to the top ten finishers, silver to runners under 7:30, and bronze to finishers under 11 hours. Elite runners are often referenced by their total of golds, and silver clearly earmarks near-elite status. On average only five percent of the field earns silver. The bronze is also highly respected, in part because a portion of the field that embarks at the 6:00 a.m. start does not reach the finish by the 5:00 p.m. finish.

And the race does indeed *finish* at 5:00 p.m. At *exactly* that time, an honorary race official (normally a former winner) stands with his back to the runners and fires a gun into the air to signify the end of the race. Runners falling even meters short of the clock at this point go unrecognized. The stadium doors are closed, annually leaving hundreds of heartbroken runners behind. While this tradition may seem harsh, it creates a clear, unequivocal goal for many "backmarkers." In many years, nearly half of the field crosses the line in the final hour.

And make no mistake about it, 11 hours for the 90-km course is a solid achievement. Without a strong training base, this mark can be difficult indeed. Some of the Comrades' most dramatic moments have occurred as runners desperately lunged for the finish line in the final seconds before either 7:30 or 11:00 expired on the clock.

The year 2000 marked the 75th running of the Comrades, a race originally established to honor comrades in arms from World War One. The popularity of this race, combined with its steep tradition, will no doubt keep the Comrades in it position as the most prestigious in the world for years to come. *Note: In 2003 the Comrades implemented a new final finishing cut-off of 12 hours.*

The Trail of Misfortunes That Created the Western States 100 Mile

By Gordy Ainsleigh

Life-success counselors are forever urging us to turn lemons into lemonade. Certainly, that is what happened in the creation of the Western States 100 Mile Endurance Run; sometimes I think, despite my best efforts. Social scientists long ago established that normal, comfortable people rarely accomplish extraordinary things. So maybe I should be grateful that my Mom and Dad, two of the most stubborn people I have ever met, split up before I was born, leaving me to be raised by my Mom and Grandma, who dedicated themselves to the task of making my brother and I into two of God's "separate and peculiar people," because *the end* was coming at any moment.

So there I was in the 1950s, fatherless in an age when few got divorced, going to church on the "wrong day," and forced to wear long-john underwear into June. One day when I was seven or eight, I walked out onto the playground for lunch and felt so out of place and lonely that I ran all the way home for lunch a mile across the deep creek canyon and steep hills of Nevada City. My grandmother was surprised and delighted. She made me lunch, treated me like a hero, and sent me running back to school. It felt so good I did it again and again. That was the start of my running career.

In my senior year at Colfax High School, I missed winning the league championship in the two-mile by about two seconds, leaving me with "unfinished business" in running, a never-to-be-filled empty spot that spurred me ever onward toward the Western States 100 Mile.

Another bitter disappointment occurred when my application to University of California at Berkeley was turned down. I had to settle for Santa Barbara (UCSB), where I started renting horses from the recreation department. I bought my first horse from the university stables, and eventually saw a Western States Trail Ride (Tevis Cup) brochure on the bulletin board when I came in to feed my nag. I sent in an application in April of 1970, but was turned down (yet again) in a polite letter from Drucilla Barner, the ride secretary, advising me to apply next the November, before the ride filled up. So I applied again.

I was so ignorant in 1971 that I did the ride on a bareback pad, without stirrups. From that excruciating experience, I learned that I could tolerate the pain of doing 70 miles on foot, when the alternative was an even more painful horseback experience. Relief came 10 days later, when I could finally walk without limping.

I went into the savings and loan commanded by Wendell Robie, the founder and president of the Tevis Cup, to get the ride results, and was promptly ushered into Wendell and Drucilla's office. It turned out that they were greatly amused by my wild display of masochistic ignorance; they said they respected me for sticking out my self-inflicted ordeal. I was welcomed into their circle of friends.

Rebel, that first horse I bought at UCSB in 1970, turned out to be a pretty good endurance horse. With a sturdy horse like Rebel, I might have gone on to finish 10 Tevis Cup Rides in a row, and the Western States 100 Mile run might never have happened. So after the 1972 ride, which Rebel and I completed with relative ease, what I obviously needed—if I was ever to become the so-called "father of the sport" of 100-mile trail running—was to get rid of that sturdy horse and find another steed that proved highly unreliable. That irresistible opportunity came in the form of one of the prettiest little hippie chicks to come out of Southern California in the days of "make love, not war" and $75-a-kilo weed. She loved beer and pot, camping and parties, horses in general, and my horse Rebel in particular. She always told me she loved me too, until she talked me into giving her my horse Rebel, and then left me for a short, fat bow-legged married guy with a gift for gab.

At that point, I had to get another horse. Of course, if I had gotten another durable horse like Rebel, there might never have been a Western States 100 Mile. Divine Providence intervened in the form of a guy I chose to be my best friend during the winter of 1972, a person so morally decrepit that, in our hour of need (his need for money, my need for a horse), he sold me a horse that the ride vets had told him had a permanent lameness problem, with the words, "She's never even offered to take a lame step."

The following summer, 1973, my new horse went lame, of course, on my last training ride a week before the "big event of the year." I was disconsolately trudging up Robie Drive on my way to the finish at the fairgrounds, leading my newly lame new horse, when a cheery voice came from Drucilla's house on the left side of the road: "Hello Gordy! How are things?"

I started to tell Drucilla about how awful things were, when she stopped me, and said "Don't go away; I'll be right back." She went into her house and came out with a bottle of excellent white wine (Robert Mondavi Johannesburg Riesling, I believe) and two glasses. She sat me down on the bench next to the hitching post alongside her driveway, listened to my long, sad story, advised me to get my horse re-shod by a professional (I had installed the shoes), and then observed cheerily "And even if your horse does go lame next week on the ride, it's not the end of the world. In fact, it might even be a blessing in disguise."

She commented that I spent more time on foot each year than on my horse, and let me know that she and Wendell had been wondering when I was going to leave my horse at home and just do the entire course on foot. She concluded with "Next year will be the 20th anniversary of the ride, and I think that would be a wonderful time for you to run the whole race on foot."

Still, it might never have been, but for one of my greatest gifts—a real talent, if you will—my ability to procrastinate extravagantly. Consequently, when the summer of 1974 rolled around, I still had the same lame horse, and had no choice but to either run the 100 miles or sit on the sidelines and be a spectator. I've never been much of a spectator.

On August 3, 1974, the temperature was 107 degrees F, and two horses died from their struggles on that day. I suffered terribly too. But that was the day I ran into history, founding the Western States 100 Mile Endurance Run; that day of inferno and night of strange happenings and even stranger mental functionings forever changed my life. In addition, in the world of unintended consequences, a whole bunch of lives of a whole bunch of people were also changed, most of whom I will never know.

It had to happen this way: A kid who (1) was made to feel peculiar, and had to (2) start running home for lunch out of loneliness, and then (3) fail to win the two-mile run in his senior year high school track league championship, and then (4) get rejected by the University of California Berkeley, and then (5) be forced to go to a less-prestigious University of California Santa Barbara, where there were horses, and (6) be so ignorant that he would try to ride 100 miles on a bareback pad, then (7) be so dumb that he would give away his good horse to a girlfriend who was leaving him, and (8) be such a bad judge of character that he would choose for his best friend a guy who would deliberately sell him a lame horse, and (9) be such a procrastinator that he would let a whole year pass by without replacing that lame horse, even though he was (10) the kind of guy who hated being a spectator, even on (11) a day when it was dangerously hot for the horses.

Today, because of the suggestions I made to Wendell on the placement of veterinarian checkpoints after my day in the inferno, horses no longer die of heat and exhaustion on this trail. And because of all those bad things that happened in my life for all those years, one can go almost anywhere in North America and run a wonderful trail through some of the most beautiful places on earth. As Buddha is reputed to have said, "The most beautiful lotus flower will be the one that grows out of a dung heap." Thus, we have the Western States 100 Mile Endurance Run and 100-mile trail running—the glorious fruits that grew out of the manure pile of my early life.

A Greek History Lesson at the Spartathlon

By Jackson Griffiths

This race is, quite literally, a legend. It claims to retrace the best known footsteps of Athenian foot messenger Pheidippides, he who gave birth to the phenomenon that is the modern 26.2-mile marathon, with his well publicized journey from the plains of Marathon to the city of Athens, Greece.

Little is heard however, of his more incredible journey circa 490 B.C. from the Greek Capital to the military stronghold of the mighty Spartans. That journey wound its way through coastal trails, passed by undulating vineyards, and took in a number of hills and mountain passes to cover an amazing distance of 246 km, or 153 miles. The storyteller of the day, Herodotus, recounted in writing *The Histories* that Pheidippides arrived in Sparta approximately 36 hours after leaving Athens; quite a feat given that he was wearing nothing but flip flops and a toga, let alone modern day Nikes and all the best electrolytes our chemists can muster. Thus, the modern day challenge of The Spartathlon was set: race the 153 miles from Athens to the town of Sparta as Pheidippides once did, in less than 36 hours.

Even I could tell at a quick glance that on paper that was a serious challenge. But what would it really be like? Would the good surface underfoot help me gain more speed over time? Or would the incessant pounding underfoot on tarmac gradually wear me down? Why do so many athletes herald this as the toughest race on the circuit? Why do so many fail to finish (on average, only 30 to 40 percent of the field make it) yet return time and again? Could I, average Joe ultrarunner, succeed? I set out to be enlightened.

First things first; this race is superb value for money. An entry fee of 250 euros embarrasses many other well known races and buys you 75 checkpoints with drop bags facilities and water and snack supplies at each, several nights' full board hotel accommodation, and Greek sunshine and hospitality in spades. All that remains is for you to get yourself a cheap flight to Athens and you are set.

On arrival at the hotel, race registration was relaxed to the point of negligence, but the entry qualification criteria leave you under no illusions that this is a serious event, and that only those with considerable pedigree and speed over distance need turn up. The easiest route in is to prove a 100 km time of less than 10 hours 30 minutes, still a pretty formidable accomplishment.

Should you still have any lingering doubts as to the intensity of this challenge, just show up at the start line and take a look around at those brave enough to make it there. I would say that 95-percent of entrants trained upwards of 80 miles per week, take on many ultras each year, and possess marginally less body fat than your average household toothbrush. With all that in mind, more than 60-percent of such a crowd failed to reach the finish line the previous year. Get the picture? On a lighter note, nearly one-third of the field was from Japan and Korea, bringing their usual infectious zest for adventure and sport as they always do.

Doing the math, 153 miles in 36 hours gives you various ways to pace the course, but race directors (as ever) like to throw in the odd twist. For Spartathlon, the twist comes in the shape of enforced cutoff times to ensure a relatively quick early pace. The first 43 km, for example, need to be done in four hours and 30 minutes; the first 81 km no slower than nine hours 30 minutes, all in daytime temperatures of 30 degrees C, and climbing. Where this little gem of a race tactic was recorded in the annals of Greek mythology I have yet to learn. I'm quite sure that Pheidippides wasn't subject to a ticking stopwatch with every step, but hey, that's progress.

The start of the race is dramatic, taking place at 7:00 a.m. just at the very moment dawn emerges among the shadows of the Acropolis, with the imposing structure of the Parthenon overhead. From there both the conditions and the scenery quickly deteriorate as you make you way through urban Athens and its surrounding industrial areas and all the noise and pollution that comes with it.

After you get the first 26 miles under your belt, you traverse coastal village roads leading up to the strategic town of Corinth. The sun is hot there, magnified in ferocity by the white rocks and black tarmac, much of which has been freshly laid in recent years. Further reflecting the sun's rays is the Mediterranean Sea to your left and mountains to your right, a stunning setting that lasts for 20 km or so on decently undulating roads.

As you approach and then cross the dizzying heights of the Corinth Canal, the first major milestone is in sight—81 km into the race, one-third of the distance—a place a surprisingly high number of runners retire from the race, and as I sadly did this year. Suffering from dehydration and loss of energy was my own fault for not bringing enough electrolytes with me early on during the race, a real schoolboy error. Despite feeling cool and comfortable for the first 60 km, by 81 km I was sitting on a bench, my head between my knees, suffering from stomach problems as the race clock ticked away.

In any other race, I could have taken a 30-minute break to recover, emptying the contents of my stomach by the graceful art of vomiting and then slowly re-hydrating. The problem is that in the Spartathlon you get no second chances. The timing is just too tight. I arrived at the 81-km checkpoint with about 20 minutes in hand over the cutoff time, well on schedule, but with a bad case of dehydration and no time to make amends, recover and continue. And so I duly collected a DNF. A few hours later, I was almost fighting fit again.

What dropping out did allow me to do however, was have a wonderful view of the rear end of the race, as the sweeper coach collected numerous DNFs. Given the tight cutoff times, the rear end of this race was actually the bulk of the field (well over half the runners that do finish the race, do so between 34 and 36 hours). The sweeper coach I got on was the second bus, the first already full and on its way to Sparta.

Interestingly, in talking to a few fellow runners falling behind time in the first half of the race, a high percentage of them were almost quite used to pulling out, as if they never expected to reach the end anyhow and just came along to see how far they could get. Given that this is an inexpensive race and a thoroughly enjoyable trip through some wonderful countryside, that may be understandable.

In any event, when my sweeper coach made it to a major checkpoint later on, I had the opportunity to spend two hours there watching runners come through and help with some of the supporting. Most were running without a support crew. There was water and simple snacks available at all checkpoints, but hot food was in short supply and those who needed specific grub and drinks were advised to bring a support crew. After that stop, my sweeper coach of "disqualified" runners was overflowing and thus took a direct line ahead to Sparta. Arriving there at about 2:00 a.m. I checked in, showered, and hit the sack within minutes. I awoke at about 8:00 a.m., ate a quick breakfast in the hotel and headed outdoors to the finish line, just a few minutes walk.

Sparta is not a big town, perhaps 10,000 in population, but is set in an awesome location, towering hillsides and mountains surrounding the village, glazed in bright sunshine. The finish line is just as wonderful, preceded by a teasingly long approach along an upward sloping road culminating in your arrival at the towering statue of the celebrated Spartan ruler, Emperor Leonidas. It was he that Herodotus writes of Pheidippides bringing his messages of battle to, hence the finish line for the race is to simply approach the statue and touch the foot of the Emperor. This is a lovely way to end such a great race.

As I arrived, the race clock was at 27 hours and there had already been two finishers, the winner coming home in a staggering 25 hours. That is a truly amazing performance when you consider some of the challenges faced during this race, particularly the mountainous scrambling over the peak of Mount Parthenio that strategically marks the 100-mile point in this race, which typically takes place at nighttime. The loose scree and hair-raising inclines make it a challenge not for the faint hearted.

It wasn't long before more finishers arrived, two runners approaching the statue together in third and fourth place. The organizers arrange for all runners to be escorted from the outskirts of Sparta to the finish line by local young runners, often with a handful of schoolboys unofficially joining the escort by bike. The lead runners are afforded special treatment: escorts on horseback dressed in traditional clothes from the days of Leonidas, presumably similar to the fanfare afforded Pheidippides as he approached the ancient town to address the Emperor.

As I stood by the statue on a day hotter even than the one before, the trickle of finishers was very slow, only 12 coming home inside 30 hours. The spectacle of the finishing ritual was one of the most poignant and wonderful I've seen.

As exhausted and highly emotional runners approached the finish and touched the foot of Emperor Leonidas, they were immediately offered water from the sacred Evrotas River by local Spartan girls dressed in traditional gowns and crowned with an olive wreath. Photo opportunities then abounded for runners in their moment of glory, as doctors waited the wings with wheelchairs to rush exhausted them to the nearby medical tent, a mandatory measure for all. At that point I understood why so many runners return without any real hope of completing the challenge, but feeling duty bound to try their luck and their fitness against this grueling challenge once more in the faint hope that they can experience such a momentous entry into this ancient town. The 36-hour time limit came and went, strictly enforced by the organizers; 73 finishers out of the 185 starters made it to the finish line.

My feelings having missed the time cutoff at 81 km were of both certainty that this race was beyond me and that I would not return, to feelings of how could I not fail to try again next year with improved fitness and the invaluable experience of this years attempt. Is this one of the best races ? Certainly. Could it be one of the truly toughest races ? Without a doubt. Will I be returning ? My head says no, but my heart says, inevitably, yes.

In The Shadow of Giants
By Patrick Johns

"Leave nothing but your footprints—take nothing but your memories."
Cruising at 35,000 feet and snacking on one of my last curry chicken and rice meals in India, I realized that a difficult journey was coming to an oddly comfortable close. I was returning to Delhi from Bagdogra, India. My newly acquired friend, Urs Weber, from Germany, tapped me on the shoulder and pointed out the window. Just off the wing tip, stabbing up through the clouds was the southern face of Mount Everest, along with a saw-blade array of some of the tallest peaks in the world. It was a remarkable view, similar to what we had worked so hard to see a few days before. Urs and I had recently finished the final leg of the five-day Himalayan 100 Mile Stage Race and Mount Everest Challenge Marathon. It seemed odd that we should now enjoy this majestic view without first having to expend a huge amount of energy.

Our conversation drifted back to the experience that we had just shared. Six days before, in the hamlet of Maneybhanjyang, in the Bengal Region of India, 58 participants from around the world met to begin this shared adventure. Of course, their personal starting points and experiences would be different, but ultimately we would end up at the same place.

For me, the journey started several years before, when a friend and I decided to attend the race, which we did. This year, I came better prepared and on a mission; not only to participate in the race, but also curious to identify a common thread between this small but diverse group of athletes. Who were these unique people, and what motivated them to travel the world? Was there one characteristic we all had in common, other than the desire to go to a place where we could enjoy a pre-race coffee while gazing at four of five of the world's tallest mountain peaks?

To open my fellow runners' personal vaults would take some effort—a little rooting around in the unique minds of those who chose to do this equally unique race. But, hey, I'm not shy. Since my first Himalayan 100, I have had plenty of people ask about my motives. I was curious to find out if I'd be better prepared to answer that question after the second time around.

Pre-Race coffee with World's Tallest Peaks
Like a pack of adventure loving hounds, this year's group, the second-largest in the event's 13-year history, would sniff their way to the "fox" in India. In years past, it was typical for about half of the participants to come from the U.S., but

this year would be quite different. Only a small and ragtag contingent of six would journey out from the security of the U.S. shores to attend this international shindig, yet in this warm and friendly country of India, the only thing I ever felt threatened by was the challenge of completing the race.

Although the mix of runners has changed over the last few years, the course has not. It follows a trail built in the early 1900s when the Aga Khan, ruler of much of India, told his men to build him a path. He had heard great tales of a place high in the Himalayas from where it was possible to see four giants, and he wished to travel there. The giants go by the names Everest, Lhotse, Makalu, and Kanchanjunga, four of the five world's tallest peaks. The place is called Sandakpu, and Khan's trail still exists. Much of the Himalayan 100 Mile Stage Race runs on this trail.

This five day, 100-mile adventure run is divided into 24, 20, 26, 13, and 17-mile stages. Much of the running is done on the border of India and Nepal, at an elevation of 12,000 feet. If you run on the left side of the trail, you are in Nepal, on the right, India. The first and third days are considered the hardest, but none of the days are what would be called easy.

Up and Up We Climbed

Stage one: Thought to be the most difficult stage, the trail climbed more than 8,000 vertical feet over 24 miles, following switchbacks steadily upward on what could best be described as a dangerous path of slippery boulders. On the top at Sandukpa, each runner punched through the daily finish ribbon before stopping his or her clock for the day. After being led to your assigned hut, you located the gear and sleeping bag you packed the night before. Everything needed for the remaining days was there on your bunk. There was plenty of food and the infamous "bucket bath" of hot water if you chose to be so bold in the cold mountain air.

Stage two: This day started early with an incredible photo op at sunrise, the first chance to see the peaks—and they were awesome! Then it was off to the races, starting at 12,000 feet with a 20-mile out-and-back run on a rollercoaster grade. Everest was on our left and Kanchanjunga on our right. The third tallest mountain in the world, Kanchanjunga is little known outside the climbing community, for it is a highly technical climb, and therefore doesn't get the press bestowed to Everest. Starting early and finishing early made this a good day for that "bucket bath," and a offered chance to reload badly needed calories.

Stage three: On this day the Mount Everest Challenge Marathon was run. No, we didn't climb or run the 26.2 miles on Mount Everest, but certainly enjoyed its view while we set out on the still frozen trail at 6:30 a.m. Who needs sleep anyway?

Most of the others hadn't slept either; my snoring was to blame for that. This day started early so the runners could complete the standard marathon distance before sunset. The course repeated the first part of stage two, winding out along the trail as it spooled out like The Great Wall of China. Then we "dropped for ten" (miles that is), down a steep washed out rut that also serves as a creek bed during the monsoon season. The day finished in the quaint mountain village of Rimbik. Hearing the sounds from the jungle of birds and rushing water was a great way to compensate for the inevitable "marathon wall." Running down through "the jungle rut," giving back much of the punishing altitude, was the perfect way to finish. The stark contrast between the time at the top with the peaks in view, and the jungle-like finish, was amazing.

The "Evil Twin" Awaits

Stage four: We started out on six miles of rough road that was all downhill. But wait! There was the evil twin waiting up the road in the form of six uphill miles. This was just another reminder that even on the easiest day–if you can call it that—there was no free lunch on this course. With a steady climb up the other side of the valley to what would be the starting point for the next and last day's race, the day was complete.

Stage five: After climbing out of the bus with stiff and cramped legs, we were welcomed with the realization that after completing six miles virtually straight up the winding valley wall, we would reach a pass that signaled the end of all the "up stuff." Ten more miles to the finish line in Maneybangjang where we started, and *it was all downhill!* Time to pick 'em up and take it to the house. High fives, hugs, lunch, and adult beverages waited for those so inclined. Boarding the bus and returning back to Mirik Lake for a hot shower, meal, and the awards ceremony were all that was left to round out this perfect five-day spanking.

The Most Difficult Marathon? Or the Most Beautiful?

The Himalayan 100 is usually described by two very subjective claims: "One of the most difficult marathons," and "the most beautiful marathon in the world." About the first: many of the participants in this event over the years have competed in other grueling events such as the Marathon Des Sables (a 150-mile stage race across the Sahara). I didn't hear even the most hard-core runners say that "The Himalayan 100" was a cakewalk. It is considered by many of the "desert runners" to be the flipside adventure to the desolate, stark, 150-mile run in the sand that has become internationally popular. Anyway you cut it, the words "ultramarathon" and "easy" have never co-existed in the same sentence for me. As for whether or not it's the hardest, I don't have that answer, other than to say, it's the hardest race that I have ever done.

As for the second claim, it just might be true, considering that for much of the race you are surrounded by the natural elements of the tallest mountains in the world, as well as animals, rivers, streams, and a lush jungle. When you frost this already delicious cake with the smiling native people along the trail, along with villages, shrines, and prayer flags flapping in the wind, it might be difficult to beat this claim. Many runners maxed out their digital memory cards or used up their film well in advance of the last day of the race.

Namaste! Namaste! Namaste!

The race director, Mr. Pandey, demonstrated to all his skills in organizing one of the most difficult logistical events in the world. He treated each of his guests with true hospitality and through his actions was subliminally teaching us the meaning of the word "namaste," the same word that we were showered with by the local villagers along the trail. "Namaste" has much deeper significance than simply "hello."

The Himalayan 100 boasts a 95-percent completion rate, which is even more amazing given that participants have ranged in age from 13 to 75. Doing what it takes to insure the satisfaction of a safe completion by all participants is a major goal of the always-present race doctor and Mr. Pandey. After all, participants had traveled a long way to get there. Here is a story for the books: Several years ago, a Japanese runner had become dehydrated during the very last stages of the ascent in stage one. Under the constant supervision of the race doctor, she was allowed a jeep-mounted moving intravenous drip. She slowly advanced behind the vehicle up the mountain to the finish line for stage one. Then a hot meal, more fluids, and some rest were all she needed to go on. After four more days of racing, she enjoyed a successful finish. It is an extreme case, but still very cool.

Back to the Original Question

This does however, make me stop and think once again about my original question. The curiosity I had about a common thread or motivation among the group didn't take much rooting around to satisfy. Call it what you like, but I could see it in the eyes; focus seemed to be an obvious attribute, seasoned with a good amount of determination. This was no real surprise, however, since adventure trail running, requires concentration with each step. Some came to win and others just to finish, but we would all leave India changed on some level.

I wouldn't be so foolish as to recommend this event to everyone, because it does truly possess many of the elements of a good old fashioned "butt whipping." We all know that rarely do the special things in life come without some sort of a price tag. If you are willing to endure a little hardship, commit to maximum effort for a few days, and use a little common sense, you will finish the race and your life will be changed. There is little doubt that if you push to the end of your own "effort spectrum," you are guaranteed to reexamine your definition of "hard" and in so doing, make other challenges seem easier. This is a group of people who believe this and are willing to pay that price. You will also grant yourself the privilege of making lifelong friends from around the world, friends who might speak a completely different language, but still are connected in very special way. And yes, for me, although no less difficult, it was much better the second time around. Namaste!

An Arctic Adventure
(Or What I Did on My Winter Vacation)
by Eric Clifton

First, the bare facts. The Iditasport competition in mid-February in Alaska has several different divisions—the Iditarun (running) and Iditashoe (snowshoeing), both on a half loop of about 72 miles, and the Iditabike (cycling) Iditaski (skiing) and Iditatri (triathlon)—all on the full 115-mile loop.

All divisions start together on the frozen surface of Big Lake, and make their way westward over snowmobile trails for 27 miles to the checkpoint at the frozen Big Susitna River. At Big Su the course joins the historic Iditarod Trail and follows it, with one slight detour, 15 miles to the Alexander Creek checkpoint and then a relatively short jaunt of ten miles to the Rabbit Lake checkpoint.

Rabbit Lake is the last checkpoint before the long 20-mile stretch to Skwentna, the official finish line for the runners and snowshoe racers (and unintended finishes for some cyclists and skiers!). Skiers and cyclists continue on, returning to Big Su via the frozen Yentna River and then embark upon 27 miles on the snowmobile trail back to their finish at Big Lake.

Due to the truly hostile environment, race organizers have a list of mandatory gear that all racers must have with them at all times: A minus 25 degree cold-rated sleeping bag, tent or bivy sac, insulated pad, stove with fuel, waterproof matches, a two-quart pot, a headlamp (or flashlight for runners and snowshoe racers), a full day's supply of food above what one plans to eat during the event, two quarts of water in insulated containers, and a $100 deposit for a bush pilot for evacuation if needed. The runners and snowshoe racers are flown back to Big Lake from the Skwentna finish, but that flight is included in the entry fee (which is on the high side, especially if you are a late entrant, as I was). To emphasize the seriousness of the risks, organizers require entries to be notarized.

All of this gear must be transported somehow. Before the race I borrowed the required lightweight tent and sleeping bag, bought a backpack large enough to stuff the sleeping bag into, got the rest of the stuff together, plus whatever other stuff I felt I would use, mostly clothes and more food, then I weighed it all, ready to go. Twenty-five pounds. Twenty-five pounds sounds like a small number. Add 25 pounds to my body weight and I still weigh less than several top ultrarunners, so I was seriously considering just wearing the pack the whole way and blitzing through the course.

As all ultrarunners know, numbers by themselves are deceiving. Sure, 15 miles is not a long way to go—except at the end of a 100-mile. Similarly, 25 pounds is not a great weight—until it's crammed into a backpack and put on one's back. To completely shatter my plan of wearing the pack the whole way, I did an eight-mile trail run in slippery conditions with the pack. My time was actually not very bad in an absolute sense, but in a relative sense it was terrible! I expended about a 90-percent effort for a 67-percent time, and I was sore all over. My shoulders were bruised, my lower back hurt, I could not breathe adequately for all the supporting straps and cinches, and my legs were wiped out.

Because of the snowy and icy trail conditions, gear can be hauled on a plastic two-child kid's sled. This is towed behind you, connected to a padded backpack waist belt by either rigid poles or bungee-cord threaded pipes. This is by far the most preferable method, even though it has its drawbacks. On flat terrain, which this course mostly is, the sled and load are almost negligible. On a downhill the sled gives a push that is not really the benefit that it seems at first glance. Uphills are a bear, but no worse than they would be with the pack on the back. Thankfully, there were few real uphills in the race. I decided that I would haul my gear by sled.

I arrived in Alaska already excited to be in my 50th state. I have been to all 50 states now, and raced in more than half of them. This is not a big deal to most people, but it was always a goal of mine, even as a kid, to see all 50 states. Simply by showing up in Anchorage I had reached a 30-year goal. I had good feelings from the beginning. There I was—in Alaska, in the wintertime, in some of the harshest conditions on the planet and, as icing on the cake, I was going to do an ultra! After an abysmally bad running year, I felt I needed to recover the spark, the challenge, that running had always given me. I hoped this race would do it.

I have had difficulty with cold races. Perhaps I was daft to think of trying Iditarun. My feeling is that when the easy becomes difficult, go after the impossible. It was precisely because I do not do well at cold races that I decided to do this Alaskan race in the middle of winter. It was a challenge that might or might not defeat me. It would be a serious mental challenge, offer physical hardships I had never endured before, plus have the not insubstantial financial hurdle of transportation costs, gear purchases, and so on.

Once I had committed myself mentally, I approached my only occasional sponsor, Thomas Ash (better known as Fish), of Ash and Associates, a freelance technical writer, and asked for some assistance. I do not know if it's possible, but I think he got more excited about the race than I did—and I was excited. While Fish's help did not cover all expenses, I was able to scrape up enough to do the race on a tight budget. Since a crew was a ludicrous thing to have on a course with no access for people not flown in by bush pilots, and with my wife not interested in Alaska, I saved a lot of money by going alone, although I regretted her absence, since it was an unshared experience.

With the fiscal burden allayed, I could concentrate on the physical and mental challenges that awaited. Physically, I was already fit early in the season. Two weeks before Iditarun, I did the Uwharrie 40 Mile. I ran well the whole way, despite flirting with hypothermia, and recovered quickly. Mentally I prepared by re-reading a cold weather survival book, all the pre-race Iditasport information (including a copy of Jack London's *To Build a Fire* and newspaper accounts of a moose trampling) and talked with experienced runners from Alaska. I was extremely lucky to have a chain of friends that led to a national-class miler and his wife and family living in Anchorage, who, on the strength of their own good character and one brief encounter more than a year previously, agreed to let me stay with them. They not only put me up, but also showed me around, gave me tons of advice, let me use their car, took me on runs, and otherwise entertained, educated, and tolerated me. I am greatly indebted to these people. Alaska and Alaskans are great.

I ran into an unexpected dilemma before the race. Not wanting to risk checking a sled on board the plane, I chose to buy my sled rig in Anchorage. Unfortunately, after driving all over Anchorage, (several times) I was only able to get the hardware for the sled rig, but I could not find a sled. I called Brooks and Rita Wade, Alaskans and fellow Iditarunners, and asked them where sleds were available. They had an old rig I could use, and they brought it to the pre-race meeting on Thursday. I was set to go.

By race morning I was well rested, had practiced twice with the sled, had watched dog-sled races and ice sculptures being made, had screws screwed into the soles of my shoes for snow and ice traction, and was well versed and aware of all potential cold-weather problems. I hitched a ride to the race start with a fellow Iditarunner doing only his second ultra. After the gear inspection I had about an hour and a half wait before the start, which I spent drinking Gatorade and eating. I was so nervous that I was shivering indoors. I was not cold, just trembling from excitement. The temperature outside was a comfortable 12 degrees F.

Finally—the start. What a zoo. What chaos. I loved it! We all lined up behind the banner for pictures. The day was clear, crisp, and beautiful. A nervous electric current thrummed among the athletes. With all our gear, the 60-plus racers took up a lot of room. The majority were cyclists lined up front, since they would be the fastest off. After them were the skiers with their sleds, then runners and snowshoe racers with our sleds behind us. Everything was so new and different. I was joyous just starting. I had already recaptured the feeling I had lost the previous year of participating in something grand with a similar group of special people. For me, there was magic in the air. All that remained to be seen was if the reality could equal the build-up.

We were off. Running across the frozen expanse of Big Lake I looked ahead to Mt. Susitna. That mountain gave me a rough bearing as we headed toward it and the Big Su checkpoint near its base. It seemed to rise white and majestic on the horizon, an impossible distance away, yet only about one-third of the total distance to travel.

I was unable to fully appreciate the Big Lake section, as I discovered, first, that I had consumed way too much pre-race Gatorade and had to stop frequently to urinate and, second, training twice with the sled did not teach me everything I needed to know about the nuances, tricks, and traps of sled pulling. For instance, my sled would sometimes flip on a flat section over an insignificant ski-skate track, but sometimes not flip after hitting a stump. If you do not believe in the animation of tools, I suggest you haul a sled around Alaska. It decidedly does have a mind of its own. After spending 12 miles working the kinks out of my sled handling and loading, I was finally able to concentrate on the race.

I was wearing thick cotton tights, double layered socks, Reebok Marathon Racers with screws in the soles, and a rubber overshoe strap thing with forefoot spikes called Spiky's over them. I had on a thick polypro long-sleeve shirt, a polar fleece vest, polypro mittens, and a polar fleece jester's hat. My body temperature was perfect—warm without sweating. I was constantly monitoring my hands, feet, and exposed facial areas for frostbite symptoms. Luckily, I had done several sub-fifteen degree runs, so this was not really new territory for me. That would come later, after dark. For now I was enjoying every second of being out on such a sharp day with company.

It appeared that many cyclists had much the same type of problems I had with my sled, as I would occasionally pass groups working on a bike, stowing gear, or getting gear out. At around 18 miles I caught up with Rob DeVelice, defending champion and course record holder; he was going along quite well. I had enjoyed getting his advice at the pre-race meeting, and we had run some on Big Lake together at the start. It was hard to talk clearly, as the sleds made a lot of noise behind us both, so with well wishes on both sides we separated.

The stretch to the Big Su River was, I believe, the toughest terrain. There were longer (50-yard) hills on this section, and they were often icy, making them difficult to negotiate. This stretch also had the most of what I call "speed bumps." Speed bumps are a series of roller coaster hills, up to about four feet high. For those that have run the Mountain Masochist 50 Mile, the speed bumps are similar to that race's "tank traps," except these speed bumps were much closer together and there were a whole lot more of them.

The speed bumps might even have been fun, were it not for the heavy bungee-corded sled behind me. During the last two steps up, the sled would slow down and stretch the bungee cords; it would still be dragging the first step down (it was still going up), but then on the first step up the next bump, the sled poles would rubber band into my lower back with the full downhill weight of the sled. It was irritating, until I looked at it as completely idiosyncratic to this one particular race; as such, it was simply an enrichment of my Alaskan trail racing experience. All other minor nuisances I looked at the same way; this turned the negatives into positives, or at least neutrals. It may have been uncomfortable, but it was just part of my Alaskan challenge.

I spent a lot of time searching for moose as I trekked along, but with no success. The race was still very new and fresh to me all the way to Big Su, encounters with the other racers not occurring too often. I was able to enjoy the ultra quiet, threat-laden serenity with just the right amount of distractions. On the steep, icy downhill to the frozen Big Su River, knowing the sled would flip anyway, I disconnected it and let it go ahead of me. It careened off an icy bump, built up speed, smashed into an icy snow bank, bounced off it, and finally shot out onto the river. It never once flipped! I hooked it back up once I got down, knowing I just had to cross the river and then I would be at the first checkpoint. I did not go more than ten yards before, for no obvious reason, it flipped on the flat surface. I had to laugh.

Pulling into the tent checkpoint, I took the opportunity to mix one and one-half liters of grape Gatorade, eat some of my cheese sandwich, and chew on a Stoker bar (they are softer in cold weather than Powerbars). There was a lot of hubbub going on and bikes in the way, the kind of homey disorder that lets you know there are good things in the world, and this was one of them. Later aid check stations maintained this feeling, although it generally got less crowded as the race wore on. After 11 minutes I was off, headed out to Alexander Creek.

There we started running on more frozen swamps and small pond and lake surfaces. Swamps were mostly clear areas where the headwinds blew and cooled us off; dead flat, fairly smooth running, but with a slight post-holing effect. The cyclists had chewed this up some when they also broke through crusty surface snow. The swamps—and there were a lot of swamps—were wet, but not bad for running. I liked them. You could see the competition both ahead and behind from sometimes greater distances (a half-mile or more); you could watch them falter at bad spots and hustle at good spots. The mountains to the left (south) were visible and inviting, and when I was lucky I could look to the right and make out Mt. McKinley. Visibility was exceptional.

When not on a swamp or lake surface, the course went through the woods. This meant hills, either in speed bump form or in longer, winding climbs with sled-flipping descents. Running over a frozen swamp it seemed as if the snow was only inches deep, because everything was so flat (except for infrequent drifts where it is quite deep, which I discovered often by punching through to ankle, shin, and knee depth). On the woods sections snow was softer, less scoured, and deeper, often accumulating in weird places and weird ways. Hearing that racers frequently hallucinate during the race, I thought it silly, but there is a sensory deprivation effect from running constantly in all that white. I could imagine the mind wanting to make patterns from all the macabre snow forms all around. It often appeared as if I was running through an enormous eerie modern art gallery full of sculptures, all on a white or white and brown theme, quite beautiful.

For me this part of the course was perfect. Just when I became tired of running across open swamps, there would be a section of more arduous woods running, and just when that started getting old, it was back to the easier running across a swamp. Savoring all of this I pulled into Alexander Creek.

There I spent more time eating some dried fruit, a Stoker bar, and replenishing my Gatorade. I switched from sunglasses to my regular glasses. I also put on a polar fleece jacket over everything else, plus put on another pair of tights, changed my polypro mitts to polypro gloves and then put neoprene gloves over them. I was determined not to get cold. I spent a frustrating 15 minutes searching for my primary flashlight that I must have lost, lithium batteries and all, somewhere during my first hectic 12 miles. I grabbed my backup light, stuffed it in my fanny pack, and took off. Then it was on to Rabbit Lake, the last checkpoint before the finish.

I went about 30 minutes on this stretch before it got dark, but with a little more than a half-moon, an abundance of white surfaces, and the mostly open terrain, I discovered I never needed my flashlight at all. The course did become much lonelier, as athletes were more spread out and congregated only at checkpoints. One advantage to the night running and long horizons was that it was easier to see racers ahead and behind (assuming they were using lights). I had only recently adjusted to the dark and was moseying along, head tripping on the snow shapes, when I saw a glimmer ahead in the distance. I gave chase just for fun. Gradually closing I noticed an even stronger light ahead, one that was not moving around. I closed enough to see the first light disappear into the tent. A few minutes later I arrived at the Rabbit Lake checkpoint.

During that last stretch I became aware that my fingers were getting nippy. The neoprene gloves were not cutting it. Pulling into the checkpoint I put away the neoprene gloves and put on the polypro mitts over the polypro gloves. Instant warmth. Aaahh! I pulled my shoes off to check my socks. The toes were only slightly damp and warm, so no worries there. I drank a cup of hot chocolate, ate some more dried fruit, a bite of Stoker bar, fixed my Gatorade, put on my GoreTex wind jacket, and took off. I was very excited. My next stop would be the finish line. My quest was almost over.

The adrenaline rush lasted about five miles, and got me ahead of the first two skiers and one cyclist. Then the "cold" reality of 15 more miles sank in, so I backed off the pace, ate some more dried fruit, drank some more, and tried to see the sources of occasional twig snapping in the shadow-shrouded forests. The temperature felt as if it had really dropped, although it only went to minus five. I could tell it was colder, as I had a mustache icicle extending well past my chin and so much ice clustered on the mustache that I could not rub my nose. The wind was strong coming off the frozen swamps.

As I neared the finish the course seemed to change somewhat. It became a straight line. I could look past one upcoming swamp and see the trail cut straight through the trees on a small hill on the other side. From that hilltop I could see the course go straight down across another swamp, straight up another small hill on the other side. On and on it went.

I was so into watching my footing and looking for moose that I did not realize I had not seen a trail marker for a while. So I started looking. I ran about two hours before I saw a clear trail marker. I was not too concerned, as I was following bike tracks. Had I used my flashlight, I would probably have seen many, but I wanted to do it the hard way. Also, I observed a light in the background catching up on me. The area was way too sparse to explain bike tracks in front and a light behind if I was not on the correct course. Finally, I started seeing frequent markings. What a relief. I knew I was right, but still, feeling near done and having the fear of a closing competitor, I picked up the pace.

My finish line "sprint" lasted around two hours, but that was good enough to hold off the cyclist that caught me just before crossing the Skwentna River. I was lucky to be able to watch a good display of Northern Lights ahead of me. What a treat to watch the flowing, glowing clouds dance across the sky in their rapid slow-motion movement.

Feeling like I had run an eternity since Rabbit Lake, I knew at the river crossing I was almost done. Like all really good things, my Iditarun was coming to an end. Thankfully, I approached the Skwentna lodges. I had done it. Not only had I done it, but it was a perfect race. My body temperature was just right the whole way. I finished dry and warm. My fingers were a little nippy, but all right on inspection.

I was very satisfied accepting the congratulations of the volunteers and the few resting cyclists. I had run at least 98 percent of the course, felt strong the whole way, and never once felt nauseous. The only way it could have been better would have been if I had broken Rob's course record, but that time was well out of my reach. I gave it my best shot, but was more than an hour and a half slower.

Contentedly, I went about changing shoes in the comfort of the lodge. After yanking off my shoes and socks I had a disquieting revelation. Even with a total lack of any prior symptoms my toes had frostbite. Since I had checked my feet at Rabbit Lake and because they had never felt cold or numb, the frostbite must have been a result of restricted cutaneous circulation, due to the tight forefoot shoe covering (the Spiky's) that I never removed throughout the race. Not wanting to raise an alarm, I quickly re-dressed my feet in warm socks and roomy shoes, and solemnly waited for daylight and the morning flight out to Big Lake and then back to Anchorage. I spent a good night of conversation among fellow racers and volunteers. I congratulated Rob, who came in second in the Iditarun, a little ahead of Shawn Lyons, the first Iditashoe athlete, avenging his narrow second-place finish the previous year.

In the morning, in case we had forgotten we were in a wilderness, Mother Nature had a surprise for us. Despite our relative calm there were extremely high, gusty winds in Anchorage. The planes could not leave to get to Skwentna. So we were stuck in the lodges for another day and a night. So it was with trepidation that I told the nurse about my frostbite, whereupon I was excessively babied and pampered. I found it an ironic humor that here I was the fastest from Big Lake to Skwentna on foot (that year) and yet all these people were willingly running all over the place for me. The really bad part was that except for the frostbite, which was not very painful but awfully ugly, I felt great. Even the usual ankle tendonitis that I took for granted would flare up did not bother me. I guess that was good, since my ordeal of frostbite was just beginning.

As the day and night wore on, the three small lodges accumulated more than 25 people. The Iditarun division had 11 starters and 11 finishers, a 100-percent completion rate. How tough can it be? There were two snowshoe finishers: Shawn Lyons, longtime Iditasport competitor and previous winner, and Ron Hoffman from Boston. Ron's bindings were a little tight in some areas like my Spiky's were, and he got some minor frostbite.

Sitting around the lodge trying to find a temperature comfort zone was difficult: If the area around the stove was comfortable, the area near the door (and the two were not far separated) was frigid. The conversations were fascinating. A *Jeopardy!* contestant search would have been overwhelmed. I knew I was overwhelmed, so I listened and tried not to appear any dumber than I was. No one appeared discomfited in the slightest about being stranded in the middle of nowhere. To most it seemed like just a good excuse to rest, talk, and eat more.

On one trip out of the stultifying heat into the clarity of early morning sub-zero air outside I noticed a brilliant display of Northern Lights directly overhead. It covered the whole sky. The phosphorescent mist would glide, quicken, and intensify, then fade, glide, quicken and intensify somewhere else in a stately surreal procession on the world's ceiling. It seemed so close that I felt I could reach up and grab a handful of fairy dust. I even tried. By itself this moment was worth the trip.

Later that morning the planes finally arrived, and we traveled back to Big Lake. The plane ride was an adventure in itself; I was happily clicking pictures away like any tourist. The course sure looks shorter from the air. I saw a couple of moose from the plane, but not one during the run. Arriving at Big Lake I gave foot photos—"Don't let this happen to you!" —to be used as further testament on the hazards of this race, and then hitched a ride back to Anchorage with Ron Hoffman and his wife.

Home less than two weeks. I started running again, (painfully) still trying to coax life back into my erstwhile frozen toes and to limit the amount of permanently damaged tissue. Was it worth it? Every cent and dollar, every wince and scream. It may have been expensive financially and more so physically, but any time I accomplish something I am proud of, it is worth it. In fact, the frostbite adds to the experience in a positive way. It has given me an even more tangible long-term memory of the whole positive experience.

I approached this race as an adventure, and no true adventure exists without risks. So I did not escape this adventure unscathed. In the future all I need to do to wax nostalgic about the Iditarun is simply to look at my feet. The race director expressed concern about the future of the Iditarun, largely because of the damage I suffered, and implored me to warn readers. O.K., you are warned. Frostbite can occur in the absence of symptoms (feeling extremely cold and then growing numb) if cutaneous circulation is restricted (tight socks, tight shoes, tight bindings, both snowshoes and Spiky's).

I know he is concerned about the athlete's welfare, but he is putting on a race in the middle of winter in Alaska. The checkpoints were frequent enough and the care adequate enough at them that the race, race officials, and volunteers were in no way at fault for my injury. Actually, the runners are probably the best suited for this course. We only go half as far as the skiers and cyclists, and are more likely to take our time at the checkpoints for better care.

Out on the snow and ice I ran a perfect race. I proved something to myself. Even though this was a competition, the real competitors were not fellow runners, but the whistling wind blowing ice crystals in my face and through my clothes; the white soft surface I floundered and fell in; the short, icy hill I slipped on and slid back to the bottom; the lack of food, shelter, or aid of any kind in the remote isolation between checkpoints; and always present, the numbing cold hovering constantly, patiently, waiting to bite. It was a great race, and a great experience.

Badwater: Inside the World's Longest, Hottest, Toughest, Baddest Endurance Race

By Roy Wallack

To understand the history and culture of the Badwater Ultramarathon, a 135-mile foot race from the depths of Death Valley to the flanks of Mount Whitney, you must be clear about one thing: This is not the Ironman of ultrarunning. This is not merely an extraordinarily long, extra-hard run. This is not the annual focus of all of the world's greatest ultrarunners. In fact, most top ultrarunners don't even compete in this race—or even regard it as running at all.

"It's more of a hike, a 130-degree-in-a-sandstorm hike, a torture-fest that I don't want to repeat," says the great Ann Trason, a 13-time winner of the Western States 100 Mile who participated in Badwater once—as a crew member. "I like adventure, but this is an out-of-this-world experience. I drank more *crewing* Badwater than I did *running* Western States. I felt like I was in *Star Trek*—and I wanted to be beamed out."

In a nutshell, Badwater is a different planet. In this unique world, rubber soles melt, air-sole heel cushions explode, gel oozes out of shoes. Sweat dries before it wets your skin. Cans of soup are already warm when you open them. Hotel air conditioning lowers the temperature to 90. Outside, it feels like you've got a hair dryer in your face, or you're in an oven. To put it mildly, Badwater is not for everybody. In fact, it's safe to say that it's only for people who, like Badwater itself, are *out there*.

The Pioneer

Consider Al Arnold, the man who started it all. "I've always been the type who thought, 'If the world's going one way, then I'm going the other,'" says Arnold, now 75 and living in Walnut Creek, California. Arnold was always trying something just to prove it could be done. At age 21, he was a muscle-bound six foot, five inch brute who, just for fun, would lift up the rear ends of small cars. He tried out for the 1948 U.S. Olympic boxing team as a light-heavyweight. During a University of California at Berkeley science project, he and a friend rode a teeter-totter for 72 hours straight, setting a world record of 45,159 up-and-downs. After taking 12 years to graduate with a business degree, he worked as a technician, building ocean wave force-measuring devices. He married twice, enjoyed the good life, and morphed "from jock to fat slob" (his words), ballooning to 275 pounds.

Then, at age 39, Arnold got some life-changing news: he had glaucoma. He could no longer see well enough to hit a tennis ball. He was told by a doctor that "I'd soon have a tag on my toe." But he didn't really get motivated to change his life until he got word of the upcoming 1968 U.S. vs. World Masters Invitational Track and Field Championships. Just to prove it could be done, Arnold was running stadium steps with 100 pounds of weights strapped to his body. In 18 months, he'd dropped to a solid 225 pounds. At the masters championships, he won the half-mile. Before long, Arnold was working as an athletic director at a health club, and before most people had heard of the term, he was an ultrarunner.

In 1973, Arnold heard about Paxton Beale and Ken Crutchlow, who completed a 150-mile relay run from Badwater, the lowest point in the Western Hemisphere at 282 feet below sea level, all the way to the top of 14,496-foot Mount Whitney, the highest point in the contiguous United States. Crutchlow, an Englishman from Santa Rosa, California who imported London cabs for a living, did a lot of crazy stuff in his time—including riding a bike from San Francisco to Alaska on a bet. Scanning a map of California, he'd noticed how close the "lowest" and "highest" points were. According to one report, he considered it "outrageous" to think that any man could complete that trek alone.

Arnold was electrified when he heard about the tag-team's achievement. Death Valley fascinated him. Growing up in the 1940s, his favorite radio show was *Death Valley Days*. He'd imagined old prospectors, battles with Indians, noble pioneers struggling for existence. "Immediately, I knew that I had to do that run, too," says Arnold. "But I wasn't about to leap-frog." He did plan to run with a partner—his dentist David Gabor, a former Hungarian freedom fighter—but both would not complete the entire route.

In 1974, the pair pushed off at Badwater. Several hours later, the mercury topped out at more than 130 degrees. They lasted 18 miles—until Gabor went into shock. "My buddy almost died," said Arnold. "His whole body shut down. Blood flow to the arms and legs stopped. We had put him into an ice-filled bathtub at the Furnace Creek Ranch. Took him months to recover." From that point on, Arnold knew he had to go it alone. "When you do something like this, as far-out as Badwater, your mind has to be focused. You can't feel responsible for someone." So a year later, the 47-year-old Arnold was back. Unfortunately, his knee was not cooperative. Its grotesque swelling stopped his second attempt at mile 36, just before beginning the ascent of 4,956-foot high Townes Pass.

But 1977 would be different. For two years, Arnold trained like a man possessed. He pedaled a bike in a 200-degree sauna for two hours a day. Carrying no water and living off the land, he ran 200 to 250 miles a week up and down 3,800-foot Mount Diablo, a Bay Area landmark near his home. He once jogged for 36 hours straight. "I became so much a part of the land that I could walk through a pack of deer without them moving," he says. "Once, I shared a water hole and its surrounding shade with the 'resident mountain lion.' I never saw it again. It was one of those moments that you never forget."

On August 3, 1977, Death Valley recorded its highest known temperature that year: 124 degrees F. While the nearly 50-year-old Al Arnold jogged and power-walked, the super-heated road surface radiated nearly 200 degrees. He left Badwater before dawn, along with a two-man support crew, photographer Erik Rakonen and friend Glenn Phillips, and 30 gallons of a self-concocted electrolyte solution of fructose and water. He drank it all.

Arnold covered the first 40 miles in 10 hours, developed knee trouble on the 15-mile climb over the Panamints, stopped to stretch for a couple hours, then kept going, very slowly. "At least I'd learned one thing over the years: go fast and you die," he says. Amazingly, Arnold ran an extra 45 miles over the second half of the route. Concerned over the disappearance of his support vehicle, he actually *ran back* 22 miles to find Rakonen, now crewing alone, asleep and "dead to the world" in the car. A purist, he refused a ride 22 miles back up the course and instead just resumed running towards Whitney.

Searing winds blasted Arnold with sand and silt on the climb over the Inyo Mountains, but it didn't matter. In his mind he had become Olympic decathlon champion Bruce Jenner, immortalized on a box of Wheaties. As he descended into the Owens Valley, he gazed at Mount Whitney for the first time. The sight so moved him that he stopped and spoke directly to the mountain. "You probably thought you'd never see me, but soon I'm going to be on top of you," Arnold warned the peak, according to a profile in the 1978 issue of *Marathoner* magazine. "She's a very powerful lady," he explained, "and I didn't want to conquer her, just be part of a relationship."

Approaching the little town of Lone Pine, the last stop before the final climb, people started coming out onto Highway 136 to take pictures of the "crazy man who had just run from Death Valley." A Highway Patrolman handed him a hamburger and chips. He ate only the bun and headed uphill into the Sierra Foothills, dodging two wild donkeys on the way to the Mount Whitney Portal at 8,400 feet.

The pavement ended and the 11-mile climb up the Mount Whitney trail began. "As I got closer and closer to the top, the hikers, forewarned of my arrival, all cheered for me," says Arnold. "It was like a ticker-tape parade." About 192 miles after he'd began his quest, Arnold reached 14,496 feet—the Mount Whitney summit. He burst into tears and couldn't stop. He'd lost 17 pounds, eight percent of his body weight. He'd been on the road for 84 hours.

Yet there was no time to spare. As dusk fell, Arnold staggered down to the Trail Camp campsite at 12,000 feet. A tent, sleeping bag and warm clothing were to have been stored for him there. Instead, there was nothing left but a plastic tarp. Everything else had been stolen. After nearly roasting alive in 130 to 120-degree temperatures for more than three days, Arnold spent the fourth night in his running shorts, rolled up in plastic, shivering in 20-degree temperatures.

A couple of days later, Arnold's wife suggested a way to warm her man up: a trip to Maui. It would lead to a test more challenging than his amazing run. On his tenth day of bodysurfing, a 25-foot wave torpedoed Arnold into the sand, dislocating the cervical area of his neck, separating both shoulders and leaving a severe contusion on his spinal cord. Paralyzed below the neck, gulping for air, Arnold went under seven times before washing up on the shore. Doctors told him he'd never be able to walk again without a walker, but Arnold left it on the sidewalk when the cab drove him to the airport for the flight home. A mere four months later he ran the five-loop Paul Masson Winery Marathon, stopping every five miles to run into the fire station to clean his running shorts. The accident had left him without bladder or bowel control, a condition that wouldn't clear up for nearly 15 years. Nonetheless, he finished in 4:59:59, much to the amusement of those who trailed him. "'I'll never live it down,' my friend Stan Pletz told me," said Arnold, "'I was beaten by a paralyzed man.' "A year later, he ran 99 miles around Lake Tahoe in 19 hours.

Despite his continued running, Arnold never fully recovered from his paralysis. "My body feels like my foot's been asleep for 25 years," he says. As for Badwater, Arnold's never considered trying it again. "I did it to prove it could be done—like Roger Bannister breaking the four-minute mile," he said. "Now, I just sit back amazed at the world-class names who do it now. I'm not in their league." True. Al Arnold is in a league all his own.

The Race Is On

In 1980, 34-year-old Jay Birmingham, a running-store owner from Jacksonville, Florida, ran from Los Angeles to New York wearing a small backpack in 71 days, 22 hours, and 59 minutes, the fastest non-supported transcontinental crossing in history. That run, mainly along old U.S. 60, taught him a lot, but especially one thing: "I was a good hot-weather runner," he said. He'd easily cruised through a heat wave that stretched from Texas to Indiana.

Birmingham had read the article in *Marathoner* magazine about Al Arnold's Badwater trek and felt 84 hours would be an easy record to break. He'd also gotten advice from Badwater wannabe Gary Morris, who only got as far as Townes Pass in 1980. So in August of 1981, Birmingham embarked on a family road trip through North Carolina, Colorado, Las Vegas, and other places, getting in his training miles along the way. They eventually arrived in Death Valley and he started running from Badwater at 6:00 a.m. on August 15. He summited Mount Whitney 75 hours and 34 minutes later.

Other than "terrible pain in my heel" from Townes Pass to Lone Pine due to a heat-bloated lump in his shoe, the run went smoothly. Birmingham never ran past 10:00 p.m., slept at least six hours a night, and climbed Whitney with his entire family without experiencing any altitude problems. He found the dry heat of Death Valley to be much easier to handle than the draining humidity of his Florida training ground; a week spent in the Rockies just before the run acclimatized him to high elevations.

Birmingham's feat didn't gain him national fame, but he did become the first person to publish a book about Badwater, *The Longest Hill*, released in 1983. He also put his name in the *Guinness Book of World Records* and set off a slow-building land rush that saw 30 people complete the lowest-to-highest course during the next decade. In 1982, Max Telford of New Zealand blitzed the blistering course in just 56:33. American Gill Cornell, starting at night, ran it in 45:15 in 1987. The very next day, Badwater godfather Ken Crutchlow returned with two Americans and a Brit to stage the first actual head-to-head race on the course, the U.S. versus the U.K.

As the buzz about Badwater began to grow, the course got the attention of the Hi-Tec shoe company. Seeing the race as a good promotional vehicle for its new running shoe, appropriately named the "Badwater 146," it began sponsoring and producing the event in 1988. It stuck to the long-established "gentlemen's rule" that Badwater must be held in the two-month July-August window, when the temperature is hottest. "Nothing else I've done since compares to Badwater," says David Pompel, who directed the race for three years while working at Hi-Tec and is now a manager at Timberland. "To go from lowest to highest, to be at 119 degrees at 6:00 p.m., to see the gel melting out of a (running) shoe, to have an elevation gain of 24,000 feet, it looked like something out of *Mad Max: Beyond Thunderdome*," he said. "Remember, there was no Eco-Challenge then. Most people looked at us like we'd lost our minds."

One of Pompel's most memorable moments came that first year, when he watched Adrian Crane—later to gain fame for bagging all 50 of the highest points in each U.S. state in one year—set off across the Death Valley salt flats with modified cross-country skis. "He made the rest of the runners seem normal."

In 1988, eight racers competed in the first Hi-Tec-sponsored race; four finished. American Tom Possert won in 45:10, a figure in dispute because he was photographed being dragged uphill by his support crew. In 1989, seven finished and the race scored its biggest media coup: five minutes on *The Today Show* with Bryant Gumbel.

One big change in 1989 was moving to a 6:00 p.m. start time, to avoid the hottest part of the day in Death Valley. This rankled the purists, who wanted maximum heat exposure in Death Valley, so the race was eventually switched back to an a.m. start for the 1996 race and those held since. In 1990, the Forest Service forced the race to conclude at the Whitney Portal, creating the 135-mile distance that has been the official route to this day. Over the years, many runners continued onto the mountain unofficially after securing permits. That year, Possert set a new record to the Portal of 27:56. That time shrank quickly over the following decade: to Marshall Ulrich's still current p.m. start record of 26:18 in 1992, then a slew of a.m. start records, such as Gabriel Flores' 28:09 in 1998, Eric Clifton's 27:09 in 1999, and the current a.m. and overall record of 25:09:05, set in 2000 by Russian superhero Anatoli Kruglikov.

Angelika Castaneda and her twin sister Barbara Alvarez were the only women to finish Badwater in 1989 and 1990, but by 1991 were being challenged by the likes of Bonnie Boyer, who set the women's p.m. start record that year, 36:19. The field grew to seven women by 1999, when all female participants proudly finished. A record 17 women registered to compete in 2002. The current course record was set in 2002 by Pam Reed, in a time of 27:56:47. That was nine hours faster than Castaneda's 1999 record of 36:58, which was, in turn, three minutes faster than Lisa Smith's 1997 record of 37:01.

Smith, a massage therapist and running and triathlon coach from Victor, Idaho, exhibits the typical ultra career path; tiring of triathlon after seven Ironmans, she heard about Badwater from Ulrich at the 1995 Eco-Challenge. When she lined up in 1995, the longest run she'd ever done was four hours. Luckily, she loves the heat. She finished in 41:24. After winning three times, she married cameraman Jay Batchen in 2000, and naturally persuaded her husband to run with her. They set a couple's record of 43:23:56 in 2000.

The Supermen

One night in early 1989, Richard Benyo, a marathoner, author, *San Francisco Chronicle* columnist, and former *Runner's World* managing editor, was getting drunk with Tom Crawford, the fifth person to complete Badwater and a two-time finisher. "Listen, man," Benyo slurred, "since you already had to come 12 miles down from the peak, why the heck didn't you just run back all the way (back) to Badwater and finish it?" Badwater was suddenly taken to a new level: the double. Round-trip. Back-to-back.

For three months beforehand, Benyo and Crawford ran in a dry sauna for up to an hour a day. They doubled their bodies' water processing ability from two quarts to one gallon per hour. They camped for a week in Panamint Springs before the event, running in the heat for four or five hours a day to teach their bodies to conserve water and salt. "Untrained people lose more salt than trained people," he explained. "So we developed a ritual—licking each others' arms. After the third day, they wouldn't taste so salty anymore."

During the run, everything went smoothly until the descent from the Mount Whitney summit, when hail and lightning storms reigned terror on the duo. Benyo, slowed by destroyed toes and quads, hobbled back to Badwater in 170 hours and 58 minutes, two days after Crawford, who doubled in 126:34. Every inch of the agonizing way is detailed in Benyo's acclaimed book, *The Death Valley 300*.

Two months after the double, Benyo and Crawford began planning another attempt. Benyo completed the double again in 1992 in 157:58. Over the next four years, six others doubled, including Benyo's wife, Rhonda Provost, who became the first woman to do a double in 1995, in a time of 143:45. In 1996, Milan Milanovich of Switzerland set the double record of 110:26. In 1994, American Scott Weber did a triple: Whitney to Badwater to Whitney to Badwater, in 257:32.

Marshall Ulrich felt the need to push the boundaries of human endurance even further. A long-time marathoner and ultrarunner from Fort Morgan, Colorado, Ulrich wholesales boneless frozen beef to dog food manufacturers. In 1990, he was looking for a new challenge. Naturally, that led to Badwater. Having never driven the course, Ulrich figured it would cool off once he left the Death Valley floor. "I had no idea," he said. After leading the race for 117 miles, Ulrich was passed by 1988 winner Possert. Vowing to return and win, Ulrich set a new p.m. start record of 26:32 in 1991 and lowered that to 26:18 in '92. At this writing, Ulrich has done the Badwater race ten times, won it four times, never stopped at the Portal, and still holds the unofficial record of 33 hours to the Whitney summit.

But all that was just a warm-up for a feat that astounded the ultrarunning world. On July 3, 1999, just ten days before the race, Ulrich became the first person to complete the Badwater course *unassisted*. Pulling a specially designed, two-wheeled, solar panel-equipped cart that initially weighed 212 pounds and held 21.5 gallons, he reached the Portal, and then continued with a backpack to the top of Mount Whitney. The total time: 77 hours and 48 minutes. "It's the hardest thing I've ever done," he told the *Fort Morgan Times*. "I don't know how many times I thought of quitting. I was reduced to a desert animal, crawling under mesquite bushes to get away from the heat."

As if that wasn't enough, in 2001 Ulrich commemorated his 50th birthday with something else that had never been done before, a quad: a double up-and-back; 584 miles with 48,000 feet of elevation gain. Starting on July 20, 2001 at 6:10 a.m., Ulrich ran continuously for the first four days, stopping only for short naps totaling one-and-a-half hours per day. He broke the old double record by almost nine hours, finishing in 96:07, attended the pre-race meeting, went to sleep, then woke up in time to start the official Badwater Ultramarathon with 70 other contestants the next morning.

Wracked by severe tendinitis on his shins, Ulrich's crew had to ice and wrap his legs every 20 to 30 minutes during the third and fourth crossings He summited Whitney for a second time with the clock ticking at 185 hours, setting a new triple-crossing record. Nearly wearing through his second pair of shoes, which had to be cut on the sides to relieve several huge, painful, blisters, Ulrich hobbled into Badwater after 253 hours (10 days and 13 hours).

The effort paid off. Ulrich, growing increasingly spiritual over the years, managed to raise $65,000 for Teachers Fillipinni, a Rome-based order of nuns dedicated to helping starving children. On April 17, 2002 he and Lisa Smith, his Quad crew chief, had an audience with the Pope at the Vatican.

But Ulrich is not finished. In 2002, both he and 67-year-old Englishman Jack Denness, a retired Lloyd's of London driver, became the first people to complete 10 Badwater races. This milestone was also Ulrich's 100th ultra, with an average distance per outing of 110 miles. From there, he plans to make what he calls "a logical progression": combining hot weather ultrarunning with snowbound mountain climbing. In 2003, he'll take it to the extreme: The Everest Summit to Sea—the longest, fastest descent ever from the world's highest place, Mount Everest, to Calcutta and the Indian Ocean, 600 miles away. Through it all, though, he won't forget his roots. "When I'm 100, I'll still be doing Badwater," he says.

The Organizers

When Hi-Tec employee Matt Frederick took over as Badwater 135 race director in 1996, the participation limit was gradually raised from 25 to 40. The time to "buckle"—to earn the prized Badwater belt buckle that signifies you finished well under the overall time limit of 60 hours—was raised from 45 hours to 48. He was also at the helm when Hollywood immortalized the race in the award-winning feature-length documentary *Running on the Sun*, directed by Mel Stuart of *Willy Wonka and the Chocolate Factory* fame.

Frederick enjoyed the quirkiness of the event. In a statistical irony that rankles purists, he discovered that walkers have a higher finishing percentage than runners. He found that older runners finish more frequently than younger ones. He laughs when he tells of driving all the way to Beatty, Nevada, cleaning out a little store and driving back with 200 pounds of ice. Most of all, he remembers the characters: California dentist Dale Sutton, who raced in pajamas from head to toe, and kept cool by sewing extra pockets on his pants and filling them with ice; Major Maples, a U.S. Marine who DNF'd every other year, but finally finished with a whole crew of Corpsmen as his support crew in 1997 and 2000; and Charlie Liskey, who crawled across the finish line in 1996. His favorites are the three-time finishers he calls his "virtual grandparents," Ben and Denise Jones, known to most as the "mayor" and "first lady" of Badwater.

The couple officially received their titles in a special ceremony at Badwater on July 4, 1992, in recognition of their generous support of the event. Ben, the sole doctor in Lone Pine, has provided medical assistance, served as the race's historian (see his many race reports on the web site), and, with Denise, hosts annual race-course training clinics on Memorial Day and Fourth of July weekends. They also are enthusiastic participants. In 1991, then-58-year-old Ben became the only runner to conduct an autopsy in the middle of the race. He arrived at the Portal that year in 49:00, and at the Whitney Summit in 72:58. He completed Badwater again in 1992 and 1993, with a support truck carrying plastic palm trees and an ice-filled casket in which to cool off. Denise, known as the "blister queen" because of her expertise in dealing with Badwater runners' feet, is also a three-time finisher (1994, 1996, and 1999). By late 1999, having long since dropped their "Badwater 146" running and hiking shoe lines, Hi-Tec decided to abandon all support of the race.

Into the void stepped Chris Kostman's AdventureCORPS, producers of the annual Furnace Creek 508 bicycle race through Death Valley, and creator of the Los Angeles Marathon Bike Tour, Earth Journey Triathlon Stage Race, and the relay division of the Race Across America bicycle race. No desk jockey, Kostman is a record-setting ultramarathon cyclist who has done the Race Across America, Triple Ironman, Iditasport, and other endurance events. In 1995, in recognition of the kindred spirit between the Badwater 135 and his own Furnace Creek 508, he created the "Death Valley Cup," to be awarded to the first or fastest athlete to complete both events in the same calendar year. Not surprisingly, Marshall Ulrich completed both in 1996 and became the first recipient. Angelika Castaneda took the first women's cup in 1999.

"When Ben Jones suggested that I should step in to fill the void left by Hi-

Tec's pullout, I saw an opportunity to give a fantastic, yet under-publicized event the energy and organization it deserves," says Kostman. "It wasn't hard to do; Death Valley is one of the world's great ultra athlete meeting grounds and is an incomparable natural sports arena."

Recent years have seen noticeable additions to what is now called the Badwater Ultramarathon: the first official race website, www.badwaterultra.com; an annual web cast during the race and a new title sponsor in the form of Sun Precautions, the Everett, Washington based makers of Solumbra 30+ SPF sun protective clothing, medically accepted sun protection for sun sensitive and sun sensible people. Also, with a history of successful events in Death Valley, Kostman lobbied the Park Service to double the maximum field size.

The years 2005 and 2006 saw a new force at Badwater, as Seattle, Washington's Scott Jurek took the race by storm. In 2005, Jurek took the course record into unchartered territory, clocking 24:36:08. He returned in 2006 to defend his title in 25:41:18; not a record, but a time only matched by his own the previous year.

Now, the first time, there is instant worldwide access to Badwater information and applications. In recent years, more than a dozen countries have been represented, including Russia, Italy, France, Japan, Brazil, and Hong Kong. Despite raising runner qualification and selection standards each year, the field has grown. Finally, with the establishment of the Badwater Hall of Fame, Kostman has brought a sense of history to the event. Fittingly, the first person inducted into the Hall, moments before the 2002 race began, was the man who started it all 25 years ago, Al Arnold. When told of his upcoming induction, the George Washington of running in 130-degree temperatures, now 75 and unable to run due to a bum knee, was moved to tell a story. "I just always liked doing things that others might have thought were crazy, and they weren't always grand things like Badwater," says Arnold. "I once ran around a 10-by-10 wrestling mat for 10 hours. Even now, I hike a lot in a small area in the hills that most people just pass through quickly, all except for one 14-year-old kid. He'd seen me there a few times, and finally stopped to ask me, 'Why do you come here?' I answered, 'Because it's my cave.' The boy then asked me, 'How big is your cave?' I looked at him and said, 'How big is your mind?' The boy was silent for a few seconds. Then he said, 'Can I hike with you again?'"

Across the Desert: The Marathon Des Sables

By Kevin Setnes and Kurt Barkley

Kurt Barkley is certainly not a household name in the world of ultrarunning. In fact, his only ultra credentials prior to this past April came from two minor 50-km trail races. Kurt is an ultrarunner on the rise however, as evidenced by his best-ever showing by an American in the recent Marathon Des Sables (MDS) in Morocco.

What inspired him to take on such a tough challenge? Three years ago, Kurt read an article in Outside *magazine, which referred to the Marathon Des Sables as the "toughest footrace in the world." As he says, "I just fell for it. I really wanted to challenge myself mentally more than physically. Also, the Sahara Desert holds its own mystique."*

His quest to run the race in Morocco began in earnest when he contacted me about training last fall. Having run the Marathon des Sables only in my dreams, and usually deferring to accomplished Marathon Des Sables veterans such as Cathy Tibbetts or others, I felt Kurt needed to first learn the skills of an accomplished ultrarunner, since he clearly indicated that he wanted to do more than just finish. He wanted to be competitive with the field. That's a tall order for a first-timer!

Through the winter and months leading up to the event, his principal focus was on establishing a solid base of miles, coupled with enough quality to maintain his already established speed. Added to this was the necessary logistical preparation, as well as longer runs with a pack loaded with a weight similar to what he would have to carry in the MDS.

Kurt also had to learn the finer points of energy management, as well as the recovery mechanisms that are so critical to stage races of this nature. He credits this preparation to his finishing so high in the field. When others were sick or nauseated, he was hungry and actually was able to sponge food items off others who could not stomach what they had brought. This prevented him from "bonking" or ever feeling entirely depleted.

I asked Kurt what surprised him most about the event. He said, "The miles and miles of rocks. Also I didn't expect the camaraderie and friendships made, which was probably the best part of the whole experience." When asked what area he would improve upon, he answered, "Navigation skills; learning how to run faster on rocks." Kurt's next goals are a 100-mile in the fall adding, "I really enjoy the "ultra culture" as opposed to the road race atmosphere." Here are some details from a diary he kept of the six-day experience from the Marathon Des Sables.

Sunday, April 7: Stage one: Oued Draa to Oued Mird, 26 km

9:38 a.m. I planned to go out slowly until first checkpoint (CP); it was very rocky terrain, so I had to watch every step. This first stage had one mile of dunes, which was just a preview of things to come. Although the dunes were very hard to run, they were beautiful. A tailwind pushed us through and helped cool the 85 to 90 degree F day. I had stomach cramps and did not run as hard as I would have liked. I felt like going harder, but my stomach would not let me. Diarrhea set in after the stage finish. My placing was 48th overall and third American, in 2:15:32.

I took some medicine for stomach and went to bed at 7:30 p.m., sleeping on a cardboard box, tossing and turning. My lightweight sleeping bag (one pound, seven ounces) kept me warm. I shared a Berber tent with seven others, two of whom snored loudly. I was jealous of their sound slumber, still awake at 11:30 p.m.

Stage two: Oued Mird to Bounou, 36 km

6:00 a.m. The tents were taken down by the Berbers and we were left cold and windblown in the open bivouac. I found a trash bag, using the old runner's trick of turning it into a windbreaker. Some children came up to the bivouac; I gave them all of my gin-gin candies and showed them a picture of my kids. I had to wonder how they got there, as I saw no signs of a village anywhere around.

8:50 a.m. I had to run up to the start, as the race director counted down in French to begin the stage. We encountered an immediate headwind. I started out faster than the previous day, as my stomach was feeling somewhat better. After CP1 we went into a four-km section of dunes—very tough. The course was very rocky and sand was blowing in my face, so I used a buff (scarf) over my mouth as a face mask. I caught Doug from the Clif Bar team and ran with him for a while, then paced a guy from Guatemala. More beautiful scenery of desert cliffs and mesas passed before us. At CP2, I saw Eric Bindner from Denver, grabbed water and scooted. For another five to six kilometers of dunes we formed a paceline group, with Ferg Hawke from Canada and a guy named Albert from France. At six feet, four inches Ferg provided a good wall from the headwind; we three took turns pulling each other through the brutal 35 to 40 mile-per-hour headwinds. There were a couple of times I dropped off the end of the group and had to sprint to catch back up, as I did not want to have to face those headwinds alone. At one time I thought we were lost, as visibility was greatly reduced due to a sandstorm. Albert, the Frenchman, was the "boss" of the group, giving marching orders in French, along with animated hand signals. All three of us were very tired, but we pushed on, passing several runners during the closing miles. Finally we could see the bivouac through the blowing sand. I felt relief that this effort would soon be over, but although we could see the tents, they were still about two miles away.

During the last mile the headwinds and sand picked up so much that I thought I would drop in my tracks. I finished in 3:36:02, seventh overall in the stage and moving up to 15th overall, second American.

It took us 90 minutes to fix the tent by staking it down with wooden pegs and positioning it out of the direct line of the wind. Fine sand still filtered through the sisal coffee sacks, which were sewn together to make the Berber tent. A layer of sand formed on everything: my face, mouth, nose, arms, and hands. I could wash it, off but in 15 minutes it would return. I went to sleep early (7:15 p.m.), pulling my sleeping bag over my head to escape the sand. At 3:00 a.m. the winds died down and a sense of peace returned to the bivouac. The stars were beautiful; they looked as if you could just pluck one from the sky.

Stage three: Bounou to Oued N'am, 31 km

The stage started slowly for me, due to recovery from the previous day's effort and the thought of the next day's stage (71 km). We ran through dunes and the heat started rising, but fortunately it was not as windy as the previous day, but still very hot. We ran through a small village built in a palm grove; kids cheered us in French as we passed. At 17 km we came upon another village, entering a casbah. Several hundred people cheered us on. My spirits were lifted and a result I ran faster. A headwind picked up during last two miles, but I finished strong in 2:51:14, tied for 15th in the stage, moving up to 13th overall, second American.

Stage four: Oued N'am to Lac Iriqui, 71 km

9:00 a.m. The main field started, while the top 50 overall and top five females were left in bivouac to start two and a half hours later. I was in tent with Lahcen and Mohammed Ahansal, brothers from Zagora, Morocco who have won six MDS races between them. It was interesting to see them eat a breakfast of rice and tea heated on a small fire of dried sticks, and watch them prepare for the stage. The winds started at 8:30 a.m. and quickly picked up to 30 to 35 miles per hour. By the time we started at 11:30, they had increased to gale force. A slow start by lead group allowed me a brief run in the lead (then I quickly got back in my paceline). I stayed in the second pack with Albert and four other Frenchman. At CP3, after running 22 hard miles, we were faced with 13 miles of high dunes and fierce headwinds and blowing sand. Our pack of six was down to just Albert and me. I employed a technique of using my hands to help me "crawl" up the dunes, which reach 75 to 80 feet in height. Still, the process was slow because every step seemed to spin out in the sand.

At CP4, we were halfway through the dunes. We filled our water bottles and continued. I was trying to tell Albert through hand motions that I wanted to take a picture at the rise of one of the dunes. He continued, while I stopped for a brief moment to take snapshots of the beautiful landscape before me. The dunes seemed to go on forever in every direction. I had to surge to catch back up with the crazy little Frenchman who was leading me through this vast land. I noticed a runner with a buff that said "Desert Cup," an ultra in Jordan. I figured he would know how best to navigate the unmarked section of dunes ahead. After briefly going off course we met some other Frenchmen. They tried to figure our direction to CP5. As we ran for what seemed an eternity, I realized my fate in this race was in their hands. None of them spoke English, so I had no idea what was being discussed. At that point I was simply along for the ride. We finally found CP5 as dusk was falling.

We were faced with 12 kilometers of soft sand to the finish. My right eye was swollen shut due to the constant bombardment of sand and my left eye was barely open. All I wanted to do at that point was complete the stage. I followed the Frenchmen in a paceline, trying to keep my eyes closed for as long as possible. Eventually Albert and I were dropped by this group. He helped me get out my headlamp, which helped very little, due to my not being able to open my eyes. He then forged ahead, so I was left without a pacer or navigator. I could see headlights ahead at one point and thought it was the finish, only to find out it was a course vehicle. The last two miles I ran blindly to the finish and probably would have run off the end of a cliff had one been there. It seemed to take forever; every step was a major effort. Finally I saw the lights again and this time it really was the finish. I crossed the line in nine hours and one minute. I was in glycogen depletion at the finish, and headed straight to the medical tent to have my eyes irrigated. As I waited to be treated I thought, "this is the hardest most challenging thing I have ever done," and realized this was what I had come here for. My dream and preparation of two years had become a reality. I moved into ninth place overall and first American.

No stage was run on Thursday, as people were still finishing from the previous stage. The windstorm was still in full force. A rain shower arrived and the wind died down for 15 minutes, then the storm raged back, worse than ever. This day was supposed to be one of "rest," but it was nearly impossible to achieve because we were pinned down by the storm, so no one left the tent. The tent was miserable, as sand poured in by the bucket. I ate a meal out of a zip-lock bag, just accepting the grit, hoping it would provide some needed minerals. One of my tent mates wondered if we all would end up with brown lung, finding the irony in participating in such a "healthy" sport.

Stage five: Lac Iriqui to Nord Jebel Amsailikh, 42 km

I ran with three others, including Eric Bindner and Ferg Hawke. We worked together, keeping a good pace into the headwinds. This stage was very rocky like the others and became hotter as the day went on. We were feeling good and passed others in the later miles. We passed a small stream and ran through an oasis, which was quite remarkable in this vast desert. We decided to cross the finish with our hands joined and raised. A feeling of relief overcame me, as I did not expect to run as hard in the final stage of 20 km. We were welcomed to the bivouac with more sand and a cold wind.

Stage six: Nord Jebel Amsailikh to Foum Zguit, 20 km

Our tents were taken down one more time by the Berbers. We presented gifts of thanks to Mohammed, who helped take care of our tent all week. Our band of eight lined up in front of tent 36 for a parting shot. We all looked pretty rough, but the mood was light. My mood turned serious when I saw in the standings that I had a one minute, 50 second lead on the tenth overall competitor from the Ivory Coast. I knew it would not be easy to protect my lead. Mary Gadams, the U.S. representative, asked if I would carry the American flag at the finish. This flag had been to the summit of several major mountains and had been carried in this race for ten years. I said I would be honored. She mentioned that if it came down to losing a spot in the standings not to worry about it. I pondered this for a moment and realized that carrying the flag of my country was more important than finishing ninth or tenth.

At the start of the stage I saw the runner from the Ivory Coast warming up; it was clear he was preparing to run all out. My strategy was to just stay with him and do my best to hang on. As the final stage was counted down, he sprinted off the line at a very fast pace. I did my best to keep up with him, but he pulled away. I was running as hard as I could and felt the lactic acid burn in my legs. The course was level and fast, with the exception of soft sand and several long rocky sections. Finally after about two miles he began to slow; I caught back up, eventually passing him. I just had to hang on and not crash. This stage was the hottest yet, but I decided to run without water, except at CP1. I was trying to be as fast and light as possible.

I finally saw the town of Foum Zguit up ahead; it seemed to be carved out of the side of a mountain. It was a beautiful day with sunny blue skies and no wind. As I entered the town and turned left down a paved street (the first paved road we had run on all week) the course was lined with cheering spectators. I reached behind me to pull the American flag from my pack; as I did a Frenchman motioned for me to go ahead of him as a gesture of sportsmanship. I thanked him and sprinted to the finish line with the flag furling overhead. I don't think I have ever been more proud in my life, except at the birth of my four children. I had carried a small picture of them with me and looked at it before and after every stage. I was greeted at the finish by Patrick Bauer, the race director. After the traditional kiss of each cheek I received my finisher's medallion. I was so full of adrenaline and endorphins I felt I could run the race all over again. I walked back up the street, clapping and cheering for every finisher. The mood was high for all finishers. Soon we boarded busses for the return trip to Quarzazate. Overall winner Lahcen Ahansal sat beside me. We talked for most of the four hours on the return trip. He was very gracious and unassuming. This is his fifth win at this race.

On Sunday we went to a movie studio and had an awards ceremony on the steps of a huge set that looked like the entrance to the Parthenon. I did not expect to receive an award, but did so as the ninth overall finisher. It was announced that this was the highest ever overall finish by an American.

The Grand Canyon
By Janice Anderson

No matter what you have been told, read in a book, or even seen in pictures, nothing truly prepares you for the experience when you stand on the edge of the Grand Canyon for the first time. The Grand Canyon is so overwhelming, its astonishing beauty so vast and deep, that it seems at first to be a far off world, unknown and inexplicable. The experience is personal and different for everyone; some can stand on the edge and simply view the grandeur and geological phenomenon from afar, while others are drawn to it, pulled into the spell that has enticed adventurers and explorers for centuries.

I recently stood on the Canyon's South Rim, preparing for my third running into the canyon. I was joined by a number of friends, whom I had convinced the experience would be unforgettable. We were a group of eight, including four women. Our trip had been inconvenienced by late flights, long drives and early wakeup calls. Collectively, we spent hours agonizing over what to bring in, how much fluid to carry, and how extreme the anticipated temperatures in the canyon would be. The trip seemed difficult and the run daunting. As I stood on the edge, I wondered about the women who had trekked here before me. I wondered about the hardships they faced and the lack of accessibility to the Canyon they must have dealt with, and marveled at the motivation that brought these women to the Canyon.

The Grand Canyon was largely unknown until after the Civil War. In 1869, Major John Wesley Powell, a one-armed Civil War veteran, completed the first journey through the canyon on the Colorado River, bringing the Canyon national attention and notoriety for the first time. In the late 19th century the primary interest in the region was its promise of mineral resources; thus, the first pioneer settlements sprang up in the area. These early residents soon discovered that tourism was destined to be more profitable than mining, and by the turn of the century the Grand Canyon had become a well-known tourist destination. Most of the early tourist accommodations were not much different from the mining camps from which they developed. Many visitors made the grueling trip to the South Rim via stagecoach. Even today's long security lines and airport delays (or the endless drive from the Las Vegas airport), couldn't hold a candle to the rough rides experienced by those earliest tourists.

One such tourist was Ada Diefendorf from East Worcester, New York. In 1893, she traveled to Prescott to visit relatives, where she learned that a William W. Bass offered tours of the Grand Canyon. She signed up for a tour and was soon captivated by the Canyon—and her guide. She eventually returned to Arizona and married Bass. Her life with the man who became known as "The Grand Canyon Guide" was not an easy one. Nonetheless, she raised her children at the Canyon and was an active, although unwilling participant in the Bass tourist enterprise.

The Sante Fe railroad spur reached the South Rim of the Canyon in 1901 and the first automobiles arrived soon thereafter. Larger numbers of tourists soon followed, along with workers needed to meet their needs. The Fred Harvey Company, known throughout the west for its hospitality and fine food, was given exclusive rights to manage and operate restaurants, lunch stands, and hotels along the Santa Fe railroads west of the Missouri River. By 1905 the company had completed El Tovar, a world-class hotel perched on the Canyon's southern rim, and continued to develop other facilities and services, including Phantom Ranch. They still operate the shops and some concessions today. When Fred Harvey advertised for "young women 18 to 30 years of age" to travel west to staff his famous hotels, thousands of young women applied.

One such woman was architect Mary Elizabeth Jane Colter. Born on the East Coast in 1869 she moved to San Francisco to attend the California School of Design. She initially became a teacher but also applied for a job with the Harvey Company. Colter was offered a job to decorate the Alvarado Hotel in Albuquerque and thus began a 40-year career with the Harvey Company. She designed and managed the construction of many of the Grand Canyon's most notable buildings, including the Hopi House, Hermit's Rest, Lookout Studio, Watchtower, Bright Angel Lodge and Phantom Ranch. Colter changed the name from Roosevelt Camp to Phantom Ranch after Phantom Creek, the narrow canyon where it is located. It cannot be seen from the rim, thus the name "Phantom." The Park Service has used her designs in many of its other national parks. She also designed interiors for other Grand Canyon facilities, as well as china service patterns, making her arguably the architect with the most impact on the Grand Canyon. As a woman working in a man's world, she was often criticized for her toughness, but she and her work have endured.

Bessie Haley Hyde dreamed of adventure as a young girl in Parkersburg, West Virginia. She moved to San Francisco after the end of a marriage to her childhood sweetheart. There she met and later married Glen Hyde, a young man who dreamed of riding the Colorado River though the Canyon in a boat. He persuaded Bessie to accompany him. He boasted that she would be the first woman to ever run the Colorado River. He talked about the money they could make on a lecture tour and suggested that Bessie write a book about the adventure. In October of 1928, they started down the Colorado River in a boat Glen had built. They almost made it—their boat was found floating at milepost 237. Their bodies were never found, however, and to this day there is speculation that Bessie killed her husband and escaped to live a long life.

Polly Mead first saw the Grand Canyon from the North Rim in 1927 as a college student. She later returned to do research for her Master's thesis in botany. Her topic was to analyze the abrupt stopping of the tree growth in the Canyon. This led her to establish weather stations, wind-recording instruments, often sleeping in the canyon with nothing but a bedroll and her pistol. After graduating, she was hired as the first female ranger at the Grand Canyon and the second female in the entire Park Service. Her career ended in 1931 when she married the assistant Grand Canyon park superintendent. In her own words, that is just what you did when you got married in those days. Many women rangers work in the park today. I almost ran into one as I climbed out of the South Rim as she walked down, carrying a jackhammer on her back for trail maintenance. I was immensely grateful for her difficult work on the trail; it made my run seem easy in comparison.

Many women had an impact on the rafting industry within the Canyon. My group felt lucky to escape any contact with water, except for an intentional dunking in Phantom Creek to cool off and an unintentional misdirection through a beaver bog. Georgie Clark came to the Colorado River in 1945 to help escape the grief from the death of her only child. Georgie later said that she immediately knew she was home, that everything she wanted was there, and like many others, that it was beautiful beyond words. She began her company, the "Royal River Rats," using rubber Army surplus material. At first, other companies disapproved and scoffed at her inflatable rafts. However, those rafts set the standard for river rafting that continues to this day. Her trips became legendary and she had more repeat customers than any other company. But Georgie Clark did not hire women guides. It was said that at that time the only women working on the river were "the girlfriends or wives of men who were guides." If the relationship ended, the women were forced to quit. In the late 1970s, Louise Teal began working because of her husband, but after they divorced, she continued to work as a guide with Arizona Raft Adventures, the first company to hire women guides. She eventually led the first all-women's rafting trip down the Colorado River.

Women entered the male domain of wranglers (mule train guides) in the mid-1950s, when a sex discrimination suit against the Fred Harvey Company forced them to hire women. Today about half the wranglers that take tourists into the Canyon are women. Patty Know has had wrangling in her blood since she was a small girl. Her father was a wrangler in the Canyon, but her parents wanted her to have a *real* career. She eventually returned and now guides the supply mule trains down the South Kaibab trail. She and her husband live in the house next to the corral at Yaki Point. It is a historic building built to traditional house the chief mule wrangler—her husband. We rejoiced missing their mule train as we started before daylight in order to escape the difficulties of passing the mules on the narrow trail.

The Grand Canyon has drawn a diverse and strong group of women into its depths, whether following a man, a dream, or both. It drew our group there too, and we did experience our own modern difficulties; ultimately however, several of us ran on our own for many miles in the Canyon with no true worries of survival. These courage and sacrifice shown by these pioneering women in the Grand Canyon built the trails we travel, the buildings we sleep in, and have made it commonplace for women to be part of the Canyon. Their adventures in the Canyon were undoubtedly tougher than ours, breaking barriers and standards, which makes it a little less startling to see women running alone through the Canyon nowadays. So off we went on our 21st century journey, but with more than 100 years of history to help us through the trek.

The Grand Canyon and the Ultrarunner

By Phil Lowry

The "Big Ditch," as locals call it, has a special allure to ultrarunners. It looks upon first viewing far more formidable than a mountain peak, and rightly so: what goes down must come up. Ever run a 50-miler with a 6,000-foot climb in the last 14 miles? You get the idea. The Canyon's draw is heightened by an overly paternalistic National Park Service, which, weary of search and rescue injuries and deaths, overstates the Canyon's risks to laughable proportions. Case in point: they consistently overstate the daily high temperature at the bottom of the Canyon by five to ten degrees. Even with such dire mythical warnings, tourists in flip-flops and a jug of water in one hand often stray too far and require extraction. Perhaps it's because of such warnings that ultrarunners run to the river and back in a day, as if to say to say, "I told you so."

Park Service and ultrarunners don't always mix well. A few years ago a double crossing (rim to rim to rim) was organized out of Vegas, complete with T-shirts. The Park Service placed a mole among the runners in the pre-run meeting and arrested the organizers for planning an event without a proper special use permit. (Races are not and never will be allowed in the Canyon under current policy.) A couple of years later Park Service called a truce and placed "free pizza!" signs at all trailheads, and after saying "just kidding" went on to tell ultrarunners that yes, they could run in the canyon, just to be nice and not organize. Since then things have been pretty peaceful, with only an occasional run-in with a mule or aggressive hiker. You know the type: "I will not move over even though I hog the trail with this ridiculously large backpack."

Here are some rules of the road (and trail) to follow in the canyon:

- Drink lots of water and stay on the main corridor trails (Bright Angel, North Kaibab and South Kaibab) unless you've been there before. I once tried to run from Indian Gardens to the Hermit Trailhead on four 20-ounce bottles and went dry 1.5 miles below the rim. In March.
- Yield to the mules. They stink and are a damned nuisance, but money makes the Grand Canyon world go 'round. Don't upset the skinners (mule guides). They'll cite you and ruin running for the rest of us. Stand aside and don't try to pass without letting the skinner know. He or she will let you go on soon enough.
- Say "hello" and "excuse me." Courtesy counts in the canyon. People are there as a "destination," sometimes after years of saving for a once-in-a-

lifetime trip. Make them feel at home.
- Bring money or credit card on the trail. You may need food or lemonade at Phantom Ranch—in fact, you're nuts not to get it. Stock up for the climb out.
- Take a camera. Last May I nailed an 11:32 big double (not the mini 42-mile North Kaibab-South Kaibab-North Kaibab, but the big 47-mile North Kaibab-Bright Angel-North Kaibab) and took 30 pictures. It's a great place; you'll want the memories later.
- Do not go anytime from June through September. It's like running Hardrock in January. Why suffer?
- The North Rim closes in about mid-November and stays closed until May 10 or so. Double-crosses are possible from April to May and October to November. It's crazy to attempt it at any other time.
- Train on hills. The Canyon is a quad-buster—all versions of the double-cross have 11,000 feet of descent. (The rim-to-rim has half that, but we don't talk about the rim-to-rim in this magazine because it's not an ultra, right?) Train for a lot of downhill running.
- Have fun!

Phil Lowry has run the double-cross in all variations a dozen times, and has had adventures east and west of the corridor trails.

New York City: The Ultimate in Urban Ultrarunning

by Don Allison

For most ultrarunners, New York City does not immediately come to mind when discussing venues for ultra distance running. Majestic mountain top views? Not here. Rugged, single-track trails? Not many. Peaceful communing with nature? Forget about it. Upon further examination, however, New York does indeed have a long history of ultrarunning. Some of the most prolific ultrarunners have come from the Big Apple, including the legendary Ted Corbitt, a man who has arguably has had more influence on the sport in America than anyone during past half-century.

Of course, there have been and continue to be many ultras held in New York City. Central Park, a huge expanse of greenery, is the most logical place for long races in the city. Loop 50-km and 50-mile events are held in the park each year, including the annual Metropolitan 50 Mile and Kurt Stiener 50 Km. The park was also the site of the 100 Km U.S. Championship, in 1993.

Running a race in the park, especially on a mild sunny day, is unlike almost any other ultra. Even with an early morning start, Central Park races share the road with a steady stream of cyclists, walkers, inline skaters, and other runners. Ultras held in the park require runners to wear numbers on their backs as well as front. The reason for this becomes evident early on, when runners not in the race, some moving along at a very fast clip, become intermingled with those who are. Depending upon your point of view, it can be comforting or disconcerting to know that the runner who just flew by you is just out for a training run.

Training is always a challenge for an ultrarunner living in New York City. The reality of millions of people living on a relatively small island presents obstacles that those living on or near remote trails just don't face. Ellen McCurtin, a several time member of the U.S. 100-km national team, lives and trains in the heart of the metropolis known as New York City. She offers a glimpse of what it is like to be an ultrarunner in the city.

"There is a lot I could say about running in the city. I lived in New York for more than 14 years and ran about 100 miles a week for about 12 of those years. There are both advantages and disadvantages to being an urban runner. On the minus side, there can be traffic (even when you have the right of way, drivers will just go for it to make one more light), too many people doing too many different things (bikers, bladers, people pushing baby joggers, power walkers, and dogs), pollution (especially in the summer when it is hot and humid), and noise (people lean on their horns before the light even turns green). All in all, just too much going on.

"Over the years, I have been jumped in Riverside Park (I got away), had 40-ounce beer bottles hurled at me (smashed at my feet, fortunately not my head), been chased by gangs of teenagers, seen naked guys masturbating in the bushes, had kids on BMX bikes throw handfuls of gravel at me, had an M-80 explode in front of me (during July 4 festivities in Central Park), seen someone shot, and seen a person jump out an apartment window. Sometimes, it can really drive one more than a little crazy.

"After that list, you might wonder what good things I could possible say about running in the city. I often wonder about it myself, but here goes. First, you can nearly always find a running partner, a nice thing, for both social and safety reasons. I've even heard stories about a group of runners who are out in Central Park at around 2:00 a.m. I do nearly all my morning runs with my friend Barbara and most of evening runs with other friends on different nights. This is fortunate or I would not have much of a social life. There is also a very active running club scene in New York for those who want that. There are several different clubs right here in the city. This means that you don't have travel far to get to group workouts. Also, there is a race nearly every weekend right in the park. Although the park is nice, I still try to get away whenever I can. Close by are the Palisades in New Jersey. There is a leafy and lovely unspoiled eight-mile long road that runs along the Hudson River. It's close enough to be convenient, but it feels nice and far from the city."

Dave Luljak, another elite New York area ultrarunner, has nothing but praise for the vistas offered up in city running. He talks of a few of his favorite runs: "One of my favorite races is the Joe Kleinerman 12 Hour Run, which is held in Crocheron Park in Queens during the summer. The course is a nearly one-mile loop that provides a great deal of variety. There are wooded sections and open areas, baseball games and tennis matches, and even a glimpse of the bay as you go by the scoring area. The only bad part is that in the afternoon when you're hot and tired an ice cream truck stops in a parking lot next to the course for hours. Could Leadville's Hope Pass or the hot canyons of Western States provide any more of a challenge than having to run by that truck?"

He adds, "One of my most memorable training routes, although I only did it three times, was to run along Route 25A from my house in Huntington, on Long Island's north shore, to New York City, a distance of about 35 miles. You'd start out on the rolling hills of Long Island's Gold Coast, passing horse farms and other trappings of the good life, then make your way through the congested suburbs of Nassau County, past Shea Stadium and the site of the 1964 World's

Fair, through various ethnic neighborhoods in Queens, to the warehouses and light industry of Long Island City, until you finally traversed the 59th Street Bridge with its spectacular skyline view. One year I ran to Central Park in order to turn in my envelope for entry into the New York City Marathon, a classic example of ultrarunning chutzpah."

Not only are there ultrarunners in New York and places for them to run, there are also an array of ultras in the city for them to run. The driving force behind these events for the past two decades has been the Broadway Ultra Society (BUS) and Rich Innamorato. Rich, along with his loyal band of volunteers, has directed hundreds of ultras in the metropolitan area, in almost every possible venue within the five boroughs and beyond. In addition to BUS, the Prospect Park Track Club also stages events, but perhaps the most prolific group of all is the Sri Chinmoy Marathon Team.

Sri Chinmoy, an Indian spiritual leader, came to New York in 1964. Viewing sports, especially running, as a vehicle for meditation and reaching one's highest potential, it was natural that the Sri Chinmoy Marathon Team (SCMT) was formed. The group conducted its first ultra in 1978 and hundreds have followed since. As most know, SCMT specializes in multi-day races on short closed loop courses. For many years, these multi-day races were held in Queens' Flushing Meadow Park, before the U.S. tennis center took over the area. Now the races are held in Jamaica Estates in Queens or on Ward's Island off of Manhattan.

Trishul Cherns, a prolific multi-day runner on the Sri Chinmoy Team, says, "Multi-day races are what we (SCMT) do best. We have the resources to manage events that last for days and weeks. With a closed loop course, we can manage the event perfectly. Our standards are very high; we have never had one complaint about one of our races." He adds, "We put on races that people can come to alone and be fully supported." Cherns has nothing but praise for BUS and Innamorato as well. "Without BUS there is no New York City ultrarunning. What he has done by himself is amazing. SCMT and BUS get along well and run in each other's races. We are one big, happy family."

What does Cherns think about being an ultrarunner in the city? "It's a great place to run," he says. "The streets are very safe to run on, aside from a few bad areas, such as parts of Brooklyn, the Bronx, and Harlem. We have nice measured courses in Queens to run on. It's a nice residential area. There are trails too, in the parks. You can do a 30-mile run in Forest Park or Van Cortlandt Park."

Given all of this, it becomes apparent that yes, ultrarunning is alive and thriving in America's biggest metropolis. While many ultrarunners aspire to international ultras, some of the big U.S. 50-milers or the Western 100-milers, an ultrarunner's resume is not totally complete without a trip to New York City for a true urban ultrarunning experience.

A Summer To Remember: 2,144 Miles on the Appalachian Trail

by David Horton

"I go forth to make new demands on life. I wish to begin this summer well, to do something in it worthy of it and to flee; to transcend my daily routine and that of my townsmen...I pray that the life of this spring and summer may ever lie fair in my memory. May I dare as I have never done! May I persevere as I have never done!"
- Henry David Thoreau

For years, I had dreamed of hiking and running the Appalachian Trail (AT). The summer of 1991 allowed me the opportunity to fulfill that dream.

The AT was officially opened in 1937. It extends from Springer Mountain, Georgia to Mt. Katahdin, Maine. It is the longest continuously marked footpath in the world. For many years, it was thought impossible to cover the entire trail in one summer. However, in 1948, Earl Shaffer became the first person to hike the entire trail in one summer. Since then, a few thousand more individuals have hiked the AT in this length of time.

From time to time, individuals have attempted to set the speed record for hiking the entire AT. However, the Appalachian Trail Conference (ATC) does not officially recognize any type of records on the AT. On the other hand, The Appalachian Long Distance Hikers Association (ALDHA) does recognize and certify the speed record for the AT. The unofficial record of 60 1/2 days was set in 1990 by Ward Leonard of Salt Lake City, although his time was not ratified by ALDHA because there were some questions about the "completeness" of his hike.

Not wanting to be away from my family any more than possible, but being a competitive ultrarunner and wanting to set a record, I determined (with my wife's somewhat reluctant permission) that I would try to complete the AT in less than 60 days. Actually, my pre-determined goal was 56 days, thus allowing for a few rest days if needed.

My initial plan was to use a very lightweight backpack (approximately 16 pounds or less) and mail food and supplies to various post offices along the way (as most through hikers do). However, through a plea in *UltraRunning* and with friends hearing about my endeavor, I was able to enlist various people who graciously gave of their time and resources to crew for me through the AT. This allowed me to approach AT as I would a typical ultra (handlers meeting me at road crossings with supplies and encouragement). Because of this, all I had to carry was a fanny pack and a water bottle. Sometimes, depending on the degree of help I had available, I only carried a water bottle. On May 9, at 6:45 a.m., I started from Springer Mountain. Two days earlier, Scott Grierson, of Bass Harbor, Maine, had started with the same goal as I had—56 days on the AT. Scott, who used the trail name "Maineak" when he signed in at shelters along the way, was an experienced hiker who only walked the trail. A typical day for him was some 16 to 17 hours walking. My trail name was "The Runner."

It rained continuously for nine of the first 12 days on the trail and was very foggy or the most part. This was good in that it kept the temperature down, yet it kept me from enjoying the views along the trail. On my last day in the Smokies, I developed shin splints (tendinitis) in my right leg. It progressively worsened and a few days later, began in my left leg as well. Both shins were swollen, red, and very painful to the touch, which produced excruciating pain while running or walking down hills. On the advice of Dr. Gary Buffington, I started taking anti-inflammatory medication and would ice down my shins for two to three hours every night.

Those problems abated somewhat, but still persisted into and through most of Virginia. I spent two weeks in Virginia, as one-fourth of the AT's mileage lies in the state in which I reside. During all this time (just under 1,000 miles from Georgia to Harper's Ferry, West Virginia), I had stayed two days behind Maineak. I was able to keep track of his progress by checking the registers at the shelters on the trail.

Even with the shin problems and other minor aches and pains, I was able to stay exactly on schedule, averaging 38.3 miles a day. My shins began to feel better as I approached West Virginia and Maryland. As a result of getting rid of these shin problems, finally getting in shape, colder weather, and easier terrain, I was able to pick up the pace, and for the next 18 days (days 26 to 43), averaged 44.4 miles per day. On two successive days in Pennsylvania, I increased my mileage to 52 and 51 miles. Part of this was due to the terrain and the fact that I was feeling good! However, the biggest factor was that I had heard that Maineak went 50 miles in one day in the same area.

With the increased mileage, I started gaining on the Maineak. On the 39th day, just inside the southern border of Vermont, I finally caught up with him, 1,574.6 miles from the start in Georgia. I had only four miles left for the day, so I walked and talked with him the rest of the way.

For the next four days, we played leapfrog. He would hike until 10:00 or 11:00 p.m. and as a result, would go beyond where I had stopped at 4:00 or 5:00

David Horton

p.m. The following days I would again pass him at earlier and earlier points. The last time I saw "Maineak" was about 15 miles east of Hanover, New Hampshire, on my 43rd day. We had become good friends and it was somewhat disappointing not seeing him each day. He was very helpful in telling me a great deal about what lay ahead for me on the trail. However, when I asked him about Maine, he would only say, "This is all a warm-up for Maine." When I asked him what he meant, he would only say, "You'll see!"

A typical day during the early stages of the run started a little after 6:00 a.m. I would run and walk for 10 to 11 hours per day. Later on, I started at around 5:30 a.m. and eventually in the last three weeks, began the day at 4:45 a.m.

I would eat a good breakfast (if available) and usually eat a turkey and cheese sandwich at around 12:30 or 1:00 p.m. During the day, I would drink about one and a half gallons of the replacement drink Conquest, and eat five to six Skor candy bars and occasionally a Powerbar. As long as I had Conquest available, I never bonked or had any trouble, and miraculously, I never became tired of it. In the evening, I would try to find a food bar or buffet. This was possible until I reached the Northeast states. Nearly all of the people who helped me were ultrarunners who understood my physical, mental, and nutritional needs to such a degree that I really did not have to worry about those things.

As I was making great progress in the section (44.4 miles per day) from Maryland to the White Mountains in New Hampshire, I was starting to get a little too self-confident, thinking I had it in the bag, with the worst behind me. I was sadly mistaken!

The White Mountains of New Hampshire were the prettiest place on the AT, but also the most difficult. I thought I knew what a rocky trail was, having run the Massanutten Mountain race. I was wrong. I thought I knew what steep hills were, having done the Barkley Marathons twice. I was wrong. The White Mountains were extremely rocky and steep. They don't seem to know what a switchback is in New Hampshire. Most of the trails go straight up and straight down the mountains. It was just as slow going down as it was going up.

To this point, my overall average daily time on the trail was 11 hours and 25 minutes. In the last ten days in New Hampshire and Maine, I averaged 13 hours and 37 minutes on the trail. It was very difficult to run at all. Walking, rather than running, was the basic mode of transportation in this area. Access for my crew was also very limited because there were so few road crossings. As a result of this, several times in the last one and a half weeks, I developed low blood sugar. The amount of sleep I was getting each night also dwindled.

After spending three unbelievably difficult days in the White Mountains, I finally made it into Maine. I thought I could just cruise easily the rest of the way to Mt. Katahdin (the northern terminus of the AT). I was again proven wrong!

The "Maineak" had warned me about Maine, but I had no idea what was in store in this last state. The mountains were not as big, but the climbs were just as steep. Much of the trail in Maine was new. Therefore, it was rocky, full of roots and swamps, and was generally very unrunable. My progress in Maine was just as slow as it was in the White Mountains.

During the last week in Maine I was a physical and emotional wreck! I would break down over the least little problem or setback. Every time I thought about my family, home, and normal life, I would completely break down and cry. I was also getting physically exhausted and would fall five to six times each day. My toes were sore and swollen. I kept stubbing them on rocks and roots. However, the thought of quitting or taking a day off never entered my mind. Even though I was getting so close to finishing in Maine, it was not until the day before I finished that I realized I was actually going to finish. For so long it had felt as if I was on a perpetual treadmill I would never get off. I was jealous of other people who were living a normal life.

One of the things that really helped me through these difficult times were all the letters, cards, and packages of "goodies" I received at the post office drops along the way. It meant so much to read how people were praying for me, encouraging me, and counting on me finishing in record time. This exerted a certain amount of pressure, so that it was very important, not only to me, but to countless others, to finish what I had started. It was especially important to all of those who came out and crewed for me through this endeavor. They were sharing in a very real part of this accomplishment as well.

Many times when I would be climbing those vertical ascents in the White Mountains, I would claim God's promise in Phil. 4:13, *"I can do all things through Christ who strengthens me"* and Phil. 4:19, *"My God shall supply all your needs according to his riches in glory by Christ Jesus."* He never failed me.

At 2:00 p.m. on June 30, 1991, I reached the Katahdin Stream Campground, 5.2 miles from the summit of the last mountain I would have to climb. After getting some Conquest, food, and warmer clothing, I began the 4,000-foot ascent (the single biggest climb on the AT).

I had thought every day for the past 52 days about this moment. And I was not to experience this moment alone. My 17-year-old son, Brandon, and crew members and friends Nancy Hamilton, Doug Young, Jack McGiffin, and Glenn Streeter accompanied me to the top of Mt. Katahdin, as my wife Nancy drove around to the other side of the mountain to wait for us.

The temperature at the base of the mountain was about 70 degrees F. At the top it was 50, with wind gusts of 40 to 50 miles per hour. The climb up was fun, yet very difficult. About 1,500 feet of the climb was technical, as evidenced by the pitons in the rocks for handholds. Getting to the top of the last mountain at 4:35 p.m. was a tremendous feeling of relief. I knew then that I could really stop. I did not have to climb another mountain, and I was free to resume a "normal" life once again.

Those 52 days, 9 hours and 41 minutes on the AT now seem like a dream. There is a tremendous feeling of satisfaction in having accomplished this goal. It was difficult to adjust the first few weeks back home. I had difficulty sleeping, as I experienced continual dreams of climbing. However, I eventually forgot how difficult it was. I still have mental flashes of people, places, and different events on the trail. It was much harder than I expected, but in other ways, it was much easier than I expected. There are many stories that I could share. I was able to keep a daily log of my activities, thoughts, and emotions before, during, and after this trip.

I owe so much to so many. The lord Jesus Christ supplied me the strength, endurance, and perseverance as never before. My wife was always there and supportive during this entire ordeal.

Many people helped me directly, and others indirectly through prayers, cards, letters, and packages to attain one of my lifetime dreams. I want to thank them as well. I would like to challenge each one of you to "chase your dreams."

Footnote: Maineak finished in 55 days, 20 hours and 34 minutes. Horton's record was broken in 1999, when Pete Palmer from Connecticut covered the AT in 48 days.

British Ultrarunning: An American Expat's Perspective

by Siri Terjesen

The United Kingdom could well be considered the epicenter of ultrarunning, given its long tradition of ultramarathon events, legends and world-record moments. England is host to the world's second oldest ultra, London to Brighton, which has been run for more than a half-century; and the world's second oldest marathon, the Windsor Polytechnic, which was held between 1909 and 2002. The scenic but hilly Isle of Wight marathon is in its 48th year and is the world's 13th oldest marathon. Other long-standing marathons are Sheffield (41 years), Manchester (31 years) and Duchy, Cornwall (27 years). In fact, the UK is host to approximately 100 marathons and 30 ultras each year—not bad for a country that, by land area, is 2.5 percent the size of either the United States or Canada. The close geographic proximity makes it easy to drive or take the train to a race in any part of the country in about five hours or less. The best list of British marathons and ultras can be found at Roger Biggs' 100 Marathon Club website (http://www.100marathonclub.org.uk).

Britain's flagship ultrarunning organization is the Road Runners Club (RRC), founded in 1952 after the first London to Brighton run, and has grown to 1,800 current members. As the club's name suggests, Britain is a *road* running country. Compared with North America, the UK is host to fewer "trail" events. In fact, "trail" is subject to different interpretations. In the States, "trail" can represent just about everything from a groomed surface to a thick briar patch. In the UK, "trail" generally denotes a very groomed path, e.g. a grassy field or one of the thousands of miles of "public footpaths" that crisscross the countryside. UK trail courses sometimes require special "ordinance survey" maps and a bit of decent orienteering. A good example of a well-marked "trail" marathon runs between two Neolithic monuments, Avebury and Stonehenge, each May.

Here is a brief description of the major ultramarathon events by time of year, location(s), and distance:

London to Brighton (October; London to Brighton; 54 miles) is the world's second oldest ultramarathon. The race starts with the 7:00 a.m. bell from Big Ben's clock tower in Westminster, London, and finishes along the oceanfront in Brighton. This race is the crown jewel of UK ultrarunning and regularly attracts runners from abroad. There is even a "Ted Corbitt" trophy for the first U.S. citizen to finish. (Note: after the 2005, the London to Brighton was discontinued as an official race.)

The UK 50 Km Championships (May; Sutton Park, Birmingham; 50 km) is a new event organized to encourage marathon runners to move up to the ultra distance. This championship serves as selection for the England team to the UK 100 Km Championship.

The Dartmoor Discovery (June; Devon, Cornwall; 32 miles) is in its sixth year in 2004 and expects to attract more than 100 runners. The 2004 race is twinned with the historic "Two Bridges" run.

The Barry 40 (March; outside Cardiff, Wales; 40 miles) is the UK's preeminent track race and Welsh championship. Fifty-four world records have been set on this course.

The UK 100 Km Championships (Summer; rotating sites; 100 km) are rotated annually among the four countries of Great Britain: Scotland, England, Wales and Northern Ireland. Members of the national teams vie for the team cup and also selection to the Great Britain team for the World 100 Km Championships. Other runners are welcome.

The Grand Union Canal Race (May; Birmingham to London; 145 miles) begins at 6:00 am in Birmingham at the Gas street basin and follows the Grand Union canal all the way to "Little Venice" in London. Runners are allowed 45 hours in this most challenging competition. (ed: See Alicja Barahona's report in this issue.)

Marathon of Britain (August; Across Britain; 175 miles) is in its second running and limited to 100 competitors. The race is modeled after the 143-mile Marathon des Sables stage race held annually in the Moroccan Sahara. In the first running, Portuguese-born, Jersey-bred Maria de Jesus finished first lady and second overall, just seven minutes behind leader Andrew Rivett. This challenge involves a lot of map reading over the six days.

Paris to London (April; Paris to London; 230 miles) is an event in which runners travel to Paris by train and then run the Paris Marathon (usually the week before London) and then back to London, completing about 28 miles a day for six days. The race concludes with at the finish of the London Marathon.

The East Hull 24 Hour (July; Hull, London; 24 hours) is the UK's preeminent 24-hour, run just outside of London, but limited to 50 competitors.

UK Ultrarunning legends

The UK's history of professional walkers, from Captain Barclay to the many female pedestriennes has been well documented. The UK is also home to a number of *living* ultra legends, such as former world record-holders Don Ritchie and Dr. Hilary Walker, who are both still running strong. A pair of two-time 100-km world champion women, Eleanor Adams-Robinson and Carolyn Hunter-Rowe, as well as 1999 100-km Champion Simon Pride all call England home. At "shorter distances," the UK's most famous running citizen is probably road running queen Paula Radcliffe.

UK Ultrarunning World Records
Finally, the United Kingdom also has a great history in terms of world record breaking moments. Jeff Norman's 30-mile and 50-km track, Eleanor Adams-Robinson's road 200-km, Hilary Walker's track 150-km, Carolyn Hunter-Rowe's track bests at 30 miles, 50 km and 50 miles, and Don Ritchie's 40-mile track, 50-mile, 100-km and six-hour marks still stand as a world records. Russians Denis Jalybin and Oleg Kharitonov broke Ritchie's 150-km and 100-mile track world records on British soil at Crystal Palace in October 2002.

Travel to the UK
Flights from North America
Internet travel search engines such as Travelocity (www.travelocity.com) and Expedia (www.expedia.com) can be useful for identifying low cost airfares to the UK. London's two major international airports, Heathrow and Gatwick, are west and south of the city, respectively. Heathrow is well connected to the city by the 15-minute Heathrow Express train to Paddington or a slower Underground service on the Piccadilly line. Gatwick is approximately an hour by train.

Accommodation
Some airlines and travel companies also offer accommodation packages, which can be a particularly good deal if you plan to spend a significant portion of your time in London. London hotels range from £50 to £300 per night, depending on the location and number of stars. Most ultras are held in the British countryside, where bed and breakfast accommodations can be had for about £25 per night per person.

Land Travel
For trips across the country, the rail network is the fastest, cheapest way to see the country, for example, London to Edinburgh (five hours) and London to Cardiff (two hours). If you know where you want to go and plan to travel for several days, the best prices can often be found by purchasing "BritRail" multi-day passes from home (http://www.britrail.net). See Railtrack (www.railtrack.co.uk) for rail schedules and prices for tickets purchased in the UK. For those more courageous

souls willing to drive on the "wrong" side of the road, renting a car can be a fun experience. Make sure to bring a valid driver's license from home!

Air Travel around UK and to Mainland Europe

The UK has an abundance of very cheap "Southwest Airlines" styled low-cost carriers around the UK and to mainland Europe. This is an excellent option for runners interested in running a UK race and another on the continent. Three of the best companies are Ryan Air (www.ryanair.com), Easy Jet (www.easyjet.com), and British Midland (www.iflybmi.com). To check UK-based trips on major carriers, Opodo (www.opodo.co.uk) is a good first stop. Besides Heathrow and Gatwick, the London airports for European travel are City (close to the city) and Luton and Stansted in the north. All are approximately an hour's train journey from central London. The most exhaustive calendars of ultrarunning in Europe can be found on the web at Ultrarunning (http://www.ultrarunning.com/calendar/Foreign.htm), the 100 Marathon Club (http://homepages.tesco.net/~roger.biggs/race-ultra.html), and in Dutch on Ultraned (http://www.ultraned.org/kalender/).

An American Field Guide to British Running Culture

As the British empire builder Cecil Rhodes once remarked, "To be born English is to win first prize in the lottery of life." British runners may still take great pride in their heritage and nationality, but they are equally a friendly and supportive, albeit eccentric bunch whom I have been lucky to run with for the past two and a half years. Here are a few cultural observations for those planning to cross the great Atlantic pond for a race.

Pre-Race: The British are well-known for having a stiffer upper lip and more reserved manner than their North American counterparts. In fact, British runners can be quite dainty. One English ultrarunner, Matt Lynas, brings a tidy wicker basket, which he turns over and uses as a nutrition stand during lap races. Britain's fastest 24-hour runner, Sharon Gayter, sports the world's cutest ultrarunning kit (known in the U.S. as a "uniform"), designed by her sponsor, Australian model Elle Macpherson.

During the Race: Brits are keen (read: avid) supporters, both as spectators or fellow competitors during a race. The North American shouts of "good job," "keep going" or "looking good" are generally met with a puzzled British face. Brits prefer to shout, although not quite as loudly, "well done," even if the runner is not even close to being "done" with the race! The Brits' need for privacy extends to nature's call, making them more likely to protect their modesty when making a pit stop along the road. This stoicism extends to challenging moments in a race. Take, for example, Hilary Walker, in November's World 100 Km Championships. At the start, I was so nervous that my heart rate monitor read 190. I turned to Hilary to enquire as to her heart rate. "Sixty" she cooed with the most serene look on her face. This was in spite of the fact that she was sporting a huge hand splint, having broken two fingers less than a week earlier in a 100-mile Himalayan stage race. In Taiwan, she fell again, but continued on, later remarking, "How many other people have skid marks on their splint?"

No British holiday is complete without a trip to the local fish and chips and Indian curry houses. Likewise, no British ultra is complete without a sample of the local "course nutrition." North American runners keen on a chocolate bar will find Mars, not Snickers the bar of choice at the food stops. Likewise, "biscuits" (not "cookies") and "Jelly babies" (not "Jellybeans") are usually available. Craving for a Twinkie will be met with a "Jaffa cake,"a spongy orangey chocolate that I have never quite been able to swallow. If you can manage it, you can wash it all down with "Squash," a fruit juice from concentrate. Remember to chuck (throw) your leftovers into a "rubbish bin." There are no "trash cans" in the UK.

Some Brits have a wonderful habit of "chatting away" during a race. If you are fortunate enough to run within earshot, you will be treated to a resplendent hour or two of the Queen's English. Beware British "humour" however, which is based on satire; it is said that no North American has ever truly gotten these jokes, Monty Python notwithstanding.

Finish and Post-Race: Unlike their North American counterparts, Brits are famous for not wishing to make a scene in public, regardless of the circumstances. Remember Paula Radcliffe's world record breaking times in London and Chicago Marathons? Seconds after crossing the finish line, she appeared more cool and composed than her ecstatic interviewers.

There is generally a kind British soul at the finish line of every race, cheerfully dispensing cupfuls of tea. Compared to North Americans, the British are more likely to scurry off quickly to the showers and then return to the scene smelling quite a bit fresher. In fact, Britain has the highest consumption of soap and deodorant in all of Europe. This is, of course, in sharp contrast to North Americans, many of whom prefer to go "au natural" until they get home (or even for a day or two later). Finally, Brits, like their North American friends, are quite prone to celebrating a good day out at the races. The post-race celebration of choice is often a "pint" of ale at the "local" (pub). Cheers!

America's 100-Mile Trail Races

by Jason Hodde and Don Allison

The trail 100-mile race is virtually unique to North America. Although a few such events are held in other countries, the U.S. has turned it into an art form. It is ironic then, to consider that 100-mile trail races got started almost by accident. The Tevis Cup, a 100-mile horse race in northern California, had been held for several years, when one of the riders, Gordy Ansleigh, found his horse had come up lame in the weeks leading up to the race. The organizers noted Gordy had spent much of previous races running alongside his horse, so why not try to run the entire distance on foot, sans horse? Ansleigh did just that and the Western States 100 Mile, and future 100-mile events across North America, were born.

Now 30 years old, 100-mile trail races are a fixture on the ultrarunning circuit. Although many runners never attempt a 100-mile, others consider such events to be the cornerstone of the sport, and a career in the sport not complete until in possession of the coveted finisher's buckle. As such, any compilation of the sport would be incomplete without a look at the many 100-mile races in North America. In the following piece, we offer concise, accurate summaries of the many 100-mile races that populate the ultrarunning calendar in North America. – Don Allison

Running 100 miles is most certainly a physical challenge, but it is also a mental test. In most cases, limits imposed by races are adequate for the specific course, with intermediate cut-offs weeding out slower runners. The real test one will face out on the trail is a test of inner drive and determination, a test of one's ability to adapt to rapidly changing conditions, a test that combines physical fitness with mental and emotional stability. While certainly physically demanding, it is my belief that with an adequate amount of physical preparation and determination, one can finish any of these courses.

The intent of this article is to offer a general overview of the various 100-mile races in North America and offer insight into the differences the trail courses present. Many people often ask about course difficulty. I have taken my personal experience on each of the courses and ranked them on a scale of one to ten, ten being the toughest. Some will not agree with my assessment, but generally I feel the rankings are in the ballpark. Some courses receive identical scores; in those cases, the more difficult race appears first.

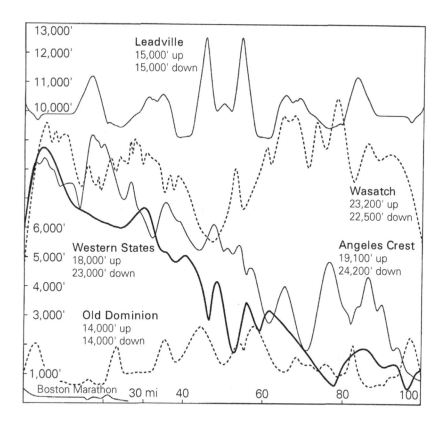

13,000'
12,000'
11,000'
10,000'
6,000'
5,000'
4,000'
3,000'
1,000'

Leadville
15,000' up
15,000' down

Wasatch
23,200' up
22,500' down

Western States
18,000' up
23,000' down

Angeles Crest
19,100' up
24,200' down

Old Dominion
14,000' up
14,000' down

Boston Marathon   30 mi   40   60   80   100

Hardrock: 10.0   Silverton, Colorado   July

The 48-hour time limit is in itself enough to indicate to the novice that this race isn't the one to try for your first 100-mile. Based in Silverton, Colorado, the Hardrock 100 is a single-loop course that covers remote, mountainous terrain from 7,700 to 14,048 feet in elevation. Aid stations are sparse, and some supplies must be brought in by pack mule. Hardrock is the most physically challenging of the 100-mile races, due to high elevation, extremes in temperature and weather conditions, steep ascents and descents on scree, difficult to follow trail markings (they are often removed by the wildlife), numerous stream and river crossings, and long distances between aid stations. At several times during the run, it is possible to be four or more hours away from aid.

Crewing for this race is a challenge. Crew points are really only accessible by four-wheel drive vehicles; passenger cars have to take the long way to the aid stations, up to more than 100 miles apart via car. Many roads are dangerous, so crews need to remain awake and alert to navigate them safely. Many aid stations are not accessible by crews, so drop bags containing extra clothes and food are essential for this run. The crew still spends a lot of time sitting and waiting, despite the driving, because most competitors take more than 40 hours to finish the 101.3-mile distance. To increase the challenge (as if all of the above were not enough!), the course alternates direction each year. Pacers are allowed from Ouray in clockwise years and from Grouse Gulch in counterclockwise years.

A wide variety of clothing, a double water pack, extra flashlights, packable food, and a tenacious spirit are required to complete the race and make it to the finish line. Because of the terrain and the trouble with animals removing the reflective aluminum course markings, arriving early to acclimate to the elevation and running on the course for a few days is the best prevention against a premature DNF.

The difficulty of the trail aside, this is by far the most scenic of the 100-mile courses, with its snowcapped mountain peaks, lush green valleys, abundant wildlife, flowing water, and quaint mountain towns, making for a vacation that an ultrarunner will never forget.

Wasatch Front: 8.5   Kaysville, Utah   September

Wasatch Front has a 36-hour time limit and is best known for two significant climbs: Chinscraper, the final push that completes the first five-mile climb out of the Salt Lake Basin, and Catherine's Pass, the high point of the run at more than 10,000 feet, which for almost all competitors occurs in the middle of the night at mile 78. Of all the races that I've done, I like this course most because of its wonderful views of the lake and the city and its meandering single-track trails through the high desert. The course is not easy, as it is comprised of many technical trails that are overgrown in spots. Run on a point-to-point course from Layton to Midway, Utah, there are many steep, sustained ascents and descents on rocky and poorly maintained trails. Course markings are more than adequate, and you will not get lost if you pay attention. While there are no water crossings on the course, the sustained ups and downs, dusty trails, high winds, rocky downhill running, and extremes in temperature offer more than enough challenge for even the most experienced 100-mile runner. Daytime temperatures in the 80s can be expected, with winter-like temperatures at night. Come prepared with warm clothes, stable shoes, and iron shins—some of the scrub oak is downright mean!

Few realize that the altitude at Wasatch is generally between 8,000 and 9,000 feet, with lower sections in the canyons, and higher sections going over mountain passes later in the race. The sustained altitude for the duration of the run adds mental and emotional fatigue to the physical exhaustion caused by the climbs.

Herein lies the true challenge for the runner attempting the Wasatch course.

Crewing for this race, like at Hardrock, is quite difficult, but is feasible if the crew has experience traveling on narrow mountain roads and a lot of patience. Many aid stations are accessible by car, as long as sufficient time is allowed for travel. Intermediate cut-offs are more than adequate for the terrain, and it is my general impression that the overall time limit is very generous for the course. Drop bags can be helpful, especially for changes of clothing, and are essential for access if no crew is available. Extra food and three bottles of water can be helpful in spots, especially during the daylight hours spent in relentless open prairies. Pacers are allowed from mile 36 to the end.

Susitna: 8.5   Big Lake, Alaska   February

It can truthfully be said that there is no 100-mile quite like the Susitna 100 Mile. The primary reason for that is that the event is held in Alaska in February! Naturally, winter-like conditions are a distinguishing feature of this event. Race organizers say, "As befits a wilderness race, expect temperatures to be anywhere in the range between 40 degrees F above zero and 40 degrees F below zero. Fortunately, (the race) usually ends up with a reasonable compromise (between the two). By 11:00 a.m. (two hours into the race) you will likely notice a 10 to 20-degree rise in temperature as the sun climbs over the Chugach Mountains. You will enjoy three or four hours of 'warmth' and then a slow but steady descent into nightfall." Needless to say, hypothermia and frostbite are real concerns, which the runner must be vigilant of throughout the duration of the race.

The course begins and ends on a plowed ice road that crosses several lakes. This surface is hard, so you will move faster on this stretch than anywhere else on the course. After nine miles, the course becomes a true wilderness trail, consisting of deep snow that has been "groomed" through recreational use by snow machines, dog teams, and occasional snowshoers, skiers, and bikers. The trail is normally firm enough to run on with regular running shoes, but soft enough to leave a track or footprint. However, there are many different weather conditions that can change this course consistency.

The Susitna course consists of a series of commonly-used snowmachine trails linked together to form a giant lollipop. The trails are put in every winter (as snow permits) by the committee and the motoring public. These trails are generally placed in the same location every year, but one of the attractions of snowmobiling in Alaska is the high degree of freedom in "going as you please." Thus, trails abound everywhere and it is quite possible to get on the wrong trail and ultimately get lost on this course. A handbook, course controls, tracks, and trail markers all help keep the runner on course.

There is a mandatory gear requirement in this event; the runner must carry 15 pounds worth of required gear throughout the race. This is done by running with a sled carrying the gear. Along with a running race, there are concurrent cycling and skiing races. There are regular aid stations to serve the participants' needs. If a winter 100-mile adventure is on your list of events to do, this is the race for you. Beware however; even the most experienced of ultrarunners will be challenged by the conditions presented in this event.

The Bear: 8.0   Preston, Idaho   October

The Bear 100 Mile offers runners the opportunity to experience the high country straddling the Utah/Idaho border in the peak of the fall color season, but the runner will have to work hard to appreciate the scenery. The last of the major mountain ultras on the annual calendar, it allows runners to get in one more run before the snow flies, or to redeem themselves from a DNF earlier in the season. It will not come easily, however. Altitude and climbs offer major challenges, along with a longer night than experienced earlier in the year. An advantage of the Bear is that heat, while possible, is usually not a major issue.

The race begins in Cub River Canyon at the Deer Creek Inn, located above Preston, Idaho, just north of the Utah/Idaho border. The area features Old West charms, including the opportunity for race participants to join in a western dance night after the race, if you are up to it! The Inn also has the added benefit of providing lodging in rustic and inexpensive ($20 to 40 per night) cabins. As the course is a loop configuration, these accommodations are especially convenient.

The course is a loop in the shape of a figure-eight, with a short out-and-back segment connecting the top and bottom loops. Much of the route follows high ridgelines that afford spectacular views, especially to the south and west. The start/finish is at approximately 5,000 feet; the course reaches 9,000 feet and at two points the course dips into the 7,000-foot range when following beautiful mountain streams along trails and primitive roadways. Daytime temperatures range from 50 to 70 F on the course, while overnight temperatures range from 30 to 50 degrees F . There are no significant water crossings. Aid stations are placed throughout the course, more numerous later in the course as runners slow their pace, and have a full complement of food and drink, similar to that offered in other ultras. There are cutoff times at many of the 15 aid stations, but aid station captains have discretion to let the runner pass through. The time limit to officially complete the course is 35 hours, indicative of the challenge this 100-mile presents.

Superior Trail: 8.0   Silver Bay, Minnesota   September

The Superior Trail 100 Mile, although somewhat on the difficult side, can be a good choice for a first 100-mile. The course runs point to point from Silver Bay to Grand Marias, Minnesota on the single-track Superior Hiking Trail. The race also occurs relatively late in the racing year, providing runners with plenty of time to train and otherwise prepare during the summer. The trail is rarely flat. The climbs and descents are short, steep, rapid, and appear to be never ending. Examples of 200 to 300-foot climbs and descents are Carlton Peak (mile 47) and Moose Mountain (mile 60; 900 feet in one mile). There is a 34-hour time limit.

Plan on going out easily and enjoying the scenery, while still paying attention to the footing—you don't want to fall, twist an ankle, or go over the cliff! Most of the aid stations are near the bottom of the ravines, so take some food and eat as you climb back up to the ridge. The lack of any big climbs might tempt you to go out too fast over the first half, but save yourself for the endless series of small hills. The first 11 miles consist of very rugged terrain with several steep hills. The first one to two hours will be run in the dark, so you will need a light of some kind at the start.

There are several streams to cross, but most have bridges. Nevertheless, plan to get wet. If it has rained recently, also expect patches of mud. The main challenges of the Superior Trail course are rocks, roots and ravines. The weather is usually not a big concern at this time of year, but the temperature can range from about 25 to 65 degrees F. Plan for cold night air in the meadows and the possibility of thunderstorms.

Pacers can start to accompany runners at the Oberg Mountain aid station, at mile 56.6. Runners over the age of 60 may have pacers from the start. Crews are allowed at all but one aid station. Three aid stations require your crew to "walk in" from a parking area, so plan for that accordingly. Some aid stations are hard to locate in the dark. Having a copy of the *Guide to the Superior Hiking Trail* will help greatly. Crews should remember they will be traveling along scenic Highway 61, a busy tourist road with poor visibility. They will encounter many people paying more attention to the colored leaves than the highway, so they should drive with caution!

Bighorn: 8.0   Sheridan, Wyoming   June

The Bighorn Mountain Wild and Scenic 100 Mile takes place in Sheridan County, Wyoming. The event, run in conjunction with two shorter distance ultras, is designed to maximize the exposure of the participants, their families, and race volunteers to an extremely scenic, wild, and primitive area of the geologically unique Bighorn Mountains.

This 100-mile is extremely challenging, due to the rugged terrain of the Bighorn Mountains. The course layout is out-and-back, run at elevations of 3,000 to 9,000 feet, among fields of wildflowers and breathtaking scenery. The majority of the course is made up of rugged mountain trails and four-wheel drive roads. In an effort to increase the number of finishers, the time limit to finish the race was extended from 31 hours to 34 hours, with modified cutoff times designed to allow a higher finisher rate, but still ensure runner safety.

Aid stations are manned with enthusiastic volunteers, strategically placed throughout the race, and stocked with ample food, electrolytes, and liquids. The Sheridan Search and Rescue provides difficult to establish communication links on the course, necessary for the safety of participants. In the tradition of other 100-milers in the West, this is not a beginner's race. Altitude, combined with mountainous terrain, will test the mettle of even the most experienced ultrarunners.

HURT: 8.0   Honolulu, Hawaii   January

Held in a nature center in tropical Hawaii while the continental U.S. is experiencing the worst of winter, how tough can the HURT 100 Mile be? Pretty tough, actually. Muddy, rooted, rocky, single-track trails make up this multiple-loop course, set in a mountainous tropical rainforest. In addition, according to the race brochure, you can expect precipitous and dangerous drop-offs in several locations. All that and 23,750 feet of climb combines to make this one of he toughest 100-milers out there. As the race suggest, this 100-miler is for the adventurous (and experienced) ultrarunner. The 36-hour time limit attests as to its difficulty level.

There is a concurrent 100-km held with the HURT 100, and runners who complete that distance but go no further are credited with a 100-km finish. There are three aid stations per 20-mile loop, five to seven miles apart. Runners are strongly encouraged to carry two large bottles of fluid or the equivalent at all times during the race. Pacers are allowed after 100-km or the onset of darkness, whichever comes first.

The HURT has developed a reputation as a welcoming event, as race staff and volunteers offer Hawaii's trademark "aloha" to all runners. Held in January, it offers a welcome diversion to many stateside ultrarunners, but a finish in this 100-mile will be hard-earned.

The Eagle: 7.5   Keremeos, British Columbia   July

With more than 15,000 feet of elevation gain and descent and challenging terrain,

The Eagle certainly ranks among the more difficult 100-milers in North America. The race was held for several years in the late 1990s, and then took a sabbatical until 2004. The start and finish is located in rural Keremeos, British Columbia, 30 miles southwest of Penticton, a ski resort and home of Canada's Ironman triathlon

The route is out and back. While there are no water crossings, one can expect heat, cold and many hills. The Rim Trail above Quinescoe Lake is only six miles long but will take most runners two to three hours to complete. The weather is unpredictable; heat can be a factor in late July in this region, but it could also be cold. Snow and/or hail are not unheard of at elevations of more than 8,000 feet.

A minimum of two large (bike) water bottles or hydration pack must be carried at all times. Crew access is available only at pacer locations, after mile 80. The time limit is 33 hours. Given its requirement for self-sufficiency and remote wilderness location, the Eagle is a race for experienced 100-mile ultrarunners. The rewards offered by the scenery in this race are balanced by its difficult course.

Angeles Crest: 7.5 Wrightwood, California September

A one-way trail from Wrightwood to Pasadena, California, the Angeles Crest traverses well-groomed trails with much altitude gain and loss. The 33-hour time limit is adequate for the terrain and allows one to admire the beauty of the Angeles National Forest from mountain ridges and the high point on the course, Mt. Baden-Powell, at more than 9,000 feet. Several of the trails are littered with fist-size rocks and boulders, adding to the challenge of the sustained descents. This is a downhill course, starting high in the San Gabriel Mountains, and ending in the foothills within the Los Angeles basin. Course markings are adequate, and as long as attention is paid to the route (there are many side trails in places), becoming lost should not be a problem.

Much of the course parallels Highway 2, the Angeles Crest Highway. Aid stations are set up at scenic turnouts and parking areas, which makes crewing for much of this event easy. There is a long drive to Chantry Flat (mile 75) from Shortcut Saddle, and crews are not permitted on the last 25 miles of the course. Aid is plentiful early in the race, and there are only two long sections to be concerned with: the Baden-Powell climb and the Cooper Canyon traverse. Baden-Powell will take most runners more than an hour to climb, and at least that long to descend. Cooper Canyon, although only eight miles long, will likely be hot. Carrying extra water in these two sections is advised.

The real challenge of the Angeles Crest is presented in the last quarter of the race. Two significant climbs, Mt. Wilson, and the Idlehour Trail, occur late in the race in the dark. There is no crew access in this section of the run, and aid stations are more spread out due to the remoteness of the terrain. It is advisable to carry extra water, especially over the last ten miles, and to pack drop bags for delivery to aid stations after Chantry Flat. I've not experienced any cool weather on this course, as the area is desert and is dry most of the year. A light jacket as a safety net should suffice for sections of cool air that may be present if the runner doesn't reach the Front Range (around mile 65) before dark.

The course is 100.53 miles long, and offers a variety of terrain. Groomed and rocky trails, high desert, steep climbs and descents, heat, and Mt. Wilson make this a challenging run, one I wouldn't advise for a novice. The only thing lacking along the course are water crossings. Pacers are allowed from Chilao, mile 53, and can greatly aid in route finding through some confusing areas later in the run.

Massanutten Mountain: 7.5   Front Royal, Virginia   May

Billed as the toughest 100-mile east of the Rockies, this course lives up to that billing. There is hardly a flat portion on these 100.43 miles of trail, which is narrow and extremely rocky. The official time limit is 36 hours, adequate for most runners. The course consists of a loop on and around Massanutten Mountain in Virginia. Most of the climbs and descents are short, and few exceed 1,000 feet in vertical climb. Altitude is not an issue on this course, as most of the area is at less than 2,500 feet; the issue is the rockiness of the trail. Course markings make the trail easy to follow, and although intersections are well marked, scarcity of ribbons on some straight sections may make some runners nervous. Since there are areas of the run over which runners pass in opposite directions, it is very important to study the course map before the run, and carry it along if you are worried about directions. The turn to climb up Waterfall Mountain, the steepest on the course, is the intersection that appears to cause the most trouble.

Temperatures can be variable, but because of long exposed sections on the ridgeline, it would be advisable to carry a light jacket for most of the run. It can be cool at night, and because the more difficult trail sections occur after dark, warm clothing is the best defense against hypothermia. There can be several stream crossings, as several of the trails are more like creek beds than trails. You will get wet.

Aid is excellent, with each aid station offering not only standard fare, but also something unique. There are 17 stations on the course, with no more than eight miles between any two stations. While eight miles may not seem like a very long way between stops, the trails that connect them are rugged and the going slow, for most. Even faster runners should allow two hours between them. Come prepared with a mental attitude that much of this race will be tough and slow. Crewing for this run is easy; the aid stations are easily accessible by road. Pacers are allowed from any point of the run after 6:00 p.m. on Saturday.

The race offers runners who reach the Visitor's Center, mile 47, but who don't complete the run, a "visitor's award." Appropriately enough, the award is a rock culled from the millions on the trail, a rock that will be a reminder of mental fatigue, emotional fragility, and physical pain one is sure to experience during this race. This course is tough enough to make even a seasoned veteran cry. Finish this one, and you will be more than prepared to tackle any of the more popular runs in the West.

Leadville: 7.0   Leadville, Colorado   August

This 100-mile out-and-back route from Leadville, Colorado, is run entirely at altitude in excess of 9,200 feet. While the trail offers fantastic footing, wide gravel roads and gently rolling terrain, there is no shortage of elements to challenge the runner along this course. There are two significant climbs in each direction, Sugarloaf Mountain and Hope Pass, with the more difficult direction occurring on the return trip from the turnaround at the ghost town of Winfield. There are more difficult courses in terms of footing and terrain, but the combination of four significant climbs, only nine full aid stations, unpredictable Colorado weather, and high altitude, certainly make this course a challenge.

Uncertainty in the weather means that the runner needs to be prepared for almost anything. Warm clothes are essential for the night sections, as temperatures in the 30s and 40s are not uncommon. Precipitation is also a concern, so a wind and water-resistant jacket should be available from start to finish. There is a single river to cross, but it must be crossed twice. The water is nothing more than snow melt, so it is cold. The water level depends on the amount of rain and the temperature; it is not uncommon for ankle-deep water to become waist-deep in the span of a few hours. Mosquitoes can be a major problem around Twin Lakes, so insect repellant is a good comfort item to pack. Be prepared for weather extremes and water by packing extra shoes, socks, and clothing.

Aid stations are few because most of the course is in very remote country, but crew access to all of these points is easily obtained. A large portion of the course is on dusty roads that are shared with crew vehicles, a frustrating experience for many runners. It would be a good idea to carry a bandana to help filter the dust on these sections; also advise your crew to carpool with others as much as possible, especially on the road to Winfield where travel is very congested. Pacers are allowed for all runners from the turnaround at mile 50.

The time limit for this run, 30 hours, adds to the challenge of the course. Strict cut-offs at each aid station are followed, and some are not as lenient as others. Since the trip back to Leadville from the turnaround is more difficult than the trip out, it is wise to try to reach Winfield with time to spare before the 14-hour cut-off; those who push this time limit stand a good chance of not finishing.

Western States: 7.0   Squaw Valley, California   June

Nearly 30 years old, Western States is the Boston Marathon of ultrarunning. Many runners worship the trails this course is run on and return year after year to test their mettle on some of the most beautiful terrain in northern California. Wide, well-groomed trails and a downhill course make Western States a very runable race. A point-to-point route from Squaw Valley to Auburn, California, the high point of the course four miles from the start (Emigrant Pass, 8,700 feet) offers splendid views of Lake Tahoe in the distance. There are several steep climbs and descents, their difficulty enhanced by the extreme temperature differences between the high country and the canyons. The trail is very runable; the canyon heat and dust are the major contributors to difficulty of this race. It is a good idea to carry a bandana to help filter dust and to dip in available springs for on-the-run cooling. Unless it is raining, your feet will stay dry and very dirty for most of the race. There is only one major river crossing, Rucky Chucky at mile 78, that will get you wet from at least the waist on down. Many runners pack a drop bag with a change of shoes on the far side of the river crossing.

Hot weather gear is needed for most of the run, except for early morning and night running. A light jacket should suffice at these times, and may not even be needed depending on the day's weather. As in all cases, it is much better to be prepared than to underdress and get cold. Two water bottles should be plenty for most runners, and should be consumed completely between each of the 10 weigh-in points along the trail. Medical checks here are strict; it is important to show that weight and hydration are being maintained. Aid stations are superbly stocked, although I found them somewhat lacking in solid food. There is, however, plenty to eat and drink. Volunteers in tuxedos and podiatry tents along the course make leaving some of the aid stations difficult for tired runners.

Because of the point-to-point nature of the course and long drives to checkpoints, Western States is a logistical nightmare for crew support. Allow at least two hours to drive from the start to the finish, and make lodging plans accordingly. In some places crews cannot get in to meet their runners easily unless they are shuttled in. In other places, they may need to walk and carry supplies for a mile or more. Because of the number of runners (usually around 400), most of whom have crew, traffic and congestion can be extreme. Avoid trying to rush into and out of aid stations to meet your runner, because you'll only get upset and frustrated. Patience here is a virtue. Dusty and winding mountain roads that make for slow driving offer the crew an ultra of their own. Pacers are allowed from Foresthill, at mile 62.

Drop bags would certainly be advantageous for this run, especially given the technical difficulties in getting crew to the aid stations. Crew members are not allowed in some of the aid station tents, so drop bags nearby are an advantage to a runner wishing to change socks and shoes. Keeping the dust away from one's feet is important in preventing blisters, and is best done by frequent sock changes at the aid tents.

The time limit for Western States is 30 hours. Intermediate cut-offs along the course are generous for the overall limit, but even these can be challenging for slower runners. The best preparation for a finish here is a lot of downhill training in the heat, as these are the real challenges faced along the Western States course. When running the race, knowledge of the course and terrain is helpful in judging when to run and when to walk. A fast pace early on will likely turn runable sections of trail later in the race into walks.

Cascade Crest Classic: 7.0   Easton, Washington   August

The Pacific Northwest has long been an ultrarunning hotbed, so it is no surprise that a successful 100-mile has now been established in the region. The Cascade Crest Classic has gained a reputation for a tough, but scenic and interesting course. Unlike most other 100-mile races, its 10:00 a.m. start time favors those who do not relish pre-dawn starts.

The run begins in the small town of Easton (about 70 miles east of Seattle) at 2,100 feet and after a few miles on roads winds towards Goat Peak on dirt roads and single-track trails. From atop Goat Peak, one can actually see the entire 100-mile course, as well as breathtaking views of Mount Rainier, a landmark in the Pacific Northwest. A unique feature of this race is the Snoqualmie Tunnel, just past halfway. The tunnel is 2.3 miles long, and is perhaps the darkest spot you will ever see, at least in any 100-mile race. Pacers are allowed at any time from this location onward. The "Cardiac Needles" late in the race consists of about five climbs and descents that will test even the hardiest of runners. After that, it is about 10 miles to the finish, most of which is downhill.

You won't go hungry at this race; 18 aid stations are fully stocked with the normal "ultra" food, although several of the more remote ones won't have the selection that the main ones have. There are four drop bag locations. The time limit is 32 hours; in addition there are two intermediate cut-offs late in the race.

Otherwise, the Cascade Crest is pretty much devoid of strict rules. There are no medical checks or weigh-ins; the runner knows whether or not he or she should be participating. The Cascade Crest is tough, but comparable to other 100-milers in the West, what with its 20,500 feet of elevation gain.

Rio Del Lago: 5.0   Granite Bay, California   September

This northern California 100-mile in Granite Bay, California, consists of an out and back for 67 miles along the American River equestrian trails, then an out back of 33 miles in the opposite direction, before returning to the finish line at the school. A full 98 percent of the race is run on groomed trails and dirt roads. Much of the course is familiar to runners who participate in other ultras run in the area. The elevation change is approximately 18,000 feet. Twenty-eight well-stocked aid stations offer support for runners. For crews, there is easy driving access to most aid stations. The time limit is 30 hours. This race is a good choice for a moderately difficult but achievable 100-mile, even for first-timers, although the weather can be a factor, as early fall can be very hot in this region. That combined with regular climbs and descents through the race offer the runner a serious challenge.

Mohican: 5.0   Loudonville, Ohio   June

A modified loop course in the Mohican River valley near Loudonville, Ohio, this 100-mile run is run on 35 miles of dirt and paved road and 65 miles of well-groomed Midwestern trail. The 30-hour cutoff is more than generous for the undulating terrain, with its multiple ascents and descents into and out of the river valley the main challenges the runner will face. The trails are virtually void of rocks, but as on many of the Midwestern trails, there are roots and stumps to deal with instead. The course is divided into a cloverleaf structure, with the major aid station at the covered bridge in the center of the leaf. This aid station is passed five separate times, offers a generous supply of traditional fare and solid food (pizza and burgers), and serves as the medical checkpoint with both emergency as well as podiatry aid available.

Course markings are more than adequate if the runner has enough mental faculties available to not become confused by the different colored markers. Each of the cloverleaf petals is marked with different colored ribbons, and following the loops in order is important to follow the course as designed. A brief reconnoiter of the covered bridge area would certainly benefit anyone easily confused by several trails converging in a single area.

Central Ohio is almost always hot in June. Warm weather clothing will be needed for the run, and will generally be sufficient for even the night sections.

There is one major crossing of the Mohican River, in addition to several stream crossings. It is a waste of time to try to stay dry, so planning to run with wet feet through mile 75 will save time and energy. The trail section is complete at about 75 miles; the rest of the course is on dirt and paved roads. If you are going to pack a change of shoes and socks, this would be the place to do so. Two drop bags, one at the end of the "red loop" and the other at the covered bridge, are more than adequate.

Crewing for this run isn't difficult, as runners pass by many aid stations more than one time. Roads in the area are only mildly congested, and although there is no parking available right at the bridge, a parking lot a quarter-mile away is available for crews. Pacers are allowed for the last 35 miles.

In addition to the heat and the multiple short climbs and descents as the major challenges to this race, black flies, mosquitoes, and poison ivy are also things to watch out for. The flies can be quite thick in places, especially in low-lying areas and along sections of the course that double as a horse trail. Recreational horse riders may be out on race day. Sections of trail are overgrown and littered with poison ivy; it is virtually impossible to avoid. Take a shower using Tecnu immediately after the run to keep the itching at bay.

Old Dominion: 4.5   Woodstock, Virginia   June

A loop course through Fort Valley in Virginia, Old Dominion is run in the same area as the Massanutten Mountain Trail 100. It is not the same course. In fact, the 80 miles of road running makes Old Dominion about eight hours faster to run than Massanutten. Some of the trail sections of Old Dominion are common to the Massanutten course, and these are tough, rocky, and technical climbs over short, steep mountains. While these trails are frustrating when running Massanutten, they are a nice alternative to the miles of paved and gravel road that make up the bulk of the Old Dominion course. Since the trails offer only a minor challenge to the runner, the major obstacles encountered are the unforgiving road surface, vehicular traffic from Fort Valley residents, and the heat of Virginia in June. Bugs are not much of a problem, except in the muddy areas around Duncan Hollow, the slowest portion of the 100 miles. Except for this low-lying area, which can be wet even when the rest of Virginia is dry, the route is free from streams and mud.

This is one of the original four 100-milers, and not much has changed over the years. Currently, the time limit is 28 hours, which should allow for all except the slowest runners ample time to finish. Aid is adequate and plentiful for the middle-of-the-packer, but faster runners may arrive before aid stations are prepared, and the slowest runners may arrive after all of the food has been eaten and the water consumed. On this course, it is best to have crew and provide for yourself, or run in the middle of the pack. I personally had none of the problems encountered by others while I was running this course, although even at my modest pace, I arrived at an aid station before it was prepared adequately.

Crewing is easy, since the route is mostly run on roads. The roads, however, are narrow and winding. Many are shared with runners, and can become congested at times. As mentioned above, the runner may count on the crew for aid at various points in the run, so help is recommended. Drop bags can be prepared for delivery to various aid stations, to ensure that personal supplies are on hand even when the race management has run out of their own.

Temperatures in Virginia in June can be extremely warm. A singlet should suffice for most of the day, with only a light shirt at night. Ticks and gnats may be encountered, so a repellant is a nice comfort item to include in a drop bag or two. The most difficult climb, Sherman Gap, is the trail section that occurs after 75 miles. Many runners will navigate the steep climb and descent in the dark. A second climb, Veach Gap, follows a few miles later. Pacers are not allowed in the run, but "running companions" are allowed for a 12-mile section beginning at the Elizabeth Furnace aid station and ending at the bottom of Veach Gap. For the most part, the runner is expected to be self-sufficient.

Aside from some problems with the aid, this run is otherwise well organized and is marked well, although the scarcity of ribbons on some stretches of road may be worrisome to some runners. The course receives a higher difficulty ranking for the undulating roads through hot and exposed terrain, tough and rocky trail sections, variable availability of aid, and the prohibition of pacer support. It is a fast course and a good one for a physically and mentally strong first-timer with crew support.

Kettle Moraine: 4.0   Whitewater, Wisconsin   June

A "moraine" is an accumulation of earth and stones carried by a glacier and usually deposited into high points, such as a ridges. The course for this race features such terrain, run entirely on trails (except for a couple hundred feet of road crossings) traversing the Ice Age National Scenic Trail. The configuration consists of two out-and-back legs of 62 and 38 miles, on about 80-percent wooded terrain, the rest meandering through gentle prairie or marsh areas. Part of the course features a rollercoaster of hills, with small rocks and roots scattered about. Other sections are gently rolling with relatively smooth running surfaces. Although the hills are not long and/or especially steep, they can take a toll if attacked too vigorously. Pacers are allowed at mile 62, and there is easy crew access throughout the race. The 100-mile has a 30-hour time limit. There is also a concurrent 100-km race. With 7,700 feet of climb and descent, the elevation is modest by 100-mile standards, thus making it a good choice for first-timers or an intermediate level 100-mile test.

Heartland: 4.0   Cassoday, Kansas   September

This event is aptly named, taking place in the heart of the continental U.S. This race in unusual in that unlike the many 100-mile races that take place in the mountains, the Heartland 100 mile embraces the open plains. The 50-mile out and back course on backcountry gravel roads has less than one mile of paved surface. Much of the course meanders through an open range with stunning views of the vast expanse of the Flint Hills tallgrass prairie. The course features rolling hills and 6,000 feet of climb and descent.

The race has a 30-hour time limit. There are 20 aid stations and crew access is available at nine locations for the 100-mile. Fourteen of the aid stations can be used for drop bags. There is a concurrent 50-mile race, on an out-and-back on a portion of the Heartland 100 course. As for the weather, the normal high is 73 F and a normal low is 48 F. In Kansas however, one must be prepared for extremes. One of those involves the wind, which so often accompanies this event, it is referred to as "Kansas mountains."

Arkansas Traveller: 4.0   Perryville, Arkansas   September

The Arkansas Traveller 100 Mile is held on a 17-mile loop, followed by an 83-mile out-and-back. A short section of the route, about eight miles, is run over the unstable and rocky footing of the Ouachita Trail; the remainder is a mix of primarily dirt and jeep roads consisting of variably adequate footing. With no especially unique challenges, the 30-hour cut-off should be more than adequate for all runners. There are no major climbs on the course, the highest point a hill called Smith Mountain that is crossed in both directions (mile 45 and 75) of the out-and-back. Since much of the course is run on dusty forest service and jeep roads, exposure to the sun should be expected. There are no stream crossings to deal with, and only a few short sections over which mud may be a concern. Since rutted jeep trails tend to hold stagnant water, breeding grounds for mosquitoes may be encountered.

The run is staged in October when daylight is getting scarce. Be sure to carry a flashlight with extra batteries if you plan to be out overnight. There is a lot of darkness on this run, which adds to the challenge of dressing properly. Warm autumn days become cool autumn nights, and if it is cold and raining, hypothermia is a distinct possibility. Be sure to carry at least a light jacket for night running, as the trees in the forest make for cold nights. Drop bags are really a comfort item on this course, and are only needed if the runner wants to provide special supplies or a change of socks. I would suggest, however, that a bag with a warm jacket or a blanket be placed at the Lake Sylvia aid station for use upon completing the run.

Crewing for this race is not difficult, as most aid stations offer full crew support and easy access via forest service roads. The forest service roads, although passable, are fairly well maintained, but may be rutted. Be sure to carry a spare tire, as FS114 (one of the two access roads) has a long history of causing flats. Pacers are allowed from the Powerline aid station at mile 49.1, and are welcome to partake in the excellent aid station fare at all of the checkpoints. Aid stations are superbly stocked and offer a wide variety of standard fare. No two aid stations are the same, but all are excellently staffed and prepared with unique food. The burritos and beer tasted good in the middle of the night!

Vermont: 3.0 South Woodstock, Vermont July

Based in South Woodstock, Vermont, this 100-mile course is run on a beautiful loop course, consisting of well groomed trails (25 percent) and roads (75 percent). Vermont's Green Mountains offer challenging, undulating hills and a few unstable and rocky trails. The lush green pastures and quaint New England farms offer a spectacular setting that can be enjoyed because the runner doesn't have to constantly watch his or her feet for rocks, roots, and ruts on the course. The main challenge here is the amount of pavement on the course; well-cushioned shoes will help protect feet from the constant pounding. Temperatures can get warm, but are usually moderate. Since nights can be slightly cool, it is a good idea to pack a light jacket for night sections run through dense forest trees. It gets cold quickly when the sun goes down.

There are approximately 36 aid stations, many of which are unmanned and offer support between the 16 fully-stocked aid stations with crew access. The frequency of aid means that the runner need not worry about carrying his or her own personal supplies between aid stations; a single bottle should suffice. Crew access is good, but many of the roads tend to be narrow. Parking can be a problem, because most of the 250 runners have crew. With aid so frequent, it is easy to get caught up at the aid stations. Don't fall into the habit of spending too much time at each one. Get what you need and move on.

The course is one of the best-marked trails of all the 100s, and maps and directions found in the entry confirmation are not as hard to follow as they appear.

The biggest challenge in following this course is in finding the start. I tried to do it at 3:00 a.m. and got lost three times. It is much better to do, at least for the first time, in daylight.

Many runners camp for free at the start and finish. The pre- and post-race gatherings in a large barn that serves as the finish line provide a real party atmosphere to the race, and serves as one of the best introductions to the world of 100-mile races for the novice. If you choose Vermont as your first attempt at 100 miles, you won't be alone.

Haliburton: 2.5   Haliburton Forest, Ontario   September

The Haliburton Forest 100 Mile course is very runner-friendly, a double out-and-back configuration run on country roads, forest service roads, and trails in Haliburton Forest, a private forest in central Ontario. The private forest surroundings ensure that traffic is minimal; most race-day traffic consists of crews shuttling supplies from aid station to aid station.

The total climb and descent is 6,782 feet each way. The highest elevation on the run is 1,542 feet; the start is at 1,345 feet and the low point is 1,247 feet. There are many short and steep climbs. The steepest section (and worst footing) is on the Krista Trail, a three-mile segment from miles five to eight. The trail sections are quite narrow, and some places on the course are overgrown. This isn't a problem if you are running, but the trails are shared with mountain bikers during the day. It is advisable to step off the trail and let them pass. The first five miles are on roads, so be sure not to go out too fast. The hills are short and rugged. Don't worry about walking them, as there are plenty of gentle road sections to run. Some rough trails with rocks make short sections very interesting to run. Steep trails obstructed with roots are more common than rocks. Low-lying areas are breeding areas for bugs, especially at night. Insect repellant is a good choice as the sun goes down.

The aid stations are close together, but some fairly rough trails can be slow in spots. A single bottle should suffice for most of the race. Much of the course is heavily wooded and remains fairly cool (50 to 60 degrees F) at its late summer date, so a light jacket may be needed at the start and at night. Short, steep hills ensure that you will work up a sweat, though, so versatile clothing is important. Aid stations offer basic fare that can sustain you throughout the event, but remember that foods in Canada can vary in taste from those routinely encountered on runs in the United States.

There is easy crew access to all of the aid stations. Much of the course is within a 15-minute drive of the base camp; most of the aid stations lie along the main forest road, making navigation to the checkpoints easy. A small grocery, phones, and restaurant are available at the base camp for some last minute supplies or a snack. Pacers may start at mile 75, at the far end of the course, to cover the final 25 miles with their runners.

The most difficult part of the run will come at mile 50. You are back at your car, have put in a good 50-mile effort, and will be forced to make the decision to stop or continue on. However, when you turn around at mile 75, you'll know you're on your last leg to your first finish! This is a small-town race with a big heart. It is low key in every way except for enthusiasm, which makes it a great event for all who participate.

Javelina: 1.5   Fountain Hills, Arizona   October

This event, which debuted in 2004, is held in Arizona's McDowell Mountain Regional Park, located 15 miles northeast of the city of Scottsdale in the lower Verde Basin. Elevation ranges from 1,550 feet at the southeastern corner, to 3,100 feet along the western boundary of the 21,000-acre park.

The course consists of six runable 15.3-mile loops on gently rolling, single-track trails. Runners complete the loops in alternating directions, a plus in that it offers a change if scenery and full panorama of the mountain views. Aid stations every five miles, with available drop bags, offer access to just about anything a runner will need during the race. This event is a good choice for beginners, as it offers a relatively easy course and is well supported by volunteers, who promote having fun, enjoying the race, and sharing the experience with other runners.

Rocky Raccoon: 1.5   Huntsville, Texas   February

This race offers a unique opportunity to run a 100-mile race in the middle of the winter. Rocky Raccoon also provides the first time 100-mile runner a course that can't get much easier in terms of terrain or design. The course is run on the trails of Huntsville State Park, mirroring many of the trails used for the Sunmart Texas Trail 50 Mile held in December. The course, a mixture of forest service roads and relatively flat and well-groomed trails, consists of five 20.2-mile loops with four well-stocked aid stations. This race has had the distinction of being run in 60-degree temperatures one year, followed by a snowstorm in the next. Being prepared for any type of weather is a good idea, as the sun can get hot during the day; nights may be cool however, even in mild years.

The course is very well marked, and the multiple loop format means that route finding after 80 miles should not be a problem. However, people still get lost. Paying attention to the marked intersections and understanding the course map are important to running the course correctly. There are several sections of out-and-back trail that can get confusing at times, and since there is a lot of course in a very small area, a flashlight a few feet to your left can mean the runner coming in your direction is miles ahead of you.

Crew access to the course is minimal, and pacers, allowed after the third loop, are really not needed. Since crew access is poor, bringing a drop bag or two would be preferable to bringing along the family. The trail can be muddy in spots, and many of the low-lying areas around the lake can be flooded. Most of the streams are bridged, but if the water level is high, the potential for wet feet is present.

This is a very low-key event, with a short trail briefing and a simple dinner available before the race. There is no post-race awards ceremony, and the 30-hour cut-off is ample time to allow for even the slowest of runners to complete 100 miles. It is an easy, fast course that is perfect for the novice 100-mile runner, but the general lack of participation and laid back atmosphere means that the hype of the 100-mile distance and running with a group of others may best be saved for another race.

Umstead: 1.5   Raleigh, North Carolina   April

The Umstead 100 Mile in North Carolina is an excellent choice for a first 100-mile attempt, since it is one of the easier courses around. It does not have the mountainous terrain of many of the 100-milers and the course is run a 10-mile loop, so the problem of getting lost is practically non-existent. Once you make it around the first loop, you will know the course.

This is really a road race, with less than two miles of trails on the loop. The footing is excellent and running on the course at night does not require an elaborate flashlight. Many ultrarunners have finished Umstead as their first 100-mile; once they do, they have the confidence to attempt some of the others.

Run the first loop at an easy pace, since you'll be running it nine more times. All of the hills are runable, but don't forget that there is 16,000 feet of elevation change. The biggest obstacle for most runners is the mental challenge of passing your car nine times and not dropping out!

The aid stations offer excellent food, but if you need your own supplies, it's easy to leave them in either of your two drop bags. You should be able to get by with one water bottle, since the intermediate station can be used to top off your bottle. The weather can be warm and humid (the normal high is 71 degrees F) during the day, but cool (the normal low is 45) and damp at night, so plan accordingly.

There are 19 aid stations and a 30-hour time limit, which should be more than sufficient for all runners attempting the 100-mile. There is also a 50-mile race, and those who pass 50 miles but drop out later in the 100-mile race are given a finishing time in the 50-mile. There is crew access at the intermediate aid station, but parking is limited, so the start/finish aid station is the best place for crewing. Access to the park between 8:00 p.m. and 5:00 a.m. is limited to once per hour, so crews should plan accordingly. It's a one-hour round trip to nearby stores and back. Bring a sleeping bag so you can wait for your runner in one of the cabins. Pacers may start anytime after 6:00 p.m. Plan on having your pacer join you at the start/finish aid station.

Summary

In this article, we have attempted to provide an accurate assessment of each of the events presented. Courses range in difficulty from easy to extreme, but there is at least one thing in common with all of them: each is 100 miles in distance, a very long way to run. Proper physical preparation, an ability to tackle mental and emotional demons that may surface during the run, and the tenacity to keep going despite discomfort, are all keys to completing the distance, no matter which course you choose to attempt. At this distance, experience will be your best teacher. Believe in yourself and your abilities, plan accordingly, work through areas of discomfort, and you can be successful on any course you run.

Ultra People

Bios and Interviews

One of the truly wonderful aspects of ultrarunning is the array of individuals who comprise the sport. It really is true that every runner has a story and that story is an interesting one. Many of these individuals have managed to carve their own unique and outstanding niche in the sport. We present biographies of and interviews with a select few of those people in this section.

In the 20th century, one true pioneer and visionary of ultrarunning was South African Arthur Newton. Larry Myers delves deep into the life and running of Newton in his profile of this outstanding runner. It is amazing how successful Newton was in pioneering training and racing methodology. Many of the practices he instituted are still widely used decades after he introduced them.

Trishul Cherns offers an insightful interview with Ted Corbitt, another of the sport's pioneers. Corbitt revitalized the ultrarunning in the 1950s after a long dormant period. He also bridged the gap between the marathon and ultras, in both of which he excelled.

No discussion of excellence and ultrarunning would be complete without mentioning Yiannis Kouros. Competing in the late 20th century, it can be said that Kouros is perhaps the greatest ultrarunner of all time. He has turned out an incredible volume of 24-hour performances that have not even been approached by any other men in the history of the sport. Many have tried to study and learn form Kouros, a true master of the sport. We present articles both about and by Kouros himself, in attempt to learn for ourselves just what sets him so far above the rest of the human race in his ultrarunning exploits.

If Kouros defines greatness on the men's side, Ann Trason is without question the finest female ultrarunner of our time. Her record, including 10 consecutive victories at the Western States 100 Mile, is truly astonishing. For much of her career, it was a foregone conclusion that she would win; the question was by how much. In profiling Ann, we learn more about just what has allowed her to compete at such a high level and transform the sport during the past decade or more.

Of course ultrarunning is about much more than winning. Many of ultrarunning's greatest ambassadors, those who have shaped the sport and inspired thousands of others, have never even come close to winning a race. One such runner is the vibrant Helen Klein. Competing at a high level at an age when most other women would never dream of running ultra distances, Helen has been a shining example of what we all can achieve with the desire and motivation to succeed. Without a doubt, Helen Klein is one of the greatest ultrarunners of all time, as we learn from James Raia's interview with her.

Micah True takes us on a fascinating journey into Mexico's Copper Canyon to study the intriguing Rarimuri, or Tarahumara Indians, for whom long distance running is not a sport, but a way of life necessary for survival. In addition, Katy Williams profiles the ritual surrounding the legendary long distance races run by the Tarahumara.

Some of the greatest American ultrarunners have achieved lofty heights after the age of 40. Sue Ellen Trapp is one of those runners. In her 40s and 50s she has routinely competed not just with women under the age of 40 , but younger men as well. Trapp, along with Sue Olsen, is one of the greatest 48-hour runners in history. Kevin Setnes tells how this pair is capable of such tremendous two-day running efforts. Another great masters ultrarunner was Bernd Heinrich, who set records in the 1980s. Heinrich is also a world class zoologist and has taken a scientific approach to his running, applying the physiological principles from the animal kingdom to his own ultrarunning. In an extensive interview, he shares some of his findings and details how he was able to set an American record at 100 km.

These are just a few individuals who have shaped the sport of ultrarunning. Were we to profile everyone whose story is unique and interesting, this volume would fill an entire library!

Arthur Newton: A Pioneer of Ultrarunning

by Larry Myers

There are many great ultrarunners on today's running scene, but perhaps the greatest of them all was Arthur Newton, "The Exceptional Mr. Newton," according to Ron Clarke in *The Lonely Breed*. Newton's techniques pioneered a new branch of long-distance running and had great influence on renowned coach Percy Cerutty and his Stotan training system. Newton, after his retirement from running, stated that Cerutty carried training and technique a step farther and forward by incorporating intensive training with a new running style, the five basic movements for varying a runner's a gait during a race.

Arthur H. Newton, the son of a clergyman in Somerset, England, emigrated to Natal, South Africa where he took up farming and won prizes for growing cotton and tobacco. After 16 years of hard work to build a prosperous business, Newton was struck a cruel blow when the Department of Native Affairs declared the area "black" and forced him to sell his farm. This, along with a bitter divorce, motivated the 39-year-old Newton to take up running as a way of gaining public support for his disagreements with the government. What began as a desperate protest later became Newton's real profession and life's work, as he pioneered a new era in ultrarunning. During the period from 1922 to 1934, Newton set world records at all distances between 40 miles and 24 hours. His 24-hour record of 152 miles was set in 1931 and not broken until 1953. Indeed, even today the 150-mile barrier is seldom reached in a 24-hour race. This article chronicles Newton's running philosophy and offers a sketch of his life.

Training

Arthur Newton began running relatively late in life with a weak heart and frail body, never having competed in sports in his formative years. Newton made a total commitment to training, often running all day from dawn to dusk. His business, social life, and hobbies all became secondary to running. Running for Arthur Newton became an escape from reality; it was a total obsession by which he expressed his frustrations with his own personal problems and the political climate in South Africa.

In Newton's first workout, he tried a long, slow run, but a stitch, caused by weak abdominal muscles, forced him to walk home after running 12 miles. Newton believed walking and hiking played an important part in building up strong primary and secondary tanks for negotiating longer distances. Only three months after his first run, during which he ran and walked 12 miles a day, Newton ran his first marathon. Years later, after setting many world records, Newton said the long walks became detrimental to his training and no longer played a crucial role, because his training had become more advanced: he had successfully established a strong secondary tank by going through many breakdowns over the years, the bitter price a runner pays for greatness.

Arthur Newton trained for five months and covered thousands of miles in preparation for his first Comrades Marathon in 1922, a 54-mile race from Durban to Pietermaritzburg. He competed in six Comrades marathons, winning five times and setting records for both directions of the steep course. He also set a London to Brighton record in 1924, finishing ahead of top English marathoners who had competed in the 1924 Paris Olympics.

Newton, a professional distance runner in every sense of the word, beat younger runners simply by being better conditioned, using superior training methods that were years ahead of his time in both theory and principle. During his illustrious 12-year career, Newton covered 102,735 miles, averaging 140 miles weekly. "Make a training schedule for one week and concentrate on one day at a time according to your day-to-day feelings," said Newton. "Every runner is different and unique in his personal makeup, and his strength and energy changes from hour to hour and from day to day. The longer the distance, the more time, work and energy are needed to prepare for the race. There is no such thing as a 'born athlete' in ultrarunning."

Newton's system taught that the ideal training distance for ultrarunning is 10 to 15 miles, concentrating on a varied pace and tempo with a six and a half to 10 mile-per-hour pace. Once or twice per month there should be a 60-mile weekend (two times 30 miles), forcing the breakdown needed to build a strong secondary tank of energy and strength, not to be confused with "second wind," which Newton thought was a myth in 100-mile and longer races. "When the runner can easily cover 60 miles without any undue signs of stress or strain," Newton said, "this is the cut-off point for eventually covering 50 to 100 miles."

Newton's long (20 to 30 miles) runs were covered at slower than race pace, but his shorter runs (10 to 15 miles) were at race pace or sometimes a little faster. He finished every workout by "whipping in" his training runs with a fast 880, and he won many races by defeating runners who were totally exhausted in the closing stages. By training mostly at slow six to seven miles per hour, as opposed to his eight to ten mile-per-hour race speed, Newton conserved strength and energy for when it counted, setting records in races. Newton was strictly against time trials at the ultra distances, and strongly advised the runner to concentrate totally on building stamina and endurance by training below race pace, but constantly varying the pace, tempo and running movements to breakup the monotony of the longer distances. Some faster running is important, he said, to avoid becoming a "plodder" who runs mile after mile with the same pace and movement during every workout. As a race approaches, there should be a sudden tapering of both distance and intensity.

Hill training

Training on the hills of the Comrades course, Newton soon learned the importance of hill training, as Cerutty and Lydiard did years later for middle-distance running. Hills simulated the exhaustion of the late stages of a race. Newton did not surge up angling sand hills as those coaches advocated, but he did use the same low arm action with forearms held low and parallel to the angle of the hill that Cerutty taught his runners. In races, Newton found he could rest while coasting down the other side of a hill. Newton said that the loss of energy during the race and the hard roads, which led to foot, ankle and knee injuries, were an ultrarunner's worst enemies. He preferred to train on dirt roads near his farm in Natal, where he did not have to compete with traffic.

When an Achilles tendon injury forced an eight-month layoff, Newton kept in shape by doing strength training, cycling, swimming, hiking and walking, which did not interfere with the neural patterns he had already conditioned for running. Newton cycled up to 100 miles in a single workout, which he casually remarked as being quite restful because he could view the scenery. Later, recovered from his injury, he said that cycling, like his earlier walking, only detracted from his running. The layoff was a terrible setback to his training, but he strongly recommended a one-month layoff each year at the end of the competitive season, which would serve to revitalize the runner for more hard training the following year. Newton experimented with his training, concluding that all running injuries were caused by poor running style, shoes without a thick, crepe-rubber sole, and running on the hard roads.

Newton might have been the greatest distance runner of the century, but Percy Cerutty believed Newton's world records would have been even faster had he properly strengthened his frail upper body and perhaps undertaken a higher quality of intensive training, as do most of today's top ultrarunners. Weight training would have easily lengthened Newton's stride and increased his strength, but I believe Newton did not lift weights because: (1) he did not want to carry any extra weight, even a small amount, on his lean frame; and (2) he failed to realize that acquiring speed, strength and power, even for an ultrarunner, is just as important as building endurance. A lack of upper body strength was Newton's weakest link.

Newton firmly believed that any dedicated distance runner could set world records provided he had: (1) dedication to sacrifice the so-called pleasures the majority of people are not willing to do; (2) sufficient time to train each day; and (3) dominating incentives and motivation to train until goals were achieved.

Neural patterns

It is a known fact a middle-distance runner excels much faster with an intensive training program by progressively reducing the distance and quickening the pace over the training year. The ultrarunner, however, achieves maximum results by doing just the opposite, following a more advanced program of endurance training, with some intensive training thrown in for balance at odd times during the year. Newton did this by gradually piling up the mileage and training below race pace with varied speeds of six and-a-half to ten miles per hour, concentrating on stretching out his aerobic capacity to fill the empty space of 50 or 100 miles, or beyond to 24 hours.

As I have previously discussed, and it is worth repeating, the ultrarunner cannot imitate the middle-distance runner and run time trials at the race distance. The basic solution to this problem is to run shorter distances, 10 to 30 miles, three times during the week, and to cover longer distances on the weekend.

Another solution to this problem is that the ultrarunner can mentally piece together the "parts of the puzzle," in his mind by practicing meditation and visualization at home in a passive state without the tension of training, and not even running at all! The best time for meditating on the neural patterns is late at night just before falling asleep and early in the morning, when the mind is totally receptive and more relaxed and able to "see" all the parts of the race. Newton said, "Parts of a 50 or 100-mile race flicker across the subconscious mind, like the frames of a motion picture, along with instant flashbacks of my childhood, farming, the marriage and subsequent divorce, and the many countless hours of preparation and training."

Newton worked hard to harness the nervous energy before and during a race. "Worrying about the race," Newton said, "uses up more energy than even racing does. Do not think too much about the race the night before, but develop a casual attitude of indifference to the pain, ultra distances and the other competitors, and you will be in the 'flow' naturally and instinctively, so the breathing and running will become automatic. Always remember when the mind gives in to the stress and strain of the longer distances, the body quits."

Running style

"The longer stride is best for the shorter distances up to the marathon," said Newton, "but a shorter stride with a greater frequency of strides per mile is more economical for ultrarunning." Arthur Newton ran with a shorter stride, using a formalized version of Cerutty's amble, trot, and modified gallop, because it conserved more strength and energy over the long run. Newton would amble or trot for seven miles, then change abruptly to the modified gallop.

Poor, inefficient running style creates pounding and jarring, which Newton said drains valuable energy, causing injuries and antagonistic muscles that ultimately force the ultrarunner to "tie up" in the closing stages of the race when faced with the walls of pain.

Newton ran flatfooted, with a soft, slithering motion, coasting lightly over the ground like a gazelle, as his feet traveled in small arcs that were supported on top with a low arm carriage. The weight from each stride shifts from the heel to the outside edge of the foot, as the small pads on the ends of the toes absorb a small amount of shock from each stride to gently "flick" the runner forward into the next stride. Knees absorb the most shock and mile after mile on hard roads can cause serious injuries, operations, and, for the unfortunate ones, permanent disabilities. All runners should avoid hard roads as they would the plague the runner over time.

Diet and Baths

Arthur Newton experimented with diet, as he did with every facet of training. His normal body weight was 138 pounds; he dropped three to four pounds in a marathon and as much as six pounds over 100 miles. To compensate for the loss during a race, he put on an extra six pounds before the race to provide extra energy reserves.

Rapid loss of perspiration during the race posed the biggest problem for Newton and most ultrarunners, because sweat dries on the skin in cold and hot weather, clogging up the pores. Newton remedied the problem by taking warm, ten-minute baths at the 50-mile mark of a 100-mile race. The clock did not stop for Newton's baths, but he was so far ahead in the race that he set world records anyway.

The warm baths were more refreshing and stimulating to the system than the liquids and full course meals Newton took at 20 or 30-mile intervals en route to 50 or 100 miles. He took quick sponge baths for shorter races but much preferred warm baths in 100-mile and 24-hour runs.

Newton's secret "magic drink" was a pint of lemonade with three teaspoons of sugar and one teaspoon of salt. He believed the salt was needed to prevent cramps, stitches, and stomach disorders. The drink was taken every 20 miles. At 30-mile intervals Newton would take another stop for a full course meal lasting 12 minutes.

His diet varied with the distance of the race. Newton found that eating big meals before a race only depleted the runner's strength by putting extra stress on the digestive organs. For the shorter races of 30, 40 and 50 miles, Newton had a small meal composed of cheese sandwiches, fruit salad, two bananas and two cups of coffee or tea with double the amount of sugar. Newton preferred sugar to honey for instant energy. The full course meals were eaten for longer distances of 60 and 100 miles or 24-hour runs, and consisted of a steak, eggs, two bananas, brown bread, and two cups of coffee or tea loaded with sugar. Newton disliked thick soups, vegetables, starches, milk, hot chocolate and, especially fish while racing, though he did eat and enjoy those foods when not racing.

Newton had to increase his normal consumption of meat and protein, as he increased his training miles, and was opposed to a vegetarian diet. The middle distance runner does not find it necessary to increase protein consumption as he increases gradually the intensity and reduces the distance of his training. Alkaline foods were always eaten days after the race to dissolve and neutralize the buildup of lactic acid in the system.

Newton was an early riser, getting up early every morning at 5:00 a.m. for an ordinary breakfast of ham and eggs, hash browns, melba toast with jam, jelly or marmalade, and two cups of coffee or tea with double sugar. During the day he would stop and buy pastries and hard candy while he was training. Lunch and dinner were balanced with many natural foods. Newton completely abstained from alcohol and he never drank his coffee or tea while he was eating the main course of his meal because it diluted the digestive juices. He enjoyed smoking a pipe in the evening while he was relaxing and reading.

Newton advised the runner to never "gulp" down his food in a hurry, because it caused indigestion, cramps and stitches. Staleness, he found, was caused by overtraining and a poor diet of dead foods. Finally, each runner must do what Newton and Cerutty did, by experimenting with his own diet to see what is best.

Clothing and shoes

Newton ran his best times in cool, damp weather with temperatures of 55 degrees F, which he called the perfect racing conditions because of the minimization of energy-draining perspiration. Nylon training suits, such as are common today, were preferred to wool and cotton by Newton, because they held in body heat. A ski cap, mask, wool socks and mittens wore worn in winter; Newton believed that if the head, hands and feet were warm, then the body would be toasty and comfortable too, during either a workout or a race.

In cold weather Newton's feet cracked, causing blisters, like chapped hands: he solved this problem by soaping the insides of his shoes and feet with ordinary toilet soap before going out for a run. He also rubbed baby oil under his arms and crotch to prevent chafing, and he used baby oil to prevent sunburn. Newton thought of everything!

In the summer heat and tropical conditions when humidity was a big factor, Newton drank more liquids and wore white cotton clothing to reflect the bright sunlight, and a painter's hat to prevent sunstroke. He also carried a handkerchief to wipe off perspiration. He advised runners to never train or race in the heat of mid-day.

Running shoes were a major problem in Newton's time, simply because there were none available with a thick crepe-rubber sole to suit his specifications. He had to have his running shoes specially hand-crafted from canvas and kangaroo leather with an extra wide toe box and tiny hole up in front and on the sides for added comfort, movement, and proper ventilation. He wore shoes a half-size too large with plenty of room to wiggle his toes, thus preventing blisters and serious injuries, since the feet expand during a long run. Newton designed his shoes for running faster times with the least amount of effort, and he cared nothing for cosmetic value. He averaged 3,000 miles in each pair of shoes!

Racing

Arthur Newton returned to England in 1924, where he set the London-to-Brighton record and all of his world records and lived out the remainder of his life. He trained and raced in South Africa, England, Canada and the United States.

Newton was invited to compete in both of C.C. Pyle's transcontinental races from New York to Los Angeles in 1928 and 1929. He dropped out at 575 miles with the Achilles tendon injury that cost him the eight-month layoff; however, he continued on as a technical advisor to aid the other runners. The race that stands out as one of Newton's greatest races took place in 1927 when he broke Hatch's 100-mile world record by running 14:43 on a dirt road. This record brought him to the attention of the running world; shortly thereafter he ran his record 152 miles in 24 hours.

Another famous Newton race took place in 1929 in Philadelphia when he and Pete Gavuzzi, along with several teams of two runners, beat two teams of stock horses over 100 miles. The race was run at seven miles per hour on a square track with 12 laps to the mile. Both runners and horses experienced nausea and giddiness after just two hours of circling the small track. Gavuzzi had to retire briefly from competition for a short rest, as Newton set a good pace and went on to win the race. "The horses quit the race," Newton recalled years later, "because they were simply bored sick with circling the track, mile after mile as runners do on a 400-meter track; they did not have the incentives to stay in the race, much less finish, as the winners did to claim the prize money of $500 for a week's work."

Arthur Newton

Pre-race

Newton believed the runner should always arrive at the racing venue a week early to acclimatize to the people and food, and get a good feeling for the course. He found that younger runners acclimatized faster. "The runner should cover the road course in a car a few times to mentally 'piece together' the race," said Newton.

Arthur Newton was also a firm believer in altitude training, and said that if the race site is more than 2,000 feet above sea level, the runner should train there for three months before the day of the race. Many athletes competing in the 1968 Olympics at Mexico City trained from six weeks to three months at altitude.

On race day, Newton was awake at 3:00 a.m. for a heavy breakfast, which consisted of eggs, oatmeal, bacon, liver, sausage and pork chops—foods that are hard on the digestive system and stay in the stomach longer for sustained energy during the race. The first 10 miles of the race were used to settle the breakfast! Newton guarded against the smallest problems that might cost him the race; he always put a new pair of laces into his shoes, whether he needed them or not.

The race

Racing tactics, such as a miler uses, are not required for ultras. Newton recommended always running one's own race and forgetting the other runners. Being able to finish is of the utmost importance, and Newton advised starting slowly, as Abebe Bikila did to win to marathons, and varying the pace during the race. Newton's race pace in a race would vary from six-and-a-half to ten miles per hour.

Rhythm, intensity, pace and tempo are crucial for running 50 to 100 miles under any conditions. Essentially the ultrarunner has to trust his basic instincts by adjusting his overall pace to naturally coincide with his strength and energy as it ebbs and flows over the race.

Newton advised the runner to gradually increase the overall pace of the race as it progresses from start to finish, ever so slowly and slightly, so the other runners will not feel a noticeable increase in speed. "If a runner passes you up," Newton said, "don't be a fool and play into his hands by going out after him and running his race. Far better to run your own race, and wait a little while; then catch him on the hills in the later stages of the race when closing the gap is crucial to winning or losing the race. The secret to winning the race, or setting a world record is to control the 'flow' of the race from start to finish with sustained energy throughout, by keeping the body energized with the proper nourishment and relying heavily on the runner's secondary tank."

To divert his mind from the boredom and drudgery of running mile after mile, Newton concentrated on the scenery. Once he played records on a phonograph in the back of Pete Gavuzzi's truck, listening to Josephine Baker, Bach, Beethoven and Mozart. He found the Sousa marches a bit too fast for his tempo of running.

In the 70 years since Newton's set his 24-hour record, only a few dozen men have surpassed his total of 152 miles, thus confirming that the legendary Arthur Newton was indeed an ultrarunner well ahead of his time.

Ted Corbitt: An Ultrarunning Pioneer
by Trishul Cherns

Ted Corbitt's distance running career has been legendary, inspiring, and pioneering. In 1952, early in his marathon career, Corbitt made the US. Olympic team, and ran the Olympic marathon in Helsinki. After ten years of distinguished marathon running (2:26:44 personal best), Corbitt decided to try his hand at the ultra distances. He finished fourth at the 1962 London to Brighton and continued to compete in ultras, setting high standards. He set an American record for 50 miles on the track (5:54 in 1966), 100 miles (13:33 in 1969; still the U.S. 45 to 49 100-mile record), and 24 hours (134.7 miles in 1973). One of his most noteworthy marks is 5:35:03 for 50 miles (1970), which is still the U.S. 50-and-over record.

These top performances were not the result of talent alone. Corbitt trained hard, and was the American pioneer of 200 and 300-mile training weeks, which prepared him for world-class results in major competitions.

Ted Corbitt played a central role in many important developments in U.S. distance running, most notably the founding of the Road Runners Club (he was the first president) and the establishment of guidelines for the accurate measurement of courses.

Looking back at this amazing man's career, we marvel at the standards he established and respect the foundation of American long distance running he created for us.

This interview touches on only a few aspects of Corbitt's life and running career. For a more detailed account, readers should consult the biography by John Chodes: Corbitt, The Story of Ted Corbitt, Long Distance Runner. *(154 pp., paperback, published by Track and Field News.)*

Personal Background

What sports did you do as a child?

Mostly, I ran. There was not much else to do, except when friends came by, I would wrestle with them. Just playing like that. This was on a farm in South Carolina. When we moved to Cincinnati, it was mostly running games: hide and seek, short races, and baseball. In high school I trained for cross-country for one year, but did not race because we never had a team. But I participated in track, running the half-mile with a best time of 2:10.

How did you start running, and when did you start running competitively?

On the farm. I ran to the store, to the mailbox and to school. I ran just about everywhere. In Cincinnati, I walked every day, first to elementary school, then to junior high school, high school, and the University of Cincinnati. My first formal race was in seventh grade in 1933: the intramural championship 60-yard dash, which I won. Then I raced in high school, (in college) at the University of Cincinnati, and afterwards. There were not many track meets in Cincinnati or the Midwest, especially when World War II was getting cranked up. That limited meets. Also, the color line was drawn even in some of the meets in Cincinnati, so I could not participate in them. In the Midwest, places like Illinois and Indiana, there were track meets, but I was a little reluctant to take part in them because I did not know what type of reception I would get, and what problems I would have getting a place to stay and getting something to eat. If I had owned a car, I would have taken part because eventually you could find a place to stay. In my sophomore and junior years in college I ran the half-mile (2:09), mile (under five minutes) and two-mile (under 11 minutes). In my senior year, I ran the quarter mile (51 seconds), mile relay, and 100-yard dash. In my best 100 (10.1) I pulled a hamstring at 70 yards, finishing third. I limped the rest of the season. In my senior year in college I ran cross-country. These were on four-mile hilly courses done in times between 23 and 32 minutes. We did not have many races, so it was difficult to get in shape and my times were slow. This was during the war. The seasons were curtailed, as was traveling, to some degree.

Did you have any interest in long-distance running in high school or college?

Yes, the idea intrigued me. In 1936 I heard of the marathon and realized for the first time that people ran that far. So I became interested in that event at that time. I was not really thinking of that when I started running in college, but I did start exploring longer distances and I found it hard to get used to. It took a lot of work to be able to run any real distance, but I started because I was interested to know if could do it.

Where there any individuals who helped you in your early years of marathon running or ultrarunning?

These individuals came in the form of books. When I got out of school, I went into a public library and tried to find out something about running. There was not much available, but I read what I could and used that as a guide. There was an article on marathon training in *The Amateur Athlete,* which was the periodical of the governing body and it advocated three workouts a week.

What people had the greatest influence on you and your running career?

Arthur Newton, through his books. One was called *Races and Training.* I don't remember the other book. And Percy Cerutty of Australia. I met him in Helsinki during the Olympic Games and corresponded with him from then until he died in 1976. Percy came through New York City in 1958 and he gave a demonstration and held some training sessions with members of the New York Road Runners Club in Van Cortlandt Park in the Bronx. Dr. William Ruthreuff from Philadelphia had a great influence on me. He spent a lot of time working with me in the late 50s and early 60s. He helped me with my form. He thought I was training too hard, which I did not believe at the time. He helped me get to some races and gave me valuable advice.

Training

People often identify Ted Corbitt as being one of the first people to use very high mileage in training. Is that true?

Well, if you say that I was one of the first, it is approximately true. Arthur Newton had done high mileage. By the time I became an ultrarunner there was a handful doing 200-mile weeks.

In your early years of marathon running, how many miles did you do a week?

I ran six or seven days a week, totaling about 100 miles. I ran all kinds of races during my training. The only slow pace I did was on my long workout. I ran hard, not racing speed, but not a jog. I also did some interval running. Believe it or not, I started that before I knew what the term was. I would run up a hill and then run back down taking a 70-yard recovery. This was all done on grass. In 1951, I met Fred Wilt at Prospect Park and he was surprised that I was doing this. He had written some articles on that training method, but I had been doing this back in Cincinnati.

Tell us about your training for your first marathon?

My first marathon was in Boston (April 19, 1951: 2:58:42). I trained for a year. I decided I wanted to master 30 miles before I would attempt a marathon, because I had difficulty getting past 20 miles in training. I wanted to be sure that whatever happened, I would finish. I finally did conquer 30 miles after a number of failures (if you can call a 20 or 22-mile workout a failure). I did it on a cold day and it was starting to snow and I realized at one point that I was sticking my tongue out to get some snow flakes and that made me think that probably I was thirsty. So after I took a good drink of water (right on the course) I felt so much better and it gave me the strength I needed to finish the workout.

How often did you do 200 miles in a week, and for how long and when?

I started this early in my marathon career but I only did it for one week. It happened on a Labor Day weekend—I would do 30 miles a day for seven consecutive days. On the weekdays I had to run after work, which made it tough. Later, I did it twice a year. In 1956, I did 200 miles a week for the months of January, February, and into March. This was a preparation for the Olympic marathon trials in 1956. In March I went to a 30-km race in New England and I did not have any speed; one of my teammates, John Connelly, beat me. I was overtrained and he apologized. It made me feel terrible.

Are you saying that the long 200-mile weeks did not necessarily pay off?

They can and they did. It is just that I had not prepared for the marathon, but that woke me up. This is one of the disadvantages of training by yourself. That is, you are not always doing what you think you are doing in terms of form and so forth and it's very easy to train too hard for too long. That's what happened to me in this March race. Coming up in April was the Boston Marathon (the first of two Olympic trials). So I started doing some speed work every day up to the day of the race, which I finished in 2:28:06 for sixth place.

So ultimately the high mileage helped you?

Yes, I think there is a place for 200-mile weeks for some runners who can build up to it. I built up to it and had great success. Some runners have observed that they run faster times after a long race. One New York ultrarunner ran a six-day race and then ran personal bests in all the shorter races that followed that summer. I ran faster after long workouts. So I continued to run 30-mile workouts, but I eventually cut down on the number of them. I always tried to run one before my first marathon of the season. At some point I realized I did not need to do this anymore, but I ran one anyway, although sometimes I delayed it until the last possible day because I really did not want to do it. By then I was running ultras and I would run to work. Sometimes I would come up to Van Cortlandt Park and run 17 miles on the track and then run downtown to work to make a 30-mile day.

Do you regret your training methods or do you think they were best for you? Would you have done anything differently?

No, I learned about the body as I went along and at the time I did the high mileage it was all right. I was doing a lot of experimenting. Looking back, I realize that I had gotten good advice, though I did not know at the time that it was good advice and I had to find it out for myself. The good advice was to rest more. I would do the long runs again, but I would make a point of breaking off.

You see, the fault of long running is that if you don't come out of it in time, then you won't run as fast as you are capable of running. For example, in 1956 I was training high mileage for Boston and, not having switched over to racing speed, I ran a poor 30-km training race. I could have run all day possibly, but I could not run any faster.

Were you working full-time when you were putting in high mileage?

Yes, 40 hours a week. (Ted was a physical therapist from 1948 until his retirement.) The only time I took off from work was to go to the Boston Marathon. Otherwise I just took my regular vacation time for trips and races. Some marathons were on Saturdays, which was not a day off in New York. So I would have to take the day off to run them.

Was all your training on paved surfaces?

No. I ran some cross-country trails in Van Cortlandt Park, and on the grass in Brooklyn's Prospect Park, where I made up a half-mile loop on the meadow that I used every time I went there. There were not many runners around and I figured it was better in terms of contact with the police to run in that area. In Highland Park in Brooklyn I also ran on the grass. I started running mostly on paved surfaces when I went to work in Manhattan. I would run through the streets in street clothes and street shoes.

Did your training include any non-running activities?

Other than weight training, no. I did stretching, but I would consider that just part of training, to warm up. I did weight training early on, before most runners would do it. It was done as part of an experimental physical therapy program. I was not the first runner to do this. The main reason other runners did not train with weights was that their coaches prevented it. At that time they did not know enough about proper training with weights.

How about any other activity, like playing baseball?

After I got out of high school, I did not play much more baseball. I did not do any other activity other than walking. I used to start each cross-country season with long walks, up to 28 miles. I had always walked to and from school and when I was injured in running I would walk to and from work and so forth.

Would you do anything specific in preparation for a 50-mile race, such as extra long workouts? Shorter races?

For races up to 30 miles my marathon training would suffice. My first

50-miler was the London to Brighton race and I would increase the amount of running that I did. By that time I was routinely running 100 miles or more per week. I gradually increased the amount and got up to 200-mile weeks. But this was probably the first time I did a 300-mile week. Manhattan Island is just over 31 miles around the edge and I started this on the Labor Day long weekend by running twice around each day. I had decided that if I could not do this, then I would not go to England. On the second lap I started getting pains at old muscle injury sites, but got to a certain point and the pain went away. On the third day the pain in my knee persisted so I stopped with ten miles to go—it was very hilly coming up the West Side and I decided I was satisfied. So most of the mileage was done in the other three days. I did this 300-mile training week at Labor Day every year after that whether I went to London or not.

If you were coaching an upcoming ultrarunner what general guidelines would you suggest?
Ideally, I would like to get the runner early, in junior high or high school. First I would have him become a good cyclist and possibly a good swimmer for general development. Then I would have him compete in track in college and do the long-distance running afterwards. Then I would put him on a weight training program to get him really strong; he would learn how to stretch properly and just progressively move up. I would make him as good a track runner as possible from the mile on up and then have him take on a marathon, but then take him up by degrees. The ultra distances can be taken on without too much specialization beyond the marathon.

Racing

What memories of your racing career stand out?
My most disappointing race—and it's a great memory—is a 24-hour run. I had hoped to do about 155 miles, which I still think was a reasonable expectation. I'd had some trouble training that summer: I had pain in one of my quadriceps so I would stop and stretch and the pain would go away; then I'd run another hour and repeat it. After a time this did not work and this accursed pain in my quadriceps was killing me. After 17 hours I realized that I was not going to achieve my goal, but I did not drop out. I ran and walked to finish the race. That is a negative memory.

During the first 50-mile championship on Staten Island in July 1956, there was a heat wave. On the day of the race, the heat had melted the glue in my running shoes so that the sole came loose. I noticed this just as I was packing my bag before

I left the house. So I got my old pair of shoes made of leather, but unfortunately they blistered my feet. My goal was to do the first marathon in 2:42 to disarm my major opponent. When the blisters started to develop, I slowed down. We still passed the marathon in 2:49 but it slowed me down. They said that if the temperature passed 85, they would stop the race. I don't know what it reached, but they did not stop the race. I got severe dehydration cramps. The second time they stopped me the muscles in my feet contracted so strongly that I just stood there. It was the first time I had ever stopped or walked in a race. I resigned myself to second place in 6:12 or something like that.

Any favorite ultras?
The greatest ultra I ever saw was the 100-mile in Flushing Meadows Park where Don Ritchie ran 11:50. That was easily the best one I have seen. I have been in three world record races, but I rate the Don Ritchie race superior. One of the best ultras I have heard about is the Comrades Marathon in South Africa, which is on a tough course.

Bronchial asthma halted your career. Do you know why this happened and whether it could have been avoided?
I am not sure why this happened. First I thought it was due to air pollutants and I am still not sure that is not the case. I told this to the doctor who was helping me and he said it was internal pollution—not enough sleep, and so on. I was burning up over 6,000 calories per day. Up until last year I thought I was the only member of my family to have had bronchial asthma but I discovered that an aunt also had it. I was a 54-year-old when I first got it. So I guess I am lucky I did not get it any earlier.

Race Relations

Judging from incidents all around the country, in colleges, in suburbia, and in working-class neighborhoods, black-white relations seem to be stagnating at a low point. What are your feelings about the state of race relations in the country?
As I mentioned previously, after I got out of college and in my senior year of college at the University of Cincinnati, traveling and finding a place to stay were problems. There were two colleges that would not permit the University of Cincinnati to bring black track men with them to meets. I read about today's problems and see it as part of evolution. There is no reason why this should go smoothly. Part of it is economics and fear. I tie this in with South Africa too. South

Africa and the United States have similar patterns in that sense. For example, in 1931, the National AAU Track and Field Championships were scheduled for New Orleans and they were not going to let the black track and field athletes compete in that championship. So the championship was moved to Lincoln, Nebraska. These were the black athletes that won medals for the United States at the Olympics the following year.

Did you encounter discrimination in your running endeavors? How did it affect you?

The only problem I can think of offhand was the junior national 10,000 meter championship in upstate Ohio in 1943. I believe they recommended two hotels. I went to one hotel and I am not even going to describe what happened. So I ended up in the gym. I was the only one who stayed there. The hotel experience was overwhelming.

Miscellaneous

What do you think of the state of ultrarunning in the United States?

As far as I am concerned it is healthy. It is almost strictly amateur in the old sense. The fact that there are pages of race listings in the magazines, that is amazing to me. After World War II you had only three or four marathons in the United States that you could count on each year.

Were you surprised by the resurgence of multi-day running? Would you have liked to have tried a six-day or longer stage race?

I did not envision it happening because there was little interest in ultras in general. I thought there would be a lot of runners who felt like we did, namely that we would finish a marathon with something left and so we wanted try longer distances. But we did not get the participation in 50-mile races that they got for 100-km races in Europe. So when multi-day running came in I did not expect it to be the attention-getter it was. I would have liked to run a six-day or longer race. I had planned to run solo across the country and received permission to take time off work, but bronchial asthma put an end to that plan.

I see a future for multi-day racing, because there are people that are interested. It is not necessary to have large fields. The British Road Runners Club put on a race for attempts to set world records and they had a very limited field. You can have a race with two people in it—it's all you need. You don't have to have a large field to be successful.

Is the sport more or less popular than you would have predicted 30 years ago?

More popular, except that I thought ultrarunning here would attract enormous fields for the 100-km races, as happens in Europe. That has not happened. It is expected that there will be more leisure time in the future, perhaps instead of 40-hour work weeks, two people will share and work 20-hour weeks or something like that. The human body, in order to function well has to be used in all ways, including the physical, and I think a lot of people with more leisure time will choose running.

Ann Trason: Ultra Wonder Woman

By Don Allison

No book about ultrarunning could be considered comprehensive without chronicling the accomplishments one of the greatest ultrarunners of the current era, Ann Trason. The diminutive Californian has not been content with becoming the world's premier female ultrarunner; she regularly competes for the overall victory in most all ultras in which she competes, something rarely seen in running or any other athletic venues. So far clear of all other female competition is Trason that in nearly every ultra distance race she has entered, the women's win was a foregone conclusion. The only question was how few—if any—men would finish before she did.

If ultrarunning is Ann Trason's domain, ultra distance trail running is her passion. The rugged Western States 100 Mile—the biggest and most well known ultra in the U.S—is stamped with her accomplishments. For ten consecutive years she won the women's division, and in two of those races she finished second overall. As if that were not challenge and accomplishment enough, she twice dominated the Western States—with some 30,000 feet of elevation change, snow at the high altitude start and baking furnace-like conditions in the canyons—less than two weeks after winning the prestigious 56-mile Comrades ultra in South Africa.

Trason developed into an age-group track star, then as a senior in high school in 1978, ran 9:58 for 3,000 meters and 35:11 for 10 km. Her college running experience (at the University of New Mexico on a track scholarship) was less than stellar, however. "I was injured and I never could run," she says. "Such disappointment. I decided to transfer schools. I went up to Berkeley and was running five miles three or four times a week. I just got involved in school and I never really thought about competing. I didn't really like running on the track. I liked cross country, but they had me run the 10-km on the track when I was in high school. It was awful. My hat goes off to those people who do it. I think it's a horrible event."

Years later, she returned to competition. "I was intrigued by endurance activities like triathlons," she explains. "I did a half-Ironman in 1984 and I almost drowned. I can't swim. After that I got hit by a car on my bike and I damaged my arm pretty badly and I couldn't swim at all. My bike was destroyed. So I started just running." There she found her niche.

"I wanted to run a marathon and I then saw an ad for a 50-mile race. It seemed like it would take a little longer, but it was the same mentality. That was in 1985. (The American River 50 Mile near home in Northern California.) So I did it."

In 1987, she worked up the nerve to try her first Western States run. She didn't make it to the finish. A year later it was the same story. Then she went to Leadville, Colorado, for the annual trail 100-mile. She finished, even with having to cross 13,000-foot Hope Pass twice. "I've finished every trail 100—knock on wood—that I've started since then. It kind of made up for those two disappointments."

Trason has proved equally adept at road and track ultras as she is on the trails. In 1995 she set the world mark for 100-km, seven hours and forty-seven seconds. That is a 6:40 pace for more than 62 miles. Or consider, it is like running a 2:55 marathon, then continuing for 36 more miles at that pace. That record stood until it was bettered by world-class marathoner Tomoe Abe in 2000. Trason's time remains as the second-fastest in history. What is her secret to running so fast over such long distances? "If you focus on the short goals, it goes by pretty fast," she says. "If you concentrate hard enough, the day goes by pretty fast."

As if just to be proven mortal, Trason has suffered her share of injuries. In the late 1990s, while undergoing exploratory surgery for another injury, doctors found her hamstring 90-percent detached at the insertion point. But she has returned to soar with the eagles, winning Western States three more times and going on to win several more trail 100-mile races around the country. Now a masters runner, she has already set a number of records in that division, with many more to come, undoubtedly.

Although she has excelled on roads, the track, and in states and countries all over the world, it is the course in her own backyard that continues to grab hold of Trason. Of her initial experience at Western States, she says, "It was beautiful. There are some places you go in life where you feel like you just belong. I felt like I was floating, floating in the clouds and the flowers. Coming home, I fell down a hill. I'd left my friend and didn't know where the course was, but I found my way. It was mystical—and I'm not a mystical person.

"There's something very romantic when you're running 100 miles in the Sierra. And you have to know a lot about yourself. You have to be in tune with your body and know when you can push it and when to back off. Your head's the coach and your body is the team, and your body has to listen to the coach about how much water to drink, how much food to eat, the pace. I find it less boring than going out and running a marathon."

Competing evenly with the top men in her sport has been both a blessing and a curse for the world's top female ultrarunner. "This sport has a lot to offer women and I don't think they should have that burden," Trason says. "The thing that's probably hardest for me is when I've won and people say I was second or third. They don't do that in the marathon. Can you imagine (women's champion) Uta

Ann Trason

Pippig finishing the Boston Marathon and being told she was 31st place or 37th or whatever? It wouldn't happen. But for whatever reason people say, 'You've done so well against the men, you deserve to win.' I just want to go out and run."

And going out and running is something she has kept on doing, year after year. What is it that has kept Trason's passion for ultrarunning alive for so long? "It's the sense of achievement," she explains. "When you finish a 10-km," Trason says, "you might look at your watch and see an improvement of 20 seconds or so from your previous time. But when you're running rugged trails over 50 or 100 miles, anything can happen. Your times vary by hours, not seconds. "When you finish 100 miles," Trason says, "I don't care what your time is—you feel like you've really accomplished something."

Former Western States 100 Mile race director Norm Klein calls Trason the finest athlete in the world today. "Look at what she does—she's competing against men because the women are no competition to her, and she's holding her own. And she's doing it and not getting anything in return. She's doing it for the love of the sport and the satisfaction she derives from it."

In sport, every once in a great while an athlete comes along who transcends his or her chosen sport, in a way that makes all others involved rethink just what is possible. In ultrarunning, Ann Trason has done that. By that standard alone, Ann Trason ranks as one of the premier runners of her time.

Ann Trason's PRs (road):	
5 km	17:11 '95
Half marathon	1:17:35 '85
Marathon	2:39:15 '92
50 miles	5:40:18 '91 (WR)
100 km	7:00:47 '95
12 hours	91 miles, 1312 yards '91 (WR)
100 miles	13:47:42 '91 (WR)
24 hours	143 miles

Yiannis Kouros: Modern Day Greek Mythology

by Andy Milroy and Dan Brannen

How good is Yiannis Kouros? Put it this way: He is the only runner for whom an accusation of cheating eventually became an honor. The quality of his run in the first Spartathlon was so far beyond what anyone thought possible that the only way to put his performance in perspective was to assume that he had cut the course. The first Spartathlon race between Athens and Sparta in Greece took place on September 10, 1983. A strong field of established international ultrarunners took part, and it was taken for granted that the winner would come from among this fraternity. Before the start organizers went to the assembled group of runners and asked if two additional runners could take part, despite the fact they had arrived after the deadline for entrants. One was a well-known British runner, and for this reason the assembled runners agreed to the request. The other runner was an unknown Greek named Yiannis Kouros. If the assembled runners had not been willing to bend the rules for a friend, then it is possible that Kouros would never have run an ultra.

When this unknown Greek won the race by more than two and a half hours, naturally great skepticism was expressed by the experienced runners, particularly as much of the race had been run in darkness; rumors were rife of competitors taking rides in cars. In the opinion of third-place finisher Alan Fairbrother from England, Kouros did not "have the experience or class to get anywhere near Dave Dowdle's 274 km world track best over a good flat surface in good climatic conditions."

One of the field, Austrian Edgar Patterman, was not quite so skeptical. He arranged a multi-day stage race along the Danube in April of 1984 and invited a large group of international runners to compete, including Yiannis Kouros. So Kouros came to Austria on Easter weekend of 1984 as the object of sincere suspicion. Three days later he left as the object of unreserved reverence. In between he averaged 66 miles per day of nonstop running at seven-minute-per-mile pace During those three days he passed more than 30 well-stocked aid stations and never stopped—or even walked—at a single one. His slowest individual mile during the three days was well under eight minutes. His only complaint was that he had no one to push him.

When he returned to defend his Spartathlon title a year later, he became the object of the most scrupulously scrutinized point-to-point ultra in history. Virtually every step he took was observed by official race personnel. In this, a 150-mile race in hot weather on gravel roads that includes climbing two mountain ranges on steep, rocky trails, he hit the 100-km mark in less than seven hours, the 100-mile mark (atop the highest mountain range) in less than 13 hours, then took less than nine hours for the remaining 50 miles.

In between these two events, the Greek god made mockery of the finest six-day field assembled in modern times in a week of bizarre weather in New York City. It was a performance that finally made the nineteenth century specialists seem just like the rest of us. What can you say about 635 miles? Well, you can say that it included 266 miles in 48 hours, and before that 163 miles in 24 hours. The single-day total made him the track world leader for that year. The two-day mark was an all-time best, despite the fact that it included more off-track time than any other performance over 220 miles.

However, Kouros found a way to top all of these prodigious exploits. Where do you go if you have demolished the all-time running records? How about the all-time recovery records? Barely a month after his Spartathlon victory Kouros returned to New York, setting a world road best for 100 miles on the way to an all-time record-breaking 24-hour of 177 miles. This on a far less than ideal road loop with no lighting and in subfreezing weather.

Not yet finished with feats of the incredible, Kouros then cut his recovery even more, starting the Colac Six Day less than three weeks later. A more cautious opening two days of 250 miles allowed him to add a little to his own six-day mark.

Kouros continued his nearly non-stop, record-breaking romp through ultrarunning during the 1980s. The year 1991 was to mark a major turning point in the Greek's life. Disenchantment with the Greek Federation, as opposed to the warmth of the welcome shown to him by the large Australian Greek community, plus greater competitive opportunities in Australia, meant that Kouros was spending more and more time away from Greece, living "down under." He moved to Australia in 1990 and, after a year in Sydney, moved to Melbourne. In 1992 he became a full-time student at La Trobe University, studying for a bachelor of arts degree in music and modern greek literature. He studied for degrees in greek literature, and became an Australian citizen.

Kouros returned to ultrarunning late in 1994. During the next few years he again returned to the top echelon ultrarunning, turning out several outstanding 24 and 48-hour races. but he was not yet satisfied. He had his sights set upon a seemingly unreachable goal and would not rest until he conquered it.

In 1997, the Greek-born Australian Yiannis Kouros produced what is probably the most phenomenal endurance feat in modern times by obliterating his own world track 24-hour record on October 4 in Adelaide. Kouros ran the equivalent of seven successive marathons in a single day, covering 303.506 kilometers, or

188 miles, 1,038 yards in the race organized by the Australian branch of the Sri Chinmoy Marathon Team.

The 41-year-old runner was frustrated earlier in the year in his decade-long desire of breaking the 300-km barrier—first by heavy rains, and then by injury. In his successful attempt, he was totally focused. In his own words, he said he would never be as fit again. This would be his ultimate effort.

Kouros cruised through the early laps, reaching 100 kilometers in 7:15. In recent years he has opted for a more even-paced approach, but not on this day. He reached 150 km (93 miles) in 11:05:02, a new Australian record, and 100 miles in 11:57:59. This put him 13 minutes ahead of his previous world record schedule.

He had covered 100.25 miles by the time he reached 12 hours, running a totally inspired race, looking strong, and pushing his limits. He reached 200-km (124.25 miles) in 15:10:27, a new absolute world best. He was beginning to feel the pain and as the race went on, he forced an increasingly unwilling body to submit to his indomitable will. In fact, he was running faster than any human ever done at that point in a 24-hour race. Covering each lap in about two minutes, and urged on by his handling crew and Sri Chinmoy organizers, Kouros drove himself relentlessly. By 17 hours into the race he had covered 138 miles, a distance that most ultrarunners would be delighted to accumulate for in an entire 24-hour race.

However, even the remarkable Kouros has his limits. Twenty hours into the race he began to find them. He had a "bad patch," his laps slowed slightly, and he stopped talking as he focused his will on maintaining his momentum. Meanwhile, his crew continued their race-long refueling, placing small pieces of food in his mouth as he passed each lap. Then, slowly, as dawn broke and the warmth of day seeped over the track, the great ultrarunner revived. He began shouting to his crew as he circled the track, seeking more "fuel" to drive his flagging body over the final crucial hours. He needed to cover 11.1 miles in the last two hours to reach the goal that had eluded him for so many years, the target on which he had set his mind and from which he would not be denied.

When he finished, he declared emphatically, "I will run no more 24-hour races. This record will stand for centuries." He complimented the Sri Chinmoy Marathon Team, saying he was determined to set his greatest 24-hour mark in one of their races because they are always so well organized and supportive. Kouros could be right about his record lasting for centuries. His new world record is 17 miles greater than the next best 24-hour distance on record, a dominance unmatched in athletics and probably in all of sport.

You will not find the secret to Kouros in either his ability or his training. His

Yiannis Kouros

marathon best is only 2:24. He has said he rarely takes a training run longer than 12 miles, and is never over 80 miles per week. He follows a strict vegetarian diet that has no red meat, poultry, fish, eggs, or dairy products. Surely the reason for his success lies beyond nutrition, but nobody now following the sport is likely to find it.

Like the Trinity, pi, and pyramid power, he is a classic mystery. The best approach to take with a mystery is to stop trying to solve it and just believe.

"A War Is Going On Between My Body And My Mind"
by Yiannis Kouros

In my youth I ran 1,500 meters and 3,000 meters, later also marathons. But at the finish I always had the feeling I could go on much longer. So I tried the 1983 Spartathlon. It was my first ultra distance event, and I won, with over three hours on the second-place finisher. It went very well and everybody was surprised. First nobody wanted to believe it, because very good runners participated.

The first great success I had was in 1984 New York Six-Day Race. This was my first great experience in a multi-day race. Already at the beginning I was running very fast and because my toes were bleeding very much, many believed I would have to drop out. There I experienced how important the mental attitude is. In the fourth night Sri Chinmoy came to the track. From others I knew a little bit about him. I stopped and went to him. He gave me his hand and said: "You will win!"

I thought he must know it. He read it from my eyes and he saw it in my face that I wanted to win. I very strongly started to believe it. I always wanted to win, but I had no security. Every day I was afraid that I would have to stop. But after Sri Chinmoy was there I had such beautiful feelings; my insecurity and my fear were gone. Sometimes I even ran very fast. I almost danced from joy. From that moment I was sure to make it. Again and again I thought of him during the race. Then I won and I eventually broke the nearly century-old record of George Littlewood.

Some may ask why I am running such long distances. There are reasons. During the ultras I come to a point where my body is almost dead. My mind has to take leadership. When it is very hard there is a war going on between the body and the mind. If my body wins, then I will have to give up; if my mind wins, I will continue. At all times, I feel that I stay outside of my body. It is as if I see my body in front of me; my mind commands and my body follows it. This is a very special feeling, which I like very much. And now I reach that point later and later. First it happened during the marathon, then at the Spartathlon, then in the 1,000-mile race and now I have to run three or four days to reach that point. It is a very beautiful feeling and the only time I experience my personality separate from my body, as two different things.

The body is like a servant to whom you have to give drink and food. You have to care about it, otherwise it will not obey you. You have a goal. When you do not care about your body you will not reach your goal. The two things have to go together. You cannot say in your mind, "Now I am flying." Your body has to reach the finish line. You cannot only be at the finish line with your mind, because the others will not be able to see it. You have to do something natural. With your mind you can maybe be at the finish line always, but the result has to come to reality through your body.

I always choose new goals. During the race I try not to have negative thoughts. You have always to feel that you have to give your best. You must never let go no matter how far ahead you are of everybody. Otherwise your ego comes forward and makes you weak. You must always feel that you are at the same level as everybody else.

I always think that I am nothing. I am not thinking that I am a champion and therefore I am winning. I need the grace and the good will of God to achieve something. But I do not sit down and wait until God gives me everything, because I believe that one has to try everything to achieve his goal. But of course, I need His help like everybody. Because I am a normal human and when I have injuries it is just bad luck. But you have to feel that you have to do something great to become a great personality. Again, you must see yourself as very little, otherwise you will not be giving your best.

Not only the goals give me very much inspiration but also the memories. I think of the great achievements of Greek athletes in ancient times, of great men who did great things. Their achievements inspire me always. It also inspires me to try something impossible and to challenge the impossibility. If you want to achieve something very much, and you believe in the goal very much, you will achieve it. Like that you can also overcome difficulties in the race. For example, at the Sri Chinmoy 24-hour race in 1985, I ran 177 miles—a new world record.

In 1986, I came back to run a new world record. But in the beginning a hurricane started. I used all my strength, not to run, but to stay on the course. After some hours the storm stopped, but my time was naturally very bad. But then I started to run faster and faster and at the end I reached the world record, 178 miles, one mile more than in the year before. And I had still one hour to go. But I stopped so as not to make the record too high, so that it would not be more difficult to break the record the next time. That shows how the hurricane had helped me. If it had been easy I would have gone slower and slower, but because it was difficult I could fight.

In 100-km runs and 24-hour races you can still run on the physical level. But multi-day races have other conditions. You need a special psychic attitude to do it. At the shorter races this is not as important. With the right attitude of the mind you can overcome the upcoming problems. This is not too different from normal life, in a profession, or in the family. You need inner peace, then you can do a good result. During the old Olympic Games in the old Greece, all wars were stopped for the duration of the Games. All fights were stopped.

Many times people ask how I can sleep so little during my runs. Can one train not to sleep? In my case it developed like this: In 1985 during the Sydney to Melbourne race I slept all together about seven hours in five days. In 1986 I slept about four hours, 1988 about three hours, and the next year I slept all together only one hour, 50 minutes in the whole race. But after the race I sleep 12 hours a day for one month.

The problem is that when you get slow, you have more desire to go to sleep. When you are running fast you keep up your determination. As an example, at the New York Six Day Race, my plan was to run 20 hours and then to sleep for four hours. But what happened? The first day I could not sleep. The second day I could not sleep. Also at a six-day race in Australia it was the same. I was so fast that I could not go to sleep. The heart was going so fast I could not go to sleep. And then during the 1,000-mile run in New York I could not sleep for four or five days.

From my races I need to recover about two months. Then I feel that I have the appetite again to go running and start again. Directly after the race I feel that I am coming from another star. Often then also real hurt starts in my legs. Before I was concentrated only on running.

In ultrarunning there are no real limits. One can go on and on. I try to achieve some something special in each race. A new world record or a new distance. I am not interested in the place. A world record makes a race something extraordinary. To do an ultra run means to go to the limits.

I believe that more and more people will start with ultrarunning, but maybe not so many as in the marathon today. And I feel I belong to the pioneers now, as Emil Zatopek was a pioneer at his time for the marathon.

Masters of the 48-Hour Race:
Sue Ellen Trapp and Sue Olsen
by Kevin Setnes

The final stages of any 24-hour run are an awkward picture of struggling runners, trying with all their might to maintain any semblance of forward motion. The majority are reduced to a walk, or perhaps "hobble" is a better choice of words. For hours they have endured the long, slow grind of lap after lap, wondering why they ever chose to subject themselves to such pain and fatigue.

In contrast to the weak and weary runners in most 24-hour events, we occasionally get a glimpse of thoroughbreds at work. These runners somehow manage to overcome the aches and pains, to simply defy whatever toll the miles might have taken. They are driven by deep inner motivation that allows them to use their physically trained bodies to overcome the difficulties brought on by running all day and night. How do they do it? How do they maintain their running form? What gives them the ability to go on and on for hours? Two runners define this ability as well as anyone I have ever seen. For them, 24 hours is not an upper limit; 48 hours is within their grasp as well. Sue Ellen Trapp of Fort Myers, Florida and Sue Olsen of Burnsville, Minnesota have been at the forefront of America's 24- and 48-hour events for many years. Both have achieved a consistent level of success most of us can only dream of.

Trapp, a four-time National Champion at 24 hours, is not only the American record holder at 24 hours (145.3 miles), but at 48 hours as well (234.8 miles). Sue Olsen has also been a regular fixture at national 24-hour events; in 1991, she won the FANS 24-Hour Run in Minneapolis outright. She gained national notoriety in 1995 by running 62 miles the day before giving birth to her first child. Her bests are 134.9 miles for 24 hours and 216 miles for 48 hours.

What makes this pair tick? Do they have a secret ingredient others do not? How have they consistently performed so well over the years? And what about those 48-hour races? If they hesitate to say that it's their favorite event, no wonder. Try a 48-hour sometime—you will see what they mean. What attracts them is the extreme challenge of 48 hours. While 24 hours can be done with little or no sleep, with only one sunrise to look forward to, 48 hours demands sleep and punishes aching legs and feet from the constant, seemingly endless grind.

Training for 48
There is no easy way to prepare for an ultra. You cannot fake success at ultras; if you try, rough times lay ahead. I have suggested the single most important part

of training is weekly mileage and long runs. The manner in which you arrange weekly miles with long training runs is even more important. Have you heard the phrase, "learn to run tired?" There is only one way to achieve tired legs that I know of—that is to go out for a very long run.

Sue Olsen and Sue Ellen Trapp, like many elite runners, go through a buildup phase that involves fairly high mileage as they near the 48-hour run. An even more common thread is the way they schedule their long training runs. Both practice back-to-back long runs. In other words, they will run a long distance on Saturday, followed by another long run of equal or longer distance on Sunday.

Olsen says the key to her training for a 48-hour event is "to do two or three back-to-back, 40-mile training runs" (40 on Saturday and 40 on Sunday). She spreads these training weekends about four weeks apart, with the last one about a month before her event. She prefers to do the Sunday 40-mile run alone, as this will train her mind for the long mental struggles that are inevitable in a 48-hour event.

Trapp has a similar pattern in her training. She will complete a stretch of four weeks of high mileage, (110 to 120 miles) focusing on back-to-back runs. In

Sue Olson

1997, Sue set the current world record of 234.8 miles. While not running as far as 40 miles, she will do a Friday through Sunday routine of 20-20-20 or 20-30-20. Both accumulate enough miles on their legs in these sessions to simulate plenty of "running tired" time. It also provides ample time to practice their important eating and drinking routines.

Strategy

Both Olsen and Trapp understand fully the enormous task at hand when running a 48-hour event. Neither woman, however, will let themselves become intimidated or psyched out by the task ahead. For this very reason, they tend not to think too much about a specific plan or strategy for running 48 hours.

Sue Olsen tends to run as she feels for the first 24 hours. Only when the second day rolls around does she start to focus on what other runners might be doing. Sue Ellen Trapp also does not like to think too much about the pace or miles being racked up until the end of the first day. She says, "It takes me about 62 miles (100 km) to get into the rhythm of the race," adding, "it is always a nice surprise to get the first mileage totals from Ron (her husband and handler). I'm really just out there meeting other runners."

Eating and Drinking

Two facets of these long runs both athletes seem to have conquered are eating and drinking routines and sleep breaks. Both are very regimented when it comes to consuming food and drink. Olsen likes to eat something substantial every four hours, with intermittent snacks every 30 minutes (a banana, cracker or cookie). She drinks frequently in small amounts. At night, she prefers hot tea or hot chocolate, especially if the weather is cold.

Trapp, like Olsen, drinks frequently, taking a sports drink every two miles. She sticks with this routine for a large portion of the race; only in the later stages does she take in bananas, cakes, juice, coffee, soup and GU.

Sleep

Both will attest that sleep is necessary, albeit in short periods. Olsen plans two major sleep breaks during the event, the first coming about 16 to 17 hours into the race. Her second break will be about 32 hours into the event. Each is planned for about one hour, and is followed by eating, walking, and then finally attempting to run. The later stages of the event (the final 12 hours) require only a few five to ten-minute naps.

Trapp gets by on less sleep, but she still tries to take one or two short naps of about 15 minutes each during the second day of the race. She claims, "It is amazing what just a short nap will do for you." In her first 48-hour event, she ran without stopping for the first 30 hours and was in pretty good shape. Shortly after that, she hit the wall—she just had to sleep before going on. "The desire was so great (to sleep), that I just had to take little 15-minute naps to keep going."

Mental Approach

Both Trapp and Olsen say, "You cannot think about the 48 hours when starting the event." The sheer amount of time you will be out there running (or walking) can be intimidating. "Breaking the race into smaller pieces is key," says Olsen. She tries to narrow her focus, looking forward to specific moments in the race when something as "momentous" as changing directions can occur. At Surgères, France, the site of all three of Sue's 48-hour runs, they change direction every six hours, in order to prevent injuries from the repetitive stress of turning in the same direction for the entire race.

She also likes to plan ahead to her eating breaks, and during the second night, look at the leader board. Sue says, "Trying to do simple calculations can take a very long time," a phenomenon that is quite commonplace near the end of long ultras. That is likely why they hold these events on tracks or small loop courses, so participants are not required to follow arrows. Some runners might be unsure of the meaning or direction of the arrows.

Sue Ellen says she will develop a strong mental bond with her handler, something that is important in every race, but is especially crucial in the 48-hour event. "Everyone has experienced it, the energy drawn from one's handler or crew. In a 48-hour, it is greatly emphasized," says Trapp.

After the Race

Thank god it's over! Now what? Both runners have experienced the joy and elation of having finished and excelled at 48 hours. But how have they recovered? Sue Olsen struggled with injuries for much of the year after running the Surgères 48 hour in early May. "My biggest problem is swollen ankles after the race," says Sue. She is adamant about taking one week off following the 48 hours. After that, she will intentionally keep her mileage low (no run over 10 miles) for a few weeks. She also acknowledges that in future events, she will allow even more time off to recover from the trauma of the event.

Sue Ellen, like Olsen, refrains from running the week following an event and, in fact, needs a couple of months to recover from such an effort. The superficial damage, such as swollen ankles or feet, are only part of the problem. The internal bodily mechanisms, like the endocrine system, are also stressed and must be given ample time to recover.

A Different Breed?

Both Sue Olsen and Sue Ellen Trapp have achieved remarkable success at not only 24 hours, but 48 hours as well. They excel at what they do for many reasons. Are they thoroughbreds? I am sure both would grant that they have been blessed with talent. They are superior, mostly however, because they have the ability to train physically at very high levels. Secondly, they have a tremendous competitive spirit that drives them not only to train, but to compete at similar levels. They both also have an excellent mental approach. They concentrate on getting into a rhythm early on, carrying out little rituals, and then letting the race evolve naturally. Lastly, they both maintain an extremely positive attitude. Both women have an outlook that evokes a smile more often than a grimace. Sure it is difficult, but that's what it's all about—isn't it?

Helen Klein: Grand Slam Grandma
by James Raia

The sprawling cactus garden in front of 11139 Mace River Court in Rancho Cordova, near Sacramento, sets the Klein home apart from the rest of the large, modern houses on the cul-de-sac. It's an immaculately tended garden, reflecting the perfectionist (and occasionally prickly) personality of its creator, former Western States 100 Mile race director and cactus hobbyist Norm Klein.

If Norm is the most prolific ultra race director in North America, his wife Helen is equally well known as one of the most inspirational of all ultrarunners. Helen is a somewhat reluctant role model to all that aspire to slow the cadence of the aging process. The retired nurse will gladly speak to any group who will have her on the value of keeping active throughout life.

She is also one of four who were the first women to complete the 100-mile Grand Slam—Old Dominion, Western States, Leadville and Wasatch—then she tossed in a fifth trail 100-mile, Angeles Crest, for kicks. She felt so good after Angeles Crest, reports husband and avid fan Norm, that "she could have turned around and run back." She shoots back: "I don't know about that." As detailed below, she also holds most world and U.S. records in her current age division, and continues to set personal bests.

Helen pours the same vigor into running that she once drew upon as a New York City emergency room nurse and as a mother of four. (Her offspring, at last count, have produced eight grandchildren and three great-grandchildren.) UltraRunning visited Helen to try to learn some of her secrets.

How did you stumble into running?

I started in 1978 at (age) 55. Prior to that I was an emergency room nurse and then Norman's oral surgery assistant, but I retired at 53. I was a slim, physically fit person, so to maintain that I started hiking and walking, because I did not want to become a sedentary person. When I was 55, we were challenged to do a 10-mile (race) in a small town in Kentucky where we lived. We had two weeks to train and had never run before. Norman likes challenges, so he decided we should both train for it. There were no women runners in that area, so it was difficult for me because I was brought up in an era when women did not participate in sports. My mother was very adamant about ladies not sweating. So the most difficult part for me was to overcome my dislike of sweat, and it was July when I was training so I really did sweat! (Laughter) I learned to sweat with the best of them. I did have fun in the race, and because I was the only woman over 40, I won my age division. It took us two hours to do that race, so we were running twelve-minute miles. But after only 10 weeks of training, I was happy with that. I did enjoy it, so I continued to train—not to race, but to stay in shape. Norman decided to run a marathon, so we went to a marathon in Chicago. I really became nervous waiting for him because he was taking longer than I anticipated, so after that I told him. "If you want to run, then I'll run too, and let you wait for me." He has been waiting for me ever since.

Helen Klein

Most marathoners, though, never move up to the ultras. Why did you?

After several marathons I was not really improving, just staying around 4:30, so I decided I would try an ultra because I did not seem to have speed. Well, I may have speed, but I did not want to train for it because I don't like to hurt. I really don't like to do anything so intense. I am a relaxed person; Norman is an intense person and one of us is enough.

Did that relaxed attitude change after you began doing well in ultras?

No, I still have the attitude. Every time I am out there just to finish. That's the goal. Some I have not finished. Anything can happen.

So you challenge yourself by trying to run farther, or over more difficult terrain rather than faster?

That's right. Of course sometimes you have to be concerned with time because of cut-off times, and move a little faster than you may be feeling up to. I really like to just go out there and enjoy it, go at my own speed and not bother competing with anyone. But when I do follow my routine—listening to myself and not getting caught up in trying to keep up with other runners—I do feel better at the end and have more left, so I invariably pass people. Some runners, including my husband, see that and attribute it to competitiveness. It's really because I pace myself better, I'm anxious to get it over, and I do have speed at the end, especially if it's downhill.

(Norm Klein) What she says isn't always so about being competitive because...

(Helen Klein) O.K., there were two times that I've been competitive, but when you consider that I've run more than 100 races of marathon or greater distance. That doesn't make me a competitive person. In a 10-km in China I tried to beat a woman because her husband had been rude to me, and the other time was my last 24-hour track run, when I ran 106 miles for the world record. That time, my motivation was by way of *UltraRunning,* because of a French lady's picture with a story about how she had taken the record away from me—104 miles. The caption said, "France's answer to Helen Klein." That made me competitive. I decided that day that I would go get the record.

Do U.S. and world age-group records motivate you?

Not really. There are not many women doing these distances. There was one West German woman who had the 24-hour track record, and I took that away from her in 1985. Then the French lady took it back, and I got it again.

Do you own all the ultra records for women 60 and over?

(*Norm Klein*) She has all the 65 to 69 records up through 24 hours, and all but one for 60 to 64, the 100-km record that Ruth Anderson broke.

What led you to do your first Western States 100?

By 1983, I was still living in Kentucky and doing some ultras around the country, and because I was 60, I was allowed to have a pacer the entire way. I would never do a trail run where I would be in the dark without a pacer, because I become lost very easily. I have no sense of direction. So in 1983, we both entered Western States, and that was the year of all the snow. There was 18 feet of snow on the road up to Emigrant Pass. I have slides of Norman in the snow where he looks like an ant. I had never run mountains, and my only trail ultra had been the Ice Age 50. It was a struggle. I fell so many times in the snow those first 26 miles. I got to Devil's Thumb and missed the cut-off time at that checkpoint. I said, "Never again." It was so tough. Then after sleeping that night in the motel, I got up the next morning to see Norman finish. As I was watching the last stragglers, I saw a lady who was 15 minutes past the cut-off, although they were letting her finish. She came around that track really slogging, hardly moving. She was so muddy, from head to toe, and someone came up to me and said, "Is that Helen Klein?" I said, "No, I'm Helen Klein and I had to drop."

When I saw that woman finish, I thought, "Boy, maybe. Maybe I'll be back." Since then I have stricken the word "never" from my vocabulary. On the way home, I said to Norman, "The only way I'll ever finish that race is to train on the trail. I could never just train in Kentucky and do it." That put a bee in his bonnet and shortly thereafter, we moved here. He just got out of his medical practice and we came. Western States was the major factor in deciding to move here. We trained on the trail and in 1984 I was successful,

Did your move to California, with its multitude of trail ultras, result in your racing more often?

Yes. I had done lots of marathons, a few 50-milers and the Ironman Triathlon before the move. My goal had been to do a marathon or ultra in every state and I was up to 21. Kentucky did not have that many races. After the move, there were so many races in California that are so great, I did not have to travel. Here it's not a matter of where to go for a race, but which race to do again.

Of all the Grand Slam 100s, which proved to be the most difficult?

I always think Wasatch is, because of the altitude and the trail conditions. Although altitude does not bother me, a lot of climbing does. I am a good downhill runner, so I like races where there is more down than up. Also, it takes longer to do Wasatch: it takes everyone longer, and the longer you are out there, the more difficult it is. Western States is also difficult because of the heat, and because it is our race. I'm really under pressure to finish it.

Could you recount your failure to achieve the Grand Slam in 1988, and subsequent success in 1989? What changed?

I discovered a problem at Old Dominion, the first race of the 1988 Grand Slam attempt. Any time I did a long climb, I had to stop a few times to breathe, and I incorrectly assumed it was my lungs. Actually, as the race medical director pointed out to me, the problem was the muscles that support my shoulders. I did not have upper body strength. I needed to work on those muscles to support me so that I had better posture going up. He said it was too late for that Grand Slam, but that after I finished that try to join a club and work out. That's what I did and I have been doing upper body and abdominal exercises ever since, and I am really strong now. Climbing is still difficult, but now I can ascend two miles without resting. That was the primary difference. There were other circumstances. It was so cold at the 1988 Wasatch that my bottles froze and I had hypothermia, so after 70 miles, I had to quit. In 1989, the weather could not have been better at every race, so you have to have a little luck as well as conditioning. I set personal bests in all the races I had done before.

Do you walk in races?

I walk all the significant uphills in training and races, no matter the distance. On the track, I also walk. I run three laps and walk one when I run 24 hours and keep that up as long as I can. The first time, it was 50 miles. The last one I did, I was able to hold up for 70 miles. Then after that I run the straights and walk the curves.

How much have you slowed in your decade of marathoning and ultrarunning?

They say after seven years you start losing it, and they say as you get older you drop a certain percentage per year. Don't believe it. I had my best year in 1989.

(Norm Klein) She has also had personal bests recently at 100-km, 100 miles and 24 hours.

Are you a high mileage trainer?

Never. I have always believed in rest, and I always take a rest day once a week. I also don't keep a log, because I don't want to see how many miles I do each week and try to top it. If I am training normally, I go out for 10 miles five or six days a week. Training for 100-milers, I do runs of 18 to 25 miles three times a week—Wednesday, Saturday and Sunday—usually in the canyons on the Western States course. The other days I just do weight training and run no more than five miles. I race frequently, though, which adds to my mileage. I never overtrain, I listen to my body, and that is why I don't get into trouble. I don't believe in "no pain, no gain."

No injuries?

Not really. I attribute that to not doing speed training, relaxing when I run, trying to keep it low-key, knowing the difference between tiredness and pain, and probably good genes, supple muscles and good strong bones. I participated in an osteoporosis study in Kentucky and had twice the calcium level of any of the 300 sedentary women who were tested, I had calcium levels of a 25 to 30-year-old. The computer determined I should be fracture-proof through age 109. The study concluded that a combination of good genes and exercise are probably the biggest factors in avoiding osteoporosis.

Do you pay attention to nutrition?

I have always had a good diet. I happen to have been raised by a mother who, without nutrition education, just happened to eat well and liked foods that were good for her. Because I was fond of my mother, I wanted to be like her so I ate what she ate. I grew up with a good diet. I did not eat sweets. I like sour things. Apples are my favorite food, plus any fresh fruits, vegetables and all the grains. For meat I just eat small portions. I ate well without knowing anything about nutrition, and as I studied nutrition, I realized I had a good diet and continued it I have always been slim. Now with all the distance I run, I weigh 110, and I have to really eat a lot to keep that 110. I eat frequently, and I have to eat huge amounts of pasta and fruits and vegetables in the days before a race. Sometimes I become bored with eating because I eat so much.

What motivates you to keep doing ultras?

Finishing races gives you such a wonderful sense of accomplishment and makes you feel good about yourself. The greatest reason is that Norman is so involved, because we have always done everything together. I really believe that you have to have similar interests in the major forces of your life or you drift apart. Actually, I have reached the point now where I have gotten a little bored with it, maybe even quite bored because it's so much of our lives. It is our entire life. Every minute of every day is running, racing, talking about it, or answering the phone about it. I don't think that's very good. There is nothing else to talk about anymore except the running. If he were to change his position today and do something else, I would probably quit running. Probably two miles a day for exercise and enjoyment, but not the long races. It does get boring.

Wouldn't you miss the trails?

I would like to hike the trails for a change, to see them, because I can't take my eyes off my feet when I am running trails. The smallest little root or pebble can throw you. I have fallen a lot I have really scarred knees.

Any advice for someone doing their first ultra?

Start out slowly. When you are feeling comfortable, keep within that range of comfort, especially when it is a long race. If you start out comfortably, as long as you make the cut-off times, you can usually finish. Your primary goal should be just finishing. Then if you still have something left the last 20 miles, you can push, and it generally happens that way. If you have higher aspirations, it is usually your downfall, because you are going so far beyond what you have done before.

Do you believe in taking breaks during a race?

No breaks. Get in and out of an aid station as fast as possible. Don't get comfortable at an aid station. Thank people, but don't take time to socialize. For instance, Western States has 26 aid stations. If you spent five minutes in each aid station, count that up and see how much time you have lost. I also seldom change socks and shoes. It is too time-consuming, and you don't feel better anyhow.

Are you comfortable with being a role model for older people?

It is one of the things that keeps me going. Because of my age, I get an awful lot of attention, and I always feel that everybody out there wants me to finish because it says something to them. It says, "I may be able to do this for many years, and if I'm enjoying it now, I can enjoy it over a good number of years, and how wonderful that will be." I think I give them that hope. It is also one of the reasons why I have not given it up and turned to something else. Usually after seven or eight years of doing anything, I become bored with it and try something different. But every time I even suggest I am going to quit and start hiking and enjoy the scenery, they all come at me with, "Oh, you can't, you inspire us." I get so many letters. Everybody inspires me, because they are so gracious on the trails. When I'm coming by and having my good downhill, they move aside for me without any grudges.

Anything you would like to conclude with?

Just that stressing yourself really does slow the aging process, not just in body, but also in mind, because you are around energetic people. It is only when you decide to become a couch potato, at whatever age, that you lose it.

Helen Klein's Personal Bests		
Marathon	4:07	(Oakland Marathon, 1984)
50 miles	9:01	(Jed Smith 50, Sacramento, 1984)
100 km	12:09	(Ruth Anderson 100 Km, Oakland, 1990)
100 miles	24:59	(Vermont 100,1989)
	22:12	(split at CSUS 24-Hour, Sacramento, 1990)
24 hours	106.75 miles	(CSUS 24 Hr, Sacramento, 1990)
WS 100	29:25	(Western States 100,1989)

The Running Tribe: Tarahumara Indians
by Micah True

The Tarahumara. For long distance runners, this tribe from the Copper Canyon in Mexico has been romanticized as a people possessing great endurance, able to run ultra distances with relative ease. Some of the mystery surrounding the Tarahumara was removed in the 1990s, when a few of the tribe was brought to the U.S. to run in 100-mile events, most notably the Leadville and Western States 100 Mile races. Wearing their trademark huaraches, they did indeed produce some startling performances, including a course record of 17:30 at Leadville by Juan Herrera that stood for eight years.

Micah True has been living in the land of the Tarahumara for several years and currently offers adventure treks into the Copper Canyon for those seeking to visit the land of the Tarahumara. Micah shared the following observations on the Tarahumara in the early 21st century.

Interactions with the Tarahumara

As a *gringo raramuri*, I have a certain insight into the life of the Tarahumara. A shy and gentle people, the Tarahumara live well away from any towns, in casas of adobe that are usually in the general vicinity of a small, localized settlement that might consist of a little store, a church, and a school where the children stay during the week before returning to their family *ranchitos* on weekends. These raramuri walk everywhere that they want to go, including the *meztizo* (larger pueblos) to work hard labor jobs or to purchase bulk supplies.

"Rarahipa:" the races

Although running is traditionally a big part of Tarahumara culture, you will rarely see a Tarahumara running. They save themselves for the occasional *rarahipa* (traditional ball race), where teams of raramuri are kept focused by passing a hand carved wooden ball between them with their huarache (sandal) clad feet. These races are big events and contribute greatly to the material gain of the village. A rarahipa is something to behold. The race starts and ends at a village where all the spectators can witness and participate by offering aid in the form of *pinole* (finely ground roasted corn), and water, as well as massages when needed later in the race, and general encouragement to the runners. For this reason the format of the race is usually run in laps that might consist of 10 miles or so. Shaman come out to cast spells on the opposing team.

There is a huge pile of booty stacked in the village plaza for the winning team. In these races everyone is expected to lay down a bet. Poorer people might bet corn, while the wealthy bet livestock. It is considered high social status to bet big (cattle or horses). The winning village takes all. Because of this, the raramuri are heroes among the Tarahumara, much like *gringo* professional sports stars in our culture. It is considered in bad taste to celebrate immediately following a race because the winners have just cleaned out the competitors. Therefore, the winners sit on the ground solemnly, saying not a word. There will be time for celebration later, dancing and drinking of the loved *suwiki* (corn beer).

When the Tarahumara see me running for 'fun,' for pleasure, just to be out in nature, as well as in my thoughts and body, they wonder what I am doing. I will run through a village, take *korima* (sharing) of pinole, saying hola to all the curious children and run on. The Tarahumara of the deep canyons think that I must be *tan loco* (good and crazy). My raramuri name is *kaweki rosakame* (white horse), although increasingly am *caballo loco* (crazy horse). That is a grand compliment here in the land of *manana* and non-pretension, where people are respected for being different, for dancing to the beat of a different *tambor* (drum).

A celebration occurs whenever there is a reason, such as a new moon's planting of corn. There is plenty of dancing of the *matachin* while drinking the blessed *suwiki*. The dancing is a prayer, as the steps to the *matachin* consist of a continuous tapping on the sacred earth (like running); it goes on all night long, an endurance event. While I am dancing in the always moving spiral of the *pascole* dance, I am moved by my surroundings. I realize that life is a gift to be appreciated at all times. May the Tarahumara and all our relations (all of them), each in our own unique ways, continue to run free.

Adventure treks into the Copper Canyon

I will say that out of respect for the people, I do not take tourists tromping through Tarahumara settlements without being specifically invited. The Sierra Madre is huge, and there is plenty to explore in the land of the Tarahumara. I also want to stress that I am no great authority on anything. I do have certain insights from having lived in the canyons for the last six winter seasons, as well as having had some respectful interactions with some of these very unique people. I do not intend to in any way romanticize the Tarahumara life—it can be hard. When the rains come, the corn harvest is good and the people thrive along with the rest of nature. When there is no rain, life becomes harder. The Tarahumara are an extremely resilient people. That is, they know how to manage discomfort and to survive—with smiles on their faces—despite the adversity. These are only my perceptions; this is what I see.

Copper Canyon, home of the Tarahumara

There are 50,000 Tarahumara Indians living in and around the vast area of Chihuahua known as La Sierra Madre and Copper Canyon. Copper Canyon is a general name for the vast canyon system of northern Mexico's Sierra Madre, which has four large *barrancas* (grand canyons) winding deep within her folds. Besides these four large *barrancas*, there are numerous side canyons feeding *las barrancas* that would be considered major canyons.

Culture and development

Most Tarahumara do not have electricity. The people of the deep canyons and more remote regions are generally more traditional. I believe that most Tarahumara land is reserved in a *ejido* system that guarantees land for the raramuri. As far as development goes, much of this land is much too remote and rugged to be developed. The story goes that in centuries past, the Spanish exploiters drove the Tarahumara off of their original land in the fertile high valleys. The Spanish wanted to enslave these beautifully free people to work in the silver mines. The Tarahumara took refuge in La Sierra Madre (the mother mountains) and her deep canyons. When the conquerors looked into the vastness of the canyons, there was no effort to follow.

There is development occurring in the areas more accessible to 'real tourists' (lazy car drivers). This is occurring at a much less accelerated rate then say, in the Front Range of Colorado. Encroachment and development are relative terms.

Living at the bottom of Batopilas Canyon, in my explorations I have seen road building projects that do encroach on 'my' favorite trails. It is depressing, but who are we to say it is better not to drive, scar the beautiful landscape, cut down the trees, mine the earth, or pollute the air with industry? Of course we could go on. These projects, of course, are planned by government. The Tarahumara have a word for non-Indian exploiters. This word is *chabochi*, and the Tarahumara have certainly seen their fair (unfair) share of exploiters.

Work, income, and schooling

All Tarahumara settlements are a good distance from any town. Many Tarahumara are subsistence farmers. Tarahumara think nothing of walking 25 miles round trip to the nearest town in order to buy bulk supplies or to work labor jobs. A good wage is about 100 pesos a day (about $11).

All settlements have a schoolhouse, where the children are taught in a loving, nurturing environment. Many Tarahumara children, as well as older people, speak only the Tarahumara language. The schools are taught in both Tarahumara and Spanish.

Diet

A Tarahumara will eat anything! Mostly, they eat a lot of corn, beans, and any kind of meat that they can muster (usually goat). They eat good, healthy, natural food, except when they get into a town, where there exists plenty of 'junk food.' Whatever they eat, they burn off! I figure one reason that the Tarahumara do not run for fun or training is because they cannot afford the caloric intake that this gringo luxury requires.

Sandals or running shoes?

Huarache sandals—always. The raramuri find running shoes hot and cumbersome. They have been running in their huaraches since childhood and are quite accustomed to them. When running with huaraches, I find my feet feel much lighter and I am much more focused on the trail and how I pick up and put down my feet. They are an acquired taste.

The fitness of the Tarahumara

There are few fat Tarahumara. Do they possess the genetics to be great endurance runners? The raramuri that finished first, third, fourth, and fifth (and three other top eleven places) in the 1994 Leadville 100 Mile were almost all from one village of 500 inhabitants. The individual that brought them to Leadville that year recruited 'his' team by asking where some good runners lived.

Women run as well. Everybody does plenty of walking. No, not all Tarahumara walk everywhere. If they happen to live near a road they will take a ride every chance they get! (Disappointing, huh?) Very few Tarahumara have cars—or would even know how to drive one.

What can we learn from the Tarahumara?

I don't know how to answer this question. We all learn our lessons (or don't), in unique, personal ways. I think that we need to be open to experience in order to assimilate knowledge. I would say that having humility in knowing that we really do not know anything, and that all people, all cultures, have a wealth of experience to share, that nobody is better than anyone else—just different.

What became of the Tarahumara who ran in Leadville and other 100-mile races in the 1990s? Will they run in the U.S. again?

Quien sabe? (Who knows). All of those runners are running free in 'La Sierra.' Victoriano is 63 years old now and still running strong. He won the Leadville race in 1993 when he was young (54). Juan broke the course record at the 1994 race (17:30). I don't think that any of the raramuri care whether or not they run in the United States. They are living in the present in the Sierra Madre. They went to the states to run because they were hungry. The early 1990s were a time of severe drought in La Sierra and the raramuri were desperate to win to earn enough to garner food for their starving families. I find the Tarahumara to be a very sensitive people and who but a chabochi would want to go where they are not invited? God bless America—god bless the mother earth in all of the four directions. All of us, are of the same earth.

Racing, Raramuri Style

by Katy Williams

A Raramuri race really begins several weeks before the actual event. Two *cabiceros*, or team leaders, are chosen. It is the responsibility of each to invite and encourage the best runners to compete on his team. The invitation process alone may take days, as it is necessary to travel by foot over rugged terrain through the canyon to reach villages that may be located 20 or more miles away. As the appointed day approaches, the level of excitement increases. Members of the community begin placing bets on their favorite team.

Race sites may vary, even within the same community, depending upon which fields are currently under cultivation and cannot be trampled. If necessary, a few of the men will clear and ready the race course several days prior to race day. This consists of removing any major obstacles; but the course will remain extremely rocky and rugged. The race course itself is a loop, ranging from approximately two to five kilometers.

Finally, race day dawns. The runners, together with their families and friends, begin traveling toward the race site. Some will walk 20 miles that morning just to reach the start. The hillsides are dotted with color as the brightly dressed people make their way over the trails. The men wear shirts in hues of turquoise, marigold, orange, emerald green, or white, and embroidered breechcloths or *tagoras*. Slightly varied styles of tagora and the type of embroidery displayed thereon distinguish different areas of the canyon. The women wear similar blouses, paired with long, full skirts. The clothes are all hand-sewn and directly descended in style from those of the Spanish conquistadors, complete with collarless necklines and billowy sleeves. As head coverings, the men often sport bright headbands, while the women usually prefer multicolored scarves, tied under the chin.

The Raramuri are known for their beautiful weavings called *lajas*, which serve as belts for the men. Sometimes bells are attached to the back of these belts that serve as a sort of runner's "metronome." Runners' pounding feet keep pace to the jingle jangle of the bells before them. Of most interest to runners in the U.S., however, would be their shoes. In our high-tech times of air and gel-filled soles, the Raramuri cover trails rivaling those of the most infamous U.S. trail runs wearing nothing more than a foot-sized piece of tire tread, held on by a leather thong. That's it—in their *huaraches* the Raramuri cover miles and miles of rocky and treacherous trail without so much as a misstep.

The two teams gather at separate locations, usually at a team member's home. Activity at each reaches a fevered pitch as the children play and women grind corn on stone *metates* and work over open fires to hurriedly prepare tortillas, beans, coffee, and pinole for runners and spectators alike. *Pinole*, a corn meal mixture that is thinned with water, is traditionally used as the primary source of nutrition during the race. As the runners gather to eat and generally prepare themselves for the race to come, an important aspect of pre-race activity consists of casting spells and hexes on the other team.

Older men come too. Their days as racers but distant memories, they perform vital functions as coaches and "medicine men" for their respective teams. The root of an agave cactus is roasted over the fire by one of the elders. He then carefully pulls apart the onion-like layers and uses a stone to pound them against a large rock. These layers, believed to contain medicinal properties, are soaked in water that is used to anoint the runners' bodies before the race begins. Later, it will be brushed on a tired runner's legs, poured over his head and upper body, or even drunk.

Another elder busies himself carving the traditional wooden balls or *bolas*. The wooden ball is central to Raramuri racing, because it is the position of the ball that determines the position of the team. Each team has a ball of approximately four inches in diameter, which is alternately kicked and chased by team members. The Bola is rolled up onto a runner's bare toes and then flung forward (ouch!). Due to the rugged terrain, the ball frequently becomes wedged between rocks or in crevasses. To disengage the ball in these cases, the racers carry long, hand-carved, spoon-shaped sticks as they run. Occasionally the ball will be lost over the side of the cliff, so the elder continues to carve new balls all afternoon.

After all the preparation, the actual start of the race is handled with surprisingly little fanfare. The teams walk slowly to an area that is not marked in any way, but appears to have been designated as the start. Suddenly, the balls are in the air and the racers take off emitting whoops and shouts that are chillingly primordial in nature.

Each team has a designated area alongside the race course similar to what we know as an aid station. The first item of business at each of these locations is the creation of a line of stones to represent the number of laps to be run. Stones are moved, one by one, to the side as the team completes a lap. This particular race course was about three kilometers and the stones indicated that they expected to complete 34 laps. Raramuri races are won when the first team completes the final lap, or when the last remaining member of the losing team drops out. As the hours wear on, and the racers begin to tire. Tacos made of tortillas and beans will be offered. The runners will not help themselves to any food or drink, and they take only what is handed directly to them.

The bright sun warms the afternoon as the race continues. Everyone takes an active interest. The hillside is dotted with spectators perched on top of boulders scattered around the race course. Children play with smaller versions of wooden balls and sticks, in preparation for the day they too will be old enough to participate. Gradually the younger and older of the men begin to drop out, leaving only the most fit to continue the challenge. They have been running for several hours, but the pace has slowed very little. The elder's role grows in importance as tiring runners turn increasingly to them for encouragement, massage, new leather thongs, or whatever else may be needed. These "medicine men" seem, almost magically, to be able to produce a variety of requested items including, in one case, a cigarette plucked from the elder's headband for the needy runner. Unbelievably, the racers will occasionally take time out for a smoking break. As with many Native Americans, however, the smoking is more a ceremonial ritual than an addiction.

As the sun moves lower in the sky, the remaining runners are few. Runners have dropped out for reasons ranging from simple fatigue or muscle aches to having been hit on the head by the wooden ball. By dusk, there are three runners left on one team and only one on the other. As darkness looms, that final runner on what will become the losing team drops out. He has carried on a valiant struggle; but after kicking the ball all afternoon, he is losing the toenail on his big toe and is in a great deal of pain. This signals the end of the race.

The remaining three runners on the winning team thankfully stop running and head back to the house serving as their team headquarters. Of the 34 laps projected to be run, 32 have been completed over the course of that day. The balls are collected and given to the elder of the winning team, who blesses them and saves them for a future race. The proceeds from the betting are distributed among the happy winners and their families. In the glow of the sunset, runners, crew and spectators from winning and losing teams gather to rest and joke and laugh and eat. As night approaches, many roll up in blankets beside the fire and prepare to spend the night before undertaking the long journey home. The beat of a distant drum echoes through the night. The sound is strangely exciting, yet at the same time comforting. We reflect upon our two divergent cultures, our victories and defeats, our lives and dreams. Perhaps we are not so very different after all.

Bernd Heinrich: The Animal Kingdom, Evolution, and Running

Bernd Heinrich has a unique place in ultrarunning. In addition to being a one-time world class ultrarunner, Heinrich is also a world renowned zoologist. He has published several books on various species of the animal kingdom. In his latest book, Why We Run: A Natural History, *Heinrich combines his knowledge of running with years of research. The result is a fascinating look back at his career and the influence his research on other members of the animal kingdom have had upon his running, both in theory and in application. In this interview Heinrich shares his thoughts on the book and other topics.*

What motivated you to write this book?
I had thought about it before many times, but never got around to doing it. A few years ago I was doing a book reading (for a previously published book) in Farmington (Maine) and someone said, "Why don't you do a book about running?" I thought, what better way to combine my interest in running and the research I had done with animals? I felt I should do it now, before I got too busy with another project. I always felt I wanted to write a book about my experience in the 100-km, even at the time I was doing it.

One of the main themes of the book is that the differentiator between humans and animals is the mind, in that intellect allows humans to achieve feats beyond that of animals, since animals only develop their endurance through evolution and what they need to survive as a species. Is that right?
Yes. One must consider though, that the mind is a product of evolution as well. We evolved a hunting strategy and our psychology reflects that adaptation. Just as dogs have developed their own hunting strategy through endurance, so have we as humans. As I point out in the book, in that way we are more like dogs than cats, who are sprinters.

If that is the case, do animals used for racing purposes, such as thoroughbred horses, push to their limits to win a race? Or will they only run as fast as they feel they need to?
That is a good question. Thoroughbred horses are bred to run as hard as they can. Through that breeding the fastest runners will always be selected. So yes, I think they will always try their hardest in a race. Those horses are bred for psychological development, as well as physical. A highly developed racehorse will be allowed to leave off many (descendants), sharing its traits.

Bernd Heinrich

Aside from the mental aspect, are there any other aspects of long distance running and endurance that are particular to humans? Have we developed a distinct physiological response to endurance through evolution that no other animal has?

I would say the magnitude of the sweat response is unusual in humans. For most people in most of their lives, the sweat mechanism is useless. But if we evolved on the African Plain (as is generally believed), then having this sweat response was very useful in that we could gain an edge on other hunters and scavengers by hunting during the day, whereas other hunters (animals) could not be subjected to the strong sun and the heat, since they had not developed this sweat mechanism.

It has been suggested that as the distance increases women will perform better than men. Do you feel there is any physiological basis in this assertion? Is there any precedent in the animal kingdom that would suggest this is true?

The theory is that women store more fat, so will be better runners, because they will be able to tap into those fat stores. But there is no empirical evidence that would suggest women are better than men at long distance running. On average, men will always come out ahead. This of course, is on average. Any one individual woman may be a world record marathon runner.

In your quest to set the 100-km record, you seemed to tap into your own instincts to train the way you thought best in order to reach the record. Do you feel that was the best way? Would you recommend it to others?

When I was training for the 100-km, I did not know any other ultrarunners, nor did I know of any training manuals on ultrarunning. I would have read anything that was available, but there was not much out there at the time. Knowledge is very important. But I was up there in the woods by myself, so I trained the way I thought I should. I felt I had to do long, hard, runs. I tried to tax myself, then allow for rest and recovery. My instinct when training was to stop at 25 miles, but knew I needed to do more than that sometimes to prepare for the race.

I was forced to my own devices back in 1981 when training for the ultra and didn't necessarily believe folk wisdom. For example, when I was running cross country in high school and college we were always told, "You need to take salt tablets. Look at your sweat—it's all salt." Well that was because we were taking in so much salt we had to sweat it all out!

You mention more than once that running is the only real way to develop as a runner and that you have never lifted weights or stretched much at all. Do you feel these additional types of supposed performance enhancements will not be of any real help for ultrarunners? If so, why do so many coaches and trainers recommend these and other practices to runners?

What animals stretch? Cats do, but they are sprinters. They need an explosive start, where stretching is really a help. I just did not see that stretching helped for long distance performance. As for weightlifting, I was injured lifting weights in college, so I shied away from it later on. Besides, I was a heavy runner, not a light runner. I was five feet, eight inches and 160 pounds. I wanted to *lose* muscle, not add it. It seemed that it would me better to be skinnier than heavier with a lot of muscle from lifting weights. I thought the safe thing was to let the body decide the right thing to do. Time was also a factor in all of this. I just did not have the time to do everything, so the 15 minutes it would take to stretch or lift weights I felt was better spent running. That was two more miles I would be able to run.

In the book you make frequent references to efficiency in long distance running and how you were attentive to not wasting any energy, right down to coordinating your arm swing with your leg cadence. You emphasize that running involves the synchronization of an incalculable number of different parts in order to work and that no one part can take precedence over another. Do you feel most runners can benefit from improving their efficiency of motion?
Yes, one should pay attention to form and efficiency. It was ingrained in me when I was at Berkley (University). I used to run on the track a lot when I was there, and at the time there was a horse trainer who would go to the track. He would analyze my style and make recommendations about my arm swing and cadence. He made me much more conscious of my stride.

One should not underestimate the coordination that is involved in running. If you watch a good runner you will realize just how much coordination is necessary in order to be a graceful and efficient runner. You can't have one muscle group working against another; otherwise you will waste energy and become inefficient. That does not mean you have to be thinking about your form all the time, but a little conscious editing can be a good thing.

In the book you make note of the extraordinary respiratory systems that have evolved in birds through millions of years and how we as humans have an inefficient respiratory mechanism in contrast to theirs. Why is it that our breathing mechanisms are so poor, comparatively speaking?
Humans have a good enough respiratory system. We have evolved the best possible respiratory system that we can, given the constraints of being mammals. Evolution can tinker with that mechanism and improve it over time, as it has, but you can't tear down everything and start over.

Birds are predisposed for flight and thus have evolved a better respiratory system. The have light bones and a hollow body cavity, which allows them to fly, and have then secondarily developed the necessary breathing capacity to do so.

Based on what you have observed from the animal kingdom, would you be able to make a guess at why certain groups of humans, such as the Kenyans, excel in long-distance running, as supposed to other groups? Is it primarily due to a genetic component, or is it attributable to their socio-economic structure, (i.e. running to school as young children and running being an income producer), geography, or a combination of different factors?

There is no one factor that will result in why we evolve as we have. It is combination of many factors. There are innumerable factors that go into the development of the ability to run long distances, the combination of which will yield very unpredictable results.

The social and cultural aspect is very great in why some African tribes have become superior runners. In a book on this subject, by native East African whose name I cannot recall, it is pointed out that only some tribes had produced great distance runners. You rarely hear of a West African becoming a great runner; it is almost always the East Africans. The black African population is very diverse. Both Pygmies and the Masai are Africans, yet distinct from each other and unique.

It is sometimes difficult to differentiate genetics from the cultural component. Look at the East African women who carry very heavy loads on their head. That, like long distance running, is an extreme physical thing, done with ease by these women. But no one would say they have a genetic gift for carrying heavy loads. There can't be a gene for that. It is though years of doing so in that culture that they have developed the ability to carry these heavy loads.

One cannot discount the genetic component however, as it is a factor (in long distance running). But as we have seen, there is a big distinction between what is average and what any one individual can do.

Do you feel participating in ultrarunning in the long-term, year after year, is good for the human body, or is their long-term irreparable damage done in some way? If so, is there anything we can learn from the animal kingdom that would help us as humans minimize that damage and/ or the decline in performance that naturally occurs with aging?

The animal lifestyle requires a long-term excuse to develop a repair mechanism. I would guess that for both animals and humans, continuous running with no rest would produce harm in the long term. The question then is how much rest one needs, and that varies from individual to individual and with age.

It has been suggested that humans are nearing their limits in terms of performance potential, that is that world records at various distances will be improved little in the foreseeable future. Do you feel this is true? Do you think for instance, a sub two-hour marathon is possible?

It is entirely possible that we are coming close to the limits. I don't know about the marathon. It seems that given the huge field of people that have now run the marathon that the limits are very close. At the longer ultra distances however I think there is still room for improvement.

Your 100-km run from 1981 seems to have had a profound effect upon your life. Would you recommend all ultrarunners to try for a "once in a lifetime" peak performance?
I can't speak for others; it worked for me. Looking back, that run was really not even as good as some others that I did later. At the time however, in order to motivate myself, I had to make myself think it would be (a lifetime peak performance) in order to run my best. A while after the race I was training again, but during the race itself I told myself that I would never, never do this again!

After studying the animal kingdom and the lessons it has taught us, for so many years, what advice would you give to a beginning ultrarunner hoping to improve his or her performance level?
I would suggest to have high but reasonable goals, and to be willing to adjust as circumstances warrant. I potentially could have been a good ultrarunner before the age of 40, but I thought it was too difficult, that I could not do it. Then I saw so many others out there doing it that I said, "I can do this too," and tried a shorter race. I did well and picked the next goal.

As humans we are inherently cautious about things we don't know, but if we try, we usually find we are capable of more than we think. It helps to have faith in ourselves and to know that we have the adaptive ability to be able to run very long distances.

Philosophy

The Philosophy of Ultrarunning: Why Do We Do It?

Among sporting endeavors, few inspire inward thoughts as much as ultrarunning does. The effort required to complete ultra distances not only stretches the limits of the body, it extends the mind as well. How many times have you heard the tenet, "It's all in the mind?" Well, it may not *all* be in the mind, but covering ultra distances does engage the mind in a manner which allows us to reflect, providing a new angle on the perception of nature and our place in it.

One question that permeates our thoughts in ultrarunning is "Why do we do it?" Runners and writers throughout the years have speculated on the reason why as individuals we would undertake such a difficult endeavor voluntarily. There must be a reason. Most of us learn early on that winning a race is not one of those reasons. Thus, the need to search the mind, heart, and soul for answers. Inevitably it comes down to a search for fulfillment in our lives that only testing our athletic limits can provide.

In his article, David Phillips draws an analogy between ultrarunning and religion. He suggests that the traditions and rituals that have been acted out in religious services throughout the years are now being expressed by many in the sporting arena. Dan Lindstrom speculates on how an aggressive outlook can be detrimental in a 100-mile run, and Kris Clark-Setnes studies the psychological and emotional responses to injury.

Bill Demestihas tells us that the philosophical approach of a back-of-the-pack runner is quite different than that of other runners and requires special considerations. Garett Graubins explores the thorny and often agonizing question of whether or not to quit an ultra. In that vein, Nathan Whiting philosophizes that learning to live with humiliation is a very important step in becoming an ultrarunner. Suzi Cope believes that adopting a training philosophy that is geared towards finishing rather than winning is the right one for most ultrarunners.

A consistent theme in all of these articles is that the mind plays on integral role in ultrarunning. Although at times ultrarunning may seem to be a completely physical undertaking, fraught with bodily concerns, if we dig a little beneath the surface we find that the mental aspect is equally important. This being the case, it is only natural that ultrarunners explore the philosophy of the sport and attempt to answer the eternal question "why?"

Rules for Being an Ultrarunner
by Keith Pippin

Ultrarunning, and in particular, ultrarunners, have been a source of continuing fascination for me since I first participated in this most unique of sports. The things that we do and accept as commonplace are truly beyond the comprehension of "others." So often ultrarunners have lamented, "Most people would just not understand."

As the years of miles, and miles of years have passed, I have spent considerable time in thought and discussion of that which we undertake. One day on the trails, that day when everything was working just right, it occurred to me that perhaps there was a common thread of philosophy or mental disposition, a mental perspective that would perhaps provide a basis for being an ultrarunner.

In effect, I was thinking, "Is there such a thing as a set of rules for being an ultrarunner?" The word "rules" seemed to be dictated by the trends of our society today, as we are smothered with an endless list of rules, regulations, and laws. Anyway, using the word with tongue in cheek, the following "rules" for being an ultrarunner seem appropriate:

- You have received a body, the genetics of which were determined by those you selected for parents. The body you received may or may not be suitable for running. You may hate it or like it, it makes no difference; this is the body you have.
- You may train as hard or as easy as you like. Your VO_2 max will not change by any appreciable amount.
- Each time you run you will receive lessons. You have enrolled in the school of ultrarunning. You may like the lessons or think them irrelevant and stupid. What you think makes no difference; the lessons will be presented until they are learned.
- When you run, there are no mistakes, only lessons. The art and science of ultrarunning is a process of trial, error, and experimentation. The failed experiments are as much a part of the successes as the combination that ultimately works.
- Lessons will be presented in various forms and intensities. Each lesson will be repeated until it is learned. When you have learned one lesson you will be presented with another.
- The learning of lessons does not end. There is no part of your running experience that does not contain lessons. Each time you run there are

lessons to be learned.

- There is no better run than the one you are presently on. Do not aspire to do better in the next run until this one is completed.
- Periodically you will be tested. The test will be presented in the form of a race. This may be an announced test such as a race to be run at a future date, or it may be in the form of a pop quiz when a "friend" calls on Friday to run on Saturday. The tests may be severe and demanding, testing you to the very limits of your mental and physical capabilities. You are the only one who will know your test score. After the test you will know which lessons require more study.
- How your running affects you and those around you is up to you. You have the ability to choose—positive or negative. The decision is yours. You will live with the consequences of the choices you make.
- Life's answers lie within. Life's questions can be answered from within. Running is the medium through which these answers will be revealed. All you have to do is look, listen, feel, and trust.
- As you advance to greater challenges, you will continue to gain knowledge of yourself, Periodically you will be required to reach ever deeper into your inner being, seeking out the strength needed to continue the endeavor of the moment. The strength you seek is layered within. The number of layers is infinite. All you have to do is believe, have faith in yourself, and expect to find that which you seek.
- You are in a process of continuing evolution. This process will take you ever closer to an acceptance of self that few others will ever experience. You will come ever closer to accepting those shortcomings and frailties that reside within, of which only you are aware. As this process is experienced, you will move ever closer to becoming that ultimate human being that only you are capable of becoming. Look, listen, feel, believe, and have faith in yourself. This process will not be completed during your present lifetime.

You must always remember: "The people dancing were judged insane by those who could not hear the music." Few people will ever hear your music. Run long and prosper.

Who are we? A Paradoxical Explanation of Ultrarunning

by Dr. Rowly Brucken

All ultrarunners struggle to explain what motivates them to undertake seemingly impossible and self-destructive quests. I have spent a fair amount of time stumbling and rambling through these inquiries, but have concluded that it is impossible to describe in a clear and concise manner why I run ultras. Instead of trying to formulate better answers, I have asked myself why it is hard for me to explain, and for others to conceptualize, the running of very long distances. After all, almost anyone can and has run at some point in their lives; it's not the activity itself that precludes understanding. I have no more innate or genetic ability to complete 100-mile races than most of my neighbors. But over the eight years that I have run ultras, I have slowly discovered a system of values and perceptions that enables me to train for endurance events. It is this world-view based on four paradoxes that allows me to enter the world of ultrarunning, to relate to many who compete alongside of me, and to keep myself motivated while running for hours at a time. For non-ultrarunners, in my mind, the difficulty in understanding lies doubly in the paradoxical nature of these points, as well as the fact that they contrast with values that permeate our current day society. If non-ultra folk could understand these four insights, I think they might gain a better understanding of the sport and its participants.

1. The fullness of silence and simplicity
Many ultrarunners are "running loners." We are often very social people at work and in informal settings: some of us are extreme extroverts and revel being in the company of others. But many of us prefer to—or by circumstance have to—run alone. It is during long runs that we discover ourselves in our surroundings. Running for hours is rarely boring and dull, a common and understandable belief of non-ultrarunners, primarily because we all live in a culture of noise and of short attention spans. At work or at home, we must accomplish many different tasks quickly. Our lives are governed by the complexities of work and family life. How could a mentally balanced person do something as simple as run for hours (without even bringing a cell phone!) and come back feeling spiritually refreshed and even energized?

Yet, that is exactly the point. Doing something as simple as running allows us *not* to think about running, to escape (for a while) the other demands on our lives, and to draw us into a world dominated only by natural sounds and our own thoughts. We move slowly and deliberately to a very personal rhythm, not according to a watch. Unless we are elite runners, many of us train by disowning the three preoccupations of sub-ultra conditioning: calculating an exact time spent, the exact distance covered, and the resulting pace per mile. We don't take the shortest or flattest route between points, so we "waste" time and energy in a world that demands efficiency. We revel in simplicity, not complexity: few pieces of equipment to buy, no advance planning needed, no perfect weather required, no rules to memorize, no colleagues or teammates to coordinate schedules. Yet the sense of peace, alertness, quiet, and solitude that training provides is irreplaceable.

2. The certainty of uncertainty and the resulting calmness in anxiety
We live in a world dominated by the fear of natural or human-made disasters, personal failure, or the unknown. Yet the caution and conservative decision-making process that understandably comes from these threats constricts our view of the possible. We are afraid to venture outside of what we conceive to be safe boundaries, whether they be physical borders or mental barriers in our career, personal lives, or hobbies. We think in worst-case scenarios of what might happen to us if we do, and we often define success narrowly as winning. Athletes, both the real and armchair variety, often define anything less than victory as failure: if you're not a competitor for first place, you're something of a secondary athlete.

In contrast, ultrarunners, no matter their level of training, expect and try to plan for the worst to happen: we will feel pain, fatigue, boredom, depression. We may have to drop out of a race. We will feel terrible when we finish and sore for days afterward. We worry about old training injuries that might surface, surgeries that make joints weak, and past races that we did not complete. That does not make us pessimists—just realists! We have the confidence, though, that we have prepared for these obstacles and can continue despite many of them.

At the starting line of every ultra, there is a lot of nervous energy, but it is expressed far more quietly and internally compared to the minutes before marathons and sub-marathons start. We feel fear and reverence. We are about to begin a largely unknown journey that will last for hours, and we will be at the mercy of things beyond our control: blisters, joint pain, sudden hormone alterations, dead flashlight batteries, and the weather. We know at some point things will go wrong, and yet the fear of the unknown calms us so that we are mentally and physically prepared for what might come. So we begin each race with the promise of doing the best that we can, not knowing exactly what that is or what will happen to us on the long journey. To finish is to win, and to finish last means often receiving a standing ovation at the post-race awards ceremony. It is a special sport!

3. The pursuit of real but invisible rewards

One of my favorite questions from friends involves explaining the rewards one gets for finishing and for placing among the top overall runners. A fleeting feeling of stupidity comes over me, since our society defines rewards as tangible: a promotion, more money, publicity—something that demands respect from others due to its prominent visibility. "Well," I reply, "with usually little if any press coverage, many ultras give out trophies to the top finishers and belt buckles for all who finish under 24 hours. When I placed ninth at the Vermont 100 Mile in 2004, I won a Montrail hat!" This reply usually ends the conversation. Why do something so demanding if there isn't fame, money, or at least valuable prizes waiting at the finish line?

The description of ultrarunning's very tangible rewards vary from person to person. As a cancer survivor who almost lost a leg, running long distances gives me a feeling of wellness, vitality, and strength. For some of us, ultrarunning provides the confidence and empowerment needed to push forward in other aspects of our personal or professional lives. For many of us, being outdoors generates a spiritual consciousness that results in a feeling of well-being and provides extended time for acknowledging a divine presence. We don't do ultras to get prizes or recognition. We do them because we seek adventure, challenge, and the unknown. We want to find unexplored areas of physical and mental consciousness, to probe the limits of muscular endurance, and to chart new voyages of accomplishment. And ultras, we know, never let us down in this quest. But we do hang on tightly to those belt buckles!

4. The arrogance and the humility

In an age of celebrity worship, mass media, and tell-all memoirs, we learn that those who speak loudly, brashly, and boldly get most of the attention and fame. Conversely, if you don't call attention to yourself and your accomplishments, they don't really exist in a meaningful way.

Ultrarunners, in contrast, generally have unique personalities: on one level, as with anyone who tries to do exceptional feats, we have to possess an inner core of arrogance. We think we are supermen and superwomen, that we are mentally and physically tougher than most, and, despite the difficulties we will encounter we possess the resources to triumph in the end. And yet ultrarunners are some of the most humble, friendly, approachable people I know. We intimately know our bodies and minds and how vulnerable and frail they can be. We know of failure, of injuries that take too long to heal, of having to drop out of a race. We know of the necessity of teamwork with pacers, supporters, race volunteers, and communion with complete strangers on the course that will get us through the dark miles. Everyone who finishes can give thanks for the love, patience, and support of others. We each know this, and we are proud of ourselves and grateful for others, knowing that the non-completion of an ultra could be only the next race away.

So we are then, a breed apart: an anthropologist might classify our tribe as one that lives in groups yet can thrive in solitude, possesses a spirit of calm and detached durability, and revels quietly in adventurous challenges. Is that so hard to understand?

DNF: When Success is a Three-Letter Word
by Garett Graubins

"Failure is the opportunity to begin again more intelligently." – Henry Ford

It's unlikely that Henry Ford ever ran an ultramarathon; he was far more likely to drive one of his innovative automobiles past the marathon distance. Yet his words echo the feelings of many an ultrarunner who has suffered the heartbreak, frustration, disappointment, and sadness of the most lamented acronyms in the sport: DNF (did not finish).

Within the pages of *UltraRunning* each month, there are stories of successes. There are the victories, the personal triumphs, and the stories of those who have successfully completed a daunting distance. With each race report, there is a list of finishers to accompany the story of the battles that took place to decide the winners.

But what about the others; the runners who toed the starting line with high hopes of winning, improving on a previous performance, proving something to themselves or somebody else, or just crossing the finish line? Consider the following:

- In the Leadville Trail 100 Mile, 246 runners who started the race did not finish.
- In the Western States 100 Mile, 133 runners failed to endure through the race's heat, canyons, and quad-pounding downhills.
- In the Hardrock 100 Mile, 42 runners—37 percent of the field—who started the race did not experience the exhilaration of "kissing the Hardrock," signifying they had conquered one of ultrarunning's most difficult races.

That adds up to more than 400 DNFs in these races alone. To put that into perspective, imagine if the entire field of the American River 50 Mile failed to finish. That would be the approximate equivalent.

DNF's are a fact of ultrarunning that virtually every ultrarunner, regardless of his or her ability or where he or she normally finishes in the placings, has experienced. In fact, many ultrarunners feel a DNF is a rite of passage on the way to becoming a stronger runner. It's akin to the adage, "That which does not kill me makes me stronger." In order to graduate to higher levels of the sport, everyone needs to experience their medical wristband being cut or the surreal moment when they hear themselves say, "I'm done" in a sport in which you're never supposed to say those words.

The process of a DNF transcends the moment of dropping out of a race. It also involves coping with both the psychological and physical ramifications, and seeking redemption. To illustrate this process, three accomplished ultrarunners recently shared their DNF stories with *UltraRunning*.

The Drop

This step of a DNF may also be known as "I quit", "I can't take no more", or "Put a fork in me, because I'm done." Recently, Deb Pero of Dublin, New Hampshire traveled to the high mountains of Colorado's San Juans for arguably the most extreme of the ultras: the Hardrock 100 Mile. Like almost everybody else standing at the starting line of the race in Silverton, she had trained like never before, researched the course, spoken with others about it, and devoted her entire year to preparing for the race. She and her soon-to-be-fiancé, Steve, even scouted the course for two weeks prior to the race, just to physically and mentally acclimate. In short, they did everything the "book" says to do when preparing for Hardrock.

Race day was not Pero's day. After battling an asthma-like condition for two weeks prior to the race—most likely caused by the chemicals sprayed on the dirt roads to control the dust—she still roughed it through the race before dropping at mile 70. She did everything possible to finish the race, battling through vomiting spells, "blind spots" in her vision caused by the altitude, and even a miscommunication that led her to think she was dangerously close to the cut-off. When she dropped, it was a painful decision, as she recalls in *Running through the Wall:* "It was gut wrenching to watch that dream slip away, then to finally give it up for good. . . I felt so guilty, like I had utterly failed and disappointed him (Steve). This was so damned unfair."

In a recent Wasatch 100 ultrarunning veteran Roch Horton also experienced the feeling of failure. Horton had prepared well for the race and entered race day healthy and injury-free. In his words, "I was trained and ready; I even ran (parts of) the course." Still, there were surprises in that year's race that caught everyone off guard, including him. That year, the middle miles of the race across Alexander Springs and Lamb's Canyon were hot. At Wasatch, that is not too unusual. However, beginning at dusk, the temperature dropped approximately 50 degrees over the course of ten hours. Horton fell victim to the weather: "At Mill Creek (mile 62), I sat comfortably by the space heater, oblivious to the nosedive in temperature. I ate and was feeling good. Then I faced a big decision. Should I bundle up in layers or head out with what I had (on)? I chose wrong when I left the station with only a long sleeve top and gloves."

Horton made a classic mistake at Wasatch and paid for it at the next major aid station, Brighton Ski Lodge (mile 75). He somberly recalls, "The ridge before Brighton (Red Lover's Ridge) was bitterly cold. And when I arrived at mile 75, I was not right. My body was shutting down." Despite these warning signs of hypothermia, Horton set out from Brighton to climb Catherine Pass in the cold of night. "It was darker than dark as I began the 1,500-foot climb and, at that point, I was barely walking," remembers Horton. He barely choked down a gel as he shivered his way up the pass, further from the warmth of the aid station. The lights of the Brighton Ski Lodge down below still beckoned him and he tried everything to warm his exhausted body. "I was cold to the core," he says.

At a distinctive fork in the trail—still well below the top of the pass—Horton made the decision. He remembers the moment of his DNF as clearly as yesterday, "I said to my pacer, Virgil, 'We need to go down. I can't go anymore.'" With that, he and his pacer turned around and struggled to return to the Brighton Ski Lodge. Back at the Lodge, Horton stuck out his wrist and watched as an aid station volunteer cut his wrist band. Horton, who had several difficult 100-mile finishes under his belt, had failed to cross a finish line for the first time.

One of the most notable DNFs in the history of ultrarunning took place in the Leadville 100 Mile. Chad Ricklefs, an accomplished ultrarunner with many notable records and titles to his name, dropped out just five miles from the finish line. After trailing for a majority of the race, Steve Peterson passed Ricklefs near mile 91 on his way to his fifth Leadville victory.

After Peterson passed him, Ricklefs continued to about mile 95. Yet Peterson only widened the gap between the two as he put on a dramatic push to the end. Ricklefs had been experiencing extreme fatigue and nausea for several miles and simply could not continue. After crossing a road and beginning down a forested hill, he discussed his decision with his pacer, former world marathon champion and physical therapist Mark Plaatjes. "I made the decision and Mark supported it. I turned around and went back to the road where my crew had a car. I hopped in, and that was it."

Acceptance

Following an unsuccessful race, most ultrarunners undergo their own versions of the soul-searching process, ridden with pangs of self-doubt, frustration and a feeling that a dream has been left unfulfilled. There is also a realization of one's mortality, a concept that is often discouraged in a sport that challenges athletes to accomplish superhuman-type feats.

For Pero, the time after the Hardrock 100 was an emotional rollercoaster. On one hand, she experienced the elation of a trip to the beautiful San Juan Mountains, her engagement (during the race itself, no less) and fiancé Steve's inspiring finish. On the other, she felt disappointment over her inability to finish the race. It had been a dream to finish the race with Steve, and this dream lingered like an unfinished book. "Leaving Silverton without a buckle, without a finisher's print, was sort of a bummer," she says, adding, "after we returned home, I think I felt the disappointment more keenly."

Pero also experienced the self-doubt common to anybody who's tasted a DNF, secretly wondering if Hardrock was beyond her capabilities as an ultrarunner. "You begin to tell yourself things like: 'Maybe if I'd just waited a little longer, then I could have recovered and gone on. If I wasn't such a wimp I could have pushed through it. Maybe I just don't have what it takes.'"

Like Pero, Horton also worked through a process of regret and self-doubt. After the Brighton Ski Lodge staff cut his wrist band, his inner psychologist went to work. "I remember telling myself—actually trying to convince myself—that dropping was an act of courage. It was a tough thing to do, but I was going to be o.k. I also had to remind myself that my friends wouldn't think any less of me," he recalls.

Even hours after experiencing early signs of hypothermia, Horton's body still felt cold. He recognized this as further evidence that he had made the right decision, albeit a difficult one. Still, he had second thoughts, just as Pero did. "When the sun was coming up, I began trying to convince myself that I still had time to go back and finish," Horton laughs. Sitting at the finish line, remorse set in as he watched more and more people crossing the finish line. "That could be me," he would think to himself. The most important part of Horton's recovery process was the acceptance that he made a poor decision in dealing with the abnormally cold temperatures at that year's Wasatch. With a heavy tone of nostalgia, he recalls, "Everybody had a cold story that year and, the more stories I heard, the less bad I felt. I had made a good decision."

Accepting the DNF and moving on was also a part of Ricklefs' post-Leadville experience. When asked if he regretted the decision to drop so late in the race, he said, "I definitely got upset . . . to work so hard and fall short. It's the failure of a goal." But Ricklefs' definition of failing to accomplish a goal is different from many others. For him, the goal at the Leadville 100 Mile—or any race, for that matter—is to win. If a race is going against his plan or if it is not his day, he adopts a big-picture perspective on his running. "If I do not feel good, there is no reason to go through extreme pain and risk causing permanent injury. There are other days." Yet dropping out of the Leadville 100 did seem to bring on some self-doubt. After the race, Ricklefs immediately shifted his sights to another major challenge, the JFK 50 Mile. "I wanted to run JFK to prove something to myself. It was a shot at immediate redemption."

Redemption

That brings us to the third step of fully experiencing a DNF. After the DNF has sunk in and a process of acceptance and realization has taken pace, most ultrarunners think about the best way to exorcise the DNF demons once and for all. A few disappear from the sport, retiring to shorter distances. But most—those who love the sport far too much to surrender—turn their sights to new challenges, chances at redemption.

Many ultrarunners who DNF will seek out another race almost immediately. Horton signed up for The Bear 100 Mile just a few days after his Wasatch experience. Ricklefs immediately turned his intense focus toward the JFK 50, later in the autumn after his Leadville DNF. Despite this, virtually every ultrarunner will not experience full recovery from a DNF until they return to the "scene of the crime," the race that stole their dream of succeeding.

Pero had to return to the Hardrock 100 Mile. She felt she had no choice. She remembers, "having experienced the DNF, I definitely felt I had something to prove, and I was not going to drop out this time, come hell or high water." But Pero had to experience an agonizing wait before taking another shot at the Hardrock course. The next year's race was canceled due to forest fires in southwestern Colorado, and she was far down the waiting list for the following year. Yet she crossed her fingers and hoped. Then, just one week prior to the event, she received a phone call notifying her that she could run the race if she could make the trip. Despite the fact she had resigned herself to not running it that year, and one week allowed little time for acclimatization to the thin air of the San Juan Mountains, she gleefully set off for Silverton, Colorado, eager to redeem herself.

Speaking about the chance to run the race with husband Steve again, Pero reviews her strategy going into the race, "The plan was to run very conservatively. We would stick together, and just try to get a finish. We didn't care about time. I was totally serious when I said that 47:59 was o.k. by me." (The final cutoff is 48 hours.) Pero's finishing time turned out to be fairly close to 47:59, but most importantly she finished. She battled through the heat, dehydration, fear of steep drop-offs, vision problems, and lingering self doubt from the earlier DNF.

Many ultrarunners who return to the site of a DNF describe an odd, almost haunting connection they feel with the place where their decision was made and they realized they would not complete the race. For Pero, this moment came at the Sherman Aid Station. "I remember distinctly that I did not want to go into the tent, the spot where I had laid down on a cot for several hours the year I dropped out. I told the aid station volunteer, 'I gotta get out of here for sure. Last time, this is where I dropped.'"

Similar to visiting a gravesite to make peace with a portion of the past, these parts of the race course hold deep, hallowed meaning for many runners. The following year, Roch Horton also returned to the site of his DNF: Wasatch. When he came to the point where the previous Wasatch race ended—the Lake Catherine trail junction—he felt a strong tie to his history at that spot. With reverence, he recalls, "When I reached that point, I felt something right there. I felt like a part of me died there, like I lost a part of my ultrarunning innocence." After a long pause at that spot, Horton continued up the pass, putting his past behind him once and for all. He went on to finish in 29th place, in a stellar time of 28:11.

In returning to Leadville the following year, Ricklefs showed that even the champions feel a need to redeem themselves after a DNF. Ricklefs remembers, "After a DNF, it's natural to take a little uncertainty into the next race. But the DNF helped me in that it was a motivating factor that day." Ricklefs ran a strong race, just as he had the previous year. In fact his splits were nearly identical the previous year. "They were within 30 seconds," he states matter-of-factly. The major difference from the previous year was that he made it past the final stages of the race without any nausea like he had experienced the previous year.

When Ricklefs passed the spot where his DNF was sealed, he didn't stop and reflect. "I did make a mental note of the spot and mentioned it to my pacer," he says, "at that point, the adrenaline was kicking and I could feel the end was near." However, it is possible that Ricklefs would have reflected if he had not been in such a hurry; his finishing time that day smashed the Leadville course record, one that had stood for eight years. That is redemption with an exclamation point!

Deb Pero, Roch Horton, and Chad Ricklefs are three very different ultrarunners. They differ in age, body type, experience, natural ability, strengths, and weaknesses. Yet there is a common bond between them that is also shared by virtually every ultrarunner who has spent any amount of time pushing the limits of endurance. This bond is the DNF. Every runner experiences one at some point. The true test of an ultrarunner, however, is not the miles of the next race, but how he or she works through the moment the myth of invincibility is shattered.

Training to Finish Makes More Sense Than Training to Win

by Suzi Cope

The book titled, *Eat to Win* was probably a success because we would all like to be capable of winning by simply eating certain foods. We are even willing to read about how to train correctly to win, although obviously only a few runners will ever win an ultra during this life, because it also requires talent. However strange it may seem, the title to this article is not as senseless as it appears. I agree, nobody consciously wants to quit, but my training philosophy is geared towards a finisher's reward, not a winner's award.

My personal achievements in ultrarunning, and those of others I have listened to, prove that the one of the most important ingredients for completing an ultra is mental attitude. Not just on race day or race weekend for a 100-miler, but during training. The "Suzi T" definition of training may reveal the secret to all my 100-mile finishes, in that I believe life is training for everything. Not that training should be your life, but that your life should count as training. When a 50-mile race turns into a 50-mile hike, I consider it a training session of grand proportions.

Setting goals you believe are attainable helps, no matter what everybody else thinks. You can't finish your chosen event if you don't honestly deep down trust your ability and your preparation. There are stories told after each run about someone doing well who "doesn't train." Well, what is training?

The components I base my plans on include the facets of everyday life. First and foremost, to finish, your head has to be on straight, which means emotionally you must be sound. Certainly I act in a less than sane manner at times, but for me that passes as normal. The relationships I have with myself, my husband, my family, my workers, my friends, and even strangers are reflected in my success possibilities. If you sacrifice your personal relationships for an all-consuming training regimen, your success ratio drops, as well as the satisfaction of a finish if it occurs.

Everything you do counts as training and you can reward yourself accordingly. When I walk to the post office instead of driving, I feel better mentally, and I count it physically as part of my training. At work in the travel agency, I often stand at my desk instead of sitting; this time on my feet is training. When I work in veterinary clinics, I consider lifting a big dog an "upper body workout." Sure, I could train more mileage and run faster during races, but what would I sacrifice to find the time and energy? Why give up rock climbing, when you can just count it as strength training? Take your kids for a bike ride, or your dog for a walk; it's life, it's training, and it counts.

Even resting is part of the plan. When I am injured, or tired, or both, I try not to begrudge the runs I am missing. Instead, I do my planning. The strategy I feel is needed to finish includes wardrobe planning, food preparation, equipment modification, and lots of daydreaming. The anticipation is half the enjoyment, and if things go right, it will not be all of the enjoyment

Give yourself credit. Count your life as training. Make your life the best you can manage and your ultra experiences will provide the satisfaction that comes with a completion.

Living With Humiliation
by Nathan Whiting

It is generally felt that humiliation is the one thing to avoid in competition, yet there are instances when it becomes part of one's game and adds to the drama and the triumph. A football lineman is pushed back by a bruising pass rusher repeatedly, but survives just long enough to allow the winning pass to be thrown. A baseball player strikes out three times in a row, then hits a long home run.

It is hard to think of a sport that offers more opportunity to battle humiliation, or greater pieces of it, than ultrarunning. There is something profound about being able to run 50 miles in seven hours and finding out it takes ten hours on another day. There is something very deep and mysterious in the middle of the night when you can no longer run and each 20-minute mile seems to last an hour. There is a truly hopeless confusion when one "bad spell" drops you from fourth place to fifteenth.

One problem we have is that humiliation can be hard to recognize. It hides in a thicket of pain and fatigue. It pretends to be some kind of injury. It pulls a netting of depression over itself. It sneaks off course and goes home, declaring itself a "bad day." It wanders around telling whoever it encounters that it's "mental, not physical." To call poor humiliation a "mental" problem as if we did not prepare ourselves for the race, is amusing. It is the humiliation we are not prepared for.

Humiliation is the face turned inside out, when we don't want it seen, when we don't want to see it. There is ego in racing; a better time, a longer distance, a higher place. There is our identity as distance heroes, an urge to brag, wear the T-shirt, show the trophy. Ego is in our plans. It underwrites our mistakes. Humiliation is the severe bending of the green stick of our ego. The support is gone, momentum delayed. We hang in a seemingly motionless nowhere, without plans, with nothing to boast of. Time and distance are suddenly much larger than we are. We can still move ahead. We can finish the race, but we must find something deeper, stronger, and more within ourselves than ego to do so.

One does not have to be a runner to know the posture of humiliation. The head hangs. Shoulders sag forward as if to hide the head. The hands curl dismally into the body. The long legs shorten with shame. The tail crawls between the legs and dies, but since we have no tail, our rear end pokes out hopelessly seeking one. This is a wonderful posture for humiliation, but a lousy way to move forward. If you want to enjoy the humiliation for a while go ahead, but if you want to get going, lift the head, pull the shoulders back, involve the arms, lengthen the stride, wag the tail and let it push you along.

Humiliation, like mountains and bad weather, should be prepared for. For some, it comes boldly and expansively in their first ultra. Others can escape with only faint tastes as they hurry through several great efforts in a row. Experienced ultrarunners say things such as "The worst that can happen is...." or, "The time limit is...." or, "All I have to do if I am in trouble is...." or, "I don't care if I am last as long as I finish." See that a goal of a race is to experience time as well as distance. Think in miles per hour as well as minutes per mile. Get rid of the idea that there is a hurry to finish or the need to have time to enjoy yourself after the race (you probably won't anyway). Remember, a slow race is easier to recover from. Pace your psychic and mental energy as well as your physical, to have good thoughts left for the low points. If you feel humiliation coming on, let a little and yield one place or a few minutes rather than sink into oblivion. Save energy for night, which is humiliation's sister. Plan to appreciate the scenery. Plan to enjoy all the humiliation given you.

Humiliation is humility. Humility and compassion are the two most saintly qualities. Compassion for one's self is the essence of humility. I think we run these things for a lot more than national rankings. We seek to discover ourselves. We want to find the emotions and truths denied to us by daily routines. The distances we run are humiliating. In many ways we look for humility in a world where "the individual" has come to mean me-ism and greed, where society is allowed to exist as group against group. Active humility is the clearest looking glass the world offers. Perhaps it explains the quietly compassionate tolerance of many distance runners, and explains our calm. Perhaps it explains our search for a larger feeling beyond the quick amusements advertised. This is a sport that honors finishers, that honors *every* finisher. We don't rate knowledge higher than humiliation.

Ultrarunning pioneer Ted Corbitt and multi-day herald Don Choi were as noted for their humility as for their achievements. I'm sure there are examples wherever you run. Simply running a lot of races or very long ones does not guarantee humility. The great New Zealand adventurer Siegfried Bauer was not usually considered humble. His strategy—to always run and have efficient sleep stops—and professional attitude tended to separate him from any prolonged humiliation. There are runners (often successful) who must either run well or quit. It is too bad to let expectations get in the way of experience and the wonderful camaraderie of fading through the field and meeting everyone. Running well does not exclude humiliation. Yiannis Kouros is a humble runner who clearly shows signs of humiliation during his record-breaking efforts. He just has the unusual ability to convert it to better uses. Ann Trason has suffered some real pits of humility, agony, and anguish, yet she does not give up her spirit or her lead. In humiliation there is always light. There are ladders and tunnels out. They lead to triumph.

Running a 100-Mile?
Leave Your Aggression at Home
by Dan Lindstrom

I first became interested in personality characteristics of distance runners as a result of my participation in the Western States 100 Mile. I wanted to find out if there were any personality differences between race finishers and non-finishers. I strained a groin muscle in the race and was forced to withdraw at the 86-mile mark. I realized then, that in order to finish the race, the strength of my personality and will to endure must be equal to or stronger than physiological demands of running the Western States. After that failure I continued in my quest to finish the Western States. In later years, I completed the race in less than 30 hours, but my own inability to finish that first race still haunted me. I kept asking myself. "Why couldn't I finish the race?" I was in better physical condition that year, ten pounds lighter, and I had faster 50 and 100-mile times. Consequently, I decided to study some personality characteristics of runners who participated in the Western States.

I sent a background questionnaire to all male participants between the ages of 38 and 46, who had trained an average of at least 62 miles per week for at least six months before the race. Competitors who took part in the study were divided into two groups: finishers (30 runners) and non-finishers (16 runners).

Reviewing the background questionnaire, I found that runners who finished the race ran significantly more training runs of at least 20 miles compared to runners who failed. Finishers' training patterns enabled them to be better prepared to endure prolonged physical exertion. Their physiological responses to exercise, along with the adaptation of their individual personality characteristics, were better suited to cope with severe stress encountered in the race.

As might be expected, I found differences in mood states that differentiated finishers from non-finishers. Non-finishers scored higher than finishers on post-race mood states of anger and depression. Generally, runners are extremely focused going into this race, to the point where it almost becomes an obsession. It stands to reason that non-finishers would have elevated anger and depression post-race scores. Non-finishers had lower post-race vigor scores than did finishers. Reduction in vigor level was the result of interaction between non-finishers not feeling good about failing to finish and their own low energy levels.

Differences in personality traits were also found that distinguished finishers from non-finishers. High levels of aggression and exhibition were more common in non-finishers than finishers. I found a relationship between the aggressiveness and exhibitionism of non-finishers and the fact that they did not finish. Non-finishers may have pent-up anger that is expressed through their starting out too quickly. Yet by starting fast, non-finishers also satisfied their urge to be the centers of attention. High levels of aggression and exhibition appear to contribute to their failure to complete the race. Starting out too fast in this race is cited by past competitors as one of the main reasons for the high dropout rate (up to 50 percent in some years) at Western States. Runners who start out too quickly tend to crash and burn later in the race. These runners choose to ignore how their bodies are performing. When there is a physical problem, they deny what is happening to them until it is too late. Consequently, a severe breakdown may occur, which can result in runners failing to finish.

According to race organizers, the Western States does not really "begin" until the 62-mile mark at Foresthill. Since most runners are running in the dark from Foresthill to the finish in Auburn it is critical to set an appropriate pace during daylight hours so there is enough reserve energy to negotiate the slower final leg of the race where visibility is limited to a narrow beam of light. Finishers may have a more realistic approach as to what it takes to finish the Western States.

The study concluded that runners have a selected personality advantage if they can effectively deal with their anger and are more reserved than exhibitionists. Finishers were characterized as being more passive and introverted than non-finishers. The identification of these characteristics may aid coaches in training athletes to be successful in ultra endurance sports and help ultrarunners acquire the desirable characteristics required of the sport.

Cheaters

by Gary Cantrell

The race had just concluded and various runners sat about the headquarters drinking beer and exchanging "war stories." The important issues of the day seemed to be the outstanding race put on by the race committee and the dominating performance of the winner.

Unfortunately for the race organizers, their enjoyment of a job well done was soon marred by controversy. A scan of the lap times revealed some times more impossible than unlikely, and the sixth-place finisher was, after much discussion and soul searching, disqualified. The situation deteriorated, as the runner in question vehemently denied any wrongdoing and the committee was faced with either accepting a performance apparently aided by cheating or disqualifying a possibly stupendous effort. Since the eight laps were not equal in length, here were his lap times in terms of average pace per mile: lap one: 8:08; lap two: 7:57; lap three: 8:15; lap four: 9:02; lap five: 9:47; lap six: 7:43; lap seven 5:32; lap eight: 9:13.

The 7:43 pace on lap six would have raised eyebrows coming as it did after 32 miles in a typical slowing pattern. But the 5:32 pace on the seventh lap equates to a 34:22 10-km; this runner's personal best for that distance was more than 41 minutes.

So unyielding was the runner's defense of his performance, attributed to yoga and mind control, that the lap times, by themselves, were not what led to his disqualification. Ultimately, it was due to the fact that not one runner in a field of veterans could report having seen anyone pass them at sub-six minute pace during the race. During the seventh lap, he would have passed about 30 runners.

Sadly, this is not an isolated case. Cheating has become one of road racing's hottest topics. Rosie Ruiz shocked us all with her unusual "race-winning" technique in the Boston Marathon, but her story has now become too familiar. A runner logs an outstanding performance and receives initial acclaim; then facts come out that lead to doubts about the time and the runner denies any wrongdoing. The performance is disqualified due to incontrovertible evidence, but the runner stands fast, even threatens legal action. Ultimately, everyone loses.

While this type of cheating has received the most attention, it is only one kind of dishonest performance and actually the least damaging to the sport. To begin with, the performance is generally not believable. Before the cheering ends, questions are being raised and inevitably, no matter how steadfast the runner's stand, his or her claims are discredited. In the one noteworthy case where the athlete was indeed as good as his surprising time indicated, Yiannis Kouros proved his ability, and no one was happier to be shown wrong than those of us who questioned that initial Spartathlon race.

Another type of cheater has plagued the ultrarunning world—fraudulent runners. Never mind the fantastic amount of publicity that one particular non-ultra runner has generated. Beyond the undeserved public acclaim as a world record holder and "most revered ultrarunner of our time," the real tragedy is his ability to generate funds. Perhaps the only man in America making a substantial income for his ultrarunning has never run an ultra. What bitter irony, since the lack of funds and sponsors severely limits our ability to put on major events. Not only are potential funds pulled away from our sport, a sponsor once burned is unlikely to respond to legitimate requests.

The third type of cheater is the worst threat to us all. The first group always gets caught. They do not make their performance believable with a better thought out plan of cheating. Whatever leads to the actions they take is beyond our understanding. Some powerful internal pressure must exist to make the end result worth such a cost. The second group avoids us. Regardless of their actions, they only affect us indirectly. However, the third group is more insidious. We really don't know who they are, because these are the runners who arrive well prepared to cheat. With small fields and sprawling courses, most ultras are easy prey for those willing to sacrifice self-respect for the respect of others.

No matter how insignificant our sport is, some motivation exists for people to cheat. We know because it happens. For some, only records and wins can satisfy the hunger for success. For a few of those, the hunger is satisfied no matter how the result is achieved. As painful as it is, race directors must now acknowledge the possibility and make plans to catch cheaters.

We can no longer hide behind the popular myth that cheating is a special province of foreigners whose cultures consider fair whatever can be gotten away with. One look at the list of colleges sanctioned for athletics violations in any given year provides clue as to what Americans actually consider fair. We cannot afford the luxury of entrusting our sport to the integrity of the participants. At least one legitimate ultrarunner has been caught course-cutting. How many (or few) have not been caught remains a matter of conjecture. The fact is that such incidents create more, and longer-lasting, bad feelings than all the good feelings generated by a first-class event. However painful the implicit distrust, we must safeguard our races against the dishonest competitor, or risk losing the fun that makes the races worthwhile.

The Back of the Packer: It's a Different Event

by Bill Demestihas

At 4:30 a.m. I was tired and sleepy. People at the aid stations would ask, "How you doin'?" and all I could think to say was, "I wish this would be over soon." These words exemplify what it really feels like 90 miles into a 100-mile run for us "Back of the Packers."

In all the issues of *UltraRunning* magazine I have read, the challenge experienced by those of us who run as "Back of the Packers" has not been fully explored. It is a very different race for us than for the winners or even the 24-hour finishers. What is also very different is the way we train.

I have read *UltraRunning* magazine for several years, and have been running ultras for years. I have pored over every issue, and have read every article about how to train for and run an ultra. While I believe that there is some important message in each article, there is a big difference between the runners/authors and me.

There are two types of runners who offer advice to novice ultrarunners. One category of runner/author talks about the relaxed training regimen. This training plan would have you not run more than 15 to 18 miles in your long runs and not more than 40 in a week. The author continues by telling you that you should stop and smell the roses and admire the scenery along the run, that the run is to be seen as a long walk in the country and not the incredible challenge that you thought it was. You then learn at the end of the article that the author has been running ultras for ten years, and runs a three-hour marathon, a 21-hour 100-mile, and has won numerous running events. Sorry, but that does not coincide with either my experience or my skill level.

The other category of runner/author is one who believes in the adage "no pain, no gain." This author describes a running regimen that begins four months before a race and includes two runs a day, 70 to 90 miles per week, at an average pace of about a seven and a half to eight minutes-per-mile for regular runs. Also included in this regimen is cross-training weight work and a diet that a full-time chef would be challenged to prepare on a daily basis. Get real, guys!

Like most of the runners, I work. I try to run five days a week, usually beginning at 4:30 to 5:00 a.m. before I go to work, and before 4:00 a.m. on Saturday for my long run. I could not run more than that without jeopardizing my job, my health, and my marriage. The most I have run in any week is 54 miles, 25 miles of that on a Saturday. This is the reality for many ultrarunners. We love to run and we enjoy the races, especially the company of other ultrarunners, but most of us are not three-hour marathoners, nor do we have unlimited time to train.

For Back of the Packers, the race is not about speed or beating other runners. We are obviously not trying to win the race; we are just trying to survive the course and the maximum time limit. We know we are going to be out there running for a long time. Couple that with the anxiety of not making a cut-off time or other fears we create for ourselves, like being eaten by a wild animal while running in the middle of the night, and you begin to get a feel for our experience.

There should be an appreciation for anyone who will knowingly enter a race that they acknowledge will not end for them until sometime in the late morning of the next day. I certainly appreciate crews that are willing to stay up and patiently watch over their runners as they painfully trudge on mile after mile, hour after hour. It's amazing to me that crews are able to keep their enthusiasm and good cheer long after most are exhausted and wishing they were in bed, asleep.

The people who work aid stations, bless their hearts, are almost without fail wonderful and always try to be helpful, cheerful and supportive. However, after twenty-something hours at an aid station, we often find these dedicated workers looking and feeling almost as tired as we are. It is unfortunate, but when you are at the tail end of the pack you sometimes get the tail end of their enthusiasm. At many aid stations food is gone, or at least in short supply. Supportive words are still there from race personnel, but as one might suspect, somewhat subdued by 3:00 a.m.

A Back of the Packer runs all night and then some. We are exhausted and wishing for the sun to rise so we can see again without a flashlight. The light of the morning sun is what we are waiting for. We begin to think of the first rays of the sun in mystical proportions and know that it will be the most glorious event of the decade. These thoughts begin to take form about two hours after sunset and build in anticipation for several hours.

During those dark lonely hours, I keep saying to myself, "If I make it to see the sun, I will make it." That sun, however, does take its sweet time rising. You sometimes imagine you see those first glorious rays of light, only to have your hopes dashed by the lights of a car coming over a rise.

The finish is the thing we most anticipate and pray for. When we do finish, it is the most wonderful, powerful feeling you can imagine. I still remember seeing my disbelieving brother's smile when he saw me coming into sight and the sound of his cheering me on in the last few hundred yards. I remember hearing the chatter of runners, equally as exhausted as me, giggling in delight to have the race finally over, still be in one piece, and glad to be walking. I do not really understand it, but somehow it makes it all seem worth it. I immediately began to recall parts of the race that I thought I might have run better; that just maybe I could have run a little faster or run an uphill instead of having walked. I even began to think of how I could run better or faster the next year. Then nature and a loving wife took hold, and before the hour was up, I was asleep for what would probably be ten hours, although not necessarily restful sleep. I vividly remember leg cramps that made me wake screaming.

After all the running, fatigue, anxiety and pain, the wonderful thing about time is that it will play tricks. I do not recall as well the pain and fatigue. I feel as much as I recall the great feeling of finishing the race. I do not recall how sleepy I felt at 25 hours as well as I do the warmth and camaraderie I felt for my crew and them for me. I do not recall the nausea I experienced as much as the look of admiration and pride I saw in my wife's and brother's eyes when I came running across the finish line.

When it is all over but the soreness, it really does feel as if it was worth the training, the sleeplessness, the fatigue, and the sacrifice. I will trust my own instincts for how much I should train, how many miles I will run per week, and at what pace I will run. While all the articles I read add to my understanding of the sport and the demands I might encounter, I cannot run someone else's run or train by someone else's methods. What I can do is listen to my body and listen to what it is trying to tell me. I can cherish and take good care of my wonderful friends who are willing to stay up all day and night to help me complete my race, and I can remember the love and warm feelings I got from everyone who helped me to get to and run those last few hundred yards. Most of all, I can be glad I survived it to tell the tale.

The Older Ultrarunner: A View from Over the Hill
by Pete Stringer

You've all heard this one before: a 65-year-old looks at a photograph of a local group, perhaps in his hometown newspaper. He recalls the event, then focuses on the strangely familiar features of the old gent right there in the middle. He squints a bit, blushing in increasing embarrassment from his slow take. He gulps. Tiny alarms going off now that there's full recognition. "My God! Can that wrinkled up old geezer right there amid those athletes possibly be me?" he cries in horror. "Mine own self?"

Ah, yes. 'Tis the sad truth: the black-and-white image reveals the world's all too correct perception. The once smooth face and rippling muscles of yesteryear live on only in the old warrior's memory. Perhaps this is not so sad, however. Perhaps it is even remarkable. For if it's a photo based on an actual endurance running event, where results, not style, count, the casual reader's initial perception can change, growing to real astonishment if he reads on. For while the camera was trying its best, the real story lies in the printed page below. Because geez, it seems that in many instances "the old guy" has somehow finished this very long race (100 miles? Can this really be?) in the upper half of the field!

Nowhere in sports is the joy of combat and actual participation allowed to ferment and prosper (well, at least stick around) and be so doggoned welcomed, as in our beloved sport of ultrarunning. Those explosive herky-jerky muscles that once allowed us to sprint so fast and jump so high have long since gone and split the party, plumb vanished. But the slow-twitches, the chuggers, they're a more relaxed, laid-back lot. They have lasting power. Give us a goal line that stretches out to the horizon and those repetitive, reliable old pistons seem to still get the job done. Quite nicely, in fact. And they have so darn much fun doing it.

Like any old machine, you gotta check the oil often (hydrate!), grease her up (glucosomine the joints), and keep it out of the cold (remember the thermals). Regular tune-ups at the doc's office help too. Adjusting prescriptions becomes a fine art. Gradual, incremental, and steady become the oft-used mantras of our daily lexicon. And always and forever, the motor…the cardio pusher…with a little loving care the damn thing still works, too good an instrument to retire just yet. A bit less lard around the belly might help the ticker on its daily rounds. The diet may need a little more attention to detail, for no longer can the old guy expect to roll out of bed after a night on the town and be ready to race as soon as he laces up the sneakers. That's history. Just yesterday was spent wandering the laxative aisle at the CVS, and one does not transpose that anxious senior citizen to a supple athlete with an easy twitch of the wand. Perhaps a long-range stealth plan, best devised by a canny old codger with miles of experience, works best.

Most regular readers are well aware of the exploits of the vanguard of the over-60 set: the incredible Ted Corbitt, Helen Klein, Dick Opsahl, Ephraim Romesburg, Ed Williams, Stuart Nelson, Ray Piva, Karsten Solheim, Richard Busa, Carol LaPlant, Roy Pirrung, and way too many others to mention. (In truth, the last two are about to become 60, but too impressive to leave off the list). Just recently, the Grand Slam completed in September added yet another sexagenarian to its most exclusive list: 62-year-old Gary Knipling. And surely, any current notation of extraordinary older ultrarunners' accomplishments must include the astonishing Hans-Dieter Weisshaar, who, depending on when this comes to print, nears his 100th 100-miler. (That is not a misprint!)

However, while paying respect to the great talents of the leaders of the senior set, this column would also like to acknowledge the great majority of veterans who so love the sport that they doggedly run on, refusing to depart when there is still the slimmest of chances to complete the course. The challenge becomes entirely different once one enters the freefall that is associated with life as an athlete past age 60. Please believe me on this one. If you ain't been there, you don't know what I'm talkin' about.

Somehow my vision of 75-year-old Dan Baglione fruitlessly slugging it out at The Barkley (yeah, that very walk in the park) this past spring comes to the forefront of my heroes of the moment. Does this man love ultrarunning? His shining shield fairly gleams in the sun! It makes me want to try harder. I need this kind of inspiration—Old Don Quixote tilting at the friggin' windmill.

Just last month I wrote about my ineffectual attempt to conquer Leadville, ruminating about how "smart" it would be to ever try the race again. My history there, a woeful one in six, effectively mirrors the odds of my age group's annual percentage of entrants-versus-finishing success.

But doesn't that actually say something more important? Like truly loving something? Like hanging in there when something's so dear and sweet we want the dance to last forever? That a group with such daunting odds never allow that silly narrow window to slide shut just because the challenge appears so formidable? Isn't that the epitome of flying-in-your-face cool? That there were more than 30 hoary old souls lined up at 4:00 a.m. on that Colorado morning knowing this history, yet just delighted to cross the starting line to try? Well, that warms my heart, and makes me proud to say these are my people, the very motley crew I want to hang with. Screw the odds. Prudence and wisdom can be overrated.

Why Don't More Young Runners Run Ultras?

by Tony Krupicka

In Fyodor Dostoyevsky's classic tome *The Brothers Karamazov*, one of the fundamental characters—Ivan Karamazov—is confronted in a feverish vision by an apparition who claims to be the Devil. Ivan's guilt-ridden nervous breakdown is caused by realizing his complicit role in the central murder of the novel, and the supposed Devil proceeds to taunt and torment Ivan with unsettling arguments that question some of Ivan's most deep-seated beliefs. This inquisition shakes Ivan to his core, but the Devil's discourse allows Ivan to ultimately emerge from the experience with a better understanding of himself and the ways in which he should engage the world.

Although all human beings are confronted with a dizzying number of choices on a weekly—even daily—basis, a member of the "twenty-something" age-group is arguably more often faced with making a decision that will ultimately affect a great influence over the lifestyle or habits that he or she will end up developing and then maintaining for the rest of his or her life. Many of the decisions that a person of this age makes simple carry a great deal of existential "weight," and the consequences of many of these choices tend to stick.

Accordingly, one of the myriad choices that may confront a *runner* of this age is deciding exactly what direction he wants his or her running to take now that he or she is no longer running and/or competing under the auspices of a high school or collegiate cross country or track program.

A typical runner who emerges from either the secondary or collegiate running ranks would likely have zero experience with ultrarunning and very little experience with trail running. Confronted with this reality, it is much less of a risk—much more within one's given comfort zone—to confine oneself to the relative tameness and general familiarity that road running and racing provides, when compared with the domesticated environs of a groomed cross-country course or rubberized track that has provided the arena for any battles of self-realization thus far in the young runner's life. If one has spent the past five or so years trying to run five kilometers as quickly as possible, it is just simply a lot easier to transition onto the paved roads, on which one has a legitimate shot at achieving continued satisfaction from running fast, than it is to foray into the unknown realm of ultrarunning, trails, and a markedly longer, slower pace.

However, if a young runner does want to enter the arena of ultrarunning, there is a decided change in running attitude that one would have to undergo (assuming that a 20-year-old has any conventional experience in competitive running). This country has no ultrarunning or trail running "leagues" for adolescents to join as an alternative to a local soccer team (this, actually, is probably a good thing, Tarahumaras and East Africans notwithstanding), no accolades to be awarded for winning a nonexistent secondary school city championship of running all day, no scholarships offered at the collegiate level for possessing the ability to run through the night while navigating a precipitous mountain trail, and finally—once out of college—virtually no prize money for getting to the end of that mountain trail quicker than the next runner. Confronting such a stark contrast between road or track running and ultrarunning is daunting. Although it seems that the path of ultrarunning would appeal to humans' craving for variety (it's new! different! unknown!), it seems that many are actually surprisingly reluctant when it comes to change—especially change that offers no monetary compensation.

It seems the main issue is that—like when the Devil confronts Ivan—the decision regarding whether to become an ultrarunner or not is really a question about the way in which one is willing to engage the world; and this can be a gnarly, distressing, and even off-putting quandary. Ultrarunning is a sometimes scary, often irrational activity and it represents an unknown frontier that can only be authentically explored by the individual and his or her internal psyche. In ultrarunning, internal demons are confronted alone and internal battles of will are fought without the typical ammunition of reason and logic. There is simply no logical reason to force one's being through the territories of suffering and fatigue encountered in ultramarathons that could so easily be abated by a DNF—or better yet, a DNS. One can never know how he or she will react to the major metabolic systems failure or inordinate fatigue that has been known to occur on the far side of the marathon distance without actually getting out there and *experiencing* it. The self-knowledge, constitution, and resolve necessary to be successful in ultrarunning is often only found in a runner sufficiently wizened by the general ups and downs of having achieved middle age. Apparently, the task of locomoting all day and night, over and through mountain passes and canyons—when every fiber in your being is pleading for you to stop, take a rest, quit—would not readily lend itself to the fancy-free caprice and whim of an impatient, instant-gratification-raised youngster.

The rewards in ultrarunning are largely of an internal, spiritual nature rather than of an external, material variety, and it seems to be the rare twenty-something that is readily equipped—both mentally and physically—to set about the grueling, heart-rending, but ultimately spectacularly satisfying task of realizing these rewards. What ultrarunning lacks in fanfare and material benefits, however, I believe it more than compensates for with untold unquantifiable remunerations of the character-building, camaraderie, and self-realizing variety. By nature, these awards are more difficult for a younger person to value to any meaningful extent.

As a young ultrarunner myself—especially a particularly inexperienced one—it might seem strange, or at least to ring a bit hollow, for me to be making such grand, sweeping generalizations about an entire generation's motivations—or lack thereof—for competing in ultras. However, I suppose I am placing stock in the assumption that my very youth might offer a germane viewpoint, and that my own, albeit limited, experiences in the ultrarunning universe have stirred something in me that courses deeper than the largely typical and uninspiring experience I had as a young track and road athlete.

Trail running in general—and ultrarunning in particular—provides an opportunity for me to tap into a seemingly more pure, stripped down, primal existence as a human being that is largely unavailable in the banality of my daily engagements as a usual member of modern society. This unfettered state of being seems to only truly come into existence after several miles, even hours, out on the mountain trails. Of course, ultrarunning is not the only path to feeling connected and grounded, but, for me, it is a tremendous means for exploring my outer limits and for realizing that these limits are primarily a consequence of my inner proclivities and determinations. By having my senses flayed and refined—by countless twists and interminable turns of endless single-track—to a point where nothing else matters but getting to the top of the mountain pass or to the next aid station, or of coaxing more long-chain maltodextrin down my gullet or some sweet H_2O past my lips, I am finally able to quit worrying about everything that is trivial and that simply does not matter for survival and instead focus on those elements of my constitution that are undeniably mandatory for an authentic existence. When I am out running on the trails I am transformed from cosmopolitan city-dweller to Neolithic hunter-gatherer. Without my daily forays into the wilderness I would be denying myself the opportunity to realize and fulfill one of man's most basic and necessary privileges: his capacity for irrational acts.

On its surface, running 50 or 100 miles in the mountains may not seem to have any rational reason, and really, may not even be a whole lot of fun. But to folks who might value actions by the standard of how logical and reasonable they are, I would ask that they ponder the exquisite advice that the Devil finally gives Ivan in *The Brother's Karamazov*:

If everything in the universe were sensible, nothing would happen. There would be no events...and there must be events. So against the grain I serve to...do what's irrational...For all their indisputable intelligence, men take this farce as something serious, and that is their tragedy. They suffer, of course...but then they live, they live a real life, not a fantastic one, for suffering is life. Without suffering what would be the pleasure of it? It would be transformed into an endless church service; it would be holy, but tedious.

Perhaps a lack of sufficient reason is why it is difficult to attract a younger generation to ultrarunning—a generation that, for the most part, is simply trying to get its collective feet on the ground by starting careers and/or a families. However, I am not personally in the pursuit of reason, nor tedium. Although certainly not reasonable, ultrarunning is—at least for me—indubitably *real*. It may not contain any logic or conventional wisdom, as defined by society at large, but I believe ultrarunning offers a chance at an authentic, fulfilling existence not available in the standard arena of life. As a young runner and human being, I can think of no greater reward—or "reason"—to at least give ultrarunning a charitable chance.

Psychological and Emotional Responses to Injury

by Kris Setnes

Runners are frequently asked, "Why run?" Ultrarunners are often questioned why they choose to run such long distances. "What motivates you to run 50 miles, 100 miles, or 24 or 48-hour runs?" the non-runner may inquire of the ultrarunner. In his numerous publications, Dr. George Sheehan seemed to have an eloquent manner of stating the psychological and spiritual aspects of running. In his 1992 book, *Running to Win*, Dr. Sheehan states, "My sport, running, is an individual thing. My opponent is myself. There is never a question of whether I want to run in the race. Only an injury would reduce me to being a spectator. So I seldom go to watch a race. It's too painful not to be part of it. The runner always wants to be in the race. Once a person enters a race, there is never again a question of watching other people have all the fun."

While running offers many reasons to continue to pursue this sport and lifestyle, every athlete, coach, and medical professional can verify that if you have been running long, hard, or far enough, you have most likely experienced some type of injury at one time or another. No single subject seems to concern—and often obsess—the runner more than injury. Injury seems to have little relevance until it hits personally, and for most runners, painfully. Regardless of ability, an injury can be devastating. For the elite runner, an injury signifies a loss of personal identity, and sometimes a livelihood. For the serious athlete, injury is often equated to losing a dear friend. A friend of ours who just started running recently referred to his first running injury as "having one of the best things that has ever come into his life suddenly taken away." You will never realize how much your running is cherished, and the many rewards you receive from running, until it is no longer yours.

Injuries heal eventually, but with injury we gain wisdom, personal strength, and often a renewed perspective on running. Coping with injury (or a debilitating illness) is one of the many aspects of running that shows us how running is a metaphor for life, including personal adversity. The injured runner often struggles to keep things in perspective at the time of injury; therefore, it seems important to devote this article to the psychological and emotional aspects of injury.

When an injury occurs, causing an abrupt cessation of the positive benefits, athletes may experience post-injury psychological and emotional disturbance. Some sports psychologists have suggested injured athletes progress through a grief cycle similar to that which is experienced by the terminally ill (Kuebler-Ross, 1969). The Kuebler-Ross and other "loss of health" models, however, were derived from patient populations very different from injured athletes. In the terminally ill "loss of health" model, psychiatrist Kuebler-Ross (1969) determined that people preparing for death experience stages of denial, anger, bargaining, depression, and acceptance. Many injured runners experience similar stages.

Until recently, there were few reports documenting the psychological and emotional effects of athletic injury. While research has shown that consistent running results in a number of psychological benefits, there has been little focus on what happens when the running routine is interrupted due to injury. In a recent study, a group of 30 "prevented runners," who were unable to run for two weeks, compared their responses to several inquiries to a group of "continuing runners," who were able to run without an interruption in their schedules. Prevented runners showed significantly more depression, anxiety, confusion, and lower self-esteem than did continuing runners. Deprivation of consistent running may have resulted in the withdrawal of a coping strategy for those who run for stress management and depend heavily on the psychological benefits of running.

Studies completed by Little (1969, 1979) and Morgan (1979) noted that excessive motivation and persistence with exercise by some athletes exists at the risk of physical trauma or re-injury. The significant depression and tension frequently experienced by injured athletes, when exercise is terminated even temporarily, provides some understanding of why other injured athletes persist with their exercise or sport despite medical consequences. Many ultrarunners have chosen to withstand the physical discomfort of continuing running in the presence of injury to the emotional discomfort of depression and tension that accompany not being able to run. In another study on the emotional responses of athletes to injury (Smith, Scott, O'Fallon, 1990), the data measured were the athletes' perceptions of the severity of the injury, the perceived progress being made, and, subsequently, the emotional responses experienced. The athletes' perceptions of the severity of the injury and their perceived rate of recovery seemed to influence their emotional responses. The most severely injured athletes not only had a greater mood disturbance than the other athletes on the initial examination; they also failed to show significant improvement on the six mood scales (tension, depression, anger, vigor, fatigue and confusion) until one month after the injury. A limitation of this study was that no pre-injury emotional profiles were available on the injured athletes.

Tim Noakes, author of *The Lore of Running*, believes that regardless of personality types, runners will go through typical patterns of response to an injury. At first, Noakes reports, the runner will simply deny the possibility of injury. When the injury can no longer be denied, the athlete may become enraged and blame either his or her doctor, his or her spouse, or some third party. Occasionally, runners will blame their bodies for betraying them and may even subject their bodies to further abuse. Depression sets in, once denial and anger no longer work. Noakes writes, "Finally, after some months, the runner learns to accept their injuries and to modify their ambitions to accommodate the inadequacies of the mortal body. When this occurs, the runner is more likely to be over the injuries." Noakes goes on to describe how the runner's ambitions will again rise, the desire to do more will increase again, and the athlete will experience the neurotic need to train more to achieve greater running ambitions. This can be a very crucial and potentially dangerous period of time due to the chance of potential re-injury if the runner attempts to return to running too soon.

It is normal for an injured runner to feel down and experience such feelings of frustration, tension, and anger. The depression is usually proportionate to the severity of the injury, and usually resolves as the runner recovers. If you are truly invested in your sport (which most ultrarunners are), you can start by trying to put the injury and the sport into perspective. This may mean that you focus on the number of years that you can continue to participate in the sport once the injury has healed. The longer you deny or prolong the necessary need for rehabilitation and down time, the longer the time until you may experience that flow and ease of being a runner.

Down time can be a good opportunity to develop other skills and interests that may have been sacrificed to run long distances. Down time can allow you to spend more time with the friends, family, and other non-running activities that are often neglected during high-mileage days, intense training weeks, and periods of numerous races. You may also want to use this time to develop mentally as far as the sport is concerned. This can be done by reading about running, mental training, cross-training, nutrition, and studying the biomechanical aspects of running. Learn to relax, conjure up positive mental images and set realistic goals; all are good uses of down time. Runners and athletes who stay positive, relaxed, and goal-oriented tend to progress faster and have a better, quicker recovery. Putting as much time and energy into rehabilitation and recovery as we do into our training and racing will allow for a speedier return to running.

Although accepting injury is one of the great challenges of a dedicated ultrarunner, it is necessary to address the issue if and when the injury occurs. When either my husband or I have been injured, we too would go through the trauma and depressions of not being able to run. Running was too important to our lives not to be able to participate. "Playing the game" became the number one goal. Getting to the starting line healthy is more important than any other aspect of this game. It comes before winning or setting a personal best. Without it you are destined for a life of frustration as a runner first, and quite possibly a person second.

It is important for runners to remember that they did not become ultrarunners overnight. Endurance from running is acquired over time. Likewise, to lose the ability to run distances does not occur overnight. The body, and perhaps more importantly, the mind, has the ability to retain what it has learned. Learn to deal with injuries, first by understanding the causes, and secondly by being patient, being able to see the bigger picture. If you find the root cause of the injury (quite often the most difficult part), chart a path back to recovery. This will require discipline on your part, for most injuries that tend to linger or plague the runner, and because he or she tends to try to come back too quickly. If you accept your injury and are able to learn from it, you have taken the first step to being able to play this game of ours for many years to come.

24 Hours — A Run

by Jon Vonhof

The thin white lines are unending: straight gives way to curve, curve to straight, straight, curve, straight, curve, the cycle continues...seemingly forever. The surface of the tartan track is smooth and monotonous, each approaching yard the same as the one just past, one of 440, then beginning again...400 times and more. The people, their faces, the field, the markers, the status board, the aid tables, all the other elements of my 24-hour world become memorized, silent and unchanging. Sounds, although heard, are not retained, save for the dull tick of the Chronomix clock and the soft strike of my shoes. Movements, although seen, are not remembered, save for the changing numbers on the Chronomix face... hours...minutes...seconds.

Four-hundred times you search out that one special face...your lap counter... waiting for the nod, the raised hand, some word of encouragement some form of acknowledgment from this vital person...that this lap is counted; one more toward your goal...toward 100 miles. This person is a part of you, that remembers and tells you when to walk, when to run, if your pace is consistent, how far you have come...and have yet to go, since you, yourself, cannot remember...your lap counter remembers for you...thanks.

Thoughts...24 straight hours...time to think, thinking in phrases, one liners, circles, sometimes remembering, mostly forgetting...sometimes, a lot of times, just drawing a blank. Recurring thoughts? Many come and go...this fund-raiser... each lap benefits others, the challenges: physical and mental...which is the hardest? What is my body capable of? How hard? How fast? How long? A new personal record? Will my mind overrule a tired body? Satisfaction, a first 24-hour. A first 100-miler: the physical feelings: general and specific...overall feeling good...would love ice cream, baked potato...but reality dictates a banana; specific: seem to go through stages, tired legs, sore feet, tightness, family, friends, job. There is a lot to think about, and yet sometimes there is nothing...nothing is sometimes easier.

Again you stretch forth your hand...to grasp the water bottle, banana, cookie, some form of nourishment...hoping for energy, when you have none left. Your handlers care for you...replenish you...thanks.

Another lap and it's time for a short break, ten minutes in each two-hour period...squeeze the skin-lube tube coating my feet, slide searching fingers along the skin...are the blisters bigger? New ones? Reach for new socks. My mind queries the body...Chafing? Binding? Warm? Cold? A change of shorts? Shirt? Shoes? I ease my tired body from the chair, catch the eye of my lap counter...my eyes say "back on the track."

Spectators, the ever-present cheering force; they too care for us...a wave, a shout of encouragement, a smile, sometimes understanding our motives, sometimes not, but without them there is a void...for coming by...for staying with us...thanks.

Time seems different...24 hours...lived to the fullest in the sport you love, all the time in training, the preparation is over, we began at 0:00:00...fresh and eager: at 24:00:00 we will stop...empty, tired and hurting. In between, time moves...the Chronomix records every second, each lap. The sun moves across the sky, giving warmth, sometimes too much, shadows lengthen, coolness sets in. Eight hours have quickly gone by, we've kept moving, time has been constant, thoughts consistent. The sun sets, and colors the sky, now the long hours begin, the moon rises...a pretty, full moon...your night's companion...soon, midnight, still ten long hours left, the hardest, in the cold quiet darkness, in our small tent city, the crews are silent... Time goes by slower now, and still you circle, another lap, and another. It is strange. While some sleep, with few running, time seems to stand still. It is a feeling; this is my time to talk to God...in the quiet. But the numbers on the clock continue to flip over, time is moving on...the sky lightens, joyfully I share in the sunrise, the warmth and light give renewal. Thanks, Lord, for your gift of beauty. Each 24-hour day can be lived but once...this is my way to live this day to the fullest.

Another bond of caring has grown....22 runners, encircling an oval track, seemingly captive to the thin white lines...we run, walk, eat, drink, living together... sharing our goals, humor, hurts...our love of running. For a few, records are possible. The rest of us hope for personal bests. Lap by lap, through the hours, we learn each other's footsteps, rhythms and patterns, During the long, dark, cold night, our number dwindles, overcome with fatigue, we become a patched-up team... blisters, cramps, leg or stomach problems; some with taped feet are resigned to walk, enduring to the end, others are sleeping, and a few are forced to withdraw... the efforts of the medical team have given us a few more hours...thanks. We runners all began fresh, carbo-loaded, and now are depleted, empty, running on adrenaline, so close to the end, to 100 miles, to 24 hours...we have touched each other, have a new respect for each other, we needed and have supported each other...thanks.

The Chronomix says it all...23:17:29; it has recorded time, now we reach inside, elated...one last lap, run on hurting, pained feet, forget the cramping muscles, grit our teeth, try to hold form, this lap is for us. Hear the song *Winners* over the public address system. Runners, lap counters, handlers, spectators, we all savor this moment together. Past the Chronomix again, 23:59:36, tape marks the final yards; 50...60...70...80....the whistle blows, we stop...scattered around the track, 24:00:00. Success, survival, a rich experience for me. 24 hours, 103 miles and 105 yards...bent over, hands on knees, I give thanks.

The thin white lines, the track with its magnetism, which has held us in its grasp now releases us...our world of 24 hours is over, but never forgotten.

Reflections on Ultrarunning and Religion
by David Phillips

The day before the Western States 100 Mile Endurance Run, many of us who were scheduled to run hiked from the lodge at Squaw Valley to the top of Emigrant Pass. Then, and even more so now, it seemed less like a hike and more like a religious procession. All of us followed a runner who was carrying a banner. We shared simple food and drink as we ascended and it was, as it is for many who approach the Eucharist, a time of both celebration and fear and trembling. When we arrived at the pass, we were reminded that we were the descendants of those who had begun the ascetic-like life required to participate in such an event. We were reminded of those who had gone before us, the "communion of the saints" if you please. Especially revered were those of the Donner party, many of whom had died crossing these very mountains. There was a reading and much talk about the possibility of human reflection. There was a time of silence; many stayed to extend that time of reflection.

Also, and most profoundly, we had been promised a conversion-like experience. Thirty-five pages of material sent to runners before the race concluded with the following quotation by Bernard DeVoto. "What they had done, what they had seen, heard, felt, feared—the places, the sounds, the colors, the cold, the darkness, the emptiness, the bleakness, the beauty. 'Til they died, this stream of memory would set them apart, if imperceptibly to everyone but themselves, from everyone else. For they had crossed the mountain."

A friend who had run Western States the year before said that Emigrant Pass was so beautiful as the sun rose that he wanted to set up a tent and stay there. Of course, those who climbed the mountain with Jesus, and many others seeking a religious experience, have had the same thought.

Is there a religious nature to our ultrarunning, or is this just the overactive imagination of a clergy runner? As I talk with and read what other runners write, I sense that many are searching for meaning and self-understanding. Others feel a oneness with nature or are striving to live more fully and wholesomely. These are worthy goals of a religious person.

The marriage of sport and religion has always been a surprising and difficult one. Ancient Greeks could hardly get together without games being contested and sacrifices being made. Puritans dismissed sport as frivolous and irreligious. The Fellowship of Christian Athletes and other such organizations have baptized a sports persona who is a mixture of Jesus, Superman, and Uncle Sam. By the way, what is it that those professional football players are praying about in the closing seconds of the playoffs and the Super Bowl?

My desire is not to make fun of the religion of another person. God knows there is too much of that. What I do want to say is that, for me, there is something missing in these expressions of religious piety. More positively, I believe that there is something fundamentally religious about our sport which, though profoundly difficult to articulate, is felt by many of us.

My athletic journey has taken me from Little League baseball to ultrarunning with stops along the way for most of the traditional sports and a few of the nontraditional ones. My most recognized successes were as a collegiate hammer thrower and racquetball pro, and being the last official finisher at the Western States 100 Mile. Athletics have always been such an important part of my life that saying that athletics were like life or that they taught important lessons about life never seemed to be saying enough. However, athletics, like certain other physical activities, always seemed to lose something when discussed or analyzed.

How pleased I was when I read the following in Michael Novak's *The Joy of Sports*: "Sports flow outward into action from a deep natural impulse that is radically religious: an impulse for freedom, respect for ritual limits, zest for symbolic living, and a longing for perfection. There are many ways to express this radical impulse by the asceticism and dedication of preparation; by a sense of respect for the mysteries of one's own body and soul and for the powers not in one's control; by the sense of awe for the place and time of competition; by a sense of fate; by a felt sense of comradeship and destiny; by a sense of participation in the rhythms and tides of nature itself." How Novak has so well articulated what underlies ultrarunning for me is a mystery in that he is most interested in big money, spectator sports. Nevertheless, I am indebted to him.

"Asceticism and dedication." My many solo runs around the borough of Manhattan in preparation for the Western States—usually started before 4:00 a.m.—did for me what early morning prayers and meditation have done for religious ascetics through the centuries. "Mysteries of body and soul." Who can explain the renewed strength, physical and spiritual, that overcomes runners as they watch the sun rise a second time even though there are "miles to go before we rest." "Fate and powers not in one's control." This is the stuff of ultra folklore. A single rock over which 100 runners mindlessly pass is where the race ends with a twisted ankle for the one hundred and first runner. Two inches of hail on Hope Pass at the Leadville 100 Mile was beautiful for the frontrunners, safely over the pass, but painful for those who had not yet crossed. Reread Novak's words slowly and, if you are like me, a flood of memories will return. Surely, this must be one ple of what Jesus called the "abundant life."

This is not the religion that most of us grew up with. The ultrarunning community is big enough that within it most religious traditions must be represented. Most of those traditions have not always held what I like to call, "the life of the body" in high esteem. St. Augustine, upon whose writings much of Christian theology is based, is well known for phrases such as "the slimy desires of the flesh." Puritans, who have had a huge influence not only on Protestants but all Americans, were much more interested in work than play. John Calvin wrote that no one in this earthly prison of a body has sufficient strength to press on with due eagerness, and weakness so weighs down the greater number that, with wavering and limping and even creeping along the ground, they move at a feeble rate. That wavering, limping and creeping along the ground at a feeble rate does remind me of my friend Bob on Hope Pass at Leadville (he was about seven miles ahead of me), but I'm not sure that is what the good doctor from Geneva had in mind. I suspect that neither the early church fathers, nor those who molded the predominantly religious attitudes in the U.S., would be enthusiastic or even begin to understand the celebration of the flesh, of the body and spirit, that has a grip on so many ultrarunners.

Happily, there are other interpretations of religious teachings. A scholar of the Hebrew scriptures, which of course Christians recognize as authoritative, summarized the Jewish tradition's attitude toward the body as this: "The soul and body are so intimately united that a distinction cannot be made between them. They are more than united: the body is the soul in its outward form." St. John tells us, "The Word became flesh and dwelt among us, full of grace and truth." I would suggest that the fundamentally religious nature of ultrarunning is that flesh becomes a witness to the potential of human endeavor and the splendors of the physical world.

In 1944, Pierre Elliot Trudeau, who would later become Prime Minister of Canada, published an article in the French language journal, *Jeunesse Etudiante Catholique*. Happily, it was reprinted in English in *Wilderness Canada* (Borden, Spears, Clarke, Irwin and Co., Ltd. 1970) with the title, "Exhaustion and fulfillment: The Ascetic in a Canoe." In the journey of which he wrote, he and his friends were obliged, on the pain of death, to do more than 1,000 miles by canoe from Montreal to Hudson Bay. I count him worthy of quotation here. In fact, it is such an insightful article I will quote it at length:

"I do not know how to instill a taste for adventure in those who have not acquired it, and yet there are those who suddenly 'tear themselves away' from their comfortable existence and, using the energy of their bodies as an example to their brains, apply themselves to the discovery of unsuspected pleasures and places.

"What is essential at the beginning is the resolve to reach the saturation point. Ideally, the trip should end only when the members are making no forward progress within themselves. They should not be fooled though by a period of boredom, weariness or disgust; that is not the end, but the last obstacle before it. Let saturation be serene.

"For it is condition of such a trip that you entrust yourself, stripped of all worldly goods. To remove all the useless material baggage from a man's heritage is, at the same time, to free his mind from petty preoccupations, calculations, and memories.

"Nevertheless, he will have returned a more ardent believer from a time when religion, like everything else, became simple. The impossibility of scandal creates a new morality, and prayer becomes a part of everyday affairs."

I believe every idea that Trudeau has presented except that of the "impossibility of scandal." While I think that sport has occupied an honored place in virtually every society because it is fundamentally "good," it seems completely evident that sport, like everything else, is corruptible. I would like to think that we have not seen such corruption in ultrarunning because it is, and always will be, a morally superior sport. Better yet, I would like to think that ultrarunners themselves are morally superior. Is this true? The volunteers might be, but not the rest of us. I think we have not had the problems that other sports have because our sport is so young. I have some fears when I read about those who seek to make ultrarunning an Olympic event or about so-called world championships. I don't want our sport to become what the modern Olympics have become in little more than a century of existence.

Former Western States race director Norm Klein noted the irony in the happiness and goodwill that are so much a part of ultras and the lack of the same among professional athletes. I agree with him and am happy that he made such an observation, but this is not to say that our community is above reproach. Last year I saw a runner, who later finished the race, being physically pushed up Hope Pass by members of his crew. However, in a sporting world that is generally devoid of morality, and anything but a superficial religiosity, ultrarunning could be an example that there is "a more excellent way," as St. Paul said.

Both sport and religion in America are in need of rethinking, and maybe an out-and-out conversion. Sport and religion both fail to live up to their potential and high calling. Religious teachings about the body have been twisted out of shape to such an extent that many who love the life of the body feel out of place in traditional religious settings. Sport is consumed by love of money, arrogance, and nationalism. As the father of two children, I despair for them becoming involved in sports. Everyone needs the sweet taste of victory at least occasionally, but a too narrow definition of victory seems to require of many an unwholesome price.

Religion in America, and the places out of which our religious heritage grew, has always bean anti-body and, I would add, also very wordy. But it need not be that way. Despite what theologians have taken from Augustine, he recognized what many of us might consider doing. "If you find pleasure in bodily things, praise God for them, and direct your love to their maker, lest because of things that please you, you may displease him." (The *Confessions of St. Augustine*, Book 4, Chapter 12, Section 18.)

I would like to finish with a personal note. For my 40th birthday, my sister and her husband made it possible for me to run the American River 50 Mile in California. My brother-in-law ran with me for many miles, and then, on separating, I decided to run with a Walkman for the first time in a race. I guess that everyone who uses a Walkman has music they hope will provide enjoyment or diversion. I chose a tape of Robert Shaw directing his chorale and orchestra in selections from Handel's *Messiah*. If I had just run a little faster, I would have finished to Handel's musical interpretation of Isaiah:

"Every valley shall be lifted up, and every mountain shall be made low, and the rough made plain. And the glory of the Lord shall be revealed, and all flesh shall see it together, for the mouth of the Lord has spoken." Next time I will run faster.

Winners and Losers
by Gary Cantrell

There is only one winner; second place is just the first loser. Everyone who participates is a winner, just for trying. So which is it? Is it all about competition—or participation? Is ultrarunning a sport—or an activity? What is the true nature of this game we play? No matter which answer you choose, you are at least partially wrong. Ultrarunning has as many faces as there are runners.

There was a time, not so long ago, when ultrarunning was all about competition. Nearly everyone who took part was a serious, competitive athlete. Runners who became too old to contend found they no longer had a place in the sport, unless it was as a race organizer, crew, or volunteer. Times have changed. Today's ultrarunning community is peppered with runners too old or too slow to compete. Many runners collect vast numbers of finishes without ever trying to beat anyone. Others are fiercely competitive, but only with their friends, runners in their own age group, or themselves. While there are those who adhere to one or the other of the philosophies stated at the outset, most of us fall somewhere in between. Most important however, is the fact that if we are to survive over the long haul—both literally and figuratively—we must adapt as we go along.

For fast runners, and for those who have come to ultrarunning from other sports to scratch the competitive itch, some form of the "one winner" belief system is adhered to. However, even ultrarunning, with all the success that older runners can enjoy, does not afford an unlimited life expectancy for top athletes. Wear and tear, injuries, emotional fatigue, and new challengers constantly threaten the status of those at the top of their game. Life at the top, with a few notable exceptions, is tenuous and most often short. History has shown that the shortest career span in ultrarunning usually belongs to the most competitive runners. For these individuals it seems to be especially difficult to stick with it when winning is no longer a possibility. The former stars of open competition do not generally dominate age-group competition, as one might expect. Instead, age-group competition tends to be the domain of newcomers to ultrarunning, runners whose bodies are fresh, as is the thrill of victory.

Runners who come in without a background in competitive sports tend to have a less competitive mindset than former jocks. In addition, women tend to be less expressive about their competitiveness than men. I truly believe this is a product of our societal expectations of women, because in practice women can be every bit as competitive as men—they are just not as apt to admit it. But then, almost all runners are more competitive than they let on. If you want to see a runner come back to life during the late stages of a race, just tell he or she the runner up ahead is hurting and walking slowly. It doesn't matter how feel good, lovey dovey, "everyone is a winner" they were talking at the pre-race dinner, give them the opportunity, and they are likely to grab it as if it were the last cup of water at an aid station.

If we are to define competition however, we must also define winning. This discussion began with a strict definition of winning, but in reality winning means different things to different people. I have not been the first finisher in a race, at any distance, since 1980. Yet I have experienced the feeling of victory many times since. I have felt victorious after setting personal bests, running negative splits, breaking 24 hours for 100 miles (a major goal for me), or just beating my friend Linda (something I did not accomplish very often).

However satisfying these alternative victories might be, there is a definite difference between them and an outright first place finish. Even after all these years I have not forgotten the incomparable feeling that comes from passing the last runner and having no one else in front of me. What a combination: the ecstasy of being there, the pain of getting there, and the fear of someone trying to take it away.

As humans, it is our nature to think of things in absolutes, to judge those who agree with us as being correct, and all others as being wrong. But who are the "real" ultrarunners? Are they the runners who try to win every time out, even if it means frequently dropping out? Are they the runners who do 30 or 40 races a year, but never come anywhere close to a maximum effort for fear of endangering next week's finish? Or are they the runners who astound themselves by finishing at all? There is nothing written in stone about what any runner's goals must be, or how they define winning. When it comes right down to it, no matter how we define winning, there is nothing to gain by what we accomplish in the sport, other than self-satisfaction and the respect of our peers.

Is the sport somehow degraded by the incredible variation among the runners and their goals? Hardly. From the fastest record-setters, to the slowest, least competitive ultrarunners, each is a necessary component if our games are to exist at all. It is true that not so long ago that nearly everyone who ran was fast and serious. But there were only a handful of events to run, and ultrarunning careers were limited to the years during which one could perform somewhere near the top level. Without the sea change ultrarunning has undergone, I could no longer have that next race for which to prepare. Without all those different kinds of winning, there would be no more goals for me to set. That, at least, I can share with almost everyone. Only the few lonely souls at the top can run for the outright win. And even for them, if they are to enjoy long careers, they must eventually find new ways to define winning.

When my son was young, he used to ask me after every race, "Did you win?" After every race I answered "No." One day he finally asked me, "If you never win, why do you run?" I had a difficult time formulating an answer. "Because I hope to win" wouldn't do. The chances of that had become slim and none. "For the challenge" didn't cut it either. I had finished far too many races to still doubt whether I could. Even, "To see my friends" sounded weak. There are better ways to socialize than beating my toenails off my feet. Finally I told him, "For the pure joy of doing it." Eventually I had a different answer for him when I reached the finish line. "Did you win?" he asked. "Yes" I replied.

Humor

What's So Funny About Ultrarunning?

The sport of ultrarunning does have its humorous side. The sheer magnitude of attempting to complete such long distances calls for a serious and thoughtful approach. One cannot simply waltz into an ultra and expect it to be all laughs, fun, and games. However, like most all serious endeavors, it should be fun, and sometimes you just have to laugh at the absurdity of it all.

Those observing from the outside, not immersed in the middle of the sport, generally have a perspective that allows them to offer humorous commentary on ultrarunning. Spouses of ultrarunners are particularly insightful in that regard.

Living with an Ultrarunner: It's Not Always So Easy, describes with levity just what the spouse of an ultrarunner can expect to be up against. While playfully poking fun at the self-absorption of the ultrarunner, Janet Kosky also describes just how inspiring it can be to see the immense drive and motivation channeled towards achieving a goal.

Gary Cantrell is recognized as one of the great humorists of the sport. His down home Southern style points up some of the often overlooked but truly funny aspects of ultrarunning. In his piece *The Bigger They Are....* he describes in tongue-in-cheek fashion the many ways one can fall down during a trail ultra. If Gary is a Southern ultra humorist, Al Toth is his Northern counterpart. Al's articles in this section, *Ultrarunning Names and Terms*, and *Waramaug: The Movie*, display his unique, offbeat view of the sport.

Of course, the characteristics that go into making an ultrarunner have been well documented through the years. Everyone knows ultrarunners have very unusual quirks and idiosyncrasies. In the compilation *You Know You are an Ultrarunner if....* some of those characteristics are laid bare for everyone to see. Let it not be said that ultrarunners are not able to occasionally poke fun of themselves. To paraphrase a famous quote, ultrarunning is too important to be taken seriously.

Living With an Ultrarunner: It's Not Always So Easy

by Janet Kosky

After feeling guilty for so long about not sharing my husband's enthusiasm for long-distance running, I decided it was finally time to come out in the open. Perhaps registering my complaints about ultrarunners will lend support to other spouses who experience the same phenomena, and maybe poke a little fun at those of you ultrarunners who may recognize yourselves in this description. What follows are some conclusions I have drawn after being married to a running fanatic for several years, as well as advice for the newly initiated who may not know what they are in for.

1. **Expect your food bill to double.** Burning fuel at a rate of 100 calories per mile may result in consuming twice as much food as the average American. Although most athletes with endurance goals endorse a complex-carbohydrate diet, many also avoid red meat, preferring the healthier—but also more expensive—chicken breasts and fish as sources of protein.

In our case, whatever we might save by eating vegetarian foods, we spend on Gary's dietary quirks and fetishes associated with the sport. All runners, it seems, have an attachment to the food that has made the difference in a race result, or brought them through a physical crisis unscathed. For my husband, it's a box of Grape Nuts and a pint of peanut butter every week, plus the typical runner's staples: Gatorade and Powerbars, usually bought by the case.

2. **Ultrarunners need 25 to 50 percent more living space.** Because our house is so small, four pairs of running shoes, eight water bottles, and 27 T-shirts may seem more apparent than they would in a larger home. Walk into any runner's house, though, and it is immediately identifiable by the sweaty clothes hanging from every available hook; pictures, posters, and plaques from various events on the walls and shelves; and running magazines in the bathroom. Then there are the accessories to store: 15 kinds of herbs and vitamins, sun visors and hats, warm-up suits, rain gear, sun block, dog repellent, headlamps and flashlights, just to name a few items.

3. **Don't assume the ultrarunner will be the All-American lover.** Although ultrarunners are known for their vigorous appetites for food and fresh air, this does not automatically carry over to a runner's sex life. Adding seven to ten hours a week in training time to the 40 hours most people work, plus time for stretching, showering, and icing sore muscles, does not leave many magic moments for snuggling by the fire. If there is time, they are too tired. Also, since I would prefer

not standing for 24 hours on the side of a track watching my husband run in circles, many of our weekends are spent apart: me at home and him sleeping (if at all) in a tent at the finish line.

Sometimes, ultrarunners *can* show a romantic side. I proved it the time I stood naked in the living room holding a sale ad for a pair of Asics Gels. Gary's pulse rate noticeably increased. Your guess is as good as mine as to what really caused that to happen.

4. Always bring a tape recorder or witnesses with you to the finish line to document your spouse intensely proclaiming, "Never again!" This vow will be forgotten once the blisters have healed and the medal is hanging in the trophy case. "Huh? I never said that," is what you will likely hear when applications are due for the same run the next year and you have already made plans that weekend for both of you to slip out of town (see above).

This brings us to the incomprehensible topic of motivation. What drives these maniacs? As you may well have guessed, I am not a "runner" per se. I jog to simply maintain wellness and have never claimed to like it. I have about the same level of conscious enjoyment while jogging as I do while brushing my teeth; take away the opportunity to do either one, and I become very uncomfortable, but while I am able to continue the activity, I don't think of it terms of pleasure.

On the other hand, Gary will bounce out of bed at 4:30 on a Saturday morning and be instantly excited about running 25 miles through mud, snow, or poison oak. I don't understand it, and furthermore I don't think runners do themselves. When asked why they subject themselves to this kind of abuse, most merely shrug with the same attitude as mountaineers who are asked why they want to climb a particular mountain. I would have to agree that it is a kind of addiction—not just a physical one, but a mental dependency, too. They *need* to run to be satisfied and content. To support that theory, witness the withdrawal symptoms runners suffer upon injury or other circumstances that keep them from running: irritability, listlessness, and short-term depression. About the only time my husband and I

think alike about his ultrarunning is when he reaches the 80-mile mark in a 100-mile run and begins asking, "What possessed me to want to do this?" This is of course is a short-lived doubt on his part.

5. Be prepared for complaining and accounts of exaggerated suffering after it's all over. Part of the glory comes later, in the recounting with teammates all of the gory details they endured while on the trail and those resulting from completing such an arduous feat. Get a group of them together and it sounds like a post-surgery ward in the hospital, That is, if you can understand their conversations, spiked with secret codes such as PRs, DNFs. USATF, and so on.

Sometimes there is just a plain communication gap between runner and non-competitor. I am still baffled by Gary's naiveté when, the day after a particularly grueling race, he'll hobble into the room on feet swollen to twice their normal size, minus one or two toenails, with blisters rubbed raw, and say (with irritation), "I wonder why my left ankle hurts."

6. Ultrarunners are wonderful statisticians. These guys always run with a stopwatch and study race results as if they were *Playboy* centerfolds. The track star who can recite his times for every race of his career, the number of starters and finishers, records set, and so on, will always do so not only in hours, but minutes and seconds. Instead of replying to my polite inquiry with a simple, "Oh, I ran about 15 miles today," the answer will always be specific, as in 14.7 miles done in 2:10:58.

This however, does not imply accuracy with numbers in other essential areas of daily life. When asked if there is enough money in the checking account to pay the electric bill, the response is something vague like, "It probably won't bounce." When asked, "When you drove the car last, did you happen to notice how much gas was left?" the response was, "Um, no. There were some funny sputtering noises distracting me."

7. Definitely count on feeling moment of unabashed pride and gratitude.

"Just be glad he has such a healthy hobby," a friend (who smokes) once chided me. It's true—ultrarunners reach their prime in mid-life, unlike the good looks and thinning-hair optimum. In addition to the obvious cardiovascular benefits, exercise helps reduce stress. After running for 24 hours, who *cares* if the roof leaks?

Along with the highs you can also expect to experience occasions of panic when your runner does not show up at a checkpoint on schedule or neglects to call from out of town as promised when he finishes a race. When I paced my husband the last seven miles of the Western States Endurance Run, I had to literally sign my life away, releasing the race directors from any liability for "rattlesnake bites, bear attacks, or other injuries, including death." There *are* hazards out there.

Directly following the periods of worry (I wonder if they plan it that way), are the times when the hours of loneliness and misunderstandings evaporate, and I'm then joyously running with him in spirit. Like being with him at 4:00 a.m. when he sprinted across the finish line of his first 100-mile, even though I knew he had coughed all the way and had not slept for two nights before the race. Or the time he stood before hushed audience of middle school kids, explaining the reason behind his choice to do a 24-hour race. The student body responded by contributing more than $100 to be donated to the Sudden Infant Death Institute. Or knowing that he gave up his finishing position to sit with a runner, who had taken a spill and broken her leg, until a medical crew could get there.

This last axiom tends to cancel out the other six. All kidding aside, ultrarunners are pretty inspiring. A co-worker who unblinkingly stared at me when I told her Gary's results at a 24-hour run remarked in subdued awe, "Wow, think of what we are *all* capable of—mentally as well as physically—if we could only commit our total concentration and energies toward accomplishing an objective." Now if I could only get Gary to not hang his damp running shorts on the bathroom doorknob.

Unlocking the Secrets of The World's Greatest Ultrarunner (TWGU)

by Don Allison

I have been sent here by the Man. My mission is to observe Yiannis Kouros, the world's greatest ultrarunner (TWGU), to find out what makes him tick, what it is that makes him such a superior ultrarunner, with endurance beyond that of other humans. The Man says there must be a reason, something I can ferret out from 24 hours of observing TWGU that will unlock the secret to his virtually unlimited endurance.

I watch TWGU before the race. Nothing special there. As TWGU, he must meet and greet the other runners, and he does so easily, no strain or worry about the upcoming race evident on his countenance. TWGU has no crew, just the back of a station wagon from which to obtain supplies during the race. He dresses in ragged shorts, with no shirt. His shoes look worn out, like the ones I use to wash the car, years after their running usefulness has expired. I note this in my book and underline it.

I notice that TWGU starts the race at a moderate pace, letting many other runners race ahead. He seems unconcerned about the competition at this point, which is very reasonable since there are 23 hours and 55 minutes left to go. Surprisingly, TWGU does not run with a graceful stride. He looks constrained, tight. Somehow I expected TWGU to appear more regal in his movement. The Man will be surprised at this observation.

I decide to leave my post for a few hours. There is still plenty of time left to observe. When I return, nothing much has changed. TWGU is running exactly as he had in the earlier hours. Several other runners still appear to be moving along at a faster clip. This is getting tedious. I am supposed to be unlocking the secrets of TWGU, but have learned nothing. I saunter over to the leader board. Hey, TWGU is in first place. I wonder how that happened?

Nighttime comes. TWGU has put on tights and a shirt bearing only his last name. When you are TWGU, I suppose you are entitled to wear a shirt with your name on it. Onward he marches, 'round and 'round the loop. Many are walking now, but not TWGU. Only running. He weaves in and out of the slower participants, impervious to the competition. What must he be thinking?

Since it is dark now, I unobtrusively head over to his car to have a look. What a mess! Clothes and food everywhere. How can he find anything is this chaos? He's got enough food to feed an army, including something that looks suspiciously like baklava. I make a note. The Man loves baklava.

TWGU leads throughout the long hours of the night, but a couple of American runners stay close, as if being pulled to greatness by TWGU's inexorable pace. One hundred miles, 110, 120—on it goes, the totals ever increasing. The sun rises, but it is still chilly, so TWGU continues to wear long tights. His pace has slowed marginally, but only upon very close observation. Every now and then a few of the top American runners run alongside him, but TWGU does not seem to like this. He does not converse, and at the earliest opportunity he breaks free.

It appears as if TWGU will win the race. It will not be a record shattering performance, but he ends up five miles ahead of his closest competitor, racking up 167.4 miles, a total very few men in history have ever amassed in 24 hours. Could it really be? That sure seems like a lot for someone who was not running all that fast.

TWGU appears no worse for the wear at the awards ceremony. He heads over to the massage table. I wonder if the young massage therapist knows she is working on the muscles of the TWGU. Beer is his drink of preference now. The Man loves beer too. Although most other competitors move with rickety, hunched over gaits, and with the medical area pumping IVs like water, TWGU is neither sore nor sick. He is composed, relaxed, unimpressed with his run.

The festivities complete, I head back to the car for the long trip back home. I do not relish having to report back to the Man on Monday. Despite the fact that my notebook is full of remarks and data, none of it is earth shattering, or even very interesting for that matter. I was supposed to unlock the secrets of TWGU, but I am afraid I have not been successful in my mission. Could it be that there is no secret at all to becoming the TWGU? The Man would never believe that. He says there must be a secret and The Man is never wrong.

From the South: The Bigger They Are . . .
by Gary Cantrell

From the house it looked just like snow. For 36 hours, billions of tiny bits of ice had poured from the sky. By the time it finished, a six-inch sheet of ice covered everything in sight. No matter that I had listened to the unmistakable sounds of falling ice for a day and half, it looked like snow, dammit.

And it was time to run. So I slipped on my running gear, bundled up snugly against the cold wind, opened the front door quickly, and hopped out. Landing hard on the deceptive white, rather than sinking into a blanket of snow, I shot across the porch as if it were a bobsled run. Arms whirling like propellers, I somehow stayed upright as I zipped across. Then my feet dropped off the edge and broke through the surface, stopping my flight. Well, stopping my feet anyway. The rest of my body continued only far enough to leave me sprawling face down on the ice. A smarter person would have gone back inside once he or she got to his or her feet. But I'm not a smarter person—I'm a runner. Slipping, sliding, and wobbling, I made my way across the yard to the road, only to fall again and again. Eventually, by hanging onto weeds and trees, I managed to struggle back to my house.

Many ultrarunners never even consider falling. Yet, falling might well be the most popular aspect of the running sports. Consider Jim Ryun; for nearly a decade he was the most dominant middle-distance runner who ever lived. What is he remembered for? His face-first sprawl at the Munich Olympics, of course. How about Mary Decker? After setting countless records she is still best remembered for a race that was nipped in the bud by having her foot stepped on in an Olympic 3,000-meter final. Gail Devers collected a couple of gold medals in the Olympics, but garnered the majority of her press by finishing the 100-meter hurdles head first, with the last hurdle still tangled between her legs. When you think about it, the artful fall might be considered the "slam dunk" of running sports.

This is great news for ultrarunning. No one falls like tired ultrarunners, and there is nowhere better to fall than in a trail run. We just have to move the cameras. Instead of pictures of slow-moving wind-suckers grinding up a big hill (something you must experience to appreciate), we need them to capture someone coming rapidly downhill in a wild tangle of arms and legs and a cloud of dust.

Meanwhile, it is up to us runners to perfect the running fall. Given my natural gift of gracelessness, who better to instruct those less talented in the art of crashing. There are four basic falls that an ultrarunner needs to master: face-first, flat-on-your ass, over-the-edge, and step-in-a-hole.

Face-first is the most common and most easily achieved. After enough hours of running, with your feet clearing the ground by only a millimeter or two, almost any rock, root, or other obstruction will serve to stop your forward progress. Your head, however, will continue traveling forward, making a perfect arc from above where your feet stopped. Tradition dictates that you throw out both hands to catch yourself and cry out your favorite expletive.

There are those who recommend rolling out of a face-first fall, but the hands-out technique will guarantee embedding flecks of asphalt, gravel, or at least sticks and dirt in your palms, if not a broken wrist. Style points won't be awarded unless

you emerge with tangible injuries. Runners seeking an extra degree of difficulty may add their own personalized touches, such as banging their heads into tree trunks, or cracking their knees on rocks. These will add a modicum of class to even the simplest headlong plunge. (The most noteworthy face-first fall I ever witnessed was achieved by a runner snagging a toe on a root as he was approaching a switchback. The runner vanished over the end of the trail and ended up dangling upside down in the branches of a small tree. It was, I must say, a work of art.)

If face-first is the easiest, flat-on-your-ass is the most difficult maneuver for a runner to achieve. With your body traveling as fast as you can make it move, some outside assistance is usually needed in order to get those feet out front. Ice, as we all know, was invented for this purpose. Mud, algae, and wet rocks or pavement can all do the job if we achieve sufficient inattention. Most ultrarunners are (fortunately) gifted at inattention. That's how we get lost.

Once the feet are up, the important things to remember are to exclaim "Oh!" followed by your favorite expletive, and then throw your hands or elbows out behind you to bear the brunt of the fall. It is best to shoot both feet out front, because the single-foot technique often results in a painful twisting of the remaining leg. This can inflict traumatic stretching of the muscles, tendons, and ligaments in that leg. In addition, the two-foot method places you flat on your butt, right where your feet left the ground. A one-footer might result in you ending up tumbling off in almost any direction.

Over-the-edgers are simple falls, although often quite dramatic and yielding very high scores. But not just anyone can go "over the edge." It takes a determined runner to locate—and hit just right—the loose rock, crumbling overhang, or hidden crevasse that will send he or she tumbling into the unknown.

The proper cry as you disappear is an "aaah" sound. Expletives should be reserved for when you bounce off trees and rocks. After you complete the free-fall and roll-and-bounce portions of the exercise, you are supposed to spread eagle and slide to a stop among an avalanche of dirt, rocks, leaves, and sticks. While an over-the-edge is difficult to achieve, it is a real crowd pleaser.

The step-in-a-hole fall is one of the least used falls in running, perhaps because of the high injury risk involved, but more likely because it requires a certain knack for putting your feet in the wrong places. Not just any hole will do. A shallow hole is just a variation on the old face-first approach. The proper hole must be deep enough for you to go at least mid-shin, and small enough for the foot to lodge in the bottom. Depending upon what part of your leg hits the front of the hole, either the knee or hip joint will bear the full force of stopping your forward motion. Step-in-a-hole may lack the drama of an over-the-edge, and it may not have the hilarity of face-first or flat-on-your-ass. But it sure does hurt. What step-in-a-hole lacks in visual effect is more than compensated for by the genuine cries of pain.

All in all, falling is underrated and unappreciated by runners, especially those with a natural aptitude for it. If ultrarunning is going to become a big-time sport, we've got to give the public what it wants. Looking at the sports on television now, it is obvious that flying bodies and collisions could make us all famous.

So You Think You Are Slow?
by Myra J. Linden

For the past few years I have patiently endured articles by runners who claim to be slow. They complain about the agony of finishing a 50-mile ultra in the eight-hour range. They write of their view from the "back of the pack."

They go on a similar vein brilliantly, amusingly, whimsically—but always maddeningly. I seriously question whether any of those self-proclaimed slow runners *really* understands what the word *slow* means. Now, with that off my Jog Bra, I will proceed to define the word slow from the viewpoint of a truly vintage slow runner, possibly the most experienced slow ultrarunner practicing the sport.

Slow means making your first nervous kidney pit stop approximately 100 yards after the start of an ultra and running back on course, only to see the entire field vanishing in the distance, the closest straggler a half-mile ahead of you.

Slow means standing at the starting line of the Pikes Peak Marathon in your full race regalia, with your number pinned on the front of your shirt (mind you, not on the back), and having four fellow entrants walk up to you and ask, "Are you in this race?" Such experiences lead to a very low self-image.

Slow means being a middle-of-the-pack finisher for your first three race seasons—if you count all entrants, because so many trendy runners drop out—and feeling smug about your great race record.

Slow means having your middle-of-the-pack delusions shattered despite improved speeds because once the trendy runners have become trendy racquetball players and trendy rollerbladers, you are left with the hard-core runners, who trash you in every race thereafter.

Slow means moving up to ultras and then living in abject terror lest one or more of the speed demons in your new arena of horrors inadvertently runs you down and then tramples the remains lap after lap.

Slow means staggering along trying to finish your first ultra and being startled by a CB operator inquiring, "And where is the elderly woman who is in last place?" This, when you are a mere slip of a girl at 51.

Slow means having your personal bicyclist with his CB answer, "She is at the yacht harbor walking in front of a Chicago squad car," and having the first one reply, "Really? By now I thought they'd be using a cattle prod on her."

Slow means having your finish time in the race program reprinted year after year as the slowest finisher ever (a time well over 13 hours for 50 miles).

Slow means doing an unofficial 100-km in the same race the next year, with the race director and two young male ultrarunners begging you not to do the last 12 miles because you might be raped, robbed, and turn into a pumpkin (or worse) at midnight, but finishing anyway, and then having your finish time reprinted year after year in the race program as the slowest finisher for that distance.

Slow means having your brother-in-law pressure your sister into calling the police on you in your second 100-km because you and his wife (your handler) should have finished hours earlier—as if you were being perverse and enjoyed finishing the race in a snowstorm just to inconvenience and annoy him. It means having your sister actually make the call, and having the police dispatcher somehow get the impression that you and your 40-year-old babysitters are runaway teens.

Slow means being grateful to race directors and their personnel who must think they will collect Social Security benefits before you finish, but who are game enough to wait for you to finish instead of closing the course.

Best of all (if you are a 54-year-old female ultrarunner, almost 55), *slow* means finishing in last place but never having to say you are sorry, because you are still setting records—age-group records, that is. It's somewhat like being the last man in the class at Annapolis. Let the cheering begin.

A Handy Organic Training Aid
For Winter Running
by Dale Brewer

It is with relief that I realize there are only about four more weeks of winter remaining. Since today is the fifth of December you may think I'm being too optimistic. However, for me spring begins when the sun starts its slow northward migration along the horizon. It surprising, but only a few days after the Winter Solstice you can see that the sun sets a little farther north each evening. For me that ranks right up there with the appearance of redwing blackbirds and robins a few months later.

Sometimes I think I was a bear in a previous life and the hibernation instinct is still with me. Each fall depression and lethargy beset me when Daylight Savings Time ends. The ten-mile runs after work that I normally delight in become drudgery when half or more must be run in the dark. I am also partial to warm weather, so gradually falling temperatures add to my despair.

During this period my appetite soars beyond normal limits. Red meat, which I normally avoid completely, becomes a great delicacy and beckons at every meal. In my weakness, all too often I give in to fits of gluttony. People who study human behavior tell us this is a natural, instinctive reaction to the shorter days and cooler temperatures. It may be instinctive and it may be natural, but it is not without its consequences. It doesn't take much of this change in diet before the old belt starts to feel as if it has shrunk. Soon I notice this thing that resembles an organic waist pack residing just above my belt line. It must be December; the "love handles" are back! Naturally this adds to my despair, not to mention making what running I am doing more difficult.

But wait, hold that thought for a moment, "It makes running more difficult." What must one do in training in order to improve? Add stress. The usual methods of doing this are running faster, running farther, or running hills. An alternative method is adding to the load one is carrying by any number of commercially available weight devices. Perhaps we reincarnated bears have discovered a natural, organic alternative to trying to run faster, farther, or up hills in winter's snow and ice. Once you think about it, having what I've termed a "training roll" has some real advantages. Here are a few.

- It reduces the chance of injury, because unlike hand or ankle weights, it places no unnatural strain on your extremities. Riding near our center of gravity it also has little effect on our balance or agility.

- Unless you really let it get out of hand, the training roll provides a good training load, greater in fact than what hand or ankle weights can provide. Let's say that the average roll adds ten pounds to the runner's normally trim frame. Two five-pound hand or ankle weights would not make for an enjoyable run. Trust Mother Nature; she knows how to distribute the load. The training roll leaves your hands free and relaxed, so your energy can be applied to running.
- Other than the food consumed while growing it, the training roll costs you nothing. You have to eat anyway, right? A little extra here and there is all it takes.
- You never have to worry about misplacing this training aid. When visiting a friend who suggests a run, you won't be disappointed that you left your ankle weights at home.
- It's highly unlikely that your dog will turn this training aid into a chew toy and ruin it or bury it in the backyard. You won't leave it.
- Since it is winter, you will benefit from the roll's insulating effect on

those cold days. As spring approaches the training roll will add heat stress to help you more quickly develop better heat tolerance.

- Perhaps the best feature of the natural, organic training roll is that with just a tad more self control and some increased mileage, it will disappear. Once it is gone you are stronger for having trained with it, your self-image is higher, and you are once again the lean athlete your friends remember from last summer.

In short, you are ready to race. Throughout the racing season you can take comfort in the fact that your training roll is quietly with you. Whenever you need it, with the proper care and feeding it will again rise to prominence, ready to help whip you back into shape.

Ultrarunning Terms and Names
by Albert J. Toth, D.D.S.

This brief glossary of ultrarunning terms and names is specially edited for the parents, spouses, or significant others of ultrarunners to clear up confusion. It may help make their participation (voluntary or involuntary) more appropriate.

Ultrarunning. An extravagant form of exercise, in which the athlete runs, or from time to time, walks beyond the distance of 26.2 miles. Races of ultra distance are distinguished by slowness of foot, extreme garrulity, and gorging on so-called "food" they yell at their children for eating.

UltraRunning **Magazine.** A black and white monthly periodical that is the bible of long distance runners and is commented on by readers of normal magazines for lacking color, cartoons, and centerfolds. The magazine appears to have a salivating effect on its recipients, and sociologists note that runners often read this magazine cover to cover before even opening up their *Playboy* or *Victoria's Secret* catalogs.

Grizzled runner. An old guy (over 50) finishing way down on the finishing list.

Smooth runner. A younger version of the above grizzled runner.

Endorphins. Exotic chemicals secreted by the brain that act as a mild narcotic-type of pain relief. Contrary to general belief, endorphin production shuts down after 26.3 miles. Encephalographic monitors have picked up brain waves that seem to be saying, "No more, we don't do overtime here. Let them take Advil!"

50 K. A lot of money—or not such a big deal distance. Favored by some guys attempting to make an impression on female runners who have brand new running suits and matching shoes.

Aid station. Card tables set out in the sun (summer ultras) or on top of windy hills (winter ultras) peopled by volunteers who do not run more than 10 km (if they run at all), and serve kid-size portions of kids' food and sodas and are trained to say "looking good," or "nice job." Honesty on their part when experiencing a bedraggled runner at mile 78, will result in immediate dismissal.

Yiannis Kouros. No, not an army colonel who overthrew the latest Greek government. This YK is TWGU—the world's greatest ultrarunner. He lives in Australia and plays the violin or bazooka or something. Perhaps some day the Greek government will make him an honorary colonel.

Race Director. Usually a schizophrenic type of running personality—63 percent masochist, 48 percent George Patton wannabe. The best of the bunch design uphill finishes, vague course markings, sub-minimal food and fluids at aid stations, and have a huge need to do good and be loved. When not being cursed, they are often praised for doing the same things that got them cursed.

100-Mile Trail Race. Walking, and occasionally running, up and down and up and down and up and down mountains and woods and swampy places for a very long time. Parents or significant others will note that their beloveds begin as cheerful runners and finish as the modern update of Lee's walking wounded the day after Gettysburg, minus the uniforms.

Grand Slam. In baseball, a home run with the bases loaded; in ultrarunning, four of the above type or races, all in one year. Hindu theologians when told of these facts, shake their heads slowly and say that these "Grand Slams" are performed as penance for great sins in a past life.

To Buckle (v). According to Webster's, "to bend, warp, or crumble, as under pressure or in intense heat." To put it in ultrarunning terms: to do this warping and crumbling for a long time (mercifully in less than 24 hours if possible) in order to get a "buckle" (see below).

Buckle (n). A garish small slab of brass with a horse or a mountain embossed on it, given to individuals who perform the above "buckling." This item is rarely on the contested assets list in divorce proceedings. It is sometimes worn on the waist to keep a cheap imitation leather belt together, and in Texas and Oklahoma to keep string ties from slipping off.

Blisters and Black Toes. No, not a Canadian rock group. These gruesome things are the ultrarunners' red badge of courage. There is some Freudian urge to exhibit these body parts. Private viewing is preferred by some non-runners, away from dining and living rooms, other relatives, and small children.

I Was Out There Too Long. This statement is not to be confused with the Belgian administrator Kurz' cry in Conrad's *Heart of Darkness*. Kurz was crazy. These words, usually mumbled, really mean "I was out there too long." When asked further how they are feeling, they will add mystical comments such as, "I was a tiny accordion being played by the immense hands of the compassionate Buddha," or, "I was envisioning Madeleine Albright as a *Playboy* centerfold, and I found it profoundly stimulating." A smile is preferable upon hearing these epithets, to outright guffawing.

DNF. The saddest three letters in the alphabet, except for perhaps DOA. If your runner has experienced the first situation repeatedly: a) if you are a parent, consider revising your will, or: b) if you are a significant other, consider the possibility of relegating your DNFer to less significant status, or perhaps mull the word insignificant.

Awards Ceremony. Where they get rid of the food from the pre-race pasta dinner, usually in the same barn or school cafeteria. This glutinous repast is followed by the dreaded awarding of medals and buckles. This is especially painful and interminable for onlookers at trail 100-mile races as, according to researchers, the typical buckler takes three minutes and twenty eight seconds to limp from his table in the barn to the race director's platform to be handed his or her precious piece of brass. The leg-dragging is rarely for dramatic effect. Beloveds who attend this segment of the race weekend might do well to bring a book along—something thick, such as Proust, Joyce, or the revised federal tax code.

There are also things ultrarunners say that cause misunderstandings, such as, when asked if he won, the runner says, "Everyone who runs an ultra is a winner." Your aunt or the young lady at the Gap cash register will look at him or her askance. Better to say, "Participation is what is most important." Although he may get the rejoinder, the same can be said about working the bake sale at the local church.

Also, ladies, never, never, say, "Mom, I got fourth female at the JFK 50 Mile!" Because you know the response will be, "Well, that's nice, dear, but tell me, are you still engaged to that man serving a life sentence in that prison in Michigan?"

Better to say, "Mom, I ran and ran and ran and I beat hundreds of men in a very long race!" Although after a short pause Mom will probably say, "That's nice, dear. Your brother just made partner at his accounting firm and now he has his own private bathroom."

Hopefully these humble thoughts will aid the uninitiated in the understanding and caring for the soul, and soles, of their precious ultrarunners. Like the humpback whale, they aren't absolutely necessary, but the world would be less without them.

P.S. Mom, I did five thirty five and twenty five seconds for 50 km at the Nifty Fifty. It was a perfect day, the course was well marked, and the post-race meatballs and soup were great. I thought you'd want to know.

Waramaug: The Movie
By Al Toth

Due to inclement weather, the broadcast of the race normally scheduled for this time period has been cancelled. Due to heavy rain, wind and possible lightning, there will be no running, aside from a few diehards "doing a loop or two."

As when the Yankees and Red Sox are rained out, this station will air a movie. It's either that or several hours of a flapping white tent and a couple of old Jeep Cherokees, with rain falling on a card table holding three bananas and a box of cookies.

This movie took three years to produce: two weeks to film and the rest spent finding actors to work for union scale. It is gripping, tender, poignant, and not half-bad.

Scene One: *A rent-controlled apartment in Brooklyn. A dimly lit kitchen, people eating noisily at a table. Music coming from a living room (loud),* Chariots of Fire.

Father: Whaddayamean, ya gonna get a job after Waramaug? What's with this Waramaug, shwaramug stuff, huh?

Arvi: After the race, Dad, this time I'll look for a job. Really. Hey, it's only two days away and I been training so hard for so long. I can do it, really Dad. I'll finish the 50; I know I can do under nine hours. You'll be so proud of me. Then I'll get a job, Dad. Really.

Mom: Eat some more soup my son; you'll need the nourishment. You look like a skeleton in that T-shirt. It's not even your size. What does it say anyway, New York Road Runner's Club? Are there a lot of eligible women belong to that club? And why aren't you wearing normal pants, not that silly purple undershorts thing? Eat some more soup. You should put some weight on and look like your cousin Albert, the bookkeeper. He's almost an accountant, you know.

Arvi: He weighs 200 pounds, ma.

Mom: And he successful. He has a car made since the last war, and a wife.

Arvi: After I go under nine, I'll be successful too, ma.

Dad: You should be chasing that girl Laurie around her apartment instead of running around some Indian burial grounds place. It's not normal. The neighbors are talking. They see you running in the rain and up and down the subway stairs. I got to pretend I don't see them. Oye.

Mom: Have some more soup, no? How about some corned beef? I had them leave on some fat, just for you, my son the runner. It almost sounds as important as my son the lawyer.

Scene two: *A great big lake. A road. Trees, just starting to open up. Rain. Grown* *men and women running and walking, half naked, heads turned away from the wind. Forlorn men and women, sensibly dressed in plastic with hats and gloves, standing by a shaking white tent, half-heartedly saying words that sound like, "Nice going, keep it up, only six more laps."*

A pickup truck slowly passing runners and walkers. A man the audience recognizes as the race director saying words like, "Nice going, need anything?" Also saying those words to a group of elderly women walking to a church service. Window is rolled up. The audience hears him whisper, "Please Lord, don't take any of 'em, not while they're on the course. I'll go to church myself next Sunday."

More rain. A late Beethoven quartet weaving in between the sounds of rain and swirling wind.

Scene three: *The same kitchen and table as in scene one. The same soup, the same corned beef. Mozart's requiem wafting slowly from the living room.*

Arvi: I can't eat mom. I'm so depressed.

Mom: Maybe you should call your cousin Marvin the psychologist. He's almost a psychiatrist, you know. Maybe he can fix your head.

Dad: Five years in college and you can't finish some race or something? Oye. And what happened to your girlfriend? Where's she?

Arvi: I almost finished. Next time I gotta train some more. I can't have looking for a job interfering with my 80-mile training weeks.

Mom: My car doesn't go that far in a week. No wonder you look like the way you look like. So where's this Laurie, anyway?

Arvi: Ah, well, she sort of left with the guy doing the second water stop.

Mom: What, they don't have fountains out there? Aren't you worried about germs? Did you pick up something you're ashamed to tell your mother about?

Arvi: No ma. I coulda been a mensch. Forty-eight miles and I dropped out. Oh, what's the matter with me? Maybe I need vitamins or zinc or something.

Mom: You should call your cousin Sam, the Osteopath. He's almost a doctor, you know.

Arvi: I just gotta train some more. I gotta lift weights. Maybe yoga. I should sign up for a running camp. That's what I'll do. Mom and Dad, will you lend me the money?

Scene four: *Arvi and his new girlfriend sitting in his 1987 Nissan Sentra (with 184,000 miles) parked in front of a fire hydrant two miles from Prospect Park in Queens. A 50-mile race about to begin. Steam oozing from the car's hood. Music from Rocky blaring as the screen lighting fades and the credits roll.*

Arvi: Woody Allen

Father: Gene Hackman

Mom: Dame Judy Densch
Girlfriend (first): Sissy Spacek
Running partner: Bruce Willis
Race director: John Madden
Aid station volunteer: Haley Joe Osment
Girlfriend (new): Gwyneth Paltrow

Mister Allen wishes to thanks the countless runners who picked up cans and bottles during their training runs to make the financing of this film possible. Now back to our regularly scheduled programming.

Who Wants to be an Ultrarunner?

With your host Rich "Regis" Hanna, with apologies to the hit game show
Who Wants top Be A Millionaire?

$100
1. How many miles is the JFK 50?
A. 50
B. 49
C. 15
D. It depends on how fast you run.

$200
2. How many calories are contained in are in a packet of GU?
A. 33
B. 200
C. 100
D. 500

$300
3. Which one of the following races is not included in the Grand Slam of ultras?
A. Leadville 100
B. Old Dominion 100
C. Arkansas Traveller 100
D. Wasatch 100

$400
4. Which one of the following items are you least likely to find at an ultra aid station?
A. Cytomax
B. Oreos
C. Broccoli
D. GU

$500

5. What do you earn when completing the Western States 100 in less than 24 hours?

A. Trophy
B. Silver belt buckle
C. Gold watch
D. A year's supply of moleskin

$1,000

6. Which of the following questions are you least likely to hear at the finish of an ultra?

A. How about a beer?
B. Wanna do a cool down?
C. Where is the medical tent?
D. Can you untie my shoes?

$2,000

7. Which of the following acronyms is the least favorite among runners?

A. RRCA
B. PR
C. LSD
D. DNF

$4,000

8. Which one of the following ultrarunners holds the short course record at the Western States 100 mile and what is the record?

A. Eric Clifton (11:32)
B. Jim King (14:54)
C. Tom Johnson (15:54)
D. Brian Purcell (15:58)

$4,000

9. Which if the following men is often referred to as "the father of ultras?"

A. Don Ritchie
B. Bruce Fordyce
C. Yiannis Kouros
D. Ted Corbitt

$5,000

10. What is the name the world's shortest ultramarathon?

A. Saddleback Mountain Trail Marathon
B. Ice Age Trail Run
C. Sandia Wilderness Research Run
D. Pike's Peak Marathon

$10,000

11. You have an eight-mile run scheduled, but your eight-year-old daughter needs help with her homework. What do you do?

A. Get your spouse to help with the homework and go for your run.
B. Forget the run and help your daughter.
C. Run the eight miles.
D. Run ten miles.

Audience Poll:
A. 5%   B. 78%   C. 15%   D. 2%

$20,000

12. Why did the Tarahumaras try to use voodoo on Ann Trason?

A. They thought she was a witch.
B. They live in a chauvinistic society and didn't want to lose to a woman.
C. They had large incentives from tire and shoe manufacturers to beat her.
D. To boost viewer interest.

$64,000

13. Which sport is ranked most popular, according to recent newspaper survey?

A. Tractor Pulling

B. Women's Basketball

C. Ultrarunning

D. Triathlon

$125,000

14. Which of the following is the most commonly asked question or comment by a non-runner to a runner?

A. How far is a marathon?

B. I don't even drive my car that far.

C. How can you run that far?

D. Running isn't healthy. Didn't that famous runner Jim Fixx die running?

$250,000

15. Answering the question: "Why do you run 20 miles per day?" Which of the following noted ultrarunners answered "Because that's all I have time for."

A. Rae Clark

B. Ray Krolewicz

C. Stu Mittleman

D. Joe Schlereth

$500,000

16. Which of the following phrases are you least likely to hear along the Ice Age Trail 50 course?

A. Boy, I'm really looking forward to getting in an extra 20 after the race.

B. I was passing rocks and trees like they were standing still.

C. I didn't go out too fast, I just died too soon.

D. Only 49 miles to go.

And now for your final question:

$1,000,000

17. What are the keys to success in The American River 50 Mile?
A. Pacing, fueling, hydrating, and having fun.
B. Go out fast to intimidate your opponents.
C. Set your marathon PR in the first 26.2 miles.
D. Save time by drinking less.

Correct Answers:
1. A. 2. C. 3. C. 4.C. 5.B. 6.B. 7.D. 8.B. 9. D. 10. D. 11. B. 12. A.
13. A. 14. A. 15. C. 16. A. 17. A.

You Might Be An Ultrarunner If...

- from many sources

...Your wife tries to introduce you to your three children and you reply, "Three?"

...You spend more time in the drug section than the food section of the local market.

...You wonder why they don't make all running socks a dusty brown color.

...You have more dirt on your shoes than in your garden.

...You think a bagel and Ibuprofen is a balanced breakfast.

...You get more phone calls at 5:00 a.m. than at 5:00 p.m.

...You don't recognize your friends with "normal" clothes on.

...You have more belt buckles than belts.

...You keep mistaking your boss for Norm Klein.

...6:00 a.m. is sleeping in.

...Your feet look better without toenails.

...Your idea of a fun date is a 30-mile training run.

...You're tempted to look for a bush whenever there's a long line for the public restroom.

...You don't even look for the Porto-sans anymore.

...You don't think twice about eating food you've picked up off the floor.

...You can expound on the numerous virtues of eating salt.

...You wake up without the alarm at 5:00 a.m., pop out of bed and immediately think "let's hit the trails."

...You can recite the protein, carbohydrate, and fat makeup of each energy bar by heart.

...You won't eat cake frosting because of your concerns over maintaining a healthy diet, but you ingest 10 GUs in a 50-mile race.

...Your ideal way to celebrate your birthday is to run at least your age in miles   with some fellow crazies.

...You know the location of every 7-11, public restroom, and water fountain   within a 25-mile radius of your house.

...You run marathons for "speed work."

...You have more fanny packs and water bottles and flashlights than Imelda Marcos has shoes.

...You visit a national park with your family and notice a 30-mile trail connecting where you are with the place your family wants to visit next, which is a 100-mile drive away, and you think "Hmmm."

...Someone asks you how long your training run is going to be and you answer, "Seven or eight—hours."

...People at work think you're in a whole lot better shape than you think you are.

...You actually are in a whole lot better shape than you think you are.

...Your weekend runs are limited by how much time you have, not by how far you can run.

...You buy economy-sized jars of Vaseline on a regular basis.

...You tried the Hash House Harriers, but felt the trails were too short and too easy.

...You think of pavement as a necessary evil that connects trails.

...You rotate your running shoes more often than you rotate your tires.

...Your friends recognize you more easily dressed in shorts than in long pants.

...You really envied Tom Hanks' long run in *Forrest Gump*.

...You carry money around in a zip lock bag because store clerks complain that your money's usually too sweaty.

...Any time a runner talks about his or her aches and pains, you can sympathize   because you've already had that at least once.

...You put more miles on your feet than on your rental car over the weekend.

...You don't need to paint your toenails; they're already different colors.

...You start planning the family vacation around races, and vice-versa.

...You spend your entire paycheck on running gear, energy bars, and entry fees.

...You become a quasi-expert on different detergents, so as to not "hurt" your race T-shirts.

...You wear T-shirts based on whether you've had good workouts when you've   worn them before.

...You walk up stairs and run down them.

...You start wearing running clothes to work so you don't have to change after work.

...Running trails is more fun then sex.

...The start of a marathon feels like a five-km and you're wondering, "Why is   everyone in such a rush?"

...You sign up for a 10-km and you strap on your fanny pack because you never know where the aid stations might be.

...You bring your own drinks to a 10-km.

...You bring potatoes and salt to a 10-km.

...You are the only one walking the up hills in a 10-km.

...You run the 10-km for a second time because it's not far enough to call it a training run (and you were racing the first time through).

...When "next gas—36 miles" signs start sounding like a tempting run.

...Your pedicure kit includes a pair of pliers.

...You drink from a water bottle at the dinner table.

...You just found out poison and oak are words by themselves.

...You have a room in your house dedicated to old running shoes.

...Your entire casual wardrobe consists of race T-shirts.

...You go out to run on a Saturday morning—and don't get back until Sunday.

...You overeat *during* races.

...You ride an elevator to a parking garage, and drive to a park—for a 25-mile run.

...You run 100 laps around an airport parking lot to keep from taking a day off from training.

...You consider duct tape a medical supply.

...You spend an entire day in the mountains and never see anything but your feet.

...You round off your PR's to the nearest hour.

...You refer to marathon runners as "those young fast guys."

...You look at a mountain and find yourself trying to locate a good route to the top.

...The letters "WS" only mean one thing to you.

...You think 50 runners is a *big* race.

...Your mother has despaired of your ever "outgrowing this running phase."

...Your wife (or husband) has despaired of your ever "outgrowing this running   phase."

...You actually know how far 100 kilometers is.

...You think Laura Dern's father was a good 100-mile runner.

...You stay in shape to run, rather than running to stay in shape.

...You know the location of both the Wasatch Front and Ouachita Mountains.

...You have vowed to never run the Barkley.

...You actually believe that you could.

...Everyone you know has seen you go down stairs backwards.

...You have removed your shoes after a race, and then been unable to put them back on.

...You have taken a break during a race—for a nap.

...Every time you see a road sign giving distances, you tell your passengers how long it would take you to run there.

...You have a vertical leap of less than five inches.

...You consume 7,000 to 10,000 calories per day, yet can still pass through a standard doorway.

...You have never been offered a lucrative "shoe deal."

...You hear mention of the "Trail of Tears" and figure it must be a new 100-miler.

...You have finished a race more than a day behind the winner.

...You wear a wrist heart monitor instead of a watch.

...You think someone else should do trail maintenance.

...You meet a member of the opposite sex and your first thought is, "possible crew."

...You have another 30 lines you could add to this list.

Appendix I

Gear and Equipment for Ultrarunning
by Ed Tyanich

Ultrarunning is a simple sport, in which equipment often has little bearing on one's race results. Gear for ultrarunners does have its place however, as it allows a greater degree of comfort and safety when training and racing in the extremes of weather and terrain.

Short ultras, such as 50-km road races, can be trained for and raced with little more than shoes and basic clothing. More extreme events, such as the trail 100-mile trail races, require more clothing and gear, both for the race and the months of training leading up to it. I strive to carry just enough for any possible emergency, while keeping my pack as light as possible. Basic equipment used by ultrarunners is covered in the accompanying supplier's directory.

Shoes
Shoes are the most important piece of equipment for any runner. For the ultrarunner, the long distances covered emphasize proper shoes even more. Shoes must fit correctly and should be matched to an individual runner's biomechanics. Pronaters, supinators and neutral runners all require something different in their shoes. A specialty running store can be of great assistance when choosing shoes. Some of the better mail order catalogs also provide excellent customer service in shoe selection.

Often, runners find the added distance of ultra training brings about various foot and leg problems. Arch supports, whether over the counter or custom made, can alleviate many of these problems. Custom orthotics from a podiatrist or physical therapist are usually pricey, but can compensate for many biomechanical problems.

When road runners switch to the trails, they often find they damage toenails due to the steep terrain. This can usually be avoided by buying shoes a half-size larger than what they would run a short road race in. The fit of shoes can also be adjusted by wearing a thicker or thinner sock, or by adding an insole to the shoe.

Training Shoes
Most ultrarunners train and race in the same style shoe. A good training shoe will be able to withstand several hundred miles of hard training, while protecting your feet. Many shoe companies offer shoes for the high mileage runner. These are often a good value because they tend to be longer lasting. Studies have shown that by alternating two pairs of shoes, both pair will last considerably longer than the two pair would without rotation.

Racing Shoes

Top competitors often run ultras in racing flats. This isn't recommenced for everyone, however. Biomechanical problems will be exaggerated by the lightweight shoe. Unless you have a very neutral running gait, racing flats are best saved for speed work in training and short races.

Trail Shoes

Trail shoes were once a rare sight. Now they are the biggest sellers for many shoe companies. Trail shoes are designed to be supportive, while offering good foot protection and superior traction in rugged terrain. Some trail shoes are relatively light, while others are much beefier. The runner is well served to match the shoe to the terrain. Although some veteran trail runners train and race on very rugged trails wearing road shoes, I believe a good trail shoe is a definite asset. Trail shoes also are available in waterproof models and some have integrated gaiters.

Clothing

Clothing for ultrarunning is often more like that used in adventure racing and mountaineering than in a five-km. The longer time spent running places a greater emphasis on comfort and protection from the elements. Cotton is a poor material choice, due to its ability to soak and hold moisture. This can be a serious concern in cold weather, and on a hot day a cotton T-shirt will be considerably heavier. Synthetic materials wick well and do not readily absorb moisture. Of the natural fibers, wool and silk are excellent choices. My preferred running top in cool weather is a Merino wool shirt. These new wool garments bear little resemblance to granddad's wool unionsuit.

Shorts and Tights

Most ultrarunners choose a longer cut in shorts to reduce chafing. A tight fitting stretch short is popular with many runners. Pockets on shorts allow for carrying a few basic necessities. There are many stretch and loose fit tights that insulate and provide wind protection. Tights are a necessity for winter training in most areas and are sometimes needed for the night portions of 100-mile races.

Tops

Once again, synthetic, wool or silk tops are the preferred choice. Sleeveless shirts and tank tops can result in underarm chaffing when running long distances. Often, a shortsleeve model can eliminate this potential problem. Long-sleeve shirts are becoming more popular even in the heat of summer as runners are looking for solar protection. The insulative value of a shirt should be matched to the weather conditions. Some companies offer shirts with pockets designed to carry basics, such as energy gels.

Jackets and Vests

Light nylon or micro fiber jackets and vests protect against wind and light precipitation. For more extreme conditions, a waterproof, breathable shell is recommended. There are many brands and styles available. Some are not only highly effective, but also lightweight and compact. Jackets with hoods offer the utmost in weatherproof protection. Wind vests cover the body core, providing a good wind barrier, but offer little protection in the rain.

Clothing accessories

The most common hat for ultras is the baseball cap style. The bill shades your eyes and many are available with removable capes as well. These capes prevent sunburn on the sensitive neck area. A light stocking hat or an ear band will often be needed in cool weather. Thin synthetic or wool gloves protect the hands on cold days. Even if wet, they will keep your hands warmer than being bare handed.

Socks and Gaiters

Socks are available in a variety of styles and materials. Wool or synthetic socks are less prone to blistering than cotton socks. The thickness of a sock can be an asset in achieving the best fit in your shoes. Some runners use a double sock combination to lessen any friction. Short gaiters will keep stones, snow and other debris from getting into the shoe. There are several companies that make running shoe gaiters and a few shoe companies that offer integrated gaiters for their shoes.

Cold Weather Clothing

I have run in temperatures as cold as minus 30 F and in minus 50 F wind chill temperatures. Such conditions require careful selection in clothing. Fleece tops and tights with windproof outer layers function well in this extreme cold. Wind briefs are a necessity for male runners. Gloves yield to the much warmer mittens, and hats with ear flaps and scarves are also used. Hydration packs must be well insulated to keep from freezing. In these cold temperatures great care must be used to prevent frostbite.

Packs and Hydration

Proper hydration is one of the most important challenges faced by ultrarunners. Unlike in road races, aid stations in ultras are usually many miles apart. Experts believe runners should drink 20 ounces of fluid per hour of activity. The best way to stay properly hydrated is to carry fluids with you. The most basic method is to carry a water bottle in your hand. Hand straps, offered by several companies, allow one to carry the bottle with a relaxed grip. Waist packs that have pockets for water bottles are a good choice for most ultra races and training. These packs can be found in single and double bottle versions. Most also have additional cargo space for items such as rain jackets and energy bars. I like a pack that has waist belt pockets, so items such as electrolyte caps are right at hand. Some waist packs have the bottle holsters at an angle for easier access. Several makers are incorporating hydration bladders into waist packs. My personal preference is to use bottles until more than 40 ounces is being carried. Then I switch to a bladder.

Stay away from the real spacious waist packs, as they tend to be quite bouncy. If a large amount of space is necessary, a pack with shoulder straps or a vest design will be considerably more comfortable. Packs with shoulder straps allow one to carry more gear while still maintaining a good running stride. Some of the long trail races are best done while wearing this type of pack. They will hold enough fluids, clothing and safety gear to cope with the demanding conditions. Some of these packs are worn more like a vest; I find these the most comfortable of all. As with waist packs, the more pockets that can be accessed while wearing the pack, the better.

The safety of water in backcountry locations is often suspect. Using one of the several water filters housed in a water bottle is an excellent solution. These filters provide safe drinking water and most that I tried have a decent flow rate. They are as simple to use as "scoop the water and go." There are also in-line filters that attach to hydration system drink tubes. The pump type water filters used by backpackers are an option on training runs, but take too much space and time for races.

Electronic Gadgets

There is seemingly no end to the electronic gadgets being marketed toward runners. Some of these are of great use, while others are little more than conversation pieces.

Watches, Altimeters and Heart Rate Monitors

A basic sports watch with a chronograph is all that most runners really need. Features such as timers are useful to remind you to take electrolytes or energy gels. Some of these watches also have altimeters so you can keep track of how many feet of elevation has been gained and lost. Some have digital compasses as well. As a training tool, a sports watch that has a heart rate monitor is a good investment. The heart rate monitor will help you to push enough on hard days and remind you to ease up on the recovery days. Some runners use them during races as well to monitor their running intensity.

Speed and Distance Monitors

There are sports watches that display statistics such as current speed, average speed and distance traveled. They measure distance by several different methods depending on brand. Some use a sending unit that attaches to a shoe, while another has an arm band with a Global Positioning Satellite (GPS) unit that tracks your progress by satellite. In most conditions they are quite accurate, although a GPS model sometimes does not record mileage run in a dense forest.

CD Players and MP3 Players

For the runner that has to run with his or her tunes, there is a great selection of compact players available. As with any running, use caution when wearing headphones in traffic. Some races prohibit the use of personal stereos, so check the rules first.

Lights

Running a 100-mile race will likely necessitate running through the night. Some type of light will need be carried. Flashlights have the advantage of being able to keep the light farther from the eyes so depth perception is least affected. Headlamps offer hands-free lighting that follows your eyes when moving your head. Headlamps do present a depth problem for some runners. Wearing a headlamp on a billed hat will help with depth perception.

A relatively new technology has come to lights. It is the light emitting diode or LED. LED lights have many advantages. They are very durable, with no filament bulb to break or burn out. Most LED's will burn for more than 60,000 hours. The LED light also has much greater battery life. I know of one runner who completed five 100-mile races in a summer using the same light with the original batteries. The newest multiple LED lights also have enough light for nearly any running situation. A bright, halogen incandescent light is useful as a backup for those times when the LED may not reach far enough. Tiny coin cell LED lights are a good choice for emergencies and will not even be noticed in a pack pocket.

Drop Bags and Crew Gear

Drop bags at aid stations can make or break a race. Ridged plastic boxes such as those available at discount stores provide good weatherproof storage. Duffle bags or specific designed coated nylon race drop bags are also good choices. Mark the box or bag with your name and bib number for ease of locating. Also use zip lock bags to further protect and organize contents. Duct tape will keep a box lid secure and offer a convenient place for name and number, yet is easily torn for access.

Organization for crews in also very important. Knowing where the runner's socks or favorite food is located will limit time spent at aid stations. Often-used items will be lubricants such as Body Glide or Vaseline and foot care products such as tape and Compeed.

Emergency Gear and Odds and Ends

Emergency gear will usually consist of items such as extra clothing and food, basic first aid gear and possibly survival gear. I carry my emergency kit on all backcountry training runs and scale down the contents for races. The first aid kit is tailored primarily toward foot care/blister management and abrasion coverings. The survival portion of the kit has a small compass, knife, fire starters and an emergency space blanket. The key to any kit is to balance what is truly necessary while keeping the weight and bulk at a minimum.

Energy gels have become a staple food for all endurance events. The individual serving packs are messy to carry after opened. A better solution is a gel flask. A small plastic squeeze bottle holds five to six servings. They can be pre-filled at home. Some gel makers also offer the gel in bulk servings, resulting in a cost savings as well as greater convenience.

Useful items for ultrarunners can often be found in stores that carry backpacking gear. I have found small plastic containers that are excellent for carrying sun screen, Body Glide, electrolyte caps, and other small items. Such stores also will have hiker's guide books that can be a treasure of information for long trail runs. It's always fun to do a trip the guide book lists as a three-day journey in five or six hours. Many of the survival items can also be found in these mountain shops.

Mandatory Gear List

Some trail ultras have mandatory gear lists for participants. The contents are checked and a runner is disqualified if something is missing. Having started in Britain, we are beginning to see mandatory gear list appear at ultras in the U.S. The following are the requirements for the Bighorn 100 Mile:

- Three working flashlights. Additional spare batteries are advisable.
- A long sleeve, moisture-wicking material shirt.
- Long tights or long weather pants.
- A nylon jacket or similar type of upper shell.
- A plastic emergency poncho (light weight and available at Wal-Mart for approximately a dollar, a plastic garbage bag may be substituted but isn't as good).
- Gloves.
- Headwear (a stocking cap, balaclava, or some type of hood attached or attachable to their nylon jacket or upper shell).

Appendix II

Suppliers Directory

Shoes
Adidas: www.adidas.com
Asics: www.asics.com
Brooks: www.brooks.com
LaSportiva: www.sportiva.com or 303-443-8710
Montrail: www.montrail.com or 800-826-1598
Nike: www.nike.com or 800-806-6453
New Balance: www.newbalance.com or 800-622-1218
Saucony: www.saucony.com
Salomon: www.salomonsports.com or 800-225-6850
Tecnica: www.tecnicausa.com or 800-258-3897
The North Face: www.thenorthface.com or 800-447-2333

Clothing
Many shoe companies also have clothing lines.
Cloudveil: www.cloudveil.com or 888-763-5969
Ibex: www.ibex.com
Marmot: www.marmot.com
Medalist: www.medalist.com
Mountain Hardware: www.mountainhardware.com
Outdoor Research: www.outdoorresearch.com
Patagonia: www.patagonia.com or 800-638-6464
Pearl Izumi: www.pearlizumi.com or 800-328-8488
Race Ready: www.raceready.com or 800-537-6868
Road Runner Sports: www.roadrunnersports.com or 800-551-5558
Sequel: www.sequel.tm
Smartwool: www.smartwool.com
Sporthill: www.sporthill.com or 800-622-8444
The North Face: www.thenorthface.com or 800-535-3331
Thorlo: www.thorlo.com
Wigwam: www.wigwam.com

Packs and Hydration
Camelbak: www.camelbak.com or 800-767-8725
Cascade Designs: www.cascadedesigns.com/platypus
GoLite: www.golite.com or 888-546-5483
Gregory: www.gregory.com or 800-477-8545
Lowe Alpine: www.lowealpine.com
Nathan: www.nathansports.com
Safewater: www.safewater.com
The North Face: www.thenorthface.com or 800-535-3331
Ultimate Direction: www.ultimatedirection.com or 800-426-7229

Lights
Black Diamond: www.blackdiamondequipment.com or 801-278-5533
C. Crane: www.ccrane.com or 1-800-522-8863
Essential Gear: www.essentialgear.com or 1-800-582-3861
Pelican: www.pelican.com or 1-800-473-5422 or
Petzl America: www.petzl.com or 1-877-807-3805
Princeton Tec: www.princetontec.com or 1-609-298-9331
Technology Associates: www.techass.com or 1-877-techass

Electronic Gadgets
Nike: www.nike.com
Polar: www.polarusa.com
Suunto: www.suuntousa.com
Timex: www.timex.com

Appendix III

A Historical Timeline of Ultrarunning

1762: Briton John Hague is the first to cover 100 miles in less than 24 hours.

1808: Captain Robert Barclay Allardice covers 1,000 miles in 1,000 hours (a single mile completed in each of 1,000 consecutive hours).

1874: American Edward Payson Weston succeeds in covering 500 miles in six days, heralding a new era in the sport, in which six-day races gain enormous popularity in North America.

1899: The first amateur London to Brighton race is held.

1921: South African Vic Clapham dedicates the forced marches of the First World War by organizing a 50-mile plus race from Pietermaritzburg to Durban in South Africa, the first Comrades Marathon.

1928: The first professional Trans-America race is organized by C.C. Pyle. Oklahoma farm
boy Andy Payne wins and earns $25,000. The race is repeated again in 1929.

1934: Geraldine Watson is the first woman to run the Comrades, and the next year covers
100 miles in 22:22.

1953: South African Wally Hayward, the great South African ultrarunner, sets a word record in the 24-hour race in Britain, 159 miles.

1959: The inaugural Biel 100 Km race is held in Switzerland, the first of the European 100-km running races that grow in popularity in ensuing years.

1971: Natalie Cullimore runs a women's world best 16:11 for 100 miles in California.

1972: Multi-day racing starts with the Auckland to Wellington race in New Zealand, 425 miles. This followed series of solo runs over the course.

1974: Gordie Ainsleigh, a competitor in the 100-mile Tevis Cup, a horse race in northern California, finds himself without a steed in the annual horse race from Lake Tahoe to Auburn in California. He decides to run the course on foot, setting the stage for an event that will come to be known as the Western States 100 Mile.

1975: Siegfried Bauer of New Zealand and John Ball of South Africa take part in a 1,000-mile race from Pretoria to Cape Town. Bauer wins a close race in 12 days, 21:46:30 and thus begins the history of standard multi-day races in the twentieth century.

1975: At Tipton, England, a track 100-mile race, Cavin Woodward goes through 50 miles in 4:58:53, becoming the first person to break five hours for the distance. He then clocks 6:25:28 for 100 km, taking a half-hour off the previous best. After that, he 'hangs on' for an additional 38 miles to set a new 100-mile best of 11:38:54.

1976: The JFK 50 mile, with more than 1,700 entrants, has a larger field than any American marathon.

1977: Don Ritchie sets the world 100-mile record at London's Crystal Palace, clocking 11:30:51.

1978: Ritchie improves the 100-km world best to 6:10:20, a mark that still stands today.

1978: The first Sri Chinmoy ultra race, a 47-miler, is held in 1978 to celebrate founder Sri Chinmoy's 47th birthday. The first open Sri Chinmoy ultra race in November 1980 is a 24-hour track race in Greenwich, Connecticut, where American Marcy Schwam sets a wide range of ultra track world bests. From these beginnings Sri Chinmoy ultra races develop across the world, including the multi-day events in New York, for which the organization is famous.

1983: The first Spartathlon from Athens to Sparta in Greece is held. Experienced ultrarunners agree to allow the entry of a late entrant, a local Greek. He wins the race so decisively that questions are raised as to the legitimacy of his run. These questions are later answered emphatically. The runner's name was Yiannis Kouros.

1987: The first World 100 Km is won by Domingo Catalan of Spain. The venue is the European 100 Km, in Torhout, Belgium. From this beginning, the World 100 Km Challenge develops, around which the global ultra calendar is now built.

1993: South Africa rejoins the IAAF, and the Comrades Marathon becomes an internationally recognized event.

1996: The first all-women's ultra track race takes place at Nantes, France. New world bests at 50 miles and 100 km are set.

1997: The culmination of a series of successful attempts by Yiannis Kouros to extend the limits of human endurance at 24 hours results in an epic record. Kouros runs an inconceivable 188 miles, 1,038 yards (303.506 km), an average of more than seven consecutive marathons at an average pace of 3:21 per marathon.

1998: Ann Trason wins the women's race at the Western States 100 Mile for the tenth consecutive year, an unprecedented feat.

1999: At the Lake Saroma race in Japan, Tomoe Abe lowers the women's world 100-km best to 6:33:11, taking 27 minutes from Ann Trason's world record.

2002: Oleg Kharitonov sets a word record in the 100-mile, 11:28:03, breaking Don Ritchie's 25-year old mark. The record is set at the same venue at which Ritchie set the mark, London's Crystal Palace.

2005: Scott Jurek sets a course record of 24 hours at the Badwater 135 Mile ultramarathon, two weeks after winning his seventh consecutive Western Stats 100 Mile.

Appendix IV

Additional Information on Ultrarunning

Publications

UltraRunning Magazine
www.ultrarunning.com

Ultra Listserve
http://junior.apk.net/~jurczyk/ultra/minifaq

Ultrarunning in the USA
www.ultrarunner.net

Marathon and Beyond Magazine
www.marathonandbeyond.com

Trail Runner Magazine
www.trailrunnermag.com

Trails
www.trails.com

Extreme Ultrarunning
www.extremeultrarunning.com

Organizations

American Ultrarunning Association
www.americanultra.org/index.html

USA Track and Field
www.usatf.org

Road Runners Club of America
www.rrca.org

All American Trail Running Association
www.trailrunner.com

Nutrition and Fitness

National Association for Health and Fitness
www.physicalfitness.org

The Physician and Sportsmedicine
www.physsportsmed.com

American Physical Therapy Association
www.apta.org

American Chiropractic Association
www.amerchiro.org

American Massage Therapy Association
www.amtamassage.org

American Heart Association
www.americanheart.org

American Dietetic Association
www.eatright.org

Web M.D. Health
http://my.webmd.com

Appendix V

Major Ultra Races

United States

Across the Years 24/48 Hour
www.acrosstheyears.com

Litchfield Park, AZ

Angeles Crest 100 Mile
www.ac100.com

Wrightwood, CA

American River 50 Mile
www.run100s.com/AR50

American River, CA

Arkansas Traveller 100 Mile
www.runarkansas.com/AT100.htm

Perryville, AR

Around the Lake 24 Hour
http://home.att.net/~lakerun/

Somerville, MA

Avalon Benefit 50 Mile
www.avalon50.com

Catalina, CA

Badwater Ultra 135 Mile
www.badwaterultra.com

Badwater, CA

Bandera 100 Km
www.hillcountrytrailrunners.com/raceBandera.html

Bandera, TX

Bear 100 Mile
www.bear100.com

Deer Cliff Inn, ID

Bighorn Trail 100 Mile
www.bighorntrailrun.com/

Sheridan, WY

Bishop High Sierra 50 Mile
www.bhs50.com

Bishop, CA

Bull Run Run 50 Mile
www.vhtrc.org/brr/

Bull Run, VA

Capon Valley 50 Km
www.iplayoutside.com/Capon50

Yellow Valley, WV

Cascade Crest 100 Mile
www.cascadecrest100.com

Easton, WA

Chicago Lakefront 50 Km
www.chicagoultra.org/

Chicago, IL

Crown King Scramble 50 Mile
www.crownkingscramble.com

Crown King, AZ

Edmund Fitzgerald 100 Km
www.edmundfitz.com/

Duluth, MN

Dances With Dirt 100 Km
www.danceswithdirt.com/

Hell, MI

Elkhorn Mountain 100 Km
www.elkhorn100.com

Montana City, MT

FANS 24-Hour Run
www.fans24hour.org/

St. Louis Park, MN

Firetrails 50 Mile
www.firetrails50.net

Castro Valley, CA

Grand Teton 100 Mile
http://www.dreamchaserevents.com/gtr/

Alta, WY

Golden Gate Headlands 50 Km
www.headlands50k.org/

Mill Valley, CA

Hardrock Hundred Mile
www.hardrock100.com

Silverton, CO

HAT Run 50 Km
http://hatrun.com/

Susquehana Park, MD

Heartland 100 Mile
www.ultrarunners.info

Flint Hills, KS

Helen Klein 50 Mile
www.run100s.com/hk.htm

Sacramento, CA

Hellgate 100 Km
www.extremeultrarunning.com

Lynchburg, VA

High Desert 50 Km
www.othtc.com

Ridgecrest, CA

Highlands Sky 40 Mile
www.wvmtr.org/

Davis, WV

HUFF 50 Km
www.huff50k.com

Huntington, IN

H.U.R.T. Trail 100 Mile
www.run100s.com/ht100.htm

Honolulu, HI

Ice Age Trail 50 Mile
www.iceagetrail50.com

La Grange, WI

Jedediah Smith 50 Mile
www.run100s.com/jed.htm

Gibson Ranch, CA

JFK 50 Mile
www.jfk50mile.org

Hagerstown, MD

Kettle Moraine 100 Mile
www.kettle100.com/

Whitewater, WI

Leona Divide 50 Mile
www.leonadivide.com

Lake Highes, CA

Laurel Highlands 70 Mile
www.laurelultra.com

Seward, PA

Leadville Trail 100 Mile
www.leadvilletrail100.com

Leadville, CO

Lean Horse 100 Mile,
www.leanhorse.com/

Hot Springs, SD

Le Griz 50 Mile
www.cheetahherders.com/LeGrizz.html

Spotted Bear, MT

Long Island Greenbelt 50 Km
www.newyorkultrarunning.org

Plainview, NY

Massanutten 100-Mile
http://vhtrc.org/mmt/

Front Royal, VA

McDonald Forest 50 Km
www.oregontrailseries.org/mac/

Corvallis, OR

McNaughton Park 100 Mile
www.mcnaughtonparktrailruns.com

Pekin, IL

Mississippi Trail 50 Mile
www.ms50.com/

Laurel, MS

Miwok 100 Km
www.run100s.com/miwok/index.html

Sausalito, California

Mohican Trail 100 Mile
www.mohican100.org/

Loudonville, OH

Mountain Masochist 50 Mile
www.extremeultrarunning.com/

Lynchburg, VA

Mountain Mist 50 Km
www.huntsvilletrackclub.org

Huntsville, AL

Mount Hood 50 Mile
www.pctultra.com

Government Camp, OR

Mount Mitchell 40 Mile
www.blackmountainmarathon.com

Black Mountain, NC

Nifty Fifty 50 Mile
www.ultrarunning.com/Nifty50/

Coventry, RI

North Country 50 Mile
www.stridersrun.com

Manistee, MI

Ohlone Wilderness 50 Km
www.abovethefog.net/ohlone50k

Livermore, CA

Old Dominion 100 Mile
www.olddominionrun.org/

Woodstock, VA

Pacific Coast Trail Ultras
www.PCTrailruns.com

Tiburon, CA

Pemberton 50 Km
http://pembertontrail50k.blogspot.com

Fountain Hills, AZ

Plain 100 Mile
www.cascaderunningclub.com

Plain, WA

Pony Express 50 Km
www.ultrarunner.net/raceseries/pony_race.htm

Cameron Park, CA

Quicksilver 50 Km
www.quicksilver-running.com/page2.html

San Jose, CA

Quadruple Dipsea 28.4 Mile
www.run100s.com/qd.htm

Mill Valley, CA

Quivering Quads 50 Mile
www.fleetfeetstl.com

Troy, MO

Rio Del Lago 100 Mile
www.loomisrunning.com/riodellago.htm
Granite Bay, CA

Rocky Racoon 100 Mile
www.hillcountrytrailrunners.com
Huntsville, TX

Ruth Anderson 100 Km
www.run100s.com/ra.htm
Mill Valley, CA

Run to the Sun 36.2 Mile
http://www.hurthawaii.com/
Kahului Maui, HI

San Diego 100 Mile
www.members.cox.net/sandiego100/
San Diego, California

Self Transcendnece Six Day and Ten Day
www.srichinmoyraces.org/
New York, NY

Shadow of Giants 50 Km
www.shadowofthegiants50k.com
Fish Camp, CA

Silver State 50 Mile
www.silverstatestriders.com
Reno, NV

Skyline 50 Km
www.skyline50k.us
Castro Valley, CA

Squaw Peak 50 Mile
www.squawpeak50.com/sqw_mstr.htm
Provo, UT

Strolling Jim 40 Mile
http://www.tynesweb.com/sj40/
Wartrace, TN

Superior Trail 100 Mile
www.superiortrailrace.com
Lutsen, MN

Sunmart 50 Km and 50 Mile
www.petroleumwholesale.com/sunmart.web/race/default.aspx
Huntsville, TX

Susitna 100 Mile
www.susitna100.com/
Big Lake Lodge, AK

Sybil Ludington 50 Km   Lake Gleneida, NY
www.runner.org/sybil.htm

Tahoe Rim 50 Mile and 50 Km   Lake Tahoe, NV
http://tahoemtnmilers.org/trt50/

Umstead 100 Mile   Raleigh, NC
www.umstead100.org/

AUA Championship Races   Various locations
www.americanultra.org

Vermont 100 Mile   South Woodstock, VT
www.vermont100.com

Vermont 50 Mile   Brownsville, VT
www.vermont50.com

Way Too Cool 50 Km   Cool, CA
www.run100s.com/wtc.htm

Wasatch Front 100 Mile   East Layton, UT
www.wasatch100.com/

Western States 100 Mile   Auburn, CA
www.ws100.com/

White River 50 Mile   White River, WA
http://www.seattlerunningcompany.com/WR50/

Zane Grey Highline Trail 50 Mile   Payson, AZ
www.zanegrey50.com

Australia

Glasshouse Mountain Runs Brisbane
www.coolrunning.com.au/ultra/glasshouse/index.shtml

Great Lake 100 Miles Lake Taupo
www.relay.co.nz/

Canada

Eagle 100 Mile Keremeos, BC
www.eagleruns.com

Elk-Beaver Ultras Victoria, BC
http://pih.bc.ca/elk-beaver-ultra.html

Knee Knackering 30 Mile Horseshoe Bay, BC
www.kneeknacker.com/

Haliburton Forest 100 Mile West Guilford, ON
http://ouser.org/

Lost Soul 100 Mile Lethbridge, AB
www.lostsoulultra.com

Niagara Ultras Niagara, ON
http://ouser.org/

Sulphur Springs Trail Runs Dundas, ON
http://ouser.org/

Yukon Arctic Ultra 100 and 300 Miles Whitehorse, YT
www.arcticultra.com/

Ontario Ultra Series Various Locations
http://ouser.org/

South America

Chasqui Challenge 100 Mile Machu Picchu
www.andesadventures.com/run2sum.htm

Blanca and Huayhuash 150 Mile Huaraz
www.andesadventures.com/run1sum.htm

Jungle Marathon Manaus Brazil
www.dreamchaserevents.com

Europe

Biel 100 Km Biel, Switzerland
www.100km.ch/

Del Passatore 100 Km Firenza-Faenza, Italy
http://www.100kmdelpassatore.it/

Lapland Ultra 100 Adak, Finland
www.laplandultra.nu/100kmeng/100km.html

Laugavegur 55 Km H'sadalur, Iceland
www.toto.is/RMAR/ultrmar.htm

London to Brighton 55 Mile London, England
www.roadrunnersclub.org.uk/lonbrigh.htm

Mount Blanc 150 Km Chamonix, France
www.ultratrailmb.com

Swiss Jura Marathon 323 Km Geneva, Switzerland
www.swissjuramarathon.com/

Africa

Comrades 90 Km Durban/Maritzburg, South
http://www.comrades.com/

Marathon des Sables Sahara Desert, Morrocco
www.darbaroud.com

Two Oceans 56 Km Cape Town, South Africa
www.twooceansmarathon.org.za/

Asia

Mongolia Sunrise-Sunset 100 Km   Lake Hovsgol, Mongolia
www.ultramongolia.com/

Gobi March Six Day   Urumqi, China
www.racingtheplanet.com

Soochow International 24 Hour   Taipei, Taiwan
http://ultrarunning.scu.edu.tw/players.php

Trailwalker 100 Km   Hong Kong
http://www.oxfamtrailwalker.org.hk

New Zealand

Kepler Challenge 55 Km   Kepler, New Zealand
http://www.keplerchallenge.co.nz/home_page.htm

Other

Antarctica Marathon   King George Island, Antarctica
www.marathontour.com/antarctica/

North Pole Marathon   North Pole
www.northpolemarathon.com/

Appendix VI

Author Biographies

Bob Adjemian Bob is a former contributor to UltraRunning magazine. He currently manages Vedanta Publishing in Hollywood, California.

Janice Anderson Janice is a long-time ultrarunner who has excelled in the sport at the highest levels for more than a decade, having won many of the sport's top events and participated on many national teams in international competition.

Gordy Ansleigh Gordy is a long-time ultrarunner from Meadow Vista, California. In 1974 Gordy completed the Western States 100 Mile route on foot, regarded as the first person to do so, originated the era of 100-mile trail runs, now popular in North America. Gordy has gone of to finish the Western States every since its inception.

Brent Backus Brent is an ultrarunner from Foresthill, California.

Kurt Barkley Kurt is an ultrarunner from Hickory, North Carolina.

Sunny Blende Sunny is a sports nutritionist from Sausalito, California.

Bruce Boyd Bruce is an ultrarunner from Lakeville, Connecticut. He has finished all 15 Vermont 100 Mile races held, the only runner to do so.

Dan Brannen Dan is a long-time ultrarunner from Morristown, New Jersey. He has run many outstanding ultras in his several-decade long running career. He is involved in many other aspects of the sport, and is currently the executive director of the American Ultrarunning Association.

Dale Brewer Dale is an ultrarunner from Springfield, Ohio.

Rowley Brucken Rowley is an ultrarunner from Vermont. He has finished in the top ten at the Vermont 100 Mile.

Gary Cantrell Gary is a columnist for UltraRunning, having penned the From the South and now The Open Road columns. Known for his wit and Southern humor, Gary has maintained his unique perspective on the sport through several decades of having been involved in the sport. In addition, Gary is the director of the Strolling Jim 40 Mile in his hometown Wartrace, Tennessee, and also directed the legendary Barkley Marathons in the wilds of Tennessee.

Trishul Cherns Trishul is an accomplished multi-day runner from New York City and a member of the Sri Chinmoy Marathon Team. He has completed many Sri Chinmoy ultras lasting for days, and even weeks at a time.

Eric Clifton Eric is one of the legends in ultrarunning, having won countless ultras, including some of the biggest and most prestigious races in North America. Eric is known for his fearless frontrunning, a strategy that resulted in many course records. He currently lives in Albuquerque, New Mexico and is still competing as a masters runner.

Bob Cooper Bob is a freelance writer for Running Times magazine and the San Francisco Chronicle. He is also the author of the San Francisco Running Guide.

Suzi Cope Suzi is a long-time ultrarunner from Southlake, Texas. She has completed many 100-mile trail ultras in North America and is the race director of the Grasslands 50 Mile in Texas.

Bill Demesthias Bill is an ultrarunner from Salem, Oregon.

Charles L. Dumke, Ph.D. Charles is a professor of Exercise Science at Appalachian State University in Boone, North Carolina.

Peter Gagarin Peter is a long-time ultrarunner from Sunderland, Massachusetts. He is also an outstanding orienteering competitor and one of the founders of UltraRunning magazine.

Garett Graubins Garett is an accomplished ultrarunner from Boulder, Colorado, having completed and placed well in many 50 and 100-mile races across the country. Garett is also an associate editor of Trail Runner Magazine.

Rich Hanna Rich, from Sacramento, California has been one the premier ultrarunners in the U.S. for the past several years. His top performance was a second-place finish in the World 100 Km in 2001. A 2:17 marathoner, Rich is also the author of the Marathon Guide and a coach of Team in Training in the Sacramento area.

Jason Hodde Jay, from West Lafayette, Indiana, is a nationally certified athletic trainer licensed to practice in Indiana. He holds a master's degree in exercise physiology from Purdue University, with an emphasis on tissue repair and healing. He is currently pursuing a Ph.D. in physiology, where his emphasis is the repair and regeneration of soft tissues. Jay is also an accomplished ultrarunner, having completed many 100-mile trail races in the U.S. Jay writes a monthly column for UltraRunning, Body Basics.

David Horton David has long history in ultrarunning, as a runner, coach, advisor, and race director. He has won countless ultras during his long career; his list of achievements is topped by his record-setting trek of the Appalachian Trail in 1992. He also completed the trans-continental race across the U.S. He is a long-time coach of the Liberty University cross country team in his hometown of Lynchburg, and directs the Mountain Masochist 50 Mile, the Holiday Lake 50 Km, and the Promise Land 50 Km races.

Patrick Johns Patrick is a world traveler and freelance writer from Allen, Texas.

Norm Klein Norm, from Rancho Cordova, California, has been a race director in northern California for many years. He directed the Western States 100 Mile for several years, as well as the Sunmart Texas Trail 50 Mile. Norm currently directs the Rio Del Lago 100 Mile and the Sierra Nevada 52.4 Mile. Norm has run many ultras himself; his wife Helen has been one of the most prolific age-group ultrarunners in U.S. history.

Karl King Karl is a long-time ultrarunner from Wisconsin, now relocated to Colorado. Karl has also made a tremendous contribution to the sport through his electrolyte replacement product Succeed!, which is religiously used by thousands of ultrarunners.

Tom Kline Tom is an ultrarunner from Scarsdale, New York.

Janet Kosky No bio available.

Anton "Tony" Krupicka Tony is a an ultrarunner from Colorado Springs, Colorado. He was the winner of the 2006 Leadville 100 Mile in the second-fastest time in race history.

Yiannis Kouros Yiannis is one of—if not the—premier ultrarunners of all time. Born in Greece and now living in Australia, Yiannis has redefined the limits of what was once thought achievable in ultra distance running. Holder of countless world records, his crowning achievement came in 1997, when he became the first person to ever cover more than 300 km (186 miles) in a 24-hour run.

Dr Robert Lind Bob is the chief medical director of the Western States 100 Mile.

Myra Linden Myra is a former senior ultrarunner from Chicago.

Dan Lindstrom Dan is an ultrarunner from Martinez, California.

Nick Marshall Nick is an ultrarunner and a pioneer of the sport from Camp Hill, Pennsylvania. Nick guided the sport through its early years in North America during the 1970s, winning many races in the process. Nick was also the publisher of Ultradistance Summary, a predecessor to UltraRunning magazine, for which he also made many contributions.

Shawn McDonald Shawn is an ultrarunner from San Diego. Having completed more than 50 ultras, Shawn is also a race director and coach. He is also a columnist for UltraRunning.

Andy Milroy Andy is widely recognized as the preeminent statistical and historical authority in the sport of ultrarunning. He has written several books on the sport and has witnessed some of the great performances in the sport as well. Andy reports on the goings on in ultrarunning in Europe, Asia, and around the world in each issue of UltraRunning. His Global Update column tracks the globe's leading performers, as well as developments in major championship races around the world. Andy resides in Wiltshire, England.

John Medinger John is a fixture in northern California ultrarunning, having completed countless ultras in that area and beyond. He has also assisted at races in many capacities, from pacing other runners to serving as the emcee at awards ceremonies. "Tropical John" as he is known in the ultrarunning community, is also the race director of The Quad Dipsea 28 Mile. He lives in Healdsburg, California.

Barry Mink, M.D. Barry is a physician from Aspen, Colorado. Having practiced internal medicine at high altitudes for the majority of his career, Dr. Mink has cared for thousands of people suffering the ill effects of high altitude and has written several articles about it. Dr. Mink is a competitive athlete himself, and his interest and qualifications in sports medicine resulted in his being named team physician for the U.S. Olympic Team at the Lillehammer and Lake Placid Winter Games.

Larry Myers No bio available.

David C. Nieman David is a professor at the Department of Health and Exercise Science at Appalachian State University in Boone, North Carolina. He has run 58 marathons.

Jim O'Brien Jim is a retired running coach in southern California. He also won the 1989 Angeles Crest 100 Mile in course record time and was a top ten finisher in the Western States 100 Mile. He currently resides in Monrovia, California.

Joe Oakes Joe, from Portland, Oregon, is a veteran ultrarunner. He has also been involved in many other unique sporting adventures. Joe is also well known for having founded the "Fat Ass" series of ultra distance races.

David Phillips David is the pastor of Community Reformed Church in Egan, Minnesota.

Keith Pippin Keith is a runner from Sun Lakes, Arizona and a former contributor to UltraRunning magazine.

Kevin Setnes As one of the top ultrarunners in the U.S. during the past ten years, Kevin is eminently qualified to provide what readers ask for most: advice on training, nutrition, race strategy, and improving performance. Consistency has been Kevin's hallmark as an athlete. In major competitions, Kevin can be counted on to produce a solid performance. A member of the U.S. national 100-km team for nine years, Kevin was the top American and 17th overall, running 7:08 in Moscow in 1996. In addition to his 100-km exploits, Kevin has also run 15 hours in the Vermont 100 Mile Trail Run and more than 160 miles in a 24-hour track ultra. Kevin lives in Eagle, Wisconsin.

Kris Setnes Kevin's wife Kris is also an accomplished ultrarunner. She has won many national championships during her long ultrarunning career, and also represented the U.S. in the World Challenge 100 Km. She has also won several 100-mile trail races, and has served as a coach and advisor to other ultrarunners as well.

Dahn Shaulis Dahn studied the history of long distance running while a graduate student at the University of Nevada at Las Vegas.

Pete Stringer Pete is an ultrarunner from Osterville, Massachusetts.

Ian Torrence Ian, currently living in Moab, Utah, writes The Younger Ultrarunner for UltraRunning. Twenty-something runners are a minority in the ultrarunning scene, but lately there has been an influx of participation from that age group. Ian writes about what makes them tick and discusses the motivations behind a group of runners that are the future of our sport. As a veteran of 100 ultras, Ian adds an experience-based perspective on younger ultrarunners and their efforts. Ian is employed by the National Park Service in Moab. He works as a vegetation specialist for Arches National Park, Canyonlands National Park, Natural Bridges National Monument, and Hovenweep National Monument in southeastern Utah. When he's not killing non-native, invasive plant life, you can often find him running on the trails and through the washes in these high desert parks.

Al Toth Al is a long-time ultrarunner and humorist from Norwalk, Connecticut. He is a frequent contributor to UltraRunning magazine.

Micah True Micah is a veteran ultrarunner from Colorado who leads tour groups into Mexico's Copper Canyon, the land of the Tarahumara Indians.

Ed Tyanich Ed writes the On the Go column for UltraRunning on a subject he is passionate about, technical gear. Ed has been a buyer for several local outdoor shops. Whether it's the newest trail shoe, headlamp or technical fabric, Ed has tested it on the trail. Ed and his wife run Raven Enterprises Outdoor Adventures from their 100-year-old log cabin outside Helena, Montana. Ed has been running ultras for more than 10 years.

Jon Vonhof John is the author of Fixing Your Feet, a book that has helped thousands of long distance athletes with foot care. Jon is also the former race director of the Ohlone 50 Km and lives in Manteca, California.

Roy Wallack An Irvine, California-based freelancer Roy writes for many national magazines and has completed the Eco-Challenge, the 1,200-km Paris-Brest-Paris bike ride, the 400-mile TransAlp Challenge mountain bike race and other endurance events.

Nathan Whiting Nathan, from New York City, was a frequent contributor to UltraRunning magazine in its formative years. His holistic approach, using principles and theory from dance, offered a different perspective on the sport.

Kitty Williams Kitty led the tour group Wilderness Expeditions in Tucson, Arizona. She has led trips into Mexico's Copper Canyon.

Appendix VII

Bibliography

Better Training for Distance Runners
David Martin and Peter Coe, Human Kinetics, Champaign, Illinois, 1997

Eat to Win
Robert Haas, Signet Books, 1985

Fixing Your Feet
Jon Vonhof, Footworks Publications, Manteca, California, 1997

From L.A. to New York, From New York to L.A.
Harry Berry

Guinness Book of World Records
Various authors, Bantam books, 2002

Inside Running
David Costill, Brown Benchmark, Dubuque, Iowa, 1986

Lore of Running
Tim Noakes, Human Kinetics, Champaign, Illinois, 1991

Running to Win
George Sheehan, Rodale Press, 1992

The Death Valley
Rich Benyo, Specific Publications, Forestville, California, 1992

The Joy of Sports
Michael Novak, Madison, 1993

The Lonely Breed
Ron Clarke, Pelham Books, 1985

The Longest Hill: Death Valley to Mount Whitney
Jay Birmingham, Jacksonville, Florida, 1983

The Story of Ted Corbitt, Long Distance Runner
John Chodes, Track and Field News Press, 1994

Ultramarathon
James Shapiro, Bantam Books, New York, New York, 1980

Why We Run: A Natural History
Bernd Heinrich, Ecco Press, 2002

INDEX

Drugs   98, 153, 185-6, 200, 224-5, 247